TRAVELER

australia

NATIONAL
GEOGRAPHIC

T R A V E L E R

australia

by Roff Martin Smith

National Geographic
Washington, D.C.

CONTENTS

**TRAVELING WITH
EYES OPEN 6**

CHARTING YOUR TRIP 8

History & Culture 13
Australia Today 14
Food & Drink 24
The Land 26
History of Australia 32
The Arts 56
Flora & Fauna 66

Sydney 73
Introduction & Map 74
Sydney Harbour Walk 82
Feature: Cricket 90
Feature: A Sydney-style
    New Year's 98

New South Wales 101
Introduction & Map 102
Feature: Bushfires 106
Pacific Highway Drive 118

Australian Capital Territory 127
Introduction & Map 128
Feature: Anzac Day 134

Queensland 137
Introduction & Map 138
Tropic of Capricorn Drive 150
Feature: National Parks 172

Northern Territory 181
Introduction & Map 182
Feature: Aboriginal Art 202

Western Australia 211
Introduction & Map 212
Feature: Wildflowers 222
Gibb River Road Drive 238

South Australia 249
Introduction & Map 250
Feature: Australian Wines 264
Feature: Festival State 272
Stuart Highway Drive 284

Victoria 289
Introduction & Map 290
Feature: Melbourne Cup 297
Melbourne Walks 298
Great Ocean Road Drive 310
Feature: Australian Rules Football 318
Feature: Bushrangers 322

Tasmania 329
Introduction & Map 330
Huon Valley Drive 338
Feature: Tasmanian Greens 342
Scenic Loop Drive 346
Feature: Trout Fishing 352

Travelwise 355
Hotels & Restaurants 367
Shopping 386   Activities 388

INDEX 390   CREDITS 398

Pages 2–3: The Red Centre near Alice Springs
Opposite: Beach shades near Melbourne

TRAVELING WITH EYES OPEN

Alert travelers go with a purpose and leave with a benefit. If you travel responsibly, you can help support wildlife conservation, historic preservation, and cultural enrichment in the places you visit. You can enrich your own travel experience as well.

To be a geo-savvy traveler:

- Recognize that your presence has an impact on the places you visit.

- Spend your time and money in ways that sustain local character. (Besides, it's more interesting that way.)

- Value the destination's natural and cultural heritage.

- Respect the local customs and traditions.

- Express appreciation to local people about things you find interesting and unique to the place: its nature and scenery, music and food, historic villages and buildings.

- Vote with your wallet: Support the people who support the place, patronizing businesses that make an effort to celebrate and protect what's special there. Seek out shops, local restaurants, inns, and tour operators who love their home—who love taking care of it and showing it off. Avoid businesses that detract from the character of the place.

- Enrich yourself, taking home memories and stories to tell, knowing that you have contributed to the preservation and enhancement of the destination.

That is the type of travel now called geotourism, defined as "tourism that sustains or enhances the geographical character of a place—its environment, culture, aesthetics, heritage, and the well-being of its residents." To learn more, visit National Geographic's Center for Sustainable Destinations at *nationalgeographic.com/travel/sustainable.*

australia

ABOUT THE AUTHORS

Originally a New England Yankee, **Roff Smith** has lived most of his adult life in Australia since arriving down under in 1982. He began work as a journalist for the *Sydney Morning Herald* and later for Melbourne's *Sunday Age*. Smith joined *Time* magazine in 1993, and as an award-winning senior writer he covered stories around Australia and as far afield as New Guinea, French Polynesia, and Antarctica.

In 1996, Smith set off into the Australian outback on a 10,000-mile bicycle trek. The story of his adventurous journey appeared as a three-part series in *National Geographic* magazine and was later described in more detail in *Cold Beer and Crocodiles: A Bicycle Journey into Australia*, published in 2000 by National Geographic Books. *Australia: Journey Through a Timeless Land*, was also published by National Geographic Books. His 2004 *National Geographic* magazine story on Australia's national poet, Banjo Paterson, won a North American Travel Journalist's Association award for best feature. Smith now freelances for a number of international magazines and publications, including *National Geographic*.

Peter Turner wrote the updates and sidebars for the 2010 and 2014 editions. Australian by birth, journalist by trade, and wanderer by nature, he has worked as an editor, publisher, and journalist in Australia and for newspapers in Indonesia, Thailand, and Brunei. As a travel writer and photographer specializing in Southeast Asia and the South Pacific, he has contributed to newspapers and magazines worldwide and to more than 20 guidebooks.

Charting Your Trip

Thousands of miles of glorious coastline and beaches, the world's greatest fringing coral reef, unique and varied wildlife, the rugged outback desert landscapes and lifestyles, sophisticated cities, tropical rain forest, and alpine national parks— the question is not so much what to see, but how much of it can you see.

How to Visit: If You Only Have a Week

Whether you're staying two days or two months, Australia has plenty to offer. But with a whole continent of diverse attractions to choose from, you may find planning your itinerary difficult. Given the great distances that most visitors travel just to get to Australia, the fatigue that comes with jet lag, and the fact that Australia is as large as the continental United States, it's probably best to visit only a few main destinations if your time is short.

If your trip to Australia is limited to one week, concentrate on Sydney, the awe-inspiring Great Barrier Reef, and the massive monolith of Uluru (Ayers Rock) in the Red Centre. Direct flights (Qantas is the main airline with the most extensive routes; *qantas.com.au*) make it possible to do the big three in just seven days.

First port of call for most visitors is **Sydney,** on the country's southeast coast. This lively city with a glorious harbor has fine beaches including famous Bondi, interesting historic areas, and scenic icons like Sydney Harbour Bridge and the Opera House.

After a couple days in Sydney, fly north (about three hours) to **Cairns** and take a day cruise on the **Great Barrier Reef.** The reef is everything you ever imagined— amazing giant corals and colorful fish scattered around tropical islands. If you stay in Cairns or **Port Douglas** (40 miles/64 km up the coast) for another day or two, you can rent a car and visit the ancient rain forests of **Daintree National Park,** head up into the lush mountains at **Kuranda** or the **Atherton Tablelands,** or just lie on the northern beaches, all nearby. From Cairns, a direct three-hour flight takes you to **Uluru** (Ayers Rock), where you can take a walking tour around the rock with Aboriginal guides and head to the otherworldly rock formations of nearby **Kata Tjuta** (the Olgas).

If You Have More Time

You'll need at least two weeks (preferably more) to really explore Australia. If you enjoy long road trips, car rental agencies abound throughout the country, though you'll likely want to fly a few legs to make your travels more manageable. Even so, you may not

An Australian denizen

have the time to see every region of Australia—here's an itinerary, looping around the country, from which you can pick and choose what interests you most.

Sydney & Around: After visiting Sydney, explore the panoramas and walks of the nearby **Blue Mountains** to the west. You could then drive southwest a few hours to reach **Canberra,** the country's planned, spacious capital, and on south another 100 miles (160 km) or so to the **Snowy Mountains,** for skiing in winter or fine hiking in summer.

But most visitors head north from Sydney along the **Pacific Highway** that skirts past the fine surf beaches on the coast. The lush **Hunter Valley wine district** is about 2.5 hours north of Sydney. Of the beach resorts along this coast, **Byron Bay** is a favorite, but great beaches spread all the way into Queensland.

Queensland & the Northern Territories:
The state of Queensland, home to the Great Barrier Reef, is the biggest tourist destination in the country. The coastline is truly glorious and the weather warm to hot year-round. In the south, the **Gold Coast** is a Miami-style strip of hotels, theme parks, and surf beaches that almost merges with the state capital, **Brisbane** (590 miles/950 km from Sydney). Farther north, the **Sunshine Coast** is mercifully less developed and includes the chic resort of **Noosa Heads.** Nearby **Fraser Island** is an interesting oddity—the world's largest sand island covered in rain forest.

Beyond, the Great Barrier Reef stretches north for 1,300 miles (2,100 km). Cairns/Port Douglas and the resorts of the **Whitsunday Islands** (300 miles/500 km south of Cairns) are the main bases for exploring the reef, but tours operate from towns all along the coast. The coastal range inland has rain forest, much of it protected by national parks.

NOT TO BE MISSED:

Exploring Sydney, one of the world's great harbor cities **73**

Cruising the incredible Great Barrier Reef **160**

The teeming wetlands of Kakadu National Park **188–191**

Imposing Uluru, sacred rock in the heart of the outback **204–207**

The Barossa Valley and its old-world wineries **267–268**

Driving the stunning Great Ocean Road **310–315**

Port Arthur, convict hellhole turned scenic treasure **350–351**

Koalas

Koalas are one of Australia's most popular tourist attractions, but finding koalas in the wild isn't that easy. Zoos and game parks will be your best option. You can also try evening walks through the bushy fringe suburbs of Sydney, Melbourne, or Brisbane, but your chances of encountering a wild koala are much better on Kangaroo Island, off South Australia, or on Victoria's Phillip Island.

Many visitors then fly west three hours from Cairns, across interior Queensland's vast cattle stations, to the **Northern Territory** in the center of the country. **Darwin** (2,500 miles/4,000 km from Sydney) is the tropical capital in the north of the territory and the staging point for trips to **Kakadu National Park.** Wetlands, wildlife, waterfalls, and Aboriginal rock art make this park a must-see.

From Darwin, drive south toward the **Red Centre** for gorges, stunning rock outcrops, and desert landscapes. **Katherine Gorge** in **Nitmiluk National Park,** about 150 miles (240 km) south of Darwin, is a chain of gorges carved out of the sandstone plateau by the river. Another 775 miles (1,250 km) farther south, in the center of the country, **Alice Springs** is a desert oasis and base for exploring the gorges of the **MacDonnell Ranges,** the towering **Kings Canyon,** and, of course, Uluru and Kata Tjuta.

Western Australia: Alternately, from Darwin you could head southwest into Western Australia and the **Kimberley,** a little-explored but stunning region. Travel via the gravel **Gibb River Road,** one of the great adventure drives, or take the main highway with a detour to the eerie tiger-striped rock formations of **Purnululu National Park.** Both routes reach **Broome** (1,150 miles/1,860 km from Darwin), an old pearling town turned beach resort.

Western Australia is huge and mostly desert. The coast road from Broome down to the capital, Perth—a 1,400-mile (2,255 km) jaunt—passes beaches, remote towns, and **Ningaloo Reef,** Australia's other stunning barrier reef, with fantastic diving and snorkeling. Farther south, wild dolphins come to play in the shallows at **Monkey Mia.**

Thriving **Perth** (2,450 miles/3,950 km from Sydney), in the green southwest of the state, is one of the world's most remote cities. On the city's doorstep lies the historic port of **Fremantle,** and a day's drive south brings you to **Margaret River,** a major wine district on a scenic coast. Nearby are the towering karri forests and the old whaling port of **Albany.** From Perth, the main highway heads east through the gold-mining town of **Kalgoorlie** across the **Nullarbor Plain** to Adelaide, a long, demanding drive of 1,675 miles (2,700 km), but a classic outback road trip.

South Australia & Victoria: Adelaide—870 miles (1,400 km) from Sydney—the city of churches, is the gracious capital of South Australia, ringed by beaches, hills, and wine districts. The nearby **Barossa Valley,** with its old European-style wineries,

When to Go

Winter (June–August) is the best time to visit Queensland, the Northern Territory, and Western Australia. The weather is balmy and dry, and tourism is at its peak, so book ahead. Temperatures are colder in the southern latitudes, especially in the Australian Alps and inland, where night temperatures can drop below freezing.

The coastal regions come alive in summer (December–February), when temperatures soar and the days are long and ideal for outdoor activities. Prices rise and beach resorts fill up between Christmas and the end of January, Australia's main holiday break. The northern wet season lasts from around October to March and spreads as far as southeast Queensland and northern New South Wales.

Autumn (March–May) is cooler and pleasant in much of the country, while spring (September–November) is similar if a little wetter in the south.

September–October is the best compromise for a major tour of the country.

Aboriginal guides apply traditional face paint at a homestead near the Katherine River.

is a must. The city is also the starting point for **The Ghan,** the classic trans-outback train, which heads north 950 miles (1,540 km) to Alice Springs. The **Stuart Highway** also runs north through the desert, passing **Coober Pedy,** the opal-mining town so hot in summer that residents live underground.

East of South Australia lies Victoria, the smallest and greenest of the mainland states. Gold rush wealth flowed through the elegant capital, **Melbourne,** a garden city of grand Victorian-era architecture 1.5 hours by air from Sydney. Verdant mountains, wineries, beaches, and colonies of penguins are just a day trip away from the city. The big draw in Victoria is the **Great Ocean Road,** a stunning coastal drive, to see the **Twelve Apostles,** great shafts of sandstone carved over millions of years by the sea. Other attractions include the historic goldfields towns and fine national parks such as **Wilsons Promontory.**

Tasmania: An overnight ferry or short flight away from Melbourne (or a two-hour flight from Sydney), the island of Tasmania is lush and green, with dense wilderness, superb hiking, and intriguing convict history. The island is easy to tour over a few days on a 600-mile (960 km) loop, taking in historic **Stanley,** the untamed western rivers and wilderness, the colonial capital of **Hobart,** and the old penal settlement of **Port Arthur—** before returning to Sydney for your trip home.

Currency

The national unit of currency is the Australian dollar, comprising 100 cents. It was introduced in 1966 when decimal currency replaced pounds, shillings, and pence. Notes come in $5, $10, $20, $50, and $100 denominations and are made of polymer propylene, a tough, colorful, and difficult-to-forge plastic alternative to the old paper notes. Coins in circulation are the silver-colored 5c, 10c, 20c, and multi-sided 50c pieces, and gold-colored $1 and $2 coins. Confusingly, the $2 coin is smaller than the $1.

History & Culture

Australia Today   14–23

Experience: Talkin' Aussie   19

Feature: Food & Drink   24–25

Experience: Savoring Vegemite   25

The Land   26–31

Experience: Shopping for Opals   31

History of Australia   32–55

Experience: Remembering Anzac Day   50

The Arts   56–65

Flora & Fauna   66–72

Australia's national flag incorporates the British Union Jack, a visible reminder of the country's heritage. Opposite: Sea fan, Great Barrier Reef

Australia Today

Australia has intrigued the rest of the world for more than two centuries, with its fantastic marsupials, noisy and colorful birds, and incredibly vast sweeps of outback landscape. Home to one of the world's oldest human cultures, it is also a geological marvel, famous for the haunting monolith of Uluru, the tropical wetlands of Kakadu, and of course the magnificent Great Barrier Reef.

Australia is the world's smallest continent and its largest island, a 2.9-million-square-mile (7.5 million sq km) landmass that went walkabout 65 million years ago to peaceful isolation in the South Pacific. Some of the world's most ancient landscapes are found here, dating back more than 3.5 billion years. Living examples of the world's earliest life-forms, stromatolites, can still be found on the rocks along the shore of Hamelin Pool in Western Australia. Primitive cycad palms are found nestled in gorges in the heart of the outback. In 1994, a living specimen of Wollemi pine—an ancient species of tree previously known only through fossils—was found in a dense forest close to Sydney.

Aborigines came here by rafts and little boats from Asian archipelagos more than 50,000 years ago. It was a period known to them as the Dreamtime, a central concept of Aboriginal spirituality. The magical events of that time are celebrated with an elaborate cycle of songs and enshrined in rock paintings and engravings found in thousands of rock shelters and caves throughout the country. The songs and ceremonies provide the basis for Aboriginal law and custom.

Fascination has drawn visitors here as tourists for more than 170 years. Charles Darwin remarked on Sydney's high real estate prices when he passed through in 1836. English novelist Anthony Trollope was enamored with the high Victorian architecture in the gold rush town of Ballarat. Mark Twain marveled at Tasmania's paradoxical beauty and its violent, sordid history. The millions of visitors who come through the turnstiles here today come primarily to experience Australia's sunny beach-loving lifestyle: Sydney's Opera House and Bondi Beach, Melbourne's bustling restaurant scene, the theme parks along Queensland's Gold Coast, and Adelaide's festivals and wine country of the Barossa Valley.

Australia is far more accessible now than it was in the days of steamers and the Qantas Empire flying boats that made the journey from London to Sydney's Rose Bay in "just" five days. But it is still a marathon journey: about a 15-hour flight nonstop from Los Angeles and 24 hours from London. Jet-lagged travelers step off the plane into another time, another day, and another season. The stars are strange and new, the Australian bush has a bracing, spicy tang, and even in the city a traveler can wake to the raucous screeches of cockatoos. Thankfully, in a world becoming smaller, Australia is still tinged with the romance of distance.

> **Thankfully, in a world becoming smaller, Australia is still tinged with the romance of distance.**

A nation of surfers, Australia boasts several world pros, including top-ranked Taj Burrow.

The Real Australia

In my wild erratic fancy visions come to me of Clancy;
Gone a-droving 'down the Cooper' where the western drovers go;
As the stock are slowly swinging, Clancy rides behind them singing;
For the drover's life has pleasures that the townsfolk never know.
—From "Clancy of the Overflow" (1889) by Andrew Barton "Banjo" Paterson

Ask any Australian where the real Australia is, and chances are he or she will point you toward a broad immensity of dust and sky, while sketching a verbal portrait of a sun-bronzed stockman with a tattered Akubra hat nudging a mob of sheep along a gum-shaded lane. It's a lovely, picturesque fancy, but the truth of the matter is that the real Australia is a sprawl of terra-cotta roofs in the suburbs. Typical Australians work in offices, pushing bureaucratic pens, as they did even in 1889 when Banjo Paterson wrote his much loved bush classic, "Clancy of the Overflow."

The lights of Sydney's glittering skyline reflect in the waters of its famous harbor.

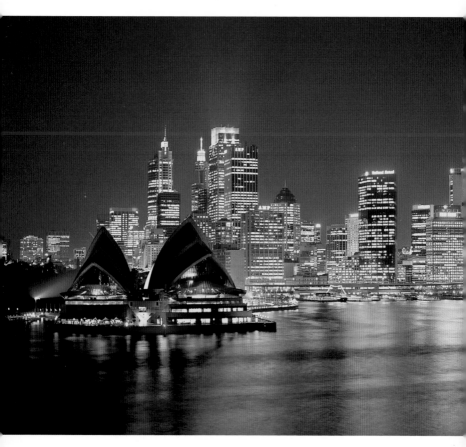

Ninety percent of Aussies live along the coast, usually within a 30-minute drive of the nearest beach. Aussie children grow up between surf-lifesaving flags, walking sidewalks bright with Lebanese, Chinese, Italian, Greek, and Vietnamese shops and dodging city traffic. They aspire to a brick veneer home in a comfortable suburb, ideally one with a quarter-acre (0.1 ha) backyard, a Hills Hoist (an ingenious Australian clothesline), and a barbecue. Although real estate is expensive—hideously so in Sydney—Australians have the highest rate of home ownership in the world. Home improvement and gardening shows have long been popular staples of Australian TV, with their cheerfully middle-class do-it-yourself advice, remodeling ideas, and landscaping tips. Cities tend to spread outward rather than upward. Sydney's sprawl reaches nearly 80 miles (128 km) from end to end. There are tough neighborhoods, but few slums. By and large this is a safe country, with a murder rate of 1 in 100,000 population—about a quarter that of the U.S.

This is an easygoing, generally permissive society, with a belief that everybody ought to have a "fair go" at leading life the way they see fit.

Australians generally spend their lives close to the neighborhood where they grew up. Although shopping malls, American fast-food chains, and supermarkets have made huge inroads, a lot of shopping in country towns and inner cities is still done the old-fashioned way: People walk along a main street and stop into the butcher's, the baker's, the fishmonger's, and the greengrocer's shops. Or they visit a bustling market, where vendors shout and thrifty shoppers haggle over prices.

This is an easygoing, generally permissive society, with a belief that everybody ought to have a "fair go" at leading life the way they see fit. Despite the presence of more than 160 different nationalities, everyone gets along pretty well. Sydney has a higher percentage of gay people than San Francisco, and its Gay and Lesbian Mardi Gras is the single biggest fete in Australia, attracting crowds of more than 500,000—gay and straight—from around the country and overseas.

Surveys show that three-quarters of Australians believe in God, but on a typical Sunday morning only 20 percent will be in church. Most will be sleeping late, perusing a newspaper, or gearing up to play (or watch) some kind of sport. This is a nation of weekend warriors. Flick on the TV news Saturday or Sunday evening and you'll see a litany of horse-race results, footy or cricket highlights, and sporting news from overseas, often followed by reports of the rescue of a hiker from the bottom of a gorge, a Jet Ski collision, or a fisherman swept off a rock by a "freak" wave of the sort that claimed another life at that very spot the previous week.

Weekends and vacations are the only times most Australians ever actually visit the "bush," the Australian term for countrified landscapes. Even then they are mighty particular where they go. Kakadu, Uluru, the Great Barrier Reef, the Flinders Ranges, and the Snowy Mountains (for skiing) are favorites. Or maybe day trips to the Dandenong Ranges, if one lives in Melbourne, or the Blue Mountains, near Sydney.

Adventurous young Aussies usually head for Europe when they want to do some wandering, but a few go to the gold mines or the remote iron-ore ports on Australia's northwest coast. Adventurous retirees increasingly haul their caravans on a several-month loop around the continent. But by and large, Australians are content to let the bush remain a comfortably distant place, something from the pages of Henry Lawson or Banjo Paterson (see pp. 56 & 58). Go to a suburban footy match on a rainy winter's day in Melbourne and a lot of the crowd will be wearing Driza-Bones, the traditional stockman's oilskin. In the parking lot will be gleaming, fully equipped Land Cruisers with four-wheel drive, kangaroo (bull) bars, and cellular phones. It's not that Australians don't love the bush; they treasure it deeply—but they prefer to live in the city or suburbs.

The Outback & Its Stations

When you talk to graziers in the outback and hear their descriptions of bushfires, floods, and droughts, it's easy to understand why most Australians prefer the suburbs. The outback landscape is often windswept and hauntingly barren. The nearest town might be 250 miles (400 km) away. The work is tough, dirty, and sometimes hazardous: Wild bulls, rolling tractors, and dirt bike accidents during livestock musters (Aussie for "round ups") help make farming the most dangerous occupation in Australia. The workdays are long, frequently stretching from dawn to dusk and beyond. On the other hand, once you've felt the camaraderie and buzz of a woolshed at shearing time, with a team of shearers toiling like demons, family and friends pitching in as roustabouts and sorters while the smallest kids play on the wool bales, it's hard to imagine wanting anything else.

> It's not that Australians don't love the bush; they treasure it deeply —but they prefer to live in the city or suburbs.

The Australian economy relies on its 190,000 farmers to the tune of about A$49 billion a year. Australia is the world's second largest exporter of beef and veal behind Brazil, having a national herd of 30 million or so cattle. It is also a major producer of wheat. But traditionally wool is king. Since the first merinos were introduced in 1795, Australia has built up a flock of around 100 million sheep and supplies about 25 percent of the wool used by the world's clothing industry. The Golden Fleece of legend seems a little less remarkable when you consider some of the ultrafine fleeces produced on specialist farms in Victoria and Tasmania. These can literally be worth more than their weight in gold and are used by top-name fashion houses for lightweight suits. Sheep that grow wool this fine (about 11 microns) are cosseted creatures that wear little coats to protect them from burrs and aren't shorn so much as given a haircut.

The rest of the nation's flock is clipped in the spring by roving teams of contract shearers. This is brutally tough and competitive work. Because shearers are paid per fleece, both money and pride rest on getting the highest total possible in a day.

EXPERIENCE: Talkin' Aussie

Australian English—called Strine, from the clipped pronunciation of "Australian"—is characterized by nasalized vowels, abbreviated words, and the addition of suffixes. Thus "utility" becomes "ute," "tin" becomes "tinnie," and "David" becomes "Davo." Australians also use many words of unique meaning. Common Strine words include:

agro—aggressive

arvo—afternoon

barbie—BBQ

billabong—water hole or cut-off branch of a river

blowie—blowfly

bludger—work-shy person

boomer—large male kangaroo; anything large or successful

chook—chicken

cobber—see "mate"

crikey—exclamation of surprise

crook—sick, bad, inferior

digger—see "mate"; also, World War I soldier

drongo—fool, simpleton

dunny—toilet

fair dinkum—true, genuine

galah—fool; pink and gray parrot

g'day—greeting, often accompanied by "mate"

grog—alcohol

hoon—lout, show-off

mate—buddy; general term of familiarity

milk bar—convenience store

no worries—no problem, good, fine

ocker—stereotypical uncultured Australian, redneck (also "yobbo")

piker—someone who chickens out or shirks their duty

ratbag—rascal, eccentric

ripper—great, fantastic

roo—kangaroo

sheila—woman

snag—sausage

swag—bedroll used in the outback

thongs—flip-flops

troppo—mad, as in "gone troppo" (too long in the tropics)

tucker—food

two-up—traditional coin gambling game

walkabout—nomadic wandering, as in "gone walkabout"

Woop Woop—remote imaginary place

yonks—a long time

A top hand (a "gun shearer" in outback parlance) will regularly shear more than 150 a day, and some do many more. In the 1890s, when shearers used crude scissorlike shears, Big Jackie Howe used to draw crowds to watch him clip 250 a day. In 1892, he sheared a record 321 ewes in a union-prescribed working day of seven hours and forty minutes. This record has never been beaten, at least with hand-powered shears. Modern electric combs have changed things a bit. The world record is held by a New Zealander named Dion King, who sheared 866 lambs in nine hours in 2007.

Anyone who has read or watched *The Thorn Birds* knows that Australian ranches, called stations, can be vast. The world's largest is Anna Creek Cattle Station, owned by the long-established Kidman family, in the South Australian outback. At 6 million acres (about 9,400 square miles, 24,000 sq km) it is about the size of Connecticut and Massachusetts combined. The world's biggest sheep property, Mount Margaret, near Quilpie in Queensland, covers just 1.48 million acres (600,533 hectares), and recently sold for A$12 million. Particularly in the Northern Territory or Western Australia's rugged Kimberley region, a million-acre spread is nothing unusual.

Sometimes the scale can be a little hard for visitors to comprehend. A cattleman who ran 465,000 acres (188,325 ha) in the Great Sandy Desert tells the story of how his immigrant father returned to his home on an island off the coast of Yugoslavia and told relatives how, back in Australia, his son had a ranch bigger than their entire island. His brother simply shook his head and replied sadly, "We never thought you would come back and lie to us." But in Europe it doesn't take 50 acres (20 ha) to support one cow; out in the Great Sandy Desert, it does.

Station life is unique. A trip to town can mean a daylong trek in a four-wheel-drive vehicle or a gut-churning plane ride bouncing over the thermals rising from the hot outback scrub. Supplies come by road train, monster-size triple-trailer trucks that can be 165 feet (50 m) long and weigh 170 tons. Cattle are mustered by helicopter. Services come by air. Out here, flying priests take the sacrament to stations and outlying Aboriginal communities, and the Royal Flying Doctor Service provides medical care (see sidebar below). Station children between the ages of 6 and 11 attend another unique outback institution: the School of the Air. They receive their lessons by hands-free telephone and send in their homework by mail. A couple of times a year, they go into town to meet their teachers and classmates. Older kids go to boarding school.

Aborigines & Europeans

About 300,000 Aborigines lived in Australia in 1788, when the First Fleet arrived from England and began the uneven contest for control of the continent. Actually, at first it wasn't such a one-way game. The soldiers were starving in this strange new land, and the unwilling convict-settlers were demoralized by being so far from home. The Aborigines were home and feasting on native foods that had sustained them for generations.

Two years after the fleet arrived, an Aboriginal leader named Pemulwuy united some of the local tribes and launched a highly effective guerrilla campaign against the invaders. Colonial authorities posted large rewards for his capture. A convict who grabbed him could get a pardon and passage back to England. Pemulwuy was killed in 1802, his head pickled and sent to England. Pemulwuy's son continued the resistance movement for a few more years until the fragile alliance of tribes broke up.

Flying Doctors

Since 1928, the Royal Flying Doctor Service has tended the sick in remote communities across the outback and on the isolated islands of the Indian Ocean and Great Barrier Reef. From 21 bases around the country, 50 aircraft fly more than 14 million miles per year to tend on-site emergencies, evacuate patients to the hospital, and deliver doctors and nurses to remote clinics. Established by Presbyterian minister Rev. John Flynn, the service relied on radio (now mostly telephone and satellite communications) to advise and attend to medical matters. Until the 1990s, it also linked students in Australia's more remote areas with their teachers.

A stockman nudges a mob of cattle through the scrub in a timeless scene.

Because there were so many different, widely scattered tribes—divided by about 400 languages—Aborigines had difficulty putting up a united front against the invaders. The latter soon gained the upper hand, using rifles against spears. The most appalling instances were in Tasmania, where farmers simply shot Aborigines on sight. In the 1830s, the few who survived were rounded up and shipped off to Flinders Island in Bass Strait.

As settlers with their sheep and cattle pushed deeper into the continent, taking up huge swaths of land, Aborigines were pushed off to ever more remote pockets. Tribes that had nothing in common found themselves scratching a living together on hard-scrabble terrain many days' journey from their ancestral grounds. Ancient traditions and cultures built over 50,000 years crumbled and vanished.

Some Aborigines received food from church missions, others worked on the stations for the new property owners. Although raising animals and riding horses had never been part of their culture, Aborigines quickly became superb stockmen and riders and made it possible for the early stations to prosper. They were generally paid in food and tobacco. By the 1930s, the authorities had settled on a program of assimilation to bring half-caste Aborigines into society. One breathtakingly cruel policy was to rob Aboriginal mothers of their babies and foster them out to white parents. Incredibly, this practice went on until the 1960s. It left a ghastly legacy of broken families and heartbreak, but Aboriginal culture refused to disappear.

The 1960s were a time of radical change all over the world, including even the remotest stretches of the outback. There were sit-ins, a prominent strike by Aborigine stockmen at the Wave Hill Cattle Station in the Northern Territory, and freedom buses traversing Queensland. Aborigines and their supporters set up a tent embassy outside Parliament House in Canberra. A constitutional referendum in 1967 gave Aborigines

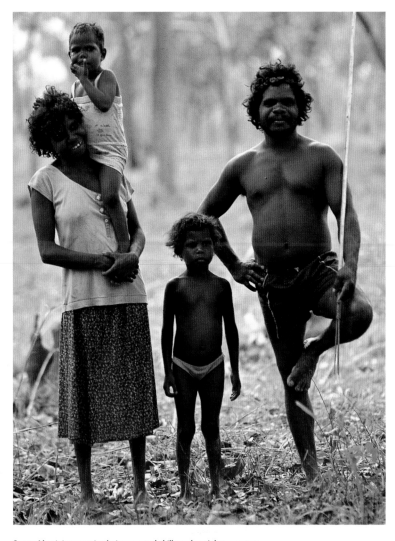

Some Aborigines retain their ancestral skills and social structures.

full Australian citizenship and voting rights. An Aboriginal flag was designed that same year. It comprised a red-and-black field with a yellow circle in the center and has come to symbolize the struggle for land rights.

A quarter of a century passed before the next major step was taken in the recognition of Aboriginal rights. In 1992, the Australian High Court issued a landmark ruling that the continent had not, in fact, been *terra nullus* (no-man's-land) when Captain Cook claimed it in 1770, and that the indigenous people had been wrongfully dispossessed. It became known as the Mabo Ruling, after Torres Straits islander Eddie Mabo, who brought the suit against the government, and it meant that Aborigines who could prove continuous contact with their land could claim vacant Crown land.

Later, in 1996, a further landmark High Court ruling, known as the Wik Decision, established that native title could coexist with mining and pastoral leases. The ruling sparked an uproar: Farmers and miners demanded legislation that would protect their rights and investments, and Aborigines insisted that the government obey the rulings of its own High Court. The debate continues, but everyone in Australia realizes that it is no longer possible to ignore the past. The Mabo and Wik rulings have forever changed the relationship between Aborigines and the people who have arrived since 1788, and put the matter of reconciliation near the top of the political agenda.

Politics and High Court rulings notwithstanding, two centuries of "civilization" have been a steep downhill slide for Australia's indigenous people. The mortality and morbidity figures of Aborigines are shocking. Their infant mortality rate is triple that of non-Aboriginal Australians, and, as a killing diet of booze, drug abuse, and fast food takes its toll, their life expectancy is shorter by 15 years. Aborigines suffer from alcoholism, tuberculosis, heart disease, hepatitis, and diabetes at far higher rates than the rest of the population. Their unemployment rate is more than 16 percent, and they are 14 times more likely than the rest of the Australian population to be in prison.

Statistics do not tell the whole story, though. Some Aboriginal communities have preserved their heritage with vibrant arts and music and matchless knowledge of the environment. Many of the strongest communities are also the most remote. Increasingly, these communities are cautiously opening the doors to allow outsiders a glimpse of their ancient culture and to try to build bridges of understanding.

Those bridges, however, suffered a setback in 2007 after the release of a report detailing child sex abuse and chronic alcoholism in remote indigenous communities. The former government ignored the report's recommendations and instead sent in police and troops, a move that outraged Aboriginal communities. The UN called the intervention discriminatory, and while the current government promises more consultation, it remains to be seen if any progress will be made beyond rhetoric. ∎

Boomerangs

Captain James Cook thought they were wooden swords, and popular myth viewed boomerangs as hunting weapons that somehow magically hit a prey and returned to the thrower. In fact, the returning boomerang was often just a plaything. More effective nonreturning boomerangs were typically used to hunt and cripple fleeing kangaroos and other animals. Boomerang shapes vary widely, and often have one arm longer that the other. They were used for fishing, hunting, fighting, or ceremonial purposes, such as a percussion instrument in dances. Not all were thrown; some were used as weapons in hand-to-hand combat.

Food & Drink

There was a time when "Australian cuisine" rated with "Holy War" as one of the English language's great oxymorons. Aussie tucker conjured up visions of Vegemite sandwiches, gristly meat pies, and a stodgy dinner of lamb chops, three watery vegetables, and a bowl of ice cream for dessert. Pizza was regarded as ethnic fare.

Fresh seafood is a staple of Australian cuisine.

Then came the great melting-pot decades of the 1970s and '80s, when immigrants from virtually every country could be found rubbing elbows in jostling city markets. Australians became curious about the herbs, spices, and exotic foods their new neighbors were cooking and found clever ways of adapting them to local fare. Out of this cultural mélange a unique cuisine evolved—a blend of Asian and Mediterranean styles, complemented by some of the world's best wines. These days Australia's top chefs enjoy celebrity status, and the vibrant restaurant and café scene is one of the highlights of a visit down under.

Asian & Mediterranean Influences

Asia is the dominating influence in this new Australian cuisine, although Australians are doing much more than merely aping Asian styles. With its large Mediterranean population and burgeoning vineyards, Australia has a strong wine culture—something Asia doesn't have. "Consequently we use Asian spices and ingredients in nontraditional ways that really surprise Asian visitors when they come here," says Neil Perry, one of Australia's most famous chefs and owner of Sydney's Rockpool restaurant. "It is very much an Australian style."

It helps, too, that Australia has some of the world's best produce: Sydney's rock oysters, handcrafted cheeses from King Island, olive oil from the Adelaide Hills, venison from Tasmania, corn-fed chickens from Kangaroo Island, and scallops and abalone from Coffin Bay, for example. Australia is a horn of plenty, and it is also largely unpolluted.

Native Cuisine

In recent years Australia's unique native fare—kangaroo, for instance—has been appearing more frequently on the menu. Once disdained by white Australians as the "bush tucker" that older rural Australians remember eating in the grimmest days of the Depression, kangaroo is now celebrated as a lean and delicate-tasting alternative to beef or lamb at the barbecue. It often appears on trendy city menus as well. Although it could be a long time before the Aboriginal delicacies of goanna, Bogong moths, or witchety grubs make regular appearances on the carte du jour, other native foods such as quandong berries, wild bush tomatoes, and wattle seeds are popular enough to be found in supermarkets. They sit beside cardamom, wasabi paste, lemongrass, and tabbouleh. Australians are settling into their own uniqueness. Anyone for smoked emu prosciutto?

Dining Out

Australia's restaurant scene is incredibly diverse, from Singaporean-style food stands and Japanese sushi bars to elegant French restaurants and Lebanese takeouts. There are more than 160 nationalities in Australia, and when you walk down some of the crowded "eat streets" you get a sense that every one of them has brought a thriving ethnic cuisine.

Melbourne, Adelaide, and Sydney in particular are famous for their eateries. Lygon Street in Melbourne has Italian restaurants, cafés, and gelaterias, and the inner suburb Richmond is crammed with little hole-in-the-wall Vietnamese eateries. Adelaide has Australia's highest concentration of restaurants, with polyglot Gouger Street alone counting more than 40. Sydney is famed for its seafood, with elegant restaurants at The Rocks and around the harbor, but also has its jumble of Asian, Indian, Italian, Greek, and Lebanese eateries and coffeehouses in inner suburbs such as Newtown, Glebe, and Paddington.

Even the sandwich shops are getting in on the act, serving focaccia sandwiches, Greek salads, and venison meat pies. And what of the traditional Aussie barbecue, with its burned lamb chops, sausages, and potato salad? It is still alive and well and very popular, but now it is just one of hundreds of possibilities.

EXPERIENCE: Savoring Vegemite

Resembling axle grease and with a taste some compare to undiluted beef bouillon, Vegemite is widely regarded as the national food. An Australian icon, despite being manufactured by the U.S. company Kraft, Vegemite is a very popular breakfast spread, usually eaten on buttered toast. Made from brewers yeast, a by-product of the beer industry, it closely resembles the British spread Marmite. Try it at your own peril.

If you give it a try in Australia and find you just can't live without it upon your return home, an order is no more than a click away at aussiecatalog.com, about-australia-shop.com, or simplyoz.com.

The Land

With the Pacific Ocean on one side and the Indian Ocean on the other, Australia seems smaller than it actually is. However, at just under 3 million square miles (7.8 million sq km), it is roughly the same size as the continental United States, but with a population of 23 million, not much more than the state of Florida.

Climate & Terrain

There's a reason for the low head count. With the exception of the fertile crescent along the eastern coast and a green pocket in the southwestern corner, most of this continent is arid and inhospitable scrub, if not outright desert. The ragged northern coasts are fringed with brackish mangrove swamps, inhabited by crocodiles, and lashed by tropical cyclones.

The Northern Territory's haunting sandstone mass of Uluru

Australia is the driest inhabited continent. The tropical north has a wet-dry climate, with winters that are sunny and dry followed by torrid summers, punctuated by monsoon rains and occasional cyclones. Bone-dry central Australia gets scorching heat in the summer and sharp cold winter nights. Most of Australia's rain falls in Tasmania or along the east coast, where rain forests flank the mountains. Perth and Adelaide enjoy a sunny Mediterranean climate. Australia does get snow—dustings have been recorded even in southern Queensland—but only the Snowy Mountains in New South Wales, the Victorian Alps, and the highlands in Tasmania receive regular snowfalls. It is sun that draws most visitors, and the majority enjoy it near the sea. Australia has more than 7,000 named beaches on nearly 37,000 miles (59,533 km) of coastline, and it also has the 1,300-mile-long (2,092 km) Great Barrier Reef.

Around 65 million years ago, Australia broke away . . . and began a slow migration to its isolation in the southern Indian and Pacific Oceans.

How the Land Was Made

Sometime around 65 million years ago, Australia broke away from the vast supercontinent called Gondwanaland

and began a slow migration to its isolation in the southern Indian and Pacific Oceans. It was an ancient land even then. Some formations along the northwest coast are among the oldest on the planet—well over three billion years old. One series of 3.4-billion-year-old rocks, found near the remote town of Marble Bar, contains stromatolites, primitive blue-green algae that are the oldest known form of life on the planet. Tracks in the red sandstones of Kalbarri National Park, not far off the North West Coastal Highway in Western Australia, mark the first recorded instance of creatures—nightmarish amphibious scorpions 6 feet long (2 m) and aquatic centipedes even longer—stepping onto land about 420 million years ago. A fossil found nearby, of a 6-inch-long (152 mm) cockroach-like animal named *Kalbarria,* is the oldest of its kind by far and could prove to be the ancestor of all insects.

Australia is the flattest continent. Because the landscape is so ancient, wind and rain have had millions of years to erode once-towering mountains to nubs. The most significant mountain range is the Great Dividing Range, which forms a spine along the eastern coastline from Victoria's Grampian Ranges to the rain forest–clad mountains in far northern Queensland. The range contains the highest point on the continent, Mount Kosciuszko (7,317 feet/2,230 m) in New South Wales. West of these mountains, flatness reigns virtually all the way across the continent to the Indian Ocean. Notable exceptions are the Flinders Ranges in South Australia, the craggy mountains of Western Australia's rugged northwest, and those world-famous stony protrusions known as Uluru and Kata Tjuta (aka Ayers Rock and the Olgas, respectively). Although there are occasional fits of seismic activity, most notably a lethal earthquake measuring 5.6 on the Richter scale near the New South Wales town of Newcastle in 1989, the continent is one of the world's most stable landmasses. Geologically speaking, Australia is a finished product.

The largest and only navigable river on the continent is the Murray-Darling, which stretches 1,650 miles (2,655 km) from the Victorian mountains to the coast of South Australia, through four states. It drains one-seventh of the continent's surface and nourishes much of its farmland. Although the outback is harsh and dry, it lies atop the Great Artesian Basin, a huge water source that helps support Australia's millions of sheep and cattle.

Export Boom

As Australia's manufacturing shifts offshore to labor-cheap Asia and drought and falling world prices hit the farm sector, mining has emerged as the country's economic savior. Even when the global financial crisis of 2008–2009 sent the world into economic meltdown, Australia's growth held, due largely to mining exports to China, Japan, Korea, and India.

Melbourne was once the country's busiest port. Now remote Dampier and Port Hedland take the title, shipping out Western Australia's massive deposits of iron ore and gas, followed by coal ports on the east coast.

Iron ore is Australia's biggest export, worth U.S. $66 billion a year, followed by coal ($44 billion). Gold ($14 billion), gas ($10.2 billion), oil ($11 billion), alumina ($5.5 billion), and aluminum ($4.7 billion) are all major earners. Other important mineral exports are copper, nickel, zinc, lead, manganese, titanium, uranium, and diamonds.

Mineral Wealth

Fickle geology may have left Australia alone in one of the globe's most isolated corners, and left much of it uninhabitable, but it has more than compensated for these inconveniences by making this land a virtual treasure trove of precious metals, coal, natural gas, diamonds, uranium, and opals.

The fabulous gold rushes in Victoria during the 1850s were the richest Australian strikes in history and changed the face of the country forever. Lured by gold, tens of thousands of prospectors flocked to Australia from all over the world. Some found vast fortunes; most didn't, but often stayed on anyway, establishing families, farms, businesses, and towns. Victoria's gold rushes were followed by rich strikes in Western Australia and Queensland. To this day Australia is one of the world's richest sources of gold, producing nearly 300 tons a year. Much of the gold comes from huge opencut mines in Western Australia, northern Queensland, and the Northern Territory's remote Tanami Desert. The Super Pit Mine, near the historic Western Australian town of Kalgoorlie, is one of the world's largest mines, producing more than 800,000 ounces (22,676 kg) of gold each year. There are plans to boost that total to more than a million. Tours of the mine are available.

In 1883, at Broken Hill in far western New South Wales, a cowboy stumbled on the world's biggest known lode of silver-lead-zinc, a single chunk of rock containing more than 280 million tons (284 million tonnes) of incredibly rich ore. It spawned Australia's greatest mining companies and is still being mined to this day. The rollicking old mining town, with its gracious two-story pubs and grand Victorian and Italianate

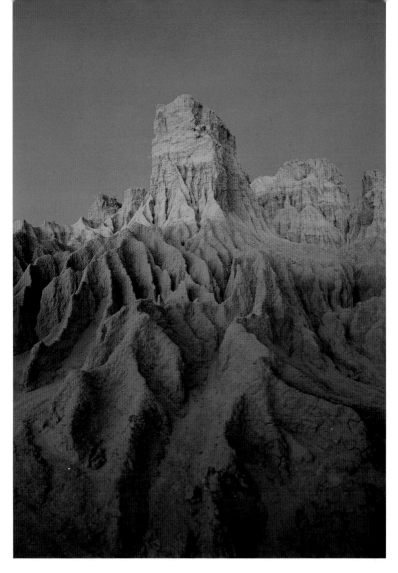

The Walls of China, a range of wind-sculpted dunes, are a dramatic feature in Mungo National Park, New South Wales.

architecture, is popular with tourists, artists, and, increasingly, film crews shooting commercials and movies in its clear desert light. Underground mine tours are available, and for claustrophobics who don't wish to go below, there is an excellent mock-up of a mine in town.

Mount Isa, in northwestern Queensland, is another rich deposit of silver, lead, zinc, and copper and has been mined since 1923. Visitors here also have the opportunity to go underground. Untapped as yet is another fabulously rich deposit, known as the Century Zinc deposit. It was discovered about 200 miles (320 km) northwest of Mount Isa.

South Australia made its early fortunes in copper, with rich diggings at Kapunda, at Burra, and around the Yorke Peninsula. More recently, the giant Olympic Dam Mine in the state's desert outback has been found to have such enormous reserves of copper and uranium that mining could continue for hundreds of years. Again, tourists have the opportunity to inspect this mine, if they care to take the detour off the Stuart Highway on the drive from Adelaide to Alice Springs.

Coober Pedy, which is on the Stuart Highway and about eight hours' drive north of Adelaide (528 miles/850 km), accounts for almost 70 percent of the world's opals. Roadside shops sell opals, tours of the diggings can be arranged, and, if you have the time and the inclination to do some digging yourself, a miner's permit is readily obtained.

> **Western Australia is perhaps the richest mineralized zone on Earth, with vast reserves of gold, nickel, and mineral sands.**

Western Australia is perhaps the richest mineralized zone on Earth, with vast reserves of gold, nickel, and mineral sands. The iron-rich Pilbara makes Australia one of the largest exporters of iron ore. The Argyle Diamond Mine in the state's remote Kimberley region is the world's fourth biggest. It produces about 8 million carats a year, including much of the world's ultrarare pink diamonds, which can fetch a cool million dollars a carat in trading rooms in Antwerp. Tours of this remote, high-security operation can be arranged in the town of Kununurra, about 120 miles (192 km) north of the mine.

Fog rises from the rain forest in Daintree National Park in Queensland.

EXPERIENCE: Shopping for Opals

Australia's fiery opals are lovely and make wonderful souvenirs, but buying them in Coober Pedy (Australia's opal capital; see pp. 280–281) or city jewelry shops requires care. You need to know what you are looking for.

Opal is made of delicate layers of silica that refract light like a prism and give the stone its distinctive sparkle. Like other gems, opals are valued by their size, the strength and brilliance of their color, and their clarity. Flaws or cracks in a stone detract from its value. The brighter and clearer the stone, the higher the value.

Black and crystal opals are the rarest and most valuable, followed by semiblack opals. Milky opals, although still pretty, are the least valuable because they lack that special dark fire.

Shape is also a very important consideration. There are three categories of opal. A "cabochon" is a solid, domed piece of opal that is the most valuable shape. A less valuable "doublet" is a thin wafer of opal against a dark background, while a "triplet" has a quartz lens as well and is the least expensive.

Unless you know opals very well, avoid deals with any kippered old characters you might meet down at the pub, however colorful such a transaction may seem. Stick to reputable dealers, shop around, and ask a lot of questions.

Coober Pedy has plenty of spots to buy opals. In Sydney, try **National Opal Collection** (60 Pitt St., tel 02/9247-6344), which stocks opal jewelry as well as loose opals, and **Opal Fields** (119 George St., The Rocks, tel 02/9251-8353), which offers opals for sale and also has a museum of opal fossils and specimens. See p. 387 for more information.

The seabed off the Western Australian coast is the habitat for countless numbers of pearl-bearing oysters. The historic pearling port of Broome, now a popular resort, is the hub of a modern pearling industry that is now worth about A$200 million a year. Beneath the turquoise waters of the Timor Sea, off Australia's remote northwest coast, are sandstone formations that are estimated to contain billions, possibly trillions, of cubic feet of natural gas.

The craggy mountain ranges of Western Australia's isolated Pilbara region, about 1,000 miles (1,600 km) north of Perth, contain some of the world's largest iron mines, at Mount Newman, Tom Price, and Paraburdoo. They turn out 120 million tons of high-grade iron ore each year. The ore is loaded into the world's longest freight trains, up to a mile (1.6 km) in length, and are hauled almost 300 miles (480 km) to the wharves at Port Hedland and Karratha. As with almost all of Australia's great mining projects, these operations can be visited, although tourists with limited time on their itineraries will find them too remote.

New South Wales and Queensland have vast seams of coal, not only of high quality but also conveniently close to the coast, helping make Australia the world's largest exporter of coal.

Off the coast of Western Australia, the giant North West Shelf venture accounts for more than 40 percent of the country's oil and gas production. There are zinc, gold, tin, and copper deposits in Tasmania. Some of the world's richest deposits of bauxite (source of aluminum) lie near Weipa on the Gulf of Carpentaria side of Queensland's Cape York Peninsula, only a few miles away from where the first Dutch ship made landfall and whose captain dismissed the continent as barren. ■

History of Australia

The first Australians arrived at least 50,000 years ago—some say as far back as 120,000 years—coming south from Asia in one of prehistory's great migrations. They came on foot and in small boats, making a series of short hops. Because the sea level was as much as 400 feet (122 m) lower than it is today, it was possible to walk across the Torres Strait from New Guinea to Australia.

Nobody knows why these people came. Restlessness or famine may have driven them; perhaps they were pushed out by stronger tribes to the north. Over thousands of years several more migrations occurred, the last one about 5,000 years ago. At least two types of people made the journey: a very heavily framed people

Aboriginal rock paintings at Obiri Rock in Arnhem Land

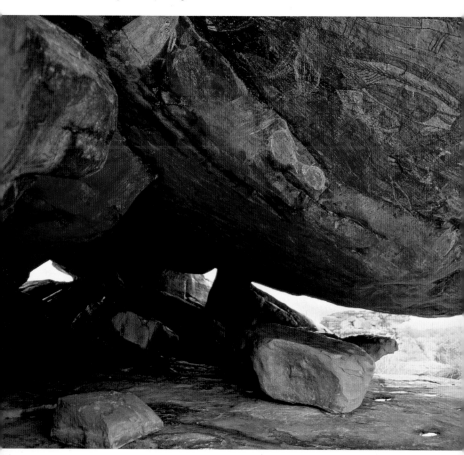

anthropologists call "Robust," and a slender race called "Gracile." Today's Aborigines are descendants of the Gracile people.

They scattered themselves widely around the unpeopled continent, which in those days contained such bizarre creatures as giant kangaroos up to 10 feet (3 m) tall and rhinoceros-size wombats. Archaeologists have found 40,000-year-old campsites near Melbourne's Tullamarine Airport, stone tools dating from 45,000 years ago in the Nepean Valley outside Sydney, and skeletal remains 35,000 years old in a cave as far south as Hobart. (In those days it was possible also to walk from today's mainland Australia to Tasmania without getting your feet wet.) At Lake Mungo National Park in far western New South Wales, anthropologists discovered the cremated remains of a woman 35,000 years old, the world's earliest known cremation. Much of what we know about these early Australians comes from

> **The first Australians arrived at least 50,000 years ago . . . coming south from Asia in one of prehistory's great migrations.**

stone tools, campsite remains, and rock art. Some of these sacred sites, burial grounds, and rock-art galleries are off-limits to non-Aborigines, but there are many thousands of rock-art murals, particularly in Kakadu and the Cape York Peninsula in the north, that are open to tourists, often with the benefit of an Aboriginal guide.

About 8,000 years ago, the Earth began to warm. As the ice sheets melted, sea levels began to rise, and the broad plains where many generations of Aborigines had camped and hunted became shallow seas—the Gulf of Carpentaria, Torres Strait, and Bass Strait.

Vast galleries of rock art in Kakadu National Park in the Northern Territory and remote locations in the rugged Kimberley appear to tell the story of those days. Desert scenes give way to coastal ones filled with trees. Dancing figures yield to people brandishing spears. Perhaps these scenes represent conflict as lowlanders were pushed by the rising waters onto their high-ground neighbors' territory. When the water stopped rising and Australia assumed its present shape, the Aborigines were locked away on their island, hardly to be disturbed until a hot summer day in 1788 when a fleet of 11 English ships—now known as the First Fleet—sailed into Botany Bay. The first recorded words spoken by an Aboriginal to a white man were *"Warra Warra!"* or "Go away!"

Early Navigators

Australia's "discovery" by Capt. James Cook in 1770, its stolidly British-to-the-bootstraps past, and the Union Jack on the flag make it easy to overlook

The routes of European traders and explorers around Australia

the fact that the English were relative latecomers when it came to exploring the antipodes. Others were here first, although they left behind only scattered artifacts, shipwrecks, and place-names.

Look at a modern map of Australia and you can read which Europeans unveiled the continent. Tasmania, Western Australia's Cape Leeuwin, and Queensland's Groote Island are all Dutch names from the 17th century, when the continent was known as New Holland. The Northern Territory's Bonaparte Archipelago and South Australia's Fleurieu Peninsula were christened by the French. Western Australia's Houtman Abrolhos Islands, the site of early shipwrecks, is a corruption of the Portuguese phrase for "keep your eyes open." Torres Strait, which separates the tip of Queensland's Cape York from Papua New Guinea, is named for the Spaniard Luis Torres, who sailed this narrow stretch of sea in 1607 and somehow missed sighting the continent.

That is the story of this continent's earliest European history: a 3-million-square-mile (7.8 million sq km) landmass in the emptiest quarter of the South Pacific found and

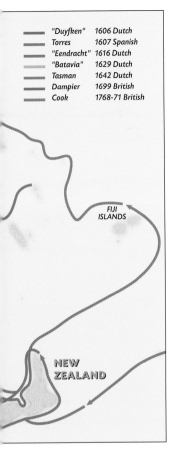

"Duyfken"	1606 Dutch
Torres	1607 Spanish
"Eendracht"	1616 Dutch
"Batavia"	1629 Dutch
Tasman	1642 Dutch
Dampier	1699 British
Cook	1768-71 British

FIJI
ISLANDS

NEW
ZEALAND

charted by a series of accidents, chance landings, missed opportunities, and coincidences.

The Great South Land

People have wondered about Australia for centuries. The ancient Greek geographer Ptolemy speculated about the existence of a great southern land, believing the weight of such a continent was necessary to balance the globe. Early Arab merchants may have pulled into Australian waters in the 13th century when they were spreading the word of Islam through Indonesia. Chinese and Malay ships may also have come here around the same time, fishing for trepang, or sea slugs, a delicacy in the markets of Canton. Fishermen from Macassar, on the Indonesian island of Sulawesi, are known to have come here since the early 16th century, catching boatloads of trepang, which they boiled and then smoked on shore while waiting for the southerly winds that would carry them back home.

Although no records exist to prove it, the Portuguese may have been the first Europeans to visit Australia. This may have occured sometime in the late 15th or early 16th century. By 1516, the Portuguese had established a stronghold on the island of Timor, less than 300 miles (480 km) from the Australian coastline. From there they traded throughout the Indonesian archipelago, buying pepper, nutmeg, and sandalwood and spreading the Catholic faith. It seems inconceivable that fortune-seeking Portuguese sea captains did not venture south. They would have known the legends of the Great South Land and heard tales from the Macassar fishermen who had been there. If their curiosity did not bring them, the fickle weather must have done so. For three months a year—from January through March—the monsoons blow strongly from the north. Sooner or later a Timor-bound ship would have been blown off course to within sight of the Australian coast. Tantalizing clues include a 15th-century-style brass cannon found near Broome, on the northwest coast of Australia, and the Dieppe Maps.

The Dieppe Maps are believed to have been copied from Portuguese sources in 1536 and suggest that the Portuguese were acquainted with Australia's eastern seaboard. It remains a matter of debate whether the lines on the map were based on exploration or were a lucky coincidence for a cartographer who sketched

> Although no records exist to prove it, the Portuguese may have been the first Europeans to visit Australia.

in the mythical Great South Land. The original map and notes were destroyed when a great earthquake struck Lisbon in 1755.

The honor of the first undisputed European sighting of the continent goes to the Dutch. In 1606, Willem Jansz sailed the *Duyfken* (meaning "Dove") from Java, entered the Gulf of Carpentaria, and landed on the western shore of the Cape York Peninsula. Like all employees of the Dutch East India Company, Jansz hoped for ivory, silks, and spices, but found instead shimmering, heat-warped horizons, a parched coast, and "wild, cruel black savages." He left unimpressed, having lost several of his men to the Aborigines. His experience set the pattern for the Dutch contact with Australia: brief landings and hurried departures.

The directors of the Dutch East India Company disapproved of idle exploration. They wanted a clear potential for profit before committing company funds or ships. From early reports, at least, that seemed to rule out the Great South Land, or New Holland as the Dutch had taken to calling it. Nonetheless, this same brusque efficiency was ultimately responsible for their mapping much of the western two-thirds of the coast.

Company navigators had discovered that the quickest way to reach Java was to sail into the Roaring Forties, south of Africa, ride the strong west winds of those latitudes across the Indian Ocean, and then turn north and sail to Indonesia. But storms and powerful westerlies often drove ships too far, too fast, and onto the west Australian coast.

The first of these was Dirk Hartog's ship, the *Eendracht,* which in 1616 landed near Shark Bay, about halfway up the coast. Hartog nailed a pewter plate to a tree to mark the occasion. (The plate was taken as a souvenir by another Dutch seaman, Willem de Vlamingh, who landed in 1697. He, in turn, left a plate of his own that was taken a century later by an errant French explorer.)

Plenty of others followed suit. In 1627 one captain badly overshot his cue to head for Java and found himself sailing near the cliffs flanking the Great Australian Bight, more than 1,000 miles (1,600 km) off course.

Two years later another ship, the *Batavia,* was wrecked off the Houtman Abrolhos Islands, near present-day Geraldton, Western Australia. While its captain, François

Captain Cook

Born in Yorkshire of humble origins, James Cook (1728–1779) found his sea legs as a merchant navy apprentice before joining the Royal Navy and rising through the ranks during the Seven Years' War in North America.

In Tahiti, after observing the transit of the planet Venus for the Royal Society in 1769, Cook read his secret Admiralty instructions to search for Terra Australis Incognita. Although he never found the mythical Great South Land, he charted New Zealand and Australia's east coast on his epic voyage before returning to England a hero two years later.

Two more Pacific expeditions (1772–1775 and 1776–1779) cemented Cook's place as the greatest British explorer. He was hailed as an enlightened leader, a man of science, and a chronicler of Pacific cultures. However, judgment deserted him in 1779, when he tried to abduct the King of Hawaii in a dispute over a stolen dinghy and was stabbed to death.

Popularly hailed as the discoverer of Australia, Cook is honored with monuments and place-names across the country. Cook's Cottage, his parents' home, now lies in Melbourne, where it is a popular tourist attraction.

Pelseart, took a few men in an open boat to Java to summon aid, the crew he left behind mutinied and murdered 125 of their shipmates and passengers. They planned to seize any rescue ship and embark on careers as pirates. Instead, Pelseart returned in force, rounded them up, and meted out savage justice. Two of the younger mutineers were spared hanging but were abandoned as castaways, earning them the dubious distinction of being Australia's first convict exiles. Their fate is unknown.

Captain Cook claimed Possession Island, northern Queensland, for Britain in 1770.

The directors of the Dutch East India Company decided to give New Holland another chance, although the only things reported by their captains were cliffs, desolate coasts, and the smoke of Aborigines' campfires. In 1642, they sent Abel Tasman to sail around the continent. He sailed the wild coastline of Tasmania (which he christened Van Diemen's Land, after the Dutch East Indies governor-general, Anthony Van Diemen), discovered the coast of New Zealand, and went on to the Fiji Islands. Tasman's voyage may rank among the great sea adventures of all time, but the directors were unimpressed. They wanted spices, bustling markets, gold, or at least a few willing souls to save. In 1644, they sent Tasman back again, but when he returned with more tales of waves crashing on cliffs, scrubby forests, and savages, they had had enough. For the next century Australia was largely left alone by the Dutch, undisturbed except for the occasional East Indies bound ship driven by storms onto the west coast.

English buccaneer and explorer William Dampier arrived in 1688 and again in 1699, with the notion of using New Holland as a staging post cum watering hole for English ships in the Pacific. He landed on the cheerless, treeless, sun-blasted coast of northwest Australia, and like the Dutch before him, went away shaking his head.

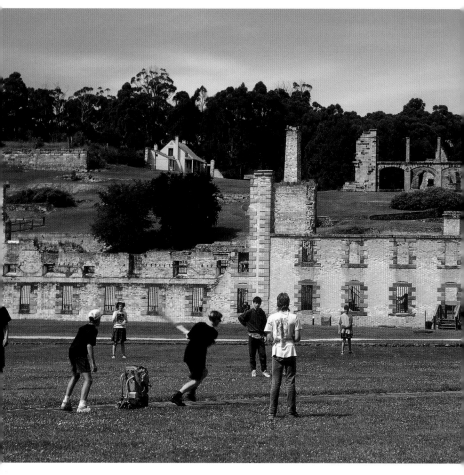

Local boys play cricket on the island of Tasmania, near the ruins of notorious Port Arthur prison.

Voyage of the *Endeavour*

In 1768, the British Admiralty and the Royal Society decided to send an expedition to Tahiti to record the transit of Venus across the face of the sun. As the transit would occur on the morning of June 3, 1769, and wouldn't happen again for another 105 years, this was a once-in-a-lifetime opportunity. A distinguished 41-year-old Royal Navy lieutenant named James Cook (see sidebar p. 36) was selected to captain the ship, a 368-ton (334 metric tons) barque called *Endeavour*. Cook was a proud, stern man, with a strong sense of duty and an equally strong sense of fair play, who had advanced on merit alone. Leading the scientific party was 25-year-old Joseph Banks—soon to be Sir Joseph Banks—an extremely wealthy young man, educated at Harrow, Eton, and Oxford and already on his way to becoming the preeminent botanist in England. Onto this crowded ship he brought his Swedish colleague Daniel Solander, artists Sydney Parkinson and Alexander Buchan, and four assistants. The ship sailed out of Plymouth on August 25, 1768, bound for the southern tip of South America and then across the Pacific. They were to record the transit of Venus, explore the South Pacific, and investigate the fabled great southern continent. In size and scope, the *Endeavour*'s expedition was the 18th-century equivalent of a moon shot.

After wrapping up their astronomical business in Tahiti, the expedition spent six months charting the coast of New Zealand. From there they turned toward the unknown east coast of New Holland. On April 19, 1770, they sighted land that is not far from the present-day border of New South Wales and Victoria. After sailing up the coast, they turned into a large bay and dropped anchor. Here they encountered so many species of plants, ferns, herbs, shrubs, and trees never before seen by European eyes that Cook decided to name the place Botany Bay. They also found rich black soils, lush meadows, and rushing creeks. The *Endeavour* continued up the coast of Australia, running aground on the Great Barrier Reef, but filling in the blank parts of the map. After repairing the *Endeavour* near present-day Cooktown, Cook claimed the eastern half of the continent in the name of George III and called it New South Wales.

Convict Colony

Despite all Captain Cook's efforts, Australia might still have been left alone had it not been for events taking place on the other side of the planet. Britain's 13 American colonies declared their independence on July 4, 1776, which meant that England could no longer ship convicts to Georgia, Virginia, and the Carolinas. A backlog of prisoners built up at the rate of about a thousand a year. In 1779, Sir Joseph Banks suggested that the Crown consider sending the prison riffraff to colonize Botany Bay. The idea drew a skeptical response. Dispatching shiploads of felons halfway around the world to New South Wales seemed an expensive way to clean out prisons. But French ambitions in the Pacific provided the government in London with a good reason to act. With America gone, England had to focus on its colonies to the east. The age-old enemy France was busily widening its sphere, establishing ports in Madagascar, combing the Indian Ocean,

[In 1770, Capt. James Cook] claimed the eastern half of the continent in the name of George III and called it New South Wales.

and sailing along the coast of Australia. A British colony in Botany Bay could be a useful foothold. The timing was impeccable: Shortly after the First Fleet landed at Botany Bay, two French ships, captained by the Comte de la Perouse, just happened to drop by.

The First Fleet

What in America was a fine piece of rhetoric to inscribe at the base of the Statue of Liberty was harsh fact down under: This nation was literally settled by huddled masses yearning to breathe free. Who wouldn't be yearning to breathe free after spending eight months chained in a stinking hold of a ship? But along with the relief at taking that first breath of fresh air and blinking in the dazzling Australian sunshine came the terror of the unknown and the grim certainty that life here was going to be rough.

On January 18, 1788, a flotilla of 11 ships, known as the First Fleet, arrived in Botany Bay. It carried 778 convicts—men, women, and children as young as nine—and 250 soldiers and colonial administrators under the command of Capt. Arthur Phillip, who became the first governor of New South Wales.

A quick look around was enough to tell the newcomers that they had no chance of establishing a settlement at Botany Bay. Cook had visited in autumn, when rains had freshened the place up, but this was summer and Botany Bay was anything but green

The routes of Australia's inland explorers slowly filled in the center of the map.

and lush. The creeks were dry, the bay was exposed, and rich meadows described by Cook were just scrub shimmering in blinding white heat. The fleet sailed 12 miles (19 km) north along the coast, between two sandstone heads that Cook had sighted but not entered. In it they discovered "the finest harbour in the world in which a thousand ships of the line may ride with the most perfect security," as Phillip put it to Lord Sydney, for whom he named the new settlement. The date was January 26, known now as Australia Day. Phillip then dispatched a ship to claim Norfolk Island, establishing an English presence and penal colony there.

Times were tough. The little colony was racked with hunger and scurvy. The soil was thin, the seed wheat had gone moldy at sea, the livestock wandered off or died. Many of the prisoners were products of London's slums and knew nothing of farming. Others were too old, ill, or weakened by the voyage to perform much work. A ship had to be sent to Cape Town, the nearest port, for emergency supplies. The Aborigines made their feelings known by spearing Phillip in the shoulder, an act that stunned the governor, who had apparently never considered that the colonists were trespassing.

> Most [convicts] were petty criminals . . . although the Irish Rebellion of 1798 provided a few genuine political prisoners.

As time passed and no supplies arrived from England, more and more convicts were shifted to Norfolk Island, where the soil was better and more fish could be caught. In 1791, the Second Fleet arrived and struggling Sydney Town began to gain its feet.

Who were the convicts? Novels such as *For the Term of His Natural Life* by Marcus Clarke (1874), an Australian classic, often portray early convicts as innocent victims who were wrongly convicted, political prisoners, or starving wretches who had stolen a cabbage to feed their children. Most, in fact, were petty criminals who had committed the kinds of crimes that might draw jail time today—or juvenile hall. Theft was the most common charge and most of the convicts were from the English slums—not Ireland, although the Irish Rebellion of 1798 provided a few genuine political prisoners.

About half drew sentences of seven years, although given the distance and cost of returning to England, transportation to Australia generally meant a life term. Skilled, lucky, wealthy, or well-behaved prisoners earned their ticket-of-leave early and were granted farms or were able to set up small businesses. Others did hard time. Floggings, leg irons, and soul-breaking work regimes were routine. Punishments were meted out with breathtaking severity—sometimes up to 300 lashes at a time, enough to leave backbones and shoulder blades exposed. Medical treatment was a dousing with a bucket of saltwater. Hard cases were sent to Norfolk Island, Van Diemen's Land (Tasmania), or Moreton Bay (Brisbane), where conditions were horrific. Weighted down with irons so tight the flesh was rubbed off their bones, working 16-hour days in the rain on short rations, and infested with lice and disease, convicts were known to commit murder simply so they could be hanged and released from misery.

Escape was fairly easy in Australia. The trouble was, there was no place to go. Some convicts headed toward the Blue Mountains, in the misguided belief that China was only a few days' hike beyond the horizon. For the most part, those who managed to get away then starved to death, died of exposure, or fell to Aborigines' spears. Some resorted to cannibalism, killing and eating their fellow absconders. Others talked their way onto Nantucket whalers that passed this way, although that was rarely a good bargain. Some Yankee whaling captains were even more brutal than the prison guards.

One woman, Mary Bryant, led an escape party north along the coast in a boat. They reached Indonesia before they were recaptured and taken back to England. Her heroism touched a chord in England. She and her group were pardoned, and she returned to her native Cornwall.

> **For generations, convict blood was a stain on the family tree. These days it is a point of pride.**

With the exception of South Australia, all of Australia's states were founded on convict labor. Transportation ended in 1868; in all, about 160,000 were sent to Australia. For generations, convict blood was a stain on the family tree. These days it is a point of pride. Having an ancestor on the First Fleet—either convict or guard—has the cachet of being a *Mayflower* descendant in Boston.

Settlement

Bengal rum was the currency of early Sydney, which by the early 1800s had the reputation of being one of the roughest ports anywhere on the Pacific. Most of the moneymaking enterprises in the colony were controlled by a military mafia known as the Rum Corps, named for the monopoly they held on that vital commodity. Alcoholism was rampant. Many officials were corrupt or incompetent or both, conducting business in a rummy fog. Convicts were effectively slaves, working for an elite group of profiteers and landowners, who kept them pliant with rum or the cat-o'-nine-tails.

In all, New South Wales did not have the kind of atmosphere that would induce decent men and women to migrate there, which was what this embryonic society needed to transform itself from a bawdy penal colony to a prosperous settlement. It needed a governor who knew how to run a tight ship, and the man selected was Capt. William Bligh, whose crew on the *Bounty* had so famously mutinied. He was dispatched to Sydney with a brief to clean up the place. Captain Bligh wasn't the lash-crazed disciplinarian of popular legend, though. He arrived in Sydney sympathetic to the little guys and sided with them against the Rum Corps. But the Rum Corps' members were army men and well entrenched. He was navy and a newcomer. On January 26, 1808, the 20th anniversary of the founding of the colony, Bligh suffered the second mutiny of his career. For the next two years, New South Wales was run by the army. Then a new governor arrived—a reform-minded Scot named Lachlan Macquarie. He broke the power of the

Rum Corps and established the first banks and the colony's own currency. He promoted expeditions across the Blue Mountains and began a series of public works and town planning projects for the fledgling colony. Macquarie even offered a name for the place, telling his masters in London of his plans to explore "the coasts of the Continent of Australia which I hope will be the name given to this country in the future."

Inland Explorers

In the early 19th century, mapmakers could sketch at least a rough outline of Australia. Matthew Flinders and George Bass had proved in 1799 that Tasmania was an island, not a long Florida-like peninsula, and between 1801 and 1803 they circumnavigated the continent. But what lay inside this 3-million-square-mile (7.8 million sq km) mass was anybody's guess.

"South Brisbane from the North Shore, Moreton Bay, Australia" (1868) by Thomas Baines

Although settlements had been established at Sydney and in Van Diemen's Land, nobody had ventured inland other than a handful of escaped convicts. There were hopes of an inland sea and hints of mineral wealth. One escaped convict stumbled upon a coal outcrop north of Sydney, and by the mid-1790s, the colony was already exporting small cargoes of coal to India. The first major barrier was a range called the Blue Mountains, steep hills about 3,000 feet (915 m) high just west of Sydney. Today this is a vacation area less than two hours from the city, but two centuries ago the mountains were formidable, forest-cloaked obstacles to progress. Several attempts were made to breach them before Gregory Blaxland, William Wentworth, and William Lawson finally succeeded in 1813.

Today [the Blue Mountains range] is a vacation area . . . but two centuries ago [they] were formidable, forest-cloaked obstacles to progress.

After a route was opened up through the mountains, settlers soon followed, spilling out into the flat, open grazing land beyond. In 1815, the town of Bathurst was founded 130 miles (209 km) west of Sydney, and exploration started in earnest. In 1824, explorers Hamilton Hume and William Hovell probed the Snowy Mountains to the south and chanced upon the Murray River near present-day Albury-Wodonga. The sight of the river flowing west, seemingly into the middle of the continent, rekindled dreams of an inland sea and a fertile heartland. Those hopes were dashed in 1830 when Charles Sturt followed the river more than a 1,000 miles (1,600 km) through the outback to its bitter end, a large brackish lake on South Australia's coastline. In 1840, a Polish count, Paul Edmund de Strzelecki, climbed the continent's highest mountain, the 7,310-foot (2,228 m) peak he named for Polish freedom fighter Gen. Tadeusz Kosciuszko.

The Desert Center: Early expeditions sketched in the southeastern corner of the continent, but vast empty reaches still awaited explorers. Edward Eyre was the first of these, crossing the continent east to west through the Nullarbor Plain in 1841. This 800-mile-wide (1,287 km) stretch of scabby earth was a brutal introduction to Australia's interior. Eyre and one of his Aborigine guides, Wylie, survived. They stumbled into Albany, Western Australia, after four months. Less fortunate was Ludwig Leichhardt, a Prussian-born immigrant, who, after crossing 3,000 miles (4,800 km) of outback between Brisbane and Port Essington, vanished without a trace while attempting to cross Australia's Red Centre in 1848. In 1855, Augustus Gregory successfully crossed from the Victoria River country in the Northern Territory, around the Gulf of Carpentaria, south to Rockhampton and finally Brisbane. Three years later, he and his brother Francis trekked across Queensland to learn what had happened to Leichhardt. The German's fate remained a mystery, but the brothers found a passage through the glaring salt lakes and on to Adelaide.

Burke & Wills: Australia's most famous and elaborate inland expedition left Melbourne on a midwinter's day in 1860. Robert O'Hara Burke and William John Wills led the expedition, and the government financed it lavishly in the hope that it would discover rich pastoral lands to the north. The goal was the Gulf of Carpentaria, more than 2,500 miles (4,000 km) away. At a spot called Cooper Creek in the

South Australian outback, the party divided. Four of the group remained as a sort of base camp, while Burke and Wills and two associates, John King and Charles Grey, pressed on, traveling light and fast and impatient for glory.

They reached the gulf in February—in the peak of Australia's summer heat, when the temperatures may soar to more than 120°F (50°C) and the monsoon rains soak the crocodile-infested wetlands. Their progress on the final push to the coast was painfully slow.

They began retracing their footsteps immediately, but the clock was running down. Grey died and the three survivors pressed on, weak and dazed, through the desert, traveling by moonlight, eventually throwing away most of their supplies in a frantic bid to get back to base camp. Burke, Wills, and King arrived seven hours too late. They found a message carved into a giant coolabah tree instructing them to dig for a cache of supplies their colleagues had left on the off chance they returned. They discovered the supplies but lacked the strength to push on to Melbourne. The expedition's two celebrated leaders perished. King was nursed back to health by passing Aborigines. The famous "Dig Tree" still stands and can be seen by expeditions traveling on the Strzelecki Track.

Stuart & Other Explorers: At around the same time, a tough Scot named John McDouall Stuart was trying to complete his own crossing of the continent. He had traveled north from Adelaide bound for near where Darwin is today, but disease, hostile Aborigines, and unbearable heat had held him back. He finally reached the Arafura Sea on July 24, 1862. Burke and Wills had performed the first south-to-north trek, but Stuart managed the more difficult feat of returning. Even so, he barely survived, staggering back blind and hardly able to stand. His journey marked the apex of inland exploration and resolved the matter of an inland lake: There was none. It also established a route that would be followed fairly closely in 1872 by the telegraph line and later the Stuart Highway, the trucking lifeline between Adelaide and Darwin.

Expeditions struggled through the Western Australian deserts in the 1870s. Ernest Giles explored the Great Victorian Desert in 1875 and the Gibson Desert the following year, the latter named for his partner, Alfred Gibson, who died on the journey. Giles's two expeditions were the last gasps of Australia's heroic age of exploration. By the 1880s, most of the interior had been explored, although some isolated pockets still remained untouched for another 50 years. As recently as the 1980s, clans of desert Aborigines were still leading a traditional lifestyle, as they had for 50,000 years.

Burke & Wills

Of all the explorers of Australia, Burke and Wills are the most fêted, despite the disastrous end to their expedition. Although Irish-born Robert O'Hara Burke lacked exploration experience, he was chosen as leader, and massive funds backed the expedition. Camels were imported from India and four Indian camel drivers joined the party of 19 men, 26 camels, 23 horses, 6 wagons, and 20 tons (18 tonnes) of supplies, enough for two years.

A crowd of 15,000 gathered in Melbourne on August 20, 1860, to bid farewell to the explorers they expected to bring glory to the colony. When news of the expedition's failure came back (one newspaper called it "one prolonged blunder throughout"), a Commission of Enquiry issued a scathing report but applauded the bravery of Burke and Wills, who were given state funerals.

Gold

Gold was the single biggest force in Australia's transformation from a clutter of struggling settlements on the rim of the world into one of Britain's most prosperous colonies. The first real gold rush began in May 1851 after a prospector named Edward Hargraves found gold at Ophir, near Bathurst, New South Wales, and bragged about it. Almost overnight a tent city of more than a thousand diggers sprang up in the mud, and thousands more fortune-seekers from around Australia quit their jobs and raced for the diggings. The human stampede was so big that employers in Melbourne, alarmed at the sudden loss of workers and envious at New South Wales's sudden prosperity, offered a reward for anybody who succeeded in finding gold close to their city.

They didn't have long to wait. Within weeks gold was discovered at Clunes, and then came the fabulous finds around Ballarat. Gold seemed to be everywhere in Victoria. Before the end of the year, people made enormously rich finds at Castlemaine and Bendigo, and 20,000 prospectors were scouring the hills looking for more. Word quickly spread overseas, and soon Chinese, English, Irish, and Americans were pouring into Australia at a rate of 90,000 a year.

Eureka Stockade: Anybody could do it. For the first time in Australia's history, the common man had a shot at serious wealth. There were no big mining companies, just small operators. To try to keep control of events, the authorities imposed a stiff tax of 30 shillings a month ($7.50, a sizeable sum at that time) on prospectors, whether they were successful or not. Resentment at this tax smoldered in the camps and finally boiled over in November 1854 in an uprising at Eureka Stockade, a hastily built fort near the Irish diggings just east of Ballarat. This was the closest thing Australia ever had to outright civil war.

> Gold was the single biggest force in Australia's transformation ... into one of Britain's most prosperous colonies.

Prospectors were already simmering over the murder of one of their number because the authorities had discharged the hotelkeeper whom they believed was responsible. The volatile mix of gold diggers included German and Italian revolutionaries, Irish Republicans, and hot-tempered Americans. At a rally they burned their licenses, proclaimed their defiance of the law, and set up a barricade. They raised a flag—a white Southern Cross on a blue field (notably without the Union Jack). The government responded savagely and on December 3 crushed the rebellion. The 10-minute fight left 6 soldiers and as many as 30 miners dead. A number

"Australian Gold Diggings," circa 1855, by Edwin Stocqueler (1829–circa 1880)

of miners were arrested and charged with high treason. Melbourne juries, however, refused to convict. In the political fallout after the Eureka Stockade fight, miners won many of the rights they had campaigned for: the abolition of the hated licenses and the right to vote and run for office. The following year their leader, Peter Lalor, who had lost an arm in the battle, was elected to Parliament.

To this day the Eureka Stockade flag remains a symbol of defiance to overbearing authority, and a spacious new museum dedicated to the uprising and the early life of Ballarat stands on the site of the battle. The prodigious wealth pouring in from the gold diggings quickly transformed muddy shantytowns into elegant cities, with gardens, wide streets, mansions, and grand public buildings. Victoria's gold rushes were the biggest, but the 1860s and '70s brought finds in New South Wales, at Forbes and Young. Queensland had the white quartz reefs of Gympie, then the rich beds of Charters

Australians waded into history and a hail of bullets at Gallipoli, Turkey, on April 25, 1915.

Towers, Palmer River, and Cape York. Prospectors went on to Pine Creek in the Northern Territory, and by the 1880s, Halls Creek in the Kimberley, in the remote northwest. Prospectors scrambled for the Pilbara, then the Murchison field and Western Australia's Southern Cross. The last of the huge gold strikes was at Coolgardie and Kalgoorlie in the 1890s. Most of the sites are marked, and the towns' ornate goldfield-style architecture, which characterized the optimism and wealth, are monuments to these early days.

Federation

On New Year's Day, 1901, a crowd gathered in Sydney's Centennial Park to witness the birth of a nation: the Commonwealth of Australia. Until then, the continent had been a patchwork of colonies, each of which stubbornly set its own time zone, issued its own postage stamps, and imposed confiscatory customs duties on goods crossing its borders. There was little cooperation, only competition. Colonies could not even agree on which railway gauge to use, a "mental paralysis" that dumbfounded humorist Mark Twain when he swung through this part of the world in 1895.

After years of painstaking diplomacy, with the help of compromises and nudged along by a particularly destructive drought and recession, the colonies agreed to federate in 1901. The new constitution, thrashed out in a second-floor suite in Melbourne's Windsor Hotel, was not exactly a radical piece of legislation. Queen Victoria and her successors would remain head of state, the Crown's local representative would still be a regally appointed governor-general, and Britain's parliamentary style of government would prevail. In fact, the British Parliament could still override any legislation passed in the Australian Parliament, and for legal matters the final court of appeal would be the Privy Council in London. In essence, Mother England's six Australian colonies had simply agreed to cease their sibling rivalry. Edmund Barton, a Sydney lawyer, became the first prime minister. He put aside whatever native New South Wales parochialism he may have harbored and moved to rival Melbourne, which was to be the capital until a neutral city could be agreed upon. The six states (the present states, less the Northern Territory, which was a part of New South Wales) remained powerful, but shared a vision: Australia would be stable, white, prosperous, white, protected by trade tariffs and social welfare legislation—and white. One of the first laws they passed was to restrict Asian immigration, the beginning of the infamous White Australia policy that lasted until the late 1960s. As Australia's second prime minister, Alfred Deakin, put it in a remarkably candid moment: "It is not the bad qualities but the good qualities of these alien races that make them dangerous to us. It is their inexhaustible energy, their power of applying themselves to new tasks, their endurance, and their low standard of living that make them such competitors." And so would-be migrants from Asia had to take a literacy test, in any European language the immigration officer cared to name. Gaelic was a favorite. Not surprisingly, few passed.

Because nobody could agree on which city should be the capital, the fledgling government decided to create one from scratch. In 1909, they settled on a bit of pastureland on the Monaro Tablelands, about 200 miles (320 km) southwest of Sydney. Two years later, the New South Wales government ceded the 9,650-square-mile (25,000 sq km) parcel of land to the federal government. Chicago architect Walter Burley-Griffin was selected to design the city; it would be called Canberra, from an Aboriginal word meaning either "meeting place" or "women's breasts," depending on who is doing the telling.

World War I & Gallipoli

After a good deal of bureaucratic haggling and compromise, Australia achieved nationhood by a stroke of the royal pen. There had been no death-or-glory freedom fighters, no midnight rides by a Paul Revere, no Bunker Hill battle to forge a unifying national myth in blood. But Australia didn't have long to wait.

> On New Year's Day, 1901, a crowd gathered in Sydney's Centennial Park to witness the birth of a nation: the Commonwealth of Australia. Until then, the continent had been a patchwork of colonies.

In August 1914, Britain went to war with Germany, which meant that Australia, as part of the British Empire, was at war also. In a frenzy of patriotism, more than 20,000 Aussies enlisted in the first two months, eager for bold overseas adventure. They got it starting at 4:30 a.m. on April 25, 1915, on a cliff-lined coast in Turkey, near a town called Gallipoli. Winston Churchill, who was then First Lord of the Admiralty, had decided to open a new front by taking the Dardanelles and ordered a multinational force to attack from the sea. The Turks directed withering fire onto the beaches. For the next eight months the allied troops clung to the exposed beachhead.

Both sides saw desperate fighting and horrific carnage. Although Australians had fought for Britain in the Sudan campaign and in the Boer War, this was the first time

EXPERIENCE: Remembering Anzac Day

The first Anzac Day march took place a couple of years after World War I ended, and the occasion grew in stature with the passing of the years. The motto for the day is "Lest We Forget." Ceremonies all over the country begin before dawn with a solemn religious service—always well attended despite the cold early hour—that progresses into a parade.

If the word "parade" makes you think of floats and fire trucks on the Fourth of July, think again. There are a few martial bands, but mostly you see row after row of war veterans in Sunday suits and regimental ties, wearing their war medals and marching in step with their battalions. Crowds gather on the sidewalks, waving flags and calling out their thanks. It can be a haunting spectacle. Sometimes the only sound is the rasp of shoe leather and the clinking of hundreds of campaign medals.

Later the gray-haired vets will gather at the local pubs, drink, and remember.

The dawn ceremonies that start off Anzac Day are held at war memorials across the country. Well-known services are at the **Australian War Memorial** in Canberra, the **Shrine** in Melbourne, and the **Cenotaph** in Sydney's Martin Place. The service is generally only for veterans and invited dignitaries, but in recent years, veterans' families have been encouraged to attend. The same applies to the march, but anyone is welcome to join the spectators who line the streets. Newspapers print march gathering points and routes, and the **Returned Services League** *(rsl.org.au)* is instrumental in organizing marches. Other details can be found on government defense and war veteran websites: *dva.gov.au, awm.gov.au,* and *defence.gov.au.*

they had fought as Australians. Australia's national myths were born at Gallipoli, out of courage, mateship, and the understated heroics of men such as John Simpson Kirkpatrick, who with his donkey braved the open ground to retrieve those who had been wounded, until he himself was killed by a sniper. In all, 8,587 men from the Australian and New Zealand Army Corps (ANZAC) were killed. The French, English, Indians, and especially the Turks suffered far greater losses at Gallipoli, something Australians often overlook in their patriotic fervor on Anzac Day (April 25). They also tend to overlook Australia's much greater losses in France, at the Somme (23,000) and Ypres (38,000).

World War II

World War II marked a turning point in Australia's view of the world. "Without inhibitions of any kind, I make it quite clear that Australia looks to America, free of any pangs as to our traditional links or kinship with the United Kingdom," said John Curtin, Australia's prime minister, after Singapore fell to the Japanese in February 1942. Japanese planes began bombing Darwin that same month and Broome in March.

Australia was faced with the very real possibility of a Japanese invasion. For the United States, Australia offered a last-chance Pacific foothold near Asia. Three months later a combined U.S. and Australian naval force stopped the Japanese fleet in the Battle of the Coral Sea. Australian slouch-hatted infantry soldiers then fought a brutal guerrilla war in the Papua New Guinea Highlands to save Australia's colonial outpost at Port Moresby. Its fall would have given the Japanese a springboard into mainland Australia.

Although the Japanese came within 30 miles (48 km) of the town, the Australians fought a hand-to-hand campaign and repelled them to the island's north coast. They were assisted by Papua New Guinea inhabitants, known as the Fuzzy Wuzzy Angels. In Thailand, thousands of Australian prisoners of war died of abuse, starvation, and disease while being forced to build the infamous Burma Railway. Others were saved by the unflagging efforts of Edward "Weary" Dunlop, their fellow prisoner and an army surgeon who became a symbol of Australia's unflinching yet soft-spoken style of heroism.

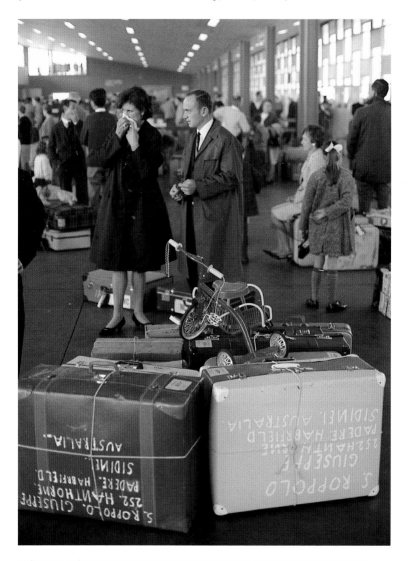

In the 1950s and '60s, more than two million New Australians arrived at steamship terminals.

Started as a service to safeguard swimmers, surf rescue quickly became a sport.

New Australians

After World War II, Australia went through enormous changes. When the government launched one of the greatest migration programs of the 20th century, more than two million immigrants poured into the country. According to the census of 1947, about 98 percent of Australians were Anglo-Saxon. Now "New Australians" were coming in from all over war-ravaged Europe—Italy, Germany, Yugoslavia, Greece, and the Baltic countries. As long as they were white, they were welcome, and the government would underwrite the cost of their passage. A berth on one of the liners could be had for as little as ten English pounds (A$23 at the current exchange rate).

The newcomers settled in with surprisingly little friction. For one thing, plenty of jobs could be had all around in those prosperous postwar years, so nobody felt cheated.

Factories were sprouting up, steel mills and coal mines were busy, and the government was spending big money on major public works such as the Snowy Mountains Hydroelectric Scheme, an enormous project. There were also thousands of new suburban houses to build for this booming population. The country positively oozed good health and high spirits. Bronzed Aussie tennis players won at Wimbledon, and the nation's swimmers were the finest in the world. When the Olympics came to Melbourne in 1956, the home team walked off with 35 medals—an unheard-of success for such a small population.

The age was also an artless one. Australians wince today when they see old newsreel footage and hear the narrator's cheerfully jingoistic, sexist, and racist observations. Blokes were blokes, and the women stayed home. Aborigines were not citizens and could not vote until 1967. For all the influx of other peoples after the war, Australia remained culturally a stodgy pocket of the British Empire.

Time for Change

It wasn't all sunny isolation. Always obliging to its allies, Canberra signed up for the Korean War and conflicts in Malaya and Borneo. It let Britain use a patch of South Australian desert to test atomic bombs and allowed the United States to set up spy-satellite monitoring posts around the continent. In 1962, Australia followed the U.S. into Vietnam. But as the body bags came back—Australia lost about 500 lives in Vietnam—a vocal antiwar movement sprang up. In Australia, as elsewhere, the late sixties blossomed into a time of liberalization, questioning, and protest. Australia was changing rapidly. A charismatic, bushy-browed giant named Gough Whitlam emerged to lead the Australian Labor Party to victory in 1972 with the slogan, "It's time." The time brought healthcare reforms, free college education, the formal end of the White Australia policy, widespread new social programs, and increased support for the arts. Like Camelot of the U.S., the Australian version lasted about three years, ending abruptly in November 1975, although with considerably less brutality. Whitlam's administration could not pass through Parliament the spending legislation necessary to keep the government running. On November 11, the governor-general, Sir John Kerr, exercised a rarely

After World War II, Australia went through enormous changes. . . . "New Australians" were coming in from all over war-ravaged Europe.

used and highly controversial prerogative: He sacked the Whitlam government and declared a general election. Conspiracy theorists have dined out on it ever since. Was it a coup d'état? Was the CIA involved? What really happened? The only thing beyond dispute is that four weeks later Whitlam lost the election in a landslide, and Malcolm Fraser, an equally physically towering but very conservative sheep grazier from Victoria, became Australia's next prime minister.

Pacific Rim & Republic

Alarm clocks rang all over Australia at four o'clock one morning in September 1983, and a sleepy nation got out of bed to watch live TV coverage of a yacht race on the other side of the world. Australians held their collective breath while their yacht, *Australia II,* knifed through the waters of Narragansett Bay in Rhode Island. An American yacht was bobbing somewhere astern. A horn blared. The race was over. Australia had won the America's Cup.

Back in Sydney, people danced in the streets, free beer flowed in the pubs, and Bob Hawke, the new Labor prime minister, crowed on national TV that any boss who didn't give his workers this historic day off was "a bum." For Australians this was more than a great sporting triumph. It was a catharsis, dispelling lingering doubts about whether their remote country, with its tiny, fiercely blue-collar population and convict roots, could make it in the glamour leagues. For many it seemed to kick-start the roaring eighties. A confident, outward-looking Australia strode onto the world stage as a player in its own right, not as England's wild colonial cousin.

It was the time of the global bull market, and Australia dealt itself in with alacrity. The dollar was floated on the world exchange, trade barriers were lowered, and foreign banks were allowed to set up shop in Australia. Meanwhile, Australians headed overseas, buying 20th Century Fox, the London *Times,* and the national telephone company in Chile. *Crocodile Dundee,* Foster's lager, and "tossing another shrimp on the barbie" became part of the world's vernacular.

The clock could not be turned back. In 1988, as the country started its third century since colonization, Australians began to ask themselves questions about who they were and where they belonged in the world. After 200 years of being distracted by links to Europe, they suddenly realized they had box seats to the economic theater where it seemed much of the global monetary action was going to be in the 21st century—Asia. They began to think of themselves in Asian terms, rather than as a far-flung corner of England.

Asian countries had already devoured the majority of Australia's exports, Asian

Poms

Pom or Pommy is a slang term for British, as in "thrash the Poms," a common cry when British cricket or rugby teams tour. Akin to Limey, it is primarily used as a good-hearted gibe, though many Brits regard Pom as derogatory, reflecting the love-hate relationship between Australians and the British. Because Australia was first settled by exiled convicts and then waves of British migrants, many Australians identified themselves as British subjects well into the 1950s, despite being scorned as uncouth colonials. Broad postwar migration strengthened a divergent national identity, but strong ties, with a hint of resentment, linger. The origins of the word are disputed, though Pom most likely comes from pomegranate, early Australian rhyming slang for immigrant.

immigration flourished, and an Australian initiative drove the founding of the Asian-Pacific Economic Cooperation Forum. The Labor government exhorted Australians to look East and promoted multiculturalism to break down the barriers of xenophobia, but out in the broad sunny suburbs of the cities, disquiet grew at this rapid shift in the national identity.

Promising an end to modern Australia's growing climate of political correctness, the conservative government of John Howard came to power and changed the political landscape over the next decade, taking a harder line against refugees, unions, Aborigines, and welfare. At the same time, it turned away from multiculturalism and reaffirmed

"Tinnies" or "stubbies" of beer quench the thirst at the William Creek hotel, near Oodnadatta.

traditional ties to the U.S. and Britain, even though many Australians questioned why the Union Jack was still on the flag and the English monarch on the currency. Opinion polls suggested the majority of Australians favored a republic, but a 1999 referendum to dump the Queen was defeated when republicans split the vote by bickering over the best model for a republic.

Although the cultural focus swung away from Asia, trade was unstoppable. The China boom drove a resurgent Australian economy into the 21st century, as the country scrambled to dig up and ship out coal, iron ore, and other highly profitable minerals.

Going forward, a prosperous Australia brims with optimism and an independent spirit. In 2007, a new Labor government under Mandarin-fluent prime minister Kevin Rudd promised a new direction. Rudd was replaced in 2010 by Australia's first female leader, Julia Gillard, before regaining power in 2013. Regardless of who rules, there seems no stopping Australia's economic success story. ∎

The Arts

Anyone who still thinks that Australians are simply sports-mad Philistines should consider that touring art exhibitions regularly attract more than 500,000 visitors. Or they could listen to the squabbling over which painting should really have won the Archibald Prize—Australia's most prestigious art award, given to the best portrait painted within the previous year.

Literature

Aborigines were the earliest storytellers on the continent, with a rich heritage of Dreamtime tales to draw upon. Their oral tradition was handed down through stories told around campfires. The first Aborigine to have work published was David Unaipon, whose book *Native Legends* came out in 1929. Since then several translations of Dreamtime legends have been published, such as *Joe Nangan's Dreaming: Aboriginal Legends of the Northwest* (1976) and a variety of children's books illustrated by Aboriginal artists. One good source of Aboriginal literature, both modern and ancient, is Magabala Books, an Aboriginal publishing house based in Broome on the remote northwest coast of Western Australia. Paul Marshall's *Raparapa: Stories from the Fitzroy River Drovers* (1995) gives an Aborigine's perspective on life on the remote Kimberley stations. Some of the best books about Aborigines are *The Chant of Jimmie Blacksmith* (1972) by Thomas Kenneally, Bruce Chatwin's offbeat *The Songlines* (1988), and David Malouf's *Remembering Babylon* (1994).

White Australia's literature began with the journals of such explorers as Edward Eyre, Charles Sturt, and Ernest Giles. Some are still available in bookshops (look under Australiana) and make a nice read if you're crossing the country on the Indian Pacific Railway or traveling up to Alice Springs on the Ghan. It wasn't until the latter part of the 19th century that Australian writers began to tackle their bizarre landscapes and convict heritage. Marcus Clarke's *For the Term of His Natural Life* (1874) tells the tale of Rufus Dawes, a wealthy young gentleman wrongfully convicted of murder and sentenced to transportation to Australia. He endures the penal colonies at Port Arthur and Macquarie Harbour but in the end retrieves name and fortune. Gold rushes and bushrangers provided material for Rolf Boldrewood's *Robbery Under Arms* (1888), another Australian classic.

> Aborigines were the earliest storytellers on the continent, with a rich heritage of Dreamtime tales to draw upon.

In the 1890s, Australia's strongest national myths were forged by a handful of journalists and poets. Perhaps the best known is the balladeer and humorist Andrew Barton Paterson, who borrowed his pen name "Banjo" from a family racehorse. His ballads and yarns of swagmen, shearers, outlaws, and squatters celebrated a freedom that Australians, and the rest of the world, still like to imagine exists. He is best known for "The Man from Snowy River" (1890), "Clancy of the Overflow" (1889), and the lyrics of Australia's unofficial national anthem, "Waltzing Matilda." Henry Lawson, a dour and

Aboriginal rock group Yothu Yindi's lead singer, Mandawuy Yunupingu

much less folksy contemporary of Paterson's, is arguably Australia's finest short-story writer. While he could be as ironically humorous as Banjo, his social commentary goes much deeper. "The Drover's Wife" (1892), about a woman sitting up all night to protect her young children against a snake that has crawled into a crack in the wall of their bush shack, is a haunting story of strength, struggle, and aching loneliness.

Arthur Hoey Davis, writing under the name Steele Rudd, created two of Australia's best loved characters, Dad and Dave, in *On Our Selection* (1899). These two wide-eyed bumpkins went on to greater glory in a radio serial and in novels, plays, and films.

Poet, essayist, and songwriter Andrew Barton "Banjo" Paterson (1864–1941)

Coupled with C. J. Dennis's verse novel about a city-bred larrikin (mischievous young chap), *The Sentimental Bloke,* it reinforced the popular image of the good-hearted Aussie battler.

Australia's outback landscapes began to find their way into novels in the 1920s, helped along by English novelist D. H. Lawrence, who published *Kangaroo* in 1923. Fifteen years later came Xavier Herbert's sweeping epic *In Capricornia* (1938), with its vivid and often brutal descriptions of life in the tropical landscapes of Australia's far north. Nobel Prize winner Patrick White used the outback as a backdrop for such major works as *Voss* (1957), a novel about a mad explorer trying to cross a desert, supposedly based on the life of Ludwig Leichhardt.

If you are looking for something evocative but a trifle easier to read, try Nevil Shute's 1950 classic *A Town Like Alice* or Colleen McCullough's *The Thorn Birds* (1979).

Among the nonfiction, Robert Hughes's *The Fatal Shore* (1987) is a gripping and deeply thought-out history of Australia's years as a convict colony. Sarah Murgatroyd's lively and engaging *The Dig Tree* (2002) reads like a novel and tells the tale of the ill-fated Burke and Wills expedition in 1860. In the rugged Kimberley, Mary Durack chronicled three generations of her family history in the 1959 outback classic *Kings in Grass Castles* and its 1983 sequel, *Sons in the Saddle*. In 1981, 87-year-old A. B. Facey stepped seemingly out of nowhere with an autobiography that began when he went to work at the age of eight on a farm in the outback and followed his adventures through Gallipoli and his life in Western Australia. *A Fortunate Life* went on to sell more than 600,000 copies—a blockbuster in the tiny Australian market.

Over the past 55 years Australians have shifted their literary gaze from the outback that few of them really know to the cities and suburbs where they live. Ruth Park's *Harp in the South* (1948) and *A Poor Man's Orange* (1949) are set in the inner Sydney slums and have never been out of print. Helen Garner's 1984 novel *Monkey Grip* is about sex and drugs in the inner Melbourne suburb of Carlton during the 1970s. Australian writers achieving international success are headed by Nobel Prize winner Patrick White (1912–1990), while the 2009 literature winner, South African-born J. M. Coetzee

(1940–) now lives in Adelaide and is an Australian citizen. Peter Carey (1943–) has won the Booker Prize twice and explores Australian themes in novels such as *Oscar and Lucinda* (1988) and *True History of the Kelly Gang* (2000). Thomas Keneally (1935–) is another Booker winner and leading contemporary with works such as *Schindler's Ark* (1982; made into the film *Schindler's List* by Steven Spielberg). Authors exploring Australian society include Christos Tsiolkas (1965–), whose *The Slap* (2008) is an unflattering portrait of modern, multicultural, middle-class Australia.

Theater & Dance

For most of its history, Australia was dismissed as a cultural wasteland by the rest of the world and even by Australians themselves. This "cultural cringe" was partly a hangover from colonial days, when sophistication was considered an inverse ratio of distance from Europe. Certainly Sydney is about as far as you can go from London's West End theaters or the gilt of the Paris Opéra. Australians who aspired to careers in theater and opera were obliged to head overseas. Opera singers Dame Nellie Melba and, much later, Dame Joan Sutherland did just that. So did pianist Percy Grainger, best known for his 1908 composition "In an English Country Garden." "Sing 'em muck," Dame Nellie reportedly told a performer heading down under, "that's all they understand."

If that was ever the case, it isn't anymore. Australia not only has a world-famous opera house, it also has homegrown talent to put in it. The Australian Opera Company, the Australian Ballet, and the Sydney Dance Company—New South Wales's first profes-sional ballet troupe, founded in 1971—are all based at the Sydney Opera House.

Across the bay from the Opera House, the Aboriginal Islander Dance Theatre performs traditional and modern Aboriginal dance. Melbourne competes with Sydney to be the theater capital of Australia, and Adelaide's Festival Centre is said to have even better acoustics than Sydney's Opera House. Adelaide's biennial Festival of the Arts is huge.

Formed as a training ground for actors, directors, and set designers, the National Insti-tute for Dramatic Arts (NIDA) has launched Mel Gibson and other international stars. In Melbourne's suburb of Carlton, experimental theaters La Mama and the Pram Factory give fledgling playwrights an opportunity to stage their works. Alumni include David Williamson (1942–), Australia's most successful playwright. His credits include *Don's Party, The Club,* and the screenplay for the 1981 film *Gallipoli.*

Music

Australia's mainstream musical tastes tend to revolve around American-style light rock, with major radio stations playing a familiar

Rock Stars

Australia has contributed enormously to the global talent pool, from Johnny O'Keefe in the 1950s ("Real Wild Child") to superstar rock groups such as INXS, AC/DC, Silverchair, Men at Work, Little River Band, the Bee Gees, Black Sorrows, and Midnight Oil. Pop leading lights range from Olivia Newton-John and Kylie Minogue to Grammy-grabbing Gotye. Not everyone looked overseas for success, however. Cold Chisel, an iconic band of the 1970s and '80s, is scarcely known outside of Australia but is arguably its greatest rock group. On the indigenous front, Aboriginal rock group Yothu Yindi successfully incorporated age-old tribal rhythms and the didgeridoo into the mainstream with politically charged songs such as "Treaty."

blend of Top 40 hits and baby boomers' golden oldies. Government efforts to stem this cultural tide by requiring stations to include at least 20 percent local music in their programs, for example, have come to little because much of the local sound is indistinguishable from that produced in the United States or Europe.

Country: Country music has deep roots in Australia as it does in America. As with rock, it was strongly influenced by American stars in the early years—Aussie performers used to give themselves names like "Tex"—although Australians have always included a healthy dose of outback humor and bush themes in their music.

Tamworth, a modest-size town in rural New South Wales, about 200 miles (322 km) northwest of Sydney, is Australia's version of Nashville. Every January it hosts a popular country music festival at which the coveted Golden Guitar award is given to the year's top performer. One former winner who has gone on to a successful recording career in Nashville is Kasey Chambers, who grew up on Australia's desolate Nullarbor Plain.

Probably the best known Australian country star was Slim Dusty, who died in 2003 at the age of 76, after a lifetime of touring outback towns and Aborigine communities. He wrote hundreds of songs about living in the bush, the most famous being his iconic 1957 hit, "The Pub with No Beer," which the congregation sang at his funeral.

The 2,679-seat concert hall is the heart of the Sydney Opera House.

Jazz & Classical: Australia has world-class jazz musicians such as trumpeters James Morrison and Bob Barnard, pianist Graeme Bell, and multi-instrumented Don Burrows. Barry Tuckwell, one of the world's leading virtuosos on the French horn, is an Australian, and Australia's composers include Richard Meale, Peter Sculthorpe, Nigel Butterley, and Anne Boyd. The Australian Broadcasting Corporation maintains six independent symphony orchestras around the country.

Cinema

Australia got off to a quick start in the film industry. A cinema opened on Pitt Street, Sydney, in 1896, only a year after the Lumière brothers opened the world's first cinema in Paris. Four years later, in Melbourne, a Salvation Army officer named Joseph Perry produced *Soldiers of the Cross,* which film historians regard as the world's first genuine movie in the sense that it relied on a plot, not just visuals. It premiered at the Melbourne Town Hall in 1901 and was shown in the United States the following year. In 1906, the world's first feature film, *The Story of the Kelly Gang,* was also produced in Melbourne.

Although it lasted only 40 minutes, short by today's standards, it was considerably longer and more involved than the typical ten-minute offerings of the age.

Australia had a thriving film industry throughout the silent film era, and more than 250 movies were produced here. Perhaps the most popular was an adaptation of C. J. Dennis's verse novel, *The Sentimental Bloke,* in 1919. But Hollywood outshone the Australian film industry in the 1930s and helped to establish the American cultural hegemony in movies, pop music, and TV that Australia has never been able to shake.

Cinematic high points during World War II included Charles Chauval's *Forty Thousand Horsemen* (1940), about the charge of the Australian Light Horse at Beersheba in 1917, and the 1942 documentary *Kokoda Front Line!,* which captured the toughness of the New Guinea campaign and earned cameraman Damien Parer an Oscar. It wasn't until 1968, and the establishment of the Australian Film Institute to promote Australian cinema, that local filmmaking began a renaissance that continues to this day. The 1970s saw an emphasis on introspective productions, such as Peter Weir's *Picnic at Hanging Rock* (1975) and *My Brilliant Career* (1979), which launched the international career of actress Judy Davis. In the 1980s, Australian filmmaking became more commercial, with *Gallipoli* (1981), *Breaker Morant* (1980), *The Man from Snowy River* movies, and *Mad Max* (1979) and its sequels. In 1986, Paul Hogan's *Crocodile Dundee* became Australia's first international blockbuster, and it remains the most profitable Australian film ever made.

Over the past few years, Australian filmmakers have relied on Australia's unique brand of offbeat humor, with quirky films like *Strictly Ballroom* (1992); *The Adventures of Priscilla, Queen of the Desert* (1994); *Muriel's Wedding* (1994); *Babe* (1995); and *The Castle* (1997). A moving recent film, *Rabbitproof Fence* (2002) tells the story of three Aboriginal children who find their way home through the bush after being taken from their parents by the authorities. *Japanese Story* (2003), starring Toni Collette, is a skillful romance set in Western Australia's rugged Pilbara region. But the biggest thing to hit Australian cinemas in recent years is Baz Luhrmann's *Australia* (2008). Part social commentary, part western cliché, mostly rousing historical romance, it pitted Nicole Kidman and Hugh Jackman against the stunning backdrop of Western Australia's Kimberley region.

Aussiewood

Australia is immensely proud of its many actors, directors, cinematographers, and other film technicians who have found success in Hollywood. National pride swells when Nicole Kidman, Russell Crowe, Cate Blanchett, Naomi Watts, Hugh Jackman, Eric Bana, Geoffrey Rush, or Mel Gibson—dubbed the Gumleaf Mafia—shine at the Oscars. Many well-known actors, like Gibson, are graduates of the prestigious National Institute of Dramatic Arts in Sydney, and film schools across the country continue to pump out graduates who eye Hollywood as the main prize.

Television

The first image on Australian TV was of Brisbane's old convict-built windmill, broadcast to Ipswich, Queensland, in 1934. Regular television broadcasting did not begin until 1956, and color TV reached Australia only in 1974.

From the start, American fare dominated Australian television, with early lineups including *Lassie, Father Knows Best,* and *Hopalong Cassidy.* So it remains today.

Australian television producers have also tended to borrow heavily from successful American themes. Late-night shows have hosts who shamelessly style themselves after David Letterman, Jay Leno, or Conan O'Brien, and medical dramas bear a striking resemblance to *ER*. The Australian versions of *60 Minutes, Wheel of Fortune,* and *Big Brother,* as well as *Australian Idol,* are straightforward syndications.

This is a young nation. A 19th-century building rates as "old" here, and 18th-century structures are almost unknown.

For years Australians were vaguely embarrassed by their own locally conceived television, which seemed amateurish in comparison with slick American productions. No longer. Smartly produced Australian shows are gaining ground, and although American fare still takes up many broadcasting hours, more of the top-rated shows are homegrown. One top-rating comedy-drama is family-based *Packed to the Rafters,* though cheaper lifestyle and reality television programs dominate local production, such as TV cook-off *MasterChef.* Reality-based *Bondi Rescue,* following the exploits of lifesavers on Bondi Beach, is now shown around the world.

Other popular Aussie TV exports include the evergreen children's show *Bananas in Pajamas,* the soap opera *Home & Away,* and *Neighbours,* the show where pop singer Kylie Minogue got her start. Australia's best known TV star was the late Steve Irwin, aka the Crocodile Hunter, whose wildlife shows were a hit around the world.

Australians are pretty frank and don't shirk from discussing the mechanics of sex on programs, showing bare breasts, or salting dialogue with a modest number of expletives. Janet Jackson's famous flash of breast at the Super Bowl, which scandalized America, would scarcely have raised an eyebrow in Australia. The episode of *Ellen* that turned America on its ear, when the title character acknowledged she was gay, drew a yawn here. That had already been explored back in the early 1970s with the racy Sydney soap opera *Number 96,* which had an openly gay character. (*Number 96* also featured full-frontal nudity, something American TV is still unlikely to show.)

That said, Australian TV is not one big bawdy cavalcade. Years ago, Channel Nine ran a show called *Australia's Naughtiest Home Videos*—or rather, they started to do so. When the network's proprietor, the late billionaire Kerry Packer, got a glimpse of what was airing on his TV screen, he called the producers and ordered them to take it off the air immediately. Suddenly a rerun of *Cheers* appeared, and the next morning switchboards at talk-back radio stations around the nation lit up with calls congratulating Packer and asking him to be Australia's next prime minister.

TV Channels: Australia has three major commercial networks—Seven, Nine, and Ten—and they command the lion's share of the audience. Next in line comes the government-owned Australian Broadcasting Corporation (ABC), affectionately known as "Aunty" in TV's early days. It has a lock on the "quality" end of news and current affairs shows, as well as some of the best locally produced dramas. Foreign fare on the ABC tends to come from Britain. Last in the ratings stakes comes SBS. This station is devoted almost exclusively to foreign-language broadcasts and arts movies and has an audience share of about 4 percent. Its evening news is superb, covering all parts of the globe. All of these networks have expanded with extra channels since the introduction of digital television. There is also a cable network, and regional stations in rural centers. NITV, part of the SBS network, is devoted to indigenous programming, primarily Aboriginal news and content, but it also shows indigenous programs from around the world.

Architecture

This is a young nation. A 19th-century building rates as "old" here, and 18th-century structures are almost unknown. A convicted forger named Francis Greenway laid the foundations of Australia's architecture. He arrived in New South Wales in 1814 and was appointed civil architect two years later by Lachlan Macquarie, the high-minded governor who was embarking on an ambitious public works program.

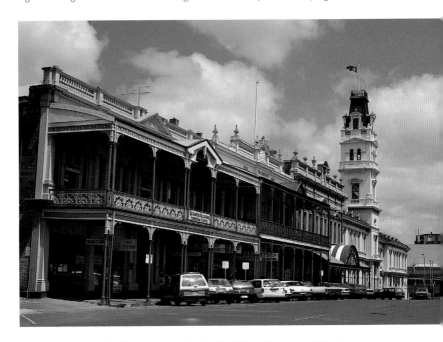

The balconied streets of Ballarat, Victoria, epitomize classic Australian town architecture.

Over the next six years, Greenway designed 40 buildings—including the Hyde Park Barracks, St. James Church, and the courthouse in Windsor—often using the honey-colored sandstone from the nearby Hawkesbury Valley. Although his classic Georgian lines were crisp and harmonious, Greenway himself was argumentative and hot tempered; he was dismissed by Governor Brisbane in 1822. (A footnote to history: Greenway's portrait appeared until recently on Australia's ten-dollar note, giving him the distinction of being the only forger honored on a nation's currency.)

For the most part Australia's civil architecture through the 19th century simply borrowed Europe's neo-Gothic, Renaissance, and classical styles. The University of Sydney was patterned on Oxford. Melbourne and the goldfield towns of Ballarat and Bendigo used the ornate styles of Victorian England to display their mid-19th-century wealth.

Domestic buildings, on the other hand, began to reflect their unique surroundings—after all, Australians had to live in them. In tropical Queensland, settlers elevated their homes and opened them up to allow cooling air to circulate. Verandas appeared all over Australia. So did the classic Aussie pub, with its double-decked veranda and lacy ornamental ironwork. Row houses, embellished with similar ironwork, mushroomed in the inner cities. Out in the suburbs, the bungalow came into its own in the 1920s.

The Old Elizabeth Farm

The oldest building in Australia is Elizabeth Farm, a brick farmhouse built for the MacArthur family in Parramatta, west of Sydney, in 1793. The MacArthur family was responsible for the early development of Australia's wool industry. The house, with its simple lines and wide veranda, is open to visitors (tel 02/9635-9488, hht.net.au).

Around this time Australian civil architects began experimenting with their own style. The Sydney Harbour Bridge, completed in 1932, was the country's first quintessentially Australian landmark. It was to have been the world's longest single-arch bridge, but by the time it opened, New York's Bayonne Bridge had beaten it by 2 feet (0.6 m). Sitting opposite its southern pylons, over on Bennelong Point, is that other great Australian architectural marvel, the Sydney Opera House, designed by Danish architect Jørn Utzon in 1955. Other buildings of note include Melbourne's sprawling new Federation Square building, built along the banks of the Yarra River, which houses the National Gallery of Victoria, theaters, and a suite of galleries and museums.

The principal designer for the Olympic Games site was Phillip Cox, designer of Darling Harbour, the Sydney Football Stadium, and Yulara Resort near Uluru (Ayers Rock).

Painting

Australia's first European artists did not know what to make of the prehistoric landscapes that spread before them, so they did what came naturally to 19th-century European minds: They rendered Arcadia, with noble savages and gum tree–lined lanes that look suspiciously like those in English villages.

In the late 1880s, Australian artists began to confront their country's harsh open spaces and blinding sun. A group of Melbourne artists, influenced by French plein air painters and the Japanese aesthetic movement, took their easels out of their studios and into the sunshine. They went to villages like Box Hill and Heidelberg, now suburbia, where they painted Australian bush scenes, refusing to succumb either to Australia's 100°F (38°C) summer heat or to the old-world notion that landscapes must be lush to be beautiful. They embraced sunburned scrub with nationalist zeal. They became known as the Heidelberg school—after the village in the Yarra Valley, not the German city—although they painted in other areas as well. Tom Roberts, Arthur Streeton, Charles Condor, and Frederick McCubbin were among the school's biggest names. Their works, found in most major art galleries in the country, are some of Australia's masterpieces. Roberts's "Shearing the Rams," which he painted in 1890 at a shearing shed in Brocklesby, New South Wales, is an Australian icon. Equally iconic is Condor's "A Holiday at Mentone," a beach scene at a resort town (now suburb) south of Melbourne that captured Australia's heat probably better than any previous painting.

Landscapes and the bush have continued to be major themes in Australian art. Some of the biggest names are Sidney Nolan (who made a classic series of portraits of the bushranger Ned Kelly), Arthur Boyd, Clifton Pugh, Lloyd Rees, and Fred Williams. Albert Namatjira, an Aboriginal watercolorist who died in poverty in 1959, had one of the surest eyes in capturing the harsh light of the central Australian deserts.

The National Gallery in Canberra houses Australia's largest art collection. Although the building was opened in 1982, the national collection was started in 1968. In the early days, there was a great deal of controversy about some of the purchases—most notably the million-dollar sum paid for American artist Jackson Pollock's "Blue Poles." Lately, Australian artists have been nudging their way into the seven-figure bracket. In 1988, "Nuit de Canicule" by Rupert Bunny, a landscape artist in 1920s Melbourne, brought A$1.25 million at auction. You won't see it hanging anywhere, however, as it was destroyed in a fire. To date, the record for an Australian painting is the A$5.4 million paid in 2010 for "First-Class Marksman" by Sidney Nolan, part of his famous Ned Kelly series.

Who is Australia's best known modern artist? That depends. The cognoscenti in Sydney's art circles will almost invariably point to the late Brett Whiteley, who died of a heroin overdose in 1992. Down in The Rocks neighborhood of Sydney, however, a large gallery sells the splashy works of Ken Done. Decried as kitsch by Australia's "serious" art world, Done is regarded as a living treasure in Japan, where he has been accorded rare honors. Displays of his work there attract the same size of crowd as rock concerts do. ■

The art deco "Australian Beach Pattern" (1940) by Charles Meere

Flora & Fauna

Undisturbed by outside influences for millions of years, Aussie wildlife evolved into the strangest assortment of creatures on the planet. Only Australia has monotremes (egg-laying mammals)—the platypus and echidna. It also has prehistoric landscapes with termite mounds 50 feet tall (15 m), boab trees, and ancient cycad palms, a species that dates back to the time of the dinosaurs.

Most of Australia's mammals are marsupials, a primitive family of animals that vanished long ago from most other parts of the world. A female marsupial gives birth to an embryo that continues its development in a separate pouch on the mother's belly (or back, depending on the species). As the offspring grows older and larger, it can climb in and out of the pouch, riding piggyback on its mother. Kangaroos

A boab tree stands solitary in the Kimberley bush near Wyndham, Western Australia.

are best known for this, and you may see surprisingly large joeys—baby kangaroos—bundling themselves into their mother's pouches for a fast bound across the plains. There are 150 species of marsupials, in a variety of sizes, from tiny kangaroo mice to powerful western gray kangaroos that can be well over 6 feet (1.8 m) tall. Koalas and wombats are also marsupials. As with the animals, the flora here often seems like a variation on a theme, with more than 600 species of eucalyptus and a similar variety of acacias found in the bush.

Australia is also full of surprises. In 1994, a ranger rappelled into a narrow 2,000-foot-deep (600 m) gorge in Wollemi National Park, less than 100 miles (160 km) from Sydney, and discovered an ancient species of pine tree thought to have been extinct for 170 million years. Until that moment it had been known only through fossils.

Only a month later came the discovery of a unique stand of Huon pines, which appears to be more than 10,000 years old, on the jungly flanks of Tasmania's Mount Read.

> **Undisturbed by outside influences . . . Aussie wildlife evolved into the strangest assortment of creatures on the planet.**

The pines, all male, have apparently been cloning themselves, their bent branches touching the earth and giving rise to new trees. Although no individual is more than 1,100 years old, the DNA—identical to that of 10,000-year-old fossilized pollen found nearby—makes this stand a contender for the world's oldest living organism.

The deep, dripping forests of Tasmania give rise to periodic—but unconfirmed—sightings of the thylacine, a striped, wolf-size, carnivorous marsupial known as the Tasmanian tiger, believed to have been extinct since the 1930s. While this mystery captures the public's imagination, rangers in the central deserts have recently found several supposedly extinct mouse-size marsupials with far less fanfare.

If you travel in the outback up north, you might hear about the night parrot, thought to have been extinct for more than a century. A dead specimen was found in Queensland more than a decade ago. Although large rewards have been posted for (living) proof of another night parrot, the noctural, shy bird has proved elusive.

Kangaroos & Koalas

Although 17 species of mammals are thought to have become extinct since the First Fleet arrived, kangaroos are believed to be more numerous now than 200 years ago, with a population of about 35–50 million, depending on seasonal conditions. This is because graziers have made water so much more plentiful out on the plains. Farmers regard kangaroos as pests, and the government permits a cull of around three million yearly. Many are shot for food (see p. 25). If you want to see them, just take a drive at dusk

Australia's famous red kangaroos can stand 6 feet (1.8 m) tall and weigh up to 145 pounds (66 kg).

out in grazing country beyond the coastal ranges. Carry collision insurance, though, because kangaroos blend in splendidly along the roadside. They look left, look right, and then hop out anyway.

While 'roos might be easy to spot in the wild, koalas are not. In fact, most Australians have never seen a koala in the wild. Estimates of koala numbers vary from 40,000 to 100,000, a far cry from the 1920s, when more than three million koalas were killed for their pelts. They have been protected since 1927, but expanding suburbs have swallowed their habitats. Although tree-planting and koala relocation programs are under way, suburban spread continues. These days, koalas are also plagued by chlamydia infections, blamed partly on stress, which cause infertility and blindness.

Kangaroo Island, off South Australia, gives probably the best chance of seeing a koala in the wild. Look in the forks of blue gums or manna gums—two of their favorite tree species—along the riverbanks. Victoria's Phillip Island is another possibility. Or go to zoos or game parks, such as Cleland in the Adelaide Hills, Healesville near Melbourne, or Eastern Creek Wildlife Park near Sydney. Private game parks used to let visitors cuddle the tubby little creatures, but many discourage that now because it stresses the animals. As former Australian tourism minister John Brown said, "It stinks, it scratches you, and it's covered with fleas." His point was that they are wild animals, not toys.

You are unlikely to see Australia's other special creatures—wombats, Tasmanian devils, echidnas, and platypuses—outside a zoo or game park. It is not that they are endangered or rare, but they are shy, nocturnal creatures and keep to themselves in forests and scrub or quiet little streams.

Birds

More than 750 species of birds live in Australia, and many of them are found nowhere else. Galahs, brolgas, jabirus, and parrots, bright as rainbows, flit through the bush, and in the summer it's not unusual to see a large gum tree virtually white with sulfur-crested cockatoos, cackling and screeching in the branches. Bird fanciers overseas pay thousands of dollars for a pair of these cockatoos, making smuggling and poaching major problems.

The Aussie birds best known outside the country are the kookaburra and the emu. The hooting laughter of a kookaburra is the sound effect Hollywood uses to evoke monkeys in the jungle. Emus, which can grow to 6 feet (1.8 m) tall and 130 pounds (59 kg), strut the outback and are a haunting sight when silhouetted against a dying sun. Like kangaroos, they also find their way onto the dinner plates of the discerning, but the smoked emu prosciutto served in trendy city bistros will have been farmed, not shot in the wild. The emu is paired with the kangaroo on Australia's national coat of arms.

Killers

Australia is also home to deadly snakes, poisonous spiders, venomous sea life, saltwater crocodiles, and the great white shark. All can kill, although fatalities are rare, newsworthy events. The taipan, the world's most toxic land snake, lives in the remote deserts of northern Australia and carries enough neurotoxin to kill 100,000 mice. The brown snake, death adder, and tiger snake also rate among the world's deadliest and are more common, but you are unlikely to see them. As a rule, snakes are shy. Treat any that you see as potentially poisonous, though, and give them a wide berth. If you happen to be one of the 300 or so people who get bitten each year, stay calm, wrap the wound snugly, and head for the nearest hospital. Don't wash the bite; doctors will need a sample of the venom.

Most of Australia's deadly critters inhabit remote pockets of bush, but the country's most poisonous spider—the funnel web—lives in Sydney's suburbs. A relative of the trapdoor spider, it lurks in rocks and cracks in brick, sometimes around swimming pools, and springs on its prey. Funnel webs are found across southeast Australia, but the most toxic varieties are near Sydney. The redback, cousin to the black widow, is found throughout the country. Antivenoms are available for both.

In the Water

Northern Australia, north of the Tropic of Capricorn, has some of Australia's loveliest beaches and most inviting turquoise waters. Summers are crushingly hot and muggy, so it is deeply disappointing to see signs forbidding swimming from November through March. There are several very good reasons. Sea wasps, which are a highly toxic box jellyfish with nearly invisible tentacles up to 10 feet (3 m) long, killed about 60 swimmers in the past century. (Diehard surfers usually wear nylon stockings to help protect them from stings.) Bluebottles, another variety of jellyfish, are painful, but not deadly, nuisances. Stonefish lurk in tidal pools, and their spines can kill if stepped upon. The shy blueringed octopus, which is actually brown until it gets upset, is found all around Australia. It has a gentle nibble, but its toxin causes respiratory failure within 12 hours. Given all that, the hotel pool starts to look pretty good.

Giant Lizards

Australia has a good selection of lizards, about 400 species ranging from harmless little skinks that scamper around backyards to the goanna, a monitor lizard that can grow to a powerfully built 7 feet (over 2 m) long. They are astoundingly fast, have large, strong, and razor-sharp claws, and if spooked will scamper up the highest thing they see. Out on the plains, that's likely to be you. The goanna is a much prized delicacy among desert Aborigines. The largest species of goanna is the perenties, second in size only to the Komodo dragon. Perenties are found in the central deserts and should be left alone. For sheer comic-nightmare quality, the frill-necked lizard is hard to top. Looking like an animated gargoyle, it scampers across the desert on its hind legs with a wide frill of leathery skin extended to frighten potential predators.

Farther out along the Queensland coast lies the Great Barrier Reef, at 1,300 miles (2,092 km) long the world's largest living organism. Made of around 300 species of hard reef coral polyps, it grows as successive generations build on their predecessors. Around it live 1,500 species of tropical fish, 4,000 species of shellfish, and 400 species of sponge. There are giant clams, tortoises, whales, black marlins, and dugongs (relatives of the manatee). Exploring it is an otherworldly experience.

The largest shark ever caught with rod and reel, a 2,664-pound (1,208 kg) white pointer, was taken in the waters off Ceduna, South Australia, in 1959. An even larger one was caught more recently near Albany, Western Australia, but was disallowed for record purposes because whale meat was used as bait. Steven Spielberg got his live shark footage for *Jaws* near Port Lincoln, South Australia. This is frightening stuff, but actually these magnificent creatures have been victims of bad press. Honeybees kill three times as many Australians as sharks do. There have only been about 690 known shark attacks in Australia since European settlement, according to the shark-attack file at Sydney's Taronga Zoo. Of these about 200 were fatal, a very small number considering the millions of Australians who swim in the ocean every weekend. The last fatal shark attack in Sydney Harbour was in 1937. South Australia put sharks on its protected species list in 1997, and today ecotourists flock to places like Port Lincoln for opportunities to dive, in protective cages, with these amazing animals.

Crocodiles are the other monsters in Australian waters. At the Shire Offices, in the northern Queensland town of Normanton, is a plaster cast of possibly the world's largest crocodile—28 feet 4 inches (8.6 m) long, with the build of a modest-size dinosaur. It was shot in 1957 in the Norman River, which flows past this rough outback town into the Gulf of Carpentaria. Saltwater crocodiles inhabit the estuaries, rivers, and mangrove swamps along the coast of tropical Australia, but they sometimes appear in pools up to 60 miles (96 km) inland. They are extremely sly and dangerous, using a high degree of skill to stalk prey, which includes anything up to and including packhorses, cattle, and sometimes people. It is extremely unwise to swim in these rivers and estuaries. Some victims, sadly, didn't know any better because tourists had taken the "Beware of Crocodile" signs as souvenirs. To thwart that, copies of the signs are available for sale.

Freshwater crocodiles are also found in the tropics. They are smaller and shy, although on rare occasions they, too, have been known to attack people. They have slightly different snouts than saltwater ones, although this can be rather a fine distinction to try to make if you are swimming in a pond and see a "log" puttering along the bank.

> **Laymen tend to divide Australian trees into two broad categories: those that are eucalyptuses and those that are not.**

Trees, Shrubs, & Flowers

Laymen tend to divide Australian trees into two broad categories: those that are eucalyptuses and those that are not. After you have asked a dozen locals to identify scores of different trees and learned that nearly all are some form of eucalyptus— blue gum, manna gum, red gum, snow gum, ghost gum, and so on—it comes as no surprise that there are about 600 different species of gum, found everywhere from harsh outback desert to mountain snowfields. They range from stunted mallee gums to towering mountain ash trees in southern Australia, which at more than 300 feet (91 m) tall are the world's tallest hardwoods. The coolabah tree, under which the jolly swagman camps in the song "Waltzing Matilda," is another form of gum tree.

Australia also has more then 660 species of acacias, commonly known as wattle trees because the early settlers used the supple branches to build wattle-and-daub cottages like the ones they used to make in England. One variety of this flowering tree, known as mulga, dominates large parts of the outback. Another, golden wattle, has become Australia's floral emblem, inspiring the green-and-gold livery of its sports teams. Banksias, named for botanist Joseph Banks, are widely found and have orange, red, or yellow flowers. Casuarinas, or shea-oaks, are nearly as widespread and varied as eucalyptuses, ranging from the desert oaks of central Australia to river shea-oaks along the banks of the Murray River.

An adventurous diver faces a great white shark at Dangerous Reef, off Australia's southern coast.

The Huon pine is an ancient and extremely slow-growing species found these days only in Tasmania. Its beautiful, dense, honey-colored wood was used to fashion cabinetry and rot-resistant boats until people realized that it could take a thousand years to replace just one big Huon pine.

The floral emblem of New South Wales is the waratah tree, famed for its flaming red flowers. Up in the floodplains of the remote Kimberley are bizarre boab trees, which look as though they've been planted upside down. Although they do not grow exceptionally high—60 feet (18 m) is a tall one—their bulbous trunks can grow more than 80 feet (24 m) in circumference. The hollowed shell of one near Derby, Western Australia, was used as a jail.

Much of Australia's interior is covered with low grasses and shrubs. Spinifex is ubiquitous north of the Tropic of Capricorn. From a distance these spiny shrubs look downy, but they were the torment of early desert explorers. Their needlelike leaves are capable of easily penetrating blue jeans and scratching your skin. Snakes and lizards love them.

Cattle flourish on the Mitchell grass that covers vast areas of the tropics. During the rainy season, these grasses can grow up to 30 feet (9 m) in a month. In the south, silvery-green saltbush covers much of the open country and supports most of the cattle and sheep in this arid landscape. Thousands of species of wildflowers grow in Australia, and many are found nowhere else on Earth. Western Australia is particularly rich, with more than 7,000 varieties (see pp. 222–223).

Alien Invaders

Australia's native flora and fauna had the continent to themselves for millions of years, during which they adapted to the changing moods of the land. Then newcomers arrived, and Australia's landscape was changed forever by sheep, cattle, wheat, barley, blackberry vines, carp, cats, and foxes. Crown of Thorns starfish invaded Australia's waters, while in 2004 it was discovered that Argentine ants had set up a vast (and harmless to humans) colony in the soil beneath Melbourne.

Rabbits may be the most destructive of the introduced species (see sidebar below), but they are far from alone. In the past two centuries, settlers have let loose an army of plants, fish, reptiles, and mammals that have wreaked havoc on the environment. Some, such as foxes and trout, were introduced for sport. Others, such as the American cane toad, were brought in to control pests—in this case, insects that ravaged sugarcane—only to became noxious pests themselves (see sidebar p. 180).

The domestic cat is believed to be responsible for endangering many species of native birds and smaller mammals. Some city councils have passed ordinances requiring cats to be neutered and locked up at night, but cat owners are vocal lobbyists. The worst offenders are feral cats—descendants of pets gone wild.

Pigs, horses, and donkeys also run wild in the bush. So do camels, which were brought to Australia for the Burke and Wills expedition in 1860 and later to carry supplies to crews building the railroads and telegraph lines across the deserts. When trains and roads made the camels obsolete, they were simply slapped on the rump and chased into the bush where they have prospered ever since. ∎

The Rabbit Scourge

In 1859, Thomas Austin, a grazier in Victoria, had a dozen rabbits shipped from England to provide a bit of sporting pleasure for him and his guests. The rabbits were turned loose in the scrub, and soon their numbers were far beyond anything hunting could control.

By 1865, hunters had killed more than 20,000 rabbits, but thousands more lived in the bush. By the 1930s, the rabbit population had exploded to an estimated one billion. Their destructive nibbling had stripped bare large areas of land and endangered many native species of grasses and wildflowers.

Nothing seemed to work against this scourge until the 1950s, when scientists let loose the myxomatosis virus, which is lethal to rabbits but doesn't infect humans or native Australian species. Rabbit numbers plummeted, but then rebounded as some rabbits developed immunity to the virus.

By the early 1990s, there were an estimated 350 million rabbits hopping around the bush. In 1996, scientists released a new disease, rabbit calicivirus, which wiped out 98 percent of rabbits in parts of the outback but seems to have left other populations untouched.

Australia's oldest, largest, and wealthiest city, with one of the most beautiful harbors in the world

Sydney

Introduction & Map   74–77

Sydney Harbour   78–87

Experience: Cruising the Harbour   79

Sydney Harbour Walk   82–85

Downtown Sydney   88–89

Feature: Cricket   90–91

Darling Harbour   92–93

Bohemian Sydney   94–95

Experience: Taking a Priscilla Tour   95

Beaches   96–97

Feature: A Sydney-style New Year's   98–99

Zoos & Wildlife Parks   100

Hotels & Restaurants   368–369

Eclectic architecture in The Rocks neighborhood of Sydney

Sydney

Flying into Sydney has to be the finest introduction to Australia imaginable. Look out your window and it's all there: the dramatic city skyline, the deep blue of the harbor spread into scores of inlets and bays, and a sprawl of terra-cotta roofs stretching to the horizon. And then you see it: the graceful ironwork of the Harbour Bridge, a perfect miniature from this height, and beside it, the white tiles of the Opera House shimmering like a pearl.

You've definitely arrived. This is Australia. And it's just as they said it would be. From 1,000 feet, anyway. After you land and begin to make your way through the tangle of grubby and crowded urban streets, craning your neck to look for landmarks such as the 960-foot-tall (293 m) Sydney Tower, you realize that this city can be a little deceptive as well. Some Australians—chiefly staid Victorians from archrival Melbourne, who tend to draw morals from this sort of thing—will say you've learned your first lesson about the shallowness of Sydney's flashy money and California-style glamour.

A Sydneysider, on the other hand, will simply give you directions down to Circular Quay. The view is like a visual mantra—just sitting on an ornamental bench by the Opera House brings back the magic, as you watch the sunlight sparkle on one of the world's great harbors, the ferries coming and going, and the spread of million-dollar bungalows along the North Shore. No matter how many times you've been there before, when you go down to the quay on a sunny afternoon it's like seeing it for the first time all over again. Even the convicts supposedly cheered on their first glimpse of the harbor when the First Fleet sailed in through the Heads in 1788.

NOT TO BE MISSED:

Cruising the city's azure harbor on a ferry to Manly 78–79

A climb up the iconic Sydney Harbour Bridge 81

A walk through the city's historic district, The Rocks 84

Sydney Opera House, a World Heritage masterpiece 86–87

Darling Harbour, the rejuvenated waterfront packed with popular tourist attractions 92–93

People-watching at world-famous Bondi Beach 96–97

The Lure of the Water

Sydney's secret is this dazzling waterfront, with its ornamental palms, gleaming yachts in quiet coves, and 70 beaches. Walk along any of them and you feel like whistling something bold and adventurous. If somebody hasn't made you a vice president, they will any day now. It's this infectious waterborne confidence that lures Australia's smartest and most artistically gifted, the very rich and those who want to be. Their scramble for waterfront footage has bumped real estate prices to absurd levels, and the shock

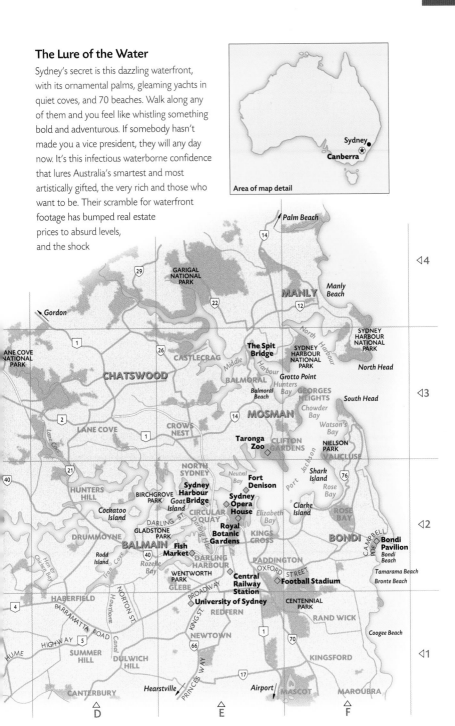

Sydney
Canberra

Area of map detail

Palm Beach

GARIGAL NATIONAL PARK

Gordon

MANLY

Manly Beach

SYDNEY HARBOUR NATIONAL PARK

The Spit Bridge

SYDNEY HARBOUR NATIONAL PARK

North Head

CASTLECRAG

CHATSWOOD

Middle Harbour

BALMORAL

Grotto Point

Hunters Bay

Balmoral Beach

GEORGES HEIGHTS

South Head

ANE COVE NATIONAL PARK

LANE COVE

CROWS NEST

MOSMAN

Chowder Bay

Watson's Bay

Taronga Zoo

CLIFTON GARDENS

NIELSON PARK

VAUCLUSE

NORTH SYDNEY

Neutral Bay

Fort Denison

Port Jackson

Shark Island

Rose Bay

HUNTERS HILL

BIRCHGROVE PARK

Sydney Harbour Bridge

Goat Island

Sydney Opera House

Clarke Island

Elizabeth Bay

ROSE BAY

Cockatoo Island

CIRCULAR QUAY

DARLING ST.

Royal Botanic Gardens

KINGS CROSS

BONDI

DRUMMOYNE

GLADSTONE PARK

BALMAIN

Fish Market

DARLING HARBOUR

PADDINGTON

OXFORD STREET

Bondi Pavilion

Bondi Beach

Rodd Island

Rozelle Bay

WENTWORTH PARK

Central Railway Station

Football Stadium

Tamarama Beach

Bronte Beach

HABERFIELD

GLEBE

BROADWAY

University of Sydney

CENTENNIAL PARK

PARRAMATTA ROAD

REDFERN

RANDWICK

HIGHWAY

NEWTOWN

Coogee Beach

HUME

SUMMER HILL

DULWICH HILL

KINGSFORD

CANTERBURY

Hearstville

PRINCES WAY

Airport

MASCOT

MAROUBRA

The downtown Sydney skyline overlooks Hyde Park.

waves can be felt in the western suburbs, where much of the population lives. A house out there can still cost A$350,000, but a comparable one along the harbor could range well into eight figures. So most of Sydney's 4.6 million residents reluctantly live away from the water, then crowd the beaches, the Manly ferry, Darling Harbour, and Circular Quay on the weekends.

City Districts

Sydney sprawls. Despite its relatively small population, it covers almost as large an area as Los Angeles and is seven times larger than Paris. It has more than 400 suburbs, the farthest being about 60 miles (96 km) from the Central Business District, or CBD.

The historic section of the city is known as **The Rocks,** a beautifully restored warren of alleyways and old stone buildings tucked away under the southern approach to the Harbour Bridge.

Pitt Street and George Street are the city's two main thoroughfares. They both begin at

The Fortune of War, at 137 George Street in The Rocks, is Sydney's oldest pub. This tiny but popular watering hole has been in continuous operation since 1828. Catch live music here on weekends.

—HOLLY SHALDERS
National Geographic contributor

Circular Quay and stretch through the heart of downtown Sydney. Both streets are lined with glittering skyscrapers and department stores, as well as gritty old shops that have somehow managed to survive the scramble for building land. This juxtaposition of styles, old and new, gives Sydney flair. For the past ten years, **North Sydney,** across the harbor, has been sprouting modernistic skyscrapers, and it now looks like an annex of downtown.

Residential suburbs in the North Shore and Sydney's ritzy east, such as **Point Piper, Double Bay,** and **Vaucluse,** rank among the priciest real estate in Australia, with harborfront mansions running into many millions of dollars. Farther east is **Bondi Beach,** the most famous of the chain of surfing beaches fronting the Pacific Ocean close to the city.

The inner east section has Kings Cross, Paddington, and Darlinghurst. **Kings Cross** is Sydney's red-light district, filled with pulsing nightclubs, fast food, and crime. Oxford Street is the main artery of trendy **Paddington** and **Darlinghurst.** With brash nightlife, stylish row houses, and great little cafés, this is the place to go if you want to soak up the city's social scene. This is also Sydney's gay center, where the Gay and Lesbian Mardi Gras draws half a million spectators, gay and straight, from Australia and around the world.

To the west is **Darling Harbour,** a pleasant walk from most places in the downtown part of the city. Filled with hugely popular museums and wildlife attractions, Darling Harbour is a great place for families and a center for harbor cruises, along with Circular Quay. Farther out are the inner west suburbs of **Glebe** and **Balmain,** old working-class docklands that have become fashionable. Also at this end of town is the raffishly chic **Newtown,** which was formerly a tough slum but today boasts a funky artistic and intellectual vibe. Neighboring **Redfern** is still tough.

Farther west are **Homebush Bay**—site of the Olympics in 2000—and **Parramatta,** Australia's second oldest city. You can reach these by ferry from Circular Quay, a better option than struggling through miles of stop-start traffic on the Parramatta Road, with its aggressive motorists, garish advertising, and tacky used car lots.

Asian Culture

Sydney is multicultural, home to more than 160 nationalities. In the past 20 years it has become a strongly Asian city, though you might be disappointed by Chinatown, which is just a token two streets on the Darling Harbour side of the city. To see Sydney's vibrant Asian community, go west to suburbs like **Cabramatta.** Here you'll find busy food stands, Asian apothecaries, sidewalks cluttered with signs in Chinese, Vietnamese, and Cambodian, cramped restaurants, and everywhere a fragrance of scorched spices and cooking oil.

Slip, Slop, Slap

This enduring health campaign slogan delivers the message to "slip on a shirt, slop on sunscreen, and slap on a hat" to avoid skin cancer. Surrounded by wonderful beaches, warm climate, and abundant sunshine, Australians reveled in their sun-bronzed image until health studies showed Australia had one of highest rates of skin cancer in the world. Visitors are also advised to follow the slogan.

Transportation

For all the urban sprawl and tangle of streets, getting about Sydney is fairly easy. Central Railway Station and bustling Circular Quay are the main transportation hubs in the city, with regular trains, buses, and ferries reaching all parts of the city, into the nearby Blue Mountains, and down the Illawarra Coast. You can also catch water taxis on the harbor, and a light rail links Central Station with Chinatown, Darling Harbour, and the inner west.

Hiking & Biking

There are nice walks to be had downtown, notably in Hyde Park and the Botanic Gardens. This is not a bicycle-friendly city, but there are spectacularly scenic bicycle lanes on the Harbour Bridge. The safe exception for riders is leafy Centennial Park, near Paddington, where there is a riding track and jogging path through the gardens and past ornamental ponds. ∎

Sydney Harbour

The best way to acquaint yourself with Sydney Harbour is to take a ferry, and the pick of the bunch is the legendary ferry to Manly. Take the slower-moving old-style ferry, rather than the speedy fast ferry, and savor the sea air on the half-hour trip. The ferry cuts its way east from Circular Quay, around the Opera House and the Botanic Gardens, past glamorous suburbs, and out toward the grand promontories—the Heads—that guard the entrance to the harbor.

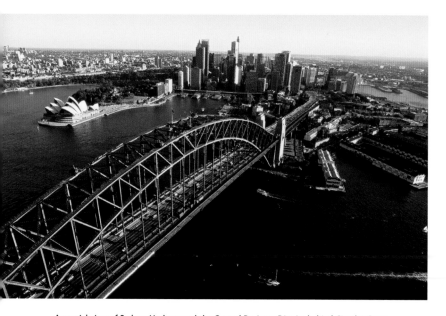

An aerial view of Sydney Harbour and the Central Business District behind Circular Quay

Sydney

Map pp. 74–75 & 83

Visitor Information

✉ Corner of Argyle St. & Playfair St., The Rocks; Palm Grove, between Cockle Bay Wharf and Harbourside, Darling Harbour

☎ 02/9240-8788

✉ Circular Quay Kiosk

☎ 02/9265-3333

sfha.nsw.gov.au/svc

Manly itself is a breezy seaside suburb on a spit of land between the north shore of the harbor and the open ocean, with a line of Norfolk pines along its esplanade and the sun-splashed Manly Corso humming with life. It's much more family-oriented than Sydney's other famous beach, Bondi. The return trip on the ferry is, if anything, even more majestic as you pass Fort Denison and draw up to the city skyline, Opera House, and Harbour Bridge.

The harbor spills into countless bays and coves. **Chowder Bay** (see map p. 75), on the north shore, was where 19th-century Yankee whalers tied up and made their chowder out of local shellfish. **Neutral Bay** was where ships of various nationalities docked. The city's earliest attempts at agriculture were at Farm Cove, now the **Royal Botanic Gardens.**

Rose Bay was where the old Empire flying boats used to take off in the 1930s on the nine-day hop to London. Reprise a bit of that golden age travel with a scenic flight on one of the classic Beaver seaplanes that take off from this same pretty bay. A variety of packages are available, including flights a short way up the coast to beautiful Pittwater, with lunch and an aerial tour of the harbor as you return *(tel 02/9388-1978, seaplanes.com.au)*.

Ferry Tours

Water travel is a way of life in this harbor city. There are ferries from Circular Quay to the Olympic grounds at **Homebush Bay, Taronga Zoo, Watson's Bay**—where you can sprawl in a manicured park eating some of Sydney's best fish and chips—and **Darling Harbour** precinct. The Hunter's Hill Ferry gives a tour of the hidden northwest arms of the harbor. All of the western ferry rides provide spectacular photo opportunities of the iconic Opera House and Botanic Gardens, framed by the Sydney Harbour Bridge, as you return to the quay.

Tours operate to some of the harbor's islands. **Fort Denison** was where poorly behaved convicts were sent to reconsider their conduct—the sharks and strong currents were efficient guards. Tours are also available to **Goat Island,** an old quarantine station and shipyard. Regular ferries visit **Cockatoo Island,** once a prison, then a shipbuilding yard. Tour the convict buildings and former dockyards, have a sunset drink at the summertime Island Bar, or take in a regular art exhibition.

Walking Tours

Landlubbers who get queasy at the very thought of being on a ship can take some fine harbor walks, including the mile-long **Hermitage Foreshore** (start from Nielson Park) around the exclusive suburbs of Vaucluse and Rose Bay. A longer hike can be had on the **Manly Scenic Walkway,** which goes 6 miles (9.6 km) from Manly Cove to the Spit Bridge *(brochures and maps from the Sydney or Manly visitor centers)*.

Sydney Harbour
- 🅰 Map pp. 74–75 & 83

Manly
- 🅰 75 F4
- **Visitor Information**
- ✉ Manly Wharf
- ☎ 02/9976-1430

Manly Ferry
- ✉ Circular Quay
- 🕐 30 minutes
- 💲 $

Fort Denison Tours
- ✉ Cadmans Cottage, 110 George St., The Rocks
- ☎ 02/9247-5033
- 🕐 60-minute tours depart No. 6 Jetty, Circular Quay, 2–3 times daily
- 💲 $$$

EXPERIENCE: Cruising the Harbour

In addition to the ferries that ply commuters around Sydney, there are several other ways to get out onto the magnificent harbor:

Captain Cook *(No. 6 Jetty, Circular Quay, tel 02/9206-1111, captaincook.com .au/sydney)* cruise ships offer everything from breakfast and high tea cruises to weekend trips.

Magistic Cruises *(King Street Wharf 5, Darling Harbour, tel 02/8296-7222, magisticcruises.com.au)* has a variety of lunch and dinner cruises.

Sydney by Sail *(Australian National Maritime Museum, Darling Harbour, tel 02/9280-1110, sydneysail.com)* offers three-hour yachting experiences that teach sailing basics.

Sydney Harbour Tall Ships *(79½ George St., tel 02/8243-7961, sydneytall ships.com.au)* has 1850s-style tall ships that depart from The Rocks.

Sydney Jet *(Cockle Bay Wharf, Darling Harbour, tel 02/9807-4333, sydneyjet.com)* combines great harbor views with high-speed thrills.

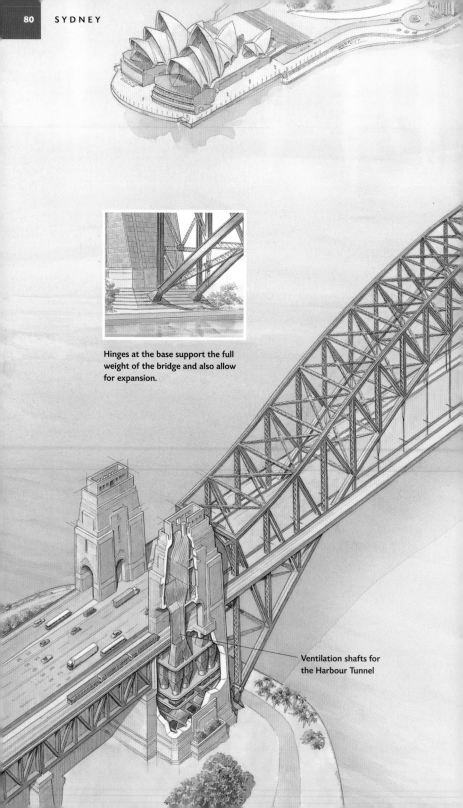

Hinges at the base support the full weight of the bridge and also allow for expansion.

Ventilation shafts for the Harbour Tunnel

Sydney Harbour Bridge

The Bridge

Sydney Harbour Bridge is instantly recognizable. This iconic structure is one of Australia's architectural and engineering wonders, and for 30 years it was the tallest structure in Sydney. The bridge was designed by Dorman Long and Co. of England to the specifications of its chief engineer, J. J. C. Bradfield. Construction started in 1923, and the bridge was completed during the Depression in 1932.

The bridge has a span of 1,650 feet (503 m), and the top of the arch is 439 feet (134 m) above the water. Originally designed to carry 6,000 cars an hour, it now tops 15,000 at peak times, in eight lanes. It also carries two railroad lines, a pedestrian walkway, and a bicycle track.

The Bridge Climb

Once a dare taken up by university students, climbing the steel arch of the Sydney Harbour Bridge is now a tourism possibility for those with a good head for heights. **Sydney Harbour Bridge Climb** (*Cumberland St., The Rocks, tel 02/8274-7777, $$$$$, bridgeclimb.com*) offers guided tours to the top of the arch. Visitors are attached by harnesses to a safety rail, used by maintenance workers, and led by experienced guides to the finest viewing spot in Sydney. There are higher points in the city (MLC Centre is 748 feet/228 m, Sydney Tower 990 feet/302 m), but nothing commands the skyline the way Sydney's "Coathanger" does.

Those who don't care for such drama can cross the bridge on the pedestrian walkway or go to the top of the southeast **Pylon Lookout** (*$$*) which, at 290 feet (88 m) above the water, gives nearly as spectacular a view.

(continued on p. 86)

Sydney Harbour Walk

With a distance of just over 4 miles (7 km), this route can be anything from a brisk hour-long walk to an all-day excursion. It can even be satisfactorily jogged because it crosses only one busy street.

Massive Corinthian columns mark the entrance to the Art Gallery of New South Wales.

Start at the **Art Gallery of New South Wales** ❶ *(Art Gallery Rd., The Domain, tel 02/9225-1744, artgallery.nsw.gov.au)*, which is located in the leafy park known as The Domain. (To get there, you can take the Explorer Bus or walk about 1,500 feet/500 m from St. James Railway Station.) This beautiful, colonnaded, sandstone building dates from 1885 and is inscribed with mood-setting names of great European artists, only a few of whom are actually represented inside. Highlights of the gallery are the extensive collection of Australian masterpieces and one of the nation's most comprehensive collections of Aboriginal and Torres Strait Islander art.

NOT TO BE MISSED:

**Mrs. Macquarie's Point •
Circular Quay • The Rocks
• Sydney Harbour Bridge**

From the gallery steps, follow the narrow road down through the Botanic Gardens and toward **Mrs. Macquarie's Point** ❷. This fig-shaded promontory was named in honor of Governor Macquarie's wife, Elizabeth, when the gardens were laid out in 1816. Supposedly she used to sit out here to watch the harbor and wait for the next ship to arrive from

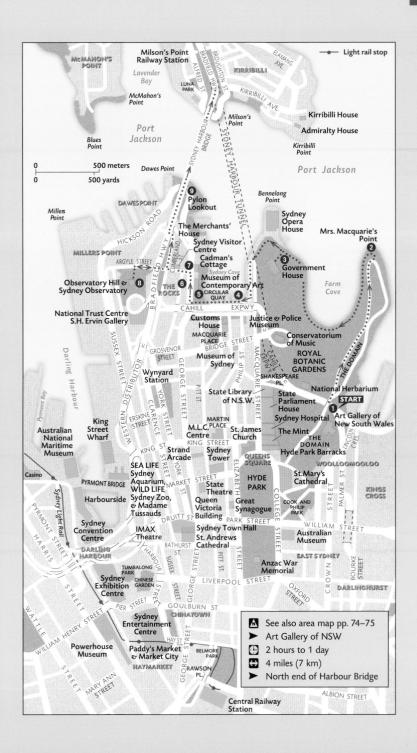

McMAHON'S POINT

Milson's Point Railway Station

Lavender Bay

KIRRIBILLI

ELAMANG AVE

KIRRIBILLI AVE

BRADFIELD HWY

BROUGHTON ST

ALFRED ST

LUNA PARK

McMahon's Point

Milson's Point

Kirribilli House

Admiralty House

Kirribilli Point

Port Jackson

Blues Point

SYDNEY HARBOUR BRIDGE

SYDNEY HARBOUR TUNNEL

Port Jackson

Dawes Point

Bennelong Point

Sydney Opera House

Mrs. Macquarie's Point
2

Millers Point

9 Pylon Lookout

DAWES POINT

HICKSON ROAD

The Merchants' House

Sydney Visitor Centre

Cadman's Cottage

Museum of Contemporary Art

Sydney Cove

Government House
3

Farm Cove

MILLERS POINT

ARGYLE STREET

CUMBERLAND ST

BRADFIELD HWY

THE ROCKS

7

6

8

5 CIRCULAR QUAY

4

Observatory Hill & Sydney Observatory

National Trust Centre S.H. Ervin Gallery

CAHILL EXPWY

Customs House

Justice & Police Museum

Conservatorium of Music

ROYAL BOTANIC GARDENS

THE DOMAIN

SUSSEX STREET

WESTERN DISTRIBUTOR

GROSVENOR STREET

MACQUARIE PLACE

BRIDGE STREET

PHILIP ST

MACQUARIE STREET

CAHILL EXPWY

Museum of Sydney

Wynyard Station

SHAKESPEARE PL.

Darling Harbour

GEORGE STREET

YORK STREET

CLARENCE STREET

ERSKINE STREET

PITT ST

State Library of N.S.W.

National Herbarium

State Parliament House

START
1

Art Gallery of New South Wales

Pyrmont Bay

Australian National Maritime Museum

King Street Wharf

KING ST

MARTIN PLACE

M.L.C. Centre

St. James Church

KING STREET

Sydney Hospital

The Mint

Sydney Tower

Strand Arcade

THE DOMAIN

Hyde Park Barracks

LINCOLN CRES

Casino

SEA LIFE Sydney Aquarium, WILD LIFE Sydney Zoo, & Madame Tussauds

PYRMONT BRIDGE

ELIZABETH STREET

QUEENS SQUARE

WOOLLOOMOOLOO

St. Mary's Cathedral

COOK AND PHILIP PARK

PALMER ST.

KINGS CROSS

Harbourside

YORK ST

MARKET STREET

State Theatre

HYDE PARK

Great Synagogue

COLLEGE STREET

Sydney Light Rail

HARRIS STREET

PYRMONT STREET

Sydney Convention Centre

IMAX Theatre

DRUITT ST

Queen Victoria Building

PARK STREET

Sydney Town Hall

St. Andrews Cathedral

Australian Museum

WILLIAM STREET

EAST SYDNEY

BOURKE STREET

CROWN STREET

DARLINGHURST

DARLING HARBOUR

BATHURST ST.

SUSSEX STREET

HARBOUR STREET

PITT STREET

LIVERPOOL STREET

OXFORD STREET

Anzac War Memorial

TUMBALONG PARK

CHINESE GARDEN

GEORGE STREET

Sydney Exhibition Centre

PIER STREET

GOULBURN ST.

CHINATOWN

WILLIAM HENRY STREET

WATTLE STREET

Sydney Entertainment Centre

HAY ST

Powerhouse Museum

Paddy's Market & Market City

HAYMARKET

BELMORE PARK

RAWSON PL.

MARY ANN STREET

ALBION STREET

Central Railway Station

Legend:

- Light rail stop
- See also area map pp. 74–75
- ▶ Art Gallery of NSW
- 2 hours to 1 day
- 4 miles (7 km)
- ▶ North end of Harbour Bridge

Scale:
0 — 500 meters
0 — 500 yards

England. The **Royal Botanic Gardens** are a wonderful place for a picnic. In addition to the ornamental trees, duck ponds, sweeping lawns, and flower beds, the gardens have a glassed-in pyramid housing a collection of tropical plants and ferns.

INSIDER TIP:

Avoid the tourist traffic and join the office workers for predinner drinks and fabulous waterfront views at the Opera Bar, outside the front of the spectacular Opera House.

—PETER TURNER
National Geographic author

From Mrs. Macquarie's chair, you can look straight across Farm Cove to the Opera House. The path hugs the waterfront, but you can take a side trip to **Government House** ❸ *(tel 02/9931-5222, house closed Mon.–Thurs.),* whose grounds lie within the Botanic Gardens. This massive two-story home in Gothic Revival style was built in 1843 for the governor of New South Wales, but the republican-minded Labor government gave it to the people in 1996. You can wander freely in the gardens or take a tour of the house, with its Australian masterpieces on the walls, ornate drawing and dining rooms, and stenciled ceilings.

The shoreline path curves around to the **Sydney Opera House** (see pp. 86–87), and from there it follows another inlet (Sydney Cove) a couple hundred yards to **Circular Quay** ❹. This stretch of footpath honors Australia's literary greats, with commemorative plaques set into the paving.

Circular Quay is the point of arrival for thousands of office workers who come daily to the city by ferry. It also attracts visitors taking sightseeing cruises and tour buses or simply

strolling the waterfront. It is probably the liveliest place for people-watching in all of Australia, with its blend of stockbrokers, secretaries, and street sweepers, tourists speaking almost every language imaginable, derelicts, peddlers, hippies, and rural Australians taking a look at "the big smoke." You usually see a gaggle of jugglers, puppeteers, and street musicians, whose talents range from brilliant to embarrassingly awful. Just beyond the quay is the **Museum of Contemporary Art** ❺ *(George St., tel 02/9245-2400),* in a restored art deco building with a fashionable outdoor café.

The area known as **The Rocks** ❻ lies between George Street and the approach road to the bridge. This is Sydney's historic district, a warren of narrow streets and old stone buildings that have been lovingly restored. It is a far cry from the way the place looked in Sydney's Dickensian days, when these alleyways were the most squalid and dangerous in Australia. Here lurked pickpockets, razor gangs, and hard-case thugs. Outbreaks of bubonic plague from 1900 forced the authorities to step in and demolish some of the rat-infested structures. More were torn down in the 1920s to make way for the approach to the Harbour Bridge. By the 1970s, the government was ready to raze what was left of Sydney's oldest structures and replace them with office blocks. Only a hard-fought campaign by left-wing unions saved the historic quarter. Militant construction workers placed the first of their famous "green bans" on the proposed redevelopment, thereby stopping work. It was a tactic they were to use throughout the 1970s to save numerous heritage buildings around Sydney.

These days, The Rocks is one of Sydney's treasured tourist precincts. It has boutiques, art dealers, cafés, upscale hotels, and pubs such as the Hero of Waterloo, one of Sydney's oldest, built in 1843. Also here is the **Rocks Markets—** a popular and relaxed weekend street fair with stalls of food, art, and various bric-a-brac. On Fridays, a food market sets up. **Cadman's Cottage** ❼, the oldest house in Sydney (built in 1816), is at 110 George Street *(tel 02/9247-5033)*. Just along the street, at No. 106, is the Sailor's Home (now Sailor's Thai Restaurant), built in 1864 to provide respectable lodgings for sailors.

From George Street you can take a short side trip along Argyle Street and then up **Observatory Hill** ⑧. It is a steep climb, but well worth it for the spectacular—and different—view of the Harbour Bridge, across to North Sydney and down to The Rocks below. Otherwise wind your way through the lanes up to the steps for the Sydney Harbour Bridge walkway on Cumberland Street.

The walk across the bridge to the North Shore is about three-quarters of a mile long (1.2 km), and every step seems to put both Sydney and the bridge's graceful ironwork in a new perspective. A small museum inside the

massive South Pylon tells the story of the building of the bridge and for a grand view of the skyline and harbor, climb to the **Pylon Lookout** ⑨ at the top. For a really stupendous view, ambitious visitors might like to attempt the Bridge Climb, right over the top of the arch itself (see p. 81).

The walk ends on the north side of the bridge, and the two options for getting back to the city are both beautifully simple. The Milson's Point train station is only a stone's throw from the northern end of the bridge walkway, and from there you can catch a train back across the bridge to Wynyard station. Or you can go the scenic way and walk a couple hundred yards down to the Luna Park amusement park or Milson's Point ferry landing then cut across the harbor back to Circular Quay.

At Circular Quay, ferries set out for waterside suburbs and ocean liners still berth.

Opera House

🗺 75 E2

✉ Bennelong Point

☎ 02/9250-7111,
reservations
02/9250-7777

💲 Tours: $$$

**sydneyoperahouse
.com**

Sydney Opera House

Sydney's Opera House, with its billowing sail roofs and breathtaking harbor setting, is one of the most potent symbols of Australia. The story of its creation is worthy of an opera itself. In fact, the Australian Opera Company recently wrote and staged just such a piece, aptly titled *The Eighth Wonder.*

The saga started in 1955 with a contest to design an opera house for the site of the old tram terminus on Bennelong Point. After looking over 233 entries, the judges selected

an innovative design by a Danish architect named Jørn Utzon. His vision for the building, which was to cost around A$7 million, resembled sails on the harbor—perfect for a breezy, yachtie-style city like Sydney. (Utzon later said he had actually been inspired by a sequence of orange segments.)

Construction began in 1959, and the trouble started almost immediately. Controversy over the radical design, as well as technical problems with its construction,

Sydney Opera House

Concert Hall

Opera Theatre

Northern
Boardwalk

Harbour
Restaurant

bogged down progress. Costs mounted, fueling the controversy. By 1966, Utzon had had enough. He withdrew from the project and returned to Denmark, bitter about what he saw as heavy-handed interference in his work.

The New South Wales government seemed glad to see Utzon go, turning the project over to a team of local architects. Costs continued to spiral. The state funded it with Opera House lotteries. By the time Queen Elizabeth II opened the building in 1973, Sydney's new landmark had cost more than ten times the original estimate, and it was ten years behind schedule. Its first production, appropriately enough, was Prokofiev's *War and Peace.*

Happily, more than 30 years after Utzon left Australia, the architect and the New South Wales government reached a rapprochement. In 1999, Utzon was appointed design consultant for remodeling the Opera House, and in 2003, the University of Sydney awarded him an honorary

Monumental Steps

Guillaume at Bennelong

Playhouse

Western Boardwalk

doctorate. Utzon died, aged 90, in 2008.

Inside are the 1,507-seat **Opera Theatre,** the 2,679-seat **Concert Hall,** two smaller theaters, a cinema, an exhibition hall, and a restaurant. The second flock of sails, the "baby" opera house beside the main complex, contains **Guillaume at Bennelong,** one of Sydney's finest restaurants (see p. 368). Take a tour to see the complex. ∎

Downtown Sydney

Once away from its dazzling waterfront, Sydney's concrete-and-glass canyons and traffic-clogged streets resemble those of cities the world over. Cranes on the skyline and construction pits between buildings speak of change. Nevertheless, a stroll through Sydney takes you shopping and sightseeing around a uniquely Australian downtown.

A good place to start is the almost ludicrously ornate Victorian-era **Sydney Town Hall** (tel 1300-651-301), on the corner of George and Druitt Streets (see map p. 83). Built of golden sandstone in 1874, it has an elaborate concert hall. Next to it is **St. Andrew's Cathedral** (tel 02/9265-1661), about the same age but simpler in style. This is the oldest cathedral in Australia, and at lunchtime on Fridays you can hear free recitals on the powerful pipe organ. The subway station of Town Hall lies beneath these two buildings.

Across Druitt Street is the beautiful **Queen Victoria Building,** built in 1898 for the city's fruit and vegetable markets. This extravagant three-story sandstone building stretches an entire city block along George Street and was carefully restored in the early 1980s, after having fallen into serious disrepair. The sculptured exterior is impressive, but the interior is even more opulent, with mosaics, stained-glass windows, and the elaborate one-ton Royal Clock, which is suspended from a central glass dome. The QVB, as it is known, houses more than 200 upscale boutiques and cafés and has some of the best shopping in Sydney. For something a bit more ostentatious, go across George Street, and in the **Strand Arcade** beneath the Hilton Hotel you'll find the exuberantly Victorian **Marble Bar.**

At the end of the QVB, turn right on Market Street. Two blocks will take you past the ornate **State Theatre** (49 Market St., tel

The Sydney Tower, built in 1981, is fast becoming an iconic landmark of the city.

The Convict Barracks

Off Hyde Park's northern end stands Hyde Park Barracks, home to 800 convicts in Sydney's bad old days. Prisoners were marched out in chains each morning, little more than slaves, to work on public projects or for one of the free settlers. After transportation to New South Wales ceased in 1848, the barracks became an immigration office and later a court building. The convict-architect Francis Greenway (see p. 63) designed this three-story structure in 1819 in a Grecian style. Today it is a museum devoted to Sydney's convict past. Aussies can check genealogical records here for any convict traces in their ancestral DNA.

13-6100), with its gilt decor, and on to the **Sydney Tower** (100 Market St., tel 02/9333-9222, $$$), on the corner of Pitt Street. Opened in 1981, the 960-foot-high (293 m) tower, with its gold minaret, is the tallest structure in the Southern Hemisphere. Few visitors pass up a chance to go to the observatory or one of the two revolving restaurants for sweeping views that stretch as far as the Blue Mountains (see pp. 104–105). If you're feeling daring, walk out onto the glass floor of the tower's **Skywalk** ($$$$$), nearly 900 feet (275 m) above the street.

Hyde Park & North

Farther down Market Street is Hyde Park, with flower beds and fountains. This is Sydney's central park. Australia's first cricket match was played here in 1803, and on sunny days the park fills up with office workers having lunch. The art deco **Anzac War Memorial,** at the southern end of the park, was built in 1934 to commemorate the dead of World War I. A worthwhile detour here is the **Australian Museum,** on the southeast corner of Hyde Park. This massive sandstone structure houses the nation's largest natural history collection, as well as displays of Aboriginal artifacts.

North of the park, next to the Hyde Park Barracks (see sidebar above), is **The Mint** (10 Macquarie St., tel 02/8239-2288, $$), which started out in 1814 as the Rum Hospital. After gold was discovered in the colonies, it became the Royal Mint, stamping out gold coins from 1854 until 1927. Today The Mint is home to the Historic Houses Trust.

Beyond the mint is New South Wales's **State Parliament House** (Macquarie St., tel 02/9230-2111). The public gallery is open when Parliament is sitting, and tours are available when it is not. Next door, the **State Library of New South Wales** houses historic records, including the ships' logs of Captains Cook and Bligh. The entryway floor has a mosaic of Capt. Abel Tasman's 17th-century chart of Australian waters.

Head past the **Museum of Sydney** and the Francis Greenway–designed **Conservatorium of Music** (tel 02/9351-1263), with free lunchtime recitals on Wednesdays, to Circular Quay. ∎

Hyde Park Barracks
- Queens Sq., Macquarie St.
- 02/8239-2311
- $$

Australian Museum
- 6 College St. (opposite Hyde Park)
- 02/9360-6000
- $$
australianmuseum.net.au

State Library of New South Wales
- Macquarie St.
- 02/9273-1414

Museum of Sydney
- 37 Philip St.
- 02/9251-5988
- $$
hht.net.au/museums/mos

Cricket

Cricket is virtually a way of life for Australians in the summer. People play it in every park, on the beaches, and even in offices, where workers playfully bat at crumpled bits of paper with rolled up magazines around the water cooler. Even airline pilots have been known to make in-flight announcements when a vital wicket falls or a batsman makes his "century"—a landmark score of a hundred runs in a single innings (at-bat).

Lee Carseldine of the Queensland Bulls bats in a 2009 cricket match in Perth.

This fascination with what appears to be one of the world's slowest games bemuses and puzzles most visitors—unless they come from South Africa, England, India, Pakistan, Sri Lanka, New Zealand, or the Caribbean. After all, this is a game that, in its "test match" version, takes five days to play, generally under a broiling sun, and as often as not results in a draw. All this time nobody ever seems to be doing much, except one bloke who keeps running across the field to hurl the ball at another well-padded bloke who slashes at it with a paddle-shaped bat. Maybe he'll hit it and run. Maybe he won't. Hours pass this way. "Baseball on Valium," is how some visiting Americans have dismissed it. But that is to miss all the game's drama and strategy.

The place to see a big-league cricket match in Sydney is the Sydney Cricket Ground (SCG), near Centennial Park in eastern Sydney. The ground holds a little more then 40,000 spectators. The nicest seating is in the elegant Members' Pavilion, built in 1886, but since this haven of politeness is open only to members and their guests, you will probably have to make do with one of the regular stands. The most atmospheric seating used to be the notorious Hill, a grassy patch opposite the Members' Pavilion, where shirtless spectators drank, brawled, and lazed away the scorching Australian afternoons, offering wittily obscene comments on the fielders. These days the Hill is gone, replaced with soulless but more comfortable seating.

There are several varieties of cricket, including the old-style, five-day-long test matches and the newer—and to traditionalists, more vulgar—one-day cricket. The game has become even more truncated with the very popular, almost frenetic, Twenty20 format, with each side bowling 20 overs in a game lasting just over three hours. "Cricket on amphetamines," anyone? The faster forms of cricket are becoming the game's moneymakers these days, and a big international match will have the most rousing atmosphere. For just a glimpse of the game, try going along to the Sydney Cricket Ground for a Sheffield Shield match—played between the states—late in the afternoon, when you can often get in for free to see the last hour's play.

Rules of the Game

The rules are hard to explain, but ask an Aussie in the stands; he or she will be happy to give you a rundown. Americans will be able to see some similarities to baseball. The game is played with a wide, flat bat made out of willow, and a red ball, slightly smaller but heavier than a baseball, with a single line of stitches around the middle. The playing area is an oval, generally much larger than a ballpark in the U.S. Each side has 11 players, and one team fields while the other bats.

Unlike baseball, cricket has two batsmen up at once, although only one at a time faces the pitcher (called a bowler). The batsman uses his bat to defend a wooden frame behind him, called "the stumps" or "wicket," upon which two pieces of wood, the bales, are balanced. If the bowler can get a ball past him and dislodge those bales, the batsman is out. To use cricket terminology, he's lost his wicket.

Bowlers hurl the ball stiff armed, making it bounce at the batter's feet. They use all manner of tricks to take a wicket, craftily putting spin on the ball so it bounces weirdly off the seam or simply relying on brute power and intimidation, racing in and hurling it at 100 miles an hour (160 kph) so that it rears up in the batsman's face. This can be a dangerous game. Strategically placed fielders wait with cupped hands to catch a nicked ball. As with baseball, anything caught on the fly is an out. The fielder behind the wicket (the wicket-keeper) wears mitts, but nobody else does. It's a game for players with lightning-fast

INSIDER TIP:

A note to globe-trotting baseball buffs: At a cricket match, it's only fair dinkum [good form] to throw back any ball hit into the stands.

—JUSTIN KAVANAGH
National Geographic
International Editions editor

reflexes and tough, calloused hands, who don't mind the odd broken finger or three.

Batsmen have to try to hit the ball and score runs. The duel between batsman and bowler can go on for hours. A ball hit to the boundary is worth four runs. One hit over the fence, home-run style, is worth six. Otherwise the batsmen scamper back and forth between the stumps for single runs. Eventually somebody loses their wicket and a new batsman comes in. When a team loses ten wickets, its innings ends and the fielding side comes in to bat. In a test match, each side gets two innings.

Although professional players are anything but choir boys—the beer drinking record of 56 cans on the flight from Sydney to London is held by an Australian—there are no pro-athlete tantrums or umpire-bullying displays on the field. After all, the pride of nations rests on the decorum of their cricketers.

Sir Donald Bradman

When polls are run to nominate the greatest Australian of all time, Sir Donald Bradman (1908–2001) regularly tops the list. The batting hero was not only the preeminent cricketer of his time, but Australians regard him as the greatest sportsman ever. Raised in Bowral, New South Wales, where he showed prodigious talent from an early age, the young Bradman first represented Australia against England in 1928 and quickly amassed record batting scores. By the time he toured England as captain for the last time in 1948, he had sealed his place as the game's greatest ever batter. His career batting average of 99.94, just short of a freakish 100, remains almost double that of any cricketer before or since.

"The Don" retired to Adelaide, where he became a statesman of the game, giving audiences to young cricketers and politicians alike. The word "Bradmanesque" has entered the Australian lexicon and means succeeding far above all others.

Darling Harbour

Once an eyesore of dilapidated wharves, Darling Harbour is now a humming tourism and leisure precinct on the waterfront. It opened in 1988, amid the fanfare of Australia's bicentennial, and the area has not looked back since. Skyscrapers have sprouted nearby, as have a convention-center-scale hotel and a glittering new casino, and businesses have shifted to the area. But Darling Harbour was designed for family-oriented entertainment—and it delivers.

The SEA LIFE Sydney Aquarium allows visitors to walk through the world of maritime life.

Darling Harbour
🅼 75 E2
Visitor Information
☎ 02/9240-0111
darlingharbour.com

SEA LIFE Sydney Aquarium
✉ Darling Harbour
☎ 02/8251-7800
💲 $$$$
sydneyaquarium .com.au

The area's two biggest family attractions are the Powerhouse Museum and the SEA LIFE Sydney Aquarium. Both are world class. The **Powerhouse Museum** is in an old generating station that used to power Sydney's tramway system. Nominally a museum of applied industry (it has superb exhibits of working steam engines), it exuberantly exceeds its brief, offering imaginatively displayed collections on Australian music, costume jewelry, trains, and

more. The museum emphasizes hands-on fun and interactive displays and makes a particularly good place to bring kids.

Darling Harbour's other blockbuster attraction is the **SEA LIFE Sydney Aquarium** (the ferry stops here). Its transparent underwater tunnels allow visitors to stroll among the sharks, eels, and stingrays of its immensely popular exhibits. The aquarium features diverse aquatic life from a wide range of marine environments that extend from the

Great Barrier Reef to the inland waterways of Australia and Sydney Harbour. Next to the aquarium, the small **WILD LIFE Sydney Zoo** *(tel 02/9333-9288, wildlifesydney .com.au, $$$$)* is home to wallabies, koalas, nocturnal marsupials, snakes, birds, and crocodiles. It provides a compact glimpse of weird Australian fauna for visitors in a hurry. **Madame Tussauds** *(tel 02/9333-9240, madametussauds .com.au, $$$$),* a franchise of the famous London attraction, rounds out the triumvirate of tourist attractions at Aquarium Pier. Waxwork figures focus on histori-cal and pop cultural icons, with an emphasis on Australian celebrities. Online discounts and combo passes are available for all three.

INSIDER TIP:

An evening ferry ride from Darling Harbour to any destination pro-vides spectacular views of the Harbour Bridge and downtown Sydney.

—DAVID KENNEDY
*National Geographic
contributor*

Around the Harbor

The aquarium is a good place to begin a walk around Darling Har-bour. Start by walking across the **Pyrmont Bridge,** built in 1902 as the world's first electrically operated swing bridge. It is used only by pedestrians today.

When you get across, the **Australian National Maritime**

Museum is on the right. It tells Australia's seagoing story from Aboriginal canoes and convict ships to 20th-century ocean liners. The broader story of Australia and the sea is also covered, from the age of exploration to surfing culture to the immigrants who have come by sea, legally and illegally. Ships moored in front include WWII craft, a Viet-namese refugee boat, and a replica of Cook's *Endeavour.* On the north-western flank of Darling Harbour behind the museum, **The Star** is a glitzy casino-hotel complex.

On the left as you step off the Pyrmont Bridge is the enormous, glass-and-steel **Harbourside.** This tourist shopping mall has a food court, restaurant, and shops, but it is probably the least interesting feature of the precinct.

Half a mile west, the bustling **Sydney Fish Market** *(Bank Street, tel 02/9004-1100)* on Blackwattle Bay is the city's main seafood mar-ket and a better spot for lunch. As well as weekly wholesale auctions, retail outlets sell fresh seafood and cheap, sumptuous platters to eat inside or at tables outside.

A stroll along the harborside, past the **Sydney Exhibition Centre,** destined for massive rede-velopment, will bring you to the **Chinese Garden** *(Harbour St., tel 02/9281-6863, $)* at the southern end of Darling Harbour. Effective at shutting out the hustle and bustle of the city, the walled enclave has a Lake of Brightness and Courtyard of Welcoming Fragrance. Chinese tea and cakes are available.

Get revved up again at the huge **IMAX Theatre** nestled in the freeway interchange nearby. ■

Powerhouse Museum

✉ 500 Harris St.
☎ 02/9217-0222
$ $$

powerhousemuseum .com

Australian National Maritime Museum

✉ Darling Harbour
☎ 02/9298-3777
$ $–$$$

anmm.gov.au

IMAX Theatre

✉ Southern Promenade, Darling Harbour
☎ 02/9281-3300

Bohemian Sydney

In a city known the world over for its breezy, beachy indolence, bohemia (in shorts, thongs, and Ray-Ban sunglasses) seems to be everywhere. Paddington and Darlinghurst, though, in the inner east, make a strong claim for primacy with their blend of seediness and sophistication. Oxford Street, the main thoroughfare, is a cavalcade of retro cafés, bookshops, nightclubs, strip joints, galleries dealing in ultracool kitsch, sex shops, and black leather.

The highlight of Sydney's Gay and Lesbian Mardi Gras is the spectacular parade down Oxford Street.

This spread-out strip has no particular social focus, although on Saturday the bustling **Paddington Markets** *(10 a.m.–4 p.m.)* comes close. One of the architectural features of Sydney's inner east is the elegantly restored Victorian-era row houses, their balconies trimmed with wrought iron that used to be known as "Paddington lace."

Darlinghurst

Darlinghurst is a trendy Little Italy, with its self-consciously cool sidewalk cafés. Stanley Street, which runs due east off Hyde Park, is the hub of the social scene here, and it is a good spot to linger over an espresso and the Sunday newspaper, soaking in the ambience and the sunshine.

Kings Cross, a few blocks farther north, is Sydney's red-light district—a weird blend of prostitution, crime, strip joints, nightclubs, fast food, and hard drugs, with a smattering of expensive restaurants and international hotels thrown in to confuse. The Cross, as it is known, was a popular R&R hangout for troops on leave during the Vietnam War, and it still attracts a lot of soldiers, along with curious tourists,

EXPERIENCE: Taking a Priscilla Tour

Stephan Elliott's 1994 film, *The Adventures of Priscilla, Queen of the Desert,* tells the tale of Sydney drag queens who take their show to the outback. An Academy Award winner for best costume design, the movie later inspired a musical. Today, it also provides the theme for flamboyant city tours by professional diva Portia

Turbo, who appeared in the movie. Fun bus tours *(tel 02/9310-0200, toursbydiva.com.au),* complete with champagne, take in the usual Sydney sights (Opera House, Harbour Bridge), as well as the gay haunts of the Oxford Strip, with opportunities to don a wig and perform.

runaways, derelicts, college students on a big night out, and bachelor parties (called Bucks' nights here). The El Alamein Fountain in Fitzroy Gardens is the area's focal point.

Just east, **Elizabeth Bay** rubs shoulders with the Cross, but it is decidedly quieter and infinitely more fashionable. This was Sydney's fashionable bohemian quarter in the 1920s, and, with its stylish period apartment blocks, it is still popular with entertainers, writers, and journalists.

Glebe & Balmain

The peninsular suburbs of Glebe and Balmain, in Sydney's inner west, used to be rough working-class neighborhoods for dockyard workers, but they have now been discovered and their houses carefully restored. Balmain is rich in Victorian-era waterfront pubs, while Glebe is a jumble of interesting hole-in-the-wall eateries, cafés, and bistros. *(Balmain is accessible by ferry from Circular Quay or bus 442 from the Queen Victoria Building. To get to Glebe, take bus 431 or 433 along George St. and up Glebe Point Rd.)*

Newtown

Newtown (take the Liverpool-City rail line) is a funky melting pot of students, gays and lesbians, intellectuals, and artists, perched on the edge of Sydney University. Thirty years ago it was regarded as a grungy slum. Now it is fashionably chic, although it still has a strong underground feel to it. King

INSIDER TIP:

A great way to see Balmain is in a kayak. Natural Wanders *[tel 0427/225-072, kayak sydney.com.au]* runs tours from Lavendar Bay near Luna Park to Balmain on weekends.

—PETER TURNER
National Geographic author

Street, the main thoroughfare, has trendy cafés, ethnic restaurants, and secondhand bookshops. The hot, sweaty, and smoky pubs here are the focus of Sydney's dwindling live band scene. ∎

Oxford Street
 Bus 333 or 380 from Circular Quay runs the length of Oxford St.

Paddington Markets
 Corner of Oxford & Newcombe Sts.

Kings Cross
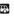 Bus 323, 324, 325, or 326 from Circular Quay. Train station on Darlinghurst Rd.

Beaches

There are more than 70 named beaches around Sydney, some of them on the harbor, others fringing the ocean. The closest ocean beach to downtown Sydney is Bondi Beach, which has become synonymous around the world with Aussie surf culture. On weekends this golden crescent of sand, located 5 miles (8 km) west of Sydney, becomes a coconut oil–scented kaleidoscope of thousands of beach towels, bronzed swimmers, surfers, and sunbathers.

Sydney's iconic Bondi Beach

Bondi Beach

As a suburb, Bondi (pronounced Bond-EYE) calls to mind a fading seaside resort. Bondi's glory days would have been in the 1920s and '30s, judging by the art deco Bondi Hotel, the jumble of 1920s apartment blocks overlooking the beach, and the gaudy Spanish-style Bondi Pavilion, which was built as deluxe changing rooms in 1928. In recent years, the town has spent a lot of money to spruce up tired facades, landscape the foreshore, and improve Campbell Street—a traffic-clogged thoroughfare of ice cream parlors, surf shops, hostels, and cafés. Bondi is more a backpackers' haunt, crowded with local and visiting beach bums, but it makes a great sunny, salty, breezy day out. If you tire of the beach and people-watching, Bondi has a good Sunday market, and a wonderful scenic 3-mile (5 km) walk wending south around the cliff tops to other beaches.

Other Beaches

South of Bondi is **Tamarama Beach,** known as Glamarama because it is where Sydney's beautiful people hang out. A mile or so farther south are **Bronte** and **Coogee Beaches,** smaller versions of Bondi.

Manly Beach, north of the harbor, is probably Sydney's second best known crescent of sand. Manly (see p. 78) occupies a narrow spit of land that ends in the dramatic sandstone cliffs at the entrance to the harbor. All these beaches are "outer beaches" facing the open Pacific.

The inner harbor has dozens of lovely beaches. One of the prettiest is **Balmoral,** on Hunters Bay. It has a genteel, Edwardian atmosphere, with palm trees and an old bandstand at the Bather's Pavilion, which is now home to a classy restaurant and café. ∎

INSIDER TIP:

Become a true local by signing up for surfing lessons at any of Sydney's popular beaches. Be prepared to be sore the next day—it's great exercise! The best surfing beaches are Bondi and Manly.

—FARNOUSH AFARINESH
National Geographic Channels International

Surf Lifesavers

Nothing evokes Sydney better than images of blue sky, golden sand, and the bronzed figures of its legendary surf lifesavers in their distinctive yellow and red caps. The world's first surf lifesaving club was formed at the Bondi Pavilion in 1907. The club was formed in response to a rising number of drownings, as an increasing number of people began to pursue the new craze called bodysurfing. Few knew anything about riptides or surf conditions then, because until around 1900, the authorities discouraged daylight swimming as an affront to public decency.

Surf lifesaving clubs quickly sprang up all around Australia. There are now 305 of them, with 25,000 active members, who rescue about 13,000 swimmers each year. Surf lifesaving has also become a sport in its own right, with colorful surf carnivals.

Bondi's lifesavers, who guard Australia's busiest and most famous beach, pluck more than 1,000 people out of the surf each year. To make sure you don't add to that tally, swim between the yellow-and-red lifesaving flags. If you do get caught in a riptide, do not try to fight it. Swim to the side to try to get out of it and raise your hand to attract a lifesaver.

A Sydney-style New Year's

If you are near Sydney over the Christmas–New Year's holiday, don't miss seeing the start of the great Sydney-to-Hobart yacht race on Boxing Day, the day after Christmas. The harbor fills with the sails of dozens of the world's fastest blue-water yachts, all jockeying for position ahead of the cannon fire that will start the annual 630-mile (1,014 km) race to Hobart, Tasmania, as well as those of thousands of spectator craft.

The sight of Sydney Harbour in full flower is unforgettable—eclipsed only by the fireworks extravaganza that ushers in the New Year. This is the celebration seen worldwide, with hundreds of skyrockets zooming off the arch of Sydney's iconic bridge, the skies above alight with starbursts and the harbor filled with hundreds of yachts.

Greeting the New Year

Australia is one of the first places in the world to greet the new year, and party-loving Sydneysiders really do it in style. Each year's celebrations follow a theme—2007, for example, marked the 75th birthday of

the Harbour Bridge, using the bridge to full effect and greatly expanding the show. In 2013, Kylie Minogue launched the Embrace theme, which included pyrotechnic bees, koalas, and octopus shells shot off in two displays: the family-friendly 9 p.m. fireworks and the midnight extravaganza.

In all, 15,400 pounds (7,000 kg) of explosives are used in these extravaganzas. They are launched by computer from a series of barges anchored in the harbor, a complex arrangement involving more than 7,500 cues and taking months to plan and choreograph.

Planning for Celebration

More than a million people will be thronging the vantage points along the waterfront, so having some idea in advance of where you want to be is a help. Designated viewpoints around Sydney begin filling well before showtime and a map can be found at the official website *(sydneynewyearseve.com)*. The Rocks has some big, popular venues. Alcohol is banned at most sites, but the Royal Botanic Gardens has two catered events *(rbgsyd.nsw.gov.au, tickets sell out weeks ahead)* and there are also two public viewing areas. For a night of family fun, ring in the New Year at the Taronga Zoo *(taronga.org.au)*, where you can bring a picnic, or buy food and drinks on-site.

The harbor islands are prime real estate for the display, and Fort Denison sells an exclusive dinner and fireworks package. Tickets for other islands and parks in the Sydney Harbour National Park go on sale at the end of November, or you can camp on Cockatoo Island for the price of a five-star hotel, but be warned any hotel is hard to find on New Year's Eve.

Another prime viewpoint is on the water. Sydney Ferries sells tickets for its cruise early in November *(book online at sydneyferries.info)* and other pricier cruises also operate.

New Year's Eve fireworks explode off the Harbour Bridge.

Zoos & Wildlife Parks

The warm breath of the bush is never far away in Sydney—long tentacles of bushland reach into the suburbs, possums come out to nibble rosebuds in backyard gardens, and, at night, hundreds of giant native fruit bats, or flying foxes, wheel in the corporate glow. However, your best chance of seeing Australia's unique wildlife up close is to visit one of the local zoos or wildlife parks.

Taronga Zoo has a lovely setting in Sydney Harbour.

Taronga Zoo

🗺 75 E3
✉ Bradleys Head Rd., Mosman
☎ 02/9969-2777
💲 $$$$$
🚢 Ferry from Circular Quay

taronga.org.au

Taronga Zoo is the easiest to reach from Sydney. It sits on a leafy hill in Mosman, overlooking Sydney Harbour, just a 15-minute ferry trip from Circular Quay. Combination zoo-ferry tickets are available at the ferry landing.

The zoo has a world-class collection of wildlife, and the spacious enclosures resemble natural habitats. Nocturnal houses and low-light enclosures reduce the stress on night-loving animals, while allowing visitors to observe them. The gorilla rain forest and the chimpanzee park are always popular, but for visitors from outside Australia the enclosures where kangaroos, wombats, and other indigenous creatures are on

display are must-sees. The koala enclosure features a walkway that winds up to these native creatures in the treetops.

Two major wildlife parks in Sydney's far western outskirts give closer, and perhaps more touristy, encounters with Australian fauna. **Featherdale Wildlife Park** (*217 Kildare Rd., Doonside, tel 02/9622-1644, featherdale.com.au, $$$$*) is the best for seeing koalas, kangaroos, wallabies, wombats, crocodiles, Tasmanian devils, kookaburras, and other birdlife. It's well worth a stop on the way to the Blue Mountains. The **Koala Park Sanctuary** (*84 Castle Hill Rd., West Pennant Hills, tel 02/9484-3141, $$$*) has a large resident population of cute koalas, with cuddling sessions, and upclose encounters with other marsupials and Australian birdlife.

On the other hand, once rare flora that you can now touch is the Wollemi pine. In one of the most startling botanical discoveries of the 20th century, a stand of 37 of these Jurassic-era trees was found in an gorge less than a hundred miles (160 km) from Sydney in 1994. A program to preserve the species proved so successful that in April 2006 the trees went on sale to the public. (Visit *wollemi pine.com* for more details.) ∎

Beyond glamorous Sydney, subtropical rain forests, high alpine grasslands, and dusty frontier outback

New South Wales

Introduction & Map   102–103

Blue Mountains   104–105

Feature: Bushfires   106–107

Jenolan Caves   108

Tamworth   109

Hunter Valley   110–111

Along the South Coast   112–113

Snowy Mountains   114–115

Experience: "The Man from Snowy River" Rides   115

Broken Hill   116–117

Pacific Highway Drive   118–121

Experience: Houseboating on the Hawkesbury   118

Outlying Territories   122–126

Experience: Getting Close to Australian Wildlife   125

Hotels & Restaurants   369–370

Alpine sunray, Kosciuszko National Park, Snowy Mountains

New South Wales

New South Wales calls itself the Premier or First State, ostensibly because it was Australia's first colony but also because it tops the rest of Australia in just about everything these days, at least in the minds of the proudly parochial New South Welsh. Sydney is here, for one thing, and Sydney is the financial and arts capital of Australia, as well as the nation's biggest population center.

In addition to Sydney, New South Wales has spectacular and diverse landscapes, from winter snowfields on the country's highest mountain (the 7,310-foot/2,228 m Mount Kosciuszko) to sultry banana plantations on the north coast and the outback to the west.

The mighty Murray River forms its southern boundary and nourishes the country's agricultural heartland. Broken Hill, one of the grand old Australian mining towns, is now an outback art colony, its clear, fragile light attracting painters and filmmakers.

For those on a time budget, this is the place to concentrate. Almost everything in Australia—rain forests, dusty outback landscapes, mountains, beaches—can be found here, including five World Heritage sites: an improbable mix of the Gondwana Rainforests; the lake beds of Willandra National Park, where Aborigines have lived for 40,000 years; Lord Howe Island,

NOT TO BE MISSED:

The spectacular panoramas from the Blue Mountains **104–105**

Line dancing at the Tamworth Country Music Festival **109**

Touring the wineries of the scenic Hunter Valley **110–111**

A horse trek or alpine hike in the Snowy Mountains **114–115**

Byron Bay, the funkiest resort along the north coast **121**

Venturing offshore to lush, tropical Lord Howe Island **122–124**

430 miles (692 km) off the central coast; the Blue Mountains just west of Sydney; and that grand architectural dame, the Sydney Opera House. New South Wales also has Tamworth, Australia's country music capital.

About an hour's drive north of Sydney, the Hunter Valley is Australia's oldest winemaking

region and a popular weekend retreat. Cessnock, the main town in the valley, is surrounded
by more than 120 wineries with ample opportunities to visit and taste. Follow the New England
Highway through the valley to Scone, home to
some of Australia's finest racehorse studs and
glamorous polo tournaments. Farther north on
the Pacific Highway are the World Heritage rain
forests of Dorrigo National Park. ■

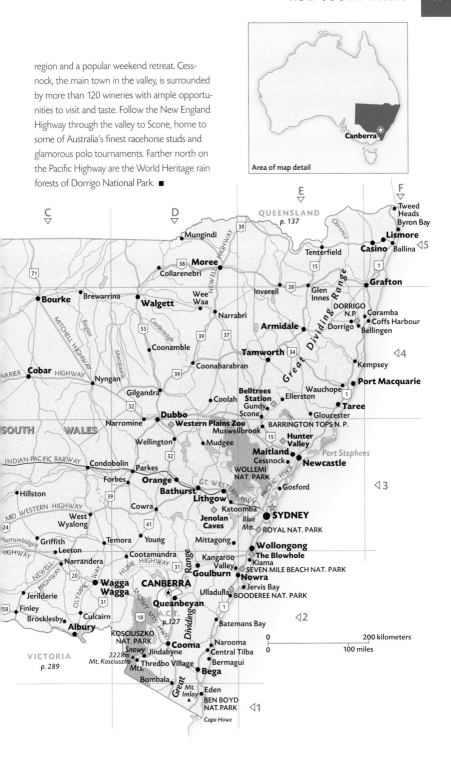

Area of map detail

Canberra

Blue Mountains

From a distance, the Blue Mountains resemble an old oil painting, with hazy blue hues that seem a trifle overdone. The blue haze is actually a fine mist of eucalyptus oil given off by dense forests. The droplets refract the sunlight, tinting the air and giving the horizon a painted-on effect. Although the Blue Mountains are only just over 3,000 feet high (915 m), they proved an impenetrable barrier for the first settlers.

It was not until 1813 that a trio of explorers—Lawson, Blaxland, and Wentworth—found a way through and opened up the wide, flat grazing country on the other side. In 1868, the railroad was built, opening up the mountains themselves. Suddenly it was possible for well-heeled Sydney-siders to escape the coastal heat and take the air in the mountains. By 1900, Katoomba, Wentworth Falls, and Mount Victoria had become fashionable resorts, with high-toned restaurants and shops and graceful Victorian hotels to cater to those who didn't have the money to build a mountain retreat themselves. The high point was reached in the 1920s, with guesthouses catering to families, while the art deco Hydro Majestic in Medlow Bath drew society's high rollers.

New Englanders may find something nookish about these leafy old resort towns—with their antiques shops, cafés, and home-made fudge—that reminds them of home. The mountains have hiking trails and tourist marvels like the Scenic Railway, which plunges into a gorge on what is said to be the world's steepest railway. It even snows here, a little, in winter. In July, the region has a Yuletide Festival, with crackling fires, roast beef and Yorkshire pudding dinners, and hot spiced wine. Afternoon tea at the **Lilianfels Blue Mountains hotel** (see p. 369) in Katoomba is a year-round tradition.

Katoomba is the main town in the Blue Mountains. It perches on the rim of the Jamison Valley, with spectacular outlooks over the wilderness below. This is the best

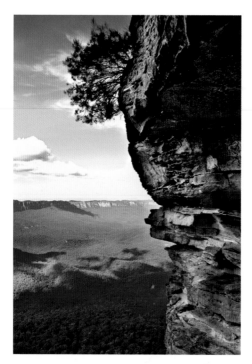

The Blue Mountains' scenic vistas are among this atmospheric area's many charms.

place to base yourself if you decide against driving through the snarl of traffic in Sydney's western suburbs and take the train. Katoomba has hotels, inns, and B&Bs. Almost everything is within walking distance of the station, and local buses serve the area as well. In fact, if you are short on time, the Blue Mountains can be a longish, but not unreasonable, day trip from Sydney. Bring a sweater because it will be cooler here than in the city.

A 20-minute walk down Katoomba Street takes you past antiques shops, galleries, and cafés to **Echo Point.** The view here is simply stunning. Off to the left are the **Three Sisters,** a formation of honey-colored sandstone nubs, floodlit at night until 11 p.m., which take their name from an Aboriginal Dreamtime legend. One version of the legend tells of a tribal leader who turned his daughters to stone rather than risk their being carried away by raiding enemies. Unfortunately, he was killed in battle and thus could not reverse his spell. Just before the lookout, you can see Aboriginal dances at the **Koomurri Aboriginal Centre** art gallery (tel 02/4782-1979, koo murriaboriginalcentre.com.au).

Easy clifftop paths are marked along the edge of the valley. Or you can take the **Giant Staircase—** a steep set of steps cut into the rock—1,000 feet (300 m) down to the valley floor. From here you can take day hikes to popular features like the **Ruined Castle** rock formation, and longer treks as far as **Jenolan Caves,** 26 miles (42 km) away (see p. 108). Or you can hike along the valley floor

to **Orphan Rock** and then take the **Scenic Railway** back up to Katoomba. The railway is part of **Scenic World** (Violet St. & Cliff Dr., tel 02/4780-0200), which includes Scenic Skyway, traversing a spur above the Jamison Valley; Scenic Cableway, a cable car running into the valley; Scenic Walkway; and even Scenic Cinema.

Leura, smaller and prettier than Katoomba, lies 2 miles (3.2 km)

INSIDER TIP:

For a taste of tranquility, take a leisurely bushwalk in the Blue Mountains. Be sure not to miss the legendary sandstone Three Sisters rock formation.

—DANIELLE WILLIAMS
National Geographic Television

to the east. It has a quaint village atmosphere that evokes its 1920s origins, with cafés, art galleries, and antiques galleries. Hiking paths lead to Leura Cascades, Bridal Veil Falls, and Gordon Falls. You can also hike along the clifftops to Katoomba.

Five miles (8 km) northwest of Katoomba is the old spa town of **Medlow Bath.** Because the eucalyptus-laden air was believed to have therapeutic powers, early 20th-century hoteliers hoped guests would come to take the waters too. The **Hydro Majestic Hotel** (hydromajestic.com.au) here still has its art deco facade. The dining room offers one of the best views of the valley. ∎

Blue Mountains
🗺 103 E3
Visitor Information
✉ Hamment Pl., Glenbrook
☎ 1300-653-408

Katoomba
🗺 103 D3
Visitor Information
✉ Echo Point
☎ 1300-653-408

Bushfires

On February 7, 2009, after prolonged drought and a severe heat wave, more than 400 bushfires broke out in the state of Victoria. Fanned by fierce winds, terrifying hundred-foot-high (30 m) flames roared through forests and towns claiming 173 lives, destroying 2,200 homes, and leaving 7,500 homeless.

A bushfire rages near Alice Springs in Australia's Red Centre.

Even to Australians, long used to bushfires, this tragedy—the country's worst natural disaster—was hard to believe. These were not isolated outback blazes but infernos that threatened the outskirts of Melbourne, Australia's second largest city. In the aftermath, the country tried to devise strategies to stop a recurrence, but this was not the first deadly bushfire. In 2003, the outskirts of Sydney and the suburbs of Canberra burned, killing four. More recently, a record heat wave in 2012–2013 saw bushfires across southeast Australia, clouding city skies with smoke.

The journals of Australia's early explorers were filled with references to bushfires and a land shrouded by smoke. Many of the fires they encountered were caused by summer lightning strikes in the tinder-dry grass, but others were deliberately set by Aborigines, who used fire as a management tool to clear scrub, drive game, and help their ancient land to renew itself.

While scorched earth and the blackened ribs of a eucalyptus forest may not be pretty to look at, such periodic wiping out and starting over is vital for the health of the Australian bush. Many of its species, such as banksias, grass trees, and cycads, are known as "fire climax" plants—those whose seeds are matured and released only by the intense heat of a bushfire. The eucalyptus even provides the tinder for its own eventual demise by continually shedding its crisp, paperlike bark. When fire comes, as it inevitably must, it sweeps away the forests' old, mature growth, allowing space for the next generation to sprout.

History of Devastation

While this may be part of the natural order, it can have awful human consequences, and not even the nation's most cosmopolitan neighborhoods are immune, as the residents of Melbourne were reminded in 2009, and Sydney and Canberra in 2003. In 1939, vast bushfires roared out of control throughout South Australia, Victoria, and New South Wales. On Ash Wednesday in 1983, South Australians suffered one of the country's most devastating bushfires, as the Adelaide Hills went up in flames, with fires claiming dozens of lives and scores of homes.

Risk & Renewal

Australians have had to learn to live with fire. Each day's fire danger is usually given with the weather report on the evening news. Homeowners prepare for the summer fire season by cutting away the bushy undergrowth from around their houses, clearing dead leaves and twigs from their guttering, and making sure their garden hoses are in good working order. Many join the volunteer fire brigade—known as the Country Fire Service (C.F.S.) in South Australia—and devote weekends to training and practice. Town councils, working alongside the C.F.S. and meteorology bureau, often arrange controlled burn-offs to clean out the drying scrub, particularly if the winter has been rainy and the undergrowth has sprouted up thick and tall. The highest risk comes on hot, windy days, late in summer, when the bush is just so many square miles of crisp, dry tinder waiting for a spark. And that can literally be all it takes—a spark, or a carelessly discarded cigarette, to start a raging fire of biblical proportions.

There are few things more terrifying than an Australian bushfire, with its roaring walls of flame. Fueled by the flammable natural oils in the leaves and wood of the eucalyptus, which make each tree a potential torch, bushfires race from treetop to treetop, like chain lightning, sweeping down a hillside faster than a man can run or a horse can gallop—sometimes too fast even for a fleeing vehicle.

There is a random quality to the destruction that Americans who live in the tornado belt of the Midwest would recognize: A car can be incinerated, while the one stranded immediately behind is untouched; one house can be razed, but its neighbor doesn't even get its gardens singed.

If the destructive power of its fires is awesome, the bushland's capacity for renewal seems nothing short of miraculous. Even with the blackened earth still warm and the air fragrant with eucalyptus smoke, there are dashes of green amid the ashes from the fire-resistant shrubs that survived the blaze. Within weeks, grasses are sprouting and the first shoots of the next generation of trees are peeking through.

Battling a 2006 blaze in Perth, Western Australia

Jenolan Caves

The Jenolan Caves are a series of 300 limestone caverns in the hillsides about 50 miles (80 km) by road southwest from Katoomba. Back in the 1920s, this was the prime honeymoon spot for adventurous young Australians, who had to drive their jalopies over hairpin roads to get here.

Jenolan Caves

- 103 D3
- 02/6359-9311
- $$$–$$$$$
- Turnoff to the caves is marked 18 miles (28 km) W of Katoomba toward Lithgow on the Great Western Highway

jenolancaves.org.au

The walls of the old Jenolan Caves House Hotel, at the caves' entrance, are lined with faded black-and-white photos of picnickers and men in straw boaters rowing lady friends on subterranean lakes. Somehow the place has managed to retain a sense of that fresh innocence: It's touristy, but delightful at the same time.

INSIDER TIP:

The final stretch of road from Katoomba into the Jenolan Valley is one-way [inbound] from 11:45 a.m.–1:45 p.m. There are alternate routes out of the valley, but plan ahead.

—ROFF SMITH
National Geographic author

The caves are located on the edge of Kanagra-Boyd National Park. In the 1830s, they were a hideout for the bushranger James McKeown, an escaped convict who preyed on the coaches traveling through the mountains. After his capture, the caves became tourist attractions, but some of the farther reaches remain unexplored.

Eleven caves are open to the public, and the caverns and features have grandiose names such as **Temple of Baal, Pool of Cerberus,** and **Imperial Diamond.** Tours run every 15–30 minutes, and the caves are graded in difficulty by how many steps they have. A "strenuous" cave may have as many as 1,575 steps, an easy one about 300. Adventure caving packages from two to six hours include rapelling and rock climbing. No experience is necessary, and overalls and a hat are provided.

Public transportation does not go to Jenolan Caves, but bus tours from Katoomba include the caves. This twisting drive through steep and dense forests is not for the faint-hearted, but the mountainside precipices give sweeping views over the pastoral country west of the ranges.

The area has fine bushwalks, from the short, scenic Carlotta Arch Track to the three-day **Six Foot Track** all the way to Katoomba. Originally cleared as a bridle path in 1884, this track begins at the Explorers Tree on the highway in Katoomba (the Katoomba visitor center has walk maps) and stretches 28 miles (45 km). There are two campsites, and guided walks are available *(lifesanadventure.com.au)* with one night in an eco-lodge. ■

Tamworth

Tamworth is Australia's country music capital, a sort of antipodean Nashville. In case you didn't know this already, a 40-foot (12 m) Big Golden Guitar will clue you in as you drive into town. Pull into the Big Golden Guitar Tourist Centre beside the giant guitar to meet some stars—at least in effigy: Chad Morgan, Slim Dusty, and Tex Morton, to name a few.

If you have the radio on during the 250-mile (400 km) drive north from Sydney (on the Pacific and New England Highways), you will no doubt figure out that country music is big in Australia.

This love affair with country music started in 1965, when local radio station 2TM began its nightly *Hoedown* program and staged live shows at the Tamworth Town Hall. These shows attracted some of Australia's top country artists and drew large crowds from around the grazing districts.

In 1973, the inaugural Country Music Awards began and quickly snowballed into the annual **Tamworth Country Music Festival.** For ten days every January, up to 50,000 country music fans, musicians, impresarios, talent scouts, agents, and bush poets descend on Tamworth. Book well in advance if you plan to stay. The festival reaches its climax on Australia Day (January 26) weekend, when the Australian country music awards—the Golden Guitars—are presented. Each year a new name is added to the **Roll of Renown,** near the Entertainment Centre.

The **Hands of Fame** on Kable Avenue has the concrete prints of more than 300

Tamworth's music festival attracts rollicking bands, including the Pigs, whose high-energy performances earn raves.

guitar-picking hands of country music stars. Music fans will also enjoy the **Walk A Country Mile** interpretive exhibit at the Tamworth Visitor Information Centre. The **Australian Country Music Hall of Fame** *(93 Brisbane St., tel 02/6766-9696)* features some of Australia's best loved country artists, as does the **Gallery of Stars Wax Museum** at the Big Golden Guitar.

Pick up a map at the visitor center and take a heritage walk around town. Out of festival time, you may not hear much country music in Tamworth, but a recording studio can be visited by appointment. Ask at the visitor center for information. ■

Tamworth

⊠ 103 E4

Visitor Information

✉ Corner of Peel & Murray Sts.

☎ 02/6767-5300

Big Golden Guitar

✉ 2 Ringers Rd. (next to the New England Hwy.)

☎ 02/6765-2688

biggoldenguitar .com.au

Hunter Valley

The Hunter Valley is an odd mix of coal-mining towns, racehorse country, and several of Australia's best known and oldest wineries. The first vines were planted here around 1830, and today there are more than 150 wineries in the valley. The region is only a three-hour drive from Sydney, so it has become a popular day trip or weekend getaway for city wine buffs and others.

The Hunter Valley produces some of Australia's most famous wines.

Hunter Valley

⛰ 103 E3

Visitor Information

✉ 455 Wine Country Dr., Pokolbin

☎ 02/4990-0900

winecountry.com.au

Singleton

Visitor Information

✉ Townhead Park, New England Hwy.

☎ 1800-449-888

The old coal-mining town of **Cessnock** on Route 82 is the gateway to the **Lower Hunter Valley.** The heart of the winemaking region is around **Pokolbin,** approximately 6 miles (9.6 km) northwest of Cessnock on McDonalds Road.

Pokolbin is home to the Hunter Valley Wine Country visitor center, a great source of brochures and maps to guide you around the wineries of the region. Some of the labels on the maps will be familiar—Rose-mount Estate and Lindemans, for example—but others will be mysteries worth exploring. Semi-llon and Shiraz are the region's signature wines, but a number

of varietals are grown. Several wineries also have restaurants.

Dozens of wineries, such as Lindemans and Tyrells, are concentrated within a few minutes' drive of each other. Almost all give free tastings. Some have barbecue and picnic facilities and winemaking museums; others such as McWilliams, Tyrells, and Hunter Estate, give tours.

Wine, food, flowers, music, and art festivals pack a busy events calendar, with something happening every month of the year. Some highlights include **Hunter Valley Wine & Food Month** in June, and **Jazz in the Vines** and **Opera in the Vines,** both in October.

Although the wineries in the Lower Valley are well known, the scenery is rather flat and uninspiring. The **Upper Hunter Valley,** 50 miles (80 km) farther north, has only a couple dozen wineries, but the scenery is better and it is far less crowded on weekends.

The scenic country around **Scone** (*visitor information: tel 02/6545-1526*) is home to some of Australia's finest racehorse studs and wealthiest grazing families. You can tour some of the stud farms (ask at the visitor center), including the **Segenhoe Stud** (famous in the horse racing world). It is best to visit in mid-May, during **Scone Horse Festival.**

About 10 miles (16 km) northeast of Scone is Gundy polo ground, where Australia's richest come to play. You can get a taste of this style of living at **Belltrees Station** (*tel 02/6546-1123*), which was the family estate of author Patrick White. Guests stay in the farmhouse, self-contained cottages, or the mountain retreat, in the cool of the Great Dividing Range. To the east of Belltrees is **Barrington Tops National Park,** part of a World Heritage area (see p. 120). ■

GETTING TO THE HUNTER VALLEY: The New England Highway is the main access route for the Hunter Valley, although back-roads enthusiasts may want to try the old Putty Road, a tortuous byway that winds more than 100 miles (160 km) through the dense forests of the Great Dividing Range between Windsor, in Sydney's outer west, and Singleton.

Top Australian Wine Regions

Australia, the world's fourth biggest exporter of wine, has more than 60 wine regions, concentrated mostly in South Australia, New South Wales, Victoria, and Western Australia.

New South Wales: Hunter Valley (see p. 110–111), 100 miles (160 km) north of Sydney, is Australia's oldest winery region and one of its largest, famous for its long-aging Semillon. Shiraz, Chardonnay, Verdelho, and others are also produced here.

South Australia: Barossa Valley (see pp. 267–268), one hour northeast of Adelaide, is Australia's largest wine region. Shiraz is its signature grape, but Cabernet Sauvignon, Grenache, Merlot, Riesling, Chardonnay, and Semillon thrive here too.

The McLaren Vale region (see p. 263), just 25 miles (40 km) south of Adelaide, produces excellent Shiraz and Cabernet Sauvignon, Merlot, Chardonnay, Sauvignon Blanc, and Riesling.

Located 80 miles (130 km) north of Adelaide, the Clare Valley (see p. 266) is the picturesque home of quality Riesling.

Coonawarra (see p. 266), 250 miles (400 km) southeast of Adelaide, is famous for its intensely flavored Cabernet Sauvignon, but it also produces Shiraz, Merlot, and Chardonnay.

Tasmania: The island produces aromatic wines unlike those of the warmer mainland. Some excellent wineries, including Pipers Brook and 9th Island in the Tamar Valley (see p. 332), produce Pinot Noir, Riesling, Pinot Grigio, and other varieties.

Victoria: Yarra Valley (see p. 308), some 30 miles (50 km) northeast of Melbourne, produces elegant cool-climate Pinot Noir and Chardonnay, and also Shiraz, Cabernet Sauvignon, Marsanne, Sauvignon Blanc, and Semillon.

Western Australia: Margaret River (see pp. 226–227), a picturesque region 175 miles (280 km) south of Perth, grows a wide variety of premium grapes but is renowned for Cabernet Sauvignon, Shiraz, Verdelho, and Australia's best Sauvignon Blanc.

Along the South Coast

Dropping south down the coast means taking it easy and escaping the rush of city life. The coast south of Sydney doesn't have the diverse scenery of the northbound Pacific Highway, but neither does it have its frantic pace. The Princes Highway rolls south through gentle farm country and placid little seaside towns.

The harbor at Wollongong, on the Illawarra Coast, south of Sydney

Royal National Park

🗺 103 E3

Visitor Information

✉ Audley Rd., Audley

☎ 02/9542-0648

Wollongong

🗺 103 E3

Visitor Information

✉ 93 Crown St.

☎ 02/4267-5910

Kiama

🗺 103 E2

Visitor Information

✉ Blowhole Point Rd.

☎ 02/4232-3322

Royal National Park, about 20 miles (32 km) south of Sydney, was established in 1879, making it the second oldest national park in the world (behind Yellowstone in the U.S.). The park is immensely popular with Sydney bushwalkers and cross-country running clubs, but surprisingly few foreigners visit. That's a pity because it has some of New South Wales's finest cliff walks and wildflower displays, and bird-watchers can find as many as 200 species. Some excellent and easily accessible trails start at the railway stations of the small towns along the Princes Highway—**Engadine, Loftus, Heathcote, Otford,** and **Waterfall.** You can also rent

canoes at the Audley boat shed (tel 02/9545-4967) if you want to float the Hacking River.

Thirty miles (48 km) south of Audley on the Princes Highway is **Wollongong,** the third largest city in New South Wales, a once heavily industrialized port looking to reinvent itself as a tourist destination. It has a particularly pleasant harbor area with a fishing fleet and lighthouse, good cafés (try along Keira Street), and some great beaches.

Kiama, 20 miles (32 km) farther, is a breezy seaside town. In 1797, explorer George Bass heard a "tremendous noise" coming from the cliffs above the bay. It occurs when big surf crashes through a rocky fissure known as the **Blowhole** and erupts as geysers up to 200 feet (61 m) tall. The sound and sight are awesome, but don't get too close; the waves can be deadly. Just west of town, a steep road leads up to the **Mount Saddleback Lookout** for sweeping views along the coast. **Jamberoo** is a pretty and historic village, 5 miles (8 km) inland.

Five miles (8 km) south of Kiama, take the turnoff to spectacular **Seven Mile Beach.** In 1933, aviator Charles Kingsford Smith took off from here on his pioneering flight across the Tasman Sea to New Zealand. The road hugs the coast for 16 miles (26 km) and joins the Princes Highway at Nowra. North of Nowra, a 15-mile (24 km) scenic detour on Route 79 goes north to the rustic **Kangaroo Valley,** which is popular with picnickers.

Jervis Bay, 20 miles (32 km) south from Nowra, has a fine sweep of coastline, white sandy beaches, and small hamlets such as Huskisson, the main center. Most of the territory is now the **Booderee National Park,** with rugged cliffs, sandy beaches, fine surf, walks, and botanic gardens.

South of Bermagui (see sidebar), the Princes Highway arcs inland to **Bega,** a cheesemaking town near the turnoff for the Snowy Mountains Highway. Come here in winter and you can surf in the morning and ski in the afternoon, if you make good time up the 100 miles (160 km) to the New South Wales snowfields.

Stay on the Princes Highway to reach the town of **Eden,** established in 1818 as Australia's first whaling port. Whaling remained the town's major industry until the 1920s. The **Killer Whale Museum** *(184 Imlay St., tel 02/6496-2094, $)* tells the story of those days, including the adventure of a Jonah-like whaler who was swallowed by a whale and regurgitated 15 hours later—still alive. Humpback and killer whales have returned to these waters and can be seen along the coast in spring.

Nearby **Ben Boyd National Park** *(contact National Parks & Wildlife Service, tel 02/6495-5000)* contains magnificent expanses of temperate rain forest and fine coastal scenery. A 2-mile (3.2 km) trail up **Mount Imlay,** 19 miles (30 km) west of Eden, rewards hikers with fine views of the wilderness coastline. The highway bends inland and continues into the forests of Victoria's Gippsland and south to Melbourne. ■

Booderee National Park
⛺ 103 D2
Visitor Information
☎ 02/4443-0977

Bega
⛺ 103 D2
Visitor Information
✉ Lagoon St.
☎ 02/6491-7645

Eden
⛺ 103 D1
Visitor Information
✉ Corner of Mitchell & Imlay Sts.
☎ 02/6496-1953

Angling in Bermagui

Bermagui lies about 100 miles (160 km) south of Booderee National Park, off the highway south of Tilba. The town has been popular with big-game anglers since Zane Grey, author of westerns and a great marlin angler, began coming in the 1930s. Big-game fishing tournaments are held here, and operators run fishing trips. Catches include black marlin and yellowfin tuna.

Snowy Mountains

The Snowy Mountains are the highest mountains in the Great Dividing Range, an ancient spine that runs along Australia's eastern coast from northern Queensland south to the Grampian Ranges in central Victoria. They are modest by world standards—the loftiest is Mount Kosciuszko, 7,310 feet (2,228 m) high—and not really very snowy, but because of their vast area they have larger snowfields in the winter season than Switzerland.

Cooma

◪ 103 D2

Visitor Information

✉ 119 Sharp St.

☎ 02/6455-1745
or
1800-636-525

On the New South Wales side of the mountains is the huge **Kosciuszko National Park,** more than 1.7 million acres (690,000 ha) of peaks, glacial lakes, meadows full of wildflowers, and deep forests. **Mount Kosciuszko** was climbed by Polish explorer Paul Edmund de

Cross-country skiers wend their way along trails near Thredbo in the aptly named Snowy Mountains.

Strzelecki in 1840, who named it in honor of the Polish freedom fighter Gen. Tadeusz Kosciuszko.

Cooma, about 250 miles (400 km) southwest of Sydney, is a good base for visiting the Snowy Mountains. Cooma was the construction headquarters for the Snowy Mountains Hydroelectric Scheme, one of Australia's great continent-taming public works projects, begun in 1949. More than 100,000 people worked on the complicated project, which included 16 major dams, seven power stations, and a vast engineering marvel of tunnels, lakes, and pipelines. When all of these were finished in 1974, the Tumut, Snowy, and Upper Murrumbidgee Rivers were providing 4 million kilowatts of electricity. The hydroelectric authority's **Snowy Hydro Discovery Centre** (*Monaro Hwy., tel 02/6453-2888*) has films and displays about how the power scheme works.

The new resort town of **Jindabyne,** 40 miles (64 km) farther south, was built along a lake that formed when the Snowy River was dammed in the early 1960s. The original 140-year-old town of Jindabyne lies under the waters of the lake. The **Snowy Region Visitor Centre** in Jindabyne is the national park headquarters

EXPERIENCE: "The Man from Snowy River" Rides

One of Australia's best loved poems, "The Man from Snowy River," written by Banjo Paterson in 1890, immortalizes the hard-riding stockmen of the high country. Though most of the cattlemen have gone, you can still ride "down by Kosciuszko . . . where air is clear as crystal, and the white stars fairly blaze."

Jindabyne Equestrian Resort *(tel 02/ 6456-7333, equestrianresort.com.au)* in Jindabyne offers one- or two-hour rides, overnight camps, lessons, and a range of accommodations. It doubles as a popular ski resort during the winter months.

Reynella Kosciuszko Rides *(tel 02/6454-2386, reynellarides.com.au)* in Adaminaby, 30 miles (50 km) northwest of Cooma, offers multiday treks into the mountains of Kosciuszko National Park from October to April.

Snowy River Horseback Adventure *(tel 02/6457-8385, snowyriverhorseback adventure.com.au)* in Jindabyne has two- to five-day horse treks though forest, meadow, and old stock routes from September to May.

and has maps and guides to Kosciuszko National Park.

Skiing & Hiking

Between mid-June and early October, visitors to the Snowy Mountains enjoy a thriving ski season. However, while the Snowy Mountains do provide the best skiing in Australia, skiers from North America and Europe are likely to find the ski slopes rather gentle and the snow wet and slushy. Still, if you want to ski among the snow gum trees—a surreal sensation—make lodging reservations well in advance. **Thredbo,** 20 miles (32 km) southwest of Jindabyne, has the longest runs in Australia—almost 2 miles (3 km) with more than 2,200 feet (670 m) of vertical drop. Perisher Valley, Charlotte Pass, and Smiggin Holes are the other main downhill resort areas, all on Kosciuszko Road in the south-center of the park.

The popularity of cross-country skiing and snowshoeing has grown in recent years. But be careful, particularly if you're tempted to venture off the groomed tracks. While these mountains may be relatively low, the weather up here can be sudden, unpredictable, and savage.

For most visitors, spring and summer are more relaxed seasons in which to visit the Snowy Mountains. Hiking is fine—either day trips or extended walks—in the high country, the wildflowers are spectacular, and trout anglers have a big choice of crystal clear lakes and mountain streams. Many ski lifts operate in the summer months, giving relatively easy access to the high country, and the ski resorts have accommodations. The summit of Mount Kosciuszko is accessible via Kosciuszko Road from Charlotte Pass (5.5 miles/ 9 km on foot, one-way), or take the Kosciuszko Express Chairlift *($$$ one-way)* from Thredbo village to one of the high ridges, and from there do an 8-mile (12.9 km) walk to the summit and back. ∎

Snowy Region Visitor Centre

✉ Kosciuszko Rd., Jindabyne

☎ 02/6450-5600

Australian Ski Areas Association

☎ 02/9326-4069

asaa.org.au

Broken Hill

If you want a taste of outback life, this is the best place to go. Broken Hill, also known as the Silver City, is one of Australia's oldest outback mining towns. For more than a century, this town, about 750 miles (1,200 km) west of Sydney, has prospered from an ore body more than 5 miles (8 km) long, containing the world's richest known reserves of silver, lead, and zinc.

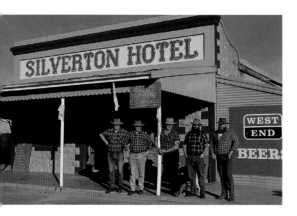

The old Silverton Hotel, a classic outback pub

Broken Hill

🅜 102 A4

Visitor Information

✉ Corner of Blende & Bromide Sts.

☎ 08/8080-3560

brokenhillaustralia.com.au

Broken Hill is filled with grand architecture such as the hugely ornate **Trades Hall building** *(Sulphide St.)*, built in 1898, with its pressed-iron ceilings and elaborate meeting hall. Built in 1891, the massive Italianate **Town Hall,** is on **Argent Street,** the city's main thoroughfare, which is lined with gracious two- and three-story hotels trimmed with iron lace.

All this opulence started in September 1883, when a boundary-riding cowboy named Charles Rasp came upon a huge boomerang-shaped ore body on a craggy rise known as the Broken Hill. Thinking the ore body was tin, he and some partners pegged it out. Only later did they learn that the 280-million-ton mass was galena-sphalerite ore, unimaginably rich in silver, lead, and zinc. It was the grandest mother lode ever found—before or since—and it went on to spawn Australia's biggest mining houses: B.H.P., C.R.A., and North Broken Hill. By 1915, the boomtown that sprang up had grown to 35,000, with 61 pubs, hotels, and grog shops. It drew prospectors, miners, con men, prostitutes, and gamblers, and it became a honeypot for union radicals.

These days, "The Hill" is a considerably tamer town of about 20,000, and unlike most outback mining towns, it is easy for tourists to visit. Trains and buses have regular schedules, and daily flights arrive from the larger cities. The highways are good, even if the drive is a little tedious.

Filmmakers have discovered the area's beautiful light and average of 320 sunny days a year. *Priscilla, Queen of the Desert* was filmed here, as were videos for INXS and other rock groups. BMW, Pepsi, and Levi's have all shot commercials in the area.

But don't come expecting cosmopolitan dining, sophisticated nightlife, or luxury resorts. This is still a working mining town, even as most of the mines themselves run out of ore. A huge slag heap looms over the city, and streets have names such as Oxide, Sulphide, and Chloride. Broken Hill is where Australia's mining empires were born and where militant miners wrote the most bruising chapters of trade union history. On top of the slag heap, the moving **Miners Memorial** is lined with plaques honoring the hundreds of miners killed on the job.

Mining doesn't drive the town as it used to, but the rise in metal prices has seen some old mines reopen, including Delprats Mine, once the premier mine tour operator, now closed to visitors. **Day Dream Mine** *(tel 08/8088-5682)*, one of Broken Hill's oldest (1881), 20 miles (33 km) north of town off the Silverton road, has tours at 10 a.m. and 11:30 a.m. Of the towns many mining and other museums, eccentric **White's Mineral Art Gallery & Mining Museum** *(1 Allendale St., tel 08/8087-2878)* has a walk-in reconstruction of a mine and a collection of artworks created by retired miner Kevin "Bushy" White using local minerals.

Twelve miles (19 km) north of Broken Hill is the ghost town of **Silverton,** where many commercials and movies, such as *Mad Max II,* were filmed. The quaint old **Silverton Hotel** has often been renamed for movies and miniseries, and its walls are lined with photos and memorabilia.

Perhaps the most haunting place to visit, however, is the **Living Desert Sculptures**—a windswept hilltop just 4 miles (6.4 km) out of town, decorated with the enormous stone works of 14 sculptors from Australia and around the world *(take Kaolin St. out of town NW, then follow signposts).* Go there at sunset. It is magical.

Broken Hill is a good place to arrange tours farther into the outback and the desert (the tourist office lists operators). If you have your own vehicle, a worthwhile two-day loop is to head 80 miles (130 km) northeast of Broken Hill to **Mutawinji National Park,** with its red outcrops, swimming hole, and Aboriginal rock art. Then

---

Outback Arts

Unlike other mining towns, Broken Hill has a flourishing arts community. The town attracted some of Australia's best known outback painters, including Hugh Schultz, John Pickup, Jack Absalom, and, most famous of all, the late Pro Hart, whose gallery *(108 Wyman St., tel 02/8087-2441)* can be visited. Painters come like moths, lured by the desert light. There are murals, artwork in the pubs, and dozens of art galleries around town.

---

continue on to **White Cliffs,** a fascinating opal mining town, where you can stay at the Underground Motel *(tel 08/8091-6677)* before heading back to Broken Hill via crumbling, colonial **Wilcannia,** once the "Queen City of the West" on the Darling River. ■

Silverton
 102 A4

Pacific Highway Drive

For deskbound Sydneysiders, the Pacific Highway is the road to adventure and sunshine, like an Australian Route 66. It meanders north along the coast toward the warmth of tropical Queensland, pausing at popular getaways such as Port Macquarie, Coffs Harbour, and Byron Bay. There is a little of everything—rain forest, empty beaches, seaside holiday towns, odd pockets of suburbia, hippie communes, and quiet farming villages.

Like the real Route 66—not the one of myth—the Pacific Highway can be narrow, heavily trafficked, tedious, and in some places downright dangerous. You may have to contend with the white-line fever of truckers making the run to Brisbane, eager families hurrying north to theme park holidays at Sea World or Movie Land on Queensland's Gold Coast, and convoys of retirees towing their campers north to softer, sunnier pastures in the tropics. Highway 1 is slowly being upgraded, with freeway or

---

NOT TO BE MISSED:

Barrington Tops National Park
• Bellingen • Dorrigo National
Park • Byron Bay

---

divided highway most of the way to Port Macquarie, and again from Byron Bay to Brisbane, but the pavement in between is mostly road travel the old-fashioned way.

Directions are simple: Cross Sydney Harbour Bridge and keep driving north on Route 1 to the Queensland border, more than 500 miles (800 km) away. Cross the picturesque Hawkesbury River, a popular boating destination, before reaching **Newcastle ❶** (visitor information: 3 Honeysuckle Dr., tel 02/4929-2588), the state's second biggest city, about 100 miles (160 km) out of Sydney. Once Australia's major steel producer, the city had to reinvent itself after the closure of the giant B.H.P. steel mills in 1999. The port still hums—it is the world's biggest coal port and export hub for the resource-rich Hunter Valley—but cleaner, greener Newcastle has imposing heritage buildings, wide tree-lined streets, thriving arts and food scenes, and good beaches. Visit historic **Fort Scratchley** (Fort Dr., tel 4974-5000), then take a fine walk along Nobbys Beach. Turn off the highway from Newcastle onto Route 15, the New England Highway, if you want to visit the **Hunter Valley ❷** wineries or the scenic horse country around Scone (see pp. 110–111).

The highway tends to run a few miles inland because the coast here has so many inlets and

---

EXPERIENCE:
Houseboating on the Hawkesbury

An idyllic way to see the Hawkesbury, and long a favorite holiday break with Sydneysiders, is to cruise the river on a fully equipped houseboat. Bookings are heavy, and prices soar during holiday periods, but are reasonable at other times, particularly midweek. Prices start at around A$500 for two nights on a 2–4 berth houseboat, A$1,000 for 8–10 berths. Operators include:

Able Hawkesbury House Boats (River Rd., Wisemans Ferry, tel 02/4566-4308, hawkesburyhouseboats.com.au)

Luxury Afloat Houseboats (Kangaroo Point Cruise Terminal, Pacific Hwy., Brooklyn, tel 02/9985-7344, luxuryafloat.org)

Ripples Houseboat Holidays (87 Brooklyn Rd., Brooklyn, tel 02/9985-5555, ripples.com.au)

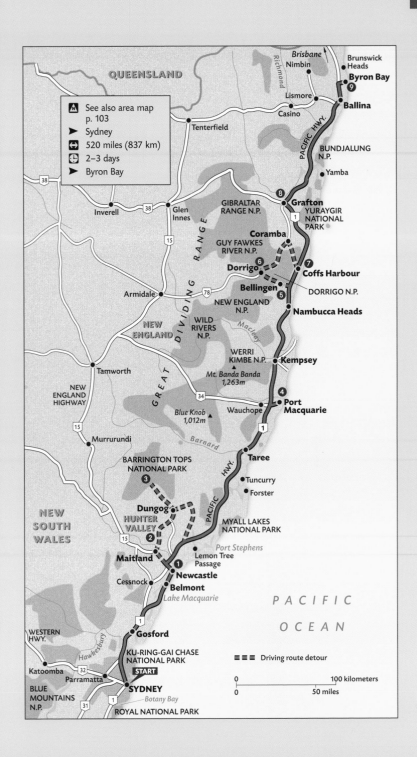

necks. Most of the interesting sights require a side trip. One of the most worthwhile is **Barrington Tops National Park ❸**, part of the Gondwana Rainforests World Heritage Area *(tel 02/6538-5300, turn north off the Pacific Hwy. to Gloucester, then take the Barrington Tops Rd.)*. The drive takes you through temperate rain forests and up onto mile-high windswept plateaus dotted with snow gums and covered with alpine bogs. This back road is not paved for much of its length, so do not attempt it in a conventional vehicle after heavy rains.

Back on the coast, you have a good chance of seeing wild koalas in the bush around Lemon Tree Passage, near Port Stephens. Farther north is the **Koala Hospital** *(off Lord St.)*, in the touristic resort town of **Port Macquarie ❹** *(visitor information: Clarence St., tel 1300-303-155)*. The hospital is run by the Koala Preservation Society of Australia on the grounds of a historic homestead. About 200 sick and injured koalas are brought here each year for convalescence. You can visit them daily.

Ninety miles (145 km) north of Port Macquarie is the turnoff for **Bellingen ❺** *(visitor information: tel 02/6655-1522)*, 7 miles (11 km) off the highway via Route 78. This laid-back and picturesque village is tucked in the rain forest at the foot of a 1,000-foot-high (300 m) escarpment. Once a major timber town, it has long been a refuge for writers, craftspeople,

and artists fleeing city life, and it is chock-full of galleries. Many of Bellingen's old buildings have been classified by the Australian National Trust. The town has regular arts and music events, and there is a market in Bellingen Park on the third Saturday of every month.

The surrounding countryside is dotted with organic farms and communes. Australia doesn't have a lot of chocolate-box scenery, but there is some here. If you can spare the time, cross the Bellingen River, on the edge of town, and drive 10 miles (16 km) or so upstream through farm country to a picnic area by the river called the Promised Land. It is spellbinding.

Equally spellbinding, although tougher on the nerves, is the drive 20 miles (32 km) up the escarpment on Route 78, from Bellingen to **Dorrigo ❻** *(visitor information: 36 Hickory St., tel 02/6657-2486)*. Lookouts along the way give views of the Pacific Ocean. On top of the plateau are the World Heritage rain forests of **Dorrigo National Park.** This is one of the best thought-out parks in the nation, with a rain forest information center *(tel 02/6657-2309)*, a skyline boardwalk through the rain forest canopy, and paths through the gloom on the forest floor. To get back to the Pacific Highway, you can return through Bellingen or follow the road to Coramba and then to Coffs Harbour.

When you reach **Coffs Harbour ❼** *(visitor information: Pacific Hwy., tel 02/6648-4990)*,

Hippie Haven

The main street of Nimbin, 45 miles (70 km) west of Byron Bay, wends though frontier wooden buildings adorned with psychedelia and Hindu iconography, past crystal shops, New Age healers, and hemp cafés. Welcome to Australia's hippie capital, a 1970s time warp of dreadlocks, bare feet, and tie-dye.

Nimbin was a sleepy dairy farming village hidden in the rain forest hills until the Aquarius Festival hit town in 1973. Organized by the Australian Union of

Students, thousands gathered for the ten-day counterculture experiment. Most returned to the "straight" world, but a few idealists decided to permanently turn on, tune in, and drop out by setting up nearby communes such as Tuntable Falls.

The experiment may not have gone exactly to plan, man; Nimbin is noted for periodic drug busts and its annual Mardi-Grass hemp festival in May. But the town remains a magnet for spiritual seekers, artists, dropouts, and tourists alike.

you're far enough north to notice the difference in climate. It's warm and sultry, and rain forests and banana plantations cling to the flanks of mountains that plunge right down to the coast. The motels are gaudier, too. Coffs is a burgeoning small city, its warm clime and fine beaches attracting residents and vacationers alike. Water sports top the many

banana movie, along with family attractions from waterslides to toboggans and ice-skating.

North of Coffs Harbour, much of the coast is national park land, and side roads lead to quiet beaches. **Grafton 8**, a genteel country town on the banks of the Clarence River, is kaleidoscopic in November (spring in Australia), when jacaranda and flame trees are in full

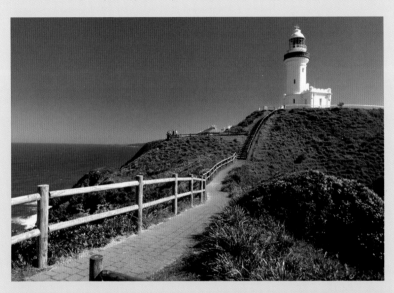

The Cape Byron lighthouse, built in 1901, protects Australia's easternmost point of land.

activities on offer, and the city is also home to the **Big Banana** *(1.5 miles, 2.5 km, north of town on Route 1)*, a monumental piece of roadside kitsch designed to draw tourists and celebrate the banana industry. Australians have a peculiar penchant for building giant objects, which you'll see dotted all around the country. So breathtakingly awful and shamelessly touristy, they demand a camera stop. The Big Crayfish (Kingston, South Australia), Big Merino (Goulburn, New South Wales), Big Pineapple (Nambour, Queensland), and Big Ned Kelly (Glenrowan, Victoria) are just a few of these tacky icons. The Big Banana is the biggest of the Big, with banana plantation tours, a banana café, a banana-themed souvenir shop, even a

flower. You are getting into lush, tropical, sugar-growing country now, and as you go farther north you'll see more houses built Queensland style, with wide wraparound verandas and elevated on stilts to let cooling air circulate.

Not far south of the Queensland border, **Byron Bay 9** *(visitor information: 80 Jonson St., tel 02/6680-8558)* is one of the prettiest places on the north coast. This was a blue-collar town whose main industry was the abattoir, but it is now a popular resort town, filled with crafts, galleries, vegetarian cafés, folk music, and markets. You can watch humpback whales off the coast of nearby Cape Byron in June and July. The lighthouse has one of the most powerful lights in the Southern Hemisphere.

Outlying Territories

Australia has a number of far-flung territories, a legacy of the British Empire when it managed, on London's behalf, a swag of colonial islands and dependencies. The easiest of these territories to visit are Norfolk Island, first occupied by an overspill of convicts from Sydney, and Lord Howe Island, an exclusive vacation destination for walkers, bird-watchers, and lovers of water sports. Accommodations are expensive, so many visitors come on a package deal.

Rising steeply from the sea, volcanic Lord Howe Island promises good snorkeling in the quiet lagoon on its western side.

Lord Howe Island
🅜 Map p. 123
Visitor Information
☎ 02/6563-2114
lordhoweisland.info

Other territories include Macquarie Island (regarded as part of Tasmania), in the subantarctic waters of the southern Indian Ocean, and Heard Island. Canberra claims nearly half of Antarctica as Australian territory, and it ruled Papua New Guinea until 1975.

Lord Howe Island

About 500 miles (800 km) northeast of Sydney, the tiny volcanic speck of Lord Howe Island is a beautiful rain forest–clad, mountainous tropical idyll. It is part of New South Wales (and a very expensive part at that), so you do not need a passport to visit from mainland Australia. There are daily flights available, but most visitors come on package tours.

The crescent-shaped island, with a wide lagoon tucked within its arms, was sighted by Lt. Henry Lidgbird Ball in 1788, on the way from Sydney to Norfolk Island. The first settlers arrived in 1833, and for the next 50 years it was a watering point for U.S. and British whaling ships. Millions of years of isolation have given rise to a unique ecology on the island, and it was listed as a World Heritage site in 1982.

Lord Howe Island is now a popular destination for ecotourists from around the world. More than 120 bird species can be seen here, including the flightless Lord Howe woodhen, one of the rarest birds in the world.

GETTING TO LORD HOWE ISLAND: **Quantas Link** (*part of Qantas; tel 13-1313*) has flights most days from Sydney, weekends from Brisbane, and from Port Macquarie, Feb.–June & Sept.–Dec.

Norfolk Island

Map p. 123

Visitor Information

Bicentennial Centre, Burnt Pine

6723-22147 or 1800-214-603

norfolkisland.com.au

GETTING TO NORFOLK ISLAND: Air New Zealand *(Burnt Pint Travel, Taylors Rd., tel 6723-22195, airnewzealand.com.au)* flies from Australia (Brisbane and Sydney) and Auckland five days a week.

The waters around the island teem with fish and contain the world's southernmost coral reef, thanks to the tropical currents from Queensland's Great Barrier Reef. Diving and snorkeling are especially good. Hikers can scale dramatic **Mount Gower** (2,850 feet/866 m) for a stunning panorama of the island and the South Pacific. The slightly lower **Mount Lidgbird** is an extremely challenging, highly technical climb that is rarely attempted.

Norfolk Island

Norfolk Island is an external, self-governing territory of Australia, a tax haven about 1,000 miles (1,600 km) northeast of Sydney. It was sighted by Captain Cook in 1774. Its sturdy Norfolk pines were made into ships' masts and its wild flax was used to make linen sails, making the island a strategically important place for the British Navy.

'Tis Mutiny, Mr. Lettuce Leaf

Thanks to the heritage of the mutineer descendants, Norfolk Island has a limited number of surnames, Christian being the most common. To help identify residents, the phone book includes an assortment of nicknames including Lettuce Leaf, Dar Bizziebee, Moochie, Loppy, Smudge, Diddles, Tardy, Frenzy, Hose, Truck, and Rubber Duck, to name a few.

The island was settled as a penal colony shortly after the First Fleet arrived in Australia in 1788, but it was abandoned in 1814 for several years. Then a new penal colony was established to be "a place of the extremest punishment short of death." In this it was wildly successful. In the hands of the sadistic governor John Giles Price, Norfolk Island became synonymous with cruelty and terror.

The penal colony was shut down in 1855, and the following year the descendants of Fletcher Christian and other mutineers of H.M.S. *Bounty* were resettled here after outgrowing Pitcairn Island. Today about 40 percent of the island's 2,000 inhabitants are descendants of the mutineers.

The chief settlement on this tiny volcanic island is **Burnt Pine. Kingston** is the island's main attraction, a historic settlement built largely by convicts. The convict cemetery is especially poignant. **Norfolk Island National Park** has bushwalks and good fishing and diving. Getting here is an international flight—bring your passport and make sure you have a visa for Australia.

Christmas Island & the Cocos Islands

Christmas Island and the Cocos lie in the Indian Ocean off the northwest coast of Western Australia. Regular flights leave from Perth, which is about 1,600 miles (2,560 km) from Christmas Island and 1,700 miles (2,720 km) from the

(continued on p. 126)

EXPERIENCE: Getting Close to Australian Wildlife

Nothing beats the thrill of seeing animals in the wild. Some prime wildlife-spotting destinations include Kakadu National Park (see pp. 188–191), particularly for crocodiles and wetland birdlife around the start of wet season in November. Other wildlife is numerous but less easy to spot, though nature tours offer a good chance.

At **Kangaroo Island** (see pp. 268–271, 274) south of Adelaide, you'll spot more wildlife—seals, sea lions, penguins, and wallabies—than anywhere else in Australia. It is your best chance of spotting koalas, whose numbers on the island have exploded since their introduction in the 1920s.

The koala conservation park on **Phillip Island** (see p. 307) in Victoria is another good place to see koalas, but the island is noted for the penguin colony that comes ashore every evening.

Australia's largest island, **Tasmania** (see pp. 330–354), has abundant wildlife such as wallabies, wombats, possums, and Tasmanian devils, but you'll have to go exploring in some of the national parks in order to find them.

Monkey Mia (see p. 229) in Western Australia is famous for dolphins that swim up to you in the shallows. Dolphins and other marine mammals thrive at **Rockingham** and **Bunbury** (see p. 226), south of Perth, and dolphin swim experiences are offered around the country. The **Eyre Peninsula** (see sidebar p. 246) in South Australia is a lesser known area to sight dolphins, seals, and sea lions without the crowds, and you can even swim with white pointer sharks (in a cage) off the coast from Port Lincoln. From June to October, whales can be sighted migrating along the southern coast, and **Hervey Bay** (see p. 148) in Queensland is the prime destination for humpback whale sightings. Of course, there's the marine wonderworlds of the **Great Barrier Reef** (see pp. 154–165) and **Ningaloo Reef** (see pp. 230–231) in Western Australia, where you can swim with whale sharks from April to July.

Wildlife Parks

If time is limited, wildlife parks across the country have all sorts of weird and wonderful marsupials, reptiles, and birdlife. Most big zoos also have natural walk-through enclosures. Some of the most popular and accessible native wildlife parks include Steve Irwin's **Australia Zoo** on Queensland's Sunshine Coast (see p. 147), **Currumbin Wildlife Sanctuary** on the Gold Coast (see p. 145) for colorful birdlife, and **Lone Pine Koala Sanctuary** (see sidebar p. 143) in Brisbane. Sydney's **Featherdale Wildlife Park** (see p. 100) has a large selection of native wildlife, and the fine **Taronga Zoo** (see p. 100) is just a ferry ride away from downtown. Melbourne also has a world-class zoo with native wildlife enclosures, and the renowned **Healesville Sanctuary** (see p. 308) is one hour away in the Yarra Valley.

A koala, one of Australia's most recognizable inhabitants

The forested slopes of Lord Howe Island offer excellent hiking.

detention center. The Australian government built the controversial facility and passed legislation excluding Christmas Island from Australia's migration zone, enabling it to detain refugees and deny them asylum.

An archipelago of 27 coral islands, the Cocos Islands *(visitor information: tel 08/9162-6790, cocos-tourism.cc)* are tranquil tropical destinations for fishing and diving. Only two are inhabited—Home Island and West Island. A Scottish seaman, John Clunies-Ross, settled here in 1827 and began a coconut industry. For more than a century, this was the fiefdom of the Clunies-Ross family, who were granted the islands "in perpetuity" by Queen Victoria. During World War II, the Cocos Islands were an important flying-boat base. In 1955, the islands became an Australian external territory and in 1978, the Clunies-Ross family sold them for A$6.25 million (then U.S. $4.75 million). In the 1980s, the 600 islanders voted for Australian citizenship over independence.

Cocos. Christmas Island *(visitor information: tel 08/9164-8382, christmas.net.au)* is covered with tropical rain forest and surrounded by coral reefs. Almost two-thirds of the island is national park. Deep-sea fishing, diving, and hiking are the main activities here. Accommodations range from basic motels to the luxurious Sanctuary.

One of the biggest things on the island is the immigration

Antarctica

If you just want to peek, Qantas (see p. 358) offers scenic flights over Antarctica over the Christmas holiday period; it is summer then, with 24 hours of daylight.

Actually getting to Australia's Antarctic Territories is more problematic and expensive. Tours from New Zealand (which may also touch base in Hobart) go into McMurdo Sound and visit Australia's Casey Base or Macquarie Island. *(For information, check out antarcticaflights.com.au.)* ■

Smaller than some outback stations, home to Australia's National Gallery, the iconic War Memorial, and the seat of government

Australian Capital Territory

Introduction & Map   128–129

Canberra   130–136

Feature: Anzac Day   134

Experience: Staying on a Farm   136

Hotels & Restaurants   371

Detail from outside the Canberra Civic Centre

Australian Capital Territory

After the six Australian colonies decided to form a nation in 1901, the next step was settling on a capital city—no easy task in a land notable for municipal jealousies, jump-and-bawl parochialism, and bickering politicians. Seven years of wrangling, two royal commissions, and numerous parliamentary debates followed as the various civic authorities put forth their arguments.

The new constitution decreed that the capital was to be somewhere in New South Wales, but at least 100 miles (160 km) from Sydney. This distance was a sop to the intense rivalry between Sydney and Melbourne, which was the stand-in capital until a permanent site was chosen.

There was no shortage of candidates for the new capital. Even tiny Wentworth, in far western New South Wales, put in its oar, using a timeless argument that its position on the confluence of the Murray and Darling Rivers—two important steamboat routes—made it a natural capital.

In 1908, a parliamentary committee settled on a site diplomatically set between Sydney and Melbourne; as wits like to put it, the place was equally inconvenient to both cities. Although Limestone Plains, as the place was called, would never otherwise have had a city on it, the setting was certainly pretty enough. Surrounded by mountains about 200 miles (320 km) southwest of Sydney, it sits on a plateau about 2,000 feet (608 m) up, high enough to get cold crisp winters and, occasionally, snow.

Two years later, New South Wales ceded the 975-square-mile (2,526 sq km) parcel of land to the Commonwealth, and the Australian Capital Territory (A.C.T.) was formed. An annex at Jervis Bay on the New South Wales coast gave the A.C.T. a seaport. The same year, an international competition was launched to find a designer for the new capital city.

The winner was Walter Burley Griffin, a Chicago landscape architect who had been Frank Lloyd Wright's chief assistant. His vision was for a city radiating out from the Parliament building and having a man-made lake at its heart. The design was controversial, and although construction began in 1913, bureaucratic resistance and World War I prevented much progress being made.

Griffin finally resigned in 1920 and went on to design several other towns: Griffith and Leeton in New South Wales, the Melbourne suburb of Eaglemont, and the Sydney suburb of Castlecrag.

Canberra's sparkling centerpiece, Lake Burley Griffin was created with the damming of the Molonglo River in 1963.

The seat of government was shifted to the new city in 1927, but Canberra's growth continued to be slow. Twenty years later it was still a country town of only 15,000. After the National Capital Development Commission was established in 1958, the city began to grow. Griffin's original vision of an artificial lake as the city's centerpiece was finally realized in 1963, when the Molonglo River was dammed to form Lake Burley Griffin. Handsome public buildings sprouted up. Suburbs grew and spread, and by 1967, Canberra was a fully fledged city of 100,000.

Today about 370,000 people live here, in what is arguably Australia's greenest city, with extensive parks coursing throughout the suburbs, giving the 90-year-old purpose-built city a respectable, established air. ∎

NOT TO BE MISSED:

Enjoying the expansive views from Black Mountain 130

Biking around Lake Burley Griffin 130–131

Taking in a free movie at the National Film & Sound Archive 132

Exploring Australian history at the National Museum 132

Parliament House, the nation's political heart 132–133

Browsing the art collection of the National Gallery 135

The Australian War Memorial, one of the great military museums in the world 135–136

Canberra

Canberra is young, smart, sporty, and generally prosperous, with plenty of restaurants, night-clubs, and a casino. It also has the National Gallery and the Parliament House, where you can watch Australia's politicians fling earthy abuse at each other—possibly the liveliest show in town. Some of Australia's best hiking and skiing are only a short drive away, and the bush wild-life is even closer. This is the only city in Australia where you might encounter a kangaroo.

Canberra, viewed from the Mount Ainslie lookout

Canberra
🅜 129 B3
Visitor Information
✉ 330 Northbourne Ave.
☎ 1300-554-144

Australian Institute of Sport
✉ Leverrier St., Bruce
☎ 02/6214-1111
🕐 Tours daily at 10 & 11:30 a.m., 1 & 2:30 p.m.
💲 $$
🚌 Bus No. 7

Black Mountain dominates the city center. Its futuristic commu-nications tower has observation galleries and a revolving restau-rant giving good views of the city. At the foot of the mountain are the **Australian National Botanic Gardens** (Clunies Ross St., Acton, tel 02/6250-9540, anbg.gov.au), which closely follow Walter Burley Griffin's original vision for a native flora garden. Their 125 acres (51 ha) hold more than 6,200 species of native trees, ferns, shrubs, and flowers, including a rain forest and 600 varieties of eucalyptus. On weekends, bus No. 981 takes you to the gardens, the

summit of Black Mountain, and the **National Zoo & Aquarium** (Lady Denman Dr., Weston Creek, tel 02/6287-8400, nationalzoo.com .au, $$$$). A walking trail winds up Black Mountain from Frith Street.

Just north of Black Mountain is the **Australian Institute of Sport.** This multimillion-dollar modernistic facility was built in 1981, at a low ebb in Australia's athletic history, to turn out world-class athletes. An interactive exhibition lets you measure your sporting fitness and aptitude. Some of Australia's top athletes lead daily tours.

Lake Burley Griffin sparkles at the center of Canberra, a bicycle-friendly city with more than

190 miles (300 km) of paths. Mr. Spokes Bicycle Hire *(near Acton Park ferry terminal, tel 02/6257-1188)*, on the north shore, rents bikes and pedal cars. Burley Griffin Boat Hire *(Acton Park ferry terminal, tel 02/6249-6861)* rents canoes and pedal boats. Beside the north end of Commonwealth Avenue Bridge, the **Captain Cook Memorial Water Jet** spurts water 460 feet (140 m) into the air. Southeast around the lakefront on Aspen Island is the **Carillon,** with 55 bells in three towers.

Parkes Place, on the lake's south bank, has the neoclassical **National Library of Australia.** Among its millions of books are the journals of the explorers Burke and Wills (see pp. 44–45) and Captain Cook's log. The library displays Australian photography, art, and a model of Cook's *Endeavour.* It also has a café with free Internet access. Just across the road, **Questacon** *(Parkes Place, tel 02/6270-2800, questacon.edu.au, $$$)*–the National Science and Technology Centre– has more than 200 hands-on exhibits. The **High Court building** sits beside the lake, a little farther east along Parkes Place, and beside it is the **National Gallery of Australia** (see p. 135).

The **Civic Centre,** around Vernon Circle on the north side of the lake, has shops, cinemas,

National Library of Australia

✉ Parkes Place

☎ 02/6262-1111

🕐 Tours daily at 10:30 a.m.

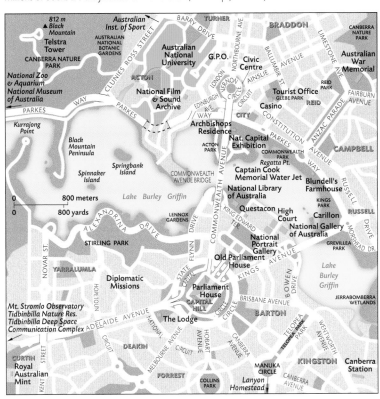

**National Film &
Sound Archive**

✉ McCoy Circuit
☎ 02/6248-2000

nfsa.gov.au

**National
Museum of
Australia**

✉ Lawson
Crescent, Acton
☎ 02/6208-5000

nma.gov.au

and restaurants, and the main post office. The casino is nearby, on Binara Street. The campus of the **Australian National University** *(Balmain Ave., tel 02/6125-5111, closed weekends, anu.edu.au)* is just west of the city center, in the inner suburb of Acton.

INSIDER TIP:

Walk or ride a bike around Lake Burley Griffin. The 3.75-mile [6 km] route around offers lots of fantastic photo ops.

—HOLLY SHALDERS
National Geographic contributor

Nearby is the **National Film & Sound Archive,** with interactive displays of Australian film and sound recordings dating back to footage from the 1896 Melbourne Cup. The **National Museum of Australia** offers a warts-and-all view of the nation's history, with eclectic exhibits, including a large collection of Aboriginal bark paintings and clothes worn by baby Azaria Chamberlain, notoriously killed by a dingo at Uluru in 1980.

Canberra Outskirts

About 20 miles (32 km) southwest of Canberra on Paddy's River Road, **Tidbinbilla Nature Reserve** *(tel 02/6205-1233, $)* has more than 15,000 acres (6,000 ha) of bushland with koalas, kangaroos, and birds; fine bushwalking trails; facilities

for picnics and barbecues; and the Sanctuary, an impressive wetlands and wildlife enclosure. The **Tidbinbilla Deep Space Communication Complex** *(tel 02/6201-7880),* a couple miles farther north, is one of the most sensitive listening posts in the world. It operates in conjunction with NASA, and its space center can be visited.

About 12 miles (19 km) south of the city and just off the Monaro Highway near Tharwa, the National Trust–listed **Lanyon Homestead** *(tel 02/6235-5677, closed Mon., $)* has a museum with exhibitions on country life.

Parliament House

Australia's billion-dollar Parliament House on Capital Hill, just south of Lake Burley Griffin, was opened in May 1988. Walter Burley Griffin's original vision for the city called for the Parliament building to be sited on this hill, and he bitterly resented the decision of the authorities to situate the "temporary" seat of government lower down on King George Terrace.

The Old Parliament House, completed in 1927, was actually used for nearly 60 years. Now the **Museum of Australian Democracy** *(King George Terrace, tel 02/6720-8222),* it is well worth a visit. The old chambers and prime minister's office, all leather and wood paneling, are just as the politicians left them in 1988.

The monumental new **Parliament House,** with its distinctive four-legged, 250-foot (76 m) flagpole, fits in beautifully with the city. Its design was the product of an international competition won in 1980 by Romaldo Giurgola from a New York firm. Parliament House took eight years to build, and naturally it was controversial.

Much of this beautiful building is open to the public. Outside the entrance is a mosaic called "Meeting Place," by Aboriginal gallery above the Great Hall was created by 500 Australians. In the heart of the building, you can see one of only four known original copies of the Magna Carta, the document signed by King John of England in 1215 that restricted royal power. The grassy lawn (which sweeps back to cover the roof of the building) makes a lovely stroll.

Parliament House

✉ Capital Hill
☎ 02/6277-5399
🚌 Bus Nos. 2, 3, 934

Stolen Generations

From the 19th century to the 1960s, as many as 100,000 Aboriginal children were deliberately removed from their families by the state and by church missions. Known as the stolen generations, the children were placed in institutions or with white families, their language and culture denied. "Half-caste" children of mixed descent were particularly targeted.

Paternalistic laws gave state governments sweeping powers to seize indigenous children without legal recourse. The policy was ostensibly for their own protection and to ensure their education, although some Aboriginal Protection Boards expressed the belief that breeding out the race was a solution to the "Aboriginal problem."

Many white Australians were unaware of the policy until the 1997 release of *Bringing Them Home*, a report commissioned by the government. It concluded that the policy was a gross violation of human rights and an "act of genocide, aimed at wiping out Indigenous families, communities and cultures."

Many saw the report as a milestone toward righting past injustices, but others balked, fearing compensation claims. Former prime minister John Howard rejected calls for a formal apology, saying Australia could not be held accountable for the actions of previous generations. Some conservatives denied it outright, claiming all the children were abandoned or given away willingly by their parents.

In 2007, new prime minister Kevin Rudd stood before Parliament and offered an apology for the loss and suffering of the Aboriginal people.

artist Michael Tjakamarra Nelson. The foyer has marble staircases and green-gray marble columns that symbolize a eucalyptus forest. The floors are made of Australian native timbers, and the marquetry panels depict Australian flora. The **Great Hall** contains a 70-foot-long (21 m) tapestry based on a painting by Arthur Boyd. The 50-foot (15 m) tapestry in the

Most of the city's 60 diplomatic missions are in **Yarralumla**, about half a mile (0.8 km) west. The U.S. Embassy is housed in a Williamsburg-style colonial building. The Thai Embassy resembles a temple. Greece's evokes the Parthenon, and New Guinea's is similar to an ornate spirit house. In the neighboring suburb of **Deakin**,

(continued on p. 135)

Anzac Day

If you visit Australia around Anzac Day—April 25— you'll quickly notice that it is not just another holiday. On this day, Australians commemorate those who served and died in their country's wars. While many countries set aside a day to pay tribute to their fallen, few do it with such style and depth of emotion as Australia.

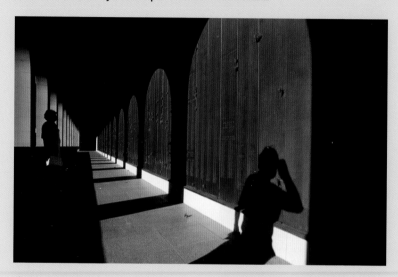

Thousands of names of the war dead etch the walls of the Australian War Memorial.

On April 25, 1915, 16,000 Australian soldiers of the Australia and New Zealand Army Corps (ANZAC) waded ashore on the Turkish coast near the town of Gallipoli. The landing was an ill-conceived part of Britain's campaign to capture the strategically important Dardanelles Strait, and by nightfall more than 2,000 Australians had died trying to capture a small bay flanked by cliffs and well-prepared Turkish soldiers. For the next eight months, the troops clung precariously to the beach without ever achieving a firm foothold. Thousands died before London issued the orders to withdraw.

The ANZAC lost 8,587 men in the fighting. What is not often mentioned is that the French lost just as many soldiers at Gallipoli, England lost three times as many, and the Turks had 86,000 dead. Those ancient nations had long ago been bloodied in conflict; Australia and New Zealand hadn't, and so this battle took on deep mythological significance.

The first parade marking Anzac Day took place soon after the end of World War I. Since then, the significance of this public memorial has steadily increased, and the parades have continued to grow larger as the children, grandchildren, and great-grandchildren put on the old campaign ribbons and step up to fill their ancestors' shoes, lest anyone forget. Ceremonies are held across the country and are open to spectators (see sidebar p. 50). The dawn service and parade are especially moving.

In 2003, the last known survivor of the Gallipoli campaign, from any army, died at age 102. Alec Campbell, an unassuming Tasmanian who had signed up for the war when he was barely 15, was given a state funeral.

the Australian prime minister lives in his or her official residence, **the Lodge.** Some of the embassies have open days, when you can visit. Ask at the Canberra visitor center (see p. 130) for details.

National Gallery of Australia

The National Gallery in Canberra stands on the south bank of Lake Burley Griffin northeast of Capital Hill. It has works by European masters (Monet, Rodin, Picasso), American pop artists such as Andy Warhol, and African and Asian art. It also has the most comprehensive collection of Australian and Aboriginal art in the country.

Twelve galleries spread over three floors. The **Art of Aboriginal Australia and the Torres Strait Islands gallery,** near the entrance, is the most popular. The displays change every few months. Typical exhibits are bark paintings from Arnhem Land, burial poles of the Tiwi Islanders, and canvas paintings from central Australia and the Kimberley.

The upper level of the building contains the Australian art collection, including early colonial watercolors, the later 19th-century Romantics, and the nationalistic art of Tom Roberts, Arthur Streeton, Russell Drysdale, and Charles Conder. These artists were among the first to capture Australia's harsh landscapes and glaring light. Their paintings soon became some of Australia's best loved icons.

Another display with iconic status is Sidney Nolan's series of 25 paintings of bushranger Ned Kelly, from the 1940s. There are also prints, photographs, ceramics, and textiles. A sculpture garden overlooks the lake. Nearby, the **National Portrait Gallery** holds the country's most significant collection of portraits in a variety of media, featuring over 400 famous Australians.

Australian War Memorial

The Australian War Memorial, with its heavy Byzantine lines and vaulted mosaic dome, is the most poignant monument in Canberra, attracting more visitors than any other building in the city. It sits at the foot of Mount Ainsley. Conceived in 1925 as a tribute to those who

National Gallery of Australia
- ✉ Parkes Place
- ☎ 02/6340-6502

National Portrait Gallery
- ✉ King Edward Terrace
- ☎ 02/6102-7000
- portrait.gov.au

Australian War Memorial
- ✉ Treloar Crescent, Campbell
- ☎ 02/6243-4211
- 🚌 Bus Nos. 10, 930

War Memorials

Virtually every town and village in Australia has a war memorial. At first glance this seems a little out of place in such an isolated country. With the exception of a few bombing raids on Darwin and Broome in 1942, the continent itself has been largely untouched by the wars of the 20th century. But Australia has never been slow to answer the call of duty, sending soldiers to every major conflict in which Britain was involved since the late 19th century— and paying heavily. More than 102,000 Australians have been killed in these conflicts—catastrophic losses in a country with such a small population.

died in World War I, it was not completed until 1941. By then the nation was in the midst of an even greater conflict and threatened with invasion. The cloisters, reflection pools, and galleries pay tribute to the dead.

The memorial also houses one of the world's great military museums. It charts Australia's involvement in conflicts from the Sudan campaign and the Boer War in the late 19th century, through both World Wars, Korea, the Malaya and Borneo campaigns of the 1950s and '60s, Vietnam, Iraq, and Afghanistan. Displays include a Lancaster bomber, a Spitfire, and one of the two Japanese midget submarines that infiltrated Sydney Harbour in World War II.

More than a million visitors shuffle through the Hall of Memory every year. It houses Australia's Tomb of the Unknown Soldier— the remains of an unidentified Aussie who was killed in France in World War I, and whose remains were returned to Australia in 1993. The ceremony was attended by the few surviving veterans of what was supposedly the "war to end all wars" and left few eyes dry when the bent old soldiers—100 years old or close to it—saluted their fallen mate.

Canberra's Anzac Day ceremonies (see p. 134) take place around the War Memorial. Tours of the War Memorial are free and quite frequent; call for details. The "Last Post" is played at closing. ■

EXPERIENCE: Staying on a Farm

Hundreds of farms all over Australia— from outback cattle stations to Tasmanian orchards—offer a great opportunity to experience rural life. Even though the country is overwhelmingly urban, ask Australians where to find the real Australia, and most likely they will say on the farm or in the outback.

Accommodations range from luxurious rooms in the homestead to something more basic in old shearers' quarters. Most farms encourage visitors to join in the activities, and some offer excursions like canoeing, bushwalking, horseback riding, and fishing.

Mowbray Park Farmstay *(tel 02/4680-9243, farmstayholidays.com.au)*, an hour southwest of Sydney, has activities from milking cows to sheepshearing. **Aldville Station** *(tel 07/4655-4814, email alanandlouise@activ8.net.au)* is an outback cattle and sheep station,

80 miles (125 km) northwest of Cunnamulla in Queensland.

Angorichina Station *(tel 08/8354-2362, angorichinastation.com)*, in South Australia's Flinders Ranges, offers luxury farm stays and flights. In southeast Queensland, **Glassford Creek Farmstay**, *(tel 07/4974-1185, gcfarmstay.com .au)* is a cattle station with horseback riding. **Oxley Farm** *(tel 08/8522-3703, oxleyfarm.com.au)* near Adelaide has family farm animal experiences.

Tourist offices will have lists of many other farm stays throughout the country. **Australian Farm Stay** *(australianfarm stay.com.au)* also offers a good selection, and **Help Exchange** *(helpx.net)* has some free and pay-per-view listings. **WWOOF** *(Willing Workers On Organic Farms, wwoof .com.au)* lists organic farms that provide the willing with accommodations and meals in exchange for work.

A tropical paradise with heartland that is classic outback, from northern savanna to the grazing lands of "Waltzing Matilda"

Queensland

Introduction & Map   138–139

Brisbane   140–143

Experience: Seeing Brisbane From
   the Water   143

Southeast Coast   144–149

Experience: Seeking Out
   Turtle Treasures   147

Tropic of Capricorn Drive   150–153

Great Barrier Reef   154–165

Experience: Cruising the Great
   Barrier Reef   160

Experience: Sailing the Whitsundays   162

Northern Queensland   166–180

Experience: Sea Kayaking   167

Experience: Diving Australia   168

Feature: National Parks   172–173

Experience: Touring the Tip   174

Experience: Horseracing in the Dust   176

Experience: Touring Mount Isa Mine   178

Hotels & Restaurants   371–376

Sweetlips swim together above reef corals.

Queensland

Queensland is where Australia goes on holiday, with thousands of miles of beaches, forest-clad mountains, and hundreds of tropical islands scattered along the Great Barrier Reef. In the south, the Gold Coast offers nightclubs and casinos, while the seaside towns and surfing beaches of the Sunshine Coast, north of Brisbane, bask in the world's "most perfect" climate.

Queensland began in 1824 as a penal colony, but by the 1840s, free settlers were streaming in, taking part in one of Australia's biggest land grabs. In 1859, Queensland became a colony in its own right and severed its ties with New South Wales. Gold, cattle, sheep, and sugar soon made it wealthy. From 1863, in one of the colony's grimmer chapters, Pacific islanders—the Kanakas—were conscripted to toil on the sugar plantations in conditions of virtual slavery. The practice, known as "blackbirding," was abolished in 1905.

For much of the 20th century, Queensland had a reputation as an antipodean Dixie. Black-birding had stopped, but the harsh treatment of Aborigines continued, as did heavy-handed policing, machine politics, and a deeply conservative outlook—particularly during the 20-year reign of archconservative premier Sir Johannes Bjelke-Petersen. A former peanut farmer from Kingaroy, he kept Queensland in what the rest of Australia regarded as a time warp until he was voted out in 1989. A cathartic royal commission followed, as did a number of indictments, and these days Queensland is one of the most open and outward-looking parts of the nation, with an easy, down-home friendliness, even in the face of adversity: Cyclones regularly hit, and in 2010–2011, a series of floods inundated the state and the capital, Brisbane. Seventy percent of Queensland was declared a disaster zone, but its residents are resilient and have quickly bounced back.

Queensland is a huge state, almost four times the size of California, with only 4.6 million people—about half of whom live in Brisbane. In addition to the southern beaches and the Great

Barrier Reef, Queensland offers much more, including sweeping expanses of dusty outback in the north, the rugged wilderness of the Cape York Peninsula, the ancient rain forests of Cape Tribulation, the lush volcanic highlands of the Atherton Tablelands, mining towns, and frontier settlements along the Gulf of Carpentaria. ∎

NOT TO BE MISSED:

The glitzy Gold Coast 144–145

Noosa Heads, the Sunshine Coast's classiest resort town 147

Fraser Island, where rain forest meets the beach 148–149

Cruising, diving, or snorkeling the Great Barrier Reef 154–165

A day sailing the tropical islands of the Whitsundays 162

Daintree National Park and its primeval rain forest 169

Lawn Hill National Park, an outback tropical surprise 179–180

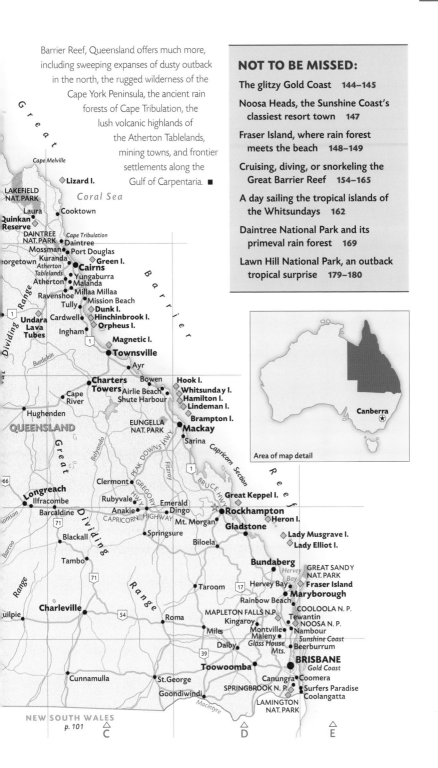

Brisbane

With its parks and gardens, jogging and bike paths, perfect winter climate and cosmopolitan style, Brisbane—with a population of 2.2 million—has a pleasant, relaxed feel despite being Australia's third largest city. It sprawls around an elbow on the Brisbane River, about 20 miles (32 km) inland from the southeast Queensland coast, making it a good base for exploration.

Office towers back Brisbane's vibrant riverfront.

Brisbane

⚑ 139 D1

Visitor Information

✉ Queen Street Mall (between Albert & Edward Sts.) & Stanley St. Plaza, Southbank

☎ 07/3006-6290

visitbrisbane.com.au

By the early 1820s, Sydney had become civilized enough to want to forget its brutal roots. Sent north to scout out a new penal colony, John Oxley, surveyor-general for Gov. Sir Thomas Brisbane, settled on Moreton Bay (20 miles/32 km from the site of the modern city). In 1824, a detachment of the 40th Regiment and a knot of Sydney's convicts set up camp near present-day Redcliffe. Unreliable water supplies and hostile Aborigines forced them to shift camp several times. They finally settled up the river where Brisbane is today.

With the exception of the Old Windmill on Wickham Terrace, built in 1828, there are very few reminders of those bad old days in modern Brisbane. A fire leveled the city in 1864, and most of its elegant buildings date from the 1880s, when gold, wool, sugar, and beef were building the state's fortunes.

Brisbane dozed away much of the 20th century, with the exception of the 1940s, when it became Gen. Douglas MacArthur's headquarters after the fall of the Philippines. It resumed its slumbers after the war, and as late as 1967 the tallest building in town was the clock tower of City Hall. The

Commonwealth Games in 1982 and the World Expo in 1988, which drew more than 18 million people, were Brisbane's coming-out parties. The city has hardly slept since.

By the early 1990s, when the rest of the nation was in recession, Brisbane's booming sunbelt economy lured thousands of job-seekers north from Sydney and Melbourne. Its suburbs were the fastest growing in Australia, luring transplants with jobs, a low cost of living, and 300-plus days of sunshine a year. Booming Brisbane took on the tongue-in-cheek moniker Brisvegas, with only the 2011 floods to dampen the party. The Brisbane River burst its banks and flooded much of the city center, though it has quickly bounced back.

Brisbane sprawls, but it's easy to get around thanks to a good public transport system of trains,

TransLink (Brisbane Transportation)
☎ 13-1230
translink.com.au

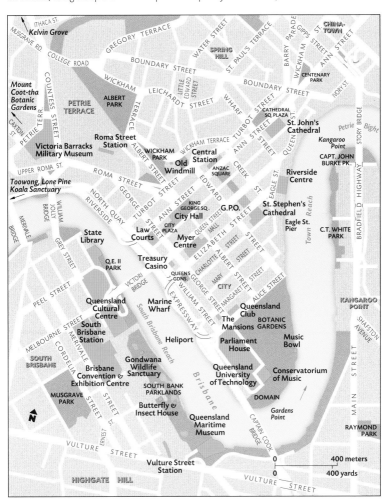

**Brisbane Botanic
Gardens**

✉ Mt. Coot-tha
   Rd., Toowong

☎ 07/3403-2535

**Sir Thomas
Brisbane
Planetarium**

☎ 07/3403-2578

💲 $$

🕐 Closed Mon.

river ferries, and buses. The downtown hub sits on a neck of land formed by a loop in the river. The city has the typical Australian blend of Victorian architecture and modern office blocks. Unique touches include bougainvillea, palms, and classic Queenslander houses—elevated wooden structures with verandas, designed to help air circulate.

behind the Gold Coast to the south, and the weird volcanic nubs of the Glass House Mountains to the north. Enjoy superb views from the restaurant and tearoom. There are also moderately strenuous bushwalking trails, the most popular being the hike to Slaughter Falls.

The **Brisbane Botanic Gardens,** at the foot of the

South Brisbane

One of the liveliest parts of Brisbane is across Victoria Bridge. On weekends, crowds flock to the 40 acres (16 ha) of **South Bank Parklands** (Stanley St. Plaza, tel 07/3867-2051, visitsouthbank.com .au) to drink caffe latte, in-line skate, watch street musicians, and stroll along the imported white sand of the artificial beach. There are also picnic and barbecue areas for public use. Another popular destination in the park is the **Queensland**

Maritime Museum, a two-level exhibition center featuring historic ship models as well as a 1900 pearling lugger and a World War II frigate. An outdoor market stretches for more than half a mile (1 km) on weekends. Nearby, along Grey Street, is the **Queensland Cultural Centre,** which includes the Queensland Art Gallery (mostly Australian artists), the Queensland Museum, the Performing Arts Complex, and the State Library.

Brisbane Sights

Perhaps the best way to get a feel for Brisbane is to drive up **Mount Coot-tha,** about 5 miles (8 km) west of the city on the Western Freeway, and up the Mount Coot-tha Road. To get here via public transportation, take bus 471 from Ann Street, near King George Square. The hill is easily noticed from the city; it's the one bristling with TV towers. The view from its 800-foot (244 m) summit is spectacular—especially in the fine light just before dusk. The Brisbane River shimmers its way through suburbs spread out like a jeweled blanket. On a clear day you can see the mountains

mountain, have tropical plants in a postmodern dome, rain forests, a display of arid-zone flora, and a Japanese garden. Also in the botanic gardens is the **Sir Thomas Brisbane Planetarium.** It is the largest in Australia and an ideal way for Northern Hemisphere visitors to get acquainted with a sky full of new stars.

It is easy to explore downtown Brisbane on foot, and the City Council has a free pamphlet of various heritage walking tours through the city. You can pick up a copy at City Hall. The commercial steel-and-glass heart of the city, and its historic districts, are in the blocks between Queen Street and the **City Botanic Gardens** at the tip of the peninsula. These park-lands have rosebushes, bamboo thickets, and poinciana trees. They are popular with walkers, bicyclists, and office workers on their lunch hours. On summer evenings, classical music recitals are given on an open-air stage.

Much of Brisbane's dignified old architecture lines George, Queen, and Elizabeth Streets. The Treasury Building on Queen Street is a massive Renaissance-style edifice built in 1890. It now houses the **Treasury Casino.** At the southern end of George Street is Queensland's **Parliament House.** It was built in 1868 in French Renaissance style, with a few tropical touches, like shuttered windows, and a dome of Mount Isa copper. Afternoon tours *(tel 07/3406-7562)* run weekdays, or watch the political action from the visitors gallery when Parliament is in session. Just up George Street on the corner of Margaret Street is a row of Brisbane's most elegant Victorian terraces, **The Mansions** (1899), with Italianate arches and cat sculptures on the parapets.

For two blocks across the city center, Queen Street becomes an upscale pedestrian mall, with flower stalls and street musicians, all dominated by the huge five-story **Myer Centre** complex of department stores, boutiques, and cinemas. Two blocks north of the mall, on Albert Street, is Brisbane's opulent **City Hall,** arguably the biggest and grandest city hall in Australia. Constructed in rich Italianate style in the Depression years, it has a beautiful circular concert hall, a cathedral-quality pipe organ, and a 300-foot-high (91 m) clock tower that gives splendid views of the city.

The elegant **Story Bridge,** where the Bradfield Highway crosses the river, was designed by Dr. John Bradfield, architect of the Sydney Harbour Bridge. A climb to the top of the 1940s cantilevered icon is rewarded with sweeping views of the city. Story Bridge Adventure Climb *(170 Main St., Kangaroo Point, tel 1300-254-627, storybridgeadventureclimb.com .au, $$$$)* offers 2.5-hour climbs by day and night. ■

City Botanic Gardens
✉ Alice St.
☎ 07/3221-4528

City Hall
☎ 07/3403-8888

EXPERIENCE: Seeing Brisbane From the Water

The sluggish Brisbane River was once Brisbane's lifeline to the outer world. These days most of the old wharves are idle, and the river is more decorative than functional. **Kookaburra River Queens** *(tel 07/3221-1300, kookaburrariverqueens .com, $$$$–$$$$$)* offers afternoon excursions and evening dinner cruises on stylish Mississippi-style paddle steamers. Or buy a ticket for just over A$3 and ride through the heart of the city, from Bretts Wharf up to the University of Queensland, on one of the large blue commuter catamarans known as the **CityCat** *(translink.com.au).*

A popular day trip with visitors is to **Lone Pine Koala Sanctuary** *(708 Jesmond Rd., Fig Tree Pocket, tel 07/3378-1366, koala.net, $$$$),* with more than 130 koalas and other wildlife. Take the **M.V. Mirimar** *(tel 04/1274-9426, mirimar.com)* upriver to the sanctuary.

Southeast Coast

The focus of southeast Queensland is the Gold Coast, Australia's answer to Miami, without the art deco and happily without the vice. But the region also includes the Sunshine Coast—a string of vacation villages, white-sand beaches, and coastal mountains about an hour's drive north of Brisbane—as well as Fraser Island, a lush paradise of wildflowers, rain forests, colored sand cliffs, freshwater lakes, and a vast array of birdlife.

Surfers Paradise is a glitzy international tourist destination with high-rises crowding the beach.

Gold Coast

⬛ 139 D1–E1

Visitor Information

✉ Cavill Ave. Mall, Surfers Paradise

☎ 07/5538-4419

goldcoasttourism .com.au

Gold Coast

Stretching from South Stradbroke Island, about 35 miles (56 km) south of Brisbane, to Tweed Heads on the New South Wales border, the Gold Coast is a relentless 25-mile (40 km) arc of surfing beaches, restaurants, motels, and developments. The glittering, brassy heart of it all is **Surfers Paradise,** where high-rise developments crowd the foreshore so closely that much of the beach is in shade in the afternoon. It doesn't seem to matter. Although warm sands and surf are still touted as

the Gold Coast's main attractions, these days they are really just backdrops for man-made amusements: nightclubs, theme parks, golf courses, boutiques, and an oversize casino.

The Gold Coast has been a vacation spot for Australians since 1884, when Cobb & Co. coaches made the trip down the coast from Brisbane to Coolangatta three times a week. The first high-rise beachfront apartments were built in the 1950s. These days more than 580,000 people live on this stretch of coast, and hundreds of hotels, hostels, and campsites cater to nearly a million overseas visitors every year, as well as several million Australians.

The Gold Coast is not for everybody, its tackiness the flip side of its glitz, but there's no denying the beauty of its beaches, and if your tastes run to high-octane entertainment, you've found the antipodean distributor. Located 35 miles (56 km) south of Brisbane, **Dreamworld** *(tel 07/5588-1111, $$$$$, dreamworld .com.au)* is a theme park in Coomera where you can ride some of the world's fastest and highest rides, play with a koala, or amuse the youngsters at Wiggles World. The adjoining **White Water World** *($$$$$, whitewater world.com.au)* has a host of water-slides, rides, and pools. A mile down the road is **Movie World** *(tel 07/5573-3999, $$$$$, movie world.com.au)*. Based on Hollywood movie sets, it offers visitors stunt and special effects shows, and Warner Brothers–franchised roller coaster rides. Nearby is **Wet 'n' Wild** *(tel 07/5556-1660, $$$$$, wetnwild.com.au)*, Australia's largest aquatic park. **Sea World,** at Main Beach *(tel 07/5588-2222, $$$$$, seaworld.com.au)* has seals, dolphins, and amusement park rides. Surfers Paradise offers the **Ripley's Believe It or Not! Museum** *(tel 07/5592-0040, $$$, ripleys.com)* and the extravagant **Jupiter's Casino** *(tel 07/5592-8100)*.

Alternatively, hang out at the beaches, learn to surf, or visit **Currumbin Wildlife Sanctuary** *(tel 07/5534-1266, $$$$$, cws.org .au)*, packed with native animals and birdlife.

National Parks

The hinterlands away from the coast are a subtropical paradise of small national parks, with rich rain forests, hidden waterfalls, and panoramic lookout views.

Burleigh Heads National Park is just off the Gold Coast Highway. **Lamington National Park,** one of Queensland's most popular, is about an hour's drive southwest of Surfers Paradise. This park has 3,900-foot-high (1,190 m) mountains in the rugged MacPherson Range and densely forested valleys with lush subtropical vegetation. Two of the park's most popular sections, **Binna Burra** and **Green Mountains,** are both accessible from Canungra. More than 84 miles (136 km) of

Crikey!

Steve Irwin (1962–2006) rose to prominence thanks to the television documentary series *Crocodile Hunter,* which aired globally. Raised around crocodiles on his parents' Queensland Reptile and Fauna Park, the young Steve had no fear of wildlife. Australia mourned when he was killed by a stingray barb that pierced his heart while filming on the Great Barrier Reef. He is survived by wife, Terri Irwin, and children, Bindi and Bob. His life's work continues at the popular **Australia Zoo** (see p. 147) and through the **Wildlife Warriors** foundation (*wildlife warriors.org.au*).

Queensland Parks & Wildlife Service

✉ Burleigh Heads National Park
☎ 1300-130-372

Lamington National Park

🅰 139 D1

Binna Burra

Visitor Information
☎ 07/5533-3584

Green Mountains

Visitor Information
☎ 07/5544-0634

walking trails lace these wilderness areas. One fine hike stretches for 13 miles (21 km) between O'Reilly's Rainforest Retreat and the Binna Burra Mountain Lodge.

Another popular national park within an hour of the Gold Coast is **Springbrook National Park,** which has 3,000-year-old beech trees, gorges, and the 200-foot-high (60 m) Purling Brook Falls.

Sunshine Coast

The Sunshine Coast starts at the Glass House Mountains and extends to the colored sands of Rainbow Beach 85 miles (140 km) farther north. Quieter than the Gold Coast,

One of the many lush coves within Noosa National Park

it has long been a vacation spot and is very popular with retirees from the cooler south. These days it is also a honeypot for families moving north from Sydney and Melbourne to enjoy Queensland's sunny promise.

Although it isn't as glitzy as the Gold Coast, the Sunshine Coast is still fairly heavily developed. It has its share of exuberantly tasteless Aussie kitsch, too: the 50-foot-high (15 m) Big Pineapple near **Nambour,** the tacky Ettamogah Pub, and the enormous Big Shell at **Tewantin.** The fashionable end of the coast is Noosa Heads, a rather exclusive seaside town flanked by Noosa National Park and Cooloola National Park. You're better off leaving the beaches alone until you get close to Noosa. In the lower part of the Sunshine Coast, the hinterlands are far prettier, with their ginger, pineapple, and sugarcane plantations and rain forests.

Fifty miles (80 km) north from Brisbane on the Bruce Highway, the Glass House Mountains Road (Steve Irwin Way) rises into tropical farmlands in the **Glass House Mountains.** This dramatic range is a series of 16 volcanic necks, as much as 1,820 feet high (556 m), rising from sugarcane plantations. Captain Cook named them for the shape, which "very much resembles a glass house." Many of the peaks are protected by forest reserves and Glass House Mountains National Park, which has fine hiking trails to some spectacular lookouts. To get into the mountains, drive northwest of Beerburrum along a scenic, winding route to the **Glass House Mountains Lookout** for views of the coast. Farther north, and west of Glass House Mountains township, walks in the national park go to several peaks, such as Mt. Ngungun or the more demanding Mt. Tibrogargan and Mt. Beerwah (the highest).

The township of Beerwah is home to one of the Sunshine Coast's main attractions, the **Australia Zoo** *(Steve Irwin Way, tel 07/5436-2000, $$$$$)*. Made famous by the Croc Hunter himself, this world-class zoo has acres of natural habitats where you can have walk-through encounters with kangaroos and other Australian wildlife; the "Crocoseum," with its famous crocodile shows; and a growing collection of exotic animals from around the world.

The tranquil villages in the nearby **Blackall Range**—for example, Mapleton, Flaxton, and Montville—have a very 19th-century English feel. You will find arts-and-craft cottages, tearooms, antiques shops, and roadside fruit stalls, in addition to several small but stunning national parks.

The 17-mile (27 km) scenic drive from Maleny to Mapleton is arguably the most beautiful in Queensland. It includes waterfalls, rain forests, and panoramic views of the mountains. Follow the Glass House Mountains Road to Landsborough and head east on the Landsborough–Maleny Road. Six winding miles (9 km) later, the Montville Road on your right is the start of the drive, but it is worth detouring 2 miles (3 km) farther east to the pretty village of **Maleny** *(visitor information: 23 Maple St., tel 07/5499-9033)*. The lookout at **Mary Cairncross Park,** near the turnoff for the Montville Road, gives fine views of the Glass House Mountains. Once at Mapleton, the northern end of the drive, stop at **Mapleton Falls National Park,** where a 400-foot

---

EXPERIENCE: Seeking Out Turtle Treasures

Visit the largest marine turtle nesting site on the east coast from late November to early March for an amazing experience. At Mon Repos, 8 miles (13 km) from Bundaberg, loggerhead and other turtles make the laborious journey up the beach to lay their eggs. The hatchlings emerge later in the season and head out to sea. **Queensland Parks & Wildlife Service** gives tours, which must be booked through the Bundaberg visitor center *(271 Bourbong St., tel 07/4153-8888, bundabergregion.info)*.

(122 m) waterfall rushes into a deep, forest-cloaked valley. From Mapleton follow the Nambour Road 8 miles (13 km) east to the Pacific Highway and turn south for Noosa.

Noosa Heads has been a surfers' hangout since the 1960s but is now a chic international resort town. With admirable foresight, the local town planners have ruled that no buildings can be higher than the trees, so though Noosa has smart restaurants and luxury hotels, it still has a small-town feel.

Noosa is protected by the headlands of **Noosa National Park,** which has rain forest trails, beaches, and views. Farther north are the beautiful colored sands of the **Cooloola National Park,** between Tewantin and Rainbow Beach. The park takes in a swath of hinterland, but it is the strikingly colored sandstone cliffs along 20 miles (32 km) of coast that catch the eye. You can see reds, ochers, yellows, and browns—more than 70 shades according

---

Noosa Heads

Visitor Information

✉ Hastings St.

☎ 07/5430-5000

Noosa National Park

🅰 139 D2

Queensland Parks & Wildlife Service

Visitor Information Centre

✉ Rainbow Beach

☎ 07/5486-3160

Fraser Island

139 E2 & 155

Visitor Information

Hervey Bay

1800-811-728

Rainbow Beach

8 Rainbow Beach Rd.

07/5486-3227

FERRIES: From Inskip Point, Rainbow Beach: *Manta Ray Barges, tel 07/5486-3935, mantarayfraser islandbarge.com.au*

From River Heads, Hervey Bay: *Fraser Venture, tel 07/4194-9300, fraserislandferry.com.au Kingfisher Bay Ferry, tel 07/4194-9300, kingfisherbay.com*

to geologists, who estimate the age of the cliffs at 40,000 years. Scientists debate whether oxides in the rock or decaying vegetable matter give these cliffs their color. Local Aborigines have a more romantic explanation: The cliffs were colored by a Rainbow Serpent who was killed by a boomerang when he came to the rescue of a young woman. Spectacular walking trails run along the coast. The visitor center, located at the northern end of the park, has details on the park and on neighboring Fraser Island.

Fraser Island

To describe Fraser Island as the world's largest sand island is accurate but misleading. Far from being just a big sandbar, this World Heritage site is, in fact, a tropical paradise dotted with crystalline lakes. The waters of this 80-mile-long (128 km) island teem with fish, and in winter, humpback whales shelter in Hervey Bay.

Located about 125 miles (200 km) north of Brisbane, Fraser Island is popular with bushwalkers, four-wheel-drive enthusiasts, and surfers. Despite the fact that up to 20,000 vehicles tour the island each year, it manages to retain its pristine wilderness feel. Ferries to the island go from **Inskip Point** *(8 miles/13 km N of Rainbow Beach)* and from **Hervey Bay,** a pleasant city of 76,000 reached by turning off the Pacific Highway at Maryborough.

Fraser Island was formed over many millions of years by currents washing sands up the coast, where they backed up against the edge of the continental shelf. Its lushness is a tribute to nature's remarkable powers of adaptation. Some trees store nutrients in their trunks, rather than rely on the sands, while others have above-ground roots capable of feeding off windblown nutrients. Still other plants obtain nitrogen from insects instead of the soil. The result is a remarkable and ancient

A Dingo Stole My Baby

The 1988 film *A Cry in the Dark,* starring Meryl Streep, detailed one of Australia's most sensational criminal cases: the disappearance of baby Azaria Chamberlain from Uluru in 1980. Although Azaria's parents reported that a dingo had taken the baby from their tent, Lindy Chamberlain, Azaria's mother, was convicted of murder and jailed. She was exonerated eight years later. Tragedy struck again in 2001, when dingoes killed a nine-year-old boy on Fraser Island.

Originally domesticated dogs brought from Asia 4,000 years ago, dingoes normally shy away from humans, but they become more brazen when accustomed to people in tourist areas. Attacks are rare, but dingoes will sometimes hunt in packs, making them a risk for children.

The dingo is conserved in some areas, notably Fraser Island, which has the purest breed. However, the world's longest fence runs 3,450 miles (5,600 km) across Queensland and South Australia and tries to keep dingoes out of southeastern Australia's farms. For the sake of the dingo and other visitors, do not feed them or encourage any interaction.

Sunlight filters through the rain forest canopy above a creek on Fraser Island.

growth of palms, ferns, and rain forest trees such as the satinay, which grows almost nowhere else and is highly sought after for its borer-resistant wood.

Fraser Island was first recorded by Captain Cook in 1770. It was named for Eliza Fraser, the wife of a sea captain whose ship foundered farther north in 1836. Aborigines killed some of the survivors—including Eliza Fraser's husband. Eliza was captured, but two months later, she was rescued by an unlikely alliance of escaped convicts and other Aborigines.

Great Sandy National Park covers all of Fraser Island and has rocky outcrops and magnificent dunes. Most of the island's 40 or so lakes—including the jewel-like and often crowded **Lake MacKenzie**—are concentrated in the south. The razor-sharp line of **Seventy-Five-Mile Beach,** along the eastern flank, has become a playground for four-wheel-drive adventurers. The forested central part of the island is comparatively untouched and offers tranquil bushwalking.

INSIDER TIP:

Fraser Island hosts Australia's last genetically pure dingoes, and dogs are forbidden lest they interbreed. Keep your distance, watch your children, and don't feed the dingoes.

—KENNY LING
National Geographic contributor

Tours of the island leave from Hervey Bay. You can also visit Fraser Island on your own. To drive on the island, you will need a four-wheel-drive vehicle and a permit (*obtainable at the Kingfisher Bay Resort ferry ticket kiosk in River Heads, Hervey Bay, or at the Rainbow Beach visitor center, among others*).

Start out at **Central Station,** a former logging camp near the island's southern end. Take a short stroll along the astoundingly clear Wanggoolba Creek, through deep forests, prehistoric ferns, and enormous satinay trees. ■

Tropic of Capricorn Drive

Just the name Tropic of Capricorn conjures up the romance of faraway and exotic places. Otherwise known as the line of latitude at 23.5° south of the Equator, it slices through the northern third of Australia on maps. Here in Queensland, you can drive along the Tropic of Capricorn for almost 500 miles (800 km).

The Capricorn Highway goes from the sparkling seas at the southern end of the Great Barrier Reef into the heart of the dusty, sunburned outback at Longreach. It starts at **Rockhampton ❶**, about a third of the way north along the Queensland coast. The Tropic of Capricorn actually runs a mile or so south of town, but enterprising locals have quietly nudged it to a more convenient location just outside the Capricorn information center on the Bruce Highway, 2 miles (3 km) south of the town center *(tel 07/4927-2055)*. A large and ornate brass sundial is out front, and at a brightly colored plaque you can stand with one foot in the Earth's southern temperate zone and the other in the torrid.

Rockhampton is a pleasant, small tropical city of about 62,000, set along the Fitzroy River about 25 miles (40 km) inland from the coast. The **Riverside Information Centre,** on elegant Quay Street, is a source of advice on local sights *(tel 07/4922-5339)*. Quay Street has ornate 19th-century architecture, thanks to the wealth that passed through here in the Mount Morgan gold rush of the 1880s and later when Rockhampton blossomed into the center for Queensland's cattle industry. The **Cattle House** at No. 180 is particularly handsome.

NOT TO BE MISSED:

Australian Workers Heritage Centre • Australian Stockman's Hall of Fame • Qantas Founders Museum

Explore Aboriginal culture at the **Dreamtime Culture Central,** on the Bruce Highway about 4 miles (6.4 km) north of town *(tel 07/4936-1655, $$)*. To the south, get to know the tropical plants of northern Queensland at the **Botanic Gardens** *(Spencer St.)*.

You should keep a couple of things in mind before you drive into the outback sunset on the Capricorn Highway. This is a genuine outback highway—paved but with long stretches of nothing between small settlements and towns. Keep an eye on the gas gauge, always carry extra drinking water, and be sure to have some cash, because banks and ATMs are scarce out here. Be prepared for the road trains—huge triple-rigged trucks of up to 170 tons (154 metric tons)—hauling supplies to lonely settlements and stations. They are nothing to be afraid of—the drivers are very skilled—but the first time one sweeps by can be a little unnerving.

The highway starts at a roundabout just south of Rockhampton and heads due west, past the sprawling cattleyards of big-time cattle country and over the Great Dividing Range. The road rolls through the timber mill town of Dingo, skirts Queensland's coalfields around Blackwater, then climbs over more ranges as it goes farther into outback Australia.

After 170 miles (274 km), you'll drive into **Emerald** *(visitor information: tel 07/4982-4142)*, a pleasant town of fig-lined streets. The town's colonial railroad station has been listed by the National Trust. West of Emerald are what used to be the largest sapphire fields in the Southern

Hemisphere. The Star of Queensland, regarded as the finest black sapphire in the world, was found at Anakie and now resides in the Smithsonian Institution in the United States. You can visit two walk-in mines at **Rubyvale ②**, and you can get a fossicking (prospecting) license if you want to try to find some gems yourself.

The highway runs from Anakie through 180 miles (290 km) of mostly empty outback before

information: Shamrock St., tel 07/4657-4637), an hour south on the Matilda Highway. Blackall was home to one of Australia's legends, Big Jackie Howe, the greatest shearer of them all. In 1892, at nearby Alice Downs Station, Howe set a record by shearing 321 ewes in the union-prescribed workday of seven hours and forty minutes, using crude iron hand shears. A statue of Howe stands near the corner of Shamrock

A quintessential outback image: saddles draped on a barn door near Winton

it reaches **Barcaldine ③** *(visitor information: Oak St., tel 07/4651-1724)*. This town of 1,600 claims to be the birthplace of the Australian Labor Party. Striking shearers gathered here in the long hot months of 1891 to plan strategy in their bitter campaign against wealthy graziers. They met beneath a 150-year-old ghost gum that became known as the Tree of Knowledge. (The tree was destroyed in an act of vandalism in 2006; a memorial in its honor opened in 2009.) The **Australian Workers Heritage Centre** on Ash Street tells the story of the struggle.

You can make an interesting detour from Barcaldine to the town of **Blackall ④** *(visitor*

and Hawthorne Streets. On Thistle Street is another icon, a reproduction of the so-called Black Stump that surveyor Thomas Frazer used as his baseline for mapping the area in 1886. Anything beyond this marker was deemed to be "outback," and Australians today still sometimes refer to the remote parts of their country as "beyond the Black Stump."

Return to the Capricorn Highway at Barcaldine and go west to **Longreach** *(visitor information: tel 07/4658-4150)*, home to the **Australian Stockman's Hall of Fame ⑤** *(tel 07/4658-2166, $$$)*. You'll see it from the highway about a mile before you get to

Longreach. It opened in 1988 with fanfare and some doubts that visitors would come this far to see it, but it has surpassed all expectations. It tells the story of Australia from the Dreamtime onward and focuses on the settlement of the outback with exhibits on pioneer explorers, outback women, shearers, and cattlemen.

INSIDER TIP:

In Longreach, be sure to visit Banjo's Outback Theatre & Woolshed [outbacknow.com .au] for dinner and a show that includes songs, skits, and sheepshearing demonstrations.

—STEPHANIE ROBICHAUX
National Geographic contributor

The Hall of Fame alone would be worth the drive out here, but Longreach has more. Qantas started operations here in 1921 as the Queensland and Northern Territory Air Service (it's the world's second oldest airline). The original hangar sits almost opposite the Stockman's Hall of Fame. Today it houses the **Qantas Founders Museum** (*tel 07/4658-3737, qfom.com.au, $$$*), which has displays of aviation history that include the airline's first plane, an Avro 504K, as well as one much more recent, a decommissioned 747; flown into Longreach in 2002, it presents a startling spectacle as you drive into town. The airline's original booking office, situated on the corner of Duck and Eagle Streets, is now Longreach's visitor information center.

Longreach marks the end of the Capricorn Highway. From here the main highway veers north, away from the Tropic of Capricorn. Known as the Landsborough Highway, at around 62 miles (100 km) from Longreach it passes the turnoff to the **Australian Age of Dinosaurs** (*tel 07/4657-0712,*

australianageofdinosaurs.com), an interesting new museum exhibiting just some of the many fossils found in the area. Next stop is **Winton** ⑥. This is where Banjo Paterson reputedly wrote "Waltzing Matilda" (see sidebar below). The truth about the origin of the song is lost in time and municipal rivalry, but according to legend it was performed publicly for the first time in Winton's North Gregory Hotel (*67 Elderslie St., tel 07/4657-1375*) in 1895. Visit the **Waltzing Matilda Centre** (*tel 07/4657-1466, $$*), an engaging museum dedicated to Australia's most popular song. It offers recordings of many of the more than 500 different renditions of the song, as well as an excellent collection of outback history and lore—every bit as good, although not as large, as the Australian Stockman's Hall of Fame in Longreach.

From Winton you can loop back to the coast via Hughenden and continue east on the Flinders Highway for 240 miles (386 km) to the gold-mining town of **Charters Towers** ⑦ and then on to **Townsville** ⑧ (see pp. 166–167) on the Coral Sea. If you don't go to Winton, you can vary the return trip by going east from Longreach on the Capricorn Highway and turning north at Emerald to follow the Gregory and Peak Downs Highways to the coast at Mackay.

Waltzing Matilda

Written by bush poet Andrew B. "Banjo" Paterson, "Waltzing Matilda" seems an odd choice as Australia's unofficial national anthem. It tells the story of a swagman (hobo) who camps by a billabong (water hole) and steals a jumbuck (sheep), only to jump into the river and drown escaping a trooper. Most likely based on the bitter shearers' strikes of the 1890s, when troops were sent in and shearers attacked sheep farms, the antiestablishment sentiment and use of colloquial language struck a deep chord with the Australian public.

Great Barrier Reef

Australia's crowning glory is the Great Barrier Reef, the chain of coral reefs and lush tropical islands that flanks the Queensland coast. No adjectives or glossy underwater photographs can adequately prepare you for that magical moment when you don a mask and poke your face into the warm tropical waters of this seductive dreamscape.

Loggerhead turtles can live for 50 years and grow to be five feet (1.5 m) long.

The Great Barrier Reef starts near **Lady Elliott Island** and stretches some 1,300 miles (2,092 km) north to **Bramble Cay,** off the coast of Papua New Guinea. Although it is generally referred to as one reef, it is in fact a mosaic of more than 2,900 distinct reefs covering almost 90,000 square miles (233,100 sq km). The reefs change character along the way. In the south they form chains of sandy cays—coral outcrops that emerge above the water and have acquired a covering of vegetation. In the north, where the coral comes closest to the coast, it runs in long ribbons.

Throughout its length, the reef is a maze of sharp corals and shallow water, and it was a navigational nightmare for Australia's early explorers. In 1768, French explorer Louis Antoine de Bougainville might have put in a claim to mainland Australia had not the sound of waves washing against the corals put him off. Describing it in his log as the "voice of

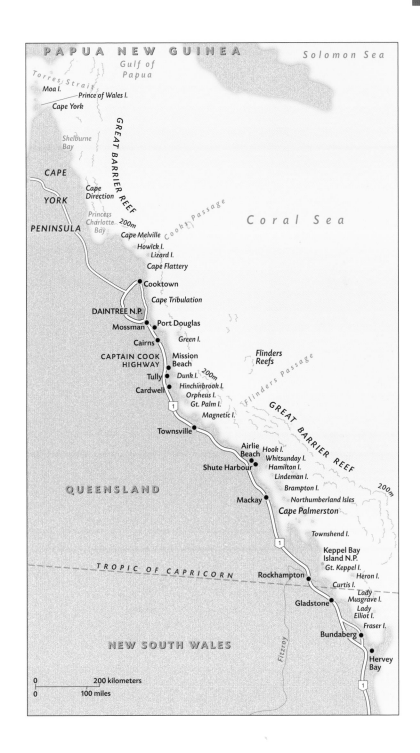

PAPUA NEW GUINEA

Solomon Sea

Gulf of Papua

Torres Strait

Moa I.
Prince of Wales I.
Cape York

Shelburne Bay

GREAT BARRIER REEF

CAPE

YORK

Cape Direction

Princess Charlotte Bay

200m

PENINSULA

Coral Sea

Cook's Passage

Cape Melville
Howick I.
Lizard I.
Cape Flattery

Cooktown

Cape Tribulation

DAINTREE N.P.

Mossman
Port Douglas

Cairns
Green I.

CAPTAIN COOK HIGHWAY
Mission Beach

Tully
Dunk I.
200m

Cardwell
Hinchinbrook I.
Orpheus I.
Gt. Palm I.
Magnetic I.

Flinders Reefs

Flinders Passage

GREAT BARRIER REEF

Townsville

Airlie Beach
Hook I.
Whitsunday I.
Hamilton I.
Lindeman I.

Shute Harbour

Brampton I.

QUEENSLAND

200m

Mackay
Northumberland Isles

Cape Palmerston

Townshend I.

TROPIC OF CAPRICORN

Keppel Bay Island N.P.
Gt. Keppel I.
Heron I.

Rockhampton
Curtis I.

Lady Musgrave I.

Gladstone
Lady Elliot I.

Fraser I.

NEW SOUTH WALES

Fitzroy

Bundaberg

Hervey Bay

0   200 kilometers
0   100 miles

Reef Formation

Coral growing in shallow water

Coastal range

As the last ice age ended and the Earth's climate warmed, Queensland's coast had a range of forested hills. Corals grew in the shallow waters of the continental shelf.

The water level rises and the coral begins to build upward.

Coral grows around submerged hills.

Glaciers and ice caps melted, raising the sea level slowly. As it rose, the coastal valleys filled, leaving islands. Coral grew upward on the old, dead coral below.

Inner reef of coral-fringed islands and coral cays

Outer reef of coral cays on the reef at the edge of the continental shelf

Coastal rain forest

Rising waters flooded farther inland. Fringing reefs grew around the inner reef islands; low coral cays developed on the spectacular reefs of the outer reef.

Creatures of the Reef

Great white shark

Green turtle

Coral polyp tentacles catch prey during the day, retract at night.

Coral cod

Featherstar

Blue sea star

Giant clam

God," he kept going. Thirty years later Matthew Flinders compared navigating the reef to threading a needle. Some couldn't do it. The reef contains more than 30 wrecks and continues to be occasionally bruised by keels and hulls today.

Natural History of the Reef

A World Heritage site, the reef was built by a simple primitive organism, a marine polyp of the family Coelenterata. Billions of polyps huddle together in warm, salty, shallow water and grow toward the sunlight like brilliant

Manta ray

Trevallies

Table coral
Acropora cytherea

Blue patch
butterfly fish

White tipped
reef shark

Nautilus

Potato cod

Blue spotted
stingray

Lionfish

Gorgonian
fan coral

Wobbegong shark

Surgeonfish

Pectinia lactuca

Staghorn coral
Acropora nobilis

Volute

Brain coral
Symphyllia radians

Turbinaria
frondens

Mushroom coral
Fungia

*Pocillopora
eydouxi*

*Leptoria
phrygia*

Plate coral
Montipora foliosa

Soft coral
Sinulara densa

flowers. When one dies, a new polyp grows on its skeleton. They are known as hard corals, for the skeletons they form. Over millions of years, a vast reef complex develops. Some parts of the Great Barrier Reef have been building for more than 18 million years. Much of the reef, however, dates from the end of the last ice age, about 15,000 years ago, when sea levels started to rise.

Reef Inhabitants

The reef is a world in itself, the coral colonies providing food, shelter, and hunting grounds for billions of other creatures. In addition to 400-odd species of corals, the Great Barrier Reef has more than 4,000 species of

Great Barrier Reef Marine Parks Authority
✉ P.O. Box 1379, Townsville
☎ 07/4750-0700

mollusks, 350 species of echinoderms—sea urchins, sea stars, and sea cucumbers—and 4,000 varieties of sponges.

About 1,500 varieties of tropical fish swim around the reef, in almost every color imaginable. There are humpback whales, stingrays, giant turtles, and dugongs—the sea cows that gave rise to myths of mermaids. No place on land, not even the wildest rain forest, supports this kind of diversity. One of nature's most spectacular sights occurs here beneath a full moon on a few nights each spring: The corals spawn, releasing billions of eggs in a rainbow of colors.

Exploring the Reef

Diving and snorkeling are the best ways to explore the reef. If you don't dive, or don't want to, it's no problem. Anyone can learn to snorkel in five minutes, and the only thing you'll miss out on is a longer period under the water. Most of the best displays are shallow anyway, and if you simply paddle facedown along the surface, you'll be treated to vivid displays of tropical color and an eerie, dreamlike sensation of flying. You don't even have to get wet: many operators have glass-bottom boats through which you can view the reef.

If you do want to learn to dive, plenty of dive courses are available along the coast, particularly in tourist hubs like **Airlie Beach** and **Cairns** (see pp. 167–168). They vary greatly in professionalism and price, so shop around. You can also do a single escorted dive with an instructor for about A$100.

Great Barrier Reef Islands

More than 700 islands dot the lee side of the Great Barrier Reef. Many of them are uninhabited, tropical paradises. Those that do have resorts

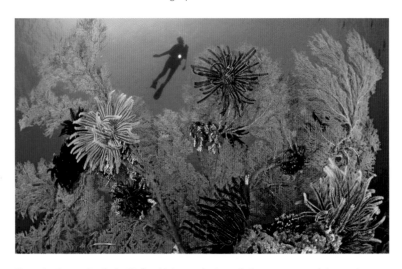

Gorgonian fan coral and crinoids flourish in a gap in the reef where currents can bring nutrients.

offer varieties of paradise to suit every taste or budget. You can choose from family retreats, ecotourist lodges, some of the world's most exclusive resorts, or no-frills college getaways known for hard partying.

Southern Islands: Most of the southern islands are clustered around the Capricorn Coast, between Bundaberg and Rockhampton. **Lady Elliott Island,** which marks the southern tip of the Great Barrier Reef,

Threats to the Reef

The Great Barrier Reef has been a protected marine park since 1975. It is managed by the Great Barrier Reef Marine Parks Authority (GBRMPA), which tries to juggle the growing demands of tourism with the critical need to protect this ecosystem. One natural threat is the crown-of-thorns sea star, which eats coral and causes severe damage in its periodic outbreaks—but the damage that people do is far worse. Any dead or broken coral that you see has probably suffered from direct human attention or from tour-boat anchors. Consider this to be the world's greatest and most fragile china shop. Look, but don't touch.

Only a very few of the Great Barrier Reef islands are on the reef itself. The majority are continental islands, which means they are ancient coastal hilltops that became islands at the end of the last ice age about 15,000 years ago, when the sea level rose. Magnificent fringing coral reefs have grown around these islands, which are often wooded, with high mountains and spectacular views of the tropical seas and other islands nearby. Some are accessible by short ferry rides, others require a longer and more expensive journey. Three island resorts are actually coral cays themselves, and at low tide visitors can walk on the body of the reef. The islands are divided into three main groups: the southern islands, the Whitsunday Islands in the center (see pp. 161–164), and the tropical northern islands (see pp. 164–165).

is a coral cay where divers stand a good chance of encountering loggerhead turtles and manta rays. In 1816 the seamen on the ship *Lady Elliott* made the first recorded sighting of the island, but it seems to have gone unsighted a little too often over the next 50 years. After an extraordinary number of ship-wrecks, an elegant lighthouse was built here in 1866. It was a lonely place to be stationed, and several early lighthouse-keepers reputedly committed suicide. The lighthouse still stands but is much less lonely these days, with the Lady Elliott Resort *(tel 1800-072-200)* catering to 140 people and daily flights, including from Bundaberg and Hervey Bay.

Neighboring **Lady Musgrave Island,** about 25 miles (40 km) farther north, is a tiny uninhabited mote popular with yachtsmen for its pretty turquoise lagoon formed by sheltering coral. It is a low island covered with grasses, pandanus palms, pisonia, and casuarina trees. In the early 1900s, goats released on Lady Musgrave and Lady Elliott Islands devastated the landscape. A revegetation program that was started in the 1970s has been fairly successful. These days Lady Musgrave is one of the best islands in the southern reef on which to camp, although light sleepers may be disturbed by the colonies of terns and other raucous seabirds. *(Arrange permits online at parks.nprsr.qld.gov.au or by phone 13-7468. Only 40 campers are allowed on the island at a time.)* Lady Musgrave Cruises *(tel 07/4974-9077, lmcruises.com.au)* day-trips to

the island from the town of 1770, not far from Gladstone.

Heron Island is another of the coral islands. Located about 70 miles (112 km) from Gladstone, it is also one of the best known islands on the reef—and with good reason. Its waters teem with coral and fish, making it a paradise for divers and snorkelers, and the island is a breeding ground for thousands of birds and turtles. Heron Island was first settled in the 1920s, when a turtle cannery was set up. In 1932, the cannery closed and a tourism industry began to evolve. The island was declared a national park in 1943. Accommodations are at the Heron Island Resort *(tel*

EXPERIENCE: Cruising the Great Barrier Reef

Cairns/Port Douglas and the Whitsunday Islands are the most popular departure points for reef tours, but cruises can also be arranged in towns along the coast such as Mission Beach, Townsville, and Bundaberg. A mind-boggling array of sailing, diving, snorkeling, and overnight to one-week tours operate, but most visitors take a day cruise.

Most day companies have their own platforms on the outer reef, about 1.5–2 hours from Cairns, slightly longer from farther south. All-day cruises include snorkeling and lunch, with extras such as undersea observatories, glass-bottom boats, and diving. Full-day cruises are A$150–250 per person. Some of the main operators include:

Cairns
Great Adventures Cruises *(Reef Fleet Terminal, 1 Spence St., greatadventures.com .au):* Big boats go to Green Island, a platform on the outer edge of the reef, or both.

Passions of Paradise *(Reef Fleet Terminal, passions.com.au):* Smaller sailing catamarans go to Michaelmas Cay and Paradise Reef.
Sunlover *(Reef Fleet Terminal, sunlover.com .au):* Fast catamarans go to Moore Reef and spend four hours.

Port Douglas
Quicksilver Connections *(Marina Mirage, tel 07/4087-2100, quicksilver-cruises.com):* Luxury catamarans visit their outer reef platform and the closer Low Isles.

Whitsundays
Cruise Whitsundays *(Abel Point Marina North, Airlie Beach, tel 07/4946-4662, cruisewhitsundays.com).* Cruises from Airlie Beach sail to pontoons at Knuckle Reef Lagoon or Hardy Reef, and those in a hurry can get a helicopter/seaplane connection. This company also runs ferries to Daydream, Hamilton, and other islands from Airlie Beach and Shute Harbour.

07/4972-9055). The island is small enough to stroll around in an hour, but you have to stay as part of a package deal.

Great Keppel Island has white-sand beaches, cabins, and camping. Great Keppel is the biggest of a chain of 19 islands that make up **Keppel Bay Islands National Park.** These hilly, eucalyptus woodland islands are remnants of the ancient Queensland coast. You can enjoy great diving, bushwalking, and camping here. Access is by boat from the Rosslyn Bay ferry terminal, northeast of Rockhampton *(tel 07/4933-6888).* Other Keppel Bay islands can be visited by water taxi from the Keppel Bay Marina *(tel 07/4933-6244).* Many of these islands are uninhabited, such as **Middle Island** and **Miall Island,** so campers have to take all supplies, including drinking water.

Whitsunday Islands: The Whitsunday Islands were named by Captain Cook, who sailed between the islands and the coast on Whitsunday in July 1770—or at least he thought he did. Although the devout captain kept meticulous logs, he had not allowed for the international dateline and was actually a day off.

The hundred or so Whitsunday Islands are perhaps the most gorgeous of Queensland's tropical paradises. These continental islands formed when the sea level rose after the last ice age, and they still resemble the mountaintops they once were. They are steep and lush, covered with

Whitehaven Beach on Whitsunday Island, one of the loveliest of the Great Barrier Reef beaches

dense pine forests. Although the islands are more than 30 miles (48 km) from the reef, they are fringed with coral. Many of them became national parks in the 1930s and now form a string of national parks, including the Whitsunday Islands, Molle Island, Lindeman Island, and the Repulse Islands. Although some of the islands have resorts on them, most

Whitsunday Islands

🗺 139 D3 & 155

Visitor Information Centre

✉ 259 Shute Harbour Rd., Airlie Beach

☎ 07/4946-5299

tourismwhitsundays .com.au

EXPERIENCE: Sailing the Whitsundays

Life doesn't get much better than sailing your yacht with friends and family around the tropical waters of the Whitsunday Islands. Cruise the calm waters sheltered by the Great Barrier Reef, drop anchor in sheltered coves, dive over the side to swim and snorkel, or cook up a seafood feast in the galley. Don't have a yacht? Never sailed? Never mind, the Whitsundays are the ideal place to go bareboating (DIY boating). A number of companies make it easy, renting fully equipped yachts, catamarans, and powerboats with from 2 to 12 berths.

Boating experience is preferred, but all new skippers are given three hours'

instruction before sailing. If preferred, a skipper is provided (at extra cost) for as long as necessary, usually the first day. Book ahead.

Cumberland Charter Yachts (Shop 2 Shingley Beach Rd., Abel Point Marina, Airlie Beach, tel 07/4946-7526, ccy.com.au)

Queensland Yacht Charters (Abel Point Marina, Airlie Beach, tel 07/4946-7400, yachtcharters.com.au)

Sunsail Australia (Front Street, Hamilton Island, tel 1800-803-988, sunsail.com.au)

Whitsunday Rent A Yacht (6 Bay Ter., Shute Harbour, tel 07/4946-9232, rentayacht.com.au)

Mackay

☒ 139 D3 & 155

Visitor Information

✉ Nebo Rd.

☎ 07/4952-2677

Queensland Parks & Wildlife Service

✉ Corner of Mandalay & Shute Harbour Rds., Airlie Beach

☎ 07/4967-7355

are uninhabited, and on several you can camp next to pristine beaches. The attractive resort town of **Airlie Beach** is the main transit point for the Whitsundays, and a good base for day-tripping to the islands, with ferries and cruises departing the town marina or nearby Shute Harbour.

Brampton Island is the southernmost of the Whitsundays, only 20 miles (32 km) northeast of the region's main city, **Mackay,** a booming coal port. Most of Brampton Island is national park, with seven coral beaches and rain forests bright with rainbow lorikeets and butterflies. You can hike to the summit of Brampton Peak (a very steep one-hour hike, so be sure to take water) for fabulous views of island-dotted seas, but until the resort reopens, there is no ferry.

Whitsunday Island is the largest of the islands—almost 30,000

INSIDER TIP:

Whitsunday's White-haven Beach, with its silica white sand, has a well-earned reputation as one of the region's finest beaches. Treat yourself: Arrive early and stay late.

—CATHERINE PEARSON
National Geographic contributor

acres (12,150 ha)—and probably looks much as it did when Captain Cook sailed past in 1770. The island has no resorts, just tropical forests, inlets, and unspoiled Whitehaven Beach—arguably the finest in the islands. If you want to go back to nature, this is one of the best places along the coast to do it. Cid Harbour, on the island's west coast, was an anchorage for part of the U.S. fleet just before the Battle of the Coral Sea (1943). Cruises from Airlie Beach to Whitehaven can drop you on the island. The national parks office at Airlie Beach can advise on the island's idyllic campsites and what to bring.

Hook Island, directly north of Whitsunday, is the second largest in the group. It has an underwater observatory and a low-key private resort, the Hook Island Wilderness Resort *(tel 07/4946-9470)*. A semi-submersible boat tours the island's spellbinding coral reefs.

Lindeman Island is another large member of the group, spanning about 5,000 acres (2,025 ha)—and all is national park. The snorkeling is superb, as is the bird-watching in the island's forests. Butterfly Valley offers a chance to see rainbow lorikeets and spectacular blue tiger butterflies, while 700-foot-high (213 m) Mount Oldfield has great sea panoramas. The Club Med Resort here became rundown, a fate of a number of island resorts, and is now closed awaiting redevelopment.

Closest to Airlie Beach, **Daydream Island** is the smallest of the developed islands, lying only 3 miles (4.8 km) from Shute Harbour on the mainland. The family-style Daydream Island Resort *(tel 07/4948-8426)* occupies all the northern end of the island. Nearby **South Molle Island** has a dilapidated resort but fine beaches and walks. It is a good day-trip option, as is forested **Long Island,** which also has upscale resorts.

Hamilton Island and **Hayman Island** are the most developed of the Whitsundays, with the most luxurious accommodations.

Nearly 5,000 species of mollusks inhabit the Great Barrier Reef, including the giant clam.

Hamilton, approximately 10 miles (16 km) southeast of Shute Harbour, is the most built-up of all, with a high-rise apartment tower, restaurants, marina, jetport, shopping boutiques, and sports complex *(tel 13-7333)*. Ferries to Hamilton Island leave from Shute Harbour, or fly direct from Sydney, Melbourne, or Brisbane. Hayman Island is the Whitsundays' most luxurious resort *(tel 1800-122-339)*, competing with the world's finest. The stunning design incorporates three swimming pools, tropical gardens, and a seawater lagoon. This place is for guests only; don't even think about day trips.

Northern Islands: In Far North Queensland (FNQ), the reef veers closest to the coast, and the coral and fish life are the most colorful and diverse. **Magnetic Island** was named by Captain Cook, who had some problems with his compass when he sailed past in 1770 and decided the island must be magnetic. Nobody else's compass has ever been troubled by it, but the name remains. You can get to it from Townsville in as little as 20 minutes—it is only about 7 miles (11 km) away. As a result, Magnetic Island is increasingly becoming a suburb of Townsville. It has more than 2,500 residents, some of whom commute to jobs across the bay. The island is ringed with white-sand beaches, and more than half of it is national park, with excellent bushwalking tracks, fine lookouts, and koalas in the wild. If you miss the wild ones, you can visit a koala park or aquarium.

Orpheus Island, a small volcanic nub fringed by kaleidoscopic coral reefs, is 50 miles (80 km)

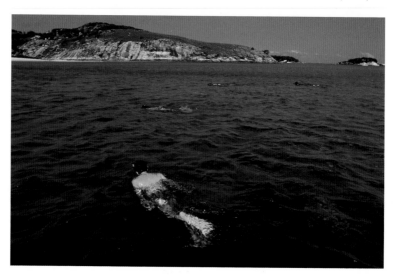

Snorkelers glide across Watson's Bay at Lizard Island.

farther northeast of Townsville. It is a national park, and its beaches have marvelous seashells.

Farther up the coast looms the formidable tree-clad mass of **Hinchinbrook Island,** just across a narrow channel from Cardwell on the mainland. It is the largest island along this stretch of coast—about 250 square miles (648 sq km)—but was never settled, and today it is a nearly pristine wilderness of mangroves and white-sand beaches dominated by a line of steep, dark mountains rising to more than 3,000 feet (914 m). With the exception of the modest Cape Richards Resort *(currently closed)*, Hinchinbrook Island is still pretty much as it was two centuries ago. It can be visited on a day trip from Cardwell, but a better option if you have the time and energy is to walk the East Coast Trail or Thorsborne Trail (see sidebar).

Dunk Island is just 3 miles (4.8 km) off the Queensland coast near Tully, about 125 miles (201 km) north of Townsville. Rich in bird life, densely forested, and bright with tropical butterflies, the island boasted a popular resort until hit by Cyclone Yasi in 2011. Until rebuilt, the only way here is by water taxi from Mission Beach. Also in this group is little **Bedarra Island,** which has a luxury resort currently undergoing renovation, or an exclusive private villa *(tel 07/4067-5311)*.

Green Island, about 15 miles (24 km) from Cairns, is part of the reef. This coral island is less than half a mile (1 km) long, and Green Island Resort *(tel 1800-673-366)*

Thorsborne Trail

This difficult 20-mile (32 km) trek on tropical Hinchinbrook Island rewards with beaches, rain forest, waterfalls, and rich birdlife. Water taxis from Cardwell drop you off at the start of the walk and pick up from George Point at the end. The Rainforest & Reef Information Centre *(tel 07/4066-8601)* **in Cardwell has details. Taking 3 to 5 days, the hike is on a rough track, traversing hills, swamps, and creeks. Keep an eye out for crocs in coastal areas. Bring all food, tents, and cooking gear. Seven campsites are spaced along the trail, and camping permits must be reserved. Trails are limited to 40 people at a time, and the walk must be booked** *(tel 13-1304 or epa.qld.gov .au)* **well in advance (up to a year for school holidays).**

takes up most of it. **Lizard Island,** among the reef's northernmost islands, has some of the finest coral reefs. It lies 60 miles (96 km) north of Cooktown. Captain Cook landed here in 1770 and climbed Cook's Lookout (as it is now called) to plot a way through the reef. He named the island for the large but harmless monitor lizards that still bask here. Lizard Island Resort *(tel 07/4043-1999)* is luxurious and pricey. An alternative is the national park campground *(reserve at Queensland Parks & Wildlife Service in Cairns, see p. 167)*. ■

Northern Queensland

Northern Queensland is home to Townsville, the region's industrial center and Australia's largest tropical city, and Cairns, the most useful base for visitors to the northern part of the Great Barrier Reef and a magnet for people who want adventurous activities—hang gliding, bungee jumping, white-water rafting, skydiving, and hot-air balloon rides. It also includes quiet resort beaches, exhilarating drives, and one of Australia's wildest corners, the Cape York Peninsula.

Cairns Harbour has long been a jumping-off point for excursions to the Great Barrier Reef.

Townsville

Townsville

⚑ 139 C4 & 155

Visitor Information

✉ Flinders Mall

☎ 07/4721-3660

Two entrepreneurs—a Scot named Melton Black and a wealthy sea captain named Robert Towns—sowed the seeds of Townsville. In 1863, they built a wharf and a rendering plant here for cattlemen who couldn't reach the port at Bowen when the Burdekin River was in flood. Gold rushes at Cape River (1867), Ravenswood (1869), and Charters Towers (1871) helped the city prosper. During World War II, Townsville was a strategic base for U.S. and Australian forces, and it was bombed three times by the Japanese in 1942. Today it is one of Australia's biggest military towns and home to James Cook University.

Although Townsville is the administrative and commercial capital of northern Queensland, it struggles to hold the interest of tourists, who prefer more fashionable Cairns and Port Douglas farther north. Visitors who expect lush rain forest are surprised to see typical olive-gray Australian scrub.

The tropical heat and humidity are here, but the rain forests don't start for 100 miles (160 km) north along the Bruce Highway.

Townsville does have elegant tropical architecture and stately figs along the **Strand,** and the city has spent millions trying to entice tourists. A casino is now on the waterfront, along with the superb **Reef HQ Aquarium** (2-68 Flinders St. East, tel 07/4750-0800, $$$), which has coral, anemones, and schools of colorful tropical fish.

Sunset views of the city lights from **Castle Hill** are outstanding, and **Billabong Sanctuary** (Bruce Highway, Nome, tel 07/4778-8344, $$$), 11 miles (18 km) southeast of town, has Aussie animal shows, feeding, and petting (but not the crocodiles). Townsville is also a base for visits to the Great Barrier Reef, and it is the only access point to Magnetic Island (see p. 164).

Cairns

Beneath a range of rain forest mountains that rise steeply from the coast, this tropical city lives for the sea, and a recent refurbishment of the seafront esplanade has made it feel sunnier and breezier than ever.

Cairns started out in the 1860s as a camp for trepang fishermen, but a succession of gold and tin strikes in the Atherton Tablelands (see pp. 170–171, 174), just over the mountain range, lured settlers from farther south, and the town was established in 1876. In 1924, the railway from Brisbane made its northern terminus at Cairns.

Until the tourism boom in the 1980s, Cairns was a sleepy sugar

town and laid-back seaside resort popular with marlin fishermen. Seemingly overnight it became a throbbing, fast-paced tourist spot. Yet while the development has made Cairns one of Australia's most popular destinations, it has virtually destroyed the tropical laziness that gave Cairns its charm. These days thriving Port Douglas, where the trains and the jumbo jets that descend on Cairns never came, has become the more fashionable vacation spot. The popular northern beaches just past the Cairns airport, such as Trinity Beach and upmarket Palm Cove, are quieter resort beaches close to Cairns.

Nevertheless, Cairns is a convenient base from which to explore the region. Visitors take day trips to the Great Barrier Reef, make excursions to the nearby islands, or charter deep-sea fishing boats. The rail/cable car to Kuranda (see p. 171) is another

Cairns

🅰 139 C4 & 155

Visitor Information

✉ 51 Esplanade

☎ 07/4051-3588

Queensland Parks & Wildlife Service

✉ 5B Sheridan St., Cairns

☎ 07/4222-5478

EXPERIENCE:
Sea Kayaking

Between Townsville and Cairns lies popular Mission Beach, a burgeoning resort with fine beaches and offshore islands. A great way to explore the Coral Sea is to kayak out to rain forested **Dunk Island,** 3 miles (4.5 km) offshore. You can hire sea kayaks and do it yourself, possibly spotting dolphins or turtles on the way, then snorkel on the island's reefs or lunch at the chic Voyages Dunk Island resort. The easiest and best option for inexperienced kayakers is a guided day trip with **Coral Sea Kayaking** (tel 07/4068-9154), which includes hotel pickup, lunch, and snorkeling gear.

EXPERIENCE: Diving Australia

The Great Barrier Reef is Australia's unrivaled diving paradise, with myriad dive sites for the experienced and dive schools all along the coast for beginners looking to gain certification with a 4–5 day open-water course. Cairns, Port Douglas, Townsville, and Airlie Beach are the main dive centers, and prices are competitive.

From Cairns or Port Douglas, top dive destinations include **Lizard Island,** noted for its giant clams, and the **Cod Hole,** where you can hand-feed potato cod. **Osprey Reef** has magnificent soft corals and giant fish, including numerous reef sharks.

From Townsville, 56 miles (90 km) south, the **Yongala Wreck** teems with marine life, including sharks, manta rays, and turtles. Perfectly round **Wheeler**

Reef on the edge of a drop-off also features spectacular large fish.

In the Whitsundays, teeming **Bait Reef** and **Hardy Reef** are top destinations. Farther south, **Heron Island** has superb snorkeling and diving, as does **Lady Elliot Island,** the southernmost island.

Australia's other standout dive destination is **Ningaloo Reef,** a lesser known but no less spectacular 160-mile (260 km) reef off the coast of Western Australia. Dive shops are in Exmouth and Coral Bay. Exmouth's Navy Pier at the end of the peninsula is one of the country's top shore dives.

Visit *australia.com* for information on diving locations, operators, centers, and local accomodations all over Australia.

Port Douglas

🄰 139 C4 & 155

Visitor Information

✉ 23 Macrossan St.

☎ 07/4099-5599

Quicksilver Catamarans: Cairns to Port Douglas

✉ Marina Mirage

☎ 07/4087-2100
Offers fast catamaran service to Cairns, also day trips to the reef

popular day trip. Local attractions include the **Cairns Historical Society Museum** (*Lake & Shields Sts., tel 07/4051-5582*), the tropical **Botanic Gardens** near the airport, and the **Tjapukai Aboriginal Cultural Park** (*Kamerunga Rd., tel 07/4042-9900, $$$$*) in the northern suburb of Smithfield, with informative day tours and evening dinner/cultural performances.

Port Douglas to Cape Tribulation

The chic resort town of Port Douglas is 40 miles (64 km) north of Cairns on the Captain Cook Highway. This is an idyllic road, one of the most beautiful in Australia, rolling past isolated beaches and lush tropical hills. If you have the time and energy, make the journey on a bicycle.

Port Douglas, 3 miles (5 km) off the highway, was a sleepy seaside fishing village until the 1980s, when it was discovered by tourists and resort developers. Set in the rain forest beside the Coral Sea, the little village of 250 people seemed to be everyone's idea of a tropical hideaway. However, large-scale development has taken its toll, and the permanent population of 2,000 quadruples at peak tourist times.

Port Douglas is noted for five-star luxury resorts, such as the Sheraton Mirage (*Davidson St., tel 07/5577-0000*), and for its golf course, marina, and upscale shopping complex. Although it seems geared to the top end of the market (former U.S. President Bill Clinton has vacationed here), it has budget accommodations and eateries as well. Port Douglas is more relaxed than Cairns and has plenty for visitors to do: walking the Mossman Gorge, taking trips into the Daintree rain forest, or exploring the northern end of the Great Barrier Reef.

Still very much a small sugar town, **Mossman** is on the Captain Cook Highway around 9 miles (14 km) north of Port Douglas. Its major attraction is the lush, waterfall-laced **Mossman Gorge** about 3 miles (5 km) west. The Kuku Yulanji people, a local Aboriginal tribe, give guided tours, or you can take a shuttle bus (*$*) from the huge new visitor center.

The quiet village of **Daintree,** 22 miles (35 km) farther up the highway, is set on the edge of the rain forests of the vast **Daintree National Park** stretching to the north. The village was established as a timber camp to cut the prized red cedars that grew here. These days, it is a base for cruises along

the mighty **Daintree River**—a chance to putter through the tropical rain forest and spot saltwater crocodiles basking in the sun along the banks. One of the larger cruise operators is Daintree River Trains *(tel 07/4090-7676, $$$).*

Cape Tribulation is 22 miles (35 km) north of Daintree. To get there, take the ferry that crosses the Daintree River about 6 miles (10 km) south of Daintree. Car ferries run every few minutes, from 6 a.m. to midnight *(tel 07/4098-7788, A$20 return).* The road beyond the ferry is paved all the way to Cape Tribulation.

The **Daintree Discovery Centre** *(tel 07/4098-9171, $$$$),* about 5 miles (8 km) past the ferry, is a popular stop, with interpretive displays, a forest walkway, and a 75-foot (23 m) canopy tower lookout. Alternatively, turn off to the **Mount Alexandra Lookout** for sweeping (and free) views

Daintree
⚠ 139 C5
Visitor Information
✉ 5 Stewart St.
☎ 07/4098-6133

Daintree National Park is one of the last strongholds of ancient Australian rain forests.

across the park to the coast. A number of excellent short walks in the park will get you out into the rain forest and the mangroves. Don't miss the **Jindalba Boardwalk,** an easy loop through magnificent forest with a good chance of spotting cassowaries.

Cape Tribulation and nearby Mount Sorrow were named by Captain Cook when his ship grounded on a coral reef, forcing him to beach it near present-day Cooktown for repairs. For much of the next two centuries this lonely stretch of coastline was seldom visited. In the 1970s, a few hippies arrived, and the area began to be better known. It still has a remote feel, although in holiday periods

INSIDER TIP:

Dive with sea turtles and sea snakes at the wreck of the passenger ship S.S. *Yongala*, which sank near Townsville in 1911. This is one of the best dive sites in the Great Barrier Reef.

—PETER FUNCH
National Geographic field researcher

you'll see plenty of tourists, and accommodations at Cape Tribulation often are full.

The Cape Tribulation section of the Daintree National Park is a spectacular paradise of mist-shrouded mountains tumbling down to the Coral Sea. One of the wettest corners on Earth, the park

has virgin tropical rain forest and coral reefs virtually side by side. It is the jewel of Queensland's 3,500 square miles (9,065 sq km) of wet tropics. Hidden in Cape Tribulation's forests are primitive varieties of plants and flowers found nowhere else. Among them are species of angiosperms that are forerunners of all flowering plants. New species of ferns are often discovered. Crocodiles lurk in the mangroves and estuaries, and the forests have 120 bird species, from rainbow honey-eaters to the flightless cassowary, which stands more than 6 feet tall (2 m). Butterflies include the cobalt blue Ulysses and the huge Hercules moth, one of world's largest.

In the 1980s, conservationists and the timber industry fought a bitter campaign over the building of the **Bloomfield Track,** a four-wheel-drive road that connects Cape Tribulation with Cooktown, 100 miles (160 km) north. The conservationists lost that battle, but the attention focused on the rain forests led the federal government to nominate the forests for the World Heritage List. Today logging is banned in the area, and because ecotourism is now the dominant industry in far northern Queensland, rain forests are a vital part of the economy.

Atherton Tablelands

Simply getting to this lush volcanic highland looming above Cairns can be as much fun as exploring it. The Kuranda Scenic Railway climbs the jungle-clad range that broods over Cairns to the cool moist heights of the Atherton Tablelands. One of the world's great short train journeys, the railway was built in 1891 to link the Herberton tin mines with the coast.

Pulled by a 125-year-old steam engine, the train skirts the coastline and then ascends the mountains in a series of switchbacks. It runs

Having arrived by train, you need to rent a car to see the glories of the tablelands. Rain forest towns such as Atherton and Ravenshoe (pronounced RAVENS-hoe) attract artists, back-to-nature types, and gypsies and have a friendly offbeat style. The little village of **Yungaburra,**

Atherton Tablelands

🗺 139 B4–C4

Visitor Information

✉ Silo Rd. & Main St., Atherton

☎ 07/4091-4222

Kuranda Scenic Railway

☎ 07/4032-3964

Kuranda

🗺 139 C4

Visitor Information

✉ Therwine St.

☎ 07/4093-9311

The high, cool rain forests of the Atherton Tablelands shelter rare orchids, ferns, and brilliant tropical butterflies.

along a 600-foot (183 m) sheer precipice above the **Barron River Gorge** and through 15 tunnels cut into the stone. The 20-mile (32 km) ride ends at **Kuranda,** a rain forest town with a famous crafts market and an arty atmosphere. Crowds and trashy souvenirs in the market are lessening its charm, but it has gorgeous rain forest walks close by. A track from the picturesque colonial station takes you into the wilds of **Barron Gorge National Park.** Another way to reach Kuranda is on the **Skyrail Rainforest Cableway** (tel 07/4038-1555), a 5-mile (8 km) cable car ride that leaves from Cairns's northern suburbs.

about 8 miles (13 km) east of Atherton on the Gillies Highway, is a central spot from which to explore. Two of the loveliest crater lakes you'll ever see—**Lake Eacham** and **Lake Barrine**—are east off the Gillies Highway. Both are national parks, with swimming holes and bushwalks around their rims. A mile (1.5 km) or so south of Yungaburra, on the road to Malanda, is the **Curtain Fig Tree,** a massive, much photographed tangle of roots and vines.

A few miles south of Atherton, off the Kennedy Highway, is **Mount Hypipamee National Park.** More than 300 species

(continued on p. 174)

National Parks

Australia has more than 500 national parks and thousands of reserves, and they cover every kind of significant natural terrain in the country, including rain forests, deserts, islands, mountain ranges, and long stretches of haunting coastal dunes. Some are extremely remote, and visitors must travel across barren desert just to reach them, a journey that may be extremely dangerous for the inexperienced or the unprepared.

Not all of Australia's wild places require expedition planning. Some of the prettiest national parks are perched on the edge of cities. Royal National Park is on the coast just south of Sydney. In 1994, a bushfire in the Sydney suburbs destroyed about 90 percent of the park.

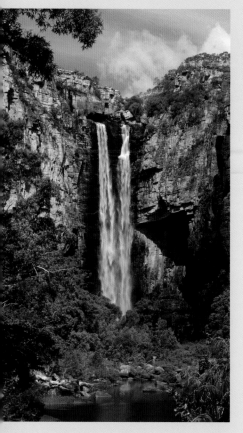

Waterfalls pour over the escarpment in Kakadu National Park, Northern Territory.

Within a year, however, green shoots had appeared in the blackened soil, and the bush now is well on the way to recovery. Lush Dandenong Ranges National Park is only a suburban train ride from Melbourne.

A string of national parks protects 14 areas on the United Nations' World Heritage List. The Great Barrier Reef is among them. So is the Northern Territory's magnificent Kakadu National Park. This tropical wetland about three hours southeast of Darwin is the biggest tourist draw in the north. The main physical feature is the dramatic Arnhem Land escarpment, a 400-mile-long (640 km) line of massive sandstone cliffs. During the summer wet season, runoff from the monsoon rains spills over the cliffs in a series of spectacular waterfalls. In the dry season, the shrinking water holes are raucous with thousands of migratory birds. Kakadu is on the World Heritage List for cultural reasons as well. Aboriginal culture here dates back more than 50,000 years, and thousands of rock-art murals decorate its gorges, rock shelters, and caves.

The haunting monoliths of Uluru–Kata Tjuta National Park (Ayers Rock and the Olgas) are also on the World Heritage List for both cultural and natural reasons. Australia's other World Heritage sites include Shark Bay in Western Australia, popular with tourists for its friendly dolphins but famous among paleobotanists for the primitive blue-green algae matting the rocks on the edge of Hamelin Pool. These algae, called stromatolites, are living fossils dating back 3.5 billion years.

Some of Australia's other World Heritage sites are wilderness islands. Fraser Island, off the southeast coast of Queensland, is the

Ten of the Best National Parks

Cradle Mountain–Lake St. Clair NP: In central Tasmania, the park features Australia's best hike, the 40-mile (65 km) Overland Track, taking in snowy peaks and alpine meadows and lakes. See pp. 344–345.

Daintree NP: Just 100 miles (160 km) north of Cairns, this park has ancient rain forest, mangroves, crocs, and white-sand beaches at Cape Tribulation. See p. 169.

Fraser Island (Great Sandy) NP: The world's largest sand island, off the Queensland coast near Hervey Bay, has rain forest, dune lakes, dingoes, and miles of pristine beach. See pp. 148–149.

Freycinet NP: Wineglass Bay is the jewel of this stunning park on Tasmania's sunny east coast, blessed with wonderful beaches and pink granite hills. See p. 348.

Kakadu NP: This World Heritage–listed park, 95 miles (153 km) from Darwin, has spectacular escarpments, waterfalls, rock art, and wetlands. See pp. 188–191.

Kosciuszko NP: Skiing in winter, fine hiking in summer, and Australia's highest peak are highlights of this alpine wonderland in the Snowy Mountains of New South Wales. See p. 114.

Nambung NP: The Pinnacles, 156 miles (251 km) north of Perth, comprise hundreds of eerie limestone pillars jutting out of the desert. See sidebar p. 216.

Port Campbell NP: This park is home to the awe-inspiring Twelve Apostles, giant arches and islands carved by the sea from sandstone cliffs, 170 miles (280 km) from Melbourne. See p. 313.

Purnululu NP: In Western Australia's Kimberley region, the tiger-striped "Bungle Bungle" has spectacular sandstone domes, cliffs, and chasms. See pp. 236–237.

Uluru–Kata Tjuta NP: The towering monolith of Uluru and nearby Kata Tjuta's strange rock domes lie 250 miles (400 km) southwest of Alice Springs. See pp. 204, 206–208.

world's largest sand island. It is forested with unique rain forest plants and trees, such as the satinay. Lord Howe Island is a tropical paradise about 430 miles (692 km) off the coast of New South Wales. The southwest corner of Tasmania, also on the World Heritage List, is cloaked by some of the world's last great stands of virgin temperate forest.

The Gondwana Rainforests of Australia are a group of 50 reserves covering about 570,000 acres (265,000 ha) in the coastal highlands of New South Wales and southeast Queensland. The Fossil Mammal sites are widely scattered: One is at Riversleigh in Queensland, and the other is more than 1,800 miles (2,896 km) away in the Narracoorte Caves of southeastern South Australia. As the name implies, these are treasure troves of fossil remains, revealing the history of Australia's unique fauna. The most obscure World Heritage site is Willandra National Park,

a sequence of dry Pleistocene lake beds that are located about 100 miles (160 km) northwest of Griffith in central New South Wales.

Visiting National Parks

National parks are administered by the individual states, and facilities vary. Some have resort accommodations inside or nearby, for example, the Flinders Ranges in South Australia and Watarrka (Kings Canyon) in the Northern Territory. Other parks have pit toilets and picnic tables, and some have no facilities at all. Contact the park in advance if you want to stay, as some parks allow only a few visitors at a time, and you may have to reserve a camping spot or accommodations. You also need to find out what equipment to take. *(The national parks agency in each state has details. For addresses and telephone numbers see p. 366.)*

Cape York Peninsula

138–139 B5–B6

Natures Powerhouse Visitor Information Centre

✉ Finch Bay Rd., Cooktown

☎ 07/4069-6004

of birds have been found in this forest. A path leads a quarter of a mile (400 m) along Dinner Creek to a sinister volcanic cavity that plunges a sheer 200 feet (61 m) into a dark, algae-covered pool. The 10-mile (16 km) "waterfall circuit" drive around nearby **Millaa Millaa** (south of Malanda) takes in the best of the area's waterfalls. Take the Theresa Creek Road off Palmerston Highway toward Millaa Millaa Falls, the first and most magnificent. Then drive through dense rain forests and farmland to Zillie, Mungali, and Elinja.

Thirty minutes from Millaa Millaa along the Palmerston Highway toward the coast, the **Mamu Rainforest Canopy Walkway** (tel 07/4064-5294, $$) is a spectacular elevated, 1,100-foot-long (350 m) walkway through the rain forest canopy to a cantilevered overhang and lookout tower.

Cape York Peninsula

Driving up to the Tip, as Aussies call the Cape York Peninsula, is one of the great four-wheel-drive adventures on the continent, a challenging 500-mile (800 km) trek to mainland Australia's most northerly point.

This is most definitely not a trip for beginners or the ill-prepared. The roads and tracks are mostly dirt, and there are many river crossings. While it is possible under favorable conditions for a

---

EXPERIENCE: Touring the Tip

The Cape York Peninsula is the Holy Grail for four-wheel-drive adventurers. Plenty do the pilgrimage, but it is only for well-equipped vehicles, which usually travel in convoy. Depending on the route you take, you'll need a winch, chains, and plenty of experience fording rivers. Riverbanks can be steep and muddy, and crocodiles lurk in the water. The main road—the Peninsula Development Road through Laura to Coen and Weipa—is unpaved but graded and easy going when dry. Serious off-roaders like to take tougher routes, such as the detour to Cape Melville. Past Weipa, a four-wheel-drive vehicle and experience using it are essential. Those after a challenge take the Old Telegraph Track. The alternative to doing it all yourself is to a take a driving tour, flight, cargo ship, or combination.

Cape York by Four-wheel Drive:
The following Cairns operators offer a wide variety of 4WD tours to Cape York,

lasting from seven days to two weeks or more:

Heritage Tours
(tel 07/4054-7750, heritagetours.com.au)

Oz Tour Safaris
(tel 1800-079-006, oztours.com.au)

Wilderness Challenge (tel 07/4035-4488, wilderness-challenge.com.au)

Cape York by Plane:
Qantas (tel 13-1313) has daily flights to Weipa and Horn Island from Cairns, while **Skytrans** (tel 1300-759-872) flies from Cairns to Bamaga, Coen, Lockhart River, and Arukun.

Cape York by Ferry:
M.V. Trinity Bay (tel 07/4035-1234, seaswift.com.au), a working cargo ship, takes vehicles and up to 38 passengers in en suite cabins from Cairns up the coast to Cape York via Horn Island, Thursday Island, and Bamaga.

On Cape York Peninsula, rainless lightning storms may set the bush ablaze.

conventional vehicle to make it as far as the mining town of **Weipa,** about two-thirds of the way north, the final leg to the top is a very rough track, strictly for four-wheel drive vehicles. During the summer monsoons, forget it. Happily enough, if you lack the experience or gear, you can take one of a number of four-wheel-drive tours to the Tip, or get there by air or barge from Cairns.

The launching pad for the cape is usually **Cooktown,** the northernmost town on the east coast. Lying on the croc-infested Endeavour River, it has a lazy frontier feel, but tourism is on the rise since the inland road from Cairns was paved in 2006. Most 4WD visitors, however, come up the more scenic Bloomfield Track from Cape Tribulation.

If air-conditioned travel to Cape York seems like rough-ing it, think how it was in 1848, when Edmund Kennedy led an ill-fated expedition to explore the peninsula. Of the 14 people who started, only three survived. Kennedy was speared by hostile Aborigines and died of his wounds. The only member of the party to reach the cape, where a ship was waiting, was the Aborigi-nal guide, Jacky Jacky.

In 1863, an adventurer named John Jardine established a pearling, coconut, and trading port called Somerset near the tip of the cape. His ambition was to make his little kingdom rival Singapore. In the following year, Jardine's sons Frank and Alexander drove a thousand head of cattle from Rockhampton all the way to the tip of the peninsula to help feed the struggling outpost. The remarkable venture opened up miles of new country, but in the end the termites and attacks by hostile Aborigines proved too much. In 1877, the Jardines gave up on Somerset and relocated the

EXPERIENCE: Horseracing in the Dust

Due south of Cape York in far southwest Queensland near the South Australia border, Birdsville is as remote as the Black Stump or mythical Woop Woop, synonymous with the outback in the Australian psyche. A mecca for four-wheel-drive adventurers, this settlement on the edge of the Simpson Desert really comes alive in the first week of September, when more than 6,000 people flock to its infamous horse races

(birdsvilleraces.com) for drinking and partying in the dust. The town can be reached via the famed Birdsville Track in South Australia, or from Charleville in Queensland, both rugged routes for the well equipped. Alternatively, **Skytrans** (tel 1300-759-872, skytrans.com.au) flies to Birdsville on its Brisbane–Mount Isa run. The colorful **Birdsville Hotel** (tel 07/4656-3244), right next to the airstrip, is the place to stay and swap yarns.

Gulf of Carpentaria

Map pp. 138–139

Visitor Information

Caroline St., Normanton

07/4745-1065

ROCK-ART TOURS:
Trezise Bush Guide Service, tel 07/4060-3236

little community of 200 to nearby Thursday Island.

By then, all the action on the Cape York Peninsula was taking place much farther south, along the Palmer River, where a gold rush drew thousands of prospectors. The diggings were marked by racial strife between the Australian and Chinese prospectors, and the Aborigines who did not care for either in their territory.

Laura, about 200 miles (320 km) north of Cairns, was at the heart of the diggings, and 20,000 people a year passed through at the height of the boom. Laura is on the Peninsula Developmental Road, which you can join at **Mareeba,** west of Cairns on the Kennedy Highway. It is an easy drive, unless there has been heavy rain. There is not much to Laura itself, but it is the nearest township to the **Quinkan Reserve Aboriginal rock-art galleries** near Split Rock, about 7 miles (11 km) south. The galleries are among the world's largest collections of rock art, with tens of thousands of paintings

dating back more than 13,000 years. Most haunting are the Quinkans—gaunt, angular, sinister figures with staring eyes, whom the Aborigines believe lurk in cracks in the rocks. Tours to the galleries can be arranged through the Quinkan Reserves Trust (tel 07/4060-3457). The **Aboriginal Dance Festival,** held in Laura in June of odd-numbered years, is a riveting spectacle, worth arranging your itinerary around if you can be in Queensland then. The Ang-Gnarra Aboriginal Corporation in Laura (tel 07/4060-3214) has information on local rock art and on the dance festival.

Many people are attracted to **Thursday Island,** off the tip of the cape, simply because this tiny spot in the Torres Strait is the end of the line. It is the most visited of the 60-odd Torres Straits Islands. Its residents are a multicultural swirl of Aborigines, Melanesians, Malay, Papuans, Chinese, and the descendants of Japanese pearl divers who worked here when the island was a pearling center. The pace of life is slow and accommodations are limitied to a few options. Peddell's Ferry Service *(tel 07/4069-1551)* makes the crossing from Seisia, at the tip of Cape York, to Thursday Island.

Gulf of Carpentaria

The Gulf of Carpentaria and Queensland's rugged northwest are not for everyone. This is unvarnished outback, with mining towns, isolated ports, and rough pubs. The landscape is blindingly hot savanna, studded with termite mounds capable of breaking the axle of a four-wheel-drive vehicle. Crocodiles inhabit the rivers and mangroves along the edge of the gulf, and the lonely towns can be cut off for weeks when the monsoons hit in summer. Despite all that, the area has an odd frontier appeal that pulls you on.

It's about 450 miles (720 km) from Cairns to Normanton on the lonely and evocative **Gulf Developmental Highway,** which runs down the western flank of the Atherton Tablelands and into the savanna country. Here, you're on a lonely highway into an outback barely changed from the days when explorers such as Burke

and Wills passed this way. About 150 miles (240 km) southwest of Cairns, the highway passes the **Undara Lava Tubes,** a vast series of hollow basalt chambers through which massive amounts of lava flowed in a volcanic eruption about 200,000 years ago. They are the largest such formation in the world and are well worth a visit.

INSIDER TIP:

Consider a 4WD safari from Cairns to get the most out of little-known and remote Cape York and the Gulf of Carpentaria. [See sidebar p. 174.]

—ROFF SMITH
National Geographic author

Normanton is a rough old river port that over the decades has served the local cattle stations, the 1880s goldfields around Croydon, and the silver mines in Cloncurry. The Norman River is rich with barramundi, tropical Australia's magnificent sweet-eating game fish. Catching their first barramundi is the goal of many Australian anglers heading to the tropics. If you'd like to try your hand, guided game-fishing trips can be arranged in town. If you decide to do a little fishing or boating, remember that these waters are home to some of the world's most dangerous saltwater crocodiles. Check out the 28-foot (8.5 m) statue of what was reputedly the biggest of them all—shot

Undara Lava Tubes
   139 B4

Lava Lodge Undara
☎   Accommodations & tours of the lava tubes: 07/4097-1900 or 1800-990-992

Morning Glory

The atmospheric phenomenon called Morning Glory—a bizarre tubular cloud formation in the dawn skies in spring—is often visible over the Gulf of Carpentaria during the spring months, September to November.

Mount Isa

 138 A3

Visitor Information

✉ 19 Marian St.

☎ 07/4749-1555

outbackisa.com.au

in the Norman River in 1957—near the town's garishly painted Purple Pub.

A 45-mile (72 km) side trip north from Normanton brings you to **Karumba,** a prawn-trawling port on the gulf. In the 1930s, it was a refueling stop for the Qantas Empire Flying Boats that flew between Britain and Australia. These days fishing enthusiasts flock here to try their luck at what is said to be the best light-tackle fishing in Australia. The gulf is filled with grunter, king salmon, blue salmon, and the famous barramundi. And, of course, saltwater crocodiles.

Except for the superb angling, you will find little else to do in Karumba. Sunsets over Karumba Point are gorgeous, as the blood-red sun appears to melt into the gulf. The beach is gorgeous, too, but don't even think about a dip unless you are into wrestling with a crocodile.

A 150-mile (240 km) dirt track leads west from Normanton to

Burketown, population 170, which is one of the loneliest towns in Australia, particularly during the wet season (Oct.–April), when it can be cut off for weeks. Although the road is bumpy, you normally do not need a four-wheel-drive vehicle in the dry season. The track runs through harsh spectacular country, past beautiful Leichhardt Falls.

If you are adventurous, you can drive to **Darwin** from Burketown along the **Gulf Track.** It is about 300 miles (480 km) of dirt track from Burketown to the next paved road, at Borroloola, and from there it is a farther 600 miles (960 km) to Darwin. Attempt the Gulf Track only in the dry season. The less demanding **Wills Developmental Road,** another dirt track, goes 75 miles (120 km) south from Burketown to **Gregory Downs** cattle station. There you can turn off for Lawn Hill (Boodjamulla) National Park (see p. 179) or take the Wills Highway 90 miles (145 km) southeast and turn south to Cloncurry.

The **Flinders Highway** runs east from Cloncurry to Townsville and the coast. West of Cloncurry, the highway runs 75 miles (120 km) to the sprawling mining town of **Mount Isa.** One of Australia's largest outback cities, with a population of 22,000 (marginally fewer than Alice Springs), Mount Isa claims to be the biggest city or municipal area in the world, covering almost 16,800 square miles (43,348 sq km). The main industry here is the giant silver-lead-zinc mine, also one of the biggest in the world.

EXPERIENCE:
Touring Mount Isa Mine

The big attraction in Mount Isa is **Outback at Isa** *(19 Marian St., tel 07/4749-1555, outbackatisa.com.au, $$$$$)*, featuring a multimedia gallery, outback park exhibiting Mount Isa's natural and indigenous heritage, and the fascinating Riversleigh Fossil Site. The highlight, however, is undoubtedly the Hard Times Mine tours. Don overalls, hard hat, and lamp, and descend underground with experienced miners to learn how it's done and to try your hand with mine machinery on the rock face.

In August, Mount Isa is host to Australia's largest rodeo.

Lawn Hill (Boodjamulla) National Park

Lawn Hill (Boodjamulla) National Park is one of Australia's jewels, an unexpected tropical oasis in the vast black those ancient rain forests. They are lined with fan palms, fig trees, and ferns. The water attracts large numbers of mammals, birds, and reptiles such as water monitors, tortoises, and shy freshwater crocodiles. The Waanyi people have been here for 30,000 years, and the park is rich in rock art.

Lawn Hill National Park

⛰ 138 A4

☎ 1300-1303-72

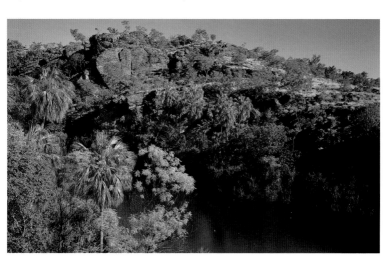

Lawn Hill Gorge is a hidden tropical oasis of fan palms, parrots, and freshwater crocodiles.

soil plains of the gulf country. Locals and many visitors claim it is at least as spectacular as Kakadu (see pp. 188–191) and arguably more so, because its lushness is so surprising in the hot bleakness that surrounds it. It is a legacy of a time when all of northern Australia was covered with dense rain forests. When the climate grew warmer and drier, the forests retreated.

These gorges, which are watered by a series of springs in the limestone hills along the nearby Northern Territory border, are the last secluded pockets of

Trails and boardwalks lead hikers to the **Wild Dog Dreaming** and **Rainbow Dreaming** rock-art sites.

The park has about 15 miles (24 km) of walking tracks in all, but most visitors prefer to explore it by canoe or inner tube, floating in its clear, lime green waters looking up at the colored sandstone walls of the gorge rising 200 feet (60 m) above the pools. Although plenty of crocodiles live here, particularly in the lower parts of the gorge, these waters are safe for swimming. Freshwater crocodiles are smaller and much more timid than their saltwater cousins.

In the southern end of the park, the staggeringly rich limestone fossil beds of the World Heritage–listed **Riversleigh Fossil Site** tell the story of the past 20 million years. The fossils reveal that this was once a scary little jungle filled with carnivorous kangaroos, marsupial lions, rhinoceros-size wombats, and relatives of the now-extinct Tasmanian tiger. Also living here were birds, bats, and prehistoric pythons up to 25 feet (7.6 m) long. The fossil beds were actually a series of lakes where creatures came to drink. Fossilized remains have been extracted by blasting chunks out of the stubborn limestone beds. A roadside display contains some of the finds at the park. The fossil areas are a protected site.

Cane Toad

The large, warty, poisonous cane toad (Bufo marinus) was introduced into the sugarcane fields of northern Queensland in 1935 to combat the cane beetle. It has spread rapidly since then and now threatens biodiversity in a huge area from Kakadu National Park in the Northern Territory to Port Macquarie, near Sydney. Its poison sacs make the toad deadly to native amphibians, reptiles, and mammals, including freshwater crocodiles and quolls. Biological solutions are elusive, and community toad roundups remain the most effective control.

In all, Lawn Hill is a hidden gem. Now comes the heartbreak part. There is a reason for the use of the adjective "hidden." This park is a long way from anywhere, and the final leg of the journey involves a long ride over a rough dirt track that is virtually impassable after heavy rains. A four-wheel-drive vehicle is recommended, although a conventional vehicle can make it through in dry weather, if the driver has experience on bush tracks. The park is about 250 miles (400 km) northwest of Mount Isa. The easiest drive there is to take the Burke Developmental Road north from Cloncurry to the Burke and Wills Roadhouse, and then go northwest on the Wills Highway. A 90-mile (145 km) drive will bring you to the Gregory Downs Hotel (tel 07/4748-5566), an old outback pub. You can buy food and fuel here, and the pub also has accommodations.

Access to the park is on a track by the pub, and this final leg is a tough 70-mile (113 km) ride. It would be nice to say that the scenery along the track into the park is stunning—but it isn't. In fact, it is positively apocalyptic in its bleakness, which is what makes Lawn Hill itself such a delightful surprise. Six miles (9.6 km) east of the park entrance is Adel's Grove Kiosk (tel 07/4748-5502), where you can buy supplies and rent canoes. A privately run campsite is here, with another in the park itself. Despite its remoteness, Lawn Hill is popular and the campsites are often booked up. Check with the park office. ■

Colloquially known as the "Never Never" and home to two cherished icons: Uluru and the wild, monsoonal wetlands of Kakadu

Northern Territory

Introduction & Map   182–183

Darwin   184–187

Kakadu National Park   188–191

Litchfield National Park   192–193

Nitmiluk National Park & Katherine   194–195

Arnhem Land & the Tiwi Islands   196–197

Alice Springs   198–201

Experience: Henley-on-Todd Regatta   199

Feature: Aboriginal Art   202–203

Experience: Buying Aboriginal Art   203

Uluru–Kata Tjuta National Park   204–208

Experience: Bushwalking   205

**Experience: Getting to Know
the Aborigines**   209

Watarrka National Park   210

Hotels & Restaurants   376–377

A traditional Aboriginal art dot pattern

Northern Territory

At 525,000 square miles (1,359,750 sq km), the Northern Territory is about the size of Alaska, but with only 234,000 inhabitants it is one of the least populated places in the world. About half of its residents live in Darwin, in the tropical north. Alice Springs, in the Red Centre, is the other main population hub. The rest of the population lives in Aboriginal communities, mining camps, or cattle stations.

The first settlements in the territory were on Melville Island and the Cobourg Peninsula in the 1820s, when the British hastened to claim the northern coastline ahead of the French and Dutch. Yet it wasn't until 1869, when Palmerston (later Darwin) was established, that Europeans took root.

The Northern Territory has the highest percentage of Aborigines in its population—about 32 percent—of any state in Australia. About 50 percent of the state is Aboriginal land. Much of it is remote, and visiting requires a permit. But some Aboriginal communities are opening up, inviting responsible tourism operators onto their lands, or starting their own operations, both to create jobs and to share their ancient knowledge and arts.

Many people visit the territory just to see Uluru (Ayers Rock) and the wetlands in Kakadu, but the Northern Territory also has Kata Tjuta (the Olgas, near Uluru), the lost world of Watarrka, the MacDonnell Ranges near Alice Springs, and Nitmiluk Gorge near Katherine.

The tropical north has two seasons. The Wet runs through the summer, when heat, humidity, and monsoonal rain make life tolerable only to a special breed of frontier lovers. Bush tracks can be washed out for months, dry creek beds turn into cataracts, and wild tropical grasses grow as much as 30 feet (9 m) in a month. The Dry begins around April. The storms clear away, and for the next six months the country bakes beneath faultless skies. Daily high temperatures are in the high 80s°F (30°C). This is the best time to visit the north, or Top End. The buildup to the Wet starts again in October, with rising heat and humidity, and

> ## NOT TO BE MISSED:
>
> **Tropical Darwin** 184–187
>
> **The wetlands marvel of Kakadu National Park** 188–191
>
> **Swimming under waterfalls in Litchfield National Park** 192–193
>
> **Experiencing indigenous culture in the Tiwi Islands** 197
>
> **Walking through shady gorges in the MacDonnell Ranges** 200–201
>
> **The sacred sites of Uluru–Kata Tjuta National Park** 204–208

dry thunderstorms that give no relief. In the central deserts, the weather is scorching during the summer and dry as parchment. Winters are cold and frosts are possible.

Visiting the Northern Territory requires planning because of the distances involved, but actually moving within it is fairly easy. The major highways are paved and even the gravel back roads are generally graded. Flights go to Alice Springs, Darwin, and Yulara (the resort near Uluru) from all parts of Australia. Alice Springs and Darwin are accessible by the Ghan train (see pp. 282–283).

Statehood—and the full right to determine its own affairs—continues to elude this last frontier. A referendum for full statehood was narrowly defeated in 1998, and although the territory is self-governing today, officially it remains answerable to the federal government in Canberra. ■

Timor Sea

Arafura Sea

Cape Wessel

6 ▷

Smith Point

Cobourg Peninsula

Bathurst Island

Melville Island

Van Diemen Gulf

WESSEL ISLANDS

Nguiu

DARWIN

Nhulunbuy

Cape Arnhem

Ubirr

Humpty Doo

Gove Peninsula

N.T. Wildlife Park

Darwin Crocodile Farm

Batchelor

Jabiru

Nourlangie Rock

LITCHFIELD NAT. PARK

KAKADU NAT. PARK

Yellow Water

Adelaide River

Jim Jim Falls

Goyder

Robin Falls

Hot Springs

Douglas

Arnhem Land

Twin Falls

Groote Eylandt

Daly River Nature Park

Daly River

Pine Creek

5 ▷

Leliyn (Edith Falls)

NITMILUK NAT. PARK

Gulf of Carpentaria

Springvale Homestead

Katherine Gorge

Roper Bar

Katherine

Cutta Cutta Caves

Elsey

Roper

SIR EDWARD PELLEW GROUP

Mataranka

Victoria River

Larrimah

Cox

Timber Creek

Borroloola

CARPENTARIA HIGHWAY

GREGORY NATIONAL PARK

Daly Waters

Cape Crawford

Top Springs

NORTHERN

4 ▷

BUCHANAN

VICTORIA HIGHWAY

TERRITORY

Elliott

Barkly Tableland

Kalkaringi

Renner Springs

Attack Creek Historical Reserve

Three Ways Roadhouse

BARKLY

HIGHWAY

3 ▷

Area of map detail

★ **Canberra**

Tennant Creek

STUART HWY

Devil's Marbles

QUEENSLAND p. 137

Wauchope

Central Mount Stuart Historical Reserve

1140m

Barrow Creek

Mt. Leichhardt

Ti-Tree

Yuendumu

Atartinga

Lake Mackay

2 ▷

WESTERN AUSTRALIA p. 211

Simpson's Gap

TREPHINA GORGE N.P.

Ormiston Gorge

Standley Chasm

Arltunga

Ross River Homestead

Hermannsburg Community

MacDonnell

Alice Springs

WATARRKA (KINGS CANYON) NAT. PARK

FINKE GORGE N.P.

Ranges

Todd

Henbury

Meteorite Craters

Lake Amadeus

1 ▷

Petermann Ranges

1069m

Yulara

Kata Tjuta

Uluru (Ayers Rock, 863m)

LASSETER HWY

Erldunda

Finke

Simpson Desert

ULURU–KATA TJUTA NATIONAL PARK

STUART HWY

GHAN RAILWAY

Finke

△ **A**   △ **B**   △ **C**   △ **D**

0 ___ 400 kilometers
0 ___ 200 miles

Darwin

This prosperous modern city of 130,000 can come as quite a shock to first-time visitors who have come to the rugged tropical north expecting a brawling frontier settlement out of the movie *Crocodile Dundee*. Darwin is Australia's most suburban city, a white-collar enclave with a low-rise skyline and sprawl of neat suburban homes, shopping malls, cinemas, a casino, and fast-food chains.

The Northern Territory's Parliament building

Darwin

🗺 183 B6

Visitor Information

✉ Corner of Smith & Bennett Sts.

☎ 08/8980-6000

generous government paychecks, live in nice subsidized homes, and work in air-conditioned office blocks downtown. Nevertheless, Territorians cherish their rough-and-tumble, maverick image, and Darwin is genuinely a magnet for the adventurous, the restless, and the outcast (and the occasional wanted-by-police). It is a town of transients, and most residents are from somewhere else. Darwin is exceptionally ethnically diverse, with more than 50 nationalities represented here.

Darwin sometimes seems to be a parody of itself, self-consciously straining to maintain its frontier image. Tempers flare during the buildup to the wet season, when heat and humidity rise and the

In its better neighborhoods, only the heat and the bright tropical flowers distinguish Darwin from a suburb of Melbourne. The elegant old-fashioned tropical-style houses, built of timber with sweeping verandas and elevated several feet off the ground in case of flooding, are mostly gone. In their place are brick ranch-style houses, less evocative but more resilient in a cyclone. Darwin is the world's lightning capital, and the frequent electric displays over the Arafura Sea beggar description.

This is a public service town at heart. Many of its citizens draw

Cyclone Tracy

Cyclone Tracy almost obliterated Darwin when it roared into town on Christmas Day in 1974, with winds that exceeded 135 mph (215 kph). The city that was rebuilt from the wreckage is brighter and more cosmopolitan— and, one hopes, sturdier— than the ramshackle trading port that had grown up previously.

police logs fill up with petty assaults. For some, Darwin's wet season is as depressing as the long Scandinavian winter; for others, it is an opportunity to see nature spring to life after the long dry season.

During the gold rushes of the 1880s, Darwin filled with fortune-seekers from all over Asia. The settlement was founded as Palmerston but renamed Port Darwin after the naturalist Charles Darwin, who passed through this harbor on the *Beagle* in 1839. In 1911, the name was simplified to Darwin. In the early days, Darwin hoped to rival Singapore, but the harsh climate, sporadic tropical cyclones,

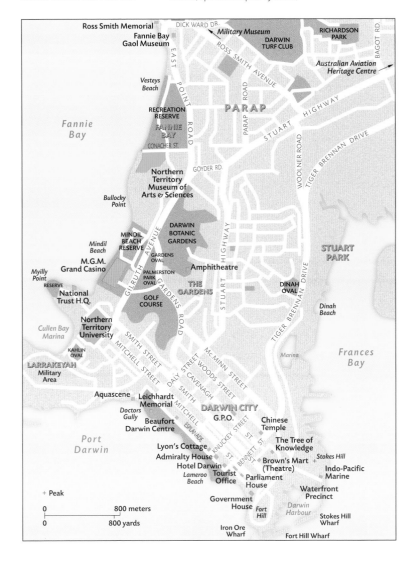

Northern Territory Museum of Arts & Sciences

✉ Conacher St.

☎ 08/8999-8264

and poor communications with the rest of the world were difficult obstacles to overcome.

During World War II, Darwin was a key base for Allied forces. Hastily built highways to Alice Springs and Mount Isa linked Darwin with the rest of Australia, and airstrips were bulldozed in the bush nearby. It was the only part of a peninsula jutting into the harbor. Although most of the early buildings were leveled, either by Japanese bombing or by Cyclone Tracy, some classic colonial tropical buildings still stand on the Esplanade—**Admiralty House** (now Char Restaurant) and **Lyon's Cottage** (both 1920s), and the restored **Government House**

Bombing of Darwin

Following the attack on Pearl Harbor on December 7, 1941, Allied ships, planes, and troops were dispatched to Darwin, a key defensive port against the Japanese. Women and children were evacuated. On February 19, 1942, 188 Japanese planes attacked Darwin's harbor, sinking eight ships, damaging many more, and destroying the town before a second raid hit the military airfield. More than 240 people were killed; the remaining civilians fled, fearing invasion. Over the next year and a half, Japan raided Darwin 64 times but never invaded, its intent being to wipe out Allied military forces capable of countering its push into Southeast Asia.

of Australia subjected to sustained attack (see sidebar above). After the war, the city was rebuilt, but it reverted to its former torpor until Cyclone Tracy (see sidebar p. 184) leveled it again in 1974.

Today, it is an administration center, with government, mining, tourism, and the military as big local employers. With the arrival of the railroad in 2004 and vast new cargo-handling facilities at its port, it is casting itself as Australia's commercial gateway to Asia.

Darwin Sights

Darwin is a base for expeditions to Kakadu, Katherine Gorge, and Litchfield National Park. There are also some worthwhile things to see while you are in town.

Downtown Darwin is a simple grid of wide streets at the end

(built in 1870). The tourist office has information on other heritage buildings. The Esplanade runs along the edge of the ocean and makes a lovely evening stroll. A huge embroidered quilt, hanging in the nearby **Northern Territory Library** in Parliament House and crafted by people who lived here in the 1940s, tells the story of Darwin during World War II.

The **Northern Territory Museum of Arts & Sciences**, overlooking Fannie Bay about 2 miles (3 km) north of the city center, is one of the best cultural attractions in Darwin. Part of the massive rebuilding program after Cyclone Tracy, it houses a major collection of Aboriginal and Pacific Islander art. The national Aboriginal Art Award ceremony is held here in September. The museum also highlights the contribution of Southeast Asia to the development of Australia's tropical north. One of the most popular exhibits is the stuffed, late, and unlamented "Sweetheart," a 17-foot (5 m), 1,700-pound (770 kg) saltwater crocodile that terrorized local fishermen by attacking the outboard motors on their boats until he was captured in 1979.

Darwin has a number of very pretty beaches, but strong tides, crocodiles, and the presence of deadly box jellyfish six months of the year (Oct.–April, during which swimming is banned) have kept it from becoming much of a beach town. Nothing prevents you from rolling out your towel and catching some sun, or swimming at the Waterfront Precinct's man-made lagoons.

Mindil Beach has a lively open-air market on winter evenings (Thurs. and Sun., May–Oct.). Scores of stands offer Asian and other food. Families set up elaborate picnics, kids play beach cricket, and crowds browse through racks of T-shirts, leather goods, bush hats, etc. The nearby **Darwin Botanic Gardens** have one of Australia's finest collections of tropical plants—including more than 400 species of palms.

Across town, the old wharf area around the Stokes Hill Wharf is now the fashionable **Waterfront Precinct,** with upscale eateries, outdoor cafés, hotels, a convention center, a wave pool, and shops. Near the convention center, living coral and tropical fish can be seen at **Indo-Pacific Marine** (tel 08/8981-1294), or

head along the Esplanade to **Aquascene,** where you can feed the fish—milkfish, rays, and many others—that come in on the tide.

Wartime Sites

Darwin holds special memories for veterans who spent time here during World War II. You can tour ($) the old oil storage tunnels on Kitchener Drive near the wharf, which were dug into the rock beneath the city to protect vital fuel during air raids. The **Darwin Military Museum** tells the story of Darwin's World War II bombings and includes the new Defence of Darwin Experience next door. The **Australian Aviation Heritage Centre** has a Japanese Zero that was shot down over Darwin on the first raid, as well as a huge

INSIDER TIP:

Darwin Harbour's outdoor Deckchair Cinema is a great place to take in a movie [every night at 7:30 from mid-April to mid-November].

—PETER TURNER
National Geographic author

B-52 bomber on loan from the U.S. Air Force.

The most poignant memories for those who served here may be triggered by driving south to the abandoned airstrips. The strips are just clearings now, with rusting fuel drums scattered in the bush, eerily still except for the birds chirping in the treetops. ∎

Darwin Botanic Gardens
- ✉ Geranium St.
- ☎ 08/8981-1958

Aquascene
- ✉ 28 Doctors Gully Rd.
- ☎ 08/8981-7837
- 🕐 Open for an hour around high tide; call for times
- 💲 $$

Darwin Military Museum
- ✉ East Point Reserve
- ☎ 08/8981-9702
- 💲 $$

Australian Aviation Heritage Centre
- ✉ Stuart Hwy. (5 miles/8 km S of Darwin)
- ☎ 08/8947-2145

Deckchair Cinema
- ✉ Darwin Harbour
- ☎ Program information: 08/8981-0700

deckchaircinema.com

Kakadu National Park

A wetlands marvel, Kakadu National Park stretches across nearly 8,000 square miles (20,000 sq km) of remote tropical wilderness, about 95 miles (153 km) southwest of Darwin. Australia's largest national park encloses the entire drainage basin of the South Alligator River—so named by Capt. Philip King, an early explorer who confused the area's many crocodiles with alligators when he surveyed Van Diemen Gulf (just to the north) in 1818.

Monsoon rains swamp Kakadu's wetlands and roads during the wet season, peaking January to March.

Kakadu contains more than 290 species of birds (about one-third of all known Australian bird species), 26 kinds of frogs, 74 species of reptiles, 68 species of mammals, and more than 10,000 varieties of insects. The list of Kakadu's flora and fauna is being lengthened all the time, and some species, such as the Oenpelli python (discovered only in 1977), are probably unique to the park. The wildlife provides some of the most enduring images of Kakadu: elegant Jabiru storks, thousands of galahs or magpie geese taking wing from a pool, and awesome giant saltwater crocodiles sunning themselves in the mud. Thousands of salties live in the park, and every tour guide seems to have an inexhaustible stock of macabre anecdotes about them. The park is not a great place for a dip.

Kakadu's human history dates back more than 20,000 years, and thousands of Aboriginal rock-art galleries can be found in the area's cliffs and rock shelters. More than 5,000 sites have been cataloged so far. Most are off-limits, either because they are too hard to reach or because they have spiritual significance to the Gagadju people, who own the land and lease it to the government. Two accessible rock-art sites, are at **Ubirr** and **Nourlangie Rock.**

Mining

Controversy has long raged over Kakadu's rich mineral resources. Some of the world's richest uranium deposits are here, as well as gold, platinum, and palladium ore bodies in nearby Coronation Hill. The **Ranger Uranium Mine** has been in operation since 1979. The company, Energy Resources of Australia (ERA), is required to operate under strict environmental guidelines and set aside a trust fund for the eventual rehabilitation of the land when mining has stopped. Rumors of the mine's closure regularly surface, along with adverse reports of contaminated water leakage from the site. Losses have hit the mine in recent years, but despite closing its huge open-cut mine, underground mining has dramatically expanded. A number of Aboriginal leaders have campaigned against the mine, though it has its supporters, with rent and royalties distributed to indigenous groups.

Four miles (6.5 km) west of the mine is the township of **Jabiru** (population about 1,200). It was built in 1981 to service the mining operation, but the growing popularity of Kakadu has made it something of a tourist center, complete with a luxury motel in the shape of a crocodile (see p. 377).

Visiting Kakadu

Getting to the park is easy. Drive along the Stuart Highway south of Darwin and make a left turn onto the Arnhem Highway. This highway takes you past the colorful old pub at Humpty Doo and through the heart of the park to Jabiru. Getting around this vast wilderness is something else. Four-wheel-drive vehicles or light aircraft are the best bets for reaching the most interesting and remote places.

INSIDER TIP:

The swimming holes and waterfalls in Kakadu are fantastic, but remember to keep an eye out for signs telling you if crocodiles are present.

—STEPHANIE ROBICHAUX
National Geographic contributor

Excellent tours leave from Darwin, and the visitor center at the park headquarters has helpful pamphlets, information on ranger-led walks, videos, and a visitor's guide to help you get the most out of your stay.

When to go is another matter. The Aborigines distinguish six different seasons in the Kakadu calendar, but choosing between the wet and dry seasons is complicated enough for most people. The dry season (May–Oct.) is by

Kakadu National Park

🗺 183 B5

Visitor Information

✉ Kakadu Hwy., Jabiru

☎ 08/8938-1120

kakadu.com.au

Freshwater crocodiles live along the tropical coastline.

far the most popular, with heat and humidity at tolerable levels and the wildlife concentrated around a few shrinking water holes. To see Kakadu during the Wet, however, is to see it in all its glory, with booming monsoonal thunderstorms sweeping over the plains, cataracts spilling over the escarpment, and lush tropical grasses running riot. Against this you have to weigh the crushing heat and humidity, the fact that the wildlife will be dispersed throughout the park, and the flash floods that make much of Kakadu inaccessible. Go when the dry season has just begun, and you may get the best of both seasons.

The most popular attractions in the park are Aboriginal rock-art sites at Nourlangie and Ubirr, the magnificent Jim Jim and Twin Falls, and Yellow Water, near the Gagadju Lodge, Cooinda, which is also the most convenient place to stay in Kakadu *(tel 08/8979-0145)*. There are no real long-distance

trails in this park—something of a disappointment to bushwalking visitors. Most of the trails are just short nature strolls, with the 7-mile (11 km) hike around Nourlangie being the most challenging.

Nourlangie is one of the easiest major sites to reach in Kakadu, only 20 miles (32 km) south of the park headquarters. It is a haunting deep-red sandstone formation, cloaked in forest, that falls away in steep cliffs with rock shelters clustered at its foot. A mile-long (1.6 km) walk takes you from the parking lot to **Anbangbang Shelter,** which has 20,000-year-old rock art. Nearby are sweeping views over the Arnhem Land Escarpment. If you want to hike, follow the 7-mile (11 km) Barrk Walk around Nourlangie. The park headquarters has a leaflet on this hike.

Ubirr, about 25 miles (40 km) north of the park headquarters on a paved road, depicts numerous animals, including tortoises, goannas, wallabies, and some that are long extinct, such as the thylacine, or Tasmanian tiger. You will also see depictions of the Rainbow Serpent—a powerful female character in the Aborigines' creation story and a frequent rock-art motif—and of mischievous Mimi spirits who dwell inside the rocks. Artistic styles vary, ranging from more than 20,000 years ago until the mid-20th century. A trail (about a mile/1.6 km round-trip) takes you from the parking lot to the rock-art galleries and includes a spectacular lookout over the East Alligator River and the rocky crags of Arnhem

Land. A less frequented 4-mile (6.4 km) hike called **Sandstone and River Walk** runs along the river. **Gulu-yambi Cruises** *(tel 1800-895-179)* has a river trip with Aboriginal guides from the start of the Sandstone and River Walk and upstream through dramatic scenery to the escarpment.

Jim Jim and **Twin Falls** are out of the way, about 70 miles (113 km) south of the park headquarters on a challenging four-wheel-drive track, but they are well worth a visit. They are best seen right at the beginning of the dry season, after the rains have stopped long enough for the road to be open and graded, but with enough water swelling Jim Jim Creek to make the falls an awesome sight. Water tumbles more than 700 feet (213 m) down the cliffs, including one unbroken 660-foot (200 m) fall, into a large pool. As the Dry takes hold, these falls can stop completely. Twin Falls is 6 miles (9.6 km) from Jim Jim, along an even trickier four-wheel-drive track and then a slippery climb up a forested gorge. The river cascades into an idyllic pool with a sandy beach. During the wet season, both of these spectacles are inaccessible.

For many people, **Yellow Water** is the highlight of their visit to Kakadu. It is a richly vegetated lagoon formed by Jim Jim Creek as it flows onto the floodplain about 30 miles (48 km) south of Jabiru. In the dry season, it teems with many species of waterfowl, and saltwater crocodiles bask in the mud. Sunrise and sunset are the best times to be on the lagoon. Regular boat cruises leave from nearby Gagudju Lodge. ■

Crocodiles

The world's largest reptiles, saltwater crocodiles *(Crocodylus porosus)*, or "salties," as they are affectionately known, average around 17 feet (5 m) and 1,000 pounds (450 kg), but can weigh double that and reach 23 feet (7 m). They inhabit the tropical coastal regions of Queensland, the Northern Territory, and Western Australia. Crocodiles prefer mangroves and river estuaries but can swim out to sea and across to islands. They can also be found in freshwater up to 62 miles (100 km) inland. Salties are not to be confused with "freshies," the smaller, less aggressive, and much less dangerous freshwater crocodiles *(Crocodylus johnstoni)*, also found in the north.

Saltwater crocodiles are very efficient killers. They lie hidden in the water until prey approaches. Then they strike, exploding from the water, driven by their powerful tails. They grab their prey and drag them under, often employing the "death roll" to break necks and ensure drowning.

Salties can run quickly in short bursts, and the danger for humans is being snatched without warning. In crocodile areas, stay away from the water's edge, where they may be lurking just below the surface. Don't swim in the water—fresh or salt—unless you know it is safe.

At Kakadu you have a good chance of seeing crocodiles in the wild, or plenty of wildlife parks offer an easier option. The late Steve Irwin made crocodile shows famous at his Australia Zoo (see p. 147), where the "Crocoseum" is a popular attraction.

Litchfield National Park

Only a two-hour drive from Darwin, Litchfield National Park is a beautiful collection of water-falls, sandstone formations, termite mounds, and crocodile-free swimming holes. Many people actually prefer this quieter and smaller park to the better known Kakadu, and it is a popular day trip for locals and can get crowded on weekends. As is usually the case in the Northern Territory, access is much easier during the dry season, from May to October.

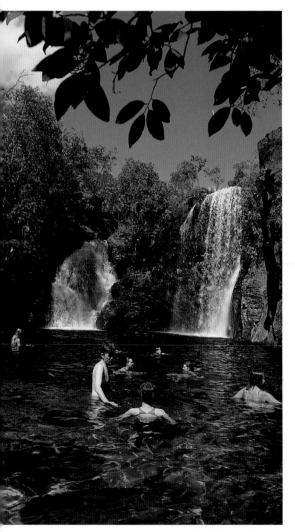

Swimmers take a dip in the waters beneath Florence Falls.

Litchfield National Park is a 580-square-mile (1,500 sq km) parcel of rugged wilderness that takes in the Tabletop Range, a vast sandstone plateau covered by eucalyptus wood-lands. A series of spring-fed rivers spills over the rim of the plateau in spectacular waterfalls that plunge into rain forest valleys below.

The park's most popular attractions are Florence Falls, Wangi Falls, Tolmer Falls, and Tjaynera (Sandy Creek) Falls. There is no entry fee or visitor center in this park, although the national parks office in Batchelor has information on bushwalks, flora and fauna, the termite mounds, and the waterfalls.

Driving to the Park

Plenty of organized tours of Litchfield National Park leave from Darwin, or you can drive there yourself, down the Stuart Highway and through the old mining town of Batchelor.

The park has two entrances. One is a gravel road from the north via the Berry Springs–Cox Peninsula Road. The other is a paved road from the east that starts in Batchelor. The two roads link up inside the park, so you can do Litchfield on a loop.

The Lost City

The Lost City, Litchfield's freestanding sandstone formations, with its narrow alleyways and domes, may look like the work of a long-lost civilization. But Mother Nature is to thank for these rock structures, carved out of wind and rain over the millennia. The sandstone is believed to be 500 million years old.

The **Northern Territory Wildlife Park,** located about 30 miles (48 km) south of Darwin *(tel 08/8988-7200, territorywildlifepark.com.au, $$$),* is a worthwhile stop along the way, complete with an outstanding aquarium, aviaries, a reptile house, and nature trails. Day tours leave for the park from Darwin.

Waterfalls

Florence Falls: If you enter Litchfield National Park through Batchelor, the 700-foot-high (212 m) Florence Falls is the first waterfall you'll come to, and the pool at the base is an excellent swimming hole. You can camp here or at the nearby Buley Rock Holes.

Tolmer Falls: You will find the turnoff to Tolmer Falls about 11 miles (17.7 km) past the turnoff for Florence Falls. In order to protect the nesting site of the rare orange horseshoe bat, visitors are forbidden to swim in the plunge pool here.

Wangi Falls: Another 4 miles (6.4 km) will bring you to Wangi Falls. The year-round waterfalls are certainly the most popular attraction in Litchfield National Park, with an idyllic tropical swimming hole and a rain forest boardwalk. The big new café at the falls attests to the park's growing popularity.

The Lost City & Sandy Creek Falls

One of the other great attractions in the park is the **Lost City,** an eerie collection of weathered sandstone columns that resemble ancient ruins (see sidebar above left). The turnoff is about 4 miles (6.4 km) past

INSIDER TIP:

Visit Litchfield with a cultural perspective and head out with Tess Atie, a local indigenous person. She'll fascinate you with stories of earlier times. Visit *ntitours.com.*

—MEREDITH BAXTER
Territory Discoveries

the turnoff for Florence Falls. To get there, you bump another 5 miles (8 km) along a steep, muddy four-wheel-drive track. Farther south, **Tjaynera (Sandy Creek) Falls** can be reached on a four-wheel-drive track leading directly off the main track through the park. ∎

Litchfield National Park
△ 183 B5
Batchelor Office
☎ 08/8976-0282

Nitmiluk National Park & Katherine

Nitmiluk, or Katherine Gorge, is one of the three sights you should not miss in the Top End of the Northern Territory (along with Kakadu and Litchfield National Parks). It is a chain of 13 gorges carved out of the surrounding sandstone plateau by the mighty Katherine River during the past 25 million years or so. In addition to the towering orange cliffs, there are spectacular Aboriginal rock-art galleries that you can see while on a canoe trip or cruising on the river.

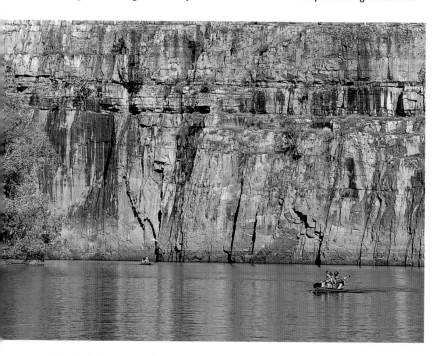

Canoeing is the most popular way to see Nitmiluk's ancient gorges.

Katherine

⚑ 183 B5

Visitor Information

✉ Lindsay St. & Katherine Ter.

☎ 08/8972-2650

Katherine

Explorer John McDouall Stuart, who came this way in 1861, named the river after the daughter of one of his friends. Ten years later, a couple named Frank and Kate Knott set up a pub and general store. The town of Knotts Crossing (later Katherine) sprang up here. It was a rough-and-tumble outback settlement when a woman named Jeannie Gunn visited on her way to Elsey Station in 1902. Gunn wrote about Katherine's old pub, the Sportsman's Arms, in her classic novel about station life and Aborigines, *We of the Never Never.* For years, the presence of reliable water made Katherine a stopover point for drovers and prospectors crossing the desert.

By Northern Territory standards, Katherine is a bustling city of 9,800. The Tindal Air Force Base here is the main tactical fighter base for northern Australia. You can tour the **School of the Air** (tel 08/8972-1833, $) on Giles Street to see how children in the outback are taught, and **Top Didj & Art Gallery** has Aboriginal cultural demonstrations and talks.

Nitmiluk National Park

Nitmiluk National Park is about 20 miles (32 km) northeast of Katherine, at the end of a highway that runs from the town center. Most visitors come on a day trip during the dry season and go no farther than the second gorge. The river is flat, low, and calm at this time of year, and canoeists are impeded by piles of boulders that require portaging. Canoes can be hired from the park visitor center at the gorge, where you can also book boat tours to the second and third gorges (two and four hours) with Nitmiluk Tours (tel 1300-146-743).

If you want to see all the gorges, plan on doing an overnight trek. The first legal campsites are **Dunlop's Swamp** and **Smitt Rock** in the fourth gorge. The uppermost gorges are best seen by beaching the canoe after the fifth gorge and scrambling over the rocks for the last couple of miles. During the wet season, however, the river becomes a formidable torrent. In 1998, Katherine was devastated

by a 1-in-500-year flood, as the river burst its banks and turned the countryside into a vast lake.

Walking trails will lead you through the park's scenic bushland and down into the gorge. The longest of these is the 50-mile (80 km) hike to **Leliyn (Edith Falls).** You can also reach the falls by taking the Stuart Highway 28 miles (45 km) north of Katherine, then 12 miles (20 km) along the paved road to Leliyn, where there is a campground. The park visitor center has the main campground. A bus shuttles between Katherine and the national park.

INSIDER TIP:

Reserve in advance if you want to take the multiday hike to Edith Falls—the campsites only accommodate ten people at a time. Note that all hikers must register before 1 p.m.

—LARRY PORGES
National Geographic Travel Books editor

Five miles (8 km) west of Katherine, just off the Victoria Highway, **Springvale Homestead** is the oldest station in the Northern Territory. Built in 1879, it offers accommodations for travelers. Still farther south is the **Cutta Cutta Caves Nature Park,** which has 500-million-year-old limestone formations and caves that contain rare orange horseshoe bats. ■

National Parks & Wildlife Service

✉ 32 Giles St., Katherine

☎ 08/8973-8888

Top Didj & Art Gallery

✉ Gorge & Jaensch Rds., Katherine

☎ 08/897-12751

Nitmiluk National Park

🗺 183 B5

Visitor Information

☎ 08/8972-1886

Arnhem Land & the Tiwi Islands

Aborigines hold big tracts of land in the Top End—the primeval wilderness of Arnhem Land, the Cobourg Peninsula, and Melville and Bathurst Islands. Much of this land is off-limits to individual tourists. Aborigines have lived in these remote places for more than 40,000 years, and for the most part they do not wish to be disturbed. They are responding to the growing interest in their culture, though, and there are a few unique opportunities for travel.

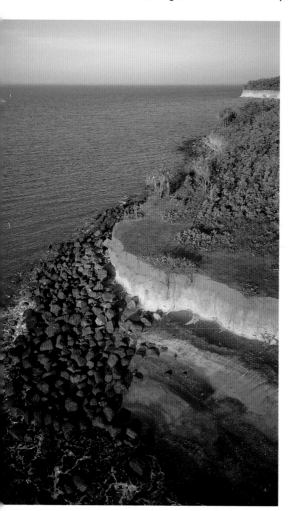

Cape Helvetius, on Bathurst Island, juts into the Timor Sea.

Arnhem Land

The vast wilderness of Arnhem Land is slowly opening its doors to controlled tourism. The main settlement is the bauxite mining town of **Gove/Nhulunbuy** in the northeast corner. You don't need a permit to fly there, but this port has little appeal. Independent tourism outside it is virtually impossible. Travel permits take up to a year to be issued, and most go to game anglers heading up to Smith Point. If you want to try anyway, contact the Northern Land Council Office.

The Aboriginal-run **Bawaka Cultural Experiences** *(tel 08/8987-3433, bawaka.com.au)* has day and overnight trips to the Bawaka homeland on the unspoiled tropical beaches south of Nhulunbuy. The emphasis is on cultural experiences, from traditional fishing to art and craft to bush food appreciation. **Davidson's Arnhemland Safaris** *(tel 08/8979-0413, arnhemland -safaris.com)* guides groups through central Arnhem Land around Mt. Borradaile, home to sandstone hills, caves, and abundant Aboriginal art.

The most luxurious way to experience Aboriginal land is to visit **Seven Spirit Bay** *(tel*

Deadly Stingers & Biters

Australia makes up for its lack of dangerous mammals with a host of creatures to keep a keen eye out for.

Common varieties of Australian snakes include the tiger snake (named for its stripes), brown snake, and red-bellied black snake. Deadliest but less common are the taipan and the suitably named death adder.

The only deadly spiders are the funnel web, found in suburban Sydney, and the red-back spider, widespread though only occasionally fatal.

Saltwater crocodiles, the world's largest reptiles, are found in far north Australia (see sidebar p. 191). Heed all signs announcing their presence. Smaller freshwater crocodiles can bite but impart no serious harm.

With all that coastline, Australia has many species of sharks. Great white, tiger, bull, and whaler sharks all feed on large sea mammals. None specifically targets humans, though they might mistake you for a seal.

From November to March, look out in northern tropical waters for the box jellyfish, which can deliver multiple, potentially fatal stings from its trailing tentacles. Other dangers include the poisonous-spined stonefish and the pretty, but often fatal, blue ring octopus.

You are much more likely to be in a car accident than encounter any of these threats. Snakes are rarely sighted, and antivenins are widely available. Sharks strike only a handful of people—usually surfers and others in deep water.

08/8988-2648), an ecotourism resort on the tip of the Cobourg Peninsula, 130 miles (209 km) northeast of Darwin. It offers guided bushwalks and fishing trips and is reached only by light aircraft or four-wheel-drive vehicle.

Tiwi Islands

Bathurst Island and **Melville Island,** about 50 miles (80 km) north of Darwin, are home to the Tiwi people. The Tiwi Land Council, which governs the islands, has opened them to small tour groups (not individuals). **Tiwi Tours** (tel 08/8923-6523) is the only accredited operator. It runs day trips from Darwin and camping in some of the most remote territory in Australia.

Tiwi language and culture developed independently of the rest of Aboriginal Australia. Features unique to this people include their *pukumani,* or burial poles, which are carved or painted with totems and motifs and set out around graves.

Tiwis have fiercely guarded their independence. The British established Fort Dundas on Melville Island in 1824, but it lasted less than five years. The Tiwis regained political control in 1978. Most Tiwis lead nontraditional lifestyles in the main settlement of Nguiu on Bathurst Island. Much of the islands remains a wilderness. Visitors can buy local artwork, meet with community leaders, and then head out to the bush. Overnight visits can include lessons in digging wild pumpkins, hunting goannas, and spearing fish. The packages are fairly expensive, but this is not an everyday trip. ■

Northern Land Visitor Information

✉ Northern Land Council Office 45 Mitchell St., Darwin

☎ 08/8920-5100

nlc.org.au

Alice Springs

Alice Springs is an oasis town in the dramatic rocky walls of the MacDonnell Ranges. It is a good base from which to visit most of the attractions in Australia's Red Centre—notably Uluru (Ayers Rock) and Kata Tjuta (the Olgas).

The boisterous Camel Cup is held in Alice Springs each July.

Alice Springs

⛰ 183 C2

Visitor Information

✉ 60 Gregory Terrace

☎ 08/8952-5800

alicesprings.nt.gov.au

Northern Territory Parks & Wildlife Service

✉ South Stuart Hwy. (3 miles/ 4.5 km S of Alice Springs)

☎ 08/8951-8211

The Alice, as it is known, was settled in 1871 as a relay station for the Overland Telegraph Line that stretched from Adelaide to Darwin. The old stone-built Telegraph Station, now a restored historical reserve a mile (1.6 km) north of town, was built near a permanent water hole in the normally dry bed of the Todd River. The station was one of 12 built along the telegraph line, which hooked up in Darwin with the undersea cable from Java to connect Australia with the rest of the world. You can walk to the station on a path by the riverbed. To drive there, take the Stuart Highway north and turn right at the sign about half a mile (1 km) out of town. The springs are a nice place for a swim or a picnic.

The town was originally gazetted as Stuart, but the name was officially changed to Alice Springs in 1933. Nevil Shute's 1950 novel *A Town Like Alice* made it known across the world, but it wasn't until 1987 that you could drive here from Adelaide on a paved road. The Alice today is a

INSIDER TIP:

Check out the Alice Springs community calendar at *alicesprings .nt.gov.au* for a complete list of upcoming local events.

—CLAIRE ASHARD
Alice Springs Town Council

modern little city of 22,000, laid out on a five-street grid between the bed of the Todd River and the Stuart Highway.

Just west of town, the **Alice Springs Desert Park** is a superb botanic gardens–style attraction with imaginative displays of the flora and fauna found in various Northern Territory ecosystems, and an entertaining show of predatory desert birds. Nearby, on Larapinta Drive, the **Araluen Cultural Precinct** is a concentration of cultural venues, museums, sacred sites, and a sculpture garden joined by a walkway. One fee ($$) covers entry to the **Araluen Arts Centre,** with its theater and art galleries, the **Central Australian Aviation Museum,** the **Museum of Central Australia,** and the **Albert Namatjira**

Gallery featuring the work of the famous Aboriginal artist and his contemporaries.

The **Royal Flying Doctor Service** delivers medical services to remote communities, and its Alice Springs base has tours, a small museum, and a café, with proceeds aiding this essential service. In a similar vein, visitors can tour the **School of the Air,** the "world's largest school," delivering lessons to isolated students across an area twice the size of Texas. Once dependent on radio transmission, students now rely mainly on satellites and the Internet.

There is a great lookout over the city and the MacDonnell Ranges from the top of Anzac Hill, a steep but convenient rocky crag near the top end of Todd Street. You can drive up to it.

Ten miles (16 km) southwest of Alice Springs, **Pyndan Camel Tracks** has camel rides. Camels were imported to Australia in the mid-19th century and then set free after trains and roads made them obsolete. Now an estimated 15,000 camels roam the Red Centre, and thousands more inhabit Western Australia. Around July, Alice Springs comes alive for the **Lasseters Cup** camel races.

Alice Springs Desert Park
- ✉ Larapinta Dr.
- ☎ 08/8951-8788
- 💲 $$
- alicespringsdesert park.com.au

Araluen Cultural Precinct
- ✉ Cnr. Larapinta Dr. & Memorial Ave.
- ☎ 08/8951-1120
- artsandmuseums .nt.gov.au

Royal Flying Doctor Service
- ✉ 8–10 Stuart Ter.
- ☎ 08/8958-8411
- 💲 $$
- flyingdoctor.org.au

School of the Air
- ✉ 80 Head St.
- ☎ 08/8951-6800
- 💲 $
- assoa.nt.edu.au

Pyndan Camel Tracks
- ✉ 21259 Jane Rd.
- ☎ 04/1617-0164
- cameltracks.com

EXPERIENCE: Henley-on-Todd Regatta

Australia is a land of irony and irreverence, and one of the country's more bizarre events, the Henley-on-Todd (*henleyontodd .com.au*) is a mock regatta held in Alice Springs on the dry Todd River in August.

Poking fun at British private school rowing regattas, teams carry metal framed "boats" and run with them in an insane race along the dry riverbed. If the river is flowing, as it does after floods, the event is canceled. Spectators at this iconic regatta need to take care at the finals, which are accompanied by flour bombs and water cannon.

Drought

Despite rain-drenched coasts and tropical wetlands, Australia is the driest continent, and drought is an ever present threat. Prolonged drought, the worst on record, affected much of Australia from 1992 until 2008. Severe water restrictions were imposed, while most of the states built desalination plants or recycled sewage for drinking water. In Queensland, one of the wetter parts of Australia, dam levels fell to an alarming 20 percent of capacity.

Prolonged droughts threaten farm incomes and have seen the Murray River slow to a trickle, its wetlands and bird populations depleted in a worsening ecological disaster. The drought broke with a flood, mostly across the north in 2009, and again in Queensland in 2013. However, in the southern part of the country the dry spell returned, temperatures hit record levels, and wildfires swept the southeast.

Many blame global warming and point to Australia's energy consumption and carbon dioxide emissions, among the highest per capita in the world, much of it due to burning coal, Australia's biggest export. Poor management of inland waterways, over-irrigation, and the failure to build new dams despite a rapidly growing population have exacerbated the problem.

Arltunga

Visitor Information

☎ 08/8956-9770

MacDonnell Ranges

The Alice is the base for some great day drives through the deep, shady gorges and along the spectacular cliffs of the Eastern and Western MacDonnell Ranges. Unless you are part of a tour, you'll need your own transportation.

There are excellent walks in **Trephina Gorge National Park,** about 40 miles (64 km) northeast of Alice Springs on the Ross Highway, and around the nearby **Ross River Homestead Resort** *(tel 1800-241-711),* southeast of

INSIDER TIP:

There are many great water holes around Western MacDonnells to enjoy on a hot day. Try Glen Helen Gorges or Ormiston.

—KENNY LING

National Geographic contributor

the highway a little farther on. Out here you'll have a good chance of seeing a perentie—at up to 7 feet long (2.1 m), the largest lizard in Australia and second biggest in the world after its cousin, Indonesia's Komodo dragon. Be careful if you encounter one. They are astoundingly fast and have powerful razor-sharp claws. If frightened they will run up the highest thing they can see—even if it is you.

The ghost town of **Arltunga** haunts the far Eastern MacDonnell Ranges, 65 miles (105 km) northeast of Alice Springs on the Ross Highway. It was settled in 1887, when gold was mined here, but abandoned in 1912, when the gold finally ran out. It has an excellent visitor center and free guided tours, May through September.

In the Western MacDonnell Ranges you will find **Simpson's Gap,** a deep cleft cut by tiny Roe Creek, about 12 miles (19 km) west of Alice Springs on Larapinta Drive. It was made famous by the paintings of Aborigine artist Albert Namatjira, one of Australia's best known outback painters and the first Aboriginal granted Australian citizenship. He died tragically of alcoholism in 1959.

Twenty miles (32 km) farther west, turn south off Larapinta Drive for about 6 miles (9 km) to reach **Standley Chasm,** an incredibly narrow gap whose near-vertical walls seem little more than shoulder-width apart, and where the sun shines only for an instant around noon. Three miles (5 km) west of the turnoff along Larapinta Drive, the road forks. The right fork is Namatjira Drive. Aptly enough for a road named after the great Aboriginal artist, it goes out to the **Ochre Pits,** 40 miles (64 km) farther on, where ancient Aboriginal artists obtained their pigments. From there the road continues 10 miles (16 km) or so to rugged **Ormiston** and **Glen Helen Gorges.**

If you stay on Larapinta Drive for 50 miles (80 km), you reach **Hermannsburg Community.** This Aboriginal community was set up by South Australian Lutheran missionaries in 1877 and still has some of the original date palms they planted. The traditional German farmhouses have now been restored.

Finke Gorge National Park is 7 miles (11 km) on from Hermannsburg, and you need a 4WD vehicle to get there. In the park is **Palm Valley,** an isolated tropical pocket filled with Australian cabbage palms. The trees are unique to this gorge and have grown here since wetter, prehistoric times.

Drive 60 miles (96 km) south on the Stuart Highway to reach the **Henbury Meteorite Craters,** a few miles west off the highway on the Ernest Giles Road. The craters were formed several thousand years ago by the chunks of a meteor. The biggest crater is almost 600 feet (183 m) across. ■

Standley Chasm in the Western MacDonnell Ranges glows red when the sun shines in briefly at midday.

Aboriginal Art

Art has always played an important role in Aboriginal culture as a way of recording human events, honoring the land, and passing on to future generations the stories of creation and the deeds of supernatural beings. There are examples of paintings and rock engravings dating back at least 50,000 years, and the work of modern Aboriginal artists is increasingly in demand.

Aboriginal artist Kathleen Wallace with bush medicine and one of her paintings

Rock Art

Aboriginal rock art gives a unique illustrated history of the continent over thousands of years. The earliest art in Kakadu, dated to the last ice age, shows an arid landscape in which hunters kill kangaroos with boomerangs. Later, trees and flowers begin to appear in the record as the ice age ended and sea levels began to rise. Hunters are shown using spears, which were more reliable than boomerangs in the newly dense scrub. One 6,000-year-old rock mural, in a remote corner of Kakadu, illustrates what some art historians believe to be the world's earliest battle scene. It shows 111 stick figures, apparently charging each other and hurling spears.

Eight have fallen, and blood is gushing from their spear wounds. Scientists speculate that conflicts such as the one depicted in the mural may have been caused by the slow rise of the sea, which over centuries forced coastal people to migrate inland and onto the higher territory of their neighbors. Aboriginal art of the 15th century represents the Macassar fishermen who arrived at that time from Indonesia, and art of the 18th and 19th centuries includes references to Europeans.

Art historians recognize several successive styles of rock art, starting with drawings of animals in what is known as the naturalist style. This was succeeded by the dynamic phase, in which motion, such as the trajectory of a spear, appears to be represented by scribbles, dashes, and dots. These paintings, the earliest of which are found in Kakadu and date from about 12,000 years ago, are the world's earliest forms of narrative art. Later came the curious "yam"-style paintings, in which humans and animals

INSIDER TIP:

Fancy a go at Aboriginal art? Try Aboriginal Culture and dot-painting classes at Daintree Eco Lodge [daintree-ecolodge.com.au].

—JUSTIN KAVANAGH
National Geographic International Editions editor

were represented with yam-shaped symbols. Next came the X-ray style, in which the skeletal frames of people and animals appear. It is a tribute to the remarkable longevity of Aboriginal culture that today's elders can often look at a piece of art created by an ancestor a hundred generations before and understand the story being told.

Visiting Rock-art Galleries

Many rock-art sites remain inaccessible to tourists, in some cases because they are so remote but also because, after two centuries of disruption to their culture, Aborigines wish to keep the sacred sites private.

The richest area for rock art is in northern Australia: in Kakadu and Arnhem Land in the Northern Territory, and in the Kimberley region of Western Australia. Motifs include simple handprints, complex hunting scenes, and fabulous renditions of Rainbow Serpents—deities who played crucial roles in Dreamtime creation stories.

Some particularly magnificent galleries that are open to the public are Ubirr and Nourlangie in Kakadu (see p. 190), rock murals near the base of Uluru (see p. 207), and two of the Quinkan rock-art galleries near the town of Laura in Queensland (see p. 176). Totally different from anything in Kakadu, Quinkan art contains paintings of the region's wildlife and illustrates the spiritual life of the Ang-Gnarra people. The spookiest images are those of the Quinkans, large and apparently malicious humanoid spirits who dwell in fissures in the rocks. Only two of the Quinkan galleries are open to the public, Split Rock and Guguyalangi.

Modern Aboriginal Art

Many of today's Aboriginal artists continue to draw on the Dreamtime for inspiration, and centuries-old practices, such as painting on bark and mixing the same natural pigments as their ancestors, remain popular. Others have adopted nontraditional media, such as acrylic paints, and adapted Western artistic styles. The art they create comes in a variety of forms and includes everything from traditional dot paintings to exquisitely carved didgeridoos, decorated boomerangs, beautiful fabrics, and pottery.

EXPERIENCE:
Buying Aboriginal Art

Since the 1980s, Aboriginal art has enjoyed something of a boom. Indigenous artists have found creative new ways to express and preserve their culture and non-Aborigines have acquired a taste for Aboriginal art's unique and powerful style. **Arnhem Land**'s bark paintings and the abstract, dot-painted murals of central Australia are tremendously popular. Expect to pay good money for good art, but be wary of imitations. Non-Aborigines have been caught in the act of turning out "Aboriginal" art. Go to reputable dealers who know about the artists, and they will give you and the artists a better deal. For a list of Aboriginal-owned art galleries throughout Australia, see p. 386.

Uluru–Kata Tjuta National Park

Uluru and the Sydney Opera House share the distinction of being the best known landmarks in Australia. Uluru (also known as Ayers Rock) attracts more than half a million visitors each year. This haunting monolith in central Australia, one of the world's largest, rising almost 1,150 feet (350 m) from the flat scrub, is a remarkable spectacle. Naturally, Aborigines consider this a holy site, and visitors should be respectful of the Rock's sacred standing in their culture.

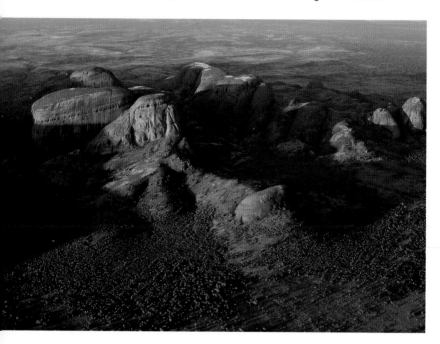

A sunset view of Kata Tjuta (the Olgas)

Uluru–Kata Tjuta National Park

 183 B1

Visitor Information

✉ Uluru National Park Entrance

☎ 08/8956-1100

Uluru (Ayers Rock)

The Rock lies about 250 miles (400 km) southwest of Alice Springs. It is the summit of a massive underground chunk of sandstone about 600 million years old. Geologists believe that only the top 10 percent of the rock is visible. Erosion over many millions of years has slowly exposed its mass,

and weathering has revealed its characteristic red hue. Explorer Ernest Giles was the first European to set eyes on this wonder, back in 1872. The following year another adventurer, William Gosse, scaled the monolith with an Afghan camel driver and named it Ayers Rock after the premier of South Australia, Henry Ayers. In 1985, Ayers

EXPERIENCE: Bushwalking

From ten-minute riverside strolls to the 715-mile (1,144 km) Heysen Trail, thousands of walking trails cross the country. The best walks tend to be in national parks, where the trails are often well marked, but not always. Bushwalking in Australia tends to be a wilderness experience. The most popular trails get lots of traffic at peak times, but there are plenty of opportunities to have nature to yourself.

The best time to bushwalk in northern Australia is during the dry season (May–Sept.), while October–April is better for hiking in the southern states. The southern mountains can be snowed under in winter (June–Sept.) but are wonderful in summer (Dec.–Feb.), when temperatures can soar elsewhere. Spring and autumn are the overall best times to walk in much of the country.

Planning is required, especially for overnight hikes. Always check local conditions with park authorities and be fully equipped. Many bushwalks require some outdoors experience.

Guided Walks

If you prefer guided walks, plenty of companies can transport your gear, cook your meals, set up your tent, or put you up in luxury accommodations. Tasmania has the pick of the luxury walks. Cradle Mountain Huts (tel 03/6392-2211, cradlehuts.com.au) operates **Cradle Mountain Huts Walk** and **Bay of Fires Walk** (see sidebars pp. 345 & 347), while **Maria Island Walk** (tel 03/6234-2999, mariaisland walk.com.au) is a wonderful four-day coastal walk with stays in beach camps and a historic homestead. Good tour operators for guided walks throughout the country include: **Auswalk** (tel 03/5356-4971, auswalk.com.au), **Parktrek** (tel 03/9877-9540, parktrek .com), and **World Expeditions** (tel 1300-720-000, worldexpeditions.com).

INSIDER TIP:

On the Overland Track bushwalk, be sure to allow time to hike to Mount Oakley for some of Tasmania's most stunning views.

—JOHN & LYN DALY
Bushwalkers & authors of the Take a Walk book series

Some of Australia's best bushwalks include:

Australian Alps Walking Track. A 406-mile (650 km) trek from Walhalla in Victoria to Tharwa near Canberra; or do just part, like Mount Bogong or Feathertop.

Bondi–Bronte, Sydney. A stunning 3-mile (5 km), one-hour stroll from Bondi Beach around the headlands.

Cape to Cape Track, Western Australia. See wild beaches, cliffs, and whales on this 85-mile (135 km), seven-day walk from Cape Naturaliste to Cape Leeuwin near Margaret River.

Flinders Chase Coastal Trek, South Australia. A 12-mile (19 km), daylong walk on Kangaroo Island with rugged coastal scenery, beaches, and lots of wildlife.

Larapinta Track, Northern Territory. Glorious gorges, chasms, and outback scenery along this 140-mile (223 km), 13-day trail west of Alice Springs.

Mt. Kosciuszko Summit, New South Wales. Take the chairlift in summer, then walk 4 miles (6.5 km), two hours, to the top of Australia's highest peak.

Overland Track, Tasmania. Australia's premier wilderness walk from Cradle Mountain to Lake St. Clair, 45 miles (73 km), six days, with huts along the way.

Thorsborne Trail, Queensland. Tropical wonders define this 20-mile (32 km), three-to-four-day walk on Hinchinbrook Island.

Wineglass Bay Circuit, Tasmania. A 7.5-mile (12 km), four-hour walk in Freycinet National Park to idyllic Wineglass Bay and Hazard Beach, then back around the coast.

Rock was handed back to the Pitjantjatjara and Yankunytjatjara Aborigines, who promptly restored its ancient name of Uluru and then leased it back to the government for use as a national park. The local Aboriginal communities get 25 percent of the gate takings and a royalty of A$75,000 per year.

Tourism at the rock has boomed since the elaborate Yulara resort complex opened in 1984. A local airstrip handles Qantas and Virgin jets from Cairns, Sydney, and Alice Springs. Philip Cox, creator of Sydney's Darling Harbour Exhibition Centre and a major force in the 2000 Olympic Games, designed the resort village, whose canopies resemble sails in the desert. Yulara has a wide range of accommodations, from the five-star opulence of Longitude 131, with its luxurious safari tents, down to plain-old do-it-yourself camping. The village is just outside the park boundaries, about 12 miles (19 km) from Uluru and a little more than 30 miles (48 km) from Kata Tjuta.

The **Cultural Centre,** 8 miles (13 km) into the park near the base of Uluru, makes an excellent first stop and focuses on Tjukurpa, the traditional law that guides Anangu culture. Park rangers at the information desk can fill you in on visiting the park, and you can book tours with Uluru Aboriginal Tours (tel 0447/878-851, uluru aboriginaltours.com.au).

To Climb or Not to Climb? There Is No Question.

Would you pitch a tent on the fields of Gettysburg? Would you skydive onto Jerusalem's Temple Mount or into Mecca? Yet for more than a century, tourists have clambered up the steep flank of Uluru without asking if the Aborigines minded people climbing on their sacred monolith. When somebody finally posed the obvious question, the answer, naturally, turned out to be an emphatic yes.

Local Aborigines, who took possession of Uluru in 1985, have posted signs asking visitors not to climb the Rock, but almost one-fifth of its 350,000 annual visitors ignore the plea. The government is considering a proposal to ban the climb and impose other restrictions to protect the park from the crush of tourists.

The climb is nothing memorable for adventure buffs in any case. The initial pitch is extremely steep and exposed—terrifying to anyone with a fear of heights—and the strain has induced several heart attacks. Every year, on average, somebody dies on the Rock, either from heart failure or in accidents while straying off the track. Now removed, crosses at the foot of the climb commemorated those who died and served as a warning. Inevitably, they also served as a challenge for egoists, who posed for pictures by them before starting their climb.

Climbing the Rock is a good way to lose sight of the Rock, both spiritually and literally. With its haunting mass under your feet, not before your eyes, you cannot truly experience its power and mystique.

The gentle, 6-mile (9.7 km) walk—or jog for the running enthusiast—around the base of Uluru (see p. 207) gives you a better sense of its size, shape, texture, and character as it rises up almost vertically from the desert floor. Best of all, you'll be respecting the wishes of the people who have revered and understood this natural marvel for many thousands of years.

Seeing Uluru: Everything here is about seeing Uluru. When all is said and done, you can do so in two ways. You can gaze up at it or see it from the air with the flat red desert spreading out to the curve of the horizon. Scenic flights over Uluru and Kata Tjuta are organized locally by Ayers Rock Helicopters *(tel 08/8956-2077)* and others. The 7-mile (11 km) driving loop around the rock has a sunset viewing area on the west side and a

INSIDER TIP:

Check out the Cultural Centre in Uluru-Kata Tjuta National Park. This chronicles the return of Uluru to the Aboriginal people.

—DAVID KENNEDY
National Geographic contributor

good sunrise viewing spot on the southeast. About 30 percent of visitors attempt to climb Uluru despite requests not to (see sidebar p. 206).

A far better alternative to climbing Uluru is to take the pleasant and flat **Base Walk** that circles the Rock. Walkers see some of the flora and fauna, and there is Aboriginal rock art in shelters near the base of the Rock. A good place to begin the walk is at the Mala parking area, near the climbing trail up Uluru. The park visitor center supplies a brochure on this walk and

Water cascades from Uluru during a spring rainstorm.

on shorter hikes near the base. You can also join a free morning tour on the Mala Walk led by a park ranger and learn about the park, rock art, and the traditional Aboriginal way of life.

Kata Tjuta (The Olgas)

Kata Tjuta, or the Olgas, is a collection of sandstone and arkose (sedimentary rock formed from granite sands)

Yulara Resort
- 🏕 183 B1
- ☎ Reservations
  1800-809-622

Anangu Tours Nighttime Sky Show
- ☎ 1800-803-174
- 💲 $$, includes transportation

monoliths about 20 miles (32 km) west of Uluru on the Docker River Road. They form an eerie, hole-in-the-wall maze, and though they are not as well known as their world-famous neighbor, many visitors find them much more intriguing.

to Aboriginal women, for it is a men's sacred site.

Because much of the park is sacred, there are only two hiking paths through Kata Tjuta. The main attraction is the **Valley of the Winds Walk,** a spectacular 4.5-mile (7.4 km) loop that winds

The Dreamtime

Natural formations such as Uluru and Kata Tjuta often play key roles in Aboriginal stories of the Dreamtime. A central concept of Aboriginal spirituality, the Dreamtime is the time of creation, when the ancestral spirits rose up from the barren earth. Taking many supernatural forms, some part human and some animal, the spirits traveled, hunted, and

fought across the landscape, creating mountains, rivers, plants, the elements, animals, and eventually humans, who trace their ancestry back to different totemic spirits. The paths the spirits took are known as dreaming tracks, which link sacred sites. Ceremonies and songs often tell of the Dreamtime and provide the basis for Aboriginal law and custom.

In 1873, English-born explorer Ernest Giles (see p. 45) was the first European to see Kata Tjuta. He waxed lyrical about these "rounded minarets, giant cupolas and monstrous domes" and named them after Queen Olga of Württemburg. To the local Aborigines the rocks had always been Kata Tjuta, or "many heads," and they restored the ancient name once they regained possession of this site.

The largest of the many towering heads—there are 36 in all—is **Mount Olga,** which rises about 3,500 feet (1,069 m). Geologists believe the whole collection was once part of an enormous monolith ten times the size of Uluru. As with Uluru, the Aborigines regarded Kata Tjuta as a holy place, and the eastern side of the formation remains off-limits to visitors—as well as

through ocher-red chasms, gorges, and cliffs. The way to the trailhead of this walk is clearly marked. For a shorter hike, there is a straightforward, well-marked trail into the Walpa Gorge.

Taking Photos

Photographing Uluru or Kata Tjuta is fast becoming a thorny issue. Because Aborigines hold these places to be sacred, they believe that capturing images of them on film, other than at certain prescribed locations, is a form of desecration. Signs posted around the sites indicate where photography is permitted, and you should only take shots at these points. Any visitor who is planning to photograph the Rock for professional purposes must be pre-approved by the local council, which often charges hefty fees. ∎

EXPERIENCE: Getting to Know the Aborigines

Aboriginal culture is at its strongest in the outback, particularly the Northern Territory and Western Australia. Parts of the Northern Territory did not have contact with Europeans until the 1940s, and some remote communities still live a semitraditional lifestyle. Permits are required to enter Aboriginal lands, and the best way to experience indigenous culture is on a tour.

Northern Territory

In the Northern Territory at **Kakadu National Park,** Kakadu Culture Camp *(tel 04/2879-2048, kakadu culturecamp.com)* offers bush food tours, followed by a traditional campfire dinner, and night boat cruises. Or get dropped into the **East Alligator River** region by helicopter (no roads) with a guide and have this slice of Arnhem Land to yourself.

In **East Arnhem Land,** Lirrwi Yolngu Tourism *(tel 08/8987-2828, lirrwitourism .com.au)* has overnight trips to the Bawaka homeland south of Nhulunbuy. The emphasis is on cultural experiences, from fishing to arts and crafts, dance, and bush tucker appreciation.

At **Uluru–Kata Tjuta National Park,** the traditional owners, the Anangu people, offer a variety of tours through Uluru Aboriginal Tours *(tel 04/4787-8851, uluruaboriginaltours.com.au).* Desert Tracks *(tel 04/3950-0419, deserttracks.com.au)* has one-day tours of Cave Hill with Pitjantjatjara guides.

Western Australia

In Western Australia, Kepa Kurl Discovery Tours *(tel 08/9072-1688, kepakurl .com.au)* has 4WD eco-cultural tours along the white beaches of **Esperance,** explaining the Noongar's relationship to the land.

Broome is a good place to organize Aboriginal tours, and 125 miles (200 km) north on the superb beaches of remote **Dampier Peninsula,** an Aboriginal-owned wilderness camp, Kooljaman at Cape Leveque *(tel 08/9192-4970, kooljaman.com.au)* has tents and cabin accommodations. Or stay at the nearby Lombadina Community *(tel 08/9192-4936, lombadina .com.au),* where tours can also be arranged. At **Wyndham,** Wundagoordie Aboriginal Safaris *(tel 08/9161-1145, wundargoodie.com.au)* offers 4WD tours into the remote north Kimberley to explore rarely visited landscapes and rock-art sites.

South Australia

In South Australia, Bookabee Tours *(tel 08/8235-9954, bookabee.com.au)* has two- to five-day adventures in the **Flinders Ranges,** taking in rock art and regional indigenous history. Iga Warta *(tel 08/8648-3737, igawarta .com),* in the northern Flinders Ranges, has bush meals, wildlife, and Adnyamathanha cultural tours.

Many other tours operate, and many museums have excellent indigenous arts and crafts galleries. Numerous Aboriginal cultural centers—from the Brambuk Cultural Centre in Victoria's Grampians National Park to the excellent Tjupakai Aboriginal Cultural Park in Cairns—offer the visitor interesting and educational insights.

Australians of Aboriginal heritage

Watarrka National Park

Watarrka National Park (formerly Kings Canyon) contains the deepest and most spectacular gorge in central Australia, with rocky pools, palms, and beehive-shaped outcrops that call to mind the Bungle Bungle (see pp. 236–237). The park has some superb walking trails, both around the rim of the canyon and up the gorge.

Visitors on the rim of the 310-foot-high (95 m) walls of Watarrka

Watarrka National Park

🅰 183 B2

Visitor Information

✉ South Stuart Hwy. (3 miles/ 4.5 km S of Alice Springs)

☎ 08/8951-8250

This desert canyon had been virtually inaccessible until recent years, although it is only about 150 miles (240 km) southwest of Alice Springs. Even in the early 1990s, getting here meant traveling a rough dirt track, and facilities were few. That changed with the building of the **Kings Canyon Resort** (tel 1300-863-248). A paved highway now links Kings Canyon with the Yulara resort complex (see p. 206).

Two major walking trails both begin at the parking lot by the park entrance. The **Canyon Walk** is a three-hour hike that winds around the rim of the canyon, through a maze of rocky outcrops and the palm-filled Garden of Eden. Very different is the hourlong **Kings Creek Walk**, a scramble up the narrow gorge, with its boulders and ghost gums, to the idyllic pool and waterfall at its head. ■

Australia's wild west, a colorful blend of frontier styles and famous for its deep karri forests and shining capital city of Perth

Western Australia

Introduction & Map   212–213

Perth   214–216

Experience: Day-tripping from Perth   216

Fremantle   217–218

Experience: Cooking Australia   218

New Norcia   219

Rottnest Island   220–221

Feature: Wildflowers   222–223

The Southwest   224–225

Margaret River   226–227

Shark Bay   228–229

Ningaloo Marine Park   230–231

Experience: Swim With Whale Sharks   231

Broome   232–233

Experience: Camel Treks   233

The Kimberley   234–235

Purnululu (Bungle Bungle) National Park   236–237

An Australian bottlebrush wildflower

Gibb River Road Drive   238–239

Kalgoorlie-Boulder   240–241

Experience: Exploring Australia's Outback   242

Eyre Highway & the Nullarbor Plain   243–248

Experience: For the Birds   245

Hotels & Restaurants   377–379

Western Australia

The fortune-seeking Dutch navigators who sailed along Western Australia's coasts early in the 17th century did not suspect that behind a mask of low, flat, sunburned scrub lay one of the world's greatest mineralized zones. They merely mapped the coast and moved on. So, too, did English buccaneer William Dampier, when he visited in 1688 and 1699. It was almost a century before any European expressed interest in the place.

France laid claim to this dry, barren land in 1779, but interest wasn't high enough to establish a colony. By the mid-1820s, Britain had claimed the land and set up a colony near present-day Albany. However, because of its remoteness, vast size, and inhospitable deserts, Western Australia was the slowest of the colonies to develop. Not until the gold rushes of the 1880s and '90s did the colony begin to prosper. Even so, it retained its provincial, frontier atmosphere.

It is still a long, desolate hike across the continent to Perth, one of the world's most isolated cities. The enormous empty distances around the state mean that visitors to Western Australia have to give some thought and planning to where they want to go. This state covers almost a million square miles (2.6 million sq km)—one-third of the entire continent—yet has only 10 percent of Australia's population.

The majority of Western Australia's 2.1 million inhabitants live within 50 miles (80 km) of Perth, the state's capital. Almost all the rest live along the coast. With its parks and gardens; dry, sunny Mediterranean climate; and yachtie Fremantle nearby, easygoing Perth is a bit like a nautical version of Adelaide.

The southwest corner of the state is a green jewel, with forests of majestic karri and jarrah trees, fabulous caves, and some of Australia's finest surfing beaches. The small but prestigious wine region around Margaret River, 150 miles (240 km) south of Perth, has gained a following among connoisseurs. Albany, the oldest settlement in Western Australia, is a fine old whaling port lying close to the dramatic wildflower-covered peaks of the Stirling Range.

NOT TO BE MISSED:

Historic Fremantle   217–218

Spending time with the quokkas on sunny Rottnest Island   221

The wineries of Margaret River   227

The dolphins at Monkey Mia   229

Swimming with the whale sharks on Ningaloo Reef   230–231

Camel-trekking on Cable Beach   233

The stunning sandstone mounds of Purnululu National Park   236–237

Driving through the Kimberley on the Gibb River Road   238–239

A wheat belt surrounds Perth. Beyond it, to the east, are the goldfields and the brawling, redneck mining town of Kalgoorlie. Still farther out lies the empty, waterless waste known as the Nullarbor Plain, stretching more than 500 miles (800 km) to the South Australian border. It is crossed by the lonely Eyre Highway and the Indian Pacific Railway.

The northern part of the state is rugged wilderness, leavened with scattered mining settlements, cattle stations, old pearling ports, and Aboriginal communities. Some of its most dramatic scenery—for example, the gorges in the Pilbara—is too remote for most visitors. Other places, such as the pearling port of Broome, the wilderness of the Kimberley, the otherworldly Purnululu (Bungle Bungle), and the beach at Monkey Mia have developed a must-see cachet despite their isolation. ■

Area of map detail

Canberra ☆

INDIAN

OCEAN

6 ▷

Cape Londonderry

Joseph Bonaparte Gulf

Kalumburu Mission

Cambridge Gulf

DRYSDALE RIVER NAT. PARK

Drysdale River Homestead

Wyndham

Ord MIRIMA N.P.

El Questro

Kununurra ☆

Collier Bay

Kimberley

Gibb River Road

King Sound

WINDJANA GORGE NAT. PARK

King Leopold Ranges

Durack Range

Turkey Creek

Argyle Diamond Mine

Derby

PURNULULU (BUNGLE BUNGLE) NAT. PARK

TUNNEL CREEK NAT. PARK

Broome

Fitzroy

Halls Creek

5 ▷

Tanami Desert

p. 181

Great Sandy Desert

• Balgo

Port Hedland

Goldsworthy

Dampier

Roebourne

Marble Bar

Percival Lakes

Telfer

Barrow Island

Onslow

Wittenoom

North West Cape

CAPE RANGE N.P.

Ningaloo Marine Park

Exmouth

Pilbara

Tom Price

Hamersley Range

Newman

RUDALL RIVER NAT. PARK

Lake Mackay

CANNING STOCK ROUTE

NORTHERN TERRITORY

4 ▷

Coral Bay

Lake MacLeod

Ashburton

Little Sandy Desert

Lake Disappointment

Gibson Desert

Carnarvon

Gascoyne

Shark Bay

WESTERN

irk Hartog I.

Hamelin Pool

Denham

Monkey Mia

Meekatharra

• Wiluna

AUSTRALIA

Lake Carnegie

Warburton

3 ▷

Murchison

Sanford

Mount Magnet

Great Victoria Desert

Kalbarri

Lake Barlee

Laverton

SOUTH AUSTRALIA

p. 249

KALBARRI NAT. PARK

Geraldton

Mullewa

Leonora

Lake Carey

91

Morawa

Lake Moore

Lake Rebecca

Dalwallinu

Kalgoorlie-Boulder

INDIAN PACIFIC RAILWAY

NAMBUNG NAT. PARK (THE PINNACLES)

Coolgardie

Nullarbor Plain

Madura Pass

Eucla

2 ▷

YANCHEP N.P.

New Norcia

Southern Cross

Cocklebiddy

Caiguna

Mundrabilla

Eyre Telegraph Station

PERTH

Northam

Rottnest I.

JOHN FORREST NAT. PARK

Norseman

Balladonia

EYRE HWY.

Great Australian Bight

Fremantle

Wave Rock

Hyden

YALGORUP NAT. PARK

Ravensthorpe

Esperance

Bunbury

Katanning

CAPE LE GRAND NAT. PARK

Cape Naturaliste

Yallingup

Busselton

STIRLING RANGE N.P.

Margaret River

Manjimup

FITZGERALD RIVER NAT. PARK

Pemberton

Denmark

Albany

1 ▷

Cape Leeuwin

WALPOLE-NORNALUP NAT. PARK

TORNDIRRUP NAT. PARK

0　　　　　400 kilometers

0　　　200 miles

△ A　　　△ B　　　△ C　　　△ D

Perth

In the 1980s, Perth was the base of high-rolling entrepreneurs whose dubious deals and shenanigans became known collectively as W. A. Inc. The music stopped after the stock market crash in 1987, but the city recovered to ride an even bigger boom, this time without the scandals, driven by massive mining exports to China and elsewhere. Today, mining dollars fund a perpetual building frenzy, the skyline eternally decked with cranes.

Perth
 213 B2

Visitor Information

✉ Cnr. Wellington St. & Forrest Place

☎ 08/9483-1111

Perth is a city of 1.9 million inhabitants, with a futuristic skyline overlooking the Swan River and a Mediterranean lifestyle. It is frequently described as the loneliest city in the world. Adelaide, the nearest comparable Australian city, is almost 1,500 miles (2,400 km) away, and Canberra is more distant than the Indonesian capital of Jakarta. Perth's isolation has shaped the city's history and created a spirit

INSIDER TIP:

Getting around Perth is easy with the free CAT buses, which run three routes around the city center. The tourist office carries maps.

—PETER TURNER
National Geographic author

of independence among Western Australians, who occasionally talk of seceding from the rest of the country.

Perth was founded by Capt. James Stirling on August 12, 1829, as the Swan River Settlement. It had an inauspicious beginning. The idea was that the colony would be made up entirely of free

settlers, but when word spread that the isolated settlement was surrounded by swamps and mudflats humming with mosquitoes, migration slowed to a trickle. By

1850, a chronic labor shortage saw the colonists abandon their lofty ambitions and start importing convict laborers. Many of the city's grandest buildings—the **Town Hall, Supreme Court buildings,** and **Government House**—were built by convict labor. In 1856, Perth was proclaimed a city. Gold strikes in the 1890s caused the population to jump 700 percent and sparked a construction boom. Unfortunately, most of Perth's grand Victorian buildings were demolished during the 1960s, '70s, and '80s to make way for the skyscrapers that dominate the city today.

Finding your way around Perth is fairly easy. The compact city is set out along the banks of the Swan River, which is its southern boundary. City Sightseeing Perth *(tel 08/9203-8882, citysightseeing perth.com)* has a hop-on/hop-off double-decker bus taking in Perth's major attractions, with a Fremantle add-on.

Transperth (Perth Transportation)
✉ Perth Station, Wellington St.
☎ 13-6213
transperth.wa.gov.au

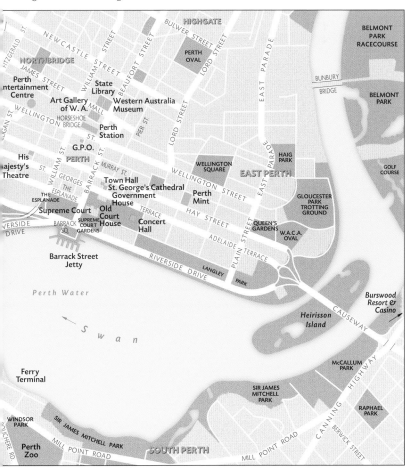

Western Australian Museum

✉ Francis St., Northbridge

☎ 08/9212-3700

museum.wa.gov.au

Art Gallery of Western Australia

✉ James St., Northbridge

☎ 08/9492-6622

artgallery.wa.gov.au

Botanic Garden

✉ Kings Park

☎ 08/9480-3600

💲 Free guided tours

bgpa.gov.au

Perth's main shopping and tourist thoroughfares are the Hay Street and Murray Street pedestrian malls, which are linked by modern arcades and department stores. St. Georges Terrace is where the mining and oil companies have their headquarters. **Parliament House** is at the western end of this street, and you can tour the building when Parliament is not sitting.

Perth's railroad lines mark the northern boundary of the city. William Street arches over the downtown railway station via the Horseshoe Bridge and leads into raffish Northbridge, with its cafés, pubs, nightclubs, and bistros. The **Perth Cultural Centre** with the state art gallery and museum are here as well. The **Western Australian Museum** includes displays on Aboriginal culture, the marine life of the Western Australian coast, and meteorites (many have been found in the outback).

The **Art Gallery of Western Australia** has collections of Australian, Pacific, and European art.

Green Perth

In Perth's early days, steep Mount Eliza was regarded as a barrier to progress, and the city grew around it. As a result, Perth now has a beautiful 2,500-acre (1,013 ha) park on its western edge. This is **Kings Park,** one of Perth's most scenic attractions. Within it is the 40-acre (16 ha) **Botanic Garden** with more than 2,500 different Western Australian plants. The park's noisy flocks of birds and dazzling display of native wildflowers in spring are pleasing reminders that Perth is perched on the edge of the outback. Kings Park and much of the Swan River foreshore have excellent bicycle trails. Bikes can be rented in Kings Park at Koala Bicycle Hire (*tel 08/9321-3061*).

The **Swan River** is the focus of the city, and it is set off by the green of Langley Park and the Esplanade. Although Perth is about 12 miles (19 km) inland, the river here is almost three-quarters of a mile (1.25 km) wide. Ferries from **Barrack Street Jetty** (off the Esplanade) go to **Fremantle** (see pp. 217–218) and **Rottnest Island** (see pp. 220–221). The Narrows Bridge (and ferries from Barrack Street) cross to South Perth, where the **Perth Zoo** (*20 Labouchere Road, tel 08/9474-0444, $$$*) is set on well-landscaped grounds. A mile or so upstream, **Burswood Resort & Casino** is a rollicking 1980s memento. ∎

EXPERIENCE:
Day-tripping from Perth

Popular excursions from Perth and Fremantle include **Rottnest Island** (see pp. 220–221). Farther afield, but still an easy day trip, is **New Norcia** (see p. 219). The Pinnacles in **Nambung National Park** are 156 miles (251 km) north along the coast. Here, hundreds of limestone pillars, from a few inches to 15 feet (5 m) high, stick up from the desert floor. Once thought to be fossilized trees, they are now considered the result of wind erosion. **Wave Rock** (see p. 225) can be visited in a day (barely), but allow longer for the southwest (see pp. 224–225) and **Margaret River** (see pp. 226–227).

Fremantle

A touch of Western Australia's colonial maritime flavor survives in Fremantle, a dockyard city about 12 miles (19 km) west of Perth, where the Swan River enters the Indian Ocean. Renovations for the unsuccessful defense of the America's Cup in 1987 helped transform "Freo" from a working-class port into an artistic vibrant city, a favorite Perth playground.

Elegant colonial streetscapes make Fremantle one of Australia's most fascinating port cities.

Although engulfed by Perth's sprawl over the years, Fremantle has retained enough of its identity to keep it from becoming just another suburb. It was founded in 1829, a few weeks before Perth, and has more local color and sense of history, and a far more relaxed atmosphere, than its busier neighbor.

Fremantle was an almost useless port until 1890, when a brilliant engineer named Charles O'Conner blasted out a rocky bar and built an artificial harbor to accommodate larger trading vessels. Today a statue of O'Conner gazes out over his creation. Although known as a smart seaside town, Fremantle is still a working port with more than 2 miles (3 km) of docks.

This once blue-collar city of 29,000 exudes a sort of raffishness—but that's nothing new. This is where Australia's only recorded formal duel took place, in 1832. But for the most part, Fremantle is a leisurely, sun-splashed town in which to stroll, take in the galleries and old buildings, sip cappuccino in the cafés on **South Terrace,** and unwind. Friday to Sunday, **Fremantle Markets,** on South

Fremantle
🅰 213 B2
Visitor Information
✉ King Sq.
☎ 08/9431-7878

EXPERIENCE: Cooking Australia

Food has become something of a national obsession in Australia. The barbie might still be king, but the prawns are doused in wine, and all manner of exotic Asian and Mediterranean flavors abound to excite the expandingly adventurous Australian palate. Celebrity chefs are worshipped, reality TV cooking shows regularly top the ratings, and cooking classes have popped up everywhere.

In the Margaret River wine region, celeb chef Tony Howell runs cooking classes at the **Cape Lodge** hotel *(tel 08/9755-6311, capelodge.com.au)*. Nearby, overlooking the ocean, **Wildwood Valley** *(tel 08/9755-2120, wildwoodvalley.com.au)* in Yallingup has a variety of classes focussing mainly on Thai and Italian cuisines.

In Sydney, the **Sydney Seafood School** *(tel 02/9004-1111, sydneyfish market.com.au)* is a great place to try your hand at cooking Aussie style.

Simon Johnson *(tel 02/8244-8220, simon johnson.com.au)*, a gourmet food store, has popular classes on food and wine. **Cucina Italiana** *(tel 8021-2699, cucinaitaliana.com.au)* emphasizes Italian home cooking in classes at its historic Annandale villa.

In Queensland, the **Spirit House** *(tel 07/5446-8977, spirithouse.com.au)* teaches Thai cooking in a lovely rain forest garden setting at Noosa. At **Mondo Organics** *(tel 07/3844-1132, mondo-organics.com.au)*, a Brisbane restaurant, courses emphasize healthy cooking.

In Melbourne, **Queen Victoria Market** *(tel 03/9320-5822, qvm.com.au)* has food and tasting tours as well as classes.

Wine leader South Australia also fancies itself a food capital. **Chapel Hill Winery Retreat** *(tel 08/8323-9182, chapel hillwine.com.au)* combines cooking classes with wine at a McLaren Vale winery.

Fremantle Prison

 1 The Terrace

☎ 08/9336-9200

fremantleprison.com.au

Western Australian Maritime Museum

✉ Victoria Quay (Shipwreck Galleries on Cliff St.)

☎ 08/9431-8444

$ $

museum.wa.gov.au/maritime/

Fremantle Arts Centre

✉ 1 Finnerty St.

☎ 08/9432-9555

fac.org.au

Terrace at the corner of Henderson Street, is a colorful, noisy bazaar where you can buy crafts, clothes, food, and other items. The town has several good restaurants and, as you might expect, the seafood is excellent. Sardines are a local specialty. The Fremantle Tram makes a 50-minute loop through the city from the Town Hall, near the intersection of High and Adelaide Streets.

City sights include the 12-sided **Round House** *(High St.)*, built in 1831 and used as a jail. The imposing **Fremantle Prison** has gruesome reminders of its long history from early convict days until it was decommissioned in 1991. Visit the small museum and shop for free. Tours *($$)* go on the half hour.

The **Western Australian Maritime Museum,** on the harbor, tells the story of international maritime travel and the history of seamanship along the Western Australian coast right up to the America's Cup era. The related **Shipwreck Galleries** on Cliff Street includes the remains of the *Batavia,* wrecked off the coast near Geraldton in 1629 (see p. 228).

The sturdy-looking **Fremantle Arts Centre,** which was originally designed as the colony's lunatic asylum, was built by convicts in the 1860s. Worth a visit for its cool courtyard garden and shop, events include the Bazaar art and design market in December and free Sunday concerts from October to March. ∎

New Norcia

Established by Spanish monks in 1846, the Benedictine mission at New Norcia makes a truly fascinating—and unusual—day trip from Perth. Its blend of Byzantine, Gothic, and classical Spanish architecture is an exotic contrast to the miles of wheat fields and Australian scrub around it.

The mission's purpose was to convert Aborigines to Christianity, teach them European-style agriculture, and rescue them from persecution. The monastery's gentle approach worked well with the Aborigines, producing a harmonious agricultural community in the 19th century. The flour mill opened here in 1879 is still going, the oldest operating mill in Western Australia. By the turn of the century, the emphasis turned to education of European children. These days it is a meditative community, known for its museum and fine art gallery.

The monks have succeeded in balancing the needs of a contemplative religious community with those of a popular tourist attraction. Visitors can tour the **chapel,** take accommodations in old convent and college buildings, and browse in shops that sell olive oil pressed at the mission. A more monastic-style retreat can be found at the **Monastery Guesthouse.** The museum and art gallery have priceless collections of religious art and manuscripts. Many of the pieces were given by Spain's Queen Isabella II (r. 1833–1870). A signposted heritage walk goes through the grounds of the monastery, starting just outside the museum, or take a two-hour guided walk.

The 80-mile (129 km) drive to New Norcia on the Great Northern Highway is particularly rewarding in spring, when Western Australia's wildflowers are in bloom (see pp. 222–223). The highway north of New Norcia rambles through Dalwallinu, Morawa, and Mullewa, all part of the **Wildflower Way,** which runs through a carpet of foxgloves, everlastings, and wattles. ■

New Norcia

🅰 213 B2

Visitor Information

☎ 08/9654-8056

💲 $$

The architecture at New Norcia is a unique mix of styles.

Rottnest Island

Although he described it as a terrestrial paradise, Dutch mariner Willem de Vlamingh clearly did not have tourism marketing in mind when he visited this little island just off the southern coast of New Holland in 1696 and named it Rottnest ("rat's nest," in Dutch). The "giant rats" he saw are actually quokkas, smallish cousins to wallabies—not rats at all. He pegged the scenery correctly, though.

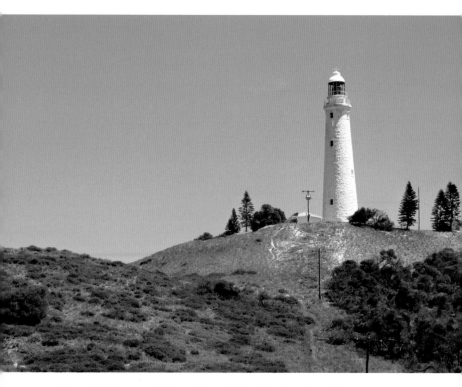

Bathurst's lighthouse guards the coastline on Rottnest Island's northern flank.

Rottnest Island
🏕 213 B2
Visitor Information
✉ Ferry Landing, Thompson Bay
☎ 08/9372-9730
rottnestisland.com

Rottnest Island is low and sandy, surrounded by turquoise waters with sparkling white beaches, and cooled by sea breezes. It has been a getaway for Perth's well-to-do population since the mid-19th century. Construction of Governor's Cottage, a summer retreat for the governor of Western Australia, was completed here in 1864. The building opened to tourists in 1917, and it was converted into the Rottnest Hotel in 1953.

The peaceful little island is about 10 miles (16 km) off the coast from Fremantle. Cars are not permitted, but wonderful bicycle and walking trails are available (you can rent bicycles on the

INSIDER TIP:

While the many quokkas ambling around Rottnest Island's visitor center are friendly to the point of being brazen, you'll need to be alert to spot them on the rest of the island, as they are much more shy in the wild.

—LARRY PORGES
*National Geographic
Travel Books editor*

island), and buses run around the island. Or you can take a tour. The island is only 7 miles (11 km) long and 3 miles (5 km) across at its widest. The main settlement is at **Thompson Bay.** The visitor center is here, next to the ferry landing. You can pick up brochures on the island's activities and arrange walking tours of the heritage buildings.

Island Activities

Visitors come here to unwind, mostly on day trips from Perth, though the island has camping, cabins, houses to rent, and other accommodations. Sprawling on the beach is the single most popular activity, although snorkeling on some of the world's southernmost coral is also big. There are dive shops on the island, a dive and snorkeling trail on **Pocillopora Reef,** just south of the island, and sailing or speed boat tours. A historic train runs 5 miles (8 km) from Thompson Bay to the **Oliver Hill Battery,** in the center of the island, which was the site of gun emplacements in World War II. There are spectacular views from **Vlamingh's Lookout,** just south of the town.

Getting to Rottnest Island

Regular ferries run from both Fremantle and Perth, or you can fly here on the Rottnest Air Taxi *(tel 04/1126-4547)* from Perth's Jandakot airport. This is a hugely popular place—more than 250,000 people visit every year—and it can be very crowded on sunny weekends. Be sure to make a reservation if you plan to stay on the island. ∎

Quokkas

Once found throughout the southwest of Western Australia, the quokka is now confined to a small protected colony on the mainland and on a few islands, notably Rottnest Island, which has the largest population of quokkas—around 10,000.

The size of a cat and somewhat similar in appearance to a wallaby, the cute quokka is the only member of the genus *Setonix.* Like other marsupials, it carries its young in its pouch.

Many quokkas show no fear of humans. You'll see plenty of them in Thompson Bay, often begging for food, but it is important not to feed them. Quokkas can fall very ill eating foods such as bread, potato chips, and meat.

Wildflowers

Spring (Oct.–Nov.) is a magical time to visit Western Australia. More than 7,000 species of wildflowers burst into life, carpeting the deserts, plains, and mountains in a kaleidoscopic blaze of color. The rich golds of the feather flowers blend with the reds and pinks of boronias, and red-and-yellow clumps of blossoms glow on the banksia trees. Most of the species are unique to Western Australia, a legacy of the area's long periods of isolation.

Blushing mountain bells, *Darwinia lejostyla*

While you are still in Perth, you can get a taste of what lies over the horizon by viewing the brilliant displays of wildflowers in Kings Park between August and October. Then head into the deserts, the wheat belt, or the Stirling Range in the mountainous southwest. Out in these places, the flowering trees, bushes, and shrubs run riot. Jarrah forests, like those in John Forrest National Park, only 15 miles (24 km) east of the city, are particularly rich. Red and green kangaroo paws, blue leschenaultia, and pink calytrix are the most prominent, but there are hundreds of other varieties. Yanchep National Park, about 30 miles (48 km) north of Perth, is another good bet.

Or you can follow the Great Northern Highway 100 miles (160 km) northeast of Perth to the wheat-belt town of Dalwallinu, then drive along the Wildflower Way another 150 miles (240 km) to Mullewa. For much of this drive, the roadside will be carpeted by wildflowers, particularly a type known as everlastings, whose petals endure after the flower itself has died. Farther north, Kalbarri National Park is vibrant with flowering banksia, grevillea, and melaleuca, and the forest floor is littered with flowering twine rushes and sedges. This beautiful coastal park, at the mouth of the ancient Murchison River, is famed for its magnificent gorges and sweeping coastal views—the spring wildflower display only gilds the lily, so to speak.

Some of the finest displays can be found in the southwest corner of the state. The jagged peaks of Stirling Range National Park are rich with pink, red, and gold flowers beautifully offset by bald granite. More than 50 species of orchid are found in the karri forests, and some of the *Dryandras* and species of *Darwinia* grow nowhere else.

The heaths at Torndirrup National Park and Walpole-Nornalup National Park, near the windswept coast of Albany, become a carpet of flowers each spring and seem to illuminate nearby dunes and granite outcrops. Fitzgerald River National Park, between Albany and Esperance, harbors more than 2,000 species of flowering plants. Of these, about 80 or so species, including oddities such as the flame orange royal hakea and the delicate pink quaalup bell, are found nowhere else in the world. In 1978, this spectacular park was declared a World Biosphere Reserve by UNESCO.

The Western Australia Visitor Centre in Perth (see p. 214) has a pamphlet on the state's wildflower trails. Most bookstores have illustrated guides to the myriad species and varieties you can see in the state. Remember that

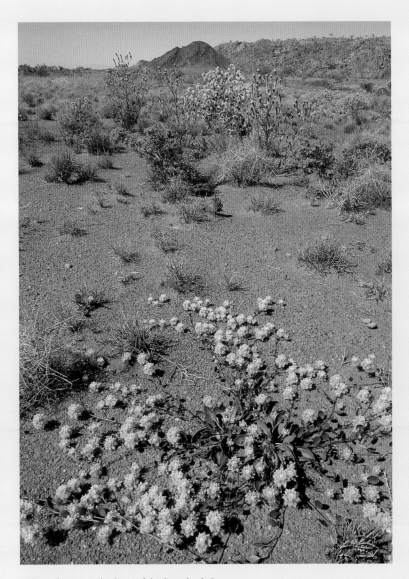

Mulla mullas among the dunes of the Great Sandy Desert

tempting as it may be to pluck a few beauties, Western Australia's wildflowers are protected under the Native Flora Protection Act. Leave them for others to enjoy.

There are, however, increasing numbers of commercial wildflower farms around Australia—particularly Western Australia—as locals begin to capitalize on the growing international interest in Australian flowers. Australia now exports millions of dollars' worth of wildflowers, such as kangaroo paw and Geraldton wax flowers, every year.

The Southwest

One of the most beautiful pockets of forest in Australia is in the southwest corner of Western Australia. This region has towering forests of karri and jarrah trees, gentle dairy country, rocky coasts, and the jagged expanse of the Stirling Range that are a riot of wildflowers every spring.

The Bicentennial Tree offers a spectacular view over the towering karri forests near Pemberton.

A nice tour of the area can be had by driving the 150 miles (240 km) along the coast south of Perth to the lovely Margaret River wine and surf region. Meander another 200 miles (320 km) farther through the forests to the historic whaling port of Albany.

Nannup, Manjimup, and **Pemberton** are pleasant old timber towns, surrounded by forests of karri and jarrah trees. The pale-barked karri are among the world's tallest trees and can reach more than 300 feet (90 m) in height. What you don't see when you drive through these ostensibly virgin forests is the clear-cutting that

goes on out of sight. For more than a century, these ancient, majestic giants were subject to wholesale logging—a practice that largely came to an end in 2001 after a long and bitter public debate between industry forces and environmentalists, with a number of local celebrities becoming involved (such as Booker Prize–nominated author Tim Winton; see sidebar p. 225).

One of the most spectacular trees is the **Gloucester Tree,** north of Pemberton. If you have the nerve, you can make the exposed climb almost 200 feet (60 m) up its trunk into what is said to be the world's highest treetop fire lookout.

The truly scary climb follows 153 spiraling rungs around the trunk. Not many people try to reach the top, but the view is remarkable. The tree was 50 feet (15 m) higher until 1947, when the top was lopped off to make way for the platform. Pemberton claims the tallest karri tree ever felled: a 343-foot (105 m) titan brought down in the last century. South of Pemberton, you can also climb the **Bicentennial Tree,** even higher at 246 feet (75 m) but without the crowds.

Seventy miles (113 km) southeast of Pemberton is the **Valley of the Giants,** in Walpole National Forest, part of **Walpole-Nornalup National Park** near the town of **Denmark.** The forest is filled with karri trees. Several species of eucalyptus grow here and nowhere else, including rare red, yellow, and Rates tingle trees, and the red flowering gum. Walking trails here include the **Tree Top Walk,** a swaying wooden walkway (wheelchair accessible) through the canopy in the Valley of the Giants.

Albany is where the British laid claim to the western half of New Holland on Christmas Day in 1826. Soon this became a bustling whaling station, with French, American, and Australian whalers putting in here. Albany was Australia's last whaling port, ceasing operations in 1978. The old Whaling Station, about 15 miles (24 km) to the southeast, is now **Whale World** (Frenchman's Bay Rd., tel 08/9844-4021, whale world.org, $$$), a museum that gives an account of the days when around 850 whales were killed each season in these waters. Happily the whales have begun returning, and southern right whales are often seen from the cliffs along the shore.

Albany itself, a pretty town of 34,000, with a vaguely New England–like, nautical feel, is one of Western Australia's most popular holiday destinations. It has a rugged coast, and the dramatic **Stirling Range** rises abruptly about 40 miles (65 km) northeast.

Another popular sight is **Wave Rock,** which is located about 220 miles (350 km) east of Perth, near the wheat-farming town of Hyden. It is a block of granite, sculpted by three billion years of wind and rain to a perfect surfer's wave about 50 feet (15 m) high. ∎

Denmark
🅰 213 B1

Visitor Information
✉ 73 South Coast Hwy.
☎ 08/9848-2055

Albany
🅰 213 B1

Visitor Information
✉ 55 Proudlove Parade
☎ 08/9841-9290

Tim Winton

One of Australia's best loved authors, Tim Winton (1960–), born in Perth and raised in Albany, celebrates Western Australian landscapes in his novels. The southwest features especially strongly in his works, which give a great sense of place if you are looking for a read while in the region.

Winton's novel *Breath* (2008) is set in the fictional southwest logging town of Sawyer and is a 1970s coming-of-age tale, told through flashbacks, about teenage surfers who take increasing risks to escape their ordinary lives. *Shallows* (1984) is based in Angelus (read Albany), where whalers and conservationists confront each other. His best known book, *Cloudstreet* (1991), is a modern Australian classic chronicling the lives of working-class families in the suburbs of Perth.

Margaret River

Margaret River is one of Western Australia's delights, an area of world-class wineries, karri forests, wildflowers, spectacular caves, and some of Australia's best surf beaches, only 150 miles (240 km) south of Perth. The region stretches about 60 miles (100 km) from Cape Naturaliste to Cape Leeuwin at the southwest tip of Australia, but skilled marketing has made the centrally located village of Margaret River the buzzword for the area.

Margaret River
🅰 213 B1
Visitor Information
✉ 100 Bussell Hwy.
☎ 08/9780-5911

The past 30 years have seen this dairy-farming area discovered by successive waves of hippies, surfers, upscale winemakers, artists, and urbanites seeking an alternative lifestyle. Most recently it has become a weekend getaway for Perth's well-to-do. It is still a major surfing hangout, because the beaches between Cape Leeuwin and Cape Naturaliste have some of the most powerful breaks in Australia.

Surfing blurs the social lines here. In any one of the beach parking lots you may see late-model Mercedes parked beside impossibly battered vintage Kombi vans. Everybody looks the same in a wetsuit. Basically two kinds of people live here: surfers and windsurfers. Those with boards go out first thing in the morning, and those with sails head out in the afternoon. Life's that simple and sunny.

The spectacular coast is a lovely drive. Just follow the Bussell Highway south out of Perth, 140 miles (225 km) or so through the beach towns of Mandurah, Bunbury, and Busselton, and from there onto the scenic Caves Road. On the way south, you might stop at **Bunbury** for a swim with dolphins. Bunbury has a resident population of around 100 bottlenose dolphins, which can usually be seen in the harbor. Dolphins often swim up to the front of the **Dolphin Discovery Centre,** which has an interpretive center and offers dolphin swim and eco-cruise tours.

The turnoff to Caves Road is 5 miles (8 km) west of Busselton and takes you to the pleasant

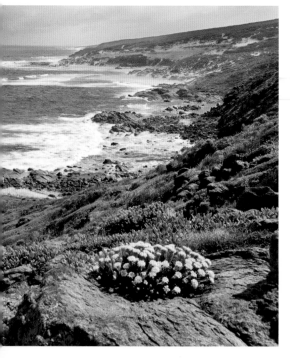

Scenery along the coast near Yallingup is a pleasing mix of cliffs and sheltered bays.

seaside town of **Dunsborough.**
A worthwhile detour is the 8-mile
(13 km) excursion down the Cape
Naturaliste Road to the historic
lighthouse (tel 08/9755-3955,
tours daily, $$) on Cape Naturaliste
and its sweeping views of the cape
and Geographe Bay. In winter, this
is a good spot for seeing humpback
and southern right whales.

Five miles (8 km) farther along,
the Caves Road from Dunsborough
brings you to **Yallingup,** where
huge Indian Ocean surf crashes
almost constantly onto the beach.
Just before Yallingup, **Ngili Cave**
is the area's most renowned cave,
popular with tourists since 1899
and offering a range of adventure
tours. The Caves House Hotel
(Caves Rd., tel 08/9750-1888)
opened in 1905. The **Gunyulgup
Galleries** represent a number of
local craftspeople and sell fine pot-
tery, paintings, and furniture made
from prized jarrah wood.

Wineries

Wineries can be found all along
scenic Caves Road as it winds
beside the coast. Although the
wine region is generically called
Margaret River, most of the win-
eries are concentrated in a knot
about 10 miles (16 km) south of
Yallingup. Local visitor informa-
tion centers have maps and
information on the region's many
fine wineries and wine tours.

The wines from Margaret River
wineries tend to be fairly expensive
compared with those of Australia's
other premier wine districts, but
there's no doubt about the quality.
Names to look for include Cape
Mentelle, Leeuwin Estate, Voyager,

Vasse Felix, and Evans & Tate.
Leeuwin Estate, which is just west
of Margaret River, has particularly
lovely grounds. Most of the winer-
ies give free tastings. **Margaret
River** is a funky village of artists,
surfers, and aging hippies about
3 miles (5 km) off Caves Road.

Caves

Because some of the most
spectacular scenery south of
Margaret River is underground,
the scenic route through the
region is called Caves Road.
The limestone that helps make
this a superb wine region is
riddled with more than 150
caves. The best is **Jewel Cave,**
about 25 miles (40 km) south of
Margaret River, with its baroque
formations and needle-like
helictites. Fossilized remains
of Tasmanian tigers have been
found in nearby **Moondyne
Cave,** which is unlit. **Lake
Cave,** about 15 miles (24 km)
south of Margaret River, has a
Tolkienesque entrance. Despite
its name, **Mammoth Cave,**
close to Lake Cave, is the least
interesting. Guided tours are the
only way to view these caves
($$$–$$$$$); obtain information from the **CaveWorks Eco
Centre** (Lake Cave, Caves Rd.,
tel 08/9757-7411).

Augusta is an old timber port.
Continue south another 5 miles
(8 km), and you'll come to **Cape
Leeuwin** lighthouse. Between
May and September, the cape is
good for whale-watching. It often
feels like the last place on Earth,
particularly when the sky is dark
and threatening. ■

Bunbury
🗺 213 B2
Visitor Information
✉ Carmody Place
☎ 08/9792-7205

**Dolphin
Discovery Centre**
✉ Lot 830
Koombana Dr.,
Bunbury
☎ 08/9791-3088
dolphindiscovery
.com.au

Ngili Cave
✉ Caves Rd.
☎ 08/9755-2152
💲 $$$–$$$$$

Shark Bay

Sheltered by the Peron Peninsula and a chain of desolate islands, Shark Bay is a World Heritage site 450 lonely miles (725 km) north of Perth. It has ancient life-forms and some of Australia's oldest European history. The Dutch navigator Dirk Hartog landed here in 1616 on the island that now bears his name.

Winter mornings are generally the best time to encounter dolphins at Monkey Mia. As many as a dozen of these marine mammals have been recorded here at one time.

Shark Bay

🗺 213 A3

Visitor Information

✉ Knight Terrace, Denham

☎ 08/9948-1590

Shark Bay is best known today for the bottlenose dolphins that swim in the shallows to play with humans. The drive from Perth, on the Northwest Coastal Highway through the seaport of **Geraldton,** is bleak and windy, and in summer searingly hot. The coastline north of Geraldton was the scene of several Dutch shipwrecks in the 17th and 18th centuries, including the *Batavia* in 1629. The impressive **WA Museum Geraldton** has relics and other exhibits.

Kalbarri National Park is a worthwhile detour on the trek north. The turnoff is about 60 miles (96 km) north of Geraldton on the Northwest Coastal

Highway. The Murchison River runs through a spectacular series of deeply hewed gorges before it reaches the coast at Kalbarri, and the national park includes both gorges and coast. The park is particularly beautiful in spring, when the wildflowers are in bloom.

Visiting Shark Bay

The turnoff to Shark Bay is about 110 miles (177 km) farther north on the Northwest Coastal Highway. The scenery along Shark Bay itself is lovely in an arid, understated way.

The first turn off the road to Shark Bay goes 4 miles (6.4 km) to **Hamelin Pool.** The turquoise waters and the rocky coastline here are lovely, but what makes this place remarkable are the stromatolites, primitive blue-green algae that were one of the first life-forms on Earth. These living fossils in Hamelin Pool are one of the most readily accessible populations of stromatolites in the world, and their presence was a big factor in giving Shark Bay its World Heritage listing. They thrive here because the sheltered waters are extremely clear and unusually saline. Fascinating as they undoubtedly are to paleontologists, the stromatolites look like blackened chunks of concrete matting. Information is available at the nearby historic **Telegraph Station** (tel 08/9942-5905).

Past the turnoff to Hamelin Pool, the road runs to Denham along the spectacular **Shell Beach,** a unique 70-mile (112 km) coastline made up of countless shells

packed in some places almost 50 feet (15 m) deep. **Denham,** the most westerly town in Australia, was once a pearling port and has become the main tourist town on the peninsula.

Monkey Mia

Fifteen miles (24 km) east of Denham is Monkey Mia and its famous beach where dolphins play. The dolphins' interaction with humans began in the 1960s, when a small pod of dolphins allowed themselves to be petted. As a result of this contact, and the apparent willingness on the part of the dolphins, a great deal of valuable marine research took place. Then a major tourism industry

INSIDER TIP:

Although Monkey Mia is a long haul north from Perth, wading among the wild dolphins there is a magical experience most visitors never forget.

—BARBARA A. NOE
National Geographic Travel Books
senior editor

developed. Dolphins are coaxed into the bay with regular feedings, appearing most mornings in the winter months—less often in summer—while staff try to keep tourists from doing anything silly. Sometimes you'll see just a solitary dolphin, and other times you can see a dozen. ■

Geraldton
⚠ 213 A3
Visitor Information
✉ Corner of Bayly St. & Chapman Rd.
☎ 08/9921-3999

WA Museum Geraldton
✉ Marine Terrace, Geraldton
☎ 08/9921-5080

Kalbarri
⚠ 213 A3
Visitor Information
✉ Grey St.
☎ 08/9937-1104

Ningaloo Marine Park

Ningaloo Reef is a spectacular, 160-mile (260 km) fringe to the rugged Northwest Cape, some 700 miles (1,125 km) north of Perth. Much shorter than the Great Barrier Reef, it is no less impressive. Unlike its better known cousin, it is easily accessible from shore—never more than 2 miles (3 km) out and in some places only a couple hundred yards. The reef has been designated a national marine park, and the dry hills of the cape form Cape Range National Park.

**Ningaloo
Marine Park**
🅰 213 A4

Coral Bay
🅰 213 A4
Visitor Information
✉ Coral Bay
   Arcade,
   Robinson St.
☎ 08/9942-5988

Getting to Ningaloo Reef from Perth is simple. Drive about 670 miles (1,080 km) north on the Northwest Coastal Highway to the isolated Minilya Road-house. From there a paved high-way runs north, along the North West Cape, 50 miles (80 km) to pretty Coral Bay and another 90 miles (145 km) to Exmouth. Or you can take a Qantas or Skywest plane *(tel 1300-660-088)* from Perth to Learmouth, then on to Broome.

The quiet seaside resort of **Coral Bay** is at the southern end of the reef. It has pretty white beaches and is popular with divers and snorkelers. Glass-bottom boat tours cater to nonswimmers.

Ningaloo Reef

Ningaloo Reef is Australia's longest continuous fringing coral reef. It is one of only two reefs anywhere in the world on a western coast. Among its rare marine life are dugongs, humpback whales, manta rays, and greenback turtles. But perhaps the most impressive creatures are the whale sharks.

A whale shark and a scuba diver go for a swim along Ningaloo Reef.

The largest fish in the sea, these gentle plankton-eating giants grow up to 60 feet (18 m) long and weigh up to 15 tons. Swimming with the whale sharks and "flying" with the manta rays are becoming popular things for tourists to do.

The waters of **Ningaloo Marine Park** are divided into recreational, general, and sanctuary zones. The sanctuary zones are completely protected, allowing visitors to see these delicate reefs and the cycle of rare marine life. Manta rays are around the peninsula from May to November, and humpback whales pass through in June and July. Turtles lumber

INSIDER TIP:

For a real taste of the scorching Western Australian sun, visit Marble Bar, halfway between Ningaloo and Broome. On average, the town hits 100°F [37°C] more than 150 days per year.

—PETER TURNER
National Geographic author

onto the beaches at night, in the summer between November and January, to lay their eggs.

Whale sharks can be observed here from April to the end of July, when the coral spawns and plankton bloom to give the behemoths a big feed. The best way to see them is with one of the specialist

EXPERIENCE:
Swim With Whale Sharks

Whale sharks (*Rhincodon typus*) are the world's largest fish, growing up to 60 feet (18 m) in length and weighing more than 15 tons (13.6 metric tons). Every year from April to July, large numbers of them arrive at Ningaloo Reef. Following regulations, snorkeling tours get to within 10 feet (3 m) for the reef's most amazing experience.

To see these gentle giants up close, full-day reef snorkeling tours including lunch and gear cost from around A$390. Divers are also well cared for and spotter planes are used to locate the whale sharks. The **Exmouth Visitor Center** (*tel 08/9949-1176, exmouthwa.com.au*) handles reservations for Ningaloo Blue and Ocean Eco Adventures in Exmouth, and Coral Bay Eco Tours and Ningaloo Reef Dive in Coral Bay. These and a host of other operators offer diving, snorkelling, whale-watching, and other wildlife tours.

charter operators, which send up spotting planes to find them. The experience is expensive but truly unforgettable.

Exmouth

Exmouth, 90 miles (145 km) farther north up the peninsula, was built in 1967 to service the U.S. Navy's top-secret radio base, which communicated with American nuclear submarines patrolling the Indian Ocean. The Navy no longer operates the base, and today tourism is the main industry, with whale shark, whale-spotting, and diving tours leaving from the town marina. Otherwise, Exmouth is a sleepy town with not much else to do but swim and snorkel. ∎

Exmouth
◪ 213 A4
Visitor Information
✉ Murat Rd.
☎ 08/9949-1176
exmouthwa.com.au

Broome

Broome is a fascinating old pearling port on Western Australia's remote northwest coast. One of the classiest outback towns, it has a lifestyle as lazy as tropical sin. Its chief attraction is Cable Beach, regarded by aficionados as one of the world's most beautiful beaches. Imagine a 20-mile (32 km) stretch of golden sand almost half a mile (.8 km) wide at low tide, offset against a warm, shimmering turquoise sea. All this only 2 miles (3.2 km) from the center of town.

Camel rides along Broome's shoreline are offered in the early morning and at sunset.

Broome

🅰 213 C5

Visitor Information

✉ 1 Hammersley St.

☎ 08/9195-2200

Pearl Luggers

✉ 31 Dampier Ter.

☎ 08/9192-2059

🕐 Closed Sun.

💲 $$

pearlluggers.com.au

English buccaneer William Dampier was the first European known to have landed here, when he was dodging a Spanish fleet in 1699. Almost 200 years passed before anyone realized what treasures lay on the seabeds. The discovery of pearl shells sparked a pearl rush in the 1880s, and the new coastal settlement was named for Frederick Broome, then governor of Western Australia.

By 1910, Broome was the world's pearling capital, accounting for more than 80 percent of the world's pearl shell (used to make buttons). The town itself was a brawling, bustling, multicultural mix of Malays, Chinese, Japanese, Filipinos, Timorese, Arabs, Aborigines, and Europeans, with a fleet of more than 400 pearling luggers. The best pearl divers came from Japan, and the 600 graves in the picturesque **Japanese cemetery** on Port Drive, at the edge of town, bear testimony to the dangers they faced. The pearling industry declined during the 1930s, but can be recalled thanks to **Pearl Luggers**—a historical exhibition of Broome's pearling past complete with a few original pearling luggers.

The Japanese bombed Broome in World War II, and the wrecks of a number of Dutch boats sunk in the harbor during the raids can be seen occasionally. One boat was supposedly carrying a secret diamond shipment from Java. Some of the diamonds were recovered, but most were never found. A beachcomber named Jack Palmer was found with some of the diamonds and arrested, but the charges were dropped. After the war, however, Palmer developed a taste for expensive cars. He died in 1958, taking his secret with him.

Modern Broome still has much of the flavor of the old days, with its airy bungalows, palm-lined streets, and Chinese roofs. It went through a redevelopment phase in the early 1980s, thanks to English-man Lord Alistair McAlpine, who built, among other things, the luxu-rious Cable Beach Club. Economic recession stalled McAlpine's plans, but Broome has bounced back with a tourism boom that sees the population of 16,000 treble in the peak winter tourist season. A host of tours, upmarket accom-modations, and direct flights from the capital cities is transforming Broome into a chic resort.

The heart of downtown is so-called **Chinatown** (really only Carnarvon Street and Dampier Terrace), which has old-fashioned trading-post grocery stores, modern boutiques, and cafés. Here, in the hushed elegance of Paspaley's Pearls (*2 Short St.*), you can buy a necklace of perfectly matched Broome pearls—for a small fortune. The **Broome Museum** gives a good insight into the town's history, including the pearl industry.

The quaint **Sun Pictures,** on Carnarvon Street, is reputedly the world's oldest outdoor movie theater. It was built by a pearling captain in 1916 and has barely changed since. You sit in old canvas sling chairs and take in the movie on a screen framed by palm fronds.

Gantheaume Point, about 2 miles (3.5 km) west of town on Gantheaume Point Road, has a red sandstone headland, lighthouse, and 130-million-year-old dinosaur tracks that are visible at low tides.

Cable Beach

But Broome's best attraction is still Cable Beach, the place where the first overseas telegraph cable was brought ashore in 1889, linking Australia with Java and London. The beach faces the Indian Ocean rather than the bay. A crowd usually assembles on the grassy knoll overlooking the beach to watch the incredible sunset. Or you can go for gentle camel rides along the sands (see sidebar below). Don't be in a hurry to leave after the rim of the sun slides below the horizon—the most vibrant colors appear a few minutes later. If you are in Broome at full moon, you can see the Staircase to the Moon, an odd effect caused by reflected moonlight on the tidal flats. It resembles a golden staircase. ∎

Broome Museum
✉ Robinson St.
☎ 08/9192-2075
$ $

EXPERIENCE:
Camel Treks

The classic Broome photo shows a camel train walking along the sands of Cable Beach at sunset. Camel rides are now offered all over the outback—from Alice Springs and Uluru, in the Flinders Range, and at Silverton near Broken Hill—but the Cable Beach rides remain the most famous. **Broome Camel Safaris** (*tel 04/1991-6101*), **Red Sun Camels** (*tel 08/9193-7423*), and **Ships of the Desert** (*tel 04/1995-4022*) all have sunset rides.

The Kimberley

The Kimberley in Western Australia's wild northwest is generally regarded as Australia's last frontier. It is an ancient plateau, dissected by deep gorges, the craggy mountain strongholds of the Durack and King Leopold Ranges, and the bizarre sandstone formations of Purnululu (Bungle Bungle). The climate is savage, with violent storms during the summer monsoons. Lightning strikes in the dry season can spark awesome bushfires.

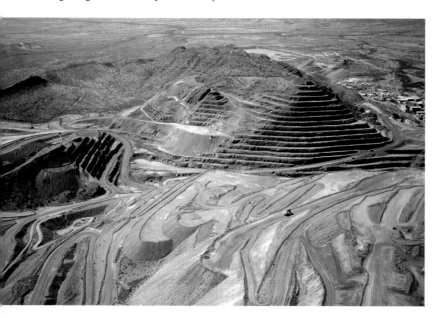

The giant Argyle Diamond Mine nestles in the southern edge of the Ragged Range.

The Kimberley
🗺 213 C5–D5
Visitor Information
✉ Coolibah Dr., Kununurra
☎ 08/9168-1177

Few people live in the Kimberley permanently—about 41,000 in an area larger than California. Most residents have come up for a few years of adventure or good paychecks at one of the mines. The region has a few scattered settlements, some far-flung Aboriginal communities, and a sprinkling of lonely cattle stations that can be bigger than some U.S. states. Saltwater crocodiles live in the rivers and estuaries along this ragged and barely explored coast, and

bizarre boab trees dot the landscape. The Kimberley is hard to reach and challenging to explore, but is one of the world's truly wild places.

The frontier region's main road is the Great Northern Highway, which was paved only as recently as 1986. It links the Kimberley's three main towns—Kununurra, Derby (actually 20 miles/32 km off the highway), and Broome (see pp. 232–233)—with the cities of Perth and Darwin. The only other route through the

Kimberley is the Gibb River Road, which crosses 400 miles (645 km) of wilderness (see pp. 238–239).

Kununurra

Kununurra—population 6,000—is the major town in the eastern part of the Kimberley and the best base for visiting the otherworldly Purnululu (see pp. 236–237) and the Argyle Diamond Mine. It is also a good jumping-off point for the Gibb River Road, which begins off the Great Northern Highway about 30 miles (48 km) west of town.

Kununurra is the area's newest town, built from scratch in 1961 to service the Ord River Irrigation Project that dammed the mighty Ord River. During the summer monsoon, the Ord was pouring more than 15 million gallons (59 million liters) of water into the sea every second. By holding back some of that water in the giant man-made Lake Argyle and using it to irrigate crops, the project has since turned about 29,000 acres (11,700 ha) of arid scrub into sugarcane and banana plantations, mango orchards, peanut and melon fields, and vegetable gardens.

One of the most spectacular and easily accessible hikes in the Kimberley is within easy walking distance of Kununurra. **Hidden Valley,** in **Mirima National Park,** is a miniature version of Purnululu, yet is only a mile from the center of the town. Just follow Barringtonia Avenue to the edge of town and you will find it, a maze of tiger-striped sandstone formations.

The **Argyle Diamond Mine** (*argylediamonds.com.au*), which is located about 100 miles (160 km) south of Kununurra, is one of the world's largest producers of diamonds. About 8 million carats a year come out of this giant open-cut mine. Most of its output is industrial quality, but it also produces spectacular jewels. They come in a suite of brilliant colors: champagne and topaz hues, blues, greens, and, rarest of all, pinks, lilacs, and reds. The mine has no public access, but the Kununurra tourist office can arrange tours. ■

Australia: The Movie

Few Australians have visited the Kimberley, but the Baz Luhrmann film *Australia* (2008) has prompted a mini tourist rush to see the sweeping landscapes where much of the film was shot. Located 25 miles (40 km) off the Gibb River Road, **Diggers Rest Station** was a key filming location, particularly the boab trees on the property. The movie's Faraway Downs Homestead was a set built on the **Carlton Hill Station** (*not open to the public*), about 12 miles (20 km) west of Kununurra. The **Cockburn Range,** rising 2,000 feet (600 m) above the plains, features in the movie, which also used the **Home Valley Station,** at the base of the range, and **El Questro Wilderness Park** (see pp. 238–239) for several filming locations.

Purnululu (Bungle Bungle) National Park

It speaks volumes for the remoteness and inaccessibility of the Kimberley that these spectacular sandstone ranges were virtually unknown to non-Aboriginal Australians until the early 1980s, when a filmmaker who was doing a documentary for the Western Australian government shot some aerial footage of them at dusk. The haunting images seized the public's imagination, and Purnululu's striped formations are now a symbol of the Kimberley.

The striated sandstone formations at Purnululu's Piccaninny Creek

Aborigines have been coming into these eerie ranges for more than 20,000 years. The park's name, Purnululu, is the local Aborigine term for "sandstone"; the name Bungle Bungle may refer to a type of grass.

In Australia these rock formations are almost as well recognized an outback icon as Uluru.

The first European to see the ranges was Alexander Forrest, who explored the Kimberley in 1879. As he was looking for prospective cattle-grazing land, he dismissed the spectacular ranges as useless wasteland and moved on. Over the next century, some of the big Kimberley pastoral leases included parts of the Bungle Bungle.

Getting to the Park

Many people who see images of Purnululu resolve to go there, but getting into this remote 750,000-acre (304,000 ha) national park is no mean feat. It is accessible only during the dry season, and even then you need a four-wheel-drive vehicle or a helicopter and must carry all supplies. Scenic flights and tours are easier. About 45,000 tourists see Purnululu each year, almost

to the park visitor center. Here you can either head north to **Echidna Chasm** (about 12 miles/19 km) or go south to **Piccaninny Creek** (about 20 miles/32 km). The Echidna Chasm area has tall, narrow gorges and dramatic

INSIDER TIP:

Camp at Kurrajong for Purnululu's northern attractions and at Walardi for those in the south.

—STEPHANIE ROBICHAUX
*National Geographic
contributor*

Purnululu National Park

 213 D5

Visitor Information

✉ Department of Environment & Conservation, Kununurra

☎ 08/9168-7300

🕐 Open Apr. through Dec.

Outback Driving

Remoteness and weather extremes in the outback require drivers to take extra precautions. Check local road and weather conditions, particularly in the wet season, and report your route to relatives or local authorities if heading off the main highways. Carry plenty of extra water, food, and fuel. If traveling off-road,

consider renting a GPS and satellite phone or high-frequency radio. If you get lost or break down, stay with the vehicle. Stories abound of motorists who walked out for help and perished. It may take a day or two for someone to come along, but increasing tourism now means the outback is not as isolated as it used to be.

---

half of them on sightseeing flights out of Kununurra, Turkey Creek, or Bellburn (in the park). The tourist office in Kununurra has details on flights and tours into the park.

Park Attractions

The vehicle turnoff to Purnululu is about 150 miles (240 km) south of Kununurra on the Great Northern Highway. From there you follow a rough, bouncing 33-mile (53 km) track

cliffs, while at the Piccaninny Creek area you will see the tiger-striped beehive-shaped sandstone formations for which the park is famous. The tiger striping is the result of orange silica being interspersed with thin layers of black lichens. Climbing the ancient and fragile sandstone formations is forbidden.

Once in the park, visitors can stay in Kurrajong Camp or Walardi Camp. Bungle Bungle is closed in the wet season (Jan.–March). ∎

Gibb River Road Drive

On a map of the Kimberley, the Gibb River Road looks like a handy shortcut between Kununurra and Derby, cutting 150 miles (240 km) off the Great Northern Highway route. But this rough track is emphatically not a shortcut; it is one of the great adventure drives on the continent. In the wet season (Oct.–March), it is impassable.

Created in 1964 to bring cattle on outlying stations to market, the Gibb River Road cuts 420 miles (676 km) through the heart of the Kimberley. It is still known as the "beef road" among locals, and travelers on it should keep an eye out for the massive road trains, loaded with cattle, booming along in a shower of gravel and dust. Also be wary of river crossings—this is crocodile country.

A conventional vehicle can make it along the Gibb River Road, with care, but a 4WD vehicle is far preferable. Food, fuel, and accommodations are available en route, but the distance between them can be great, so carry plenty of supplies, basic tools, and spares. If you don't want to drive yourself, you can join a four-wheel-drive safari from either end. Ask for information at the tourist office at Kununurra (see p. 235) or Derby (tel 08/9191-1426).

Kununurra to El Questro

From **Kununurra ①**, take the Great Northern Highway west for 25 miles (40 km) or so to the marked turnoff to the old seaport of **Wyndham ②**. The Gibb River Road goes left off this road a couple of miles north of the turning, but before you take it, Wyndham is worth a visit. A quintessential Kimberley frontier town, Wyndham is surrounded by miles of shimmering tidal flats. It used to be known for bloodthirsty crocodiles that lurked in the marshes near the abattoir, waiting for offal. The meatworks closed in 1985, but Wyndham's tidal flats are still good for crocodile spotting.

One of the most spectacular views on Australia's wild north coast is from the **Five Rivers Lookout** on Mount Bastion, immediately behind Wyndham. Drive up to the lookout

1,082 feet (330 m) above the tidal flats and see five major rivers—the Ord, Pentecost, Durack, Forrest, and King—empty slowly into Cambridge Gulf. Kimberley Motors (tel 08/9161-1281) has local information. About 12 miles (19 km) south of town on the King River Road is the 2,000-year-old hollow boab tree that served as a prison in Wyndham's bad old frontier days.

The roughest stretch of the Gibb River Road is the first 150 miles (240 km). Some of the river crossings, such as the one through the Pentecost River, are potentially treacherous in the wet season until around May, but the countryside is magnificent.

Fifteen miles (24 km) west along the Gibb River Road is a turnoff for **El Questro Wilderness Park ③** (tel 08/9426-7550, open

INDIAN OCEAN

⚠	See also area map p. 213 C5–D5
▶	Kununurra
↻	420 miles (675 km)
⏱	2 days
▶	Derby

King Sound

Mount Hart

Tunnel Creek

Windjana Gorge

Derby ⑥

Meda

Fraser

WINDJANA GORGE N.P.

TUNNEL CREEK N.P.

GREAT NORTHERN HWY.

April–Oct., www.elquestro.com.au, $$), one million acres (400,000 ha) of cattle station turned massive tourist resort. Fishing trips, horseback rides, gorge cruises, Aboriginal rock art, and hiking tours are all offered to visitors. Accommodations range from high-priced homestead rooms cantilevered over Chamberlain Gorge, one of 50 gorges on the property, to upmarket tents at fern-filled Emma Gorge and budget camping sites at the Station Township. Another accommodation option for tourists is the nearby **Home Valley Station** *(tel 08/8296-8010, hrstation.com.au).*

Onward to Mount Barnett

The next refueling point is the **Mount Barnett Roadhouse** *(tel 08/9191-7007),* which is 140 miles (225 km) farther on. APT *(tel 1300-334-872, kimberleywilderness.com.au),* the main Kimberley bus tour company, has two more accommodations on tracks off the road: near Imintji Store *(tel 08/9191-7471)* and the turnoff to pretty Bell Creek Gorge. **Bell Gorge Wilderness Lodge** has

NOT TO BE MISSED:

Wyndham • Five Rivers Lookout
• El Questro Wilderness Park
• Windjana Gorge National Park

tented accommodations. Farther along is the turnoff to **Mount Hart Homestead,** offering full-board and basic rooms.

The Road to Derby

West of Mount Barnett Roadhouse, the road enters the dramatic King Leopold Ranges. A turnoff goes 15 miles (24 km) to the **Windjana Gorge National Park** ❹ and 25 miles (40 km) farther to **Tunnel Creek National Park** ❺. This was once part of a vast coral reef; over eons, the Lennard River cut its way through the rock to form gorges. Wade through Tunnel Creek to see flying foxes. The final 40 miles (64 km) of the road into **Derby** ❻ are paved.

Kalgoorlie-Boulder

Kalgoorlie sits on the Golden Mile, Australia's richest vein of gold-bearing ore. This frontier mining town is in the old outback tradition, with tattooed, shirtless miners, and "skimpies" (scantily clad barmaids) in its pubs. It is also a much anticipated stop on the Indian Pacific train journey after the long westward trek across the Nullarbor Plain.

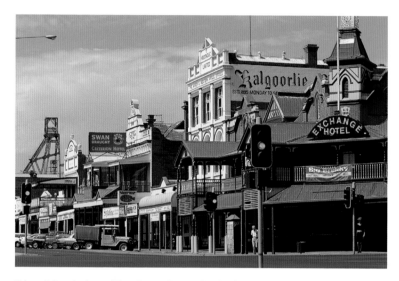

Kalgoorlie's main thoroughfare, Hannan Street, is lined with elaborate gold-rush architecture.

Kalgoorlie

🅼 213 C2

Visitor Information

✉ Corner of Hannan & Wilson Sts.

☎ 08/9021-1966

The town got its start in 1893, when an Irish prospector named Paddy Hannan stumbled across nuggets lying on the ground beneath the tree where he had stopped with two of his mates to rest a lame horse. Having spent fruitless months at the gold diggings in nearby Coolgardie, the men could hardly believe their luck. They scooped up more than 100 ounces (2.8 kg) of gold in a few days and sparked the last of Australia's great gold rushes. Within a couple of months more than a thousand fortune-seekers came to the place known as Hannan's Find.

Later the fledgling town was given back its Aboriginal name, Kalgoorlie. By 1896, the town had a population of nearly 6,000 and a neatly arranged grid of tree-lined streets wide enough to allow camel trains to turn around. It was also providing the economic oomph to assure Western Australia's autonomy and eventual statehood. That year, authorities began building a 350-mile (560 km) pipeline from Mundaring Weir to bring clean water to this desperately dry desert town. The pipeline was completed in 1903, by which time Kalgoorlie had grown to a small city of

30,000, with more than 40 hotels and eight breweries (it wasn't just water they thirsted for). The extended rail line to neighboring Boulder was the busiest in the state.

Kalgoorlie's luck as well as its ore has lasted longer than that of any of the early eastern gold towns. While it is very much alive today, Kalgoorlie had a brush with oblivion in the years after World War I, when rising costs and the falling price of gold depressed the outback community. A commodities boom in the 1970s, and new technology that enabled trace quantities of gold to be profitably extracted, gave Kalgoorlie a fresh lease on life. Today it is a bustling community of 30,000 (linked by a hyphen and municipal amalgamation to nearby **Boulder** in 1989). The town is Australia's largest gold producer and one of the richest sources of gold in the world.

Kalgoorlie Sights

Hannan Street is lined with glorious gold-rush architecture, elegant old pubs, and the grandiose Town Hall. Kalgoorlie is very much a blue-collar town, although tourism is becoming important. The **WA Museum Kalgoorlie-Boulder** has excellent displays on the town's gold-rush heyday, Aboriginal history, and the region's days as a sandalwood supplier.

The underground tour of the **Hannan's North Tourist Mine** (*Goldfields Hwy., tel 08/9026-2700, $$, mininghall.com*) is one of the biggest draws in Kalgoorlie.

The **Super Pit** is the world's biggest open-cut gold mine—virtually a canyon. It is presently about 1,200 feet (370 m) deep and produces 800,000 ounces (22,676 kg) of gold each year. The mine is 2.2 miles (3.6 km) long by one mile (1.6 km) wide and growing by the day.

You can drive to the **Super Pit Lookout** at the end of Outram Street just outside Boulder. For a sense of scale, consider the fact that the "tiny" yellow dump trucks in the pit are the size of houses and carry more than 200 tons (181 metric tonnes) of ore. The lookout is open from 7 a.m. to 9 p.m.—but is closed when blasting is being done in the mine. ■

WA Museum Kalgoorlie-Boulder

✉ 17 Hannan St.
☎ 08/9021-8533
$ Donation

Coolgardie

▲ 213 C2

Visitor Information

✉ Bayley St.
☎ 08/9026-6090

Coolgardie

The area's first gold diggings began in 1892 in Coolgardie, about 25 miles (40 km) south of Kalgoorlie. Today, it's practically a ghost town—a sort of town-size mining museum, well worth a visit. The **Warden's Court Building,** the **Town Hall,** the **Post Office,** and the opulent **Marvel Bar Hotel** attest to the prosperity this gold-rush boomtown once enjoyed. The Old Courthouse on Bayley Street houses the **Goldfields Museum,** an interesting collection of early goldfield artifacts. The 1895 **old mining warden's residence** has been restored and listed by the National Trust.

EXPERIENCE: Exploring Australia's Outback

The outback is harsh and isolated, a vast region of desert and tropical wilderness, fascinating for its tales of human adaptation as much as the varied landscapes. There are many ways to explore and appreciate this unique part of the world, ranging from short flights to multiday camping excursions and four-wheel-drive adventures.

The easiest way to get into the outback is to fly to Alice Springs and Uluru, or drive through the Red Centre on the paved Stuart Highway. Alternatively, take the Ghan, the train named after the Afghan camel drivers who once plied this remote route (see pp. 282–283).

Adventure lies off the main highways. You can muster cattle (see sidebar p. 281), stay on an outback station (see sidebar p. 136), fly to impossibly remote pubs, or drive some of the old cattle tracks deep into the Never Never, as the outback is known in Australia.

Driving the Outback

Though not to be undertaken lightly, nor in the blistering summer months, a four-wheel-drive adventure into the heart of Australia is an unforgettable experience. Classic routes include the **Oodnadatta Track,** following the old Ghan rail line north to Alice Springs, and the **Birdsville Track,** a famous stock route to the remote Queensland town of Birdsville. Both are now well-maintained gravel roads in the dry season, starting from Marree in South Australia. The nearby **Strzelecki Track** heads to Innamincka on Cooper Creek, where Burke and Wills died (carry plenty of food and water), and you can continue on to **Broken Hill,** another center for exploring the outback.

In the north, the **Gibb River Road** (see pp. 238–239) is one of the great adventure drives, and **Kakadu National Park** (see pp. 188–191) is an outback wonderland.

If you drive yourself, it is essential to plan ahead in detail. A great reference is

INSIDER TIP:

Be sure to read the fine print when researching outback tours. Accommodations and flights are not always included in the price.

—LARRY PORGES
National Geographic Travel Books editor

exploroz.com. Alice Springs, Darwin, and Broken Hill are good places to rent vehicles, and lots of operators in these centers run tours.

Tour Operators

In Alice Springs, **Ossies Outback 4WD Tours** *(tel 08/8956-9884, ossies .com.au)* goes off-road through the MacDonnell Ranges to Uluru, across the Simpson Desert, and elsewhere. **Wayoutback Safaris** *(tel 08/8952-4324, wayoutback.com.au)* heads to Uluru, Kings Canyon, and the MacDonnell Ranges.

In Darwin, **Venture North Australia** *(tel 08/8927-5500, venturenorth .com.au)* has tours to Kakadu, Arnhem Land, the remote Cobourg Peninsula, and the Kimberley. **Aussie Adventure** *(tel 08/8923-6523, aussieadventure.com.au)* can take you on tours of the Red Centre, Kakadu, and the Tiwi Islands.

In Broken Hill, **Tri State Safaris** *(tel 08/8088-2389, tristate.com.au)* has a great selection of trips right across the outback, while **Corner Country Adventure Tours** *(tel 02/8087-6956, cornercountryadventure.com .au)* goes to Birdsville and the desert regions.

Sightseeing in the Air

Not a fan of dust? No worries. You can see the outback from the air. Take a day flight to the Birdsville pub for a burger and beer with **Outback Air Tours** *(tel 07/4654-3033, outback airtours.com)* or a 12-day luxury tour in a De Havilland Dash 8 with **Bill Peach Journeys** *(tel 02/9693-2233, billpeachjourneys.com.au).*

Eyre Highway &
the Nullarbor Plain

Driving the Eyre Highway along the edge of the Nullarbor Plain is the classic outback road trip—almost 1,500 miles (2,400 km) from Perth to Adelaide and most of it empty desert highway. Yet for all the barrenness of the landscape, you can enjoy remarkable views—the expanse of saltbush from Madura Pass, the Bunda Cliffs along the Great Australian Bight. But it is the steady humming of tires on pavement that brings home the awesome size of the continent.

In a cloud of steam and coal smoke, the first Transcontinental Express pulls into Kalgoorlie in 1917.

Strictly speaking, the Eyre Highway runs just south of the Nullarbor Plain (to cut directly across it you must take the train; see sidebar, p. 248), touching the plain itself only briefly in South Australia. Australia's first transcontinental automobile journey was made in 1912 following camel tracks across the desert. World War II and the threat of invasion inspired the authorities to build a highway linking Perth with the rest of Australia. Even into the 1960s, however, the road was still little more than a rough track, and anyone who made it across in a

Norseman

213 C2

Visitor Information

✉ 68 Roberts St.

☎ 08/9039-1071

car was likely to get a mention in the Perth newspapers. In 1969, the Western Australian government paved the highway to the South Australia border, and the last parts were paved in 1976.

The first stage, if you are heading east from Perth, is the 400 miles (640 km) or so to the goldfields around Kalgoorlie. It is probably the least interesting part of the journey, a typical Australian highway through wheat fields and arid scrub with lengthening stretches between towns. To anyone coming from Europe or North America, it may even seem desolate. But this is the civilized part of the drive.

The adventure doesn't really start until you drive through **Norseman,** past the red warning sign that little or no water will be available for the next 750 miles (1,200 km), toward a heat-warped horizon. You need to have done

at least some basic preparation. Here the temperatures can soar to well over 120°F (49°C). Withering headwinds make your car work harder and chew up the gasoline, and the glare can be blinding. Be certain that your car is in good working order, that you have basic tools and spares, and above all, that you have brought extra water both for drinking and for the radiator. That said, the Eyre Highway is a reasonably well-used road that is paved and in good condition. It is the lifeline between

INSIDER TIP:

The Eyre Bird Observatory is an ornithologist's dream, but the last 7.5 miles [12 km] of the journey must be traveled by 4WD.

—STEPHANIE ROBICHAUX
National Geographic contributor

Abandoned in 1929, the old telegraph station at Eucla has been slowly engulfed by sand.

Perth and the rest of the country, and if something went wrong you probably wouldn't have long to wait, but why take chances? Food and gasoline are expensive out here. Although the roadhouses can make electronic transactions, if the lines are down you will be stuck if you don't have some cash.

Highway Roadhouses

Because no real towns are on the road between Norseman and the South Australian fishing port of **Ceduna,** 750 miles (1,200 km) away, you will find just a lonely archipelago of roadhouses, generally between 80 and 120 miles (130 and 195 km) apart. The first of these, **Balladonia,** was a telegraph station in the early days, and the ruins of the old stone buildings can be seen a few miles past the modern roadhouse complex. The early part of the drive from Norseman is surprisingly forested, but by the time you reach Balladonia you are well into the scrub. The nearby Balladonia sheep station is one of the oldest in this part of Western Australia, and it is still owned by the pioneering family that founded it. Balladonia's population is listed as nine, which gives you a hint of just how lonely the drive ahead is going to be.

Just past the old station, the road makes a beeline for the **Caiguna** roadhouse, motel, and campground (tel 08/9039-3459), about 113 miles (182 km) away. This rigid straightaway at 90 miles (144 km) is the longest in

> ## EXPERIENCE:
> ## For the Birds
>
> Birders and committed conservationists will love the **Eyre Bird Observatory** (PMB 32, Cocklebiddy via Norseman, tel 08/9039-3450, birdlife.org.au). This non-profit research station attracts birders and scientists from around the world, and you can volunteer or undertake courses in bird banding and field techniques, mammal studies, dune conservation, and other activities. Courses are usually for a week, and accommodations are basic but comfortable, with meals provided. Reservations are essential.

Australia, and while that fact may interest you for the first 10 or 20 miles, you'll have a huge sense of relief when you finally reach Caiguna. You could adjust your watch 45 minutes forward at this point to accommodate the local time zone, or just ignore it because you are passing through and time is rather meaningless out here.

Cocklebiddy, 40 miles (64 km) east of Caiguna roadhouse, is famous for the labyrinth of limestone caves beneath its flat, almost featureless plain. The system has some of the world's longest underwater caves. In 1983, a French team set what was then a world record for the world's deepest cave dive. Exploring these caves is difficult, dangerous, and best left to well-planned expeditions. More accessible here is the **Eyre Bird Observatory** (see sidebar above) at the historic Eyre Telegraph Station (tel 08/9039-3450), a few miles east of the Cocklebiddy roadhouse and down

Eyre Peninsula

An alternative to the Ceduna–Port Augusta leg of the Eyre Highway is to turn off at Ceduna and take the more scenic coast road around the Eyre Peninsula for wild beaches, cliffs, sheltered harbors, abundant seafood, and wildlife spotting.

Down the coast 55 miles (90 km) from Ceduna, **Streaky Bay** is noted for fishing, seafood, and fine beaches. Farther on, just off the highway, the otherworldly granite outcrop of **Murphy's Haystack** makes a good photo op, and the same road continues on to the **Point Labatt sea lion colony,** viewed from the cliff top. To see these lumbering beasts up close, or to swim with the dolphins, arrange tours *(tel 08/8626-5017)* at Baird Bay.

Detour off the highway for fine coastal scenery, empty beaches, and caves, before reaching the summer resort town of **Coffin Bay,** noted for its superb oysters and adjoining national park, with wild coastal scenery, birds, and other wildlife.

Similar is **Lincoln National Park,** 25 miles (40 km) away, just outside **Port Lincoln,** the thriving main town at the bottom of the peninsula. This attractive tuna-fishing port turned resort has plenty of tours for cruising, fishing, or swimming with the wildlife. The highway then heads north, skirting the quieter waters of Spencer Gulf, all the way to **Whyalla,** the state's second largest city and steel-producing port, and on to **Port Augusta.**

INSIDER TIP:

Every October, the town of Ceduna [ceduna.net] hosts Oysterfest, three festive days of parades, food, and entertainment.

—CAROLINE HICKEY
National Geographic Travel Books editor

a track to the cliff-lined coast on the Great Australian Bight.

Madura Pass is 340 miles (550 km) from Norseman. This is the most spectacular part of the drive, when the road suddenly starts down a steep, winding hill onto the **Mundrabilla Plains.** The views here are breathtaking and slam home the empty vastness of the country.

A few miles past the Mundrabilla roadhouse, the road starts to climb again, winding its way toward Eucla Pass. If it is night, you'll be greeted by the sight of the illuminated Travellers Cross on top of the craggy pass.

Eucla, 103 miles (166 km) from Madura Pass, is worth a stop. The Eucla Motor Hotel *(tel 08/9039-3468)* roadhouse and restaurant complex is dated, with outback prices, but by far the best on the route. It has a friendly bar, good meals, and a small museum on-site. The owners can direct you to some of the local sights and beaches, such as the picturesque ruins of the telegraph station, built in 1877 and now engulfed by dunes.

Beyond the haunting dunes around Eucla is the deep blue water of the **Great Australian Bight.** A weather observatory is also here—it recorded Western Australia's highest ever shade temperature (124°F/51°C) .

Entering South Australia

East of Eucla the highway dog-legs around a meteor crater and 9 miles (14.5 km) later crosses the South Australian border at **Border Village.** If you are coming from South Australia, the agriculture check-point requires you to surrender any fresh fruits, vegetables, or honey you might have with you. If you are going east, the South Australian authorities will get you just outside of Ceduna.

Border Village is the road-house, nothing more, but a good pit stop for meals, drinks, or accommodations. The big, tacky fiberglass kangaroo out front marks hole No. 6 on the Nul-labor Links golf course. Stretched the length of the Eyre Highway, you can play a hole at most road-houses; pick up a scorecard card in Kalgoorlie or Ceduna for the "world's longest golf course."

The highway clings to the Great Australian Bight for much of the next 100 miles (160 km) and has plenty of turnoffs to spectacular cliff-top lookouts. The banded **Bunda Cliffs** are up to 600 feet (180 m) high, and between June and October they make great viewing platforms for watching the annual migration of southern right whales.

The road veers inland to the Nullarbor Hotel/Motel (*tel 08/8625-6271*) and the only stretch of the Eyre Highway that actually runs on the tree-less Nullarbor Plain. It skirts it for 20 miles (32 km) or so and then takes you back into saltbush scrub. A turnoff leads to the **Head of the Bight,** the best whale-watching viewpoint between June and October.

Ceduna is about 175 miles (280 km) ahead, through lightly forested country, and the line of white wheat silos along the port is

Ceduna
🅐 251 B3

Visitor Information
✉ 58 Poynton St.
☎ 08/8625-3343

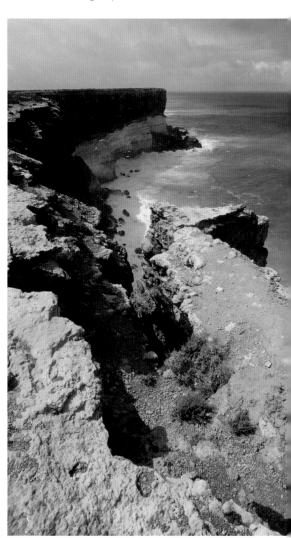

The Nullarbor Plain comes to an abrupt end at the Bunda Cliffs.

Great Southern Rail

✉ 422 King William St., Adelaide

☎ 13-2147

greatsouthernrail .com.au

a welcoming sight. This is the first town of consequence (population 3,570) after Norseman.

From here the highway crosses the arid Eyre Peninsula, which is dotted with the ruins of stone cottages of settlers who tried to scratch out a hard living on this soil in the 19th century. Your drive along Eyre Highway eventually ends at **Port Augusta**—"Porta Gutta" in local-speak. Adelaide is located about 200 miles (320 km) south, through pleasant wheat and wine country.

In Adelaide, you can catch the Indian Pacific train (see sidebar) back to Perth—your car can ride as well. For more outback driving and roadhouse burgers, make a left turn at Port Augusta and head along the lonely Stuart Highway (see pp. 284–288) toward the town of Alice Springs. ■

Rails Across the Nullarbor

The Indian Pacific train crosses the continent from Sydney to Perth. It winds its way through the Great Dividing Range and rolls across the western plains to the frontier silver mining town of Broken Hill. Then it goes on to Port Pirie and down to Adelaide, before heading westward across the Nullarbor Plain. Here the great train really hits its stride—crossing the vast and waterless expanse whose name is corrupt Latin for "no tree" *(nulla arbor)*.

For sheer size and scale, there is nowhere like it—an 80,000-square-mile (207,000 sq km) limestone plateau, scoured by desert winds and scorched by temperatures that can exceed 120°F (49°C) under a pitiless summer sun. The plateau has no surface water, although an extensive system of flooded caves lies underground. Out here lies the world's longest stretch of straight railroad track— more than 300 miles (480 km).

The first European to cross the Nullarbor Plain was explorer Edward Eyre, who barely survived his harrowing journey into ceaseless winds and deadly heat in 1841. Afghan camel drivers and telegraph linesmen helped forge a trail across it later in the century. A railroad was begun in 1911—partly as an inducement to Western Australia to join the federation. Six years later, on October 23, 1917,

the nation's first transcontinental train rolled out of the South Australian town of Port Augusta.

Building the railroad was a logistical nightmare, akin to building a space station, because nothing there could sustain life. Everything had to be taken into the desert—food, housing, water, equipment, and building materials. Provisions were sent out weekly from either Kalgoorlie or Port Augusta on what became known as the Tea and Sugar Train. Until 1996 that train still ran weekly out of Port Augusta, servicing the tiny isolated camps and the few inhabitants. The train took three days to make the crossing, bringing tankers of fresh water, freight, mail, and news of the world.

The Indian Pacific runs at a brisker pace, taking a little more than two days to cross the continent. Despite its epic stature—and in part because of it—the train lost money for many years. A few years ago, it was given an expensive face-lift in a bid to make it a sort of outback Orient Express. The result was more Aussie nouveau, although the club cars and sleepers are comfortable. But the scenery can't be replicated anywhere else. Get more information about this great train trip from Great Southern Railway *(tel 13-2147, greatsouthernrail.com.au).*

Australia's driest state, but a paradise of orchards, vineyards, and olive groves in the fertile southeast

South Australia

Introduction & Map   250–251

Adelaide   252–258

Experience: Volunteering   255

Experience: Visiting Adelaide's Markets   256

Around Adelaide   259–279

Experience: Spotting the Elusive Platypus   261

Feature: Australian Wines   264–265

Experience: Educate Your Palate   265

Experience: Taking on Seasonal Work   267

Feature: Festival State   272–273

Experience: Festival Fever   273

Experience: Renting a Houseboat   276

Coober Pedy   280–281

Experience: Cattle Mustering   281

The Ghan   282–283

Experience: Riding the Rails   283

Stuart Highway Drive   284–288

Experience: Flying Over Lake Eyre   286

Hotels & Restaurants   379–382

Bottles in the Wine Museum, Yalumba Wines, Barossa Valley

South Australia

South Australia is a cornucopia of most of the finer things in life: great food, world-class wines, and a sunny cosmopolitan lifestyle. What makes this bounty all the more remarkable is that this is Australia's driest and most barren state. South Australia has a higher proportion of desert than any other state, with more than 80 percent of its surface receiving less than 10 inches (25 cm) of rain a year.

The vast majority of South Australians live in the southeast corner of the state, a fertile pocket of land watered by the Murray River. Adelaide, perhaps Australia's most gracious capital city, is here, forming an island of elegant homes and high Victorian architecture surrounded by leafy parklands.

The climate here is Mediterranean, and the rural scenery is elegant, with stately red gums, broad vineyards, and old stone cottages. The Murray River runs through deep sandstone gorges teeming with birdlife, which you can see by steamboat. Victor Harbor, an hour or so south of Adelaide, is a popular seaside retreat, where southern right whales swim up to the coast during their winter migrations. Farther

Area of map detail

NOT TO BE MISSED:

Sampling the arts in the gracious state capital of Adelaide 252–258

The cool retreat of the Adelaide Hills and Germanic Hahndorf 260–263

Touring the old-world wineries of the Barossa Valley 267–268

Kangaroo Island, a wildlife-spotting treasure trove 268–271, 274

Cruising on a Murray River houseboat 276

Hiking the rugged Flinders Ranges, an oasis in the desert 277–279

The underground opal miners' homes in Coober Pedy 280–281

Driving though outback desert on the Stuart Highway 284–288

south, the haunting sweep of coastline known as the Coorong is a bird-watcher's paradise. Naracoorte Caves, in the far southeast, is a World Heritage–listed fossil site and home to almost half a million bats. Kangaroo Island still has unspoiled bush, old-fashioned villages, and almost tame wildlife only two hours by car and ferry from Adelaide.

Glenelg was where the first European settlers landed from the *Buffalo* in 1836. The following year Col. William Light pegged out the city of Adelaide in lines as crisp and straight as an accountant's left margin. The colony itself was the vision of entrepreneur Edward Wakefield, who wanted it to be a model settlement. Migrants purchased their land from the South Australia Company at two pounds an acre and brought along capital to invest in the colony. They were guaranteed religious and civic freedoms. No convicts here, thank you. This is the only state never to have been a penal colony.

Many early settlers came from the English gentry. By 1839, large numbers of Prussian and Silesian Lutherans had arrived, fleeing persecution, and, by 1842, were settling in the

Barossa Valley. In 1841, the colony nearly went bankrupt, and the experiment might have ended had not rich copper deposits been discovered. From then on, South Australia grew rich on copper and the steamboat traffic on the Murray River, taking wheat and wool downstream and fortune-seekers upstream to the goldfields. South Australia held to its tradition of libertarianism. In 1894, women here became the first in the world to stand for Parliament and the second (after New Zealand) to be given the vote.

When you leave the state's southeast corner, the story changes, and South Australia quickly becomes one of the world's most inhospitable places—a scene of scrub, salt lakes, and arid mountain ranges. There are things to see here, though. The desert bursts into flower in spring, and the folded rock formations of the Flinders Ranges have interesting wildlife. The Ghan train runs across the desert from Adelaide to Darwin in the Northern Territory. Or you can drive there on the Stuart Highway, through the opal-mining town of Coober Pedy, which has such savage desert heat that some residents live underground. Adventurous travelers can explore the Oodnadatta, Strzelecki, and Birdsville Tracks. To the west, the Nullarbor Plain stretches into Western Australia (see pp. 243–248). ■

Adelaide

Adelaide, also known as the City of Churches, was planned as a utopia when Col. William Light surveyed it in 1836. He laid out a simple grid, surrounded by parklands, on a pretty site with a chain of "enchanted hills" on its western flank.

Adelaide

📷 251 C2

Visitor Information

✉ South Australian Visitor Information Centre, 108 North Terrace & Rundle Mall

☎ 08/8643-4694 or 1300-764-227

The charming setting caused some initial controversy. Gov. John Hindmarsh had ordered Light to establish the city near the mouth of the recently explored Murray River, which authorities hoped would open the Australian continent just as the Mississippi River was opening North America. Light arrived only a few months before the first settlers were due and had to make his selection quickly.

INSIDER TIP:

Be sure to take advantage of the expansive parklands surrounding central Adelaide, which give the city a "big-country-town" feel.

—LAURA RUYKYS
National Geographic field researcher

After examining the frequently silted mouth of the Murray and the treacherous coastline nearby, he decided to locate the new city about 60 miles (96 km) away, farther up the Gulf of St. Vincent on an inland plain. This action infuriated Hindmarsh and sparked bitter arguments. Nevertheless, Adelaide grew and prospered, while settlements along the exposed coastline were

troubled by numerous shipwrecks. In 1878, a railway spur linked Adelaide with the bustling inland river port of Morgan, resolving the issue. However, it was too late for Colonel Light, who had died a broken man in 1839. "The reasons that led me to fix Adelaide where it is I do not expect to be generally understood or calmly judged at present," he wrote shortly before his death. "I leave it to posterity to decide whether I am entitled to praise or blame."

Posterity has come down firmly in Light's favor. The grateful city has erected a bronze statue of him on **Montefiore Hill,** a grassy knoll in North Adelaide, just above pretty Adelaide Cricket Ground and an ideal place to get a feel for the city. From here you can see the breathing space of parklands that surround the inner city, the twin spires of magnificent St. Peter's Cathedral, the graceful **Torrens River,** and the clean lines of the city skyline. The view is known as Light's Vision.

You can easily find your way around Adelaide, which is laid out in a grid. At the center is the grassy **Victoria Square,** where you can catch the tram to the beach at Glenelg (see pp. 259–260).

The Torrens River flows past central Adelaide and its many parks and gardens.

Central Market

✉ Gouger St.

☎ 08/8203-7494

🕐 Closed Sun. & Mon.

The tram also continues through the city center then northwest to the Entertainment Centre in Hindmarsh. Tree-lined **North Terrace** is the cultural focus, with museums and fine colonial architecture. The main shopping precinct is along **Rundle Mall,** a sunny pedestrian way, bright with flower stalls and lively with street musicians and jugglers. **Hindley Street** is the town's nightlife district, seedy in its way but very tame compared with Sydney's Kings Cross. On Gouger Street is one of Adelaide's gastronomic icons, **Central Market,** a paradise of local fruits and vegetables, cheeses, seafood, and meats. Gouger Street also boasts the highest concentration of restaurants in Adelaide. **Rundle Street** is the artsy café district, lined with wine bars and bistros. This city is said to have more eateries per person than any other in Australia. O'Connell and Melbourne Streets in North Adelaide are also well-known café strips.

Adelaide's character is hard to pin down. The city has a long-standing reputation for being conservative and even has a coterie of old, moneyed families known as "the Establishment." On the other hand, its Mediterranean climate, good food, and fine wine give it a hedonistic ambience. This is perhaps Australia's most vivacious city. The calendar is full of festivals, and the two professional Australian Rules football teams are cheered by crowds whose throaty parochialism would make a football-crazed Nebraskan blush.

Adelaide Sights

On a map, downtown Adelaide resembles a lopsided hourglass set against a backdrop of green parklands. The larger portion is the commercial center, and the smaller section is North Adelaide, a leafy enclave set out by Colonel Light for the homes of the landed gentry. The elegant **Adelaide Bridge,** which spans the Torrens River, connects the two. This river, once just a seasonal trickle, has been dammed to form a long lake through this part of the city.

South of the Bridge: The best place to start exploring is south of the bridge, at the corner of King William Street and North Terrace. Virtually every major attraction is only a short stroll from here—the art gallery, festival center, South Australian Museum, Parliament House, Government House, casino, botanic gardens, and zoo. Most of them are on **North Terrace,** a grand tree-lined boulevard that showcases much of South Australia's solid colonial architecture.

Start on the west corner at the monumental **Parliament House,** with its massive marble Corinthian columns. Construction began in 1883 but took more than 50 years to complete because of a dispute about a dome (which was never built). The building is open to the public, and on days when Parliament is sitting, you can watch South Australia's representatives sort out state affairs. Beside it is the beautifully restored **Old Parliament House,** completed in 1855. Next door, farther west, is the grand old railroad station, built of honey-colored sandstone in 1929. Although its imposing neoclassic lines suggest great rail journeys, only suburban lines depart from here. The Indian Pacific (see sidebar p. 248), the Ghan (see pp. 282–283), and the Overlander (to Melbourne) all leave from the soulless Parklands

EXPERIENCE: Volunteering

Most volunteer programs in Australia relate to conservation projects and offer great opportunities to work in the outdoors monitoring wildlife, collecting rain forest samples, planting trees, and performing other activities. Willingness is more important than experience. Lodging and transportation are usually provided, but volunteers must pick up the tab, which can sometimes be expensive.

Conservation Volunteers (tel 03/5330-2600, conservationvolunteers .com.au) has projects such as tree planting, erosion and salinity control, seed collection, maintenance of walking tracks, and weed control throughout the country.

Day programs are free, and a small charge is made for overnight accommodations on longer projects.

Earthwatch (tel 03/9016-7590, earthwatch.org) has wildlife-monitoring expeditions to the Kimberley, Kangaroo Island, Ningaloo Reef, and other destinations, from 2 to 15 days (costing up to A$4,200).

Go Volunteer (tel 03/9820-4100, govolunteer.com.au) is a national volunteer recruiting body for community and other projects.

WWF Australia (tel 1800-032-551, wwf.org.au) also lists conservation projects for volunteers.

Adelaide Festival Centre
✉ King William Rd.
☎ 13-1246

South Australian Museum
✉ North Terrace
☎ 08/8207-7500

Art Gallery of South Australia
✉ North Terrace
☎ 08/8207-7000

Adelaide Botanic Gardens
✉ North Terrace
☎ 08/8222-9311
$ Free

(Keswick) Terminal at Mile End, just off Burbridge Road, west of the city.

The upper floors of the old railroad station were beautifully restored in the mid-1980s and turned into the elegant **Skycity Casino** *(open 24 hours).* Abutting the casino are the convention center and octagonal towers of the InterContinental Adelaide, one of the city's most luxurious hotels. Still farther west is the **Lion Arts Centre** *(Morphett St. at North Terrace),* a venue for the Adelaide Fringe Festival. The center is a bright and airy building with exhibition galleries, theaters, contemporary art galleries, and a cinema. The Jam Factory Craft and Design Centre behind the Lion Arts Centre has high-quality glassware, pottery, and woodwork for sale.

The **Adelaide Festival Centre** is tucked behind Parliament House and the casino, on the banks of the Torrens River. This boxy version of the Sydney Opera House has better acoustics.

EXPERIENCE:
Visiting Adelaide's Markets

If you are planning a picnic, or just enjoy the sight of wonderful produce, check out Adelaide's **Central Market** on Gouger Street. More than 250 stalls sell exotic fruits, sheep cheeses, German pastries, meats, fresh local produce, fish, and more. On Sundays from 9 a.m. to 4 p.m., the lively **Rundle Street Market** in the city's East End offers clothes, leather goods, jewelry, and crafts.

Built in 1977, the modernistic complex contains a 2,000-seat theater, smaller 600- and 350-seat theaters, and a 1,000-seat recital hall. Although the Adelaide Arts Festival runs only every other year, in February and March, the center itself is busy all year and is home to the South Australian Theatre Company, the experimental Space Theatre, and a small commercial art gallery. The sun-drenched plaza behind the complex, with its fountains and bright 1970-ish sculptures, is a popular place for office workers to bring a lunch. The manicured lawns that spill down to the riverbank are part of **Elder Park,** another popular picnic spot. There are brightly painted pedal-powered boats for rent along the bank, and a landing for the sightseeing boat *Popeye (tel 08/8223-5863),* an Adelaide institution since 1935. On Sunday mornings, bands play in the lacy, cast-iron Victorian-era rotunda.

If you head east on North Terrace from your original starting point *(corner of King William St. & North Terrace),* you'll come first to **Government House**—or rather an iron gate through which you can glimpse neoclassical stonework and ornamental gardens dating from 1836. The elegant mansion is the home of the governor of South Australia—the official representative of the British crown in the state—and is not open to the public. Nearby are the hallowed portals of the very exclusive **Adelaide Club**—the bastion of the city's old boy network.

The place next door, however, does welcome visitors: the **State**

Library *(tel 08/8207-7250, slsa.sa.gov.au)*, which houses a vast collection of books, maps, and historical material, as well as browsing sections well stocked with newspapers and free access to the Internet. It adjoins the **South Australian Museum,** where a dinosaur above the coat check greets you on arrival. The museum has the world's largest collection of Aboriginal artifacts as well as an impressive and extensive Melanesian collection.

Next door is the **Art Gallery of South Australia,** which houses one of the nation's largest collections of Australian art. Excellent free audio guides are available at the front desk. Or you can join one of the free guided tours that meet at the entrance at 11 a.m. and 2 p.m. daily.

Tucked behind the library is the **Migration Museum** *(82 Kintore Ave, tel 08/8207-7580),* a hidden gem with poignant displays about the lives of immigrants who came to South Australia. It is in the former Destitute Asylum, where homeless people of the last century were kept out of sight and out of mind. The grounds behind the museum are part of the University of Adelaide campus.

Continue along North Terrace (and across the street), and you'll come to **Ayers House** *(tel 08/8223-1234, closed Mon., $$),* which is said to be the finest example of Regency architecture in Australia. From 1855 to 1878, this 40-room bluestone mansion was the home of Henry Ayers, seven times premier of South Australia and the man for whom

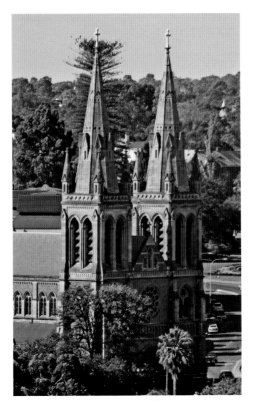

St. Peter's Cathedral's twin spires lord over Pennington Gardens in North Adelaide.

Ayers Rock (Uluru) was named. Entry is by National Trust tours, which run every half hour.

The **Adelaide Botanic Gardens** are on the eastern end of North Terrace. Established in 1855, these formal gardens have been expanded to include a palm house and the Bicentennial Conservatory, holding a modest-size rain forest. From the Botanic Gardens, you can continue to the **Adelaide Zoo**—a pleasant, if small, zoo—then return close to your starting point on the *Popeye,* along the Torrens River.

Adelaide Zoo
✉ Frome Rd.
☎ 08/8267-3255
💲 $$$$

Tandanya

✉ 253 Grenfell St.
☎ 08/8224-3200
💲 $

tandanya.com.au

On Grenfell Street, **Tandanya** is the arts center and gallery space for the National Aboriginal Cultural Institute, with rotating exhibitions, arts shop (with great didgeridoos), and performances at noon every day except Monday.

North Adelaide: Colonel Light laid out the enclave of North Adelaide as the residential part of his utopian city, a small district surrounded by leafy parklands and within an easy stroll of downtown (just across the Torrens River). Some of the city's most gracious mansions are here, as are rows of old bluestone cottages and some of the city's trendiest cafés and restaurants. The broad Adelaide Bridge is an open invitation to explore this part of the city.

The wide swath of manicured lawn to your left, after you cross the bridge, is **Pennington Gardens,** which also has walkways, ornamental trees, and flower beds. Looming above it are the twin spires of **St. Peter's Cathedral.** One of Australia's finest neo-Gothic buildings, the cathedral was built between 1869 and 1904 and has a powerful, but mellow, eight-bell carillon that is played on feast days. Up the hill, the road becomes **O'Connell Street,** the heart of North Adelaide's café scene. Alternatively, if you follow Sir Edwin Smith Avenue, to your right as you cross the bridge, you'll come to **Melbourne Street,** another cavalcade of restaurants, cafés, and bistros. Veer to the left in front of the cathedral and you'll reach the **Adelaide Cricket Ground,** regarded as one of the prettiest in the world. Saunter this way if a match is playing. In the main building, the small **Bradman Collection Museum** (closed Sat. & Sun.) displays memorabilia of Australia's greatest cricketer (see sidebar p. 91).

At the top of the hill behind the cricket ground is **Light's Vision** and the bronze statue of the city's founder. This is a great place to photograph the city, especially at dusk. Colonel Light hadn't yet created Utopia when he first gazed on the floodplain below, but he could at least see where to put it. ∎

Pie Floaters

For all the elegant and innovative dining in Adelaide, one of the things Adelaideans love most is a "pie floater." Australians everywhere love their meat pies, consuming more than 260 million of them each year. Pies are generally served in a paper bag with a squirt of tomato sauce (ketchup, to Americans) and a napkin to catch the gravy as it drips down your chin. South Australians have developed their own peculiar variation on the national dish. They float the meat pie in a bowl of pea soup, then add the tomato sauce (appetizingly called "dead horse"). You may not understand the appeal, but almost every South Australian swears a "pie floater" is food fit for gods. Pie carts all over the city once served this ambrosia, but one by one the carts disappeared. Some cafés still serve this classic, however, and it shouldn't be missed. Bon appétit.

Around Adelaide

Tucked between the sea and a range of hills, Adelaide offers plenty of options for a day out when the summer city begins to stifle. Take the tram for a half-hour ride to Glenelg, or drive up to the Mount Lofty hills for marvelous views and a fresh tang to the air.

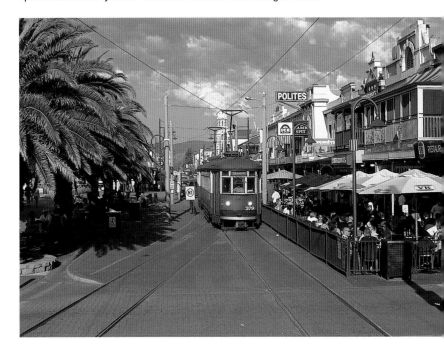

The old tram, beachside amusements, and rambling hotels give Glenelg the air of an English resort.

Glenelg & Beyond

For the quintessential Adelaide experience, take the restored 1929 tram from Victoria Square southwest to Glenelg, 6 miles (10 km) away. Fifty years ago this quaint old beach town was where Adelaide went on holiday, and even today it has the feel of an English seaside resort, despite rows of new apartment blocks.

South Australia's first settlers landed in Glenelg in 1836, and the gnarled gum tree where Gov. John Hindmarsh proclaimed it a new

colony still stands on McFarlane Street. A full-size reproduction of the settlers' ship, **H.M.S. *Buffalo,*** sits in the harbor, and on board is a popular seafood restaurant (*tel 08/8294-7000*).

Glenelg has a bustling atmosphere during the week, but on the weekends it really hums. This beach is Adelaide's most popular and most accessible. Rent umbrellas, deck chairs, boogie boards, in-line skates, and bicycles along the waterfront. Trendy cafés and bookshops cram Jetty Road.

Glenelg
🅰 251 C2
Visitor Information
✉ 12 Chappell Dr.
☎ 08/8294-5833

Adelaide Hills

251 C2

Visitor Information

✉ 41 Main St., Hahndorf

☎ 08/8388-1185

Glenelg is one of a chain of beaches along the coast—running to the north are **West Beach, Henley Beach,** and **Grange Beach; Brighton** lies to the south. All have an old-fashioned air.

Northwest of the city, **Port Adelaide,** once a working-class suburb around the old wharves, has undergone gentrification, many of its fine historic buildings now fashionable cafés, pubs, and museums. Most interesting is the **Maritime Museum** *(126 Lipson St., tel 08/8207-6255, $$),* or just spend a few hours wandering around this fascinating area.

You won't see much surf along here because these beaches are on the sheltered **Gulf of St. Vincent.** Older locals, though, can tell you about the wild storm of 1948 that virtually destroyed Glenelg's jetty. The water comes up from what Australians call the Southern Ocean, and it can be surprisingly brisk. Occasionally sharks are spotted near the beach. Use caution, but don't let *Jaws* dissuade you from taking a refreshing dip. None of the locals do. Far more dangerous and ubiquitous are the deadly ultraviolet rays of the sun, which here in South Australia regularly register as "extreme" or higher.

Adelaide Hills

A 20-minute drive east of the city on Glen Osmond Road and the Southeastern Freeway brings you to the Adelaide Hills. Called the "enchanted hills" by Colonel Light, they are leafy, green, and, on a hot day, as much as 15°F (8°C) cooler than Adelaide itself. As a consequence, they have been a retreat for Adelaide's gentility for more than a century, especially since the Southeastern Freeway has provided quick access to the city. Today, hill villages such as

Cleland Wildlife Park offers hands-on animal encounters within its 2,500-acre (1,000 ha) grounds.

EXPERIENCE: Spotting the Elusive Platypus

Of all the strange animals in Australia, none is more curious than the platypus. This semiaquatic, fur-covered mammal has a beak like a duck and a tail like a badger and lays eggs like a reptile. Males have poisonous spurs behind their webbed feet, the venom strong enough to kill a dog. When specimens first arrived in England, they were thought to be a hoax.

Platypuses inhabit rivers and streams on the east coast and throughout the Tasmanian wilderness. These mostly solitary, nocturnal animals dig burrows in riverbanks and dive to the bottom for small animals and insects, such as worms, crustaceans, and larvae.

Very few Australians have seen the shy platypus in its natural habitat. The best chance is with a guide. **Warrawong Wildlife Sanctuary** (Stock Road, Mylor, tel 08/8370-9197, warrawong.com), in the Adelaide Hills, has a breeding program where platypuses live around a lake. Call ahead to check tour times.

Eungella National Park, which is located 50 miles (80 km) west of Mackay in Queensland, is well known for platypus sightings on the Broken River. Patience and quiet are required. Dawn and dusk are the best times. **Reeforest Adventure Tours** (tel 07/4959-8360) runs eco-tours from Mackay.

Stirling feel like genteel suburbs or hobby farm country.

For visitors, the Adelaide Hills offer beautiful hiking trails and conservation parks, wineries, historic villages, and numerous festivals. Consult the helpful visitor center in Hahndorf, just off the freeway about 20 miles (32 km) southeast of the city. Pick up a copy of the *Adelaide Hills Classic Country Drive* brochure for suggestions of great day trips.

Part of the **Mount Lofty Ranges,** the Adelaide Hills are dominated by the 2,362-foot (720 m) summit of Mount Lofty. (It's the tall one with the television antennas on it.) The Mount Lofty Ranges are believed to have originally been part of the Trans-Antarctic Mountains, which existed millions of years ago before the continents broke up and drifted apart. Mount Lofty's summit is easily accessible by car and gives sweeping views over the city, the coast, and the country inland. Take the Summit Road exit off the freeway, just before the town of Crafers (about 10 miles/16 km out of Adelaide), and follow it north for about 2 miles (3 km). On the right shortly after you leave the freeway, you'll pass the beautiful **Mount Lofty Botanic Gardens** (Summit Rd., tel 08/8370-8370). The summit of Mount Lofty has a restaurant (tel 08/8339-2600) and tourist office and gift shop (tel 08/8370-1054).

Two hundred yards farther along the road, on your left, is the **Cleland Wildlife Park** (tel 08/8339-2444, $$$), a conservation park where you can cuddle a koala, hand-feed kangaroos and wallabies, or take a guided nighttime tour to see some of Australia's shy nocturnal wildlife.

Ten miles (16 km) farther east along the freeway is **Hahndorf,** the oldest German settlement in South Australia and one of the

The Cedars
✉ Heysen Rd.,
   Hahndorf
☎ 08/8388-7277
🕐 Closed Mon.

Capri Theatre
✉ 141 Goodwood
   Rd., Goodwood
☎ 08/8272-1177

capri.org.au

main attractions in the Adelaide Hills. Prussian and Silesian immigrants settled here in 1839, having come to Australia to escape religious persecution in their homelands. Today the village plays up its colorful German heritage, perhaps a little too enthusiastically for some tastes; it borders on the kitsch. It is a lively place, with German bakeries, tearooms, galleries, and craft shops. One of the town's most famous residents was the noted early 20th-century landscape painter Hans Heysen, who lived and worked in an elegant home called **The Cedars,** still owned by his descendants. About 300 of Heysen's paintings are on display in the house, located about 1.5 miles (2 km) north of town.

INSIDER TIP:

Step back in time and see a classic movie at the beautifully restored art deco Capri Theatre [capri.org.au] in the southern Adelaide suburb of Goodwood.

—ROFF SMITH
National Geographic author

In the center of town, the 1857 **Hahndorf Academy** (68 Main St., tel 08/8388-7250, hahndorfacademy .org.au) is an arts and crafts gallery with an interesting German migration museum and gallery of Heysen's drawings.

Rich with vineyards, the region has a long history of wine production (see pp. 263, 266–267).

Hiking: The area has excellent hiking, from afternoon strolls through the bush to extended treks of a week or more in the Mount Lofty Ranges. One of Australia's finest and longest trails, the 715-mile-long (1,144 km) **Heysen Trail,** named after Hans Heysen, winds through the Adelaide Hills on its way north from the tip of the Fleurieu Peninsula to the heart of the Flinders Ranges, across some of South Australia's finest countryside. Most hikers do just short sections as a day trip, but a few hardy souls have done the entire length. Maps of the trail are available in many of Adelaide's camping shops (which are concentrated on Rundle Street). Huts and campsites are regularly spaced along the route, and the Youth Hostel Association (135 Waymouth St., Adelaide, tel 08/8414-3010) has a small hostel at Mount Lofty that groups can rent. The Heysen Trail is closed in summer because of potential bushfires.

Going Farther: The Adelaide Hills are a gateway north to the vineyards of the **Barossa Valley** (see pp. 267–268). To reach them, take the Onkaparinga Road exit from the freeway near Bridgewater, about 12 miles (19 km) out of Adelaide, and go north for about 30 miles (48 km) through the villages of Oakbank, Woodside, Birdwood, and Springton.

Or, to reach the **Fleurieu Peninsula** to the south, take the

Vineyards in the McLaren Vale weave a gentle pattern in the foothills of the Mount Lofty Ranges.

Mount Barker–Strathalbyn Road south from Stirling through the stunning hills and farmland of the Adelaide Hills to Macclesfield and Strathalbyn. From there it is an easy drive along the Goolwa Road to the pretty seaside towns of **Goolwa** and **Victor Harbor** (see pp. 274–276).

Wine Districts

The Barossa Valley (see pp. 267–268) is the state's most important wine district. However, the Southern Vales, Coonawarra, the Clare Valley, and other regions are challenging its status, and new vineyards are being planted along the Murray River Valley, in the Adelaide Hills, and near Port Lincoln on the Eyre Peninsula.

The **Southern Vales,** on the Fleurieu Peninsula about 25 miles (40 km) south of Adelaide, is the state's oldest wine district. The first winery here started in 1838, and now more than 60 wineries

are in the area, which has gained a following for rich Shirazes and Cabernet Sauvignons. Chapel Hill, Hardy's Reynella, Haslegrove, and Wirra Wirra are some of the better known labels. Most of the wineries are small, family concerns. The best time to visit is during the Sea & Vines Festival in June. There are tastings, feasts, and tours; special buses go around the wineries so visitors can drink and not worry about driving. The ideal base is the pretty little village of **McLaren Vale,** a rather trendy spot that has plenty of B&Bs, galleries, and craft shops. To get to the Southern Vales, follow Main South Road out of Adelaide to Old Noarlunga and from there follow the Victor Harbor Road another 3 miles (5 km) to the turnoff for McLaren Vale.

The **Adelaide Hills** (see pp. 260–262) also have a long history of winemaking and

(continued on p. 266)

Wine District Visitor Information Centers:

Southern Vales
- ✉ Main Rd., McLaren Vale
- ☎ 08/8323-8999

Adelaide Hills
- ⓜ 251 C2
- ✉ 41 Main St., Hahndorf
- ☎ 08/8388-1185

Coonawarra
- ⓜ 251 D1
- ✉ 27 Arthur St., Penola
- ☎ 08/8737-2855

Clare Valley
- ⓜ 251 C3
- ✉ Main North Rd. & Spring Gully Rd., Clare
- ☎ 08/8842-2131

Renmark
- ⓜ 251 D2
- ✉ 84 Murray Ave.
- ☎ 1300-661-704

Australian Wines

Since the 1980s, Australia has emerged as one of the world's great winemaking nations, globally lauded for its use of innovative techniques to produce bold, fruity, and affordable wines. Connoisseurs around the world recognize regional Australian names such as Barossa Valley, Coonawarra, Margaret River, Clare Valley, and Hunter Valley. Australian labels have consistently pulled down some of the world's most prestigious awards.

Brother John May tests the wine casks at the Seven Hills Winery in the Clare Valley.

Penfolds 1990 Grange Hermitage—Australia's premier red—was judged by the influential *Wine Spectator* magazine to be the international Wine of the Year when it was released in 1995. In 1999, the magazine rated the '55 Grange among the 12 finest wines of the 20th century, ranking it with such luminaries as the '21 Château d'Yquem and the Château Mouton-Rothschild '45. Although this success seemed to come suddenly, it was not a case of Aussie nouveau. Australian wines were winning international awards as long ago as the 1870s, and Victoria's Yerinberg winery took a gold medal at the Paris Exposition of 1889.

Viticulture in Australia dates back to 1788, when the First Fleet brought vine clippings from South Africa. By the 1830s, the Hunter Valley in New South Wales was producing wine, thanks largely to the efforts of a Scot, James Busby, who had studied viticulture in France and imported hundreds of clippings from France and Spain. Prussian and Silesian immigrants began growing wine grapes in South Australia's Barossa Valley in the 1840s, almost as soon as they arrived. Victoria's wine industry was kick-started in the 1850s with 10,000 clippings from Bordeaux's Château Lafite-Rothschild.

These bold beginnings were put on hold, however, in part by the outbreak of phylloxera that ravaged much of the world's vineyards in the late 19th century, and in part by fashion. Tastes moved on to fortified wines and away from table wine. It wasn't until the 1960s that Australians began making table wine in quantity again. (Australia's total 1959 crush for Cabernet Sauvignon was 69 tons/62 tonnes, compared with 315,000 tons/286,000 tonnes in 2010.)

Australian Winemaking Today

Today, Australia is the world's fourth largest exporter of wine, after France, Italy, and Spain, with thousands of wineries, producing more than 290 million gallons (1.1 billion liters) of wine every year, two-thirds of it for export.

Grapes are grown in every state—there is even a vineyard near Alice Springs. Boutique areas such as Margaret River (located in Western Australia) and the Yarra Valley (in Victoria) are on the cutting edge of fashion, but the lion's share of premium quality wine comes from South Australia. The Barossa and Clare Valleys, the McLaren Vale, and the Coonawarra region are the best known wine districts in the nation.

One of the main reasons for Australia's success is the willingness on the part of its winemakers to use the latest technologies to blend whatever regional varieties of grapes they need to produce bold fruity flavors. The result of these so-called New World techniques is a clean-tasting wine that evokes Australia's bright sunshine and costs far less than a European

INSIDER TIP:

Penfolds's Barossa winery goes beyond the usual wine tastings. You can don a lab coat, blend your own wine, and take home a bottle of your creation. [See sidebar below.]

—JEANINE BARONE
National Geographic writer

vintage of comparable quality. Old-world wine-makers, on the other hand, have been bound by centuries-old traditions and prevented by law from taking such radical steps. But times are changing. These days Australian winemakers are in big demand in Europe, where they are help-ing some of the world's most famous houses develop their art into a science. In what would have seemed sacrilege only a few years ago, some European houses are now offering wines made "in the Australian style."

Penfolds Grange may be Australia's greatest red wine, but with a price tag of more than A$400 a bottle for the recent vintages (and into the thousands of dollars for some of the earlier ones), it is a little rich for most occa-sions. Even this outstanding red faces serious competition from other great Australian labels such as Henschke. The competition for best white wine is an open field, with runners from around the country.

EXPERIENCE: Educate Your Palate

Penfolds, one of the country's great wineries, offers a unique wine experience at its Barossa Valley cellar *(Tanunda Road, Nuriootpa, tel 08/8568-9408)*. In the winemakers' laboratory, guests can blend their own wines—from Grenache, Shiraz, and Mourvedre grapes—then bottle it to take home. Make Your Own Blend runs daily at 10 a.m. and 2 p.m.; reservations are essential. Educate Your Palate is a series of wine education courses, lasting from two hours to two weeks, with tastings of local and world wines, at the **National Wine Centre of Australia** *(Botanic Rd., Adelaide, tel 08/8222-9277, winesa.asn.au)*, an impressive complex near the city's Botanic Gardens with wine-barrel-inspired architecture.

Around Coonawarra

Located 25 miles (40 km) north of Coonawarra, **Naracoorte Caves Park**—which was featured in David Attenborough's acclaimed BBC television series *Life on Earth*—has a huge population of bats. It is also a UNESCO World Heritage site, where an astounding collection of Pleistocene fossils has been discovered, including extinct marsupials like a giant kangaroo and a rhinoceros-size wombat.

Six miles (10 km) south of Coonawarra is the village of **Penola,** where Mother Mary MacKillop, a 19th-century Catholic nun, did much of her early work on behalf of the poor and disadvantaged. Her works and the subsequent reports of miracles prompted the Roman Catholic church to beatify her in 1995—before she was canonized in 2010 to become Australia's first saint.

VISITING WINERIES: The Barossa Visitor Information Centre (see p. 267) and the South Australian Visitor Information Centre in Adelaide (see p. 252) can advise on tours and visits.

claim Australia's first known wine export—an 1845 hock from Echunga sent to England for Queen Victoria. These days, 33 wineries are in the hills, which are becoming known for their Chardonnay. Petaluma and Karl Seppelts Grand Cru Estate are two prominent local labels.

Coonawarra, about 250 miles (400 km) southeast of Adelaide, produces excellent reds. More than 20 wineries cram into this narrow region (12 miles/20 km long and a little more than a mile/2 km wide). Demand for Coonawarra's fabled *terra rossa* soil has pushed prices for land to absurd levels. Most of Australia's great Cabernet Sauvignons spring from this soil.

The **Clare Valley,** about 80 miles (128 km) north of Adelaide on Main North Road, has a lovely European feel to it and a lot less tourist hype than other districts. It was settled in the 1850s and named Clare by homesick Irish because its gentle landscape reminded them of County Clare. Winemaking in the valley began with Jesuit brothers, who grew grapes to make their own

communion wine. They named their monastery Seven Hills after the seven hills around Rome. Today, the Seven Hills winery, 6 miles (10 km) south of Clare, is still run by Jesuits, who continue their tradition of making sacramental wine but have diversified into table wines, port, and sherry. Tours of the winery and old stone cellars are available by appointment.

Seven Hills is one of 41 wineries in the region. They range from the small but highly regarded Grosset Wines, which is run out of an old butter factory in Auburn, to the giant, century-old Leasingham Wines near the town of Clare. The region is ideal for bicycling, with a number of bike trails, including the excellent 20-mile (30 km) Riesling Trail through the vineyards.

The **Murray River Valley** has long produced table grapes and cheap cask wine, but a growing number of big-name wineries are planting vines here. The Kingston Estate winery, 140 miles (225 km) northeast of Adelaide, near Barmera, is the pick of the region. Boston Bay Wineries and Delacolline Estate are the two major winemakers in Port Lincoln.

The sea view from the Boston Bay vineyard is stunning.

Barossa Valley

The Barossa Valley is South Australia's premier wine area, producing almost one-fifth of the nation's wine and accounting for about 70 percent of its wine exports. It is home to some of Australia's most respected labels, such as Penfolds, Henschke, Peter Lehman, Orlando (Jacob's Creek), Wolf Blass, Yalumba, and Seppelts—the only winery in the world with an unbroken line of vintage ports dating back to 1878. The district also produces

cost of their passage. It was the first time in Australia's history that immigrants from somewhere other than England had been actively sought. In addition to their doughty work ethic, language, and culture, the newcomers brought their winemaking skills. Within a year, they had planted grapevines along Jacob's Creek, and by 1850, the valley had begun its long tradition of winemaking. The Barossa Valley's isolation protected it from the outbreak of phylloxera in the 1870s that ravaged the rest of the world's grapevines. As a result, some of the world's oldest Shiraz vines can be found here today.

Barossa Valley

⚟ 251 D2

Visitor Information

✉ Barossa Visitor Information Centre, 68 Murray St., Tanunda

☎ 08/8563-0600

EXPERIENCE: Taking on Seasonal Work

Good for one year, Working Holiday visas enable young (18–30) travelers from Canada, the U.K., and the U.S. to undertake popular seasonal work (check *immi.gov.au* for details).

Hotels and restaurants, particularly in tourist areas, employ many overseas visitors during the high season. Picking fruit during harvest season is an easy way to help finance travels. Grape-picking work in wine areas such as the Hunter Valley, Barossa Valley, and Mildura is hot but plentiful in February and March. Peaches,

then apples, follow in the southern states, while mangoes (around Christmas in Atherton) and bananas are Queensland specialties. Prawn boats and fishing trawlers operate out of Cairns over the winter (May–Aug.). The ski resorts in the Australian Alps also have seasonal work over winter.

Websites with good information include: **Harvest Trail** (*jobsearch.gov.au/harvesttrail*), detailing harvest locations and times, and **Workabout Australia** (*workaboutaustralia.com.au*).

---

smoked meats, cheeses, and pickles that reflect its distinctive German heritage.

The valley was settled in 1842 by Prussian and Silesian Lutherans who were seeking religious freedom. They were persuaded to come to Australia by George Fife Angas, a wealthy and philanthropic South Australian landowner who underwrote the

There is still a strong German feel to the valley. Old stone Lutheran churches dot the countryside, and the villages have German bakeries and butcher shops where goods are made according to family recipes. Old German names fill the phone books, and until recently some of the valley's older residents spoke an Australianized form of German

**Barossa Valley
Cheese Company**

✉ 67b Murray St.,
Angaston

☎ 08/8564-3636

barossacheese
.com.au

Kangaroo Island

🗺 251 C2

Visitor Information

✉ Gateway Visitor
Information
Centre, Howard
Dr., Penneshaw

☎ 08/8553-1185

known as Barossa-Deutsche.

The Barossa Valley is an easy 45-mile (72 km) drive north of Adelaide on Main North Road, with ample signs to the valley's main towns of Tanunda, Nuriootpa, and Angaston.

Of the three towns, centrally located **Tanunda** is the one most geared to tourists, with a pleasant

INSIDER TIP:

Cheese lovers should follow the Barossa Valley cheese and wine trail. Start at the Barossa Valley Cheese Company in Angaston and pick up a trail map.

—JEANINE BARONE
National Geographic writer

main street and a wide selection of craft galleries, cafés, and B&Bs. **Nuriootpa** is the valley's commercial hub. The small and quiet village of **Angaston,** to the east, is perhaps the prettiest. It was founded by George Fife Angas in the 1830s. His magnificent estate, Lindsey Park, is now one of Australia's top racing stables. It is not open to visitors, but you can stay at his son's mansion, **Collingrove** *(6 miles/10 km via the road to Eden Valley southeast of Angaston),* now owned by the National Trust.

Most of the 60 cellars open to the public offer free tastings—although if you want to sample the priciest vintages and labels, you'll have to take out your wallet. Some, including **Seppelts** and

Château Yaldara, are open for tours. Seppelts is one of the best, and the drive from Nuriootpa is exceptionally scenic. The route runs along a 2-mile (3 km) avenue of ornamental date palms, with a Doric temple on the hillside (the temple is the Seppelt family mausoleum). A variety of tours is available to the wineries (you can travel by minivan, luxury Daimler, or restored 1935 Auburn convertible, among other vehicles), so everyone can partake in the tastings without violating Australia's strict drunk-driving laws.

Food is also a big attraction, the most popular place being **Maggie Beer's Farm Shop** *(Pheasant Farm Rd., Nuriootpa, tel 08/8562-4477).* This celebrity chef's gourmet outlet has local produce, food and wine tastings, and 2 p.m. cooking demonstrations.

The Barossa Vintage Festival—held over Easter week in odd-numbered years—draws thousands of visitors to the valley for a week of parades and shows. It is just one of the many festivals held here.

Kangaroo Island

If Australia has been an ark for unique flora and fauna, Kangaroo Island (or K.I.) has been its lifeboat. This surprisingly large island, barely 10 miles (16 km) off the coast of South Australia, has remained an unspoiled haven for wildlife and offers a lazy, rural lifestyle only recently invaded by luxury retreats. The roads are mostly dirt, and drivers must be careful not to dent their fenders on the high stone curbs in the villages. There are wallabies, kangaroos, koalas, platypuses, and echidnas on land, and the sea has seals, dolphins, sea lions, penguins, whales, and sharks; both host teeming birdlife.

The island has 24 national parks or conservation areas, covering about a third of its total area. The largest and best known is **Flinders Chase National Park,** which covers the western end of Kangaroo Island. The rest of the island has well-watered forests and rolling farmland, with a good reputation for such produce as sheep's milk cheeses, free-range chickens, freshwater crayfish, rock lobster, and King George whiting. Increasingly known for its honey, the island has the world's last pure strain of gentle Ligurian honeybees—brought here from Italy in the 1860s.

Australia's third largest island after Tasmania and the Northern Territory's Melville Island, Kangaroo Island is about 90 miles (155 km) long and up to 30 miles (55 km) wide. It is sparsely populated, with only 4,400 inhabitants. The dramatic cliff-lined coasts and rocky shoals have claimed more than 40 ships since English navigator Matthew Flinders set eyes on the uninhabited island in 1802. Although Aboriginal artifacts dating back 30,000 years have been found here, archaeological evidence suggests the Aborigines left around 7,000 years ago. No one knows why.

Kangaroo Island was settled in 1806 by an assortment of escaped convicts and deserters from Yankee whaling ships. They camped near present-day American River, built a 34-ton (31 tonne) schooner out of local materials, and set

FLYING TO KANGAROO ISLAND FROM ADELAIDE: Regional Express (Rex) 13-1713

CAR RENTAL: Rental companies do not usually permit their cars to be taken to Kangaroo Island from the mainland. Car rental companies such as Budget and Hertz are located in Kingscote.

Stokes Bay, on the northern coast of Kangaroo Island, is one of scores of secluded nooks and bays.

about the wholesale slaughter of the seal population. They also raided Aboriginal camps on the mainland coast. By 1827, the island had acquired such an evil reputation that the colonial authorities sent in a military expedition and dragged almost the entire population away in chains.

An official attempt was made in 1836 to set up South Australia's first colony on the island (at Kingscote), but attention switched to Adelaide instead. Throughout much of the next century, Kangaroo Island remained undeveloped. To remedy that, authorities gave free land to returned veterans from World War I and World War II.

Getting to the island is simple. You can fly daily to Kingscote from Adelaide Airport (see panel information p. 269), but most visitors go by ferry. Kangaroo Island Sealink operates two vehicular ferries from Cape Jervis, about an hour south of Adelaide at the tip of the

Kangaroo Island's Koalas

You are more likely to see a koala in the wild on Kangaroo Island than anywhere else. The koala population here has been estimated as high as 30,000—far outstripping the number of human residents on the island. The fact that the island has so many of these cuddly-looking marsupials is both a tribute to its qualities and a cautionary tale about well-meaning conservation.

Koalas are not native to the island. They were brought here in 1923, when it was obvious the species was in trouble. On the mainland, rapidly growing suburbs were gobbling up their habitat, and in Queensland they were being hunted as pests. More than three million koalas were killed after World War I, before they were finally protected in 1927. The seagirt wildlife stronghold of Kangaroo Island seemed a perfect place to relocate a few, and a group of 18 was released in Flinders Chase National Park.

The island was perfect for koalas because it had no diseases, no predators such as dingoes, and a seemingly unlimited supply of manna gums—one of their favorite foods. By 1996, however, the koala population had grown out of control, stripping the stately century-old gum trees along the rivers and creating a potential environmental nightmare. The suggestion that 2,000 or so koalas would have to be shot provoked an international uproar. Letting them denude the forests until they starved seemed little better.

Relocation was not an easy option. Koalas are exceptionally finicky eaters. Their delicate stomachs can digest the leaves of only about a dozen of the 600-plus species of eucalyptuses. Those grow on well-watered soils along the coast—prime real estate for humans. Any small fragments of koala habitat that were left on the mainland were already fully populated by koalas. So it was decided to use fertility controls to keep the population in check. Some koalas were relocated to suitable homes. Despite these efforts, the number of koalas continues to rise.

One of the best places to see koalas is in Flinders Chase National Park. Or you can visit the Cygnet River on the eastern half of the island. They can be a little difficult to spot, nestled in the forks of gum trees, because their gray coats meld perfectly with the color of the bark. Look for an irregular bump when you run your eyes over a likely gum, and slowly a koala will appear.

Fleurieu Peninsula. The crossing takes 45 minutes and delivers you to Penneshaw. A bus service goes to Cape Jervis from Adelaide's hotels *(reservations necessary, call Sealink, tel 13-1301).*

Kangaroo Island's popularity has transformed the local tourism industry, with options for visitors now ranging from good old-fashioned camping to exclusive luxury villas such as **Stone House** and the stunning **Southern Ocean Lodge** *(Hanson Bay, tel 02/9918-4355, southernoceanlodge .com.au),* with prices to match the lodge's soaring cliff-top location.

Kangaroo's Wildlife & Parks:

The main reason people come to Kangaroo Island is to see wildlife and the island's national and conservation parks, for which you need a pass (see column information). One of the best ways to catch a glimpse of the often elusive native fauna is to go on a wildlife safari. One of the most personal is **Exceptional Kangaroo Island** *(tel 08/8553-9119, exceptional kangarooisland.com),* a small firm owned and operated by expert local naturalists.

If you prefer to scout around independently, head first for **Cape Gantheaume Conservation Park** and the nearby **Seal Bay Conservation Park** to see sea lions—both about 30 miles (48 km) from Kingscote, Kangaroo Island's commercial center.

Farther to the west along the south coast are the pretty beaches at **Vivonne Bay,** the pure white dunes known as **Little Sahara,**

A koala perches in the fork of a gum tree at Flinders Chase.

and **Kelly Hill Conservation Park,** which has dunes and scrub underlaid by limestone caves *(tour bookings, tel 08/8553-4464).* The caves were discovered in the 1880s by a stockman named Kelsey and his horse Kelly, which tumbled into them through a sinkhole. The National Parks and Wildlife Service runs caving tours.

Flinders Chase National Park, in the west, has a dramatic rocky coastline, picturesque old lighthouses, and eucalyptus forests filled with wildlife. The park headquarters is at Rocky River Homestead. On the northwestern *(continued on p. 274)*

(continued on p. 274)

Festival State

South Australia's nickname is the Festival State. On its calendar are more than 400 festivals, carnivals, and sporting events, ranging from the throaty high-octane roar of V-8 motor racing to the Festival of Ideas, from the Tour Down Under—the most prestigious cycling event in the Southern Hemisphere—to the Bohemian funkiness of the Fringe Festival.

Performers pose at WOMADelaide.

Depending on when you visit South Australia, you might take in events as varied as the **Barossa Valley Vintage Festival** (Easter in odd-numbered years), the **Australian Camel Cup** race in the outback town of Maree (July), and the **Schutzenfest** (January, with oompah bands). Oakbank's **Easter Racing Carnival** is Australia's greatest picnic-day horse race, and the **Bay to Birdwood Run** antique automobile rally attracts more than 2,000 entries from Australia and around the world.

The most famous event is the **Adelaide Festival.** For glamour, excitement, and size, it easily surpasses anything else of the sort in Australia. Held over three weeks in March in even-numbered years, it attracts major artists from Australia and around the world. The festival began modestly in 1960 with 51 shows, but has burgeoned into a feast of more than 300 plays, concerts, films, dance performances,

INSIDER TIP:

Whether it's food, wine, music, arts, architecture, cycling, motoring, or writing that gives you a buzz, there's an associated festival for it in South Australia.

—LAURA RUYKYS
National Geographic field researcher

and cabaret acts. Ticket prices are quite reasonable, and for those on a tight budget, there are free weekend concerts and fireworks displays on the banks of the Torrens River. The weather in Adelaide in March is generally perfect, with hot days and warm starry nights that make outdoor performances a treat.

Coinciding with the Adelaide Festival is the even more exuberant and sometimes very strange **Fringe Festival.** Originally staged by street artists as a protest to the perceived elitism of the arts festival, the Fringe Festival is now a power in its own right, an annual event drawing thousands of visitors to the city for a month of experimental theater, jugglers, comedians, offbeat entertainers, and film festivals. If the main festival gives Adelaide a taste of Manhattan, the Fringe Festival is more like New Orleans. Walk the café-lined streets on these summer evenings and you're likely to see anything. While all this is going on, Adelaide also hosts **Writers' Week,** during which well-known authors from Australia and overseas gather to discuss their works, launch books, and give readings. This event is free.

The annual World of Music, Arts, and Dance Festival in Adelaide—**WOMADelaide**—is also a big draw, attracting acts from around the world. The **Adelaide Cabaret Festival,** held every June, has an extensive program of music and cabaret acts. The Barossa Valley also hosts **Barossa Under the Stars,** at which international stars perform in an open-air concert near one of the big wineries. This annual festival usually takes place in late February or March. The **Country Music Festival** is celebrated each June in the town of Barmera (140 miles/ 225 km northeast of Adelaide).

Gourmet festivals are another tradition in South Australia. Every August, the Barossa Valley has a **Barossa Gourmet** weekend: Visitors travel around the wineries sampling wines with dishes created by some of South Australia's best restaurateurs. The South Australian Visitor Information Centre (see p. 252) has information about these and other festivals, or check *southaustralia.com.*

EXPERIENCE: Festival Fever

Adelaide is abuzz from around mid-February to mid-March every year, when the **Adelaide Fringe Festival** *(adelaide fringe.com.au)* attracts nearly a million spectators to its performances. Featuring local and lesser known artists, the festival was born in 1960 as an alternative to the prestigious Adelaide Festival (formerly called the Adelaide Festival of the Arts).

The **Adelaide Festival** *(adelaidefestival .com.au)* has been held every other year since 1960, an era when the pubs closed at 6 p.m. and censorship of the arts was rife. Queen Elizabeth was a festival patron back then, and Dave Brubeck's jazz wowed audiences.

By the 1970s, South Australia was the most progressive state in the country, with a reform government keen to back the arts. The Adelaide Festival Centre was built, and the festivals went on to become the country's premier arts events.

Programs for both festivals are released around October. Many events are free, or you can buy tickets through Ticketek *(ticketek.com.au).*

corner of the island, about 65 miles (105 km) west of Kingscote on the island's main highway, is the square **Cape Borda Lighthouse,** built in 1858. The wild southwestern corner has the elegant **Cape de Couedic Lighthouse,** built along a line of sheer cliffs in 1906, where you can stay.

shipping, and the fickle Murray River had a habit of silting up at the mouth. Visions of an antipodean New Orleans faded completely in 1878, when a rail spur linked the river town of Morgan, 150 miles (240 km) upstream, with the deepwater harbor at Port Adelaide. The beachside villages

The Victor Harbor coastline viewed from Rosetta Head

Victor Harbor

🏛 251 C2

Visitor Information

✉ The Causeway

☎ 08/8551-0777

Victor Harbor & Goolwa

The 1870s were the glory days of the Murray River, when steamboat traffic was at its height and civic boosters hoped that settlements such as Victor Harbor and Port Elliott, near the river mouth, might rival New Orleans. Wool and grain from as far afield as Queensland floated down the river to these ports, where clipper ships whisked them off to market in London.

Unfortunately, the exposed coastline was treacherous to

found their métier instead as vacation resorts. A century later, these classic beach towns, about 60 miles (100 km) south of Adelaide, are still the getaway of choice among South Australians.

Victor Harbor: The biggest town on the Fleurieu Peninsula, this is a weekend destination for thousands of Adelaideans. Although Victor Harbor is only 50 miles (80 km) south of the city, it is generally about 10°F (5°C) cooler. The drive from

Adelaide, along Main South Road and Victor Harbor Road, takes you through the **McLaren Vale** wine country (see p. 263).

Victor Harbor sits on pretty **Encounter Bay,** where, in 1802, English navigator Matthew Flinders met his French counterpart Nicholas Baudin while both were exploring the South Australian coast. The town was founded in 1837 as a whaling station, and today the **South Australian Whale Centre** (Railway Terrace, tel 08/8551-0750, $) is the place to learn about southern right whales (an endangered species) and whaling. Better still, come to Victor Harbor between June and October and see these magnificent leviathans. No longer hunted, they come into Encounter Bay on their annual migration and can be observed from the bluffs overlooking the bay. A large colony of fairy penguins lives on nearby Granite Island. Walk out there along the causeway—a pleasant stroll—or take one of the trams pulled by Clydesdale horses.

Goolwa: With its beaches and rich beds of cockles, Goolwa became popular with homesick English migrants, who came down to gather cockles—just as they did on summer holidays back in the old country. The train bringing visitors came to be called the Cockle Train in the official railroad timetable. A restored version of the old steam-powered train still runs between Goolwa and Victor Harbor on Wednesdays, Sundays, and school holidays.

The town has a strong nautical feel. The figurehead from the wreck of the *Mozambique* is in the **Goolwa Hotel** (30 Cadell St.) dining room, and restored 19th-century steamboats do tours of the lower lengths of the Murray River. The **Goolwa Museum** (11–13 Porter St., tel 08/8555-2221) covers Murray River ecology, 19th-century river trade, and the history of the Ngarrindjeri Aborigines, who have gathered cockles on these beaches for more than 10,000 years. Spirit of the Coorong Cruises (tel 08/8555-2203) runs Murray River tours leaving from the wharf near the massive bridge to Hindmarsh Island. Built in 2001 to service a marina real estate development on the island, the bridge sparked a national political battle after Ngarrindjeri women

INSIDER TIP:

Visit Coorong National Park, two hours southeast of Adelaide, for hiking, fishing, bird-watching, and wetland boat tours.

—MCKENZIE FUNK
National Geographic writer

objected to its construction, saying it violated sacred sites. The bridge was pushed through despite widespread opposition.

Goolwa is a good base for exploring the haunting sliver of sand dunes and coastal lagoons known as the **Coorong,** which

Goolwa

▲ 251 C2

Visitor Information

✉ Cadell St. & Cutting Rd.

☎ 08/8555-3810

Coorong National Park

Visitor Information

✉ Coorong, SA 5264

☎ 08/8575-1200

Mannum

Visitor Information

✉ 6 Randell St.

☎ 08/8569-1303

extends 100 miles (160 km) along South Australia's southeast coast. Home to more than 240 species of birds, it was the setting of the 1976 film *Storm Boy*, about an Aborigine who befriends a pelican.

Lower Murray River

The Murray River is the longest and grandest river on the continent, and it is the only one that is navigable. It stretches 1,170 miles (1,883 km) from the Victorian high country to South Australia's windswept coastline. South Australia gets only the bottom 400 miles (640 km) of the river, but it gets the best scenery. The river here winds through sandstone gorges, past lagoons teeming with birdlife, and along riverbanks lined with stately Murray River gums.

By Mississippi or Amazon standards, the Murray is a trickle—barely a couple hundred yards wide. But on a continent as dry and dusty as Australia, it is life itself, accounting for more than half of the nation's fruits, vegetables, wine, meats, grains, cotton, and wool. In fact, the

quirky tasting drinking water for most of South Australia comes from the river. The river has also become the source of much debate in recent years, its waters severely depleted through over-irrigation and prolonged drought that threatens rural livelihoods and unique ecosystems alike.

The story of the Murray's steamboats began in South Australia. In 1853, a flour miller named William Randell put a crude steamboat, the *Mary Ann*, on the water near the river town of Mannum. Randell had never seen a steamboat before, but he could grasp the potential profit in being able to get his flour close to the Victorian goldfields, several hundred miles upstream. The *Mary Ann*'s makeshift boiler swelled like a football once pressure built up, causing the ship's engineer to run in terror. But these were robust times, and Randell simply bound the dodgy boiler with chain and kept on steaming up the river. A few days later, the *Mary Ann* was passed by another steamboat. The race was on. By the 1870s, more than 250 steamboats were on the river, and Randell's hometown of **Mannum** had become one of the nation's busiest inland ports, handling more than 20,000 bales of wool a year.

These days this quiet holiday town is a perfect place from which to get to know the river. It is an easy drive from Adelaide, following the Southeast Freeway 50 miles (80 km) to the old river port of **Murray Bridge** and then going 15 miles (24 km) north on the Mannum Road. A restored

---

EXPERIENCE:
Renting a Houseboat

Houseboats can be rented at Murray Bridge, Mannum, and a number of villages along the Murray River. No license or special training is required, and river charts are provided. Information about rentals on the Murray can be obtained from visitor centers or from the **Houseboat Hirer's Association** (*tel 08/8231-8466, hha.asn.au*).

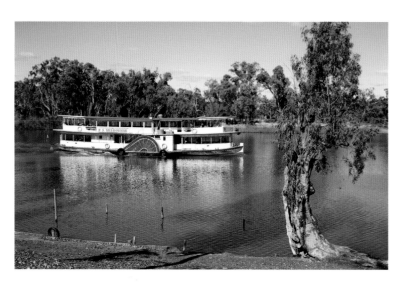

The paddle steamer *Melbourne* follows the Murray River near the town of Mildura.

1897 steamboat, the **Marion,** is part of Mannum Dock Museum (next to the visitor center) and has short and overnight cruises. The grand Mississippi-style stern-wheeler **Murray Princess** ties up here between cruises *(Captain Cook Cruises, tel 1800-804-843, captaincook.com.au).* It does three-to seven-night cruises along the river, running upstream through the sandstone gorges near Swan Reach. Another restored old steamer, the **Proud Mary** offers five-day cruises *(tel 1800-677-683)* out of Murray Bridge. It is smaller and more intimate, and serves bush tucker, such as kangaroo. Both boats have air-conditioned cabins—important in summer when temperatures soar.

Murray Bridge is also home to the **Monarto Zoo** *(3401 Old Princes Hwy., tel 08/8534-4100, $$$$),* a popular 2,500-acre (1,000 ha) big-game preserve.

The Murray is still a rural river, and the steamboats tie up at a sandbar for the night. The stars are dazzling, and you wake up in the morning to a cacophony of galahs, cockatoos, and kookaburras. The crowds tend to be very Australian—the Murray is a quint-essentially Australian holiday spot.

If you want more indepen-dence, consider renting a house-boat (see sidebar p. 276). You'll get the same dramatic gorges, stars, and noisy birdlife, but you'll have even more of a sense of freedom. The houseboats are comfortable but fairly spartan—a bit like a float-ing camper van—with a kitchen, bunks, and a living room. Naturally, most include a barbecue.

Flinders Ranges National Park

The Flinders Ranges make one of the most majestic national parks in Australia—an ancient

Flinders Ranges National Park

🏞 251 C3

Visitor Information

✉ Wilpena

☎ 08/8648-0048

Flinders Ranges Visitor Information Centre

✉ Railway Terrace, Quorn (no. 3)

☎ 08/8648-6419

folded landscape of craggy mountains and deep gorges, tinted purple and red in the clear desert light, and carpeted by wildflowers after the spring rains. With its vibrant hues, rich desert vegetation, and superb

INSIDER TIP:

Shy kangaroos are not always easy to spot, but at the Wilpena Pound campground in the Flinders Ranges they come begging for food in the morning. Look but don't feed.

—PETER TURNER
National Geographic author

hiking trails, this spectacular outback wilderness has long been a favorite haunt of hikers, photographers, and painters.

Aboriginal artists and artisans have been coming into this rocky fastness for thousands of years to collect its rich ochers and workable stones. Matthew Flinders was the first European to see these mountains, when he sailed 200 miles (320 km) up Spencer Gulf in 1802. Within 40 years, the first graziers were staking claims in the southern portion of the ranges, and by the 1870s, farm towns and wheat fields could be found deep in the mountains. The newcomers hadn't reckoned on the fickleness of South Australia's outback, however, where a few seasons of gentle rains might be followed by

a decade of implacable drought. Today the ranges are dotted with crumbling ruins of stone farmhouses and ghost towns.

The Flinders Ranges are one of those all-too-rare instances in Australia where dramatic outback landscapes can be found a convenient distance from a capital city. A four-hour drive north of Adelaide on the Princes Highway brings you to **Port Augusta.** Six miles (10 km) before town, a marked turnoff on your right leads 25 miles (40 km) to Quorn and the solitary highway that leads 70 miles (113 km) farther on, through Hawker and into the heart of **Flinders Ranges National Park.** A far more scenic (and not much longer) option is to drive north out of Adelaide on Main North Road, through the beautiful wine country around **Clare,** with scenic wheat fields and historic towns such as **Mintaro, Melrose,** and **Laura.** An additional 180 miles (290 km) brings you to Wilmington, where a sign directs you to Quorn and the Flinders Ranges. **Quorn** itself is an interesting outback town popular with vintage railroad buffs who come here to ride the Pichi Richi railroad *(tel 04/2858-1110).* This restored train makes the 20-mile (32 km) run from the town to Pichi Richi Pass. Because of fire danger in this tinder-dry region, it operates only in the cooler, wetter months (March–Nov.).

The best known feature of the Flinders Ranges is **Wilpena Pound,** a vast amphitheater of red quartzite, purple shale, and cliffs that was formed by a dramatic upheaval of the Earth's crust about 450 million years ago. A quirk in the local climate gives the interior of Wilpena Pound considerably more rainfall than the surrounding desert. The floor of this lost world is covered with grasslands, native cypresses, casuarina trees, red gums, and, between September and November, a kaleidoscope of wildflowers. The pound is also home to large numbers of wallabies, red kangaroos, and emus as well as huge flocks of rosellas, parrots, and galahs.

Wilpena comprises the Wilpena Pound Resort *(tel 08/8648-0004)* as well as a store and a campsite. The resort visitor center has information on the walking trails inside Wilpena Pound itself.

Wilpena Pound is ringed by cliffs and is accessible only by foot through a narrow gorge at Sliding Rock. Hikes can be challenging. The best known trail here is the **Heysen Trail** (see p. 262). The most spectacular are the two steep trails that lead to the summit of **St. Mary's Peak,** which, at 3,822 feet (1,165 m), is the highest point in Wilpena Pound. Other trails climb up **Mount Ohlssen Bagge** and **Wangara Lookout.** Spring is by far the best time to do any hiking. In summer, the temperatures are scorching, with the bare rocks only magnifying the desert heat. No matter what time of year, bring a hat, put on sunscreen, and carry plenty of water. Four-wheel-drive tours and scenic flights over the ranges can be booked through the Wilpena Pound Resort.

The Flinders Ranges were significant to the Adnyamathanha ("hill people"), who lived here before Europeans arrived, and the dramatic rock formations inspired some Dreamtime legends. There are rock-art galleries at **Arkaroola** and **Sacred Canyon,** both a short drive from Wilpena. ∎

Ancient coolibah trees line the valleys of the Flinders Ranges.

Coober Pedy

The apocalyptic landscape around Coober Pedy looks like the work of a disturbed mind. For miles in every direction, the ground is covered by the sharp conical piles of clayish soil left by thousands of miners in their quest for opals. Australia produces 95 percent of the world's opals, and Coober Pedy is its richest field. The settlement's name comes from the corruption of a local Aboriginal phrase Kupa Piti, which means "white fellows in a hole."

Even the pub is underground at Coober Pedy.

Coober Pedy

🅰 251 B4

Visitor Information

✉ Hutchinson St.

☎ 08/8672-5298
or
1800-637-076

Soon after opal was discovered here in 1915, this remote wasteland became a magnet for fortune-seekers, adventurers, and drifters from around the globe. It still is, although tourism has become the main industry. Exactly how much opal is mined here is a matter of great speculation because lucrative finds are kept as secret as possible.

Located about 520 miles (850 km) north of Adelaide, the town is a rare stopover on the long, empty drive along the Stuart Highway to the Northern Territory. Although nobody would ever call this dusty place charming, it has a certain fascination. Shops sell opals and galleries offer pottery made from local clay.

Summer temperatures here routinely hit 120°F (49°C). Some

of Coober Pedy's residents escape the unrelenting heat by living underground in hand-dug caves. Far from crude holes, these cave houses can be very stylish, with all the modern conveniences, and the temperature inside them stays at a constant 72°F (22°C). The tourist office can arrange visits. Several motels in town are underground or offer underground rooms. Among them are **Radeka's Downunder Motel** (tel 08/8672-5223) and the ironically named **Desert Cave Hotel** (tel 08/8672-5688, desert cave.com.au), the swankest place in town. It also has a good historic mining display, and a drink in the underground bar is de rigueur.

If you are feeling lucky, have a go at fossicking (the Australian term for "prospecting"). There is no particular logic for where opal might be. Just sink a hole and hope for the best, or pick through the mullock heaps (spoil heaps) and look for flashes of color others have missed. The best place to try your luck is at the safe **public noodling area** on Jewellers Shop Road. You can "noodle" (fossick) without danger of tumbling into an old mine shaft, a real hazard that regularly claims lives in the mining areas outside town.

Other worthwhile attractions include mine tours such as the **Old Timers Mine** (Crowders Gully Rd., tel 08/8672-5555), an old opal mine hand-dug in 1916. The **Serbian Orthodox Church** is the most photogenic of the underground churches.

The surreal **Breakaways,** 20 miles (33 km) north of Coober Pedy, are multihued mesa hills steeped in Aboriginal legend. A sunset visit is pure magic. ∎

OUTBACK MAIL RUN: For a view of the real outback, off the main highway where few venture, tag along on the **Coober Pedy Mail Run** (tel 1800-069-911, mailruntour.com, Mon. & Thurs.). Drive with the mailman on a 12-hour journey visiting outback stations, including the huge Anna Creek Station, on a loop across to Oodnadatta and William Creek. Bring a camera, sunscreen, and a big hat.

EXPERIENCE: Cattle Mustering

The iconic outback stockman, cracking a whip astride his horse, is still a reality, although the Australian beef industry has changed markedly since its heyday in the 1970s. Motorbikes and helicopters are as much a part of mustering these days.

The old outback cattle tracks are now graded four-wheel-drive roads, but you can relive the thrill of a cattle drive on horseback with the **Great Australian Outback Cattle Drive** (tel 08/8463-4694, cattledrive.com.au), based at the huge Anna Creek Station outside William Creek in South Australia. Five-day tours include two to three days of droving and comfortable tented accommodations at the station.

The **Harry Redford Cattle Drive** (tel 07/4651-3311, harryredford.com.au), at Aramac in central Queensland, is a popular 19-day outback adventure driving 600 head of cattle 124 miles (200 km) along the Redford Track around May–June. All levels of horse-riding experience are catered for, and you can tag along for as many days as you like.

Cattle station farm stays (see sidebar p. 136) offer the chance to watch and sometimes join in. **Bullo River** (tel 08/8354-2719, bulloriver.com), at Timber Creek in the Northern Territory, encourages participation from May to October. If you like dairy cattle and green fields, try farm stays in Victoria or Tasmania.

Australian Muster Experience (Kingston Rd., Whyanbeel Valley, australian musterexperience.com), near Cairns, puts on good mustering shows.

The Ghan

Every Sunday afternoon (and Wednesday in winter), the train known as the Ghan pulls out of Adelaide's Parklands Railway Station northbound on a transcontinental journey that stretches 1,850 miles (2,979 km) through the harsh deserts in the center of the continent and arrives two days later in the palmy, tropical city of Darwin, on the Arafura Sea.

The sleek silver carriages of the Ghan rumble toward the desert city of Alice Springs.

Great Southern Rail

✉ 422 King William St., Adelaide

☎ 13-2147

greatsouthernrail .com.au

The Ghan was named to honor the Afghan camel drivers whose caravans had been a lifeline to the lonely desert town of Alice Springs before the eventual coming of the railroad in 1929. The railway made the camels superfluous, and thousands of them were let loose in the desert, where their descendants still run wild today.

The original Ghan went no farther north than Alice Springs, and although for decades there was much buoyant talk of one day extending the line all the way to Darwin, nothing much was done

about it until 2001, when work started on the final 880-mile (1,420 km) stretch of track. After more than a billion dollars was spent and some 1.3 million tons (1.2 million tonnes) of steel tracks were laid, the new line opened in early 2004.

After departing Adelaide at 12:20 p.m. on Sunday, the Ghan heads north through the dry rolling wheat fields of South Australia's mid-north and then into **Port Augusta** before heading into the outback and central deserts. The train crosses the massive 15-span bridge over the

Finke River, reputedly one of the world's oldest riverbeds, before pulling into **Alice Springs** around 1:45 p.m. the next day. After a four-hour stop—during which you can take a tour of the city—the Ghan continues north to the tropics. An early morning stop is made at **Katherine**—during which you can tour the famous gorge—and the train pulls into **Darwin**'s train station at 5:30 that afternoon.

The return journey leaves Darwin each Wednesday morning at 10:00, arriving back into Adelaide on Friday at 12:30 p.m. An additional winter service operates June to August.

The Ghan has first-class sleeping cars—Platinum and Gold Service—as well as holiday-class (Red Service) sleepers and budget-priced seats. Gold passengers have access to plush club cars, where predinner drinks are served, and dine on three-course meals served in the restaurant car. Red passengers can purchase meals in the diner and buffet car. The train also carries automobiles, so you can drive one way on the Stuart Highway (see pp. 284–288), and return by rail. ■

INSIDER TIP:

Pack lightly for your Ghan train trip—you'll be charged extra if you exceed baggage weight and size limits.

—STEPHANIE ROBICHAUX
National Geographic contributor

EXPERIENCE: Riding the Rails

Since the days when the railroad was king, many rail services have ended because of competition from cheap bus travel and discount flights, but those that remain offer the comfort, scenery, and romance that only rail travel can deliver.

Australia's two iconic train journeys are the **Indian Pacific** (see sidebar p. 248) and the legendary **Ghan** (see above). **Great Southern Rail** (*tel 13/2147, greatsouthernrail.com.au*) operates both, as well as the **Overland** (Adelaide to Melbourne) and **Southern Spirit** (Brisbane to Adelaide).

Most states also have regular passenger services. Some of the main ones include Sydney–Brisbane, Sydney–Melbourne, and Sydney–Canberra. The **Sunlander,** from Brisbane to Cairns, offers a leisurely journey along the coast; the **Tilt Train** is faster for shorter hops.

Queensland Rail (*tel 13-1617, queensland rail.com.au*) operates these services and some interesting trains into the outback, including the **Spirit of the Outback** (Brisbane–Longreach), the **Westlander** (Brisbane–Charleville), the **Inlander** (Townsville–Mt. Isa), and the **Savannahlander** (Cairns–Kuranda–Forsayth). Queensland's quirkiest train is the **Gulflander,** which travels from remote Normanton to Croydon.

Popular steam-train rides include **Puffing Billy,** through Melbourne's Dandenong Ranges; the **Great Zig Zag Railway,** with its spectacular views of the Blue Mountains; the **Kuranda Scenic Railway,** from Cairns into the rain forest; and the coastal **Cockle Train,** from Goolwa to Victor Harbor.

A good website that shows all of Australia's rail services is *railmaps.com.au*.

Stuart Highway Drive

The Stuart Highway runs through the outback from Port Augusta in South Australia to the Esplanade in Darwin—almost 1,700 miles (2,735 km) through the heart of the continent. It takes its name from the explorer John McDouall Stuart, who made an epic south-to-north crossing in 1861, and approximates his route and that of the Overland Telegraph Line, built in 1872.

The gas station, shop, café, and tourist office are all in one building in settlements like Oodnadatta.

The highway rolls through the desolate saltbush country and glaring white salt pans of South Australia's deserts, into the opal-mining town of Coober Pedy, across the Red Centre to Alice Springs, and on through a lonely archipelago of outback settlements in the Northern Territory.

Port Augusta to Alice Springs

The paved, two-lane highway starts at **Port Augusta,** a truck-stop town (and the start of the Eyre Highway, see pp. 243–248). It is a good road, and unless you are venturing off onto one of the lonely bush tracks, you need no special equipment beyond spares and extra water for yourself and the car.

When Port Augusta slips beneath your rearview mirror, you are alone with your

---

NOT TO BE MISSED:

Coober Pedy • Alice Springs • Tennant Creek

---

thoughts and miles of saltbush until you reach the scruffy little settlement called **Pimba,** 110 lonely miles (177 km) later. A turnoff here leads to **Woomera,** once a top-secret rocket-testing base during the Cold War. The Heritage and Information Centre (corner of Dewrang & Banool Aves., tel 08/8673-7042) has displays about Woomera's past and can arrange tours of the still active rocket range. If you continue another 45 miles (72 km) the road will take you to the massive **Olympic Dam**

See also area map p. 251
Port Augusta
1,700 miles (2,735 km)
7 days
Darwin

Timor Sea

Darwin ⑦
LITCHFIELD N.P. Batchelor
DALY RIVER N.R. Pine Creek
Robin Falls NITMILUK N.P.
Douglas Hot Springs
Katherine
KAKADU NATIONAL PARK

DRYSDALE RIVER N.P.
Wyndham
GREGORY NATIONAL PARK

Mataranka
Larrimah
Roper Bar

Gulf of Carpentaria

Daly Waters
Borroloola

NORTHERN TERRITORY

Renner Springs

Attack Creek Hist. Res.
Three Ways Roadhouse

QUEENSLAND

Tennant Creek ⑤
STUART HIGHWAY
Central Mount Stuart Hist. Res.
Devil's Marbles Conservation Reserve ④

66 BARKLY HIGHWAY

Mount Isa

Rabbit Flat Roadhouse

TANAMI

ROAD

Lake Mackay

Ti Tree
87 PLENTY HIGHWAY
12
83

Boulia

Georgina

WESTERN AUSTRALIA

WEST MACDONNELL N.P. ③
Watarrka
Alice Springs
Arltunga

SIMPSON DESERT NATIONAL PARK

LASSETER HWY.
Warburton
Kata Tjuta
Uluru

Finke

Simpson Desert

Great Victoria Desert

Marla
OODNADATTA TRACK
Oodnadatta

Lake Eyre

STRZELECKI REGIONAL RESERVE

Cadney Homestead

TALLARINGA CONSERVATION PARK

Coober Pedy ②
William Creek
STUART HIGHWAY
Marree
Lake Blanche

SOUTH AUSTRALIA

Olympic Dam Mine ①

Lake Hart
Lake Torrens
Lake Frome

Nullarbor Plain
NULLARBOR REGIONAL RESERVE

Pimba
Woomera

NULLARBOR N.P.

LAKE GAIRDNER N.P.

87 Port Augusta

20

Great Australian Bight

1 START

Murray

ADELAIDE

NEW SOUTH WALES

8

▬ ▬ ▬ Driving route detour

0 ————— 400 kilometers
0 ————— 200 miles

copper-uranium mine ❶. For information about this giant mining facility, and to book a tour of it, contact the Roxby Downs Visitor Centre (tel 08/8671-2001).

Lake Gairdner National Park, a vast salt pan, sprawls off to the left as you drive north of Pimba. In recent years, Lake Gairdner has become a venue for land-speed record attempts. More easily visited, however, is **Lake Hart,** a blinding white salt pan just off the highway to your right, about 30 miles (48 km) northwest of Woomera.

The rough-and-tough opal-mining town of **Coober Pedy** ❷ (see pp. 280–281) appears on the horizon another 230 miles (370 km) up the highway, over a weirdly desolate landscape. Be particularly careful if you are driving this stretch of highway around dusk, because scores of kangaroos are about. Most people, whether they are going north or south on the highway, find Coober Pedy a convenient place to stop for the night. The town has plenty of good motels and some reasonably decent places to eat. (Outback Australia, as you'll quickly discover, is no gourmand's paradise. Anything more original than meat pies, sausage rolls, greasy chips, and spring rolls qualifies as haute cuisine.)

EXPERIENCE:
Flying Over Lake Eyre

Lake Eyre, about 100 miles (160 km) east of Coober Pedy, is Australia's largest lake. For the most part it is a shimmering white salt pan, but every 10 years or so, it floods and fills with water; life sprouts and thousands of birds flock to its shores. This last happened in 2009. Although you can make the drive there with a 4WD vehicle, it's a long trip. The best view is from the air, on a flight from William Creek with **Wrightsair** (tel 08/8670-7962) or Marree with **GSL Aviation** (tel 1300-475-247, winter only). Both towns lie on the Oodnadatta Track.

Coober Pedy is about 250 miles (400 km) from the Northern Territory border, with only the **Cadney Homestead** roadhouse and the tiny hamlet of **Marla** to break the scrubby monotony. The desert stretches of South Australia, it must be said, are the least interesting portions of the Stuart Highway. Marla has the dubious distinction of frequently being the hottest place in South Australia. At both Cadney Homestead and Marla you can take the rugged **Oodnadatta Track** into even more hostile—albeit scenic—outback to the lonely bush town of **Oodnadatta.** Although a standard car in good condition can do this excursion during the winter months, it is a good idea to be well prepared, have some bush experience, and let responsible people know where you intend to go and when you plan to return. Many other tracks, leading to remote national parks such as **Lake Eyre** or the **Simpson Desert,** are strictly for four-wheel-drive vehicles. Seek advice before venturing off the paved roads.

Fifty miles (80 km) after crossing the Northern Territory border, the Stuart Highway touches the Lasseter Highway, which heads 150 miles (240 km) west toward **Uluru** and **Kata Tjuta** (see pp. 204, 206–208). This paved highway was named for prospector Harold Lasseter, who supposedly found a fabulously rich gold reef out in the desert in 1897 but died trying to locate it again. The reef, if it indeed exists, has never been rediscovered, although not for want of trying. Also off this highway is the spectacular **Watarrka** (Kings Canyon, see p. 210).

Farther up the Stuart Highway, **Alice Springs** ❸ (see pp. 198–201) is an oasis town in the heart of the dramatic MacDonnell Ranges. You are now in Australia's Red Centre, and you're probably starting to feel as though you've come a long way. The Alice (as it is known) is an interesting town at the hub of a lot of outback attractions and with scenic hiking trails nearby—and it is worth spending a few days here. If you want to return to

Adelaide without driving back through South Australia's northern deserts, you can load your car onto the Ghan train and ride back in style (see pp. 282–283).

Alice Springs to Darwin

The Stuart Highway continues another 950 mostly empty miles (1,529 km) north of Alice Springs to the end of the line in Darwin. From Alice Springs the highway rolls

are a haunting spectacle, particularly in the dusk or early morning light.

Three hundred miles (480 km) north of Alice Springs is **Tennant Creek 5**. It was the site of a lonely telegraph relay station in the 1870s, and in the 1930s it was the focus of Australia's last gold rush. One of the major workings was found by a dog named Peko. Another was discovered by a one-eyed prospector named Jack Noble and his blind partner

Aborigines traditionally believe that the Devil's Marbles are the Rainbow Serpent's eggs.

north across the reddish, stony immensity of the Northern Territory outback, past the hamlet of **Ti Tree,** where Australia's first roadhouse was set up in the 1930s, and the **Central Mount Stuart Historical Reserve,** which marks the geographical center of Australia. Another 110 miles (177 km) brings you to the **Karlu Karlu/Devil's Marbles Conservation Reserve 4**. A campsite is here, and you can walk among the eerily rounded boulders. Geologists say they are the weathered remnants of a 1.5-billion-year-old granite formation. Aborigines believe the boulders are the eggs of the Rainbow Serpent. However you interpret them, they

William Weaber, and it went on to become Australia's biggest open-cut mine until it closed in 1985. The **Telegraph Station** is open for visits; so is the old **Battery Hill Mining Centre,** where gold-bearing ore was crushed and treated. Legend has it that Tennant Creek itself was settled when a wagon, loaded with beer, broke down here in 1933. The teamsters couldn't be bothered to fix it and built a pub on the spot. The **Nyinkka Nyunyu Art & Culture Centre** provides an excellent introduction to indigenous culture.

Fifteen miles (24 km) farther north, at the **Three Ways Roadhouse,** the Barkly Highway runs east off the Stuart Highway across flat, spinifex-covered tablelands to the lonely Queensland border, about 280 miles (450 km) away. An additional 25 miles (40 km) up the Stuart Highway, a sign marks the **Attack Creek Historical Reserve.** In 1860, the explorer John McDouall Stuart came here on his first attempt to cross the continent, but he was attacked by Aborigines ("tall, powerful fellows") who objected to his trespassing on their land.

The little settlement of **Renner Springs** is regarded as the point where the dry desert climate of the center yields to the seasonal wet–dry of the Top End (the north of the Northern Territory). Although scrubby, the bush becomes greener and taller as you continue north.

INSIDER TIP:

Before starting out on the long drive north along the Stuart Highway, stop off at Port Augusta's Arid Lands Botanic Gardens *[australian-aridlands-botanic-garden.org]* to learn about the beautiful and unique flora you're about to see.

—LAURA RUYKYS
National Geographic field researcher

Daly Waters—another 150 miles (240 km) north—was a vital refueling stop for early aviators such as Amy Johnson. During the 1930s, Qantas flights refueled here, and passengers were given a meal at the **Daly Waters Pub** *(tel 08/8975-9927)*, built in 1893 and said to be the oldest in the Northern Territory. It still serves good food and is filled with memorabilia from those early, seat-of-the-pants aviation days. The airfield (closed in the 1970s) and a restored World War II hangar are a legacy of its days as a staging post for Allied fighters and bombers en route to Darwin and the Dutch East Indies.

Reminders of World War II become more frequent as you near Darwin. Signs point to abandoned bush airstrips or ammo dumps. The town of **Larrimah,** 60 miles (96 km) north of Daly Waters, was a major military post during World War II and the terminus of the North Australia Railway. This narrow-gauge line had been intended to link Darwin with Alice Springs, but it had not gotten beyond Larrimah when World War II broke out. The line was abandoned after Cyclone Tracy struck in 1974, and the tracks have been torn up. Little is here now but a friendly old pub and an interesting museum covering the town's war years and the history of road trains in the Northern Territory.

Mataranka, 50 miles (80 km) to the north, has thermal springs in a pocket of rain forest about 5 miles (8 km) east of town. The film *We of the Never Never* (1982) was made near here. The relaxing hot springs can get crowded. The **Mataranka Homestead Resort** *(tel 08/8975-4544)* has accommodations and a restaurant.

Katherine ❻ (see pp. 194–195) is the next town on the highway, and with a population of almost 10,000 it is easily the biggest metropolis you've seen since Alice Springs. The big attraction is **Nitmiluk National Park** (see p. 195).

The last leg of the Stuart Highway—the 200 miles (320 km) to Darwin—crosses rolling bushland. At the old gold-mining town of Pine Creek, you can take a paved road into the heart of **Kakadu National Park** (see pp. 188–191). Ahead, turnoffs lead to scenic sites such as **Douglas Hot Springs,** the beautiful **Robin Falls,** and the **Daly River Nature Reserve.** Farther north, **Adelaide River** was a major WWII military post, and a large cemetery commemorates those killed in air raids. The Batchelor turnoff brings you to **Litchfield National Park** (see pp. 192–193). Keep going and you'll notice the houses and buildings are crowding closer together. Suddenly you are at the end of the line: **Darwin's** ❼ palm-fringed Esplanade and the Timor Sea (see pp. 184–187).

Built on the wealth of the 1850s gold rushes and Australia's most diverse state—small, pretty, and prosperous

Victoria

Introduction & Map   290–291

Melbourne   292–296

Experience: Dining by Tram   293

Experience: Photo Safari   296

Feature: Melbourne Cup   297

Melbourne Walks   298–303

St. Kilda   304

Main Yarra Trail   305

Experience: Biking Melbourne   305

Mornington Peninsula   306–307

Experience: Penguin Parade   307

Yarra Valley   308

The Dandenongs   309

Great Ocean Road Drive   310–315

Experience: Surfing   315

Victoria's Alpine Country   316–317

Feature: Australian Rules
   Football   318–319

Experience: Catch a Match   318

Goldfields   320–321

Inside Melbourne Central mall

Feature: Bushrangers   322–323

Murray River   324–325

Grampians National Park
   (Gariwerd)   326–327

Wilsons Promontory National
   Park   328

Hotels & Restaurants   382–384

Victoria

Victoria is the smallest and greenest of Australia's mainland states and the only one without much "real" outback. A history of gentlemanly farming and of vast wealth from the 19th century's fabulous gold rushes have given the state, and especially its elegant capital Melbourne, a patrician, old-money air. The richest gold diggings were in Ballarat, Castlemaine, and Bendigo, but dozens of rich strikes were made around the state.

The 19th century's heady combination of boomtime wealth and civic pride gave Victoria magnificent public architecture and elegant colonial mansions. It is not unusual in this state to drive into a farm town and see an Italianate city hall as grand as a European opera house, probably set among ornamental palms and landscaped gardens. When you see one of these grand rural palaces, just start looking for the historical marker that tells the story of the local gold rush.

No large-scale gold mining goes on here now. Victoria today is a combination of breadbasket and industrial heartland, producing about a quarter of Australia's gross domestic product. The Murray River forms its border with New South Wales and irrigates vineyards, market gardens, and vast orchards. Victoria

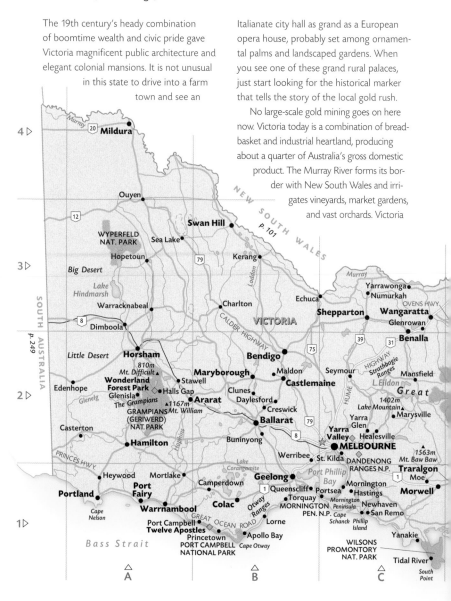

is known as the Garden State. Shepparton, in the north, is a sort of Cannery Row. The dry country in the west is golden with wheat and has some of Australia's best wool-producing regions. Dairies and cheese factories dot the state. The dense forests in Gippsland feed a timber industry, coal is mined in the La Trobe Valley, and beneath the waters of Bass Strait lurk Australia's second largest oil fields.

Victoria is Australia's smokestack industry hub, with car-manufacturing factories, chemical plants, and aluminum smelters, although, as manufacturing continues to shift offshore, the economy is dominated by service industries. Headquarters to Australia's biggest mining houses, Melbourne was for decades the nation's financial and banking center, a role it has partly conceded to Sydney.

For such a small state, Victoria has an astonishing variety of scenery, from temperate rain forests along the eastern coast to dusty outback scrub in the north to the sleek cafés of Melbourne's inner-city suburbs. Australia's best skiing is on the powdery slopes of the Victorian Alps, and some of its finest surf can be found

NOT TO BE MISSED:

Elegant Melbourne, a garden city of gracious architecture 292–296

Touring the wineries and seeing native Yarra Valley wildlife 308

Riding *Puffing Billy* through the cool, lush Dandenong Ranges 309

Driving the Great Ocean Road to see the Twelve Apostles 310–315

Hiking the Victorian Alps 316–317

Seeing a fast and furious game of Australian Rules football 318

Reliving the gold rush at Ballarat and other goldfield towns 320–321

Taking a paddle steamer at the old river port of Echuca 325

Hiking the Grampians and visiting their cultural center 326–327

on the internationally famous Bells Beach. The Great Ocean Road, just west of Melbourne, is a fabulous coastal drive.

Melbourne itself—Australia's most European capital—has theaters, museums, and a sweeping range of cultures and cuisines. Unlike the rest of Australia, where interesting sights tend to be separated by hundreds of miles of dreary scrub, Victoria's attractions form a small, neat package. Everything is an easy scenic drive from Melbourne on excellent paved roads. ■

Albury
Murray
Wodonga   Corryong
Beechworth
Myrtleford
MT. BUFFALO
N.P.   Bright
              Mt. Beauty   ALPINE
1723m   1862m   NAT. PARK
The Horn   Mt. Hotham
Dinner Plain Omeo   R a n g e
D i v i d i n g
ALPINE
NAT. PARK
              Buchan   23   Genoa
Mitchell
              Orbost   1   Cann River
Bairnsdale
              Lakes Entrance
Gippsland
Sale
         Gippsland
         Lakes
Yarram
NEW SOUTH WALES
P. 101

0 ————————— 100 kilometers
0 ————————— 50 miles

Canberra

Area of map detail

△   △
D   E

Melbourne

The 1860s gold rush transformed Melbourne from a straggling settlement on the banks of the Yarra River into a grand city of ornate public buildings, theaters, mansions, trams, and fine gardens. Stately Victorian-era architecture defined Australia's second city, banking and mining giants drove commerce, and it assumed a cultured air, looking down upon bold, brassy, nouveau riche Sydney, not without a hint of jealousy for its glorious harbor.

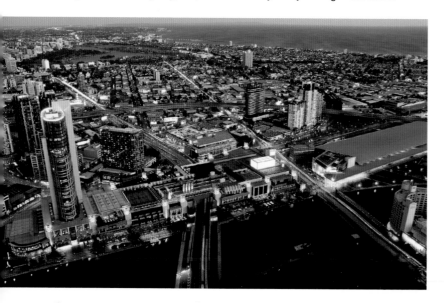

Elegant, cosmopolitan Melbourne

Melbourne

🏛 290 C2

Visitor Information

✉ Victorian Tourism Visitor Information Centre, Federation Sq., corner of Swanston & Flinders Sts.

☎ 03/9568-9658

Information Booth

✉ Bourke Street Mall

thatsmelbourne .com.au

The rivalry continues, with Sydney winning on most counts, but Melbourne seems preoccupied by a new boom of soaring real estate and migrants attracted by the city's prosperity. New development has transformed the riverfront and other enclaves in recent years, and Melbourne is kicking up its once staid heels at cosmopolitan shopping, restaurant, and nightlife precincts.

And yet the city has not lost touch with its patrician roots. This is still a city of elegant Victorian buildings, beautifully laid-out parks, and stately icons such as the Melbourne Club. Most of Australia's great mining houses are headquartered here, while the world's largest network of electric trams gives the city a pleasantly old-fashioned European flair.

Sports rule in Melbourne, which has eight professional Australian Rules football clubs. It hosts the Australian Open tennis tournament, and the Melbourne Cup—Australia's greatest horse race.

Melbourne has a vibrant mix of ethnic communities—particularly

Greek, Italian, and Asian—giving the city bustling markets, restaurants, delicatessens, and bakeries. Just choosing a restaurant in Melbourne means sifting through a United Nations of culinary styles. There is even a restaurant tram offering evening sightseeing tours around the city—a happy converging of several of Melbourne's strengths: excellent food, elegant architecture, and trams.

The city began in 1835 as a result of a dodgy land deal by two Tasmanian entrepreneurs, John Batman and John Pascoe Fawkner. They gave local Aborigines blankets, flour, axes, and trinkets in exchange for 500,000 acres (200,000 ha) of land around Port Phillip Bay. The unauthorized purchase annoyed the Colonial Office back in London, but they let it stand. Sixteen years later, fabulous goldfields were discovered around Ballarat, Bendigo, and Castlemaine, and the city's success was assured. Gold hunters flocked here—almost 2,000 a week at the boom's height—and, by 1861, gold-rush wealth had made Melbourne Australia's grandest city. You can see an audiovisual presentation on the gold-rush days in the gold vaults at the Old Treasury Building, on Spring Street.

These days, Melbourne comes a close second to archrival Sydney as the nation's financial capital and, with 4.2 million residents, is a bit smaller. But Melburnians still claim their city is the better place to live. Powerful voices support them: *The Economist* magazine regularly ranks Melbourne as the world's most livable city.

Despite Sydneysiders' claim that Melbourne's climate is drizzly and bleak, the Victorian capital actually gets less rain than Sydney. In recent years, Melbourne has challenged its brash New South Wales rival on the glamour front as well, snaring such international events as the Australian **Formula One Grand Prix** and building Australia's largest casino.

Melbourne Sights

It is easy to get around Melbourne on its network of buses, trains, and trams. A free City Circle tram (burgundy-colored no. 35) loops through downtown and on to Docklands, and the free Melbourne Visitor Shuttle bus covers a wider circle on the city's fringe.

Melbourne's Central Business District—CBD in local slang—is a pleasing mix of futuristic skyscrapers and Victorian-era stone facades. The city is set out on a grid, and you need only remember a few key streets. Excellent information booths can help you plan your explorations.

Formula One Grand Prix
☎ 03/9258-7100
grandprix.com.au

EXPERIENCE:
Dining by Tram

Trams are an icon of Melbourne and one of the best ways to tour the city. **Colonial Tramcar Restaurant** *(tel 03/9696-4000, tramrestaurant.com.au)* goes one step further, offering two-hour lunch and dinner tours. Heritage trams depart from South Melbourne near Crown Casino and trundle through the city and around the leafy, Victorian-era suburbs to the south. Reservations are essential.

Thinking Big

Australians love big things. On your travels in Victoria and the rest of Oz, keep an eye out for some of the weird, wonderful, and downright tacky oversize tourist totems that tower above the highway.

Many celebrate local farm produce, including: the Big Banana (Coffs Harbour, NSW), Big Barramundi (Daintree, QLD), Big Apple (Stanthorpe, QLD), Big Cheese (Bega, NSW), Big Lobster (Kingston, SA), Big Prawn (Ballina, NSW), Big Pineapple (Gympie, QLD), Big Ram (Wagin, WA), and Big Peanut (Atherton, QLD).

Others pay tribute to local wildlife: the Big Croc (Humpty Doo, NT), Big Tasmanian Devil (Mole Creek, TAS), Big Galah (Kimba, SA), Big Penguin (Penguin, TAS), and Big Pelican (Noosaville, QLD).

Some are just big for the heck of it: the Big Captain Cook (Cairns, QLD), Big Golden Guitar (Tamworth, NSW), Big Ned Kelly (Glenrowan, VIC), Big Stubbie (Tewantin, QLD), Big Milkshake (Warrnambool, VIC), and an all-time favorite, the Big Gumboot (Tully, QLD), awarded to the wettest town in Australia.

Queen Victoria Market

- Map p. 300
- Victoria St., West Melbourne
- Closed Mon. & Wed.

qvm.com.au

For an idea of the wealth that passed through this city in the glory days of the 19th-century gold rush and land boom, head down Collins Street to the former **Commercial Bank of Australia** building (No. 333) with its glorious high-domed banking chamber, and the ornate **ANZ "Gothic" Bank** (No. 380) with a banking museum. Bourke and Collins Streets are the city's main shopping thoroughfares, although La Trobe Street's glossy **Melbourne Central mall** boasts the city's biggest concentration of stores.

Nearby, Australia's liveliest **Chinatown** can be found on Little Bourke Street. Now mostly a throng of Chinese restaurants from budget to the renowned, fine-dining Flower Drum, this precinct dates from the arrival of Chinese gold miners in the 1850s. The district has been revived by a new wave of recent Asian migration. The interesting **Chinese Museum** (22 Cohen Pl., tel 03/9662-2888, $) showcases Chinese settlement and culture.

Queen Victoria Market, which opened in the 1870s, is a Melbourne institution and an exciting place to buy ingredients for a gourmet picnic. You will find fresh produce just off the farm, interesting cheeses, sausages, breads, meats, fish, nuts, and cakes. Shopping here is never dull or quiet. A multicultural mix of shopkeepers and standholders shout, cajole, and banter to move their goods. Saturday afternoon, when produce must be sold or thrown away, is the time for bargains. This cornucopia is on the north side of the city, only a few minutes by tram along Elizabeth Street from the center. The market is in a series of decorative old iron sheds, with food and produce spread out in a landmark building, distinctive for the livestock frieze above its portal. The biggest section behind sells all manner of cheap goods—clothes, shoes, leatherware, luggage, etc.—and is great for souvenirs, from sheepskin boots to boomerangs. Tours of the market are available (tel 03/9320-5822), as are cooking classes. Hours vary from 6 a.m. to 2–5 p.m. In summer, a Wednesday night market sets up with food and craft stalls.

Once you've bought your picnic ingredients—and you can even buy well-made baskets here—all you need is a convenient park.

INSIDER TIP:

For a great day trip and a close look at Australia's native wolf, visit the Dingo Discovery Center [dingo discovery.net], about 25 miles [40 km] from Melbourne.

—ARIAN WALLACH
National Geographic field researcher

A couple of good options are very close by. One is **Carlton Gardens** *(Victoria St.),* the grounds of the vast, high-domed Exhibition Buildings built for the Great Exhibition of 1880. Nearby is the enormous **Melbourne Museum,** opened in 2000, a postmodern architectural marvel that houses a number of huge collections and galleries—such as the **Bunjilaka Aboriginal Centre,** with its displays of Aboriginal culture; the **Melbourne Gallery,** with its focus on the history of Melbourne and Victoria; and the **Children's Gallery,** with its hands-on multimedia exhibits. The Melbourne Museum spreads over three levels and includes a vast arboretum, containing more than 120 species of trees and plants, as well as IMAX Melbourne, with its huge 3-D movie screen.

Another picnic spot is the **Melbourne Zoo,** established in 1862 and one of the oldest in the world. It is about 2 miles (3 km) north of the market, in Royal Park, and you can reach it by tram No. 55 from William Street or an Upfield line train from Flinders Street Station. The Australian fauna enclosure has a lake and bushland landscaping, where you walk among kangaroos and emus. The platypus house gives perhaps the best chance you'll have of seeing one of these elusive creatures, and the steamy tropical butterfly house is a delight. On certain summer weekend evenings, there are free jazz concerts, and the picnicker-friendly zoo even has a hamper service, where you can preorder your picnic basket while you stroll among the exhibits before you take it in to the concert.

Melbourne Museum

- Map p. 300
- 11 Nicholson St.
- 13-1122
- $$

museumvictoria .com.au

Melbourne Zoo

- Map p. 300
- Elliott Ave., Parkville
- 1300-966-784
- $$$

zoo.org.au

Picnickers near Melbourne's Yarra River

Crown Casino

- Map p. 300
- Southbank
- 03/9292-8888 or 1800-818-888
- Open 24 hours

crownmelbourne.com.au

Eureka Skydeck 88

- Map p. 300
- Eureka Tower, 7 Riverside Quay
- 03/9693-8888
- $$–$$$

eurekaskydeck.com.au

MELBOURNE—AN OVERVIEW: In general, the Yarra River forms Melbourne's social divide. Real estate southeast of the river tends to be pricier, greener, and hillier. South Yarra and Toorak are Melbourne's wealthiest enclaves, with luxurious mansions tucked away behind high walls. Land to the northwest of the Yarra is flat and dry, and it is largely filled with industry, airports, and blue-collar suburbs.

Crown Casino, on the south bank of the Yarra River, is a star-studded entertainment and gambling complex, the country's largest, with flashy restaurants, bars, nightclubs, boutiques, and a luxury hotel. It's the showpiece of the redeveloped **Southbank,** the city's bustling riverfront lined with fashionable restaurants, hotels, shops, street theater, and a great Sunday craft market. Overlooking it all, the Eureka Tower is the city's tallest skyscraper. On the 88th floor, **Eureka Skydeck 88** offers vertigo-inducing panoramas. At the lowest elevation, a host of **river cruise** operators offer insights and city views from the water. They depart from the river or Docklands (the visitor center has details). The Williamstown Ferry *(tel 9682-9555, williamstownferries.com.au, $$$)* heads downriver from Southgate out on to the bay and Williamstown (see p.302).

Like Southbank but less lively, **Docklands,** the old wharf area on the western edge of the city, now houses chic apartments, restaurants, an open-air shopping complex, and Melbourne's premier ice-skating rink.

To the east of the city, the **Melbourne Cricket Ground** *(mcg.org.au)* is the home of Australian Rules football. "The G," as the arena is called, also houses the **National Sports Museum** *(tel 03/9657-8879, nsm.org.au, $$),* showcasing Australian sporting achievements. In January, this sports-mad city plays host to the annual Australian Open tennis tournament at the nearby **Rod Laver Arena.**

Melbourne's warren of inner suburbs is notably diverse. Brunswick Street, in **Fitzroy,** has bohemian cafés, alternative bookstores, and grunge chic. It is also one of the most interesting places to have a cappuccino and people-watch during the day, or bar-crawl in the evening.

Victoria Street in **Richmond** could pass for a backstreet in Hanoi, with its bewildering jumble of Vietnamese apothecaries, family-run grocery shops, fruit stalls, and carcasses hanging in butcher-shop windows. Signs are in Vietnamese, and scores of cramped eateries line the streets. Yet just a few blocks away, on Swan Street, is a small Greek enclave. Lygon Street, in **Carlton,** is Melbourne's Little Italy, full of Italian restaurants and gelaterias.

On the south side, **Prahran** is an upscale district, its boulevards lined with bistros, nightclubs, and cool boutiques. Farther south, the bayside suburb of **St. Kilda** (see p. 304) has a profusion of bakeries along Acland Street, in addition to a breezy foreshore promenade. ■

EXPERIENCE:
Photo Safari

Photo walking tours take in famous Melbourne sights, while teaching you how to use all the functions on your camera. Expert advice shows you how to frame pictures, utilize light, and get the most out of your camera. Two-hour tours of the city center, Yarra River, or the beach suburb of St. Kilda run in the summer. Contact **Nebesky Images** *(tel 04/3204-6624, nebeskyimages.com/phototours.html).*

Melbourne Cup

The Melbourne Cup is the horse race that stops a nation. This prestigious handicap event is run on Melbourne's Flemington racetrack on the first Tuesday of every November, and for three minutes life across Australia is held in suspense. City traffic is reduced to a trickle as the post time nears.

All around Australia—even in the most remote corners of the outback—the pubs are full to bursting and latecomers stand on the sidewalk, craning their necks to see the TV screens over the crowd. Nothing beats being there at Flemington on race day, among hordes of partying racegoers, extravagant hats, and bookies surrounded by mobs of gamblers.

Run in 1861, the first Melbourne Cup was won by a horse named Archer, who won it again the next year. By 1888, the race was attracting crowds of more than 100,000.

The Melbourne Cup is the highlight of Melbourne's Spring Racing Carnival, which spreads over a few weeks and includes other top races such as the Caulfield Cup. It is a race for stayers. It started out as a 2-mile (3,218 m) event, but in deference to the metric system, the distance was shortened to 3,200 meters when Australia went metric in 1972.

The most famous Cup winner was Phar Lap, a New Zealand–born gelding who won in 1930. This phenomenal chestnut horse won 37 of his 51 starts and was taken to North America in 1932 to prove his mettle there. He died mysteriously after winning a single race in Mexico, and his death has been fertile ground for Australian conspiracy theorists ever since, with American gangsters the most popular suspects. In 1985, however, Phar Lap's trainer, Tommy Woodcock, reputedly made a death-bed confession that he feared he might have accidentally poisoned the horse with arsenic-based tonic. Today, Phar Lap's skeleton is in the National Museum of New Zealand; his hide is in the Melbourne Museum; and his huge heart rests in Canberra.

High society, bookies, gamblers, and the equine elite mix on Melbourne Cup day.

There may be some Australians who don't place a bet on the Melbourne Cup, but they are pretty rare. Even people who never normally follow horse racing, let alone place a bet, will have a flutter on The Cup. Most of those who place a bet enter the office sweepstakes, where everyone in the office kicks in a few dollars, and the horses are chosen at random. That way nobody has to study a complicated form sheet. They just kick back and wait for post time.

Melbourne Walks

Flinders Street Railway Station is a great place to start your walking tours of Melbourne. Set on a bank of the Yarra, this spectacular Edwardian railroad station, built of honey-colored sandstone in 1907, is the hub of Melbourne's commuter train system. Above its main portal is a row of clocks, and generally a knot of people sits expectantly on the steps below. "Under the clocks" has been a traditional meeting place for generations.

Melbourne's Flinders Street Railway Station is still a focal point for the city.

Those steps look out on an interesting intersection. On the opposite corner is stately **St. Paul's Cathedral,** a neo-Gothic masterpiece completed in 1892 and the headquarters of Melbourne's Anglican Church. Across the street is the **Young & Jackson Hotel,** one of the oldest pubs in Melbourne and the home of "Chloe," a full-length nude painted in Paris in 1875 by Jules Lefèbvre. In 1880, "Chloe" was sent to the Melbourne Exposition, where judges ruled the picture obscene. The drinkers in the Young & Jackson Hotel hadn't any objections, and the painting has adorned the wall ever since. It's worth going in for a beer to see this Melbourne icon, which was a mainstay of the boisterous public bar for years, but now resides upstairs in the genteel Chloe's Bar. And facing the famous clocks, just across Swanston Street, is the huge, new Federation Square complex, an architectural marvel of zinc, glass, and sandstone panels. It houses, among other things, the **Melbourne Visitor Centre** (tel 03/9658-9658); the **Australian Centre for the Moving Image** (tel 03/8663-2200, acmi.net.au), a museum dedicated to film, television, video, and digital media; and the National Gallery of Victoria's Australian art collection at the **Ian Potter Centre: NGV Australia** (tel 03/8620-2222, ngv.vic.gov.au).

There are two good walks from here (see map pp. 300–301). One walk takes you across the Yarra River to the cosmopolitan new Southgate shopping and café precinct, the botanic gardens, and some of Melbourne's oldest houses. The other explores the eclectic "real Melbourne," the downtown area north of the river.

Walk One: Over the Yarra

Begin the first walk by exploring **Federation Square ❶**, taking in the magnificent architecture in the complex itself, the scenic glimpses of the river, and the vast collection of Australian art in the **Ian Potter Centre.**

The ground floor is given over to indigenous art, with a fine collection of dot paintings by Aboriginal artists. Decorated shields, burial logs and bark paintings are scattered upstairs. The second floor houses the gallery's important collection of paintings, sculptures, drawings, and photographs from the colonial era to the 20th century. Some of Australia's best known colonial painters, such as Conrad Martens and Eugene von Guérard, are represented, along with the prized collection of famously nationalistic paintings by artists that emerged in Melbourne in the 1890s. They were known as the Heidelberg School, after the village on the Yarra River of that name in what was then the outskirts of Melbourne. These Australian Impressionists painted landscapes that celebrated the heat and dust and glare of Australia. A leading light of this school was Tom Roberts, whose 1890 painting "Shearing the Rams," capturing the camaraderie of the shearing shed, has become an Australian icon and is part of the collection

From here, cross the river on the ornate old Princes Bridge. Ahead of you, the wide, treelined St. Kilda Road slopes gently upward to the Shrine of Remembrance, a brooding gray

Romanesque war memorial. On the right over the bridge, just past the towering spire of the Arts Centre, the National Gallery of Victoria's main installation is **NGV International** (180 St. Kilda Rd., tel 03/8620-2222). It has a fine collection of European art from pre-Renaissance to contemporary, housed in a striking modernist building. The Asian, Oceanic, and decorative arts galleries are also well worth browsing, and big-name touring exhibitions show here.

Head back to the river and down to the sun-drenched promenade that follows the south bank of the Yarra, past the Melbourne Concert Hall, to the classy riverbank development known as **Southgate ❷**. One of the finest views of the skyline is to be had from along here, or see it from the water on river boat tours that depart from here and the north bank below Federation Square. Riverside redevelopment transformed what was an industrial wasteland in the 1990s and was, surprisingly, the city's first real attempt to make use of the Yarra River as a scenic water feature. It was stunningly successful. Now this whole Yarra precinct known as Southbank is a popular, fashionable focus of town, with five-star hotels, trendy boutiques, food courts and cafés, the *Polly Woodside* tall ship, the Melbourne Aquarium (melbourneaquarium.com .au), and the huge Crown Casino complex (see p. 296). Farther along, South Wharf is the latest development push into the old docks area, with shops, restaurants, and upscale apartments.

Next, retrace your steps past Princes Bridge and follow the river upstream, on paths that meander through the parkland and gardens that run along the river—Alexandra Gardens, Queen Victoria Gardens, Kings Domain, and the Royal Botanic Gardens. They all meld together to form a delightful greenbelt flanking the river. The **Royal Botanic Gardens ❸** (rbg .vic.gov.au), near the southern end of this green space, may be the finest botanic gardens in Australia. Dotted with century-old oaks and ornamental lakes, they form a lush landscape

(continued on p. 302)

NOT TO BE MISSED:

Federation Square • Southgate • Royal Botanic Gardens

Central Melbourne

VICTORIA   STREET

Flemington Racecourse
Royal Melbourne
Zoological Gardens

CARLTON

VICTORIA

Melbourne
Museum   **6**

STREET

Queen Victoria
Market   **8**

City Baths

Old
Melbourne
Gaol

7

La Trobe
Library

Wesley
Church

FRANKLIN ST.

Melbourne
Central Railway
Station

State
Library

Chinese
Museum

St. James'
Old Cathedral

Melbourne
Central mall   **9**

St. Francis'
Church

CHINATOWN

FLAGSTAFF
GARDENS

Flagstaff
Railway
Station

G.P.O.

Uniti
Chur

Centre
The Point   **2**
Walk

Georges

Town
Hall

Athenæum
Theatre

Law
Courts

Royal
Arcade

Australia
-on-Collins

CITY
SQUARE

St. Paul's
Cathedral

St. Augustine's
Roman Catholic
Church

Block
Arcade   **1**

Young &
Jackson
Hotel

Federati
Square

START
1

Docklands

Stock
Exchange

Visitor Centre

Flinders Street
Railway Station

Rialto Towers

Old Customs
House

PROMENADE

SOUTHBANK

Melbourne
Concert Hall   **2**

Southgate

Southern Cross
Railway Station

Melbourne
Aquarium

Eureka
Tower

Victorian
Arts Centre

World
Congress
Centre

Crown
Casino

SOUTHBANK   BOULEVARD

World
Trade
Centre

Crown
Casino

Yarra

'Polly Woodside'
Tall Ship

SOUTH WHARF ROAD

Exhibition
Centre

LORIMER   STREET

SOUTH
MELBOURNE

Port Melbourne

········ Walking tour route 1
••••••• Walking tour route 2

0 ┣━━━━━━━━━━━━━━┫ 600 meters

0 ┣━━━━━━━━━━━━━━┫ 600 yards

NICHOLSON STREET

Melbourne
Fire Museum

VICTORIA   PARADE

FITZROY

GISBORNE STREET

ALBERT   STREET

SPRING ST.

St. Peter's
Church

St. Patrick's
Cathedral

LANSDOWNE   STREET

CATHEDRAL
PLACE

FITZROY

GARDENS

Princess
Theatre

Parliament
House

MACARTHUR ST.

Avenue
of Elms

④

Parliament
Railway
Station

Old Treasury
Building

Windsor
Hotel

⑤

SPRING   STREET

③

Model
Tudor
Village

J. F. Kennedy
Memorial

COLLINS

COLLINS ST.

Melbourne
Club

ST.

TREASURY
GARDENS

JOLIMONT   STREET

Cook's
Cottage

Collins
Place

WELLINGTON   PARADE

EAST
MELBOURNE

FLINDERS   LANE

Conservatory

FLINDERS   STREET

WELLINGTON   PARADE   SOUTH

JOLIMONT   ROAD

JOLIMONT TERR.

National
Sports
Museum

BATMAN   AVENUE

Melbourne
Cricket
Ground

YARRA   PARK

BRUNTON   AVENUE

Yarra Bike Path

ALEXANDRA GARDENS

Rod Laver Arena

ALEXANDRA   AVENUE

MELBOURNE   PARK

QUEEN VICTORIA
GARDENS

SWAN ST.
BRIDGE

SWAN   STREET

NGV
International

LINLITHGOW   AVENUE

Sidney Myer
Music Bowl

Tan Jogging Track

Indoor Sports &
Entertainment Centre
(The Glasshouse)

Floral
Clock

ST. KILDA ROAD

KINGS

DOMAIN

Yarra

ALEXANDRA   AVENUE

BATMAN

OLYMPIC
PARK

Richmond

Victorian
College of
the Arts

Pioneer
Women's
Memorial
Garden

ALEXANDRA   AVENUE

MORELL BRIDGE

STREET

ANZAC   AVE.

Government
House

ANDERSON STREET

Toorak
S. Yarra

Victoria
Barracks

BIRDWOOD   AVENUE

Old Melbourne
Observatory

③

Governor
La Trobe's
Cottage

ROYAL   BOTANIC

GARDENS

COVENTRY   STREET

ST. KILDA ROAD

Prahran
St. Kilda
Luna Park

④

Shrine of
Remembrance

National
Herbarium

Walk One

► Flinders Street Railway Station

⬌ 2 miles (3.35 km)

🕐 Half a day

► Shrine of Remembrance

Walk Two

► Flinders Street Railway Station

⬌ 1.6 miles (2.5 km)

🕐 Half a day

► Melbourne Central Mall

that spreads over 100 acres (40 ha) by the river. They were established in 1845, but it was the late 19th-century curators Baron Sir Ferdinand von Mueller and, later, W. R. Guilfoyle who created the present masterpiece. On summer nights (Dec.–March) plays are performed in the surrounding gardens and classic films shown on an outdoor screen. For more information check with the Moonlight Cinema (moonlight.com.au).

You can explore the gardens on your own, run around them on a 2.4-mile (3.8 km) jogging track known as the Tan, or follow a self-guided walk. The elegant facade overlooking the gardens belongs to **Government House** (for tours contact the National Trust, tel 03/8663-7260), the residence of the British monarch's representative in Victoria. The house is a copy of Queen Victoria's holiday palace on the Isle of Wight. **Governor La Trobe's Cottage** (for tours contact the National Trust, tel 03/8663-7260) and the **National Herbarium** are located near the southern end of the Botanic Gardens. La Trobe's Cottage is a prefabricated dwelling that was sent over from England in 1840 to serve as the residence for the colony's first governor. The humble cottage is plainly furnished in period style, together with some of La Trobe's personal belongings.

A hundred yards (92 m) west of La Trobe's Cottage, near St. Kilda Road, is the **Shrine of Remembrance** ❹. It was built in 1934 to honor the fallen of World War I. Its eternal flame is now also a tribute to the dead of World War II, Korea, Vietnam, Malaya and Borneo, and the Gulf War. It was positioned and designed so that a sunbeam passes over the inner sanctum at 11 a.m. on November 11—the precise moment the armistice was signed in 1918 to end World War I. Galleries inside the shrine feature rotating exhibits. (Catch a tram on St. Kilda Road back to Flinders Street Station.)

Another option would be to take a cruise on the river itself. The tour boats depart from Southbank and a landing near Princes Bridge, and tickets are available at a riverside kiosk or by calling Melbourne River Cruises (tel 03/8610-2600). Various cruises go upriver past Melbourne's parks and gardens, or downriver past the city center to the docks. Alternatively, take a ferry cruise from Southgate down the river and out onto the bay to **Williamstown,** a picturesque Victorian-era seaside village. The trip takes 50 minutes, and you can get off to explore the suburb then take a later ferry back.

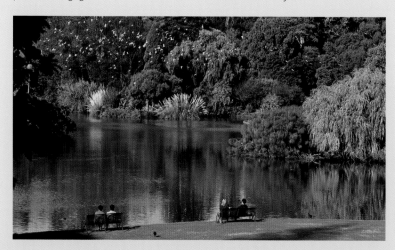

Melburnians enjoy a respite from city life at the Royal Botanic Gardens.

Walk Two: The Real Melbourne

This inner city stroll also begins beneath the clocks at Flinders Street Station. The main drag, Swanston Street, now a pedestrian mall (except for taxis, buses, delivery vehicles, and trams!), heads into the heart of downtown, but the back alleys provide a more interesting route. Melbourne celebrates its European-style alleyways and Victorian-era shopping arcades, crammed with cafés spilling tables onto cobblestones, quirky shops, street art, and pop-up bars. The visitor center has brochures detailing the most interesting alleyways, but for a quick taste, cross Flinders Street, turn left and then right down narrow Degraves Street. Café society begins here and, across Flinders Lane, intensifies down Centre Place, with its bustling eateries and side alleys spattered with street art. At the end, cross fashionable Collins Street and head left to the elegant **Block Arcade ❶**, built with gold-rush wealth in the 1880s and exquisitely restored. It has mosaic floors, an ornamental domed roof, small shops, and the venerable Hopetoun Tea Rooms (est. 1892). Behind it, the **Royal Arcade ❷**, on Little Collins Street, built in 1869, is guarded by statues of the mythical giants Gog and Magog and houses offbeat shops such as Spellbox (a speciality store for witches).

Royal Arcade emerges on the Bourke Street Mall, home to big department stores. Head up to Swanston Street, go right for one block, then up Collins Street via a gentle hill to the historic Paris End, as it is known, with fashionable shops, galleries, boutiques, and plane trees sparkling with fairy lights in the evening. The grand **Old Treasury Building ❸**, lies at the end on the far side of Spring Street. Built in 1857 to hold the fabulous wealth coming out of the goldfields, it now houses a historical museum *(tel 03/9651-2233, free)*.

Behind the Treasury Building are the beautiful **Treasury** and **Fitzroy Gardens ❹**, favorite spots for office workers to eat lunch. On weekends, Fitzroy Gardens is bright with picnickers and wedding parties having their photos

NOT TO BE MISSED:

Fitzroy Gardens • Melbourne Museum • Queen Victoria Market

taken among the flower beds or on the stately Avenue of Elms. A popular stop is Cook's Cottage ($), plucked from Captain Cook's native Yorkshire and reassembled in the gardens in 1934 to help mark Melbourne's centenary.

Return to Spring Street and turn right to reach the grand **Windsor Hotel ❺**, opened in 1883. This old-money Melbourne icon was long a favored haunt of royalty, prime ministers, and visiting dignitaries, and beneath its ornate ceilings, the nation's constitution was drafted in 1900. Though the building looks tired, as it awaits a controversial redevelopment that includes a tower block behind, afternoon tea at the Windsor is still a Melbourne tradition that is well worth trying.

Continue along Spring Street, past the ornate 1886 **Princess Theatre,** and on for another three blocks to Victoria Street, where you'll find the old Exhibition Buildings, Carlton Gardens, and the huge new **Melbourne Museum ❻** complex (see p. 295).

Turn left down Victoria Street. A short side trip two blocks later, down Russell Street, will bring you to the eerie **Old Melbourne Gaol ❼** *(Russell St., tel 03/9663-7228)*, where the notorious bushranger Ned Kelly (see pp. 322–323) met his fate on the gallows in 1880. Then continue a few blocks farther along Victoria Street to the bustling **Queen Victoria Market ❽**, a colorful Melbourne institution brimming with fresh produce, all manner of goods and souvenirs, and where you can pick up the makings for a very classy picnic—right down to the basket (see p. 294).

Now walk down Elizabeth Street to the **Melbourne Central mall ❾** shopping center. From here, you can catch either a tram or the subway back to Flinders Street Station.

St. Kilda

The suburb of St. Kilda is an old-fashioned seaside playground, with grand old hotels, a fading amusement park, and art deco apartments crowding a palm-lined esplanade and beach. Its seedy reputation has given way to cosmopolitan cool. It's also extremely popular and just a short tram ride from the city. Catch one of the trams (No. 16 or 96) clanging their way past Flinders Street Station, along St. Kilda Road, and 20 minutes later you're there.

St. Kilda's Acland Street is famous for its pastry shops, with their tempting windowfront displays.

St. Kilda
🅰 290 C2

Luna Park
✉ Lower Esplanade
☎ 03/9525-5033
lunapark.com.au

Fitzroy Street, lined with watering holes and restaurants, is the main street heading down to the sea, where the **Esplanade** curves around the beach, past the pier and iconic music venues such as the Esplanade Hotel and the grand Palais Theatre. On Sundays, a lively craft market sets up here, and around the corner, crowds flock to **Acland Street,** famous for its cake shops, ethnic eateries, and bars.

Modeled after New York's Coney Island, **Luna Park** is a small and tacky but much-loved old fairground just off the Esplanade. The rides are tame and old-fashioned—the Scenic Railway roller coaster, bumper cars, and Ghost Train are the biggest hits.

The beach is good, with a comfortable holiday atmosphere. On summer weekends, professional beach volleyball tournaments or Ironman competitions are occasionally held here. The pier, with the ornate kiosk at the end, attracts fishermen and Sunday strollers. It has a good view of the city skyline and the long curve of coastline of Melbourne's bayside suburbs. A bicycle path runs along this coast, from South Melbourne through St. Kilda and on to Brighton. ■

Main Yarra Trail

Melbourne is a bicycle-friendly city, with an extensive network of flat bicycle paths to take an inquisitive cyclist through parklands, past gritty inner-city streetscapes, and along the breezy foreshore of Port Phillip Bay. One of the most popular cycleways is the Main Yarra Trail, which runs beside the tortuous Yarra River from the heart of the city into suburban parkland. This 25-mile (40 km) path is an ideal way to get to know Melbourne; half of it is described here.

On weekends the Main Yarra Trail is cheerfully busy with cyclists and picnickers, and the river and gum trees along the way make it astonishingly easy to forget you are in a city of three million. There are plenty of bike shops and bike rental businesses in Melbourne, including one at Federation Square on the river.

The trail starts beneath the ornate Princes Bridge, across the river from the Edwardian Flinders Street Station in the heart of the city. A nice prelude to the ride is cake and cappuccino —which you'll ride off anyway— in one of the sunny cafés at the nearby Southgate complex (see p. 299). Then head upstream as the river winds its way through **Alexandra Gardens.**

The riverside path goes south and east into some of Melbourne's most fashionable inner suburbs— parklike **South Yarra, Kew,** and **Hawthorn.** It elbows around a golf course in Hawthorn, then veers abruptly north into gritty working-class suburbs such as **Collingwood,** past some of the city's earliest industrial sites.

Follow the path through more parkland, looking back occasionally for views of the Melbourne skyline, and on toward the **Fairfield Park Boathouse.** Although the path continues for many more miles, this quaint old tearoom, which overlooks the river, is a good place to stop. You can get lunch here, or rent a punt and row on the river. There is a country feel to this little enclave, and it's quite a shock to walk only a short way up a wooded path and step onto busy Heidelberg Road. Fairfield railroad station is a short ride away (across Heidelberg Road and up Station Street), and you can take the train back to Flinders Street Station. Another benefit of cycling in Melbourne is that you can take your bike on city trains for free. ∎

EXPERIENCE: Biking Melbourne

Melbourne Bike Share *(melbournebikeshare .com.au)* **is a government bike-hire initiative with 50 docking stations around the city center stacked with bikes. Swipe your credit card, grab a bike, and drop it at another station. Bike helmets ($5) are compulsory in Australia and stocked by nearby retail outlets listed at docking stations. Bicycle Network Victoria** *(Level 4, 246 Bourke St., tel 03/8376-8888, bicyclenetwork.com.au),* **a nonprofit promoting cycling, sells excellent cycling maps, and their website is a good resource. The visitor center** *(thatsmelbourne.com.au)* **lists bicycle tours.**

Mornington Peninsula

One hour south of Melbourne you'll find the fashionable beach towns of the Mornington Peninsula, where generations of Melburnians have gone to escape the rush of the city. A much loved crescent of calm beach runs nearly 60 miles (96 km) along the inner rim of the bay. The open ocean side has a dramatic rocky coastline and good surf on the "back beaches." About 60 small but superb vineyards and winemakers dot the boot-shaped peninsula.

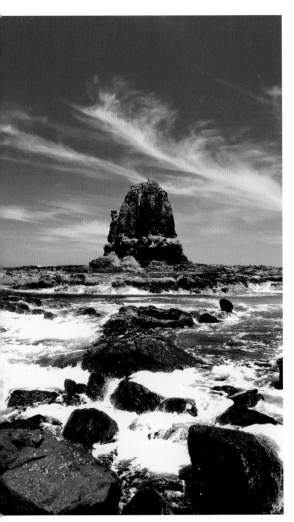

A volcanic monolith rises off the Mornington Peninsula's coast at Cape Schanck.

To get there, take the Eastlink toll road or drive south on the Nepean Highway, along the bustling southeast flank of Port Phillip Bay, past the suburb of Frankston. **Mount Eliza** marks the outermost commuter suburb. The fishing port of **Mornington,** a few miles farther south, has a scenic esplanade and the **Mornington Peninsula Art Gallery**—one of Victoria's best regional galleries. Every Wednesday there is a craft fair on Main Street.

The holiday feeling starts in **Dromana,** where the tourist office has brochures and maps for resorts down the peninsula. The bayside beaches from Dromana to Rye are bright with colored wooden shacks—bathing boxes. **Arthur's Seat State Park,** a 1,000-foot-high (300 m) granite outcrop, is nearby, with sweeping views of the bay and peninsula. In 1802, explorer Matthew Flinders climbed it to get his bearings (and learned from the view that he had sailed into the wrong bay).

Cape Schanck, a dramatic headland on the ocean side of the peninsula, is the site of an 1859 lighthouse. Excellent beach walks can be taken here, and the 16-mile (26 km) Two Bays Trail crosses the peninsula to Dromana.

INSIDER TIP:

Merricks General Wine Store, a cozy bistro and food shop, is a must-stop on your Mornington Peninsula wine tour.

—CATHERINE PEARSON
National Geographic contributor

On the bay side, **Sorrento** and **Portsea** are fashionable little towns near the toe of the boot. Even the ice cream and fish-and-chip shops along the beach are upscale. The beaches are lovely, but take care for riptides on the open ocean beaches and swim between the flags. In 1967, the Australian prime minister, Harold Holt, vanished while swimming here. Conspiracy theorists have had a ball with the incident, the most colorful theory being that he was taken aboard a Chinese submarine. The truth is that Holt disdained the rules and swam on unguarded surf beaches and was swept away by ferocious riptides.

At the tip of the peninsula, **Point Nepean National Park** has wonderful coastal scenery and the labyrinthine tunnels and crumbling fortifications of Fort Nepean, built in the 1880s to guard the narrow heads at the entrance to the bay. Walk the trails or take a shuttle bus 3 miles (4.5 km) to the fort from the old Quarantine Station, where you'll find the park visitor center *(tel 03/5984 6014),* heritage buildings, and displays. You can also drive farther into the park to Gunners Cottage.

From Sorrento you can take a ferry across the mouth of the bay to the pretty little seaside town of **Queenscliff.** The Peninsula Searoad Ferry *(tel 03/5258-3244, searoad.com.au)* carries both passengers and vehicles.

Phillip Island, at the entrance to Westernport Bay, is another popular beach destination, famed for its sunset parade of fairy penguins, which emerge in the hundreds from the water every evening and waddle up Summerland Beach to their nests. This spectacle has become a tourist must-see in Victoria, supplemented by other wildlife attractions including the **Koala Conservation Centre** and the huge **Nobbies Centre** seal lookout and displays. A bridge crosses from San Remo on the mainland to the island town of Newhaven, where a visitor center is close to the bridge, and on to the main resort town of Cowes. ∎

Mornington Peninsula

▲ 290 C1

Visitor Information

✉ Nepean Hwy., Dromana

☎ 03/5987-3078

Merricks General Wine Store

✉ 3460 Frankston-Flinders Rd., Merricks

☎ 03/5989-8088

mgwinestore.com.au

Phillip Island

▲ 290 C1

Visitor Information

✉ 895 Phillip Island Rd., Newhaven
or
91-97 Thompson Ave., Cowes

☎ 1300-366-422

visitphillipisland.com

Visitor Information on Nature Parks

penguins.org.au

EXPERIENCE:
Penguin Parade

A large colony of 4,500 little penguins, the smallest of the species at just over a foot (30 cm) high, nests at **Summerland Beach** on Phillip Island. After sunset every evening, they return to their burrows to rest or feed their young in the breeding season. The penguins are unfazed by the tour buses and packed stands, as first one animal emerges tentatively from the sea, then two, then a dozen, until a flood of cute penguins is waddling up the beach to the dunes. **Phillip Island Nature Parks** *(tel 03/5951-2800, penguins.org.au, $$$)* has details on all wildlife attractions.

Yarra Valley

Melbourne's rural fringes—the Yarra Valley and the Dandenong Ranges—are well worth exploring. They have Victoria's best wineries, excellent bushwalking, and some beautiful drives through tall forests.

Yarra Valley

🗺 290 C2

Visitor Information

✉ Old Courthouse, Harker St., Healesville

☎ 03/5962-2600

The Yarra Valley, only an hour's drive northeast from Melbourne on the Maroondah Highway, is best explored by car. This region is one of Victoria's oldest wine producers. Vines were first planted here in the 1860s by Swiss immigrants Paul and Hubert de Castella. In 1889, the region earned gold medals at the Paris Exposition. Then came the dreaded phylloxera outbreak that ravaged the world's vines in the late 19th century and struck Victoria particularly hard. Later,

INSIDER TIP:

Yering Station, the oldest Yarra Valley winery, is a must for its historic Chateau Yering hotel, restaurant, tasting room, café, art gallery, and local produce store.

—PETER TURNER
National Geographic author

Australia's palate shifted to fortified wines, and under these twin blows, winemaking in the valley seemed moribund. The last of the vines were pulled up in 1921.

These days the Yarra Valley is enjoying a renaissance, with more than 90 wineries in the region. One major presence is the French champagne-maker Moët et Chandon, whose **Domain Chandon winery,** near Coldstream, makes delectable sparkling wines. It has a delightfully airy tasting room with sweeping views of the vineyards. The **De Bortoli winery,** north of Yarra Glen on the Melba Highway, produces a dessert wine—called the Noble One—that is arguably Australia's best.

Healesville, about 12 miles (19 km) farther on the Maroondah Highway, has the **Healesville Sanctuary** *(Badger Creek Rd., tel 03/5957-2800, zoo.org.au, $$$),* established in the 1940s to care for injured or orphaned animals. Some are returned to the wild; others are used for breeding programs to help endangered species. There are more than 200 species of native birds, mammals, and reptiles here.

Beyond Healesville, the Maroondah Highway twists its way up through the deep wet forests of the **Great Dividing Range.** The incredibly tall mountain ash throw the narrow road into a welcome, cool green shade. The impression of driving through a cathedral would make you go at a stately pace even without the many hairpin turns. Giant ferns, myrtle beech, manna gums, and small sparkling waterfalls catch your eye as you pass. There are pulling-off points where you can stop and admire the scenery. ■

The Dandenongs

Tinted blue by the mist of eucalyptus oil given off by the forests, the Dandenong Ranges are Melbourne's answer to Sydney's Blue Mountains (see pp. 104–105). Drive 20 miles (32 km) southeast of town on the Burwood Highway to Upper Ferntree Gully, and then turn north on the steep and winding Mount Dandenong Tourist Road into the forests.

Puffing Billy now hauls tourists instead of its original cargo of farm produce.

The mountains rise to more than 2,000 feet (610 m) and are cloaked with dense, lush growth. Some of the gullies are shaded by huge ferns, whose fronds form an overhead canopy, blocking out the sun and sheltering a rich growth of mosses, smaller ferns, and flowers, including more than 30 species of orchids. The ranges also have 100-odd species of birds but are especially known for lyrebirds. These skillful mimics can re-create almost any sound, including other birdcalls, the motorwind on a camera, and even a chainsaw.

Ferntree Gully National Park, Sherwood Forest, Doongalla Reserve, Olinda, and Mount Evelyn forests have been combined to form the **Dandenong Ranges National Park.** Popular with bushwalkers, the park has numerous short trails, many of them with city views. **Mount Dandenong** is the top day-trip destination, with a café and unrivaled views.

The restful villages up here have tearooms, craft galleries, B&Bs, and gracious old houses with beautiful gardens. At **Belgrave** you can catch an old steam train, *Puffing Billy (reservations, tel 03/9757-0700, puffingbilly.com.au, $$$$),* which was built in 1900 to haul farm produce and now winds along an 8-mile (13 km) track to Emerald Lake Park. ■

Dandenong Ranges National Park

⬛ 290 C2

Visitor Information

✉ 1211 Burwood Hwy., Upper Ferntree Gully

☎ 03/9758-7522

EXPLORING THE DANDENONGS:
Hikers' guides to the Dandenongs, detailing paths and the flora and fauna you may see, are available in Melbourne and at *parkweb.vic.gov.au.* Belgrave can be reached by train out of Flinders Street Railway Station in Melbourne.

Great Ocean Road Drive

Simply put, the Great Ocean Road is Australia's finest coastal drive. It starts at the seaside resort town of Torquay, about 60 miles (100 km) southwest of Melbourne, and hugs Victoria's spectacular, cliff-lined Shipwreck Coast for 150 miles (240 km) to the old whaling port of Warrnambool. From Melbourne, the direct route to Torquay is through Geelong, but the road down the Mornington Peninsula is more attractive.

On view is perhaps the most magnificent mix of scenery in Australia: hauntingly long sandy beaches, miles of rugged cliffs, wildflowers, and pretty fishing ports set against the backdrop of the steep, rain forested Otway Ranges. The road's most famous landmarks are the Twelve Apostles, a series of dramatic rock pillars that rise from the sea near Port Campbell.

The road was built as a monument to the soldiers who had served in World War I. Construction began in 1918, and many of the

See also area map p. 290
► Melbourne
↔ 260 miles (418 km)
⏱ 1 day
► Warrnambool

Driving route detour
Ferry route
Walking trail route

0   40 kilometers
0   20 miles

3,000 men who worked on it were themselves war veterans. It was completed in 1932, and since then it has been hugely popular with tourists and Victorians alike.

The Great Ocean Road (*visitgreatoceanroad .org.au*) officially starts in the old vacation town of Torquay, 14 miles (23 km) south of Geelong. From Melbourne, you could cross the Westgate Bridge, follow the Princes Freeway 45 miles (72 km) to Geelong, and then take the Bypass or Surfcoast Highway to Torquay. It's a quick drive, but not particularly scenic. Instead, detour on the Nepean Highway down the Mornington Peninsula (see pp. 306–307) to Sorrento or Portsea, and then take the ferry across the

---

NOT TO BE MISSED:

Lorne • Cape Otway lighthouse • The Twelve Apostles

---

mouth of Port Phillip Bay to the old maritime town of **Queenscliff ❶**. This pretty bayside town was founded in 1838 as a pilot boat station for ships entering the bay. Later it became a naval garrison town. The railway arrived from Geelong in 1879, and the town became a fashionable resort favored for its sea breezes, yachting, and grand hotels. Even today the

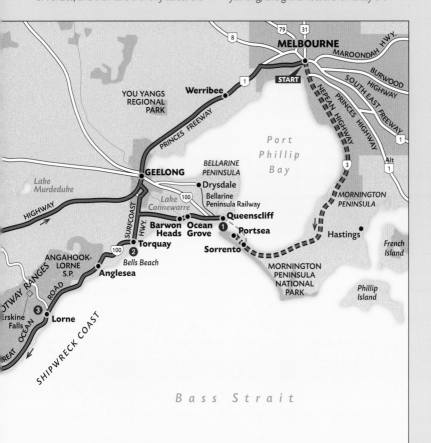

Queenscliff Hotel (see p. 384), built in 1887, and the **Vue Grand** (1884) on Hesse Street *(tel 03/5258-1544)* are very elegant retreats. From Queenscliff, it is a 28-mile (44 km) drive via Ocean Grove and Barwon Heads to the Surfcoast Highway.

Torquay ❷ *(visitor information: Surf City Plaza, Beach Rd., tel 03/5261-4219)* has been a vacation spot since the late 19th century, but the surfing culture of the 1960s made it famous. Surf conditions along these beaches can be close to perfect, and the Easter Surfing Classic, held on nearby **Bells Beach,** is a premier pro surfing event. In town, **Surf City Plaza** houses surf fashion outlets and board makers, including local companies Rip Curl and Quiksilver. Surf World surfing museum *(tel 03/5261-4606, $)* is also in the plaza.

The road veers inland for about 10 miles (16 km) before coming down to the sea again at **Anglesea,** where kangaroos graze on the golf course, but from there it diligently winds its way along the rugged coast past miles of beaches, through the picturesque seaside town of **Lorne** ❸ (about 25 miles/40 km from Torquay). Lorne has been a popular holiday resort since the 1860s, when coaches brought visitors over the Otway Ranges on muddy bush tracks. Today Lorne is one of the most fashionable retreats on the coast, popular with surfers and with bushwalkers, who can scramble up the ranges behind the town to see the delightful **Erskine Falls** or gain even more spectacular views of the coast. On a busy weekend, or around the Christmas holiday, its population can surge from 1,400 to more than 20,000. If you want to stay, avoid busy times or reserve well ahead. The Lorne Visitor Information Centre *(15 Mountjoy Parade, tel 03/5289-1152)* has details of accommodations.

The narrow and twisting 25-mile (40 km) stretch from Lorne to **Apollo Bay** *(visitor information: tel 03/5237-6529)* is one of the most dramatic sections of the Great Ocean Road. It hugs steep cliffs and winds around tight little inlets. The scenery is so beautiful that it can be hard to keep your eyes on the road—which is dangerous because the road is incredibly curvy as it picks its way along the cliffs. Happily, you can stop at plenty of lookouts.

After Apollo Bay, the road veers inland, climbing into the Otway Ranges and giving spectacular views of the ocean and rolling green hillsides spreading out behind. These steep

Shipwreck Coast

If this coast is tough on drivers, it has been much more cruel to sailors. More than 80 vessels have come to grief along here, the most famous of which was the clipper *Loch Ard*. It went down on a cold, stormy night in June 1878, and of the 53 people on board, only two survived: an 18-year-old girl named Eva Carmichael and an apprentice seaman, Tom Pearce, also 18. They were washed into a long, narrow, high-walled gorge and sheltered in a cave until morning, when Pearce scaled the cliffs to summon help. The nation was stunned by the tragedy. Eva Carmichael lost both of her parents and five siblings in the disaster, and the popular hope was that she would strike up a romance with the young seaman who had saved her life. It wasn't to be, however. She came from a prosperous family in Ireland and returned there, while Pearce went back to sea, where he survived two more shipwrecks.

Today scenic trails loop around Loch Ard Gorge, and wooden steps lead down to the tiny beach and cave—Carmichael's Cave—where the two castaways spent their miserable night. The *Loch Ard*'s anchor stands outside the visitor center in nearby Port Campbell, where the Loch Ard Shipwreck Museum tells the story of five other shipwrecks along the coast.

Despite their name, the powerful and impressive Twelve Apostles actually comprise eight sea stacks.

mountains, clad in temperate rain forests, are the wettest parts of Victoria, averaging more than 80 inches (200 cm) of rainfall a year.

If you've brought a stout pair of walking boots, Apollo Bay is the beginning of the **Great Ocean Walk,** a spectacular trail that hugs the coastline most of the way to the Twelve Apostles, 57 miles (91 km) away. The trail can be done as a whole or in stages, with maps and information on accommodations along the way available from Parks Victoria *(tel 13-1963, parkweb.vic.gov.au).*

About 12 miles (19 km) after Apollo Bay, turn left (south) on a sealed road to the **Cape Otway lighthouse ❹,** built out of local sandstone by convicts in 1848, in response to a series of shipwrecks on the reefs. The lighthouse is a paragon of reliability, but that is no protection from bad luck or poor judgment. At front you can see the rusting anchor of *Eric the Red,* which foundered in 1880 with the loss of four lives. The lighthouse has a café, tours, and accommodations *(lightstation.com).*

The Great Ocean Road winds past the small but lovely **Melba Gully State Park,** with its luxuriant ferns, dense rain forests, and eerie evening displays of glowworms, and on through the old timber town of **Lavers Hill.** The highway rejoins the coast at **Princetown** and follows it for several miles through **Port Campbell National Park,** a strip of spectacular coastline *(visitor information: tel 03/5598-6089).* Storms over millions of years have eaten away at this coast, leaving the **Twelve Apostles ❺** — enormous rock pillars, more than 200 feet (60 m) tall—in the sea. To view these striking formations, park at the Twelve Apostles Centre and take the walkway under the highway to the cliff-top lookout points connected by a boardwalk. Early morning and late afternoon are best for spectacular pictures.

The Great Ocean Road ends where it joins the Princes Highway, east of the old whaling town of **Warrnambool ❻** *(visitor information: Flagstaff Hill, Merri St., tel 1800-637-725, visitwarrnambool.com.au).* In winter months (June–Sept.), the southern right whales that use the shallows here as a nursery are a popular attraction. Once hunted almost to extinction, their numbers are now slowly rebuilding, although there are still probably fewer than 10,000. Warrnambool's days as a

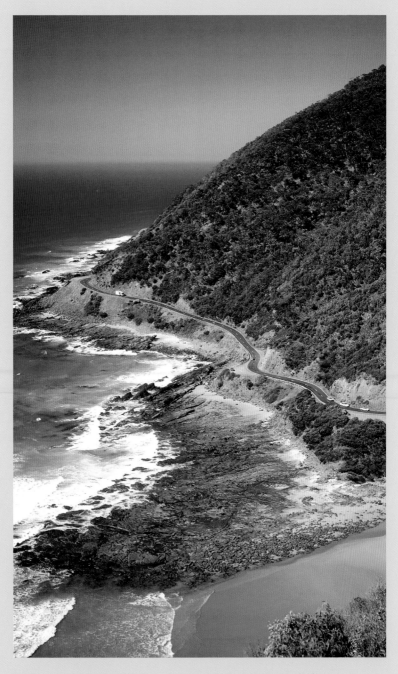

The Great Ocean Road threads between the sea and the Otway Ranges south of Lorne.

EXPERIENCE: Surfing

Victoria's **Bells Beach** (see p. 312) is the home of Australian surfing, or at least the home of the Australian surf industry's major brands like Quiksilver and Rip Curl. The big swells at Bells are renowned, but good surf can also be found elsewhere along the Great Ocean Road, and on the Mornington Peninsula and Phillip Island.

Sydney lays claim to the country's most popular surf beaches. Bondi has decent surf, but the best waves are on the northern beaches stretching north from Manly.

For warmer water, head north. **Byron Bay** to **Surfers Paradise** is Australia's premier beach holiday stretch, with plenty of good surf spots. At the top is the **Gold Coast**'s Superbank, where theme parks proliferate. The council inadvertently made a theme park for surfers when it dredged the Tweed River to form this sand bank. On a good day, legend has it, you can catch a wave for more than a mile (2 km). The **Sunshine Coast** north of Brisbane also has good surf, but the Great Barrier Reef shelters most of the Queensland coastline.

In **Western Australia**, the coast from Cape Naturaliste to Cape Leeuwin has some of the biggest and most consistent surf in Australia. The westerlies here push huge swells along the Great Australian Bight to the **Eyre Peninsula**, which has noted waves at Streaky Bay, among others.

Surf lessons are offered almost anywhere a surf scene exists. Big-name beaches like Bondi and Noosa are most popular, but you might find smaller classes elsewhere.

See *surfingaustralia.com* or *australia.com* for more information.

---

whaling station are re-created at **Flagstaff Hill Maritime Village** (*tel 03/5559-4600*), based around the lighthouse, lighthouse keeper's cottage, and fortifications built in 1887.

One of Australia's most intriguing shipwrecks is the "Mahogany Ship," reputedly buried in the sand between Warrnambool and Port Fairy. A couple of whalers first sighted it in 1836; upon examination, the Port Fairy harbormaster thought its design antiquated and its timbers unlike any he'd ever seen, "like mahogany." No record existed of such a ship being lost in the area, and local Aborigines said the wreck had always been there. Then, in 1880, a series of great storms obliterated the mysterious wreck, and it has never been seen since. Some historians believe it may have been a 16th-century caravel sent by the Portuguese government to secretly reconnoiter the south seas, in violation of a treaty with Spain. The ancient Dauphin Map, reputedly based on information from Portuguese archives, appears to show the south coast of Australia. The archives were destroyed in the Lisbon earthquake of 1755, so the question of which Europeans first saw Australia remains open.

The **Mahogany Walking Trail 7**, a 14-mile (22 km) coastal walk to Port Fairy, takes you past the area where the Mahogany Ship was last seen 120 years ago. Warrnambool's Visitor Information Centre has information on local walks and sights.

The historic seaside village of **Port Fairy** has picturesque streets lined with heritage buildings and stone cottages, many of them now B&Bs. This popular holiday spot also hosts the Port Fairy Folk Festival in March, one of the country's premier music events.

You can take the Princes Highway directly back to Melbourne, or continue on to Portland, Victoria's first town, and then along the coast to Adelaide.

Victoria's Alpine Country

The high country of Victoria is great for hiking in summer and offers some of Australia's best skiing in winter. It stretches from Mansfield—about 100 miles (160 km) northeast of Melbourne—to the New South Wales border. Most of the state's ski resorts are in this area. Picturesque villages, wineries, and small farms nestle in the valleys at the foot of the 6,000-foot-high (1,800 m) mountains and make it a delightful place to tour.

Known as Australia's powder capital, Mount Hotham is one of Victoria's most popular ski resorts.

Beechworth

🄰 291 D3

Visitor Information

✉ 103 Ford St.

☎ 03/5728-8065

The heart of the alpine country is around the **Bogong High Plains,** a four-hour drive northeast of Melbourne on the Hume Highway. The route runs through Kelly Country, where bushranger Ned Kelly and his gang hid out (see pp. 322–323). In winter, you can see the snow-capped mountains from the town of **Glenrowan,** where they fought their last battle.

At **Wangaratta,** leave the Hume Highway and follow the Ovens Highway up the pictur-esque Ovens River Valley. As with much of Victoria, it was gold that opened up this neck of the woods. The town of **Beechworth** *(visitor information: Ford St., 1300-366-321, beechworth.com)*—north of the highway—was founded in 1852 on the heels of a big strike that produced more than 4 million ounces (113,400 kg) in the first 14 years alone. In its heyday, it was a town of 42,000 with 61 pubs, famous for its gaudy politics. Amid the brass bands, free drinks, may-hem, and vote-buying of the 1855 election, one candidate, Daniel Cameron, reputedly paraded to the polls on a horse shod with solid gold.

These days Beechworth is one of the prettiest and best preserved of Victoria's gold towns, its wide streets lined with honey-colored buildings, classy restaurants, and museums. The **Burke Museum** (*Loch St.*)–named for explorer Robert Burke (see pp. 44–45), who was the town's police commissioner–tells the story of the gold rush. The 3-mile-long (5 km) **Gorge Scenic Drive** is best experienced on a bicycle. It takes you through old digging areas and past the Powder Magazine, now a museum. Beechworth is also on the **Murray to the Mountains Rail Trail,** from Wangaratta to Bright, the country's premier rail trail. The easy bitumen track runs past scenic wineries and farms.

Into the Mountains

The mountains start just past Myrtleford, with the spectacular **Mount Buffalo National Park,** known for its wildflowers and waterfalls. One notable waterfall, Crystal Brook, plummets almost 800 feet (243 m) in a single drop. There are nearly 90 miles (144 km) of hiking and cross-country ski trails on this mile-high (1.6 km) granite massif. You can drive to near the summit of the Horn and then walk to the top for a sweeping panorama.

The 20-mile (32 km) drive up the valley from Myrtleford to **Bright** is lined with small farms growing tobacco, peppermint, hops, and flowers. Bright has many European trees and in autumn is famous for its New England–like foliage. Bright's tourist information center has a leaflet on some of the lovely bushwalks in the area.

Beyond Bright the road forks. One branch leads to Mount Beauty and the ski resort of **Falls Creek.** The other winds its way to the 6,128-foot (1,862 m) summit of **Mount Hotham** and on to the village of Dinner Plain. Mount Hotham has perhaps the best powder skiing in Australia, while Falls Creek has the best cross-country skiing. It is the only ski village in Australia where everyone can ski directly from their lodges to the ski slopes.

In summer, there are magnificent hiking opportunities up here. **Mount Bogong** is a particularly nice–if somewhat steep–hike. Hikers with enough time and experience can tackle the 406-mile (650 km) **Alpine Walking Track,** which runs from Walhalla to the outskirts of Canberra. ∎

Bright
🅰 291 D2
Visitor Information
✉ 76a Gavan St.
☎ 03/5755-2275

Bogong High Plains

The Bogong High Plains in the Victorian Alps are a wonderland for cross-country skiers in winter and for hikers in summer, with huts scattered along the Alpine Walking Track and nearby walks to Mount Bogong and Mount Feathertop.

Easily accessed from the ski resorts of Falls Creek and Mount Hotham, the plains are home to some unique flora and fauna, including the rare mountain pygmy possum, thought to be extinct until one wandered into a ski hut in the 1960s. The Bogong moth also migrates here every year from November to March, when Aboriginal tribes once gathered to feast on the moths, which they called Bogong. Huge clouds of the large moths descend on Canberra and other southeast cities during their great summer migration away from the heat of the plains.

Australian Rules Football

For seven months each year, suburban Melbourne becomes a patchwork of jealous footy fiefdoms—Collingwood, Essendon, North Melbourne, Carlton, and St. Kilda, to name a few. In all, this sports-mad city supports nine professional, big-league Aussie Rules football clubs—ten if you count neighboring Geelong—and just as many professional minor-league ones. Some clubs date back to the 1850s, which makes them the world's oldest.

Club allegiances run in families, and after so many generations, team colors can form far sharper social distinctions than race, class, or money. During the footy season, about the only thing all these footy fanatics agree on is that it's sweet to see a Victorian team clobber one from interstate—especially one from South Australia.

There is no more quintessentially Melburnian activity than bundling up against the winter weather and heading down to the footy. If you're visiting Melbourne during the season, which runs roughly from March through September, go! This is the real Victoria: a bleacher seat, a meat pie, and bone-crunching action.

The "Rules" of the Game

The plot can be a little hard for novices to follow, because there don't appear to be any rules in Aussie Rules, other than that each side has 18 players on the field.

In a nutshell the object is to kick, bounce, and punch the ball up the field until you are close enough to boot it between the goalposts for six points. When that happens, the goalpost referee—who looks like he or she is wearing a lab coat—struts between the posts and quick-draws two imaginary pistols. The crowd then goes wild. If the player misses the two narrowest uprights, but gets it between the two wider ones, he gets a point for almost.

EXPERIENCE:
Catch a Match

Don't miss the chance to see a fast and furious Australian Rules game. The antics of the fanatical crowd are worth the entry ticket alone. Finals are sold out weeks before, but regular weekend and Friday night games from March to September are easy to catch. In Melbourne, head for the M.C.G. or Etihad Stadium at Docklands, near Southern Cross train station. Tickets can be booked at Ticketmaster (ticketmaster.com.au), advisable for one of the big games, but otherwise just line up at the stadium ticket window. Alternatively, the gates are opened for free entry in the last quarter (about two hours after the start time) if the stadium isn't full.

Nonstop Action & Athleticism

No doubt about it, this is one gutsy game. The players, who are built like basketball players with attitude, wear neither pads nor helmets, and they collide with reckless abandon—eyes only on the ball. They play at full tilt over four 20-minute quarters, leaping, kicking, chasing, wrestling, and tackling. Their athleticism is amazing. Imagine a bloke, maybe six feet eight (2 m) and 225 pounds (102 kg), leaping like a ballet dancer to snatch a football out of the air, then sprinting up the field, dodging tacklers, and booting the ball on a dead run 60 yards (55 m) for a goal. Injuries are common, but the action never stops, not even when someone is being stretchered off.

Weekly Clashes

The big game of the week is usually played at the Melbourne Cricket Ground (M.C.G.,

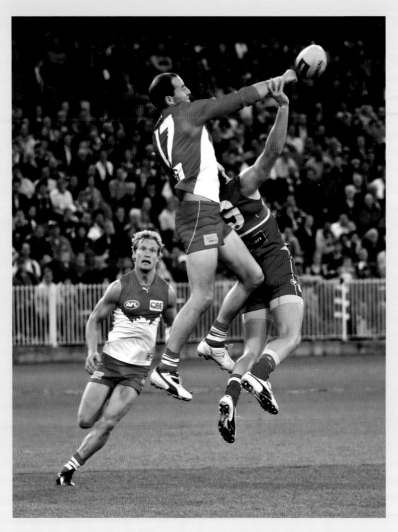

Melbourne's Western Bulldogs take on the Sydney Swans in an Australian Football League match.

see p. 296)—a sort of no-man's-land on the footy map, where both teams are visitors and 100,000-plus seats accommodate the crowd. Some of these clashes go down in footy history. The atmosphere is throbbing, blindly parochial, yet still quite friendly. There's none of the hooliganism that plagues English and European soccer. The physical contact stays on the field. Aussies generally conduct their footy feuds with barbed wisecracks—often hilariously funny, even to the recipient.

The season stretches into the last week of September and culminates with the Grand Final. If you are lucky enough to be here then and get a chance to go, or find yourself invited to a Grand Final party at a local's house—don't pass it up.

Goldfields

A string of fabulous gold discoveries in the mid-19th century transformed Victoria's economy and created huge wealth in gold-rush towns such as Ballarat, Castlemaine, and Bendigo. The nouveau riche towns flaunted their incredible wealth with elaborate gardens, bandstands, statuary, and grandly frivolous architecture. A tour of the cities and the Victorian goldfields makes a delightful three-day (or longer) drive from Melbourne.

Sovereign Hill at Ballarat is a living museum, re-creating life in gold-rush days.

Ballarat

🗺 290 B2

Visitor Information

✉ 43 Lydiard St. N.

☎ 03/5320-5741

visitballarat.com.au

Ballarat

Ballarat, the scene of the 1854 Eureka Stockade battle (see pp. 46–48), is only an hour or so west of Melbourne. Entering from the east, the ornamental trees, ornate buildings, and brilliant flowerbeds give a taste of the city's elegance and wealth. On the other side of town, the Western Highway runs along a 14-mile (22.5 km) Avenue of Honor, flanked with trees commemorating soldiers who died in World War I.

Gold was found at Ballarat in 1851, one of a series of strikes that sprang up like wildfires around central Victoria, and mining continued until 1918. Today, mining companies are exploring the area again, armed with computer-age technology that could make this a gold town once again.

The town has many old buildings, among them the classical revival **Town Hall,** the **Mining Exchange** building (1888), and the **Art Gallery of Ballarat** (1884; *40 Lydiard St. N.),* which has a fine collection of Heidelberg school and colonial art (see p. 64), and the Eureka Stockade Flag. Museums include the new **Museum of Australian Democracy at Eureka** *(Stawell St. S., tel 1800-287-113)* on the site of the uprising.

Ballarat's main attraction is the living museum at **Sovereign Hill** *(Bradshaw St., tel 03/5337-1100,* *sovereignhill.com.au, $$$$$).* It re-creates the Ballarat of the gold-rush days, with coaches clattering down cobbled streets, old shops open for business, and gold diggings where you can try your luck. There's also a Gold Museum, and Blood on the Southern Cross is a nighttime sound-and-light spectacular retelling the Eureka rebellion story.

Follow the Midland Highway northeast to the gold-mining town of **Daylesford,** better known today as a spa town. Eighty percent of Australia's known mineral springs bubble up in this old volcanic area, and for more than a century, Victorians have come here to take the water. The town has organic eateries, alternative bookstores, chic cafés, and fine dining on the lake.

Castlemaine

Castlemaine is farther north along the Midlands Highway. Reputed to have once had the richest shallow deposits of gold ever known, it is now one of Victoria's prettiest towns. Its streetscapes have not changed much since the 19th century.

Built in 1862, the superb neoclassic **Castlemaine Market** is topped by a statue of Ceres, the Roman goddess of the harvest. The restored building now houses the visitor center. An example of colonial architecture, **Buda** *(corner of Urquhart and Hunter Sts., tel 03/5472-1032)* is now in the hands of the National Trust.

The nearby town of **Maldon** is considered to have the best preserved architecture of

Victoria's goldfield towns. In 1966, the National Trust classified it as a "notable town" for its unspoiled and intact streetscapes.

Bendigo

Bendigo is where the gold rush began in 1851. Its reputation for spectacular finds spread to China, luring thousands of Chinese prospectors in its boom days. Their legacy is celebrated at the **Golden Dragon Museum** *(5-11 Bridge Street, tel 03/5441-5044, $$).* After the initial alluvial strikes, gold was mined in deep quartz reefs until the last large mine closed in 1956.

INSIDER TIP:

Don't miss Theatre Royal *[theatreroyal .info].* This Castlemaine institution is *the* place to see the latest movies in comfort while wining and dining.

—PETER TURNER
National Geographic author

Great wealth and civic pride combined to make Bendigo an architectural jewel. One of its most elegant buildings is the **Shamrock Hotel,** built in 1897 on the corner of Pall Mall and Williamson Street, which features a marble staircase, polished wood, and stained glass in its lobby.

For a taste of life in a mine, try the 200-foot-deep (60 m) **Central Deborah Mine** *(76 Violet St., tel 03/5443-8322, $$$).* ∎

Daylesford
⚠ 290 B2
Visitor Information
✉ 98 Vincent St.
☎ 03/5321-6123

Castlemaine
⚠ 290 B2
Visitor Information
✉ 44 Mostyn St.
☎ 03/5471-1795
maldoncastlemaine.com.au

Maldon
⚠ 290 B2
Visitor Information
✉ 93 High St.
☎ 03/5475-2569
maldoncastlemaine.com

Bendigo
⚠ 290 B2
Visitor Information
✉ Old Post Office building, 51–67 Pall Mall
☎ 03/5434-6060
bendigotourism.com

Bushrangers

The gold-rush days were also the glory days of the bushrangers, or highway robbers. Whether recent immigrants or descendants of convicts who had been transported for political reasons, Irish people had little reason to love English authority. They frequently sheltered and supplied the bushrangers, kept them apprised of police movements, and built them into folk heroes. Many bushrangers were of Irish stock themselves.

Sidney Nolan did a series of Ned Kelly paintings, including "Death of Constable Scanlon" (1946).

Australia's first bushrangers were commonly known as "bolters," escaped convicts who took to the bush and lived by robbing passersby. By 1814, the dripping rain forests of Tasmania had come to shelter so many armed bolters that the government declared martial law, fearing that the outlaws would help the captive convicts rebel and take over the island.

According to legend, the bushrangers were dapper gentleman-robbers, but in reality they were frequently violent and thuggish. In the setting of Australia's brutal penal colonies, however, any flouting of authority must have seemed heroic. Some bushrangers really did have a certain gallant style. When Tasmania's Matthew Brady learned that there was a reward on his head, he jauntily tacked up notices offering

20 gallons (90 liters) of rum for the capture of the colony's lieutenant-governor. Brady went to the gallows a hero in 1824, his cell filled with flowers, cakes, and letters from admirers. "Bold Jack" Donohoe was lionized by poorer Australians for his escapades. When he died in a shootout with New South Wales police in 1830, he became a martyr, remembered in ballads and in Bold Jack souvenir tobacco pipes.

Ned Kelly & His Gang

These heroes were eclipsed when Ned Kelly rode onto the scene. He was born in 1854 on a dirt-poor farm in northern Victoria, the son of an Irish convict. By the time he was 15, Ned had a conviction for assault. The next year he was sentenced to three years for horse theft, and in 1878 he gunned down three police officers who were coming to arrest him. With his brother Dan and two mates—Joe Byrne and Steve Hart—he fled into the Strathbogie Ranges. Over the next 18 months, the Kelly Gang conducted a series of dramatic raids. They once took over the town of Jerilderie, New South Wales, and held its citizens hostage. Here Ned dictated a rambling 10,000-word letter to the authorities justifying his actions, describing himself as an Irish Republican political activist. The authorities saw him as a murderous thief who had to be stopped.

In June 1880, the Victoria government dispatched a trainload of armed constables to track down the Kelly Gang. Tipped off that the law was coming, Ned and his cohorts took over the railroad town of Glenrowan and ordered workers to tear up the tracks. One of the hostages managed to get away and signal a warning to the troopers. A gun battle erupted between the lawmen and the Kelly Gang, who were holed up in the Glenrowan Hotel. The fighting lasted all night, and toward dawn the police torched the place. Ned tried to escape in the suit of armor he had made for himself, but he was wounded and captured. The rest of the gang perished in the flames, although popular myth has one (or more) of them escaping and living in quiet anonymity. Old men were still claiming to be Dan Kelly as late as the 1930s.

Romantic Martyr

Ned Kelly was taken to Melbourne for trial, found guilty, and hanged at the Melbourne Gaol on November 11, 1880. His last words were either "Such is life" or "So it has come to this." The authorities soon learned that Ned was bigger and more romantic in martyrdom than he had ever been in life (see sidebar below). A writer in the *Bulletin* magazine noted: "These splendid bushrangers never came within a hundred yards of a woman without taking off their hats." In 1906 the Kelly Gang was the subject of the world's first feature film. It was so sympathetic to Ned and his friends that the Victorian authorities banned it in Kelly's old stomping grounds for fear that it would cause a riot.

Ned Kelly's Legacy in Australian Pop Culture

Ned Kelly is as big in death as he ever was in life. He has been the subject of several movies (one starred Mick Jagger as Kelly) since the 1906 *Story of the Kelly Gang*, as well as many books, songs, and paintings. Australian artist Sidney Nolan created an entire series of paintings in the 1940s on major Kelly gang events. Nolan's paintings can be viewed at the National Gallery of Australia in Canberra. *The True History of the Ned Kelly Gang*, a novel by Peter Carey, won the prestigious Booker Prize in 2001.

In spite of the fact that Kelly was a murderer, many remember him for embodying the rebellious qualities that are part of Australia's national character. A popular Aussie expression is to be "as game as Ned Kelly," or audaciously heroic.

Murray River

The Murray River—with a colorful history of paddle steamers and bellicose steamboat captains—is Australia's longest river, running 1,170 miles (1,883 km) from Victoria's alpine country to South Australia's coastline, the Coorong. For much of its length it forms the border between New South Wales and Victoria. In 1824, explorers Hamilton Hume and William Hovell were the first Europeans to see the river, near the site of modern Albury-Wodonga.

Built 42 feet (12.7 m) above the river, Echuca's massive old wharf is still in business.

Mildura

🅰 290 A4

Visitor Information

✉ 180–190 Deakin Ave.

☎ 03/5018-8380 or 1800-039-043

visitmildura.com.au

By the 1860s, hard-riding cattlemen had claimed much of the land along the river's upper reaches. Among them was Jack Riley, the model for Banjo Paterson's "The Man from Snowy River." Dozens of steamboats puttered up the river's lower reaches and along its major tributary, the Darling, bringing supplies to what had seemed useless land.

In 1887, George and William Chaffee were invited by the Victorian government to set up an irrigation system in northern Victoria. Since then, the Murray has become the lifeblood for a good deal of Australia's agriculture. Controlled by a series of locks and dams, its muddy waters support thousands of acres of orchards, vineyards, and cotton fields.

Although it is at most a couple hundred yards wide, the red gums along its bank, its serpentine curves, and the bright sunshine have made the Murray River a classic vacation spot. Anytime but the staggeringly hot summer are good seasons to visit here.

Mildura

Mildura, about a six-hour drive north from Melbourne on the Calder Highway, is the river town where the irrigation scheme began. It is an oasis, with ornamental palms along the waterfront, landscaped gardens, golf courses, and lawn tennis courts that Australia's Davis Cup players have compared favorably with Wimbledon. Lush orange orchards and vineyards surround the town, and it is easy to forget that beyond the green fringe lie miles of harsh outback mallee scrub and salt pan.

Several restored 19th-century paddle steamers offer cruises from Mildura, ranging from an hour to dinner cruises. A word to visitors expecting massive Mississippi-style steamboats: These are more like the *African Queen* in size (but better appointed) because of the confines of this shallow river. Hot-air balloon flights are also available.

Echuca

Echuca is a colorful old Murray River port about three hours north of Melbourne on the Northern Highway, and it is the most interesting town on the river. An ex-convict named Henry Hopwood founded the town in 1853. He set a ferry crossing and, in 1859, built the Bridge Hotel. He shrewdly fixed his ferry schedule so that travelers had to wait for their crossing, and they generally waited in the pub, buying drinks. Hopwood prospered, and so did Echuca.

The gold rushes and the booming wheat trade made it one of Australia's biggest inland ports, with a massive wharf more than half a mile (800 m) long built out of red gum beams. When the railroads came, the river trade declined and Echuca faded, but it has found new life in tourism. The wharf has been restored, and there are fine restaurants and craft and gift shops. A number of restored steamboats tie up at the old wharf for cruises along this pretty stretch of river, including one-hour excursions, lunch and dinner cruises, and overnight trips. Houseboats and canoe rentals are also available. ∎

Echuca

▲ 290 C3

Visitor Information

✉ Corner of Heygarth St. & Cobb Hwy.

☎ 03/5480-7555 or 1800-804-446

echucamoama.com

Mungo Man & the Walls of China

Mildura is a good base for visiting Mungo National Park, located about 70 miles (112 km) northeast in New South Wales. This significant World Heritage area has spectacular wind-sculpted dune formations known as the Walls of China, and is home to the earliest known human on the continent, Mungo Man. Found in 1974 at Lake Mungo, the fossilized remains, sprinkled in ochre and ritually cremated, date from at least 40,000 years ago.

Ancient, dried-up Lake Mungo once teemed with wildlife and attracted Aboriginal hunters, who camped on the shores. Rich fossil beds have also given palaeontologists a glimpse of the bizarre fauna that once roamed the lakeshores, including 10-foot-tall (3 m) kangaroos.

The dirt road to the park can be impassable when it rains (*contact the park office at tel 03/5021-8900 in Buronga, just over the river from Mildura, for road conditions*). Local Paakantyi Aboriginal guide Harry Nanya (*tel 03/5027-2076, harrynanyatours.com.au*) runs very informative tours of the park.

Grampians National Park (Gariwerd)

The Grampians—also known by their Aboriginal name, Gariwerd—are a formidable series of sandstone ridges that rise to more than 3,830 feet (1,167 m) in western Victoria. A national park of 500,000 acres (200,000 ha) incorporates the ranges, with cliffs, waterfalls, ancient rock shelters with Aboriginal art, and a kaleidoscope of wildflowers. The park offers scenic drives, bushwalking trails, great rock climbing, and the opportunity to see a lot of Australian fauna.

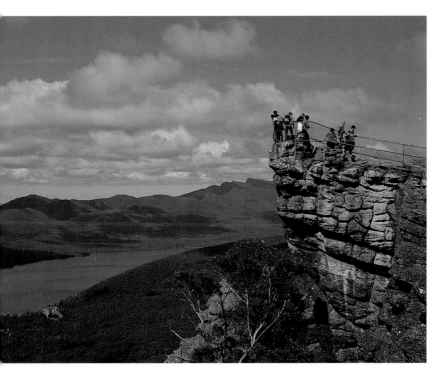

Wonderland Lookout offers a spectacular view.

It is an easy 150-mile (250 km) drive from Melbourne to Grampians National Park. The route passes through the goldfield town of Ballarat (see pp. 320–321) and the Great Western sparkling wine district, as well as the wheat and grazing country in western Victoria. **Halls Gap** is the only town actually in the park. A picturesque spot, settled in 1840, it is a great place to base yourself while you explore the park. The national park visitor center has brochures, maps, and information about the Grampians' 400-million-year history.

The Grampians are actually a collection of mountain ranges bunched together, and a diversity of landscapes is found within the park: hot, arid mallee scrub in the north; deep forests of stringy bark and red gums in the south; lush, fern-filled gullies in the Wonderland Range; and even sub-alpine vegetation near the craggy summit of Mount William. Hiking trails vary from half-hour strolls to strenuous overnight hikes on the aptly named **Mount Difficult.**

The best known drives and trails in the park take in the **Wonderland Range,** close to Halls Gap. Many of the best viewpoints are accessible by car, with only a short hike to lookouts. The most popular viewpoint is the **Pinnacle,** hundreds of feet above the plains. It is a demanding 3.5-mile (5.5 km) circuit from the Wonderland parking lot and goes via the majestic Grand Canyon. Another heart-stopping lookout is called the Jaws of Death. **Mackenzie Falls,** off Mount Victory Road, is awesome, particularly when rains swell the river in winter months.

Rock Art

The ranges have the best Aboriginal rock-art galleries in Victoria. More than 4,000 motifs, painted in red and white, can be seen in rock shelters and caves throughout the park. Some are easily accessible. At **Gulgurn Manja,** in the northern tip of the park near Mount Zero, a short signposted hike from the roadside goes to a shelter with depictions of Kartuk, the carpet snake. In the

Tug-of-War

The first European to explore these ranges (in 1836), Maj. Thomas Mitchell was also one of few early surveyors who tried to maintain Aboriginal place-names. However, he named these ranges after the Grampian Mountains in his native Scotland, presumably unaware that the Aborigines called them Gariwerd. The ranges have been the center of a name-based cultural tug-of-war. In 1991, the Victorian government formally revived the Aboriginal name, but a new administration changed it back to the Grampians, before both names were adopted.

west, along the Henty Highway near **Glenisla,** the Billimina and Wab Manja shelters have handprints and figures of fish and lizards. The **Brambuk Cultural Centre** (tel 03/5361-4000), run by local Aboriginal communities, arranges tours of the rock-art sites. The park's visitor center is also here. The center has cultural displays and a café with bush foods.

The best time to visit the park is in the wet months of spring, when the waterfalls are flowing and the wildflowers are at their best. The park has more than a thousand species of ferns and wildflowers, and the Grampians Wildflower Show is held here every October. ∎

Grampians National Park

🗺 290 A2

Visitor Information

✉ Grampians Rd., Halls Gap

☎ 03/5361-4444

visitgrampions .com.au

Wilsons Promontory National Park

One of Victoria's most popular national parks, Wilsons Promontory lies about 150 miles (240 km) southeast of Melbourne on the South Gippsland Highway and draws thousands of hikers and nature lovers. It is the extreme southern tip of mainland Australia, jutting into Bass Strait and taking the full fury of its waters on the western flank while sheltering lovely beaches on the east. Much of the park was burned in the 2009 bushfires, then flooded in 2011.

Wilsons Promontory National Park

🗺 290 C1

Visitor Information

✉ Tidal River

☎ 03/5680-9555 or 13-1963

parkweb.vic.gov.au

Wilsons Promontory has an astonishing variety of landscapes for its relatively small size. It is also rich in wildlife, with kangaroos, wombats, wallabies, and koalas aplenty. It even has emus, which can often be seen feeding on the grasslands near the park entrance at Yanakie Isthmus, and many other birds—among them lorikeets, rosellas, and kookaburras.

INSIDER TIP:

Accommodations at Wilsons Promontory include cabins, lodges, and campsites. Space is limited, so be sure to reserve well in advance.

—STEPHANIE ROBICHAUX
National Geographic contributor

Bushwalking is the best way to see Wilsons Promontory. Those who do not have the time or energy for such pursuits can still get a taste of the place—one of the best views over Bass Strait and some of the tiny coastal islands is from **Sparkes Lookout,** just off the road to the town of

Tidal River. The national park office is at Tidal River. Hiking possibilities range from half-hour strolls to overnight hikes down to the old lighthouse, built in 1859.

Three very popular shorter hikes from Tidal River are the **Squeaky Beach Track,** where half an hour of walking brings you to a beach of quartz sand so pure it squeaks underfoot. The **Lilly Pilly Gully Nature Walk** is a bit longer—about three hours round-trip—with rain forest, ferns, and gum-studded bushland where you may spot a koala.

Another popular hike is to the top of **Mount Oberon.** The enjoyable 4-mile (6.4 km) round-trip hike takes about two hours. From the Mount Oberon parking lot it is possible to hike out to the lighthouse at South Point. It is a 12-mile (19 km) walk, so start early. You can overnight at the old lighthouse keepers' cottages, which have fully equipped kitchens. Bring food, water, and a sleeping bag. Spaces are limited; make reservations at the Tidal River visitor center. Reserve Tidal River campsites, huts, and cabins well in advance at holiday times. In January, the park is overrun with vacationers. ∎

An island state with two personalities: gentle English-style countryside and brooding Gothic mountains, cloaked in forests

Tasmania

Introduction & Map   330–333

Hobart   334–337

Huon Valley Drive   338–339

Southwest Wilderness   340–341

Experience: Tracking the Tasmanian Devil   341

Feature: Tasmanian Greens   342

Franklin-Gordon Wild Rivers
    National Park   343

Cradle Mountain–Lake St. Clair
    National Park   344–345

Experience: Hike Oz's Most Famous Track   345

Scenic Loop Drive   346–349

Experience: Bay of Fires Walk   347

Port Arthur   350–351

Feature: Trout Fishing   352–353

Experience: Fishing in Tasmania   353

Bass Strait Islands   354

Hotels & Restaurants   384–385

The sturdy Tasmanian devil, a carnivore

Tasmania

Tasmania is one of those rare islands that really feels like an island. The cities and towns along its storm-lashed coasts all have a strongly maritime flavor and a history of whalers, sealers, clipper ships, and, often, tragedy. It is aloof, far beyond the 200 or so miles (320 km) that separate it from mainland Australia.

After a few days here, it becomes apparent that this is an island with two distinct personalities. There is the dark and tragic Tasmania of brooding mountains, rainy forests, and sandstone ruins left from a violent colonial past. The other Tasmania, existing cheerily, if schizophrenically, beside it, is the one of gentle English villages with apple orchards and sheep grazing on the common, quiet lanes. Both are unlike anything you'll find elsewhere in Australia.

Dutch navigator Abel Tasman was the first European known to have sighted the island. He swept along its west coast in 1642, believing it to be a peninsula jutting out from mainland Australia, and named it Van Diemen's Land, after the governor of the Dutch East Indies. His tales of rainy coasts, forbidding mountains, and savages on the beaches did nothing to kindle any enthusiasm for the place among his masters in Amsterdam and Java, and when his subsequent voyage in 1644 turned up pretty much the same things, the Dutch gave up on Australia altogether.

In 1803, the British decided to establish a penal colony on Van Diemen's Land, partly to forestall French interest in the place. Hobart Town was established the following year as a place to send convicts who had re-offended. Van Diemen's Land quickly became a byword for sadism and terror, rum and the lash, a reputation augmented by the barbaric prison camps established at Macquarie Harbour in 1821 and Port Arthur in 1832. By the time convicts ceased to be transported here in 1852, the island's reputation was so ghastly that its residents decided to change its name to the friendlier-sounding Tasmania.

Tasmania is a compact state, about the size of Scotland or Ireland. A third of its half-million residents live in Hobart. It is still very much an Anglo-Saxon community, with a deep social divide between the Greens and the predominantly blue-collar supporters of logging and mining. On the one hand, Tasmania has a higher percentage of its forests devoted to

NOT TO BE MISSED:

The colonial-era buildings and scenic harbor of Hobart **334–337**

Driving through Huon Valley farmland to the tall trees **338–339**

The rain forests of Southwest National Park **340–341**

Cruising the wilderness of the Gordon River **343**

Cradle Mountain–Lake St. Clair and the Overland Track **344–345**

Taking a chairlift to the top of the Nut in historic Stanley **346–347**

Sweeping Wineglass Bay on the sunny east coast **348–349**

Port Arthur, once a convict hellhole now a scenic treasure **350–351**

Canberra ★

Area of map detail

E ▽

Killiecrankie Bay
Stanley Point
Flinders Island

FURNEAUX ISLANDS

Whitemark
STRZELECKI NAT. PARK
Lady Barron
Cape Barren Island ◁5

Franklin Sound

Banks Strait

Clarke Island

C ▽   D ▽

Bass Strait

◁6

Cape Portland

bbins I.   Stanley
Montagu   ROCKY CAPE NAT. PARK
Smithton
A2   Wynyard
Somerset   Burnie
Yolla   Ulverstone   Devonport
Latrobe
784m
Mt. Bischoff
A10   Sheffield
Savage River
Mole Creek
1545m
Cradle Mt.
Cradle Valley
Corinna   Rosebery
Overland Track
Zeehan
CRADLE MT.-   1617m
LAKE ST. CLAIR   Mt Ossa
Mt. Lyell   NAT. PARK
Copper Mines
Queenstown
Strahan   A10   Derwent Bridge
FRANKLIN-GORDON
Sarah Island
1443m
Frenchmans Cap
WILD RIVERS NAT. PARK

ASBESTOS RANGE NAT. PARK
George Town
Bridport
Gladstone
MT. WILLIAM NAT. PARK

Beaconsfield
A8
A7   A3
Launceston   1
Deloraine
Longford

Scottsdale   Derby
A3

St. Helens
Mathinna

TASMAN HWY

BEN LOMOND NAT. PARK

WALLS OF JERUSALEM NAT. PARK
Great Lake

Lake
Arthurs Lake
Lake Country
Macquarie
Lake Sorell
1
Lake Crescent

South Esk
Avoca
A4

Campbell Town
Ross

DOUGLAS APSLEY NATIONAL PARK
Bicheno

Swansea

Coles Bay
FREYCINET NATIONAL PARK

◁4

◁3

TASMANIA
Lake St. Clair
Cynthia Bay
King William
Bronte Park
A5

Tarraleah
Bothwell

Oatlands

Great Oyster Bay
Schouten Island

Lake Gordon

SOUTHWEST CONSERVATION AREA
Strathgordon

Frankland Range

Lake Pedder

Hamilton
Kempton
MT. FIELD NAT. PARK
A10
Maydena   Brighton
New Norfolk   Plenty
1425m   1270m
Mt. Anne   Mt. Wellington
Huonville
A6

Orford   Triabunna
A3

Richmond
Sorell
Cambridge
HOBART
Lauderdale
Kingston

MARIA ISLAND NATIONAL PARK

◁2

Tasman Peninsula
Island of the Dead

SOUTHWEST NATIONAL PARK

Arthur Range

Port Davey

South West Cape

Kettering
Geeveston   Cygnet
HARTZ MTS. NAT. PARK

Huon

Southport

Port Arthur

Bruny Island
Adventure Bay

Tasman Head

Cockle Creek
South East Cape

- - - Track

0   60 kilometers
0   30 miles   ◁1

national parks and conservation than any other Australian state, and it gave rise to the Wilderness Society, one of Australia's most left-leaning Green groups. On the other hand, it is also a lumberjack state that consistently produces world-champion axmen—300 pounds (135 kg) of hard red flesh and an awesome sight to see competing at the agricultural shows. Tensions continue to smolder.

Tasmania is small enough to drive across in a couple of hours, yet varied enough to hold your interest indefinitely. Hobart has gracious

pretty villages in the eastern half of the state evoke old Britain, with names like Swansea, Brighton, and Somerset, and have cream teas, antiques shops, and colonial B&Bs. The east coast has excellent surfing and the haunting ruins of Port Arthur.

Tasmania's Aborigines

Some of the ugliest chapters of Australian history were written in Tasmania in the 19th century, when the settlers made a concerted and largely successful attempt at genocide.

Grapevines climb a Tasmanian hillside in the Tamar River Valley near Launceston.

Georgian architecture and a scent of the sea, and it lies just a short drive from the scenic Huon Valley, which spills along the coast. The southwest coast bears the brunt of the Roaring Forties gales and storms driven north from Antarctica. This is a vast World Heritage–listed wilderness, still barely explored. There is challenging bushwalking around Cradle Mountain and Lake St. Clair, and the central highlands have lakes filled with trophy-size trout. The

When the first Europeans arrived in 1803, an estimated 4,000 to 5,000 Aborigines were living on the island. These were the descendants of the original inhabitants who came here more than 11,000 years ago during the last ice age, when it was possible to walk across the shallow plain that is now Bass Strait. The Aborigines' early grudging distrust of the newcomers turned to outright hostility when they realized that these interlopers had not come to share their land but to seize it. They fought, and the settlers fought back—brutally.

By the 1820s, Aborigines were being shot on sight, poisoned with "gifts" of flour, or trapped like animals. Their children were used for forced labor. Aboriginal women were raped and killed. In 1830, the authorities formed the infamous Black Line of more than 2,000 armed citizens, who for three weeks beat the bush, shoulder to shoulder, driving out the Aborigines. The 150 Aborigines who survived were transported in 1834 to stormy Flinders Island on Bass Strait, where they were forced to become Christians and faded away in disease, grief, and malnutrition. The pitiful handful who survived were later allowed to return to Oyster Cove on Tasmania. The last of the full-blooded Tasmanian Aborigines—a woman named Truganini—died in 1856. For the next 120 years, her skeleton was in the Tasmanian Museum, until it was finally cremated and laid to rest on the waters of the D'Entrecasteaux Channel, off Oyster Cove, near where her people had lived.

Tasmanian Ferry

You can fly to Tasmania, but the most dramatic way to approach this storm-tossed island is by sea. On the sea you get a feel for its rocky fastness and insularity, not to mention a taste of the Roaring Forties—the region of heavy westerly winds between latitudes 40° and 50° south, which old mariners wrote about and feared. The English navigator Matthew Flinders discovered the strait between Tasmania and Australia in 1798, when he circumnavigated the island and established that it was not a peninsula. He named the waters for the ship's surgeon, George Bass. The new, stormy passage cut the sailing time between Sydney and India or Cape Town by a week.

Every evening at six o'clock (and extra 9 a.m. sailings late Dec.–April) the *Spirit of Tasmania* slips away from Melbourne's Station Pier to make the 10-hour crossing over the Bass Strait to Devonport, Tasmania. The ship can accommodate 1,140 passengers and 500 vehicles and has something of a cruise atmosphere with its pubs, restaurant, poker machines, and promenade decks. A Tasmanian tourism office is on board, along with cinemas, a games arcade, and an Internet kiosk. Reserve your ticket early, particularly during school vacations or if you want to take a vehicle *(tel 1800-634-906, spiritoftasmania.com.au).*

INSIDER TIP:

Fees apply for entry to Tasmania's national parks and can add up quickly. The best value is a Holiday Pass [A$60 per vehicle], valid for all parks, which is available at park offices and visitor information centers.

—PETER TURNER
National Geographic author

The ferry gives fine views of Port Phillip Bay, and if you are heading to Tasmania in autumn or winter, the lights of the receding Melbourne skyline are particularly pretty. The waters in the bay make smooth sailing, but this starts to change as the ship goes through the choppy seas out of the bay and into Bass Strait. If you are not a good sailor—or at least do not respond well to seasickness tablets—this voyage is not for you. The sea may be as smooth as a mill pond, but it can be rolling heavily, if not downright rough. Bass Strait has some of the world's stormiest seas because it acts as a funnel, compressing the full strength of the Roaring Forties gales.

The *Spirit of Tasmania* has accommodations from luxury suites to hostel-style bunks and reclining chairs. Meals are available too, if your stomach proves seaworthy. Rise early the next morning to catch your first glimpse of Tasmania's rocky coastline and green hills. ∎

Hobart

Australia's second oldest city (after Sydney), Hobart looks far older because it has so many elegant, albeit convict-built, 19th-century buildings. Situated at the foot and lower flanks of Mount Wellington, it spreads out along both banks of the Derwent River, about 12 miles (19 km) from its mouth. Hobart's houses are mostly of timber, painted soft pastels, and call to mind places like Halifax, Nova Scotia, or St. John's, Newfoundland.

Hobart's skyline and harbor with cloud-shrouded Mount Wellington rising behind

Hobart

🅰 331 D2

Visitor Information:

✉ 20 Davey St.

☎ 03/6238-4222
&
1800-990-440

**hobarttravelcentre
.com.au**

The city's focus is its harbor as well as the century-old stone warehouses and wharves that are located near Constitution Dock. Many of these buildings have been restored and converted into restaurants and pubs. This quarter of town becomes one of the most boisterous spots in Australia over the Christmas–New Year's holiday, when the Sydney–Hobart Yacht Race enters the dock.

Hobart was founded in 1804 after an earlier attempt to settle at Risdon Cove, on the eastern side of the harbor, had failed. The new town, built on Sullivans Cove, was named Hobart Town after Lord Hobart, then Britain's colonial secretary. The name was streamlined in 1881. Although its founder, Lt. Col. David Collins, had a poet's eye when it came to selecting a lovely setting for the city, he had a laissez-faire attitude to town planning. When Lachlan Macquarie, the public works–minded governor of New South Wales, visited in 1811, he lamented the town's chaos and ordered that a simple grid of streets be laid out. Thanks to him,

Hobart is today a very easy city to get about, with its downtown streets arranged in a grid around Elizabeth Street Mall. No place in the center is more than a few minutes' walk from the waterfront.

Sullivans Cove and the bustling Franklin Wharf have been the town's commercial heart since the 1830s, when Hobart was one of the world's whaling capitals. Fortunes were made in whale oil, shipbuilding, and trading in wool, meat, and flour. Between 1835 and 1860, as the town grew wealthier, a new line of handsome

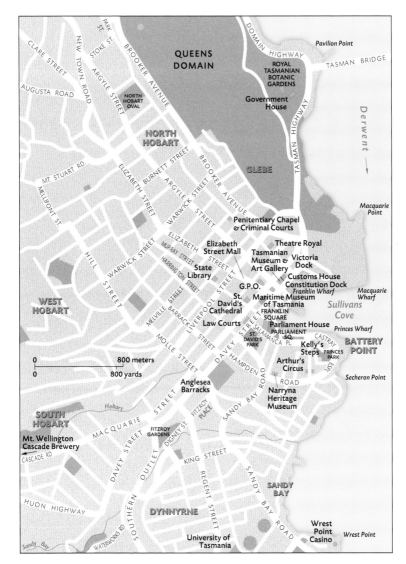

Tasmanian Museum & Art Gallery

⛰ Map p. 335

✉ 5 Argyle St.

☎ 03/6211-4134

tmag.tas.gov.au

Narryna Heritage Museum

⛰ Map p. 335

✉ 103 Hampden Rd.

☎ 03/6234-2791

🕐 Closed Mon. in winter

💲 $

narryna.com.au

Maritime Museum of Tasmania

⛰ Map p. 335

✉ Corner of Davey & Argyle Sts.

☎ 03/6234-1427

💲 $

maritimetas.org

MONA

✉ 655 Main Rd., Berriedale

☎ 03/6277-9900

💲 $$

mona.net.au

sandstone warehouses was erected on Salamanca Place. These beautiful old buildings have been sensitively restored and converted into craft galleries, cafés, vegetable markets, and gourmet shops.

On Saturday mornings, on the plaza in front of **Salamanca Place,** a crowded market sells anything from healing crystals to

INSIDER TIP:

Stroll Hobart's quaint streets and sample diverse cuisine from Cambodian fare to a flat white [coffee] and a vegemite sandwich.

—DAVID KENNEDY
National Geographic contributor

timber cutting boards. Alternatively, you can always nurse a cappuccino at one of the sidewalk cafés and watch the Tasmanians.

A narrow stairway, known as **Kelly's Steps,** leads between two of the warehouses on Salamanca Place up to **Battery Point.** Named for the cannon that were set up in 1818 to protect the city's harbor, Battery Point became a blue-collar neighborhood for mariners, shipwrights, sailmakers, coopers, and longshoremen. Later, as Hobart continued to prosper, wealthy merchants began building in this area too. Hobart in general, and Battery Point in particular, has escaped the wrecking ball of development. Wander the 150-year-old tangled alleyways,

with their stone churches, corner shops, and workers cottages, little changed from the days of whaling.

Hobart's city center has about 60 buildings listed by the National Trust, including some of Australia's finest examples of Georgian architecture along Macquarie and Davey Streets. Hobart's earliest surviving building is the Commissariat Store, built by convict labor in 1808. Now it houses the **Tasmanian Museum & Art Gallery.** The gallery has fine displays on Tasmania's Aborigines and a good collection of colonial art.

The **Narryna Heritage Museum** is an elegant 1836 Georgian mansion in Battery Point with a fine collection of 19th-century items. The **Maritime Museum of Tasmania,** in the historic Carnegie Building, is near Constitution Dock, the maritime heart of the city. The visitor center has heritage building brochures, and Hobart Historic Tours *(tel 03/6238-42222)* has walking tours leaving from the visitor center.

In contrast to all that history, the stunning modern architecture of **MONA (Museum of Old and New Art)** and its vast collection of modern art are not to be missed. This private museum, the brainchild of collector David Walsh, is a world-class facility on the Derwent River, 7.5 miles (12 km) north of the city. As well as its collection of provocative art, it has a cinema, restaurants, winery, brewery, accommodations, and tours. The scenic option for reaching MONA is to hop aboard the museum ferry from Brooke St. in downtown Hobart.

Mount Wellington

The best overview of Hobart is from the top of Mount Wellington, which looms more than 4,000 feet (1,270 m) above the city to the west and is sometimes covered with snow. This mountain dominates the city and draws visitors like a magnet, one of the most famous to climb it being Charles Darwin, who scaled it in 1836.

There are walking trails to the summit (it's about a two-hour climb), or you can drive up the winding road that turns off the Huon Highway. Just head inland, southwest of Hobart, along Cascade Road. On the way you'll pass Cascade Gardens and the **Cascade Brewery,** which looks like a grand French château nestled in the foothills. This is Australia's oldest brewery—and its best, according to many beer lovers. It began in 1832 and still makes beer in a traditional way, using the cold clear water that cascades down the mountainside. Nearby, at the ruins of the **Cascades Female Factory,** 11 a.m. theatrical tours re-enact the grim life of the convict women imprisoned here.

The stone **Pinnacle Observatory Shelter** on the craggy summit of Mount Wellington gives a stunning view of the city, out to the mouth of the Derwent River and over the wild countryside stretching out for miles in every direction.

The first European to climb this peak was navy surgeon and explorer George Bass, who stopped here in 1798 (and whose name was given to the Bass Strait; see p. 333). The road to the summit was opened in 1937. The view is particularly dramatic when the valleys below are in broken mists or rain, as they often are. No matter what the weather, bring a jacket or sweater, even if it seems warm down in Hobart. ∎

Cascade Brewery

✉ 140 Cascade Rd.
☎ 03/6224-1117
💲 Tours $$$

cascadebrewery
.com.au

Cascades Female Factory

✉ 16 Degraves St., South Hobart
☎ 03/6233-6656
💲 Free, tours $$

cascadefemalefactory
.wordpress.com

English novelist Anthony Trollope once dismissed Mount Wellington as "just enough of a mountain to give excitement to ladies and gentlemen in middle life."

Huon Valley Drive

This is the heart of Tasmania's picturesque apple orchard district and where the valuable Huon pines were first discovered. You'll find fishing villages, dairies, tranquil island beaches, and the savage wilderness strongholds of the Hartz Mountains. You can see the valley on a pleasant day trip or over several days, depending on your pace and time.

To begin, follow Davey Street south out of Hobart, where it becomes the Huon Highway, for a hilly and scenic drive down into the valley.

The first apple orchard was planted in the Huon Valley in 1841, and within ten years apples were being exported to New Zealand and India. By the 1920s, nearly 30,000 acres (12,150 ha) of orchards were growing more than 500 varieties of apples. These days the valley has diversified with wine, salmon, and tourism, although apples and cider mills are still big. (Only eight varieties are grown these days, with Red Delicious the mainstay.) The valley is also Tasmania's cherry-growing center. In Grove, 20 miles (32 km) out of Hobart, you can visit the **Apple Museum ❶** (tel 03/6266-4345).

The town of **Huonville ❷**, 5 miles (8 km) farther south on the highway, is the valley's commercial center (visitor information: tel 03/6264-0326, huonvalley.tas.gov.au). Timber became a big industry here when settlers discovered the Huon pines—"green gold," in the eyes of pioneers. This slow-growing softwood, unique to Tasmania, is nearly rot-proof and quickly became popular with 19th-century shipbuilders. Thousand-year-old trees are hard to replace, and few Huon pines are left in the valley today. You can arrange an exhilarating jet boat ride through the falls on the Huon River with Huon River Jet Boats (tel 03/6264-1838).

Another 15 miles (24 km) south on the Huon Highway brings you to **Geeveston,** an old timber town and the gateway to the Hartz Mountain wilderness. The **Forest and Heritage Centre** (Church St., tel 1300-720-502, adventureforests.com.au) has displays on the timber industry and walking guides to **Tahune Forest Reserve,** where you can see magnificent stands of ancient Huon pines. The reserve is about 15 miles (24 km) west

NOT TO BE MISSED:

The Apple Museum • Waratah Lookout • Adventure Bay

of Geeveston on a partially paved, marked road. By the road are picnic grounds, walking trails, and several good viewpoints. The popular **Tahune Airwalk and Visitor Centre** (tel 1300-720-507, $$$) offers spectacular walks through the old-growth Huon pine forest at canopy height, on a 2,000-foot (600 m) treetop walkway that offers stunning views over the rivers and to the Hartz Mountains. A scenic off-road detour leads to the **Arve Valley** and some of the world's largest hardwood trees, eucalyptuses that rise over 250 feet (76 m).

Described by Sir Edmund Hillary as some of the wildest country he'd ever seen, the magnificent Hartz Mountains loom just to the west. Part of Tasmania's World Heritage area, **Hartz Mountains National Park ❸** has dense rain forests, snow-covered dolerite peaks, and rugged alpine moors. The spectacular **Waratah Lookout,** about 15 miles (24 km) from Geeveston, is reached by a graded road off the road to the Tahune Forest Reserve. The park's trails are challenging but recommended, especially a six-hour (round-trip) hike to the 4,117-foot (1,255 m) summit of Hartz Peak. If you decide to hike, be prepared for sudden and extreme changes of weather, and carry warm, waterproof clothing no matter how nice the day appears when you leave Hobart. For information on trails, contact the Forest and Heritage Centre in Geeveston.

Retrace your route as far as Huonville and then take the Channel Highway. It runs along

See also area map p. 331
► Hobart
◄► 214 miles (325 km)
⏱ 1 day
► Hobart

the eastern bank of the Huon River, through the orchard town of **Cygnet,** which has black swans and old timber cottages, and along the D'Entrecasteaux Channel to **Kettering** ❹, about a 40-mile (64 km) drive from Huonville. Orchards and fields of strawberries and raspberries surround this old fishing port. The waters of **Oyster Cove,** 3 miles (5 km) northeast of Kettering, supported generations of Aborigines, and it was here that the last few Tasmanian Aborigines were allowed to return.

From Kettering, regular ferries make the short hop to **Bruny Island** ❺. Buy tickets at the Bruny D'Entrecasteaux Visitors Centre (*tel 03/6267-4494*), next to the ferry terminal. Sighted by Abel Tasman in 1642, this island was a veritable crossroads for 18th-century explorers: James Cook, Captain Bligh, Matthew Flinders,

John Cox, Bruni D'Entrecasteaux (for whom the island is named), and Nicholas Baudin visited here. A botanist on one of Bligh's expeditions is believed to have planted the first of Tasmania's apple trees. Later, the island was a base for whalers. Today it is tranquil, with rain forests, guesthouses, and seafood restaurants. The island is about 30 miles (48 km) long, and most accommodations are at **Adventure Bay,** in the southern half, which also has the best scenery. Built in 1836, the **Cape Bruny Lighthouse,** at the southwest tip reached via road B66 through Alonnah, is the second oldest in Australia.

From Kettering drive back to Hobart through Margate and **Kingston,** where the Australian Antarctic Division headquarters (*Channel Hwy.*) has interesting displays and the latest information on Antarctica.

Southwest Wilderness

Tasmania's southwest wilderness is one of the world's few remaining untouched places, with vast tracts of virgin temperate rain forests, swamp gums more than 300 feet (91 m) high, rare ferns and lichens, and wild rivers boiling through the gorges. Rain falls on more than 200 days a year. The gloomy, storm-lashed coastline of the southwest cape has remained virtually unchanged since Abel Tasman swept past these rocks in 1642.

Cushion plants on the north ridge of Mount Anne in the southwest wilderness

These days Tasmania's southwest wilderness is protected as **Southwest National Park** and the adjacent **Southwest Conservation Area**—which together compose a 2.5-million-acre (1 million ha) wilderness stronghold with some of the most challenging and remote hikes on the planet. But these hikes should be attempted only by experienced bushwalkers who are well equipped for sudden savage turns in the weather. This area is noted for violent storms, mists, and cold rain, even in summer.

The hiking trails themselves scramble up steep muddy slopes, over rocky quartzite crags that may require ropes, and across miles of swampy buttongrass marshes infested by leeches. You'll have to carry everything with you, although you can arrange an airdrop of extra supplies if you are planning an extended hike.

The reward for all this hardship is immersing yourself in the solitude and isolation of a primeval world so fresh and new it seems to have the first dew still on it. If this sounds like something you are interested in, consider tackling the **South Coast Track,** a 55-mile (88 km) trail that stretches from Cockle Creek to Malaleuca. This moderate-to-difficult route is maintained and generally takes about a week to ten days to traverse. Most hikers fly into Malaleuca airstrip and hike east, back to Cockle Creek. Other, even more imposing challenges include the **Port Davey Track,** the **Western Arthurs Traverse,** and the **Mount Anne Circuit.** Some of these trails can be linked up for an expedition-length trek.

INSIDER TIP:

Hiking in the southwest wilderness is amazing but isn't for casual day-trippers. Be prepared for rough conditions and terrain.

—BARBARA A. NOE
National Geographic Travel Books
senior editor

The alternative to flying in is to drive into the park via the Strathgordon Road and the rough sidetrack to Scotts Peak Dam, and walk the Port Davey Track to Malaleuca (70 km, three to five extra days). The park office at Huonville (tel 03/6264-8460) has up-to-date information on the park. This walk is only for experienced hikers. Specialist hiking maps and guidebooks are on sale in shops in Hobart. Par Avion *(tel 03/6248-5390, paravion.com.au)* flies hikers in and out of the park, and can arrange pick up by bus from Cockle Creek.

Scenic flights are a less strenuous way of enjoying this wilderness. Par Avion also operates a wilderness camp and runs a tour boat on the Davey River that goes into the heart of the park. ∎

Southwest National Park
🄰 331 C2–D1
Visitor Information:

Parks & Wildlife Service
✉ 134 Macquarie St., Hobart
☎ 1300-135-313
parks.tas.gov.au

Forest & Heritage Centre
✉ Church St., Geeveston
☎ 1300-720-502

EXPERIENCE: Tracking the Tasmanian Devil

The Tasmanian devil is a carnivorous marsupial found only in Tasmania, although it once inhabited the mainland. Primarily a carrion eater, it has the most powerful jaws of any mammal and uses them to crush bones. It has a squat body about the size of a small dog and emits a ferocious snarling when feeding or threatened. Although not the cutest of Australia's marsupials, it bears little resemblance to its crazed, whirling Looney Tunes cartoon counterpart.

Seen as a threat to livestock, devils were hunted by Tasmanian farmers until they were protected in 1941. Since then, a new threat has killed up to 50 percent of the population—devil facial tumor disease. DFTD is a rare and contagious cancer that causes tumors and swelling on the face, usually resulting in death within a year. No cure has been found. As insurance, devils are being bred in quarantined areas and sent to the mainland to ensure survival of the species. Devils favor dry forests and coastal heaths, but you might spot them anywhere you drive—they like to live dangerously by feeding off roadkill, especially at night.

For a guaranteed sighting of a devil, maybe even eating a dead wallaby, stop by the **Tasmanian Devil Conservation Park** *(tel 03/6250-3230, tasmaniandevilpark .com)*, in Taranna on the highway to Port Arthur. This wildlife park has lots of native wildlife and its disease-free habitat is helping to ensure the devils' survival. You can also help by becoming a "Friend of the Devil" as a donor or volunteer.

Tasmanian Greens

When you look at a map of Tasmania, the first thing you notice is the huge swath of green covering the lower left quarter of the state. Tasmania has a higher percentage of its land set aside for conservation and national parks, much of it World Heritage listed, than any other state in Australia—and a legacy of bitter environmental protests.

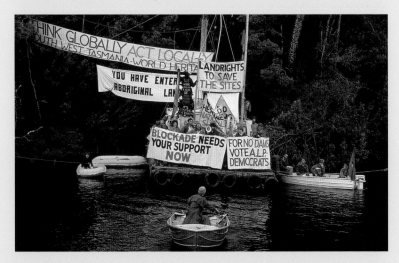

Protestors take to the water in 1982 to demonstrate against the Franklin River dam.

Tasmania's strident environmental movement began at Lake Pedder, which sprawls along the edge of the southwest wilderness. Before 1972, this tiny jewel was accessible only by light plane. But then the Tasmanian Hydro Electric Commission dammed the nearby Gordon River, flooding the lake and surrounding valleys to create Australia's largest inland freshwater catchment. Conservationists, who had lost their battle to stop the dam, formed the Wilderness Society in 1976 to better organize for the next confrontation. They didn't have to wait long.

The Hydro Electric Commission's next plan was to dam the Franklin River, the last major wild river in Tasmania. This sparked a divisive campaign in Tasmania, which snowballed into international protest when the Tasmanian government continued with its proposal even after the river and surrounding wilderness received

World Heritage listing in 1982. Protesters came from around Australia and overseas to throw up a human blockade to the bulldozers. Hundreds were arrested. The new Labor government that came to power in Canberra in March 1983 stopped the building of the dam.

Tasmania elected two Green senators to the federal Parliament, including Greens leader Bob Brown. He has since retired but the party he founded has become a significant national force in Australian politics. In the 2010 election, the Greens garnered 13 percent of the national vote, with senators elected from each of the six states. The support of the sole Green lower house member, Adam Bandt, was crucial for the minority Labor government to form power. Pulp mills and wood chipping are still the big Green topics in Tasmania these days, but the Greens have taken environmental issues to a whole new level in Australian politics.

Franklin-Gordon Wild Rivers National Park

Franklin-Gordon Wild Rivers National Park exists pretty much for itself. Many of its million acres (400,000 ha) are covered by dense rain forest and rugged mountains, and they are virtually inaccessible on foot. Boats or scenic flights are really the only way to see the park.

Gordon River

Scenic cruises go out of **Strahan,** a remote town of 600 on the central west coast near Macquarie Harbour. Most visit **Sarah Island** and the ruins of its notorious prison camp, then putter up the tannin-rich waters of the Gordon River another 20 miles (32 km) or so. The Gordon is Tasmania's largest river, and reflections of ancient Huon pines on its mirror-smooth surface make evocative photographs. Strahan Seaplanes & Helicopters *(tel 03/6471-7718)* has scenic flights over the Gordon River and the Southwest National Park. The West Coast Visitor Information Center *(tel 1800-353-200)* on the Esplanade in Strahan offers information on the park.

Franklin River

More adventurous visitors may wish to raft the wild Franklin River. The full trip takes up to 14 days, through some of the world's most challenging white water. It starts on the Collingwood River, 30 miles (48 km) west of Derwent Bridge, and ends at Heritage Landing, where a seaplane retrieves you.

This is not a trip to attempt independently, unless everyone in your party is very experienced.

A number of outfits run river trips (see Rafting, right) that do not require experience. Those on a time limit can do an eight-day trip.

Hiking

The trail up the spectacular, 4,734-foot-high (1,443 m) Frenchmans Cap gives breathtaking views. The southeast face is a sheer 1,500-foot (457 m) cliff of white quartzite, and the mountain is prone to mists and violent storms. The hike is for experienced bushwalkers only. It starts at the Lyell Highway, 19 miles (30 km) west of Derwent Bridge. The 29-mile (46 km) round-trip hike takes three to five days. ∎

Franklin-Gordon Wild Rivers National Park
🏕 331 C3

RAFTING: Tour operators offering rafting packages on the Franklin include: **Rafting Tasmania,** P.O. Box 403, Sandy Bay, 03/6239-1080, raftingtasmania.com; **Water by Nature (Tasmania),** 1800-111-142, franklinrivertasmania.com; and **World Expeditions,** 1300-720-000, worldexpeditions.com.

The Franklin River draws adventurers from around the globe.

Cradle Mountain–Lake St. Clair National Park

Cradle Mountain–Lake St. Clair National Park is Tasmania's most popular wilderness park. Its deep gorges, mountain peaks, glacier lakes, and broad expanses of alpine moorland are challenging enough to excite any bushwalker, yet it is still (at least by Tasmanian wilderness standards) fairly accessible. Its southern end is only a two-hour drive north from Hobart on the Lyell Highway, and its northern one is about 50 miles (80 km) from Devonport.

Cradle Mountain–Lake St. Clair National Park

⚐ 331 C3

parks.tas.gov.au

The first person to begin campaigning for the area's preservation was an Austrian naturalist, who built himself a chalet in the Cradle Valley in 1912. He lived long enough to see 130,000 acres (52,650 ha) of the valley set aside as a scenic reserve in 1927. The World Heritage–listed park has since grown to 400,000 acres (162,000 ha). It contains

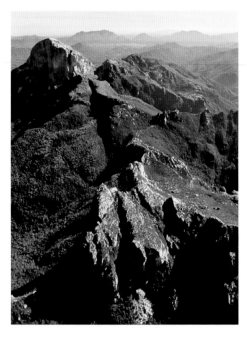

Cradle Mountain rises 5,069 feet (1,545 m) above sea level.

5,305-foot (1,617 m) **Mount Ossa,** Tasmania's highest peak, and beautiful **Lake St. Clair,** Australia's deepest freshwater lake (600 feet/183 m deep).

Many exciting trails cross through these mountains, but the **Overland Track** (see sidebar p. 345) is the biggest draw. Hundreds of bushwalkers flock here each summer to trek the 40 miles (65 km) from Cradle Mountain in the north to the southern tip of Lake St. Clair. It is a stunning trail, through wildflower-dotted high-country meadows, buttongrass marshes, and deep forests of beech, Tasmanian myrtle, and pandanus. The Overland Track typically takes six days and is a satisfying challenge for experienced and well-equipped hikers. Side trips—up Mount Ossa, for example—can easily double your time in the wilderness. You're limited only by the amount of supplies you can carry. Half a dozen main huts along the trail provide accommodations, but it's essential to bring a tent because bad weather or fatigue may force an unscheduled stop.

The weather here is notoriously fickle, and sudden storms on these exposed ridges can easily trap the

EXPERIENCE: Hike Oz's Most Famous Track

The Overland Track—Australia's most famous hike—normally takes six days and boasts stunning scenery. You must carry food, a fuel stove, tent, and sleeping bag with you, and be prepared for freezing conditions, even in summer. Alternatively, Cradle Mountain Huts (tel 03/6392-2211, cradlehuts.com.au) provides all gear on guided trips staying in exclusive huts.

Permits & Bookings: The hike requires a Parks Pass and payment of a hiking fee. From Nov. to May, you must hike from north to south. A limited number of 34 places are available, so book well in advance (overlandtrack.com.au), especially during Dec. and Jan.

Accessing the Trailheads: Tassielink (tel 1300-300-520, tassielink.com.au) has buses to/from Launceston and Hobart to both ends of the trail and **McDermotts Coaches** (tel 03/6330-3717, mcdermotts.com.au) has buses from Launceston to Cradle Mountain. Some other tour operators offer on-demand hikers' transport to the trailheads, usually for a minimum group charge.

Walking the Track: A typical itinerary includes: **Day 1,** Ronny Creek (or Wald-heim Hut) to Waterfall Valley Hut, 6.2 miles (10 km), 6 hours (side trip: Cradle Mountain). **Day 2,** to Lake Windermere Hut, 4.6 miles (7.5 km), 3 hours (side trip: Lake Will, or Barn Bluff). **Day 3,** to Pelion Hut, 10.2 miles (16.5 km), 6 hours. **Day 4,** to Kia-Ora Hut, 5.5 miles (9 km), 3 hours (side trip: Mount Ossa). **Day 5,** to Bert Nichols Hut, 6.2 miles (10 km), 4 hours, (side trips: D'Alton and Fergusson Waterfalls, or Hartnett Falls). **Day 6,** to Narcissus Hut, 5.5 miles (9 km), 3 hours, then take the boat to Cynthia Bay or walk (9.3 miles/15 km, 4 hours, along the lake).

---

unwary or the foolish. Snow is possible even in summer. Rain, mud, and leeches are near certainties at all times. However, the scenery and sheer exhilaration of being in this wilderness is well worth any hardships. Late summer is the best time to go, although some exceptionally experienced hikers have enjoyed the challenge of winter traverses.

Most hikers start at the northern end of the park and go south to Lake St. Clair. If you want to avoid the last day's hike around the lake, you can arrange to have a launch (tel 03/6289-1137) pick you up at Narcissus Hut and take you to the trailhead at Cynthia Bay.

The stunning lake cruise is also a great way to get a taste of the Tasmanian wilderness. Or you can do a day trip on the Overland Track by taking the boat to the northern end of the lake and hiking back—a very scenic six-hour walk. **Cynthia Bay,** at the southern entrance, has a ranger station, restaurant, and a lodge with the choice of luxury and budget accommodations.

At the northern end of the park, buses run between Launceston, Devonport, and Burnie to the entrance in Cradle Valley (most days in summer, less frequently in winter). This end of the park has several excellent ways to savor the wilderness. The spectacular half-mile (800 m) **Visitor Centre Rainforest Walk** is wheelchair accessible. Scenic flights are flown by Cradle Mountain Helicopters (tel 03/6492-1132). Information on shorter day and half-day hikes is available at the interpretive center. ∎

Cradle Mountain Northern Entrance
🗺 331 C3
Visitor Information
✉ Cradle Valley
☎ 03/6492-1110

Southern Entrance
🗺 331 C3
Interpretive Center
✉ Cynthia Bay, Lake St. Clair
☎ 03/6289-1172

Scenic Loop Drive

Tasmania's compactness, the fact that it is an island, and the scenic loop of highway that stands out on the map make circling the island by car the most obvious and rewarding way of seeing the place. The scenic loop is about 600 miles (960 km) in all, although with side trips to the Huon Valley (see pp. 338–339), Port Arthur (see pp. 350–351), and Macquarie Harbour on the rugged west coast, you'll likely add a bit more.

Secluded Wineglass Bay in Freycinet National Park is accessible by foot or by boat.

The drive takes in primeval rain forests and brooding mountain ranges, wild rivers, towering trees, and lakes filled with trout. There are mining ghost towns, ruined penal colonies, and the maritime charm of Hobart. Along the north and in the midlands, gentle landscapes with old stone churches and cottages call to mind England.

North & West Coasts

You could begin this tour almost anywhere in Tasmania—Hobart, Launceston, or straight off the ferry at Devonport, if you brought a car. This description starts in **Devonport ❶**, a bustling port and tourist town, and goes counterclockwise.

Follow the coastal highway northwest out of town to the logging and paper-milling port of **Burnie,** named after William Burnie, a director of the Van Diemen's Land Company, an enterprise founded in London in 1825, with a million pounds (U.S. $1.6 million) in capital and a grant of about 300,000 acres (121,500 ha) in northwest Tasmania.

The company got off to a rocky start. Prized sheep, horses, and cattle died, European agricultural equipment—imported at great cost—proved unsuitable, and the Aborigines fought bitterly to keep their land. In its first 32 years, the company paid only two small dividends. While shareholders lost money, the company's exploration of the rugged wilderness opened up the northwest. The discovery of tin at nearby Mount Bischoff sparked a rush to the northwest, and the deepwater seaport at Burnie flourished. Unfortunately, Burnie itself is a dreary smokestack city despite its beautiful pastoral surrounds. Better to skate through the old port and onto **Wynyard** *(visitor information: 8 Exhibition Link, tel 03/6443-8330),* a pleasant seaside community just 12 miles (19 km) farther along the highway. This dairy town is a good place to catch a flight to King Island (see p. 354), or visit **Rocky Cape National Park ❷**, with its profusion of wildflowers, including rare native orchids, and white sandy beaches. The place has a long human history. For more than 8,000 years Aborigines sheltered in caves in these quartzite hills. Two major caves—**North** and **South Caves**—contain huge shell middens, bones, and tools. There are many trails in the park, but limited facilities and no water supplies.

Take a detour by following the Bass Highway northwest for about 40 miles (64 km) to reach **Stanley,** a picturesque fishing village at the foot of a dramatic volcanic neck known as the **Nut.**

The Van Diemen's Land Company set up its headquarters here in 1826 and built its slate-roofed store in 1844. The restored building is now open to the public. The **Nut Chairlift** (Browns Rd., tel 03/6458-1286, $) gives access to the top of the Nut. The view is spectacular.

The loop drive goes south on the Murchison Highway, which leaves the Bass Highway between Wynyard and Burnie. After about 30 miles (48 km) you will reach the **Hellyer Gorge State Reserve ❸**, with its deep rain forest of sassafras, giant myrtle, and huge ferns. Forests such as these used to be the haunts of the Tasmanian tiger. At one time, many of these striped, carnivorous marsupials roamed the wilderness. The Van Diemen's Land Company placed a bounty on them and they were hunted to extinction, with the last supposedly dying in a Hobart zoo in 1936. But there have been persistent reportings of Tasmanian tigers, so just maybe a few still live in the wilder corners of the northwest. If so, one likely spot is the almost untouched **Arthur-Pieman Conservation Area,** a rain forest wilderness on the west coast. It is accessible by a 45-mile (72 km) detour

each way off the highway to the nearly deserted gold-mining town of **Corinna ❹,** where you can take wilderness cruises (Pieman River Cruise, tel 03/6446-1170) through the spectacular deep gorges on the Pieman River.

The Murchison Highway becomes the Zeehan Highway 50 miles (80 km) farther south of the turning to Corinna. A turnoff at this point leads to the colorful old mining town of **Zeehan.** This was a boomtown mining silver, lead, and zinc around the turn of the 20th century, with enough money for the local Gaiety Theatre to draw the likes of Enrico Caruso and Harry Houdini. Today it is a quiet village of 900. You can continue through Zeehan to **Macquarie Harbour** and **Strahan ❺** (visitor information: tel 1800-352-200), the only town on the west coast and the base for visiting the remains of the penal colony on **Sarah Island** and the Gordon River (see p. 343).

The Zeehan Highway continues 20 miles (32 km) south to **Queenstown ❻,** a mining center built up around the **Mount Lyell Copper Mine.** The apocalyptic moonscape left by its busy mining and smelting industry has

---

EXPERIENCE: Bay of Fires Walk

When the Bay of Fires topped a world's hottest travel destination list, locals objected, saying they didn't want the attention. That sums up this remote, pristine part of Tasmania's east coast, where virgin forest and turquoise seas bound dazzling white-sand beaches.

The area is protected by **Mount William National Park** (St. Helens office: tel 03/6376-1550). Hikers can walk along the beach and stay at basic campsites, but the big attraction is the guided **Bay of Fires Lodge Walk** (tel 03/6392-2211, bayoffires.com.au).

The walk begins at **Boulder Point,** a three-hour bus ride from Launceston. The **Bass Strait Islands** lie on the horizon, and the 6-mile (9 km), four-hour walk

along the beach passes layers of shells from thousands of years of Aboriginal feasts. Capt. Tobias Furneaux gave the bay its name in 1773 for the string of Aboriginal fires spread out along the beach.

The first night's stay is in twin-share tented accommodations at the **Forester Beach Camp,** where hikers enjoy dinner served with Tasmanian wine.

The highlight of the trip is the next day, when you explore beach and sand dunes on a 9-mile (14 km), seven-hour walk to the **Bay of Fires Lodge.** This award-winning lodge is a masterpiece of understated eco-elegance. Hikers spend two nights at the lodge, with an option of kayaking on the third day, before the walk out and transportation back on the fourth day.

NOT TO BE MISSED:

Rocky Cape National Park • Hellyer Gorge State Reserve • Lake St. Clair • Richmond • Freycinet National Park

become an attraction in its own right: bare hills tinted pink, gold, gray, and purple.

From Queenstown the highway winds a tortuous 50 miles (80 km) through mountains to Derwent Bridge. A very short–3-mile (4.8 km)–detour here will bring you to the jewel-like **Lake St. Clair 7**. A lodge has accommodations and meals, and the launch trip across the lake gives some breathtaking glimpses of Tasmania's pristine wilderness.

The highway continues to **Hobart 8** (see pp. 334–337) through the hop-growing center around **New Norfolk,** settled in 1808 and now an English-style town. Take the Tasman Highway out of Hobart. A very worthwhile short detour (8 miles/13 km, north from Lindisfarne) goes to **Richmond 9** *(visitor information: 48 Bridge St., tel 03/6260-2502),* a well-preserved colonial village, with Georgian cottages and old stores. The four-span stone bridge, built by convicts between 1823 and 1825, is the oldest in Australia. A short drive back to the highway leads to **Sorell,** a historic village founded in 1805. If you have time for a detour, take the road south to **Port Arthur** to visit Tasmanian devils at the conservation park (see sidebar p. 341).

East Coast

A drive along Tasmania's east coast is nothing like a drive through the west. The eastern countryside is gentle, with a mild climate and seaside villages around secluded beaches. Forty miles (65 km) north of Sorell on the Tasman Highway is **Orford,** a pleasant seaside town and the jumping-off point for the ferry *(Triabunna Bookings, tel 04/1974-6668)* to **Maria Island National Park 10**—an 1820 penal colony but today a wildlife reserve

popular with bird-watchers *(ranger's office: tel 03/6257-1420, parks.tas.gov.au).*

The highlight of the east coast is **Freycinet National Park 11** *(visitor information: tel 03/6256-7000),* which includes Schouten Island and the Friendly Beaches. To get there follow the highway 50 miles (80 km) past Orford, through Swansea, to a turnoff on your right to Coles Bay, the park headquarters. Cape Freycinet has hiking, birdlife, and camping on **Richardsons Beach**. Sheltered **Wineglass Bay,** with shimmering beaches of white quartzite

Stanley

ROCKY CAPE N.P. 2

Wynyard

Arthur

Hellyer Gorge 3 A10
State Reserve

ARTHUR-PIEMAN CONSERVATION AREA

Mt. Bischoff 784m

MURCHISON HIGHWAY

4
Corinna   Pieman

Zeehan

ZEEHAN HWY

Mt. Lyell Copper Mine

Queenstown

6
Strahan 5

1,146m Mt. Owen

Macquarie Harbour

Sarah Island

INDIAN OCEAN

SOUTHWEST CONSERVATION AREA

🅰 See also area map pp. 330–331
▶ Devonport
↔ 600 miles (960 km)
🕓 4 days
▶ Devonport

sand, is a two-hour hike from the parking lot.

Going north, the highway hugs the coast for 40 miles (64 km), then veers through an old whaling town, **St. Helens,** and inland through farmland, dairies, and rain forests. After 100 miles (160 km) you reach **Launceston ⑫,** with a population of about 106,000 *(visitor information: Cornwall Sq., 12–14 St. John St., tel 03/6336-3133, visitlaunceston.com.au).* It sits near the confluence of the North Esk, South Esk, and Tamar Rivers. **Cataract Gorge,** where the South Esk tumbles into the Tamar, is ten

minutes out of town. Although almost as old as Hobart, Launceston (founded 1805) is a high-Victorian town—a legacy of its glory days when prospectors came to Tasmania in the hopes that its forests hid gold. For information on the town's architecture, go to the **Old Umbrella Shop** *(60 George St., tel 03/6331-9248),* now a National Trust center, built in the 1860s and lined with rare Tasmanian blackwood.

From Launceston the highway circles back toward Devonport, about 70 miles (112 km) west, and closes the scenic loop of Tasmania.

Port Arthur

"It was all out of keeping with the place, a sort of bringing together of heaven and hell," wrote American novelist Mark Twain when he visited Port Arthur on a world tour in the 1890s. Certainly it is hard to reconcile the gentle beauty of the countryside with the brutal past of the prison camp on this peninsula, 59 miles (94 km) southeast of Hobart.

The old Gothic-style church adds a touch of gentle melancholy to the ruins of Port Arthur.

Port Arthur
🗺 331 E2
Visitor Information
✉ Port Arthur Historic Site
☎ 03/6251-2371
💲 $$$$–$$$$$
portarthur.org.au

From 1832 until it was closed in 1877, Port Arthur was the final stop for many of the colony's most dangerous offenders. Its founder, George Arthur, decreed that "the most unceasing labour is to be extracted from the convicts, and the most harassing vigilance over them is to be observed." More than 12,000 passed through. Escape was almost impossible. The peninsula is linked to the mainland by a narrow isthmus barely 100 yards (92 m) wide, which was patrolled by guards and lined with savage dogs. The frigid waters that crash at the foot of these dolerite cliffs were believed to be filled with sharks.

Things got even worse in 1852, with the construction of the Model Prison based on a new concept of punishment devised in Britain: total sensory deprivation. Prisoners who had previously had the comfort of casting their eyes on soft green hills were now kept in tiny isolation cells for 23 hours a day. They were never permitted to speak, and during their solitary hour of exercise they were forced to wear hoods and shuffle around the yard in chains. Not surprisingly, many of the men went insane. No matter—the prison opened its own mental ward. The decision finally to close the prison is said to have been influenced by the dreadful publicity it received from Marcus Clarke's novel *For the Term of His Natural Life* (1874).

Visiting Port Arthur

When fires swept through the place in the 1890s, there were few regrets, and locals hoped the flames would wipe the memories off the map completely. The major restoration effort begun in the 1970s has preserved much of Port Arthur, and more than 200,000 visitors come here each year. It is Tasmania's biggest tourist attraction. More than 60 buildings are scattered around the site, including the **Asylum,** which has a small museum chronicling the settlement and the lives of some of its prisoners. Next door, the frightening **Separate Prison** was a "model prison" where difficult prisoners were subjected to the mental torture of sensory deprivation. Some of the buildings have been fully restored, but others have been left as ruins amid the gardenlike setting.

Visitors can wander around the penal colony at will; the entry fee gives access to all buildings in the complex and includes a guided tour and boat tour from the main part of the prison to the **Isle of the Dead,** where 1,769 convicts were buried. A solitary convict used

to live on the island to dig the graves. "Australia has many parking lots but few ruins," wrote Robert Hughes in *The Fatal Shore*. "Port Arthur is our Paestum and our Dachau, rolled into one."

Even in daylight, Port Arthur can be a haunting place for a stroll, but things get eerie after dark, with ghostly apparitions and phenomena recorded since the 1870s. Guides carrying lanterns lead nightly ghost tours of the buildings and ruins. They are surprisingly spooky.

A terrible postscript to Port Arthur's brutal history was written in 1996, when a gunman killed 35 people (see sidebar below). The Broad Arrow Café, where he murdered 20 victims, was gutted and its ruins built into a memorial garden. ■

1996 Tragedy

Every Australian remembers April 28, 1996, when a 28-year-old Hobart man entered the Broad Arrow Café at Port Arthur and began firing a rifle into the Sunday lunchtime crowd. By the time the killing spree was over, 35 were dead and 21 injured. The country was horrified. Since the 1980s, Australia had witnessed a number of indiscriminate killings by disturbed men armed with semiautomatic weapons. The government decided to act and introduced some of the world's strictest gun laws. No such mass killings have occurred since.

Trout Fishing

Thanks to the persistence of the 19th-century amateur naturalists who brought brown and rainbow trout eggs from England, Tasmania is today an excellent trout-fishing destination. Its highland lakes host world fly-fishing championships.

Cold, clear waters and hard gravel riverbeds made Tasmania the perfect place to introduce trout.

Trout are not native to Australia. Amateur naturalists of the 19th century, with a Victorian-era notion that a bit of England could improve any landscape, began trying to import trout and trout eggs in the early 1860s, but they were defeated by the long sea journey. In 1864, however, a man named James Youl succeeded in getting a batch of eggs out from England in an ice chest. The eggs survived a remarkable 91-day relay of clipper ship, steamer, riverboat, and finally horseback, to be released in a few ponds near the Tasmanian town of Plenty. Youl was later knighted—in part, for his efforts in bringing this gentleman's gamefish to Tasmania. (Later, the descendants of these fish stocked New Zealand as well.) The town of Plenty, about 30 miles (48 km) northwest of Hobart, has a fishing museum (*Salmon Ponds, tel 03/6261-5663*) set on English-style grounds.

Trout occupy an unusual niche in Australia's ecology mind-set. Introduced species have been almost invariably a disaster for local wildlife. The introduction of rabbits for sport-shooting in 1859 and European carp into the rivers in 1872 are the most famous and catastrophic environmental blunders in the continent's history. These days a more environmentally aware Australia spends millions trying to eradicate nonnative species such as rabbits, foxes, carp, blackberry vines, and cane toads, which were introduced with harmless intention. But trout have a certain élan, and although they are believed responsible for putting heavy competitive pressure on already threatened native species, they nevertheless enjoy a sort of honorary "native" status. They are seen as genteel, they don't muddy the rivers and lakes they swim in, and they make a significant contribution to the Tasmanian economy. Thousands of anglers flock to the state from all over the world, where their patience can be rewarded with trophy-size brown, rainbow, and lake trout.

There are a lot of good fishing holes and a number of professional guides around the state to help you find them. Back in the early 1970s, more than 350,000 brown trout fingerlings were released into Lake Pedder, and another 500,000 rainbow trout were put into Lake Gordon (both are on the edge of the southwest wilderness area). They flourished in the nutrient-rich waters, and there are (possibly apocryphal) tales of anglers catching 45-pound (20 kg) brown trout out of Lake Pedder. Whatever the truth of those boasts, the average size for brown trout in this lake is a very respectable 10 pounds (4.5 kg).

The midlands of Tasmania have trophy fishing lakes and spectacular scenery. Great Lake, Arthurs Lake, Lake Sorell, and Lake Crescent are some of the most productive, although the area has numerous smaller lakes and fishing holes. Trout were released here not long after they arrived from England, and by 1868, trout weighing nearly 10 pounds (4.5 kg) were being caught in Arthurs Lake. To get an idea of what is in those waters, stop in at the old Castle Hotel in Bothwell. While you'll no doubt hear a lot of fisherman's lies, the stuffed and mounted 25-pound (11 kg) trout over the bar offers its own mute testimony.

Tasmania's trout season opens early in August, although a few rainbow trout waters do not open until early October. The season lasts until April. The Inland Fisheries Service *(17 Back River Rd., New Norfolk, tel 03/6261-8050, ifs.tas.gov.au)* has information on bag limits, licenses, and minimum-size regulations.

EXPERIENCE: Fishing in Tasmania

Tasmania has thousands of waters for trout fishing, particularly in the Central Highland lake country south of Deloraine. At altitudes of more than 3,300 feet (1,000 m), the area is dotted with lakes within easy access of each other and the rest of the island.

Top spots include **Arthurs Lake**, renowned for its brown trout, and **Great Lake**, teeming with rainbow and brown trout. As well as these dammed hydro lakes, smaller **Penstock Lagoon** has excellent fly-fishing while **Nineteen Lagoons** offers a wide range of fishing environments.

In the northern midlands, **Brumbys Creek**'s crystal waters are excellent for sight-fishing and **Macquarie River** is good for flood-fishing in spring. Also popular are the Meander River, South Esk River, and Lake Trevallyn near Launceston, and the Derwent and Huon Rivers near Hobart.

These outfits can put together packages, including accommodations:
Fish Wild Tasmania *(Sandy Bay, tel 03/6223-8917, fishwildtasmania.com)*
Peter Hayes *(Cressy, tel 03/6397-5073, peterhayesflyfishing.com)*
Ken Orr's Tasmanian Trout Expeditions *(Brady's Lake, Wayatinah, tel 03/6289-1191, orrsometassietrout.com.au)*
Rainbow Lodge *(Miena, tel 03/6259-8090, rainbowlodgetasmania.com.au)*
Red Tag Trout Tours *(Kingston, tel 03/6229-5896, redtagtrout.com)*
Rod & Fly Tasmania *(Mountain River, tel 03/6266-4480, rodandfly.com.au)*
Tasmanian Escape *(Youngtown, tel 03/6344-1206, tasmanianescape.com)*
Tasmanian Trout Tonic *(Ouse, tel 03/6287-1445, tasmanian-trout-tonic.com.au)*
Trout Territory *(Cressy, tel 03/6397-5001, troutterritory.com.au)*

Bass Strait Islands

Tasmania includes two outer island groups in the violent waters of Bass Strait—the Hunter Islands off the northwest coast and the Furneaux Islands off the northeast. They are well off the usual tourist routes.

GETTING TO THE ISLANDS:
Flinders Island: Furneaux Freight *(tel 03/6365-1753, furneauxfreight .com.au),* ferry from Bridport. Sharp Airlines *(tel 1300-556-694, sharpairlines .com.au),* flights from Launceston and Melbourne (Essendon)
King Island: Tasair *(tel 1800-062-900, tasair.com.au),* flights from Devonport or Burnie King Island Airlines, *(tel 03/9580-3777, kingislandair .com.au),* flights from Melbourne (Moorabbin) Regional Express *(tel 13-1713, rex.com.au),* flights from Melbourne

King Island
Visitor Information:
☎ 1800-645-014
kingisland.org.au

Hunter Islands

King Island is the largest of the Hunter Islands. This low, 40-mile-long (64 km) island is blessed with lush pasture grasses found nowhere else in Australia. It produces incredibly rich handmade cheeses and thick double creams. Legend has it the grasses came from seeds in the straw-filled mattresses washed ashore from shipwrecks, of which the island has had more than any other part of Australia. The worst was when an immigrant

INSIDER TIP:

Don't miss King Island Dairy [kingislanddairy .com.au]. Yes, it's a long way to go for cheese . . . but it sure is delicious cheese.

—LARRY PORGES
National Geographic Travel Books editor

ship, the *Cataraqui,* foundered in 1845 with the loss of 399 lives. Today the island has four lighthouses. **Cape Wickham** in the north is the tallest in the Southern Hemisphere and gives a splendid view of the island.

The island's biggest attraction, the **King Island Dairy,** on North Road about 5 miles (8 km) north of Currie, gives tours and

free tastings. The island has no public transportation. Rent a car from King Island Car Rentals *(tel 03/6462-1282)* or Cheapa Car Rentals *(tel 03/6462-1003).*

Furneaux Islands

The 52 Furneaux islands are at the eastern end of Bass Strait. In 1798, Matthew Flinders charted the biggest, **Flinders Island,** which became a base for sealers, who virtually wiped out the local seal population. In 1834, the 135 Tasmanian Aborigines who survived the Black Line were sent here (see p. 333).

Flinders Island has granite mountains, secluded beaches, and excellent fishing, scuba diving, and rock climbing. There are numerous bushwalking trails in **Strzelecki National Park,** including a hike to the wind-scoured summit of Mount Strzelecki. You can look for Killiecrankie "diamonds"—actually a form of local topaz—on the beach at Killiecrankie Bay.

Like King Island, Flinders is noted for farm produce, but also for handmade chocolates and fine woolens. The main settlements are **Whitemark** on the west coast and **Lady Barron** on the south. The **Furneaux Museum,** about 12 miles (19 km) north of Whitemark, tells the story of the Aborigines' time on the island. For car rental, contact Flinders Island Car Rentals *(tel 03/6359-2168).* ∎

Travelwise

Planning Your Trip   356–358

How to Get to Australia   358–359

Getting Around   359–361

Practical Advice   361–364

Emergencies   364–365

Information Offices   365–366

Hotels & Restaurants   367–385

Shopping   386–387

Activities   388–389

A four-wheel-drive vehicle is favored outback transportation.

TRAVELWISE

PLANNING YOUR TRIP

When to Go

Australia is good for vacations year-round. For a short trip without a fixed itinerary, spring and autumn give the most flexibility. The wildflowers in the west are particularly beautiful in the spring.

Climate

The Australian spring runs from September through November, summer from December until March, autumn from March through May, and winter from June until September. Seasonal weather varies widely in the different parts of Australia.

The best summer weather occurs in the southern states, where everyone seems to live outdoors and take to the balmy seas. The center is scorchingly hot in summer, and the flies are at their worst. In the far north, temperatures may be slightly cooler, but the tropical humidity and monsoon downpours can be depressing, while poisonous box jellyfish make the sea too dangerous for swimming. On the other hand, some choose to head north during the summer in order to escape the crowds and the cities, and to see the Top End luxuriantly green and in full flood. The electrical storms are fantastic that time of year, and the barramundi fishing is superb.

In winter the southern states have snow, and some tourists come for the skiing. In the north the humidity and water levels drop. Travel is simpler, and wildlife is easier to spot, as it clusters around the remaining watering holes. This is the best time of year to see crocodiles.

Calendar of Events

See also Holidays, p. 363

January

Perth Cup (*Perth; Jan. 1*)
A popular horse-racing event
Cygnet Folk Festival (*Cygnet, Tasmania; second weekend*)
Features folk and world music, including local performers
Sydney Festival (*Sydney*)
Three full weeks of arts, music, food, and dance
Tamworth Country Music Festival (*Tamworth, New South Wales; weekend nearest to Australia Day, Jan. 26*)
Australian Open Tennis Championships (*Melbourne*) International grand slam event
Australia Day (*Jan. 26*)
Festivities nationwide, with music concerts in the capital cities.

February

Perth International Arts Festival (*Perth*) Three weeks of opera, theater, dance, music, and art
Royal Hobart Regatta (*Hobart, Tasmania*)
Tropfest (*Nationwide*)
World's largest short-film festival, screenings in the capital cities
Sydney Gay and Lesbian Mardi Gras (*Sydney*)

March

Adelaide Festival (*Adelaide; biennially, occurring in even-numbered years*) Three-week festival of the arts
Moomba (*Melbourne*) Long weekend festival ending with a street parade
Port Fairy Folk Festival (*Port Fairy, Victoria*) Four-day celebration of music, with concerts and classes
Formula 1 Australian Grand Prix (*Melbourne*) Australia's premier motor-sport event

April

Melbourne International Comedy Festival (*Melbourne*) Three-week event
Sydney Royal Easter Show (*Sydney*) Two-week festival with livestock, sideshows, and rodeos
The Rip Curl Pro (*Bells Beach, southwest of Melbourne*) Famous competition featuring the world's top surfers

May

Ord River Muster (*Kununurra, Western Australia*) Rodeo, concerts, diamond tours, and more over two weeks

June

Laura Aboriginal Dance Festival (*Laura, Cape York Peninsula*) Hundreds of traditional performers descend on remote Laura

Vivid Sydney Light and music festival with iconic buildings illuminated over two weeks

July

Melbourne International Film Festival (*Melbourne*)
Lasseter's Camel Cup (*Alice Springs*) Camel races and carnival atmosphere
Beer Can Regatta (*Darwin*) Boats made entirely out of beer cans

August

City2Surf (*Sydney*) 8.75-mile (14 km) fun run between Hyde Park and Bondi Beach
Darwin Rodeo (*Darwin; held on third weekend*)
Henley-on-Todd Regatta (*Alice Springs, Northern Territory*) Held in dry riverbed, using leg-powered bottomless boats (see sidebar p. 199)

September

Shinju Matsuri (Festival of the Pearl) *(Broome, Western Australia)*
Royal Melbourne Show *(Melbourne)* Livestock, sideshows, and rides
Royal Adelaide Show *(Adelaide)* Weeklong agricultural and horticultural show
Perth Royal Show *(Perth)* Livestock, sideshows, and rides
Australian Rules Football League (AFL) Grand Final *(Melbourne)*
Birdsville Races *(Birdsville, Queensland)* Weekend of horse racing, in aid of the Royal Flying Doctor Service (see sidebar p. 176)
Melbourne Fringe Festival *(Melbourne)* Three-week alternative celebration of the arts

October

Queen's Birthday *(nearest Monday to Sept. 30)* State holiday in Western Australia
Melbourne Festival *(Melbourne)* Music, theater, dance, and visual arts
Bathurst 1000 Touring Car Race *(Bathurst, New South Wales)* Mount Panorama circuit
Royal Shows *(Hobart & Launceston, Tasmania)* Agricultural and horticultural shows
Australian Motorcycle Grand Prix *(Phillip Island, Victoria)*

November

Melbourne Cup First Tuesday *(Flemington, Melbourne)* Australia's premier horse race

December

Sydney to Hobart Yacht Race *(leaves Sydney on December 26, Boxing Day)* Australia's leading ocean race

Travel Insurance

Always take out adequate insurance when you travel, especially for medical needs. Costs for ambulance or helicopter rescue, emergency surgery, or travel home can be exorbitant. Ensure that the policy covers all activities that you plan to undertake.

Entry Formalities

Visas

Many travelers may now obtain authority to enter Australia through the Electronic Travel Authority (ETA) system, which replaces the need for an Australian visa. The tourist ETA is valid for multiple entries into Australia (each entry to a maximum of three months) over a period of one year and costs A$20 (U.S. $20). The similar eVisitor system applies to European passport holders and is free for tourist and business visits. A business ETA allows multiple entries into Australia for the life of your passport. Restrictions apply. ETAs can be obtained through your travel agent (who may charge a fee), from your airline, or online at *immi.gov.au.* Apply at least two weeks before departure.

Travelers not eligible for an ETA or eVisitor, and those wishing to stay for longer than three months or to work, must obtain a visa. Advice and application forms may be obtained from your travel agent or from the Australian Embassy, high commission, or consular office.

Customs

Items brought in for personal use, for example cameras, laptops, radios, and film, are exempt from duty. If you take a laptop, it is a good idea to register it with your own customs officials before leaving for Australia. You should also be prepared to "boot up" the laptop on request. Travelers over the age of 18 may bring 2.25 liters (0.6 gl) of alcohol into Australia, 250 cigarettes, or 250 grams (9 oz) of tobacco, and gifts to the value of A$900 (U.S. $900) duty free. Travelers under 18 may bring gifts to the value of A$450 (U.S. $450) without attracting duty.

There are no restrictions on the amount of Australian or foreign currency you can import or export, although sums exceeding A$10,000 (U.S. $10,000), or its equivalent, should be declared on the appropriate inbound customs forms.

For details on customs controls and restrictions, contact the relevant Australian high commission, embassy, or consular office listed on p. 358, or visit *customs.gov.au.*

Quarantine

Australia has very strict quarantine laws designed to keep out pests and diseases. Planes are routinely fumigated by the cabin staff. Do not attempt to bring any fruit, seeds, vegetables, foodstuffs, or animal or plant products into the country. (Similar border controls are also in place between Australian states.) If you inadvertently carry any such item into the control zone, place it in one of the many clearly labeled disposal bins. Do not attempt to take it through customs, and if in doubt, declare it. Sniffer dogs check for foodstuffs as well as drugs. If you have hiking boots, expect to produce them for inspection. Any soil adhering to the soles must be cleaned off. Also expect items such as straw hats and wooden clogs to be scrutinized.

Drugs & Narcotics

Sniffer dogs check for drugs and narcotics. Such checks are commonplace and penalties for carrying illegal substances are severe. Medicines for personal use should be clearly labeled. Obtain a statement from your doctor if you are importing a large number of pharmaceuticals or if they are of a restricted type.

Australian Embassies Abroad

United States
1601 Massachusetts Ave., NW
Washington, D.C. 20036
Tel 202/797-3000
Fax 202/797-3168
usa.embassy.gov.au
Offices also in Chicago, Denver,
Honolulu, Houston,
Los Angeles, New York, &
San Francisco

Canada
50 O'Connor St., Suite 710
Ottawa, Ontario K1P 6L2
Tel 613/216-0841
Fax 613/236-4376
canada.embassy.gov.au
Also in Toronto & Vancouver

United Kingdom
Australia House
The Strand, London WC2B 4LA
Tel 020/7379-4334
Visa information 020/7420-3690
uk.embassy.gov.au
Also in Edinburgh

Australian Dept. of Foreign Affairs & Trade
dfat.gov.au

HOW TO GET TO AUSTRALIA

Choosing a Ticket
Travel agents and online booking sites may have the cheapest deals, but it pays to check airline websites direct for specials. You may also wish to buy air and bus discount passes before you go (see Getting Around, p. 359.)

Sydney is the main destination for inbound flights to Australia, with connections to and from most countries in Asia, Europe, and North and South America. Australia's major carrier is Qantas, with connections to all continents. From the United

States, other carriers with direct flights include United Airlines, Air New Zealand, Virgin Australia, and Hawaiian Airlines. The flight time from Los Angeles is 14 hours. You can put together some interesting routes with Pacific stopovers in Honolulu, Fiji, or Auckland. From the United Kingdom and Europe, competition is greater. British Airways, Singapore Airlines, Cathay Pacific, and many other Asian and European airlines offer regular flights. Major carriers include:

Qantas
Within Australia:
Tel 13-1313 (Reservations)
qantas.com.au
Tel 800-227-4500
qantas.com

Within United Kingdom:
395 King St.,
London W6 9NJ
Tel 0845-774-7767
qantas.co.uk

Air New Zealand
United States: 800-262-1234
United Kingdom: 0800-028-4149
airnewzealand.com

British Airways
United Kingdom: 0844-493-0787
britishairways.com

Cathay Pacific
United States: 800-233-2742
cathaypacific.com

Singapore Airlines
United States: 800-742-3333
United Kingdom: 0844-800-2380
singaporeair.com

United Airlines
United States: 800-864-8331
united.com

Virgin Australia
United States: 855-253-8021
virginaustralia.com

Package Tours
There are three main options for package tours (and endless variations within them). The first is to fly independently but spend your time with a tour company, for example:

AAT Kings
aatkings.com
U.S.: 801 East Katella Ave.
3rd Floor, Anaheim, CA 92805
Tel 714-935-0040
Australia: Bondi Junction
New South Wales 2022
Tel 1300-228-546

Australian Pacific Touring
aptouring.com.au
United Kingdom: Whielden St.
Old Amersham, Buckinghamshire
Tel 0208-812-3400
Australia: Level 4, 1230 Nepean
Hwy., Cheltenham, Victoria
Tel 03/8526-1300

Second, you can buy a package that includes flights, hotels, and rental cars or sightseeing, with **Qantas, British Airways,** or **United Vacations** *(in U.S., tel 888-854-3899),* for example.

Third, there are customized package vacations. Check the newspapers, ask your travel agent, or contact companies such as:

Fishing International
fishinginternational.com
U.S.: 5510 Skylane Blvd.
Suite 200, Santa Rosa, CA 95403
Tel 800-950-4242

ITC Golf Tours
itcgolftours.com
U.S.: 2428 Lewis Ave.
Signal Hill, CA 90755
Tel 562-595-6905

Airports

Most visitors arrive in Sydney, though international flights also arrive at Perth, Melbourne, Brisbane, Adelaide, Cairns, and Darwin airports.

Sydney International Airport, Kingford Smith, is 7 miles (11 km) south of the city and can be reached by bus, rail, or taxi. International and domestic flights have separate terminals. Shuttle buses and trains link the terminals to each other and to the Central Railroad Station, Town Hall, and Circular Quay. Many city hotels operate their own shuttle buses. A taxi to the city center costs around A$50 (U.S. $50) and takes about 30 minutes. Rail services go to Central Station. *Note:* A departure tax is assessed. This is usually prepaid as part of your air ticket.

GETTING AROUND
By Air

Australia has an excellent network of domestic air services, and vigorous competition between Qantas and Virgin Australia and budget airlines Jetstar and Tiger means that you can get some very good deals, particularly if you shop via the Internet and are prepared to be flexible in your travel plans. Carriers offer substantial savings through e-tickets and website specials, and these deals are often advertised in newspapers as well. International travelers may also be able to purchase an air pass through Qantas, which will entitle them to a set number of discounted domestic flights while they are in the country. The passes must be purchased before arrival in Australia. Prices vary according to the number of flights requested. Details are available on the Qantas website. Virgin Australia also has air passes.

Jetstar
Reservation line: 13-1538
jetstar.com
Qantas
Reservation line: 13-1313
qantas.com.au
Tiger Airways
Reservation line: 03/9034-3733
tigerairways.com
Virgin Australia
Reservation line: 13-6789
virginaustralia.com

By Car

Drive on the left and pass on the right. Remember to yield to traffic coming from the right at traffic circles. (Pedestrians should remember to look right for traffic when crossing a road.) Roads are generally well kept. You need to take special care if driving long distances, though, especially if you use outback dirt tracks. (See Driving Safely, p. 360.)

Renting a Car

Rental costs vary according to season, demand, availability, and the size and type of car required. Check whether the cost covers unlimited mileage. Certain companies add an additional charge for miles traveled over a stated limit. Prices start at around A$40 (U.S. $40) a day or A$250 (U.S. $250) a week for a manual-gearshift, economy car. There may also be local or airport surcharges. Always check the condition of the car before you drive away and report any concerns immediately. Sometimes you must return the car to the place from which it was rented. Normally cars may be dropped elsewhere (for a fee).

You may get a cheaper rate if you reserve the car before you leave home. Most major agencies, for example, Avis, Hertz, and Budget, have an international booking section. They give advice on rates, restrictions, and availability at your chosen destination and, if you choose, will reserve a car for your arrival.

Avis, tel 13-6333
Budget, tel 13-2727
Europcar, tel 1300-131-390
Hertz, tel 13-3090
Thrifty, tel 1300-367-227

Rental Conditions

In order to be allowed to drive in Australia, you must have a valid driver's license and be at least 21 years of age (a premium may be charged for any driver under 25). Third-party insurance and a collision-damage waiver are compulsory and are included in the cost of the rental. Comprehensive-coverage and personal-accident insurance are available at extra cost, but check the coverage provided by your home car and travel-insurance policies. Nearly all companies will insist that you pay for the rental with a major international credit or charge card. You may well find additional insurance protection on the card you use for payment.

Four-wheel-drive Vehicles

A four-wheel-drive (4WD) vehicle is essential for outback travel. The rental and insurance costs are higher than for an ordinary car. Damage to the vehicle caused by the driver may not be covered by insurance.

Motorhomes & Camper Vans

Motorhomes and campers may be rented locally in all states. The minimum rental period is usually one week, and good reductions may be obtained for longer periods. Rates are highest in the main holiday season of December and January. Motorcycles can also be rented.

Driving Regulations

The use of seat belts is compulsory in Australia. Drivers must ensure that passengers wear them—failure to do so results in a fine. Fines may follow you home because car rental companies will supply customer address details to the authorities.

Road Signs

Signs are easy to understand. Speeds and distances are given in kilometers. Speed limits vary from 50 kph (31 mph) in residential areas to 110 kph (68 mph) on the highways. Speed limits are strictly enforced.

Fuel

Fuel (unleaded or diesel) is sold by the liter. Expect to pay from A$1.30 a liter (U.S. $4 a U.S. gallon) in the city and from A$1.70 a liter (U.S. $5 a U.S. gallon) in the outback.

Alcohol

Permitted blood-alcohol limits are low, and it is wise to avoid all alcoholic drinks when in charge of a vehicle. Police checks are frequent and the penalties severe.

Driving Safely

Long-distance driving has its own hazards in Australia. Although the main highways are well maintained, they can be very tiring. Always build sufficient rest periods into any journey time, and do not underestimate the draining power of the sun and its glare. Always carry a good supply of water and snacks.

If planning to use dirt tracks, ensure that the vehicle is suitable and that you are prepared for emergencies. Check the weather forecast and road conditions with the local police before setting out. Deep, fine "bulldust" can prove hazardous for even an experienced four-wheel driver. Flash floods and dust storms are common in season (which varies from area to area; check with local police offices for information). Be wary of animals on the road, particularly at dawn and dusk.

The need for care cannot be overemphasized. Know where you are on your maps. Breakdown or other assistance may not be easy to attract. As well as water and snack foods to sustain you in case of emergency or delay, take warm blankets. A flashlight (with spare batteries) will help if you are stranded overnight. Use common sense and have a healthy respect for an unforgiving environment. Carry a good first-aid kit, spare fuel, and adequate tools to make basic repairs to your vehicle.

If you are planning to visit a remote national park, find out from locals and police at your starting point about road conditions, what gear to take, and what to do if things go wrong. Listen to advice, and always leave word with a responsible person or the local police about where you are going and when you expect to return.

Automobile Associations

Australian automobile associations provide services to members of most foreign motoring organizations. You need to have a valid membership card from your own organization if requesting a service. Breakdown assistance may also be available.

A.A.A. (Automobile Association of Australia)
103 Northbourne Ave.
Canberra ACT 2601
Tel 06/6247-7311

NRMA Motoring & Services
74–76 King St.
Sydney 2000
Tel 13-2132

What to Do in an Accident

Take the names and addresses of any witnesses, the driver of the other vehicle, and the owner if different. Note the make, model, and registration number of the other vehicle. Exchange insurance information and contact details. Make a note of damage to the vehicle and any injuries to yourself and other persons. Record details of the scene—visibility, traffic flow, road details, and surface conditions. Record details of the collision, including speed of travel and point of impact.

All accidents, unless they are minor scrapes, must be reported to the police. Cooperate with the police officer. Make a note of the officer's name, number, and where he or she may be contacted. Draw a sketch of the accident showing the layout of the road and the position and movement of the vehicles involved. Keep all of these details for the insurance report.

Buying a Vehicle

Before you buy a motor vehicle in Australia, check that it has a current annual Roadworthiness Certificate (RWC), in addition to making the obvious safety checks. When you want to resell a car, it is advisable to return to the state in which you bought it.

By Bus
Long-distance Bus Routes

If money is a constraint, or if you have the time and want to get a feel for the immense size and geography of the country, go by bus. Traveling the long-distance bus routes is usually the cheapest way of getting around Australia. All the major cities and highways are serviced by large express companies that link up with regional operators serving smaller communities. All the major carriers have comfortable buses with onboard sanitary facilities. Air-conditioning is the norm, and drivers often run videos on overhead monitors.

The main interstate busline in Australia is Greyhound. A series of passes, with varying duration and varying degrees of flexibility, are offered. Travelers to Tasmania can use the local Tassie Link bus pass (tigerline.com.au), which offers circuits of the island in 7-, 10-, 14-, or 21-day periods.

Greyhound
United States: 800-849-8966
Australia: 1300-473-946,
greyhound.com.au

Bus Tours
Many Australian travel operators run bus, or coach, tours. These range from a few days in luxury, air-conditioned buses and hotels to several weeks camping out of a beaten-up jalopy. The former provides interesting narration, a minimum of physical activity, and every creature comfort. For the latter, everyone is expected to lend a hand and enjoy a sleep under the stars. Some of the most popular tours run out of Darwin and Adelaide to Alice Springs and Uluru (Ayers Rock). Other popular routes are Cairns–Brisbane and Brisbane–Sydney. Check with your travel agent or with Tourism Australia for further information.

By Train
Long-distance Train Routes
The Indian Pacific runs twice a week from Sydney to Perth (and vice versa) via the Nullarbor Plain, with a running time of 65 hours (see sidebar p. 248). The Ghan train runs once a week (twice in winter) from Adelaide to Darwin (via Alice Springs) through the outback (see pp. 282–283), and once a week to Alice Springs alone. The Sunlander runs daily from Brisbane to Cairns (and

vice versa) and takes 32 hours. All these services have luxury packages that include sleeper accommodations and meals (see sidebar p. 283 for more).

Service in the Ghan or Indian Pacific comes in two main classes: The Gold Service–an essential first-class sleeper, with en suite cabin and all meals in the dining car–and the less expensive Red Service–a standard sleeper service and a café car where you can purchase meals. A still cheaper option is the day-nighter seats, with meals and snacks available for purchase.

You can make reservations at the main rail stations in Alice Springs, Darwin, Katherine, Melbourne, Perth, and Adelaide's Parkland Terminal in Keswick. The main office of Great Southern Railway (Ground floor, 422 King William St., Adelaide) also takes reservations, or book online at greatwsouthernrail.com.au.

Great Southern Railway also operates the Overlander, a weekly overnight service from Adelaide to Melbourne and return.

By Boat
The only regular maritime service in Australia is the Spirit of Tasmania car ferry that sails between Melbourne and Devonport, Tasmania (see p. 333). The sailing takes around 10 hours and is often cursed by rough seas.

Some international cruise lines, for example Holland America Lines, P&O, and Princess Cruises, sail around Australia. Typically they dock at Sydney and continue along the coastline stopping at Brisbane and Cairns to the east, Melbourne, Adelaide, and Hobart to the south, or Fremantle in the west.

Numerous pleasure boats, catamarans, and yachts operate out of the mainland towns along the east coast and islands on the Great

Barrier Reef, and out of Exmouth on the west coast for Ningaloo Reef. Some give a day's island hopping, with dolphin-watching and whale-watching, snorkeling, and scuba diving. Others go for up to a week of diving and sailing out at sea.

There are river cruises along the Murray River in South Australia (see pp. 276–277) and Victoria (see pp. 324–325), Myall Lakes in New South Wales, and the Hawkesbury River north of Sydney.

PRACTICAL ADVICE
Children
Most hotels allow children under a certain age to stay in their parents' room for free or at a discounted rate. The cutoff age varies considerably (the average is 12). A few hotels still charge for children as if they were adults. The Australian suburbs have a large number of family restaurants, with special menus for children, high chairs, and booster seats.

Communications
Mail
Stamps may be purchased from post offices, hotels, and many shops. The rate for domestic letters is 60 Australian cents (60 U.S. cents). Standard rates for postcards and letters up to 1.7 ounces (50 g) is A$1.65 (U.S. $1.65) to Asia/Pacific and A$2.35 (U.S. $2.35) to the rest of the world, including North America. Parcels up to 44 pounds (20 kg) can be sent by air or sea through post offices.

Poste Restante
Larger offices have a free poste restante (general delivery) service (as do some outback offices). Take proof of identity, such as a passport or driver's license, when collecting.

Telephones

Australia has an excellent telephone system and modern exchange. There are numerous public telephones that take both coins and phone cards. Many city telephones also accept credit cards. Phone cards are readily available and are sold in 5, 10, 20, and 50 Australian dollar units. Local calls from public phones cost 50 cents for an unlimited amount of time. The same call from a private phone costs around 30 cents.

Long-distance calls can be made from public telephones but are expensive. Calls to the U.S. cost about A$4.50 (U.S. $4.50) per minute, about half that to the U.K. Rates are slightly cheaper on weekends. Far cheaper are the international calling cards sold by many convenience stores and newsagents. From any telephone, you dial a local or toll-free number then enter your PIN and the overseas number.

Toll-free numbers in Australia have the prefix 1800. Six-digit numbers starting with 1300 or 13 are charged at local rates, regardless of where the answering office might be.

Telstra and Optus operate the two main mobile networks, with Virgin and others using these networks, while Vodaphone and Three have smaller networks. Telstra has slightly better coverage, but all cover the main populated areas. Most of Australia is unpopulated, however, so cell phones are all but useless in the outback. Prepaid SIM cards can readily be bought at supermarkets, newsagents, electronics stores, and other outlets (bring ID). Local call rates are around 80 cents a minute while international calls cost around $A1 (U.S. $1) per minute to the U.S. and U.K.

To call from Australia to the U.S. or Canada prefix the number with 00-11-1. To call from Australia to the U.K. use 00-11-44.

Fax

Faxes can be sent from any hotel business center or post office, where rates are A$5 (U.S. $5) for the first page and A$1.25 (U.S. $1.25) for each subsequent page.

E-mail & Online Services

All the big cities have online services at Internet cafés. These allow you to use the Internet and send e-mail at a half-hour or hourly rate (around A$10/U.S. $10 an hour). If you have a laptop, check with your local provider before leaving for Australia. Several larger service providers, such as AOL, have local Australian numbers that you can access from your hotel. Many hotels offer Internet access at lobby terminals, or in-room with wireless or LAN connections for your laptop, but rates are usually high. Some cafés offer free wireless Internet. Cell phone companies offer 3G data with their SIMs for Internet access, which works out much cheaper than most hotel Internet rates.

Conversions

Australia uses the metric system. Useful conversions are:

Weights & Measures

1 mile = 1.61 kilometers
1 kilometer = 0.62 mile
1 pint = 0.47 liters
1 liter = 2.12 pints
1 U.S. gallon = 3.78 liters
1 pound = 0.37 kilos
1 kilo = 2.20 pounds
1 ounce = 31 grams
1 foot = 0.30 meters
1 meter = 39.37 inches

Clothing

Women's clothing
American   8 10 12 14 16 18
Australian 10 12 14 16 18 20
Men's clothing
American 36 38 40 42 44 46
Australian 92 97 102 107 112 117

Men's shirts
American 15 15.5 16 16.5 17
Australian 38 39 41 42 43
Women's shoes
American 6 6.5 7 7.5 8 8.5
Australian 6.5 7 7.5 8 8.5 9
Men's shoes
American 8 8.5 9.5 10.5 11.5 12
Australian 7 7.5 8.5 9.5 10.5 11

Electricity

Australian electrical appliances have plugs with three flat pins. Electrical voltage is 240 AC, 50 cycles. Most visitors need to use an adapter.

Gay & Lesbian Travelers

Gay and Lesbian Tourism Australia *(galta.com.au)* promotes gay and lesbian travel within Australia and is an excellent source of help and information.

Holidays

January 1 (New Year's Day)
January 26 (Australia Day)
March/April (Good Friday, Easter Saturday, Easter Sunday, and Easter Monday)
April 25 (Anzac Day)
Second Monday in June (Queen's Birthday, national holiday except in Western Australia)
December 25 and 26 (Christmas Day and Boxing Day)

Liquor Laws

It is against the law for anyone under the age of 18 to buy alcohol or consume alcohol in public. Serving hours for public bars are usually 10 a.m.–10 p.m., Monday through Saturday, Sunday hours vary. Restaurants, clubs, and hotel lounges have more flexible hours. Alcohol is sold at liquor stores, hotels, and other licensed premises (not on supermarket shelves).

Many restaurants are licensed to sell alcohol, but some may only be able to sell it to you if you are having it with a meal. Others are BYO (bring your own). Most restaurants will allow you to BYO; they may charge a small corkage fee for opening the bottle and serving it to you.

Media
Newspapers
News Corporation's *The Australian* is the only newspaper available countrywide. Otherwise, each state has its own daily paper: the *Sydney Morning Herald* and *The Age,* from Melbourne, are the best known quality papers.

Radio
There are numerous radio channels on the AM and FM bands. In Sydney, 2GB and 702ABC have news and talkback programs; 2WS, 2-DAY-FM, and MMM play popular music; jjj is the youth station; and ABC-FM and 2MBS are devoted to classical music.

TV Channels
There are three commercial networks (Seven, Nine, and Ten), plus the government-owned but substantially independent Australian Broadcasting Corporation channel (Channel Two) and the similarly established multicultural channel, SBS. Cable is provided by the dominant network, Foxtel, which feature sports channels, movie channels, and news channels such as CNN.

Money
The unit of currency is the Australian dollar, which consists of 100 cents. Coins are available in 5, 10, 20, and 50 cents, and $1 and $2. Bills are in $5, $10, $20, $50, and $100 denominations. Different colors and sizes make them easy to identify.

At the time of publication, the Australian dollar (AUD) was trading roughly at parity with the U.S. dollar (USD).

Traveler's checks are a straightforward and secure way to carry money. You may change traveler's checks at almost any bank or licensed money changer, using your passport and/or driver's license as proof of identity. Fees vary from bank to bank, as do commission charges, but are around A$5–10 per transaction.

The major international credit cards are widely accepted throughout Australia, and even small towns seem to have an ATM allowing Mastercard or Visa cash withdrawals, or through overseas savings accounts linked to the Cirrus or Plus networks. Major charge cards, such as American Express, are also widely accepted. You should carry cash on long journeys in the outback. In all cases, it is sensible to carry a mixture of traveler's checks, credit cards, and cash.

National Trust
The National Trust *(national trust.org.au)* is dedicated to the preservation of historic buildings throughout Australia, many of which are open to the public.

Membership gives you free entry to any National Trust property. Helpful leaflets on historic buildings and walks around many towns and cities are available at National Trust offices:

Australian Capital Territory
Cnr. London Circuit & Civic Square, Canberra
Tel 02/6230-0533

New South Wales
Observatory Hill, The Rocks, Sydney
Tel 02/9258-0123

Northern Territory
2 Kahlin Ave., Larrakeyah
Tel 08/8981-2848

Queensland
95 William St., Brisbane
Tel 07/3223-6666

South Australia
Beaumont House,
631 Glynburn Rd.,
Beaumont
Tel 08/8202-9200

Tasmania
413 Hobart Rd., Youngtown
Tel 03/6344-6233

Victoria
Tasma Terrace,
4 Parliament Place, Melbourne
Tel 03/9656-9800

Western Australia
Old Observatory, 4 Havelock St., West Perth
Tel 08/9321-6088

Opening Hours
Shop hours vary from state to state, but the core opening hours are Monday to Saturday 9 a.m. to 5 p.m. Many towns have late-night shopping Thursday and/or Friday to 9 p.m. Shops in many tourist areas, and shopping malls in the cities, also open on Sunday. **Banks** are open Monday to Thursday 9:30 a.m. to 4 p.m., and Friday 9:30 a.m. to 5 p.m. In some states banks are also open on Saturday mornings. **Post offices** are open Monday to Friday 9 a.m. to 5 p.m. Many post offices open on Saturday mornings as well.

Photography & Video
Quality film and processing are available throughout Australia. Take extra care in the tropical heat, which may affect the life and quality of your film and batteries. The intense glare from the sun and its reflection on the water may bleach your photographs of color. The best

light for photography generally occurs in the early morning and late afternoon.

Senior Travelers

There are various discounts for senior citizens in Australia, but senior citizens visiting from abroad cannot claim them. However, it is always worth asking about discounts or promotional rates, particularly at hotels, with tour operators, and at car rental agencies.

Swimming & Beaches

Australia has some very fine beaches and swimming holes. As always, when swimming off unfamiliar beaches, take notice of tides, currents, and forecast weather conditions. It is advisable to swim only on beaches that have lifeguard support or supervision. A red-and-yellow flag indicates that it is safe to swim. A red flag warns that you should stay out of the water because of strong currents, rough seas, or less obvious dangers such as sharks, blue-ringed octopuses, or scorpion fish.

Between October and May, the seas of the tropical north may contain poisonous box jellyfish (stingers). All year round, the saltwater crocodile poses a serious danger to swimmers. Always heed signs warning of crocodiles. If you are camping, keep at least 50 yards (46 m) back from the water's edge, and don't follow the same route each time you go to fetch water.

Time Differences

Australia has three time zones.
Eastern Standard Time
East coast states—Tasmania, Queensland, Victoria, & New South Wales: 10 hours ahead of Greenwich Mean Time (GMT) and 15 hours ahead of U.S. Eastern Standard Time.

Central Standard Time South Australia & Northern Territory: 9.5 hours ahead of GMT.
Western Standard Time Western Australia: 8 hours ahead of GMT.

During the summer most states observe Daylight Savings Time, moving the clock forward by one hour. If used, Daylight Savings Time begins in October and ends in March or April, depending on the state.

Tipping

Tipping is not an Australian tradition. It is a matter of choice. A waiter at a quality restaurant, however, would anticipate a gratuity of up to 10 percent of the total bill if you have been satisfied with the service.

Travelers with Disabilities

The Australian Tourist Commission has consumer helplines around the world and provides a fact sheet, called "Travel in Australia for People with Disabilities," with the addresses of helpful organizations in each state or territory.

N.I.C.A.N., National Information Communications Network (48 Brookes St., Mitchell, ACT, tel 02/6241-1220 or 1800-806-769, nican.com.au), provides an Australia-wide directory of accessible accommodations and sporting and recreational facilities.

A.C.R.O.D., Australian Council for the Rehabilitation of the Disabled (33 Thesiger Ct., Deakin, ACT, tel 02/6283-3200, nds.org.au), offers advice on state-based help organizations, accommodations, and specialist tour operators.

Air travel All of Australia's airports have facilities for travelers with disabilities. Certain Qantas jets carry skychairs and have an accessible toilet on board.

Car rental Avis and Hertz have cars with hand controls. They must be reserved in advance but can be collected from major airports at no extra charge.

Parking & public toilets Major city councils can provide mobility maps to visitors.

Ferry The *Spirit of Tasmania* (see p. 333) has wheelchair-accessible cabins and provides access to the public areas on the ship.

Trains Facilities vary. The Indian Pacific (Sydney–Perth) line, for example, has cabins with wheelchair access. A skychair is used for boarding and movement between carriages. Conditions may not suit everyone. For further information, contact Great Southern Railway (tel 08/8213-4592).

Volunteer Vacations
Conservation Volunteers (tel 03/5330-2600, conservation volunteers.com.au) organizes practical conservation projects for volunteers and, on longer projects, organizes food and accommodations for a reasonable contribution toward costs. For details on their programs and other organizations offering volunteer opportunities (see "Volunteering," on p. 255).

EMERGENCIES
Emergency Telephone Number
Throughout Australia, the toll-free emergency services number for fire, ambulance, or police is **000**.

Embassies & Consulates
Most countries have an embassy or high commission within Canberra and a consular office in the major cities. Visa applications are generally handled in Canberra. For consulates, consult the local telephone directory.

United States
21 Moonah Place
Yarralumla
Canberra
ACT 2600
Tel 02/6214-5600

Canada
Commonwealth Ave.
Yarralumla
Canberra
ACT 2600
Tel 02/6270-4000

United Kingdom
Commonwealth Ave.
Yarralumla
Canberra
ACT 2600
Tel 02/6270-6666

Health
Medical care in Australia is excellent and not expensive. A doctor's appointment typically costs around A$40 (U.S. $40). The U.K., New Zealand, Sweden, the Netherlands, and a few other countries have reciprocal health care arrangements with Australia, and residents from these countries are entitled to free or heavily subsidized medical treatment at public hospitals and certain clinics.

Inoculations
None are essential. Cholera, malaria, and yellow fever are unknown, though tropical diseases such as dengue fever are a problem (see Insects, below). It is sensible to be vaccinated against tetanus and hepatitis (A and B)—but that is true whether you are traveling or not.

Insects
Flies can be a horrific nuisance in the outback, where they will settle on you by the hundred, seeking moisture from your ears, eyes, and nose.

Mosquitoes can also be a real problem in Australia, not just for the irritation of their bites but also because they may be carrying the Ross River virus or dengue fever. These can be as debilitating as malaria, though they are not widespread. Ask advice locally and use an effective insect repellent or fly net when necessary.

Spiders & Snakes
Thirteen of the most poisonous snakes and spiders in the world live in Australia. Snakes live in the water as well as on the land, but both prefer to stay out of your way and usually go before you've had a chance to spot them. If you are bitten by a snake, try to remember what it looked like (but never pursue it), and go straight to the hospital for antivenom. Most snake venom needs a few hours to take hold, but the shock of the bite can be as dangerous as the bite itself.

The most dangerous spiders in Australia are the red-back and funnel web. The latter is most poisonous and most common in the suburbs of Sydney. Again, if bitten, try to remember the features of the spider and go straight to the hospital.

Sunburn
Do not underestimate the power of the sun. Australia has the highest incidence of skin cancer in the world. The hole in the ozone layer is directly above Australia, and the clear blue skies offer very little protection from the sun's burning and dangerous ultraviolet radiation. Try to stay out of the sun at its peak strength, between 11 a.m. and 3 p.m. Always wear properly applied, high-factor suntan lotion and a hat. Keep your neck and arms well covered. Protect your eyes with quality sunglasses that fit well.

INFORMATION OFFICES
Tourism Australia is the main national tourism body, with a good website for visitor information (*australia.com*) and offices in many countries.

United States
6100 Center Drive
Suite 1150
Los Angeles, CA 90045
Tel: 310-695-3200

United Kingdom
Australia Centre, Australia House
6th Floor
Melbourne Place/Strand
London WC2B 4LG
Tel: 020-7438-4600

Internet Information
For online versions of local newspapers try:

theage.com.au (Melbourne)
smh.com.au (Sydney)
news.com.au (all of Australia)

For up-to-date weather reports, visit the Bureau of Meteorology's website at *bom.gov.au.*

Telephone numbers for the whole of Australia can be checked out at *whitepages.com.au*

State Tourism Offices
Local tourist information centers are listed throughout this book. Staff know their region and can make reservations. In addition, many offices have their own websites with extensive listings of accommodations and tours. Some offices produce plenty of good handouts, others just stock advertising brochures and act primarily as booking agencies.

Every state in Australia has its own tourism body that oversees marketing and planning and coordinates visitor information centers across the state. State tourism bodies produce some very useful glossy brochures, but as a general rule, they do not service visitors. However, they do have websites that you will find useful:

Australian Capital Tourism
visitcanberra.com.au

Tourism New South Wales
visitnsw.com

Northern Territory
travelnt.com

Tourism Queensland
queenslandholidays.com.au

South Australian Tourism Commission
southaustralia.com

Tourism Tasmania
discovertasmania.com

Tourism Victoria
visitvictoria.com

Western Australia Tourist Commission
westernaustralia.com

National Parks Offices

Every state also has offices for the departments in charge of the national parks, the environment, natural resources, and heritage. These are variously named, but all offer information and advice on visiting national parks, heritage sites, and nature reserves. The larger national parks have their own information offices. Details of those are given on the relevant pages.

Increasingly, national park services charge for entry into parks and also levy camping and other fees. Entry into most parks in Queensland, Victoria, and the Northern Territory is free, for now.

Fees and park passes are listed on state park authority websites, along with information on camping, hiking, and other activities. Parks Australia, a national body, controls a handful of national parks, notably Kakadu and Uluru–Kata Tjuta.

New South Wales
National Parks & Wildlife Commission
59–61 Goulburn St.
Sydney
Tel 02/9995-5000 or
1300-361-967
environment.nsw.gov.au

Northern Territory
Parks & Wildlife Service
Goyder Centre
35 Chung Wah Terrace
Palmerston
Tel 08/8999-4555
parksandwildlife.nt.gov.au

Parks Australia
Level 1
33 Allara St.
Canberra
Tel 02/6274-1111
environment.gov.au

Queensland
Queensland Parks & Wildlife Service
400 George St.
Brisbane
Tel 13-7468
nprst.qld.gov.au

South Australia
Department of Environment, Water and Natural Resources
205 Greenhill Rd.
Eastwood
Tel 08/8273-9100
environment.sa.gov.au

Tasmania
Parks & Wildlife Service
134 Macquarie St.
Hobart
Tel 1300-135-513
parks.tas.gov.au

Victoria
Parks Victoria
Level 10/535 Bourke St.
Melbourne
Tel 03/8627-4699 or 13-1963
parkweb.vic.gov.au

Western Australia
Department of Environment and Conservation
The Atrium
168 St. Georges Terrace
Perth
Tel 08/6467-5000
dec.wa.gov.au

Hotels & Restaurants

Cities have a wide variety of hotels and restaurants. In the country, except in tourist areas, accommodations and food are much more limited. An Australian specialty is the backpackers hostel, offering cheap but clean beds, sometimes in a dormitory. Aimed at traveling students, they also accommodate many older visitors on a budget. It is worth checking hotel websites for special offers, and online booking agencies, such as *wotif.com,* offer competitive prices, often much cheaper than walk-in or phone rates, particularly at top-end hotels.

ACCOMMODATIONS
Hotels

All the state capitals in Australia have luxury hotels belonging to international chains. Hotel groups providing high-quality accommodations are easily accessible to travelers. Rooms can usually be booked through the hotel's international network. In both town and country areas throughout Australia, more modest hotel accommodations are also available. In the outback, the only hotel is the local pub. The mainland coasts and the islands of the Great Barrier Reef have resort hotels, with a wide range of recreational activities available to guests.

Hotel Rates

The ranges of prices given for hotels are based on the standard full price for a double room. Off season, many hotels are prepared to offer guests special rates. It is always worth asking if any such arrangements are available during the time you plan to visit.

Motels

Travelers on a budget find these establishments good value. They offer comfortable bedrooms, sometimes with small kitchenettes and often with a single as well as a double bed. Most are located on main roads on the outskirts of towns and cities, but some can be found in city centers. Prices range from A$80–180 (U.S. $80–180) per night per room.

Guesthouses & Homestays

These accommodations range from a simple bedroom in a family home to a fully converted barn or a romantic country house. Prices start at A$80 (U.S. $80) a night, per double room, with breakfast, but can be more than A$200 (U.S. $200) a night in boutique places. Good websites include *australianbedandbreakfast .com.au, bbbook.com.au,* and *ozbedandbreakfast.com.*

Hostels

Australia has an extensive network of hostels. The **Australian Youth Hostels Association** *(yha.com.au)* has hostels nationwide. Standards vary considerably, from the rustic cabin with water drawn from a creek to the 500-bed modern building, with air-conditioning, swimming pool, sauna, launderette, and state-of-the-art kitchen facilities. Top-end prices hover at A$40 (U.S. $40) per night for a bunk in a dorm. Hostels are aimed at young, independent travelers, although no age restrictions apply. Guests tend to be members of one or more hosteling organizations. Membership privileges include reservations, discounts on travel and activities, and basic supplies. For further details of membership and travel centers see the website above. Other hostel networks include **VIP Backpackers** *(vipback packers.com),* **Nomad Backpackers** *(nomadsworld.com),* and **Base Backpackers** *(stayatbase.com).*

Farm Stays

Visitors can watch the everyday work on a farm, explore the surroundings, and enjoy hearty farm cooking (see sidebar p. 136). Holders of a visitor's visa are not permitted to take paid work on a farm, but voluntary work is possible (see sidebar p. 255).

Camping, RVs, & Motorhomes

The majority of parks are well equipped with power hookups, hot and cold water, toilets, showers, waste disposal, and coin-operated laundry facilities. Many also have public telephones, television and recreation rooms, a swimming pool, and convenience stores. Occasionally it may be possible to rent bed linen. Site-owned RVs or cabins, often with private sanitary facilities, may also be rented. Automobile associations (see p. 360) publish annual guides to Australian camping and RV parks.

RESTAURANTS

Major cities have a huge variety of eating places: hamburger joints, vegetarian cafés, ethnic restaurants from a bewildering number of countries, and elegant, celebrity chef–owned restaurants. Small towns, particularly outback ones, will not be able to offer much more than basic eateries.

Closings for holidays may vary from year to year. It is advisable to check and to reserve a table.

Abbreviations

L = lunch
D = dinner
AE = American Express
DC = Diners Club
MC = Mastercard
V = Visa

In the following selection, hotels are listed under each location by price, then in alphabetical order, followed by restaurants also by price and alphabetical order.

■ SYDNEY

🏨 THE OBSERVATORY
$$$$$
89–113 KENT ST., THE ROCKS
TEL 02/9256-2222
FAX 02/8248-5205
observatoryhotel.com.au
Located a few minutes from downtown, this hotel has a star-ceilinged indoor pool and deep spa baths. Sumptuous guest rooms have marble bathrooms and balconies.
🛏 100 🅿 🚉 Wynyard 😊 😊
😊 😊 🎬 😊 All major cards

🏨 PARK HYATT SYDNEY
$$$$$
7 HICKSON RD., THE ROCKS
TEL 02/9241-1234
FAX 02/9256-1555
sydney.park.hyatt.com
One of the most luxurious hotels in Sydney, with good views of the Opera House. Spacious, comfortable rooms have private balconies and harbor views.
🛏 155 🅿 🚉 Circular Quay
😊 😊 😊 🎬 😊
😊 All major cards

🏨 FOUR POINTS BY
🍽 SHERATON DARLING HARBOUR
$$$–$$$$
161 SUSSEX ST.
TEL 02/9290-4000
FAX 02/9290-4040
starwoodhotels.com

This large modern hotel was designed to evoke a 1920s ocean liner, and room furnishings echo the art deco, nautical feel. The site includes two 1850s heritage buildings: the **Corn Exchange** restaurant and **Dundee Arms** pub. There are some good deals on the city-view rooms, but hard to resist the harbor views.
🛏 630 🅿 😊 😊 😊 🎬
😊 All major cards

🏨 METRO HOTEL ON PITT
$$$
300 PITT ST.
TEL 02/9283-8088
FAX 02/9283-2825
metrohotels.com.au
Art deco hotel with a modernized interior in the heart of the city. This midrange option offers value but budget rooms are small; it's worth paying extra for a standard room.
🛏 115 😊 😊 😊 😊 🏊
😊 All major cards

🏨 HOTEL ALTAMONT
$$–$$$
207 DARLINGHURST RD., DARLINGHURST
TEL 02/9360-6000
FAX 02/9360-7096
altamont.com.au
Great value with bright, spacious rooms; this funky hotel is in a lively area and a 20-minute walk from the city center. It also has apartments a few doors down.
🛏 14 😊 😊
😊 All major cards

🏨 BAYSWATER SYDNEY
$$
17 BAYSWATER RD., KINGS CROSS
TEL 02/9361-0911
FAX 02/9361-4972
sydneylodges.com
Just away from the hustle and bustle of Kings Cross, but near the train station, this new hotel offers small, high-standard budget rooms.
🛏 51 😊 😊 😊 😊 All major cards

SOMETHING SPECIAL

🍽 GUILLAUME AT BENNELONG
$$$$$
SYDNEY OPERA HOUSE, BENNELONG POINT
TEL 02/9250-7548
guillaumeatbennelong.com.au
For a special experience, dine under the iconic sails of the Sydney Opera House. The restaurant, with stunning views of the city and harbor, is under the stewardship of chef Guillaume Brahimi and has claimed a swag of international awards. The upstairs bar is open for cocktails.
🪑 140 🅿 Circular Quay
🕐 Closed D Sun.–Mon., L. Tues., Wed., & Sat.
😊 😊 😊 All major cards

🍽 QUAY
$$$$$
UPPER LEVEL, OVERSEAS

PASSENGER TERMINAL,
CIRCULAR QUAY W.
TEL 02/9251-5600
quay.com.au
Opera House views and superb modern Australian cuisine combine to make this one of Australia's finest restaurants. Dishes are delicate and inspired; leave room for desserts such as the renowned snow egg.
🍴 85 🅿 🕐 Closed L Sat.– Mon. 🚭 ❄ 🅲 All major cards

🍴 ICEBERGS DINING ROOM & BAR
$$$$
1 NOTTS AVE.,
BONDI BEACH
TEL 02/9365-9000
idrb.com
Sydney has no shortage of waterfront dining, but this is worth the trip to Bondi for ocean views and fine Italian-inspired cuisine, perched above the famed swimming club at the end of the beach.
🍴 120 🕐 Closed Mon.
🚭 🅲 All major cards

🍴 LORD NELSON
🏨 BREWERY
$$–$$$
CORNER OF ARGYLL & KENT STS., THE ROCKS
TEL 02/9251-4044
lordnelsonbrewery.com
This is one of Sydney's oldest pubs—licensed since 1841—and beside the meals in its brasserie, serves up an interesting blend of beers brewed on the premises, some of them surprisingly potent. You can also stay at midrange rooms upstairs.
🍴 80 🕐 Closed L Sat.– Wed., D Sun.–Mon. 🚭 ❄
🅲 All major cards

🍴 SAILOR'S THAI
$$–$$$
106 GEORGE ST., THE ROCKS
TEL 02/9251-2466
sailorsthai.com.au

Housed in the old Sailor's Home (1864), the restaurant downstairs serves modern Thai food with style. Or squeeze in at long tables in the cheaper canteen upstairs.
🍴 80 🚭 ❄ 🅲 All major cards

🍴 MIRO
$$
76 LIVERPOOL ST.
TEL 02/9267-3126
mirotapasbar.com.au
Hidden downstairs, and well worth seeking out, this is one of the Spanish Quarter's better tapas restaurants. Paella, seafood, and the paintings of Joan Miró also feature.
🍴 200 🚭 🅲 All major cards

🍴 OPERA KITCHEN
$$
LOWER CONCOURSE LEVEL, SYDNEY OPERA HOUSE, BENNELONG POINT
TEL 04/5009-9888
operakitchen.com.au
The fanciest food court in town has stunning harbor views, even if the wagyu burgers are a tad expensive. Try the sushi bar at Kenji, the plank-roasted king salmon at Cloudy Bay Fish Co., or tiger prawn and green mango rice paper rolls at Misschu.
🍴 150 🚭 ❄
🅲 All major cards

🍴 MAMAK
$
15 GOULBURN ST., HAYMARKET
TEL 02/9211-1668
mamak.com.au
Malaysian chefs twirl, stretch, and slap dough onto the griddle to make flaky roti bread, perfect for dipping in rich coconut curries. Satay, nasi lemak, and other Malay specialties feature at this Chinatown favorite.
🍴 90 🚭 ❄ 🅲 All major cards

■ NEW SOUTH WALES

BLUE MOUNTAINS

SOMETHING SPECIAL

🏨 LILIANFELS BLUE
🍴 MOUNTAINS
$$$$$
LILIANFELS AVE., ECHO POINT, KATOOMBA
TEL 02/4780-1200
FAX 02/4780-1300
lilianfels.com.au
Small, sumptuous resort in a turn-of-the-century guest-house. In the heart of the Blue Mountains with wonderful valley views. Elegant dining at **Darley's Restaurant.** Afternoon tea here is an institution. Reservations essential.
ℹ 85 🅿 🛏 🚭 ❄ 🏊 🍸
🅲 All major cards

🏨 ECHOES BOUTIQUE
HOTEL
$$$$–$$$$$
3 LILIANFELS AVE., KATOOMBA
TEL 02/4782-1966
echoeshotel.com.au
Magnificent mountain views, stylish rooms, fine dining, and quiet seclusion make this a wonderful boutique retreat or honeymoon indulgence.
ℹ 14 🅿 🛏 🚭 ❄
🅲 All major cards

🍴 ARJUNA
$
16 VALLEY RD., KATOOMBA
TEL 02/4782-4662
Classic north Indian and tandoori cuisine comes with spectacular Megalong and Jamison Valleys views. BYO.
🍴 80 🅿 🕐 Closed Tues.– Weds. & L 🚭
🅲 All major cards

HUNTER VALLEY

SOMETHING SPECIAL

🏨 **TOWER LODGE**

🍴 **$$$$$**

6 HALLS RD., POKOLBIN

TEL 02/4998-7022

FAX 02/4998-7164

towerlodge.com.au

Exclusive luxury lodge at the Tower Estate Winery. Rooms furnished with antiques have balconies or courtyards with fountains, and one has a private plunge pool. There is a library, golf course, heated pool, sauna, gym, massage treatment, and exclusive fine dining at **Nine Restaurant.** Iconic **Robert's Restaurant** is also on the estate.

🛈 12 🅿 🚭 🚬 🏊 ⛳ 📺

🔷 All major cards

🏨 **PEPPER'S CONVENT**

$$$

HALLS RD., POKOLBIN

TEL 02/4998-4999

FAX 02/4998-7323

peppers.com.au

Built in 1909, this former convent has spacious rooms with high ceilings; most rooms open out onto a balcony or veranda. The decor is romantic, and the formal drawing room is furnished with antiques. Swimming pool, tennis court, and mountain bikes for rent.

🛈 17 🅿 🚭 🚬 🏊

🔷 All major cards

🍴 **OLD GEORGE &**
DRAGON RESTAURANT

$$$–$$$$

48 MELBOURNE ST.,

EAST MAITLAND

TEL 02/4933-7272

FAX 02/4934-1481

oldgeorgeanddragon.com.au

The restaurant at this former convict settlement exudes old wealth and Victorian charm. Regarded as one of the best eateries outside Sydney, the Old George & Dragon Restaurant, serves classic Anglo-French dishes like sautéed kidneys with mustard sauce or gamy venison, accompanied by Hunter Valley's best wines.

🛈 25 🅿 🚭 🚬

🔷 All major cards

COAST: NORTH OF SYDNEY

🏨 **THE BYRON AT BYRON**
RESORT & SPA

$$$$$

77–97 BROKEN HEAD RD.,

BYRON BAY

TEL 07/6639-2000

FAX 07/6639-2199

thebyronatbyron.com.au

Spacious luxury in one-bedroom suites with kitchen and lounge, set in glorious rain forest. Away from the bustle of the town, this tranquil retreat is a 10-minute walk to a long stretch of white sand at Tallow Beach.

🛈 92 🚭 🚬 🏊 📺

🔷 All major cards

🏨 **OPAL COVE RESORT**

$$–$$$$

PACIFIC HWY. NORTH,

COFFS HARBOUR

TEL 1800-008-198

opalcove.com.au

On the beach near town with a big pool, the smaller hotel rooms are good value; suites and villas are more luxurious.

🛈 173 🅿 🚭 🚬 🏊 📺

🔷 All major cards

🍴 **FIG TREE RESTAURANT**

$$

4 SUNRISE LANE, EWINGSDALE

TEL 02/6684-7273

figtreerestaurant.com.au

Impressive old farmhouse serving Mediterranean-style cuisine. A few miles out of Byron Bay, but worth the drive.

🏷 80 🅿 🕐 Closed L Mon.–Fri. & D Sun.–Wed. 🚭

🔷 All major cards

SNOWY MOUNTAINS

SOMETHING SPECIAL

🏨 **COCHRAN HORSE**
TREKS

$$$$$

"YAOUK," ADAMINABY

TEL 02/6454-2470

cochranhorsetreks.com.au

Run by Peter Cochran, a fifth-generation Snowy River cattleman whose ancestor Lachie Cochran was one of the legendary horsemen who inspired Banjo Paterson's poem "The Man from Snowy River." The two- to seven-day treks run through the rugged, awe-inspiring Snowy River countryside. Meals included.

🛈 Guests stay in tents

🔷 MC, V

🏨 **BERNTI'S MOUNTAIN**

🍴 **INN & RESTAURANT**

$$$–$$$$$

MOWAMBA PL., THREDBO

TEL 02/6457-6332

FAX 02/6457-6348

berntis.com.au

This friendly inn with sauna and spa offers delightful mountain views. Also open over the summer, when rates are cheaper.

🛈 30 🅿 15 🚭

🔷 All major cards

🏨 **PERISHER VALLEY**

🍴 **HOTEL**

$$$–$$$$$

MOUNT KOSCIUSZKO RD.,

PERISHER VALLEY

TEL 02/6459-4755

FAX 02/6457-5177

perisher.com.au

This luxury hotel has sumptuous suites, fabulous food, sauna, and spa. Rates include breakfast, dinner, and transfers to the hotel. **Snowgums Restaurant** for excellent dining.

🛈 31 🕐 Open ski season only

🚬 🔷 All major cards

🏨 Hotel 🍴 Restaurant 🛈 No. of Guest Rooms 🏷 No. of Seats 🅿 Parking 🚇 Rail Station 🕐 Closed 🛗 Elevator

AUSTRALIAN CAPITAL TERRITORY

CANBERRA

🏨 CROWNE PLAZA CANBERRA
$$$$
1 BINARA ST.
TEL 02/6247-8999
FAX 02/6257-4903
crowneplazacanberra.com.au
Renovations have restored this hotel to among Canberra's best, and the central location is unbeatable.
🛈 295 P 🔁 Ⓢ 🅒 🏊 🐶
Ⓒ All major cards

🏨 HYATT HOTEL CANBERRA
$$$$
COMMONWEALTH AVE., YARRALUMLA
TEL 02/6270-1234
FAX 02/6281-5998
canberra.park.hyatt.com
Within the Parliamentary Triangle, this beautifully restored hotel is an elegant example of Australian art deco. Extensive landscaped gardens.
🛈 249 P 🔁 Ⓢ 🅒 🏊 🐶
Ⓒ All major cards

SOMETHING SPECIAL

🏨 MERCURE CANBERRA
$$$–$$$$
AINSLIE & LIMESTONE AVES., BRADDON
TEL 02/6248-5511 OR 1800-020-016
FAX 02/6247-0864
mercurecanberra.com.au
Heritage-listed, split-level executive apartments around a landscaped central courtyard. Cheaper rates on the weekend.
🛈 126 P 🔁 Ⓢ 🅒
Ⓒ All major cards

🍴 WATERS EDGE RESTAURANT
$$$$
40 PARKES PLACE, PARKES
TEL 02/6273-5066
watersedge.com.au
Fine-dining delight with French influences in a wonderful lakeside locale make this one of Canberra's best.
🍴 76 🕐 Closed Mon.–Tues.
Ⓢ 🅒 Ⓒ All major cards

🍴 THE CHAIRMAN & YIP
$$$
108 BUNDA ST., CANBERRA
TEL 02/6248-7109
chairmangroup.com.au
Innovative Chinese food is fused with Western influences in this stylish restaurant.
🍴 150 🕐 Closed L Sat.–Mon. & D Sun. Ⓢ 🅒
Ⓒ All major cards

🍴 PROMENADE CAFÉ
$$$
HYATT HOTEL CANBERRA, COMMONWEALTH AVE., YARRALUMLA
TEL 02/6269-8810
canberra.park.hyatt.com
The elegant dining room of the Hyatt Hotel complements the Hyatt's art deco style. The à la carte menu shows flair, but the buffets are most popular.
🍴 130 P 🕐 Closed D Sun.–Mon. Ⓢ 🅒 Ⓒ All major cards

OUTSIDE CANBERRA

🏨 BRINDABELLA STATION
$$$
BRINDABELLA VALLEY, BRINDABELLA
TEL 02/6236-2121
FAX 02/6236-2128
brindabellastation.com.au
This historic farm in a classic bush setting offers farm-stay experience in two-bedroom, self-contained cottages.
🛈 2 cottages P 🕐 Closed Dec. 25 Ⓢ Ⓒ MC, V

QUEENSLAND

BRISBANE

🏨 EMPORIUM HOTEL
$$$$$
1000 ANN ST., FORTITUDE VALLEY
TEL 07/3253-6999
FAX 07/3253-6966
emporiumhotel.com.au
This boutique standout has superb rooms and an attention to detail that make it Brisbane's finest luxury hotel.
🛈 106 P Ⓢ 🅒 🏊 🐶
Ⓒ All major cards

🏨 TREASURY HOTEL & CASINO
$$$$$
WILLIAM ST.
TEL 07/3306-8888
FAX 07/3306-8880
treasurybrisbane.com.au
A fine example of Edwardian baroque. Suites are individually decorated, and rooms have antique furnishings.
🛈 128 P 🔁 Ⓢ 🅒 🐶
Ⓒ All major cards

🏨 STAMFORD PLAZA
$$$$–$$$$$
BOTANIC GARDENS, EDWARD ST.
TEL 07/3221-1999
FAX 07/3221-6895
stamford.com.au
In the downtown district by the botanic gardens, this is one of Brisbane's top luxury hotels. All of the elegant guest rooms overlook the river.
🛈 252 P 🔁 Ⓢ 🅒 🏊
🐶 Ⓒ All major cards

🏨 PULLMAN BRISBANE
$$$$
KING GEORGE SQ.
TEL 07/3229-9111
FAX 07/3229-9618
pullmanbrisbanekgs.com.au
This twin-towered luxury business hotel opposite City Hall is newly refurbished.

① 438 P 🔄 🅢 🅖 🏊 🛎
🅢 All major cards

🏨 WATERMARK HOTEL
$$$–$$$$
551 WICKHAM TERRACE
TEL 07/3831-3111
FAX 07/3832-1290
watermarkhotelbrisbane
.com.au
Just a short walk from the city
center with park views. The
service is excellent and the
hotel is newly revamped.
① 95 P 🔄 🅢 🅖 🏊
🅢 All major cards

🏨 RENDEZVOUS STUDIO
HOTEL ON GEORGE
$$$
103 GEORGE ST.
TEL 07/3221-6044
FAX 07/3238-2288
rendezvoushotels.com
Good-value accommodations
right in the heart of town
(opposite the casino).
① 99 P 🔄 🅢 🅖 🏊 🛎
🅢 All major cards

🏨 DORCHESTER INN
$$
484 UPPER EDWARD ST.
TEL 07/3831-2967
FAX 07/3832-2932
dorchesterinn.com.au
Faded but comfortable motel-
style rooms with kitchen, near
the train station, offer real
budget value.
① 10 🅢 🅖 🅢 MC, V

🍴 ECCO BISTRO
$$$$$
CORNER OF BOUNDARY &
ADELAIDE STS.
TEL 07/3831-8344
eccobistro.com
Once an old tea warehouse,
now a stylish bistro with
innovative cuisine. Bug (a local
crustacean) is popular on the
changing menu.
🍴 85 🕐 Closed Sun.–Mon. &
L. Sat. 🅢 🅖 🅢 All major cards

🍴 URBANE
$$$$$
181 MARY ST.
TEL 07/3229-2271
urbanerestaurant.com
Wonderful fine-dining restau-
rant regularly tops award lists.
Reservations essential.
🍴 60 P 🕐 Closed Sun. & L
Sat. 🅢 🅖 🅢 All major cards

🍴 CHA CHA CHAR
$$$$
SHOP 5, PLAZA LEVEL,
EAGLE ST. PIER
TEL 07/3211-9944
chachachar.com.au
Stylish grill restaurant over-
looks the river in the fashion-
able Eagle St. Pier precinct.
Specializes in steaks.
🍴 90 🅢 🅖 🅢 All major cards

🍴 LIBERTINE
RESTAURANT & BAR
$$$–$$$$
THE BARRACKS,
61 PETRIE TERRACE,
PADDINGTON
TEL 07/3367-3353
libertine.net.au
Interesting Vietnamese-French
cuisine and stunning decor in
renovated heritage building is
great for intimate dining or a
drink and snack at the bar.
🍴 100 P 🕐 Closed L. Mon.
🅢 🅖 🅢 All major cards

🍴 CROSSTOWN EATING
HOUSE
$$–$$$
23 LOGAN RD.,
WOOLLOONGABBA
TEL 07/3162-3839
thecrosstown.com.au
Popular café offering informal
dining in a renovated ware-
house. Simple, well-prepared
dishes won't shred the wallet.
🍴 80 🕐 Closed Sun.–Mon.
& L Tues. 🅢 🅖
🅢 All major cards

🍴 QUAN THANH
$$
75 HARDGRAVE RD., WEST END
TEL 07/3846-3849
Ever popular, reasonably priced
Chinese and Vietnamese restaurant, now with a Malaysian
offshoot two doors down.
🍴 100 🅢 🅖
🅢 All major cards

🍴 GOVINDA'S
$
UPSTAIRS AT 99 ELIZABETH ST.
TEL 07/3210-0255
brisbanegovindas.com.au
Cheap, filling vegetarian meals.
🍴 100 🕐 Closed D Mon.–
Thurs. & L Sun. 🅢 🅢 No cards

GOLD COAST

🏨 INTERCONTINENTAL
SANCTUARY COVE
$$$$$
MANOR CIRCLE, CASEY RD.,

HOPE ISLAND
TEL 07/5530-1234
FAX 07/5577-8234
ichotelsgroup.com
This huge, but exclusive, resort
has a large number of facilities,
including two golf courses.

🛈 243 🅿 🔄 Ⓢ 🔆 🏊 🎽
🆒 All major cards

🏨 SHERATON MIRAGE
🍽 GOLD COAST
$$$$–$$$$$
SEA WORLD DR.,
BROADWATER SPIT, MAIN BEACH
TEL 07/5577-0000
FAX 07/5591-2299
starwoodhotels.com
Set among beautiful gardens,
this luxury development has
its own secluded beach and
a number of fine restaurants.
The Marina Mirage, a luxury
shopping complex, is nearby.

🛈 293 🅿 🔄 Ⓢ 🔆 🏊 🎽
🆒 All major cards

🏨 O'REILLY'S RAINFOREST
RETREAT
$$$–$$$$$
LAMINGTON NATIONAL
PARK RD.
TEL 07/5502-4911
oreillys.com.au
Elegant family-run guesthouse
dating back to the 1920s and
situated in the cool heights,
3,000 feet (915 m) up in the
Lamington National Forest
with stunning views.

🛈 65 rooms, 38 villas
🆒 All major cards

🏨 SURF PARADE RESORT
$$–$$$
210–218 SURF PARADE,
SURFERS PARADISE
TEL 07/5538-8863
FAX 07/5598-8862
surf-parade-resort.com.au
Tower-block apartments in
Surfers Paradise offer great
value, and this is one of the
best. One-bedroom apart-
ments have kitchen, spa bath,
and balconies.

🛈 96 🅿 🔄 Ⓢ 🔆 🏊 🎽
🆒 All major cards

🍽 OSKAR'S ON BURLEIGH
$$$
43 GOODWIN TERRACE,
BURLEIGH HEADS
TEL 07/5576-3722
oskars.com.au
A well-known restaurant that
overlooks the beach. Good
wine and delicious seafood.

🍴 150 🅿 Ⓢ 🔆
🆒 All major cards

🍽 SHOGUN, SURFERS
PARADISE
$$$
90 BUNDALL RD.
TEL 07/5538-2872
Classic Japanese dishes served
with flair. Teppanyaki and à la
carte are offered.

🍴 100 🕐 Closed L
Ⓢ 🔆 🆒 All major cards

SUNSHINE COAST
& FRASER ISLAND

🏨 PALMER COOLUM
RESORT
$$$$–$$$$$
WARREN RD., COOLUM
TEL 07/5446-1234 OR
1800-266-586
FAX 07/5446-2957
palmercoolumresort.com.au
Private Mediterranean-style
villas and rooms near the
beautiful Coolum beach.

🛈 324 🅿 Ⓢ 🔆 🏊 🏊
🎽 🆒 All major cards

🏨 NOOSA SHERATON
RESORT
$$$$
HASTINGS ST., NOOSA HEADS
TEL 07/5449-4888
FAX 07/5449-2230
starwoodhotels.com
Everything you expect from a
luxury hotel, plus a number of
suites and poolside villas.

🛈 221 🔄 Ⓢ 🔆 🏊 🎽
🆒 All major cards

🏨 KINGFISHER BAY
RESORT
$$$
FRASER ISLAND
TEL 1800-072-555
kingfisherbay.com
The only luxury resort on this
World Heritage island, with
modern buildings, built of
timber and finished in natural
colors, strung along a pretty
bay on the west coast.

🛈 261 🅿 Ⓢ 🔆 🏊
🆒 All major cards

🍽 BISTRO C
$$$–$$$$
49 HASTINGS ST., NOOSA HEADS
TEL 07/5447-2855
bistroc.com.au
In a town of variable dining
standards, Bistro C has
consistently good food and a
wonderful beachside aspect.

🍴 70 Ⓢ 🔆
🆒 All major cards

GREAT BARRIER REEF:
SOUTHERN

🏨 HERON ISLAND RESORT
$$$$$
TEL 07/4972-9055
heronisland.com
Right on the reef, this island
is a diver's paradise and ideal
for snorkeling, with the clear-
est waters in June and July.
Accommodations range from
standard rooms to comfort-
able suites. One beach house
is also available. Meals are
included in the basic price.

🛈 116 🏊 🆒 All major cards

🏨 LADY ELLIOT ISLAND
ECO RESORT
$$$$–$$$$$
TEL 07/4156-4444
ladyelliot.com.au
Accommodations are in
simple, waterfront cabins on
this 100-acre coral cay with
good diving and white coral
beaches. Sea turtles visit Oct.–
March. Breakfast and dinner

are included in the basic price.
🛈 49 🏊 🅶 All major cards

🏨 GREAT KEPPEL ISLAND HOLIDAY VILLAGE
$–$$$$$

TEL 07/4939-8655
gkiholidayvillage.com.au
Great Keppel's big resort is
being redeveloped, so stay at
this modest place and sample
all the island's beauty at a
fraction of the cost. Basic
rooms, tents on wooden
platforms, cabins, cottages,
and water-based activities
are offered.
🛈 17 🅶 All major cards

GREAT BARRIER REEF: WHITSUNDAY ISLANDS

🏨 HAYMAN ISLAND RESORT
$$$$$

GREAT BARRIER REEF
TEL 1800-122-339
FAX 07/4940-1567
hayman.com.au
The reef's most luxurious
resort. The very stylish, three-
level complex includes tropical
gardens, huge salt- and
freshwater pools, and lagoons.
Children welcome. The basic
price includes breakfast; full-
board packages are available.
🛈 214 🔄 🅢 🅢 🏊 🖥
🅶 All major cards

🏨 PARADISE BAY
$$$$$

SOUTH LONG ISLAND
TEL 07/4946-9777
paradisebay.com.au
Small, simple, and intimate,
this eco-retreat has crafted
wooden bungalows on a
private beach, group gourmet
meals, daily boat trips, and
helicopter transfers.
🛈 10 🅿 🅢 🅢
🅶 All major cards

🏨 HAMILTON ISLAND RESORT
$$$–$$$$$

PMB,
HAMILTON ISLAND
TEL 07/4946-9999
FAX 07/4946-8888
hamiltonisland.com.au
Accommodations range from
exclusive Qualia pavilions to
rooms in high-rise towers.
Plenty of activities and out-
standing sports facilities. The
basic price is for room only.
🛈 680 🔄 🅢 🅢 🏊 🖥
🅶 All major cards

🏨 SUMMIT APARTMENTS
$$$

15 FLAME TREE COURT,
AIRLIE BEACH
TEL 07/4946-3400
FAX 07/4946-6287
summitairliebeach.com.au
Airlie Beach has a glut of
accommodations, like these
well-equipped apartments
above town on the hill. A good
choice for day-tripping to the
islands, without paying island
resort rates.
🛈 60 🅿 🅢 🅢 🏊
🅶 All major cards

GREAT BARRIER REEF: NORTHERN

🏨 GREEN ISLAND RESORT
$$$$$

P.O. BOX 898, CAIRNS
TEL 07/4031-3300
FAX 07/4052-1511
greenislandresort.com.au
This coral cay and its surrounding reef are a national
park. The luxury resort houses
92 guests and is reached by
catamaran out of Cairns.
The only drawback is the
big number of day-trippers
on the island until 4 p.m.
🛈 46 🅢 🏊 🅶 All major cards

🏨 LIZARD ISLAND RESORT
$$$$$

PMB 40, CAIRNS

TEL 1300-863-248
lizardisland.com.au
This has everything you might
expect at an exclusive resort.
The rock-star rates include
all meals and the use of all
facilities, which include tennis
courts, Windsurfers, dinghies,
and fishing equipment.
🛈 40 🅢 🏊 🅶 All major cards

TOWNSVILLE & MAGNETIC ISLAND

🏨 JUPITERS
🍴 TOWNSVILLE HOTEL & CASINO
$$$–$$$$

BOX 1223, SIR LESLIE THIESS DR.,
TOWNSVILLE
TEL 07/4722-2333
FAX 07/4772-4741
jupiterstownsville.com.au
This busy waterfront hotel has
spacious and surprisingly quiet
rooms and a good restaurant.
Views to Magnetic Island.
🛈 192 🅿 🔄 🅢 🅢 🏊
🖥 🅶 All major cards

🏨 PEPPERS BLUE ON BLUE RESORT
$$$–$$$$$

123 SOONING ST., NELLY BAY,
MAGNETIC ISLAND
TEL 07/4758-2400
FAX 07/4758-2499
magneticresort.com
The top spot on Magnetic
Island, overlooking the marina,
with modern rooms, good
food, and a huge pool.
🛈 52 🅿 🅢 🅢 🏊
🅶 All major cards

🏨 ISLAND LEISURE RESORT
$$$

4 KELLY ST., NELLY BAY,
MAGNETIC ISLAND
TEL 07/4778-5000
FAX 07/4778-5042
islandleisure.com.au
A resort with self-contained
cabins set in tropical gardens.

🏨 Hotel 🍴 Restaurant 🛈 No. of Guest Rooms 🔄 No. of Seats 🅿 Parking 🚉 Rail Station 🕐 Closed 🔼 Elevator

ⓘ 17 cabins 🅿 Ⓢ Ⓒ ⚟
🛡 🅰 All major cards

🏨 WATERS EDGE THE STRAND

$$

63 THE STRAND, TOWNSVILLE
TEL 07/4721-1777
watersedgethestrand.com
A pleasant seafront hotel with good service. The ocean view rooms are worth paying a little extra.

ⓘ 45 🅿 ⇄ Ⓢ Ⓒ ⚟
🛡 🅰 All major cards

CAIRNS

🏨 THE REEF HOTEL
🍴 CASINO

$$$$–$$$$$

CORNER OF SPENCE &
WHARF STS.
TEL 07/4030-8888
FAX 07/4030-8788
reefcasino.com.au
Well located near the waterfront cruise terminal, this lavish hotel has good rooms, luxury suites, four restaurants, and a host of bars.

ⓘ 128 suites 🅿 ⇄ Ⓢ Ⓒ ⚟
🛡 🅰 All major cards

🏨 REEF HOUSE

$$$$–$$$$$

99 WILLIAMS ESPLANADE,
PALM COVE
TEL 07/4080-2600
FAX 07/4055-3305
reefhouse.com.au
This delightful beachfront resort sits behind a grove of paperbark trees. Veranda rooms have cane furniture, while Brigadier rooms have a nostalgic military ambience.

ⓘ 70 🅿 ⇄ Ⓒ ⚟
🅰 All major cards

🏨 ROYDON BEACHFRONT APARTMENTS

$$$–$$$$

83–87 VASEY ESPLANADE,
TRINITY BEACH

TEL 07/4057-6512
FAX 07/4055-6883
roydon.com.au
Past the airport, the good northern beaches, such as Trinity Beach and Palm Cove, are close to the city but quieter and not as developed as Port Douglas. Apartment complexes offer great value, such as this one opposite Trinity Beach with spacious one- to three-bedroom, fully self-contained apartments.

ⓘ 20 🅿 ⇄ Ⓢ Ⓒ ⚟
🅰 All major cards

🏨 PACIFIC INTERNATIONAL

$$$

ESPLANADE & SPENCE STS.
TEL 07/4051-7888 OR
1800-079-001
FAX 07/4031-4401
pacifichotelcairns.com
This former top hotel is a little dated but offers good value and location. Guest rooms are on the seafront.

ⓘ 174 🅿 ⇄ Ⓢ Ⓒ
⚟ 🅰 All major cards

🍴 TAMARIND

$$$$

35-41 WHARF STREET
TEL 07/4030-8888
reefcasino.com.au
Consistently at the top of the Cairns dining scene, modern Australian and Asian fusion dishes are served with style in an elegant setting.

🍽 60 🅿 🕐 Closed L
Ⓢ 🅰 All major cards

🍴 MONDO CAFÉ BAR & GRILL

$$$

HILTON INTERNATIONAL HOTEL,
WHARF ST.
TEL 07/4052-6782
This casual dining café (order at the bar) has cheap grills, Asian fare, and wonderful al fresco dining, with tables on the waterfront.

🍽 160 🅿 🕐 Closed L
Ⓢ Ⓒ 🅰 All major cards

PORT DOUGLAS & CAPE TRIBULATION

🏨 SHERATON MIRAGE
🍴 $$$$$

PORT DOUGLAS RD.,
PORT DOUGLAS
TEL 07/4099-5888
FAX 07/4099-5398
starwoodhotels.com
This granddaddy of Port Douglas resorts is showing signs of age, but it has every luxury, acres of blue lagoons and pools, and grounds reaching down to Four Mile Beach.

ⓘ 294 + 105 villas 🅿 ⇄ Ⓢ
Ⓒ ⚟ 🛡 🅰 All major cards

🏨 PINK FLAMINGO

$$$

115 DAVIDSON ST.,
PORT DOUGLAS
TEL 07/4099-6622
FAX 07/4099-4571
pinkflamingo.com.au
Stylish studios and one-bedroom villas are set in a delightful tropical garden at this small resort. No children.

ⓘ 12 🅿 Ⓢ Ⓒ ⚟
🅰 All major cards

🍴 HARRISON'S RESTAURANT & BAR

$$$$

22 WHARF ST., PORT DOUGLAS
TEL 07/4099-4011
A great place to head for a sophisticated dinner after a day on the reef. French-inspired modern fine dining opposite the waterfront.

🍽 100 🅿 🕐 Closed L
Ⓢ 🅰 All major cards

DAINTREE/ CAPE TRIBULATION

🏨 BLOOMFIELD LODGE

$$$$$

AYTON, WEARY BAY
TEL 07/4035-9166
FAX 07/4035-9180

 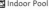

bloomfieldlodge.com.au
Isolated resort with fan-cooled wooden cabins set in the remote and beautiful Daintree rain forest along the Bloomfield River. Three-night minimum stay. Packages include gourmet meals and air transfers from Cairns.

ⓘ 17 🖼 🛇 All major cards

🏨 DAINTREE ECO LODGE & SPA
$$$$$
DAINTREE RD., DAINTREE
TEL 07/4098-6100
FAX 07/4098-6200
daintree-ecolodge.com.au
Tree house chalets set above the rain forest canopy near the Daintree River, with a range of spa treatments.

ⓘ 15 🅿 🛇 🖼 🛎
🛇 All major cards

SOMETHING SPECIAL

🏨 SILKY OAKS LODGE 🍴 & RESTAURANT
$$$$$
FINLAY VALE RD.,
MOSSMAN GORGE
TEL 07/4098-1666
FAX 07/4098-1983
silkyoakslodge.com.au
Air-conditioned colonial-style cabins sit on stilts looking out onto the rain forest or the lodge's natural rock swimming pool. Excellent **Treehouse Restaurant** and a good selection of Australian wine.

ⓘ 60 🅿 🛇 🛇 🖼
🛇 All major cards

🏨 HERITAGE LODGE & SPA
$$$$
TURPENTINE RD.,
COOPER CREEK, DAINTREE
TEL 07/4098-9138
FAX 07/4098-9004
heritagelodge.net.au
Cabin resort surrounded by rain forest adjoining Cape

Tribulation National Park.

ⓘ 20 🅿 🛇 🖼
🛇 All major cards

🏨 RED MILL HOUSE
$$$
11 STEWART ST.,
DAINTREE VILLAGE
TEL 07/4098-6233
redmillhouse.com.au
There are excellent bird-watching opportunities at this enjoyable B&B in an old Queenslander house.

ⓘ 6 🅿 🖼 🛇 MC, V

🏨 DAINTREE RAINFOREST BUNGALOWS
$$
SPURWOOD RD., COW BAY
TEL 07/4098-9229
Cabins with queen bed, two singles, and veranda in the rain forest are excellent value. A good base to explore the Daintree with beaches a short drive away. No children.

ⓘ 4 🛇 🛇 All major cards

■ NORTHERN TERRITORY

DARWIN

🏨 CROWNE PLAZA
$$$$
32 MITCHELL ST.
TEL 08/8982-0000
FAX 08/8981-1765
crowneplaza.com
Darwin's top hotel in a great location. Good value.

ⓘ 233 🅿 🛇 🛇 🛇 🖼
🛇 All major cards

🏨 HOLIDAY INN ESPLANADE
$$$–$$$$
116 THE ESPLANADE
TEL 08/8980-3600
FAX 08/8981-5701
holidayinn.com
Striking five-floor, waterfront hotel, set on tropical parkland.

PRICES

HOTELS
An indication of the cost of a double room in the high season is given by $ signs.

$$$$$	Over $280
$$$$	$200–$280
$$$	$120–$200
$$	$80–$120
$	Under $80

RESTAURANTS
An indication of the cost of a three-course meal without drinks is given by $ signs.

$$$$$	Over $90
$$$$	$70–$90
$$$	$50–$70
$$	$30–$50
$	Under $30

ⓘ 197 🅿 🛇 🛇 🛇 🖼
🛎 🛇 All major cards

🏨 NOVOTEL ATRIUM DARWIN
$$$
CORNER OF PEEL ST. & THE ESPLANADE
TEL 08/8941-0755
FAX 08/8981-9025
novotel.com
Hotel set in tropical gardens right on the Esplanade. Each of the spacious guest rooms has its own small kitchen.

ⓘ 138 🅿 🛇 🛇 🛇 🖼
🛇 All major cards

🍴 CHAR RESTAURANT
$$$$
THE ESPLANADE (CORNER OF KNUCKEY ST.)
TEL 08/8981-4544
chardarwin.com.au
In the heritage-listed Admiralty House, this stylish steak restaurant also serves vegetarian and seafood dishes. Try the

---

whole fish to share. The shade garden is a magic place to dine on a balmy evening.
🔓 300 🅒 All major cards

ALICE SPRINGS

🏨 CROWNE PLAZA
🍴 ALICE SPRINGS
$$$–$$$$$
82 BARRETT DR.
TEL 08/8950-8000
FAX 08/8952-3822
ihg.com
Set on landscaped lawns beside the Todd River, with the MacDonnell Ranges as a backdrop, this is the best hotel in Alice Springs. Its **Hanuman** restaurant is a local favorite.
🛏 236 🅿 🅒 🏊 🏋
🅒 All major cards

🏨 LASSETERS HOTEL CASINO
$$$–$$$$
BARRETT DR.
TEL 08/8950-7777 OR
1800-808-975
lhc.com.au
A sleek modern hotel just out of town that houses a casino.
🛏 76 🅿 🅒 🅒 🅒 🏊
🅒 All major cards

🏨 DIPLOMAT MOTEL
$$–$$$
CORNER OF GREGORY TERRACE
& HARTLEY ST.
TEL 08/8952-8977
FAX 08/8953-0225
diplomatmotel.com.au
A central location, friendly staff, and comfortable rooms.
🛏 81 🅿 🅒 🅒 🏊
🅒 All major cards

🍴 RED OCHRE GRILL
$$$
57 TODD MALL
TEL 08/8952-9614
redochrealice.com.au
Big plates, good service, and a wide selection including native meats such as crocodile, kangaroo, and camel. Right on

the Todd Mall.
🔓 60 🅒 🅒 🅒 All major cards

COBOURG PENINSULA

🏨 SEVEN SPIRIT BAY
$$$$$
TEL 08/8988-2648
sevenspiritbay.com.au
Luxury in the heart of Arnhem Land, Australia's most spectacularly remote region. Cottage-style hexagonal cabins, fine dining, and the opportunity to see Aboriginal rock art and wildlife. Air access arranged by the lodge.
🛏 23 🅒 🅒 🅒 All major cards

KAKADU NATIONAL PARK

SOMETHING SPECIAL

🏨 GAGUDJU CROCODILE
$$$$
FLINDERS ST., JABIRU
TEL 1800-500-401
gagudju-dreaming.com
This deluxe hotel at Kakadu is shaped like a giant crocodile. Rooms follow the curve of the croc's body and have French windows that overlook the pool in its stomach. The reception is through its mouth.
🛏 110 🅿 🅒 🏊
🅒 All major cards

YULARA (AYERS ROCK RESORT)

🏨 DESERT GARDENS
🍴 $$$$$
YULARA DR.
TEL 08/8957-7714
ayersrockresort.com.au
Set among extensive gardens with ghost gums and flowering native shrubs, this hotel offers friendly service and secluded modern rooms. **White Gums** and the smaller **Bunya Bar** serve fresh, healthy fare in a relaxed atmosphere.

🛏 160 🅿 🅒 Some
🅒 🏊 🅒 All major cards

🏨 SAILS IN THE
🍴 DESERT & KUNIYA RESTAURANT
$$$$$
YULARA DR.
TEL 08/8957-7417
ayersrockresort.com.au
Giant sails shade this airy three-story hotel. Luxurious rooms have balconies or verandas overlooking the garden. A tower offers views of Uluru. There are also deluxe suites.
🛏 228 🅿 🅒 🅒 🅒 🏊
🅒 All major cards

WATARRKA NATIONAL PARK

🏨 KINGS CANYON RESORT
$$$–$$$$$
ERNEST GILES RD.
TEL 08/8956-7442
kingscanyonresort.com.au
The hotel has well-equipped, air-conditioned rooms overlooking the desert. There are also budget rooms and a campsite. The resort offers a choice of buffet, à la carte, and barbecue meals. It is expensive for the standards but is the only option at the canyon.
🛏 96 🅿 🅒 🏊
🅒 All major cards

▦ WESTERN AUSTRALIA

PERTH

🏨 CROWN METROPOL PERTH
$$$$$
GREAT EASTERN HWY.,
VICTORIA PARK, BENTLEY
TEL 08/9362-8888
FAX 08/9367-8877
crownhotels.com.au
The guest rooms are opulent, the golf course is well

---

groomed, and the house casino is open 24 hours.

🔘405 🅿️ 🔲 🔲 🔲 🔲
🔲 🔲 🔲 All major cards

🏨 HYATT REGENCY PERTH
$$$$$
99 ADELAIDE TERRACE
TEL 08/9225-1234
FAX 08/9325-8899
perth.regency.hyatt.com
All you would expect from a luxury hotel, and in a delightful river setting. Two floors are dedicated to the Regency Club. A little dated but look out for deals.

🔘367 🅿️ 🔲 🔲 🔲 🔲
🔲 🔲 All major cards

🏨 THE RICHARDSON
🍴 $$$$$
32 RICHARDSON ST.,
WEST PERTH
TEL 08/9217-8888
FAX 08/9214-3931
therichardson.com.au
Perth's finest hotel, and one of Australia's best small luxury hotels, has spacious rooms, exceptional service, and the excellent **Opus Restaurant.**

🔘74 🅿️ 🔲 🔲 🔲 🔲 🔲
🔲 All major cards

🏨 TRAVELODGE PERTH
$$$
417 HAY ST.
TEL 08/9238-1888
FAX 08/9238-1999
Very central and affordable in expensive Perth, this is a good midrange option close to Perth's attractions with a bus stop out front.

🔘122 🅿️ 🔲 🔲 🔲 🔲
🔲 All major cards

SOMETHING SPECIAL

🍴 RESTAURANT AMUSÉ
$$$$$
64 BRONTE ST., EAST PERTH
TEL 08/9325-4900
Perth's—and one of the country's—finest restaurants

offers a great sense of occasion in food and service. The multicourse degustation menu changes with seasonal ingredients. Book well in advance.

🔲50 🕐 Closed Sun.–Mon., L
🔲 🔲 🔲 All major cards

🍴 1907
$$$$
26 QUEEN ST.
TEL 08/9436-0233
1907.com.au
Housed in a century-old building, fine dining in sumptuous, classic decor. Down an alleyway, this Perth hot spot also has a very popular bar.

🔲60 🕐 Closed L Sat.–Mon.
& D Sun.–Mon. 🔲 🔲
🔲 All major cards

🍴 PERUGINO
$$$
77 OUTRAM ST., WEST PERTH
TEL 08/9321-5420
perugino.com.au
Italian restaurant with a reputation for fine food and exemplary service. The imaginative menu takes advantage of fresh seasonal produce. Reservations essential.

🔲110 🅿️ 🕐 Closed
L Sat. & Sun.–Mon. 🔲 🔲
🔲 All major cards

🍴 LITTLE CREATURES
$$–$$$
40 MEWS RD., FREMANTLE
TEL 08/9430-5555
littlecreatures.com.au
Great pizzas, chili mussels, and tapas-style treats are offered at this landmark Fremantle boutique brewery down by the fishing docks. Reserve a table in the sun at lunchtime.

🔲500 🔲 🔲
🔲 All major cards

BROOME

🏨 CABLE BEACH CLUB
🍴 RESORT & SPA
$$$$$

CABLE BEACH RD.
TEL 08/9192-0400
FAX 08/9192-2249
cablebeachclub.com
Asian-themed luxury hotel set in landscaped oriental gardens, with rooms, bungalows, and suites, plus an elegant restaurant. Stunning views over Cable Beach.

🔘263 🅿️ 🔲 On request
🔲 🔲 🔲 All major cards

THE KIMBERLEY

🏨 TRUE NORTH
$$$$$
TEL 08/9192-1829
northstarcruises.com.au
Cruises along the north Kimberley coast are awe-inspiring, none more so than True North, a luxury vessel serving gourmet meals on 7- or 14-day trips between Broome and Wyndham, with excursions.

🔘18 cabin rooms 🔲
🔲 All major cards

SOMETHING SPECIAL

🏨 WILDERNESS
CHALLENGE
$$$$
TEL 07/4035-4488
wilderness-challenge.com.au
This company offers 6-, 9-, and 16-day overland 4WD camping (tent) safaris through the heart of the Kimberley. A 15-day option with stays in a variety of accommodations—cattle stations, bush pubs, etc.—is also available.

🔘Each 4WD holds a max of 13 people 🔲 🔲 MC, V

🏨 EL QUESTRO
$–$$$$$
TEL 08/9161-4318
elquestro.com.au
A remote million-acre (400,000 ha) cattle station in the eastern Kimberley offering everything from camping to five-star luxury and a wide

variety of activities—from fishing, swimming, and wildlife viewing to helicopter picnics at your own private billabong. Transfers arranged from Kununurra.

🅘 78 🚭 ❄️ 🌊 🄰 All major cards

NINGALOO REEF

🏨 SAL SALIS NINGALOO REEF
$$$$$

P.O. BOX 471
EXMOUTH
TEL 1300-790-561
salsalis.com.au
Award-winning, tented eco-camp only a stone's throw from one of Australia's spectacular but least viewed coral reefs. Meals, snorkeling, and sea kayaking included.

🅘 Tents ❄️ 🄰 MC, V

ROTTNEST ISLAND

🏨 HOTEL ROTTNEST
🍽 $$$$$

THOMPSON BAY SETTLEMENT
TEL 08/9292-5011
hotelrottnest.com.au
Elegant colonial mansion, built in 1864, and now a stylish hotel and restaurant. Rates include breakfast.

🅘 18 🚭 🄰 All major cards

SOUTHWEST

🏨 CAPE LODGE
$$$$$

CAVES RD., YALLINGUP,
MARGARET RIVER
TEL 08/9755-6311
FAX 08/9755-6322
capelodge.com.au
Country retreat on a plantation. Overlooking a private lake, the mansion house has luxurious guest rooms, a fine-dining restaurant, and cooking classes. The basic rate includes a wonderful breakfast. Children are discouraged.

🅘 22 🅿 🚭 ❄️ 🌊
🄰 All major cards

🏨 ALBANY FORESHORE GUEST HOUSE
$$$

86 STIRLING TERRACE, ALBANY
TEL 08/9842-8324
FAX 08/9842-8325
albanyforeshoreguesthouse
.com.au
Albany has a good selection of B&Bs such as this heritage 1888 former bank in the center of town.

🅘 5 🚭 🄰 All major cards

🍽 VOYAGER ESTATE
$$$$

STEVENS RD., MARGARET RIVER
TEL 08/9757-6354
voyagerestate.com.au
While touring the wineries, lunch at this fine winery restaurant. Try any of the innovative entrees and mains, or on weekends, high tea.

🍴 95 🕐 Closed D 🚭 ❄️
🄰 All major cards

■ SOUTH AUSTRALIA

ADELAIDE

🏨 FIRE STATION INN
$$$$$

80 TYNTE ST., NORTH ADELAIDE
TEL 08/8272-1355
adelaideheritage.com
North Adelaide's original fire station, built in 1866 and now a small and funky hotel. An immaculately restored 1942 fire truck decorates one of the suites. Breakfast included.

🅘 3 suites 🅿 Prepaid parking permit 🚭 ❄️
🄰 All major cards

🏨 INTERCONTINENTAL
$$$$–$$$$$

NORTH TERRACE
TEL 08/8231-1234

FAX 08/8231-1120
ichotelsgroup.com
Luxury hotel in the heart of town, beside the Adelaide Festival Centre.

🅘 367 🅿 🚭 ❄️ 🌊 🌊 🍸
🄰 All major cards

🏨 HILTON
🍽 INTERNATIONAL
$$$$

BOX 1871, 233 VICTORIA SQ.
TEL 08/8217-2000
FAX 08/8217-2001
hilton.com
Luxury hotel in the city center. Package deals can make this a good buy.

🅘 380 🅿 🚭 ❄️ 🌊 🌊 🍸
🄰 All major cards

🏨 STAMFORD GRAND
$$$$

MOSELEY SQ., GLENELG
TEL 08/8376-1222
FAX 08/8376-1111
stamford.com.au
A high-rise resort on Glenelg Beach with superb sea views.

🅘 220 🚭 ❄️ 🌊 🌊 🍸
🄰 All major cards

🏨 HOTEL RICHMOND
$$$

128 RUNDLE MALL
TEL 08/8215-4444
hotelrichmond.com.au
Small, chic art deco hotel, built in 1929, situated in the heart of the city. Could do with renovations but well priced.

🅘 30 🚭 ❄️ 🄰 AE, MC, V

🍽 JOLLEYS BOATHOUSE
$$$$$

1 JOLLEYS LANE
TEL 08/8223-2891
jolleysboathouse.com
Victorian-era boathouse on the banks of the Torrens River serves up trendy contemporary fare in a bright, airy conservatory setting.

🍴 120 🕐 Closed L Sat.
❄️ 🄰 All major cards

🍴 AUGE

$$$$

22 GROTE ST.

TEL 08/8410-9332

auge.com.au

Adelaide's best Italian restaurant, with fine dining flourish, in decor and cuisine, with a modern take on Italian classics.

🔟 50 🕐 Closed Sun.–Mon., L
🅢 🅕 🅐 All major cards

🍴 CHLOE'S

$$$$

36 COLLEGE RD., KENT TOWN

TEL 08/8362-2574

chloes.com.au

A glamorous restaurant with a modern French menu and a 20,000-bottle wine cellar housing some of Australia's finest wines.

🔟 100 🅿 🕐 Closed L Sat. & all Sun. 🅢 🅕
🅐 All major cards

🍴 GAUCHO'S

$$$$

91–93 GOUGER ST.

TEL 08/8231-2299

gauchos.com.au

Iconic Argentinean restaurant famed for its steaks, although seafood lovers and vegetarians are catered to as well. Excellent wine list.

🔟 210 🕐 Closed L Sat.–Sun.
🅢 🅕 🅐 All major cards

🍴 APOTHECARY 1878

$$$

118 HINDLEY STREET

TEL 08/8212-9099

theapothecary1878.com.au

Elegantly restored 19th-century pharmacy now houses the city's best wine bar and an upmarket restaurant.

🔟 50 🕐 Closed L Sat.–Tues.
🅢 🅕 🅐 All major cards

🍴 KENJI

$$$

242 HUTT ST.

TEL 08/8232-0944

Chef Kenji Ito serves up a modern take on Japanese dishes in one of Adelaide's most highly regarded restaurants. Great sashimi and innovative mains, and detoxined puffer fish if you've always wanted to try.

🔟 45 🕐 Closed Sun. & L
🅢 🅕 🅐 All major cards

🍴 PRESS FOOD & WINE

$$$

40 WAYMOUTH ST.

TEL 08/8211-8048

Warehouse fit out with interesting tasting plates and superb wood-grilled steaks. Book for the upstairs dining room, or try your luck downstairs at the bar.

🔟 40 🕐 Closed Sun.
🅢 🅕 🅐 All major cards

🍴 RUBY RED FLAMINGO

$$–$$$

142 TYNTE ST.,

NORTH ADELAIDE

TEL 08/8267-4636

rubyredflamingo.com

Elegant dining room and rustic Italian cuisine in one of Adelaide's most popular restaurant precincts. Great food and reasonable prices.

🔟 60 🕐 Closed D Sun.–Tues. & L Sat.–Tues. 🅢 🅕
🅐 All major cards

🍴 YING CHOW

$–$$

114 GOUGER ST.

TEL 08/8211-7998

Gouger Street has plenty of Asian cheap eats. This no-frills institution is always popular for good food at low prices.

🔟 60 🅢 🅐 MC, V

OUTSIDE ADELAIDE: ADELAIDE HILLS

🏨 THORNGROVE MANOR

$$$$$

GLENSIDE LANE, STIRLING

PRICES

HOTELS

An indication of the cost of a double room in the high season is given by $ signs.

$$$$$	Over $280
$$$$	$200–$280
$$$	$120–$200
$$	$80–$120
$	Under $80

RESTAURANTS

An indication of the cost of a three-course meal without drinks is given by $ signs.

$$$$$	Over $90
$$$$	$70–$90
$$$	$50–$70
$$	$30–$50
$	Under $30

TEL 08/8339-6748

FAX 08/8370-9950

thorngrove.com.au

Gothic turrets and gables outside, and an interior to match, with comfortable, well-appointed rooms. Adelaide is 20 minutes away by car.

🛈 4 🅿 🅢 🅕
🅐 All major cards

🏨 ADELAIDE HILLS COUNTRY COTTAGES

$$$$–$$$$$

29 OAKWOOD RD., BALHANNAH

TEL 08/8388-4193

ahcc.com.au

Attractive cottages with antique furnishings, in rolling countryside. Adelaide is a 40-minute drive away.

🛈 5 🅿 🅢 🅕 🅐 MC, V

🏨 GRAND MERCURE,
🍴 MOUNT LOFTY HOUSE

$$$$

74 SUMMIT RD., CRAFERS,

🏨 Hotel 🍴 Restaurant 🛈 No. of Guest Rooms 🔟 No. of Seats 🅿 Parking 🚉 Rail Station 🕐 Closed 🛗 Elevator

MOUNT LOFTY
TEL 08/8339-6777
FAX 08/8339-5656
mtloftyhouse.com.au
Sumptuous and elegant country house in a gorgeous setting. **Piccadilly Restaurant** *($$$)* has a varied menu and some of Australia's finest wines. Stunning views over the valley.
🛈 33 🅿 🔄 🚭 🛐 🏊
🛐 All major cards

SOMETHING SPECIAL

🍽 **BRIDGEWATER MILL RESTAURANT**
$$$$
MOUNT BARKER RD.,
BRIDGEWATER
TEL 08/8339-9200
bridgewatermill.com.au
This converted mill houses a stylish lunchtime restaurant run by Petaluma winery and showcasing their wines.
🪑 80 🅿 🕐 Closed D
🚭 🛐 All major cards

BAROSSA VALLEY

🏨 **COLLINGROVE HOMESTEAD**
$$$$$
EDEN VALLEY RD., ANGASTON
TEL 08/8564-2061
collingrovehomestead.com.au
Peaceful retreat in a beautiful English-style garden setting.
🛈 5 🅿 🚭 🛐
🛐 All major cards

SOMETHING SPECIAL

🏨 **THE LOUISE &**
🍽 **APPELLATION**
$$$$$
CORNER OF SEPPELTSFIELD &
STONEWELL RDS., MARANANGA
TEL 08/8562-2722
thelouise.com.au
One of the Barossa's top luxury lodges, with sweeping views over the valleys and hills. The attached **Appellation** restaurant *(reservations essential;*

tel 08/8562-4144, $$$$$) is one of the finest in the valley, if not the state.
🛈 15 🅿 🕐 Closed L Mon.–Sat. 🚭 🛐 All major cards

🏨 **NOVOTEL BAROSSA VALLEY RESORT**
$$$$
42 PIONEER AVE.,
ROWLAND FLAT
TEL 08/8524-0000
FAX 08/8524-0100
novotelbarossa.com
Next to a golf course with vineyard views, this resort is one of the valley's biggest and best equipped.
🛈 164 🅿 🔄 🚭 🛐 🏋
🛐 All major cards

🍽 **1918 BISTRO & GRILL**
$$$$
94 MURRAY ST., TANUNDA
TEL 08/8563-0405
1918.com.au
Housed in a restored villa, this delightful restaurant uses regional produce and has an outstanding wine list.
🪑 80 🚭 🛐 🛐 All major cards

🍽 **VINTNERS BAR & GRILL**
$$$$
NURIOOTPA RD., ANGASTON
TEL 08/8564-2488
vintners.com.au
Contemporary restaurant in a beautiful vineyard setting, with exquisite service, imaginative fare, and an excellent wine list. One of the best in the valley.
🪑 85 🅿 🕐 Closed D Sun.
🚭 🛐 🛐 All major cards

🍽 **BLOND COFFEE**
$$
60 MURRAY ST., ANGASTON
TEL 08/8564-3444
blondcoffee.com.au
Breakfast and lunch are served in this stylish, and extremely popular, coffee shop.
🪑 50 🕐 Closed D 🚭 🛐
🛐 MC, V

CLARE VALLEY

🏨 **CHAFF MILL VILLAGE HOLIDAY APARTMENTS**
$$$$
310 MAIN NORTH RD., CLARE
TEL 08/8842-1111
FAX 08/8842-1303
These luxury, self-contained apartments in the heart of the Clare Valley are just a stroll from shops and restaurants.
🛈 6 🅿 🚭 🛐
🛐 All major cards

FLEURIEU PENINSULA

🏨 **MCLAREN VALE STUDIO APARTMENTS**
$$$$
222 MAIN RD., MCLAREN VALE
TEL 08/8323-9536
mvsa.com.au
Modern one-bedroom apartments with all amenities, fully equipped kitchens, and private verandas with barbecue.
🛈 6 🅿 🚭 🛐
🛐 All major cards

🏨 **ANCHORAGE**
$$$
21 FLINDERS PDE.,
VICTOR HARBOR
TEL 08/8552-5970
anchorageseafronthotel.com
Grand old three-star Aussie pub opposite the waterfront.
🛈 21 🛐 All major cards

COOBER PEDY

🏨 **DESERT CAVE**
$$$$
HUTCHISON ST.
TEL 08/8672-5688
FAX 08/8672-5198
desertcave.com.au
A quality hotel—with some rooms decorated to simulate the underground dwellings typical of this opal-mining community.
🛈 50 🅿 🚭 🛐 🏊 🏋
🛐 All major cards

FLINDERS RANGES

🏨 RAWNSLEY PARK STATION
$–$$$$$
WILPENA RD., VIA HAWKER
TEL 08/8648-0030
raawnsleypark.com.au
This outback station offers a range of tours and accommodations, from camping and simple cabins to self-contained holiday units. The real standouts are the luxury eco-villas on private, secluded sites with amazing mountain views.
ⓘ 27 🅿 🛗 🚭 ☒
🗝 All major cards

🏨🍴 WILPENA POUND RESORT
$–$$$$
WILPENA POUND
TEL 08/8648-0004
FAX 08/8648-0028
wilpenapound.com.au
Wilpena Pound township is this resort, which runs the campground, shop, visitor center, restaurant, and motel-style rooms in the main building. Rooms are comfortable and the scenic position is unbeatable.
ⓘ 60 🅿 🛗 🚭 ☒
🗝 All major cards

KANGAROO ISLAND

SOMETHING SPECIAL

🏨 SOUTHERN OCEAN LODGE
$$$$$
HANSON BAY
TEL 08/8559-7347
FAX 08/8559-7350
southernoceanlodge.com.au
Breathtaking ocean views matched by stunning contemporary architecture at one of Australia's great lodges. Luxury suites are strung out along the cliff top, and the dining and lounge areas have panoramas.

ⓘ 21 🅿 🛗 🚭 ☒
🗝 All major cards

🏨 KANGAROO ISLAND SEAFRONT RESORT
$$$–$$$$
49 NORTH TERRACE, PENNESHAW
TEL 08/8553-1028
FAX 08/8553-1024
seafront.com.au
The resort overlooks a beach that has a colony of fairy penguins. Rooms, villas, and cottages available.
ⓘ 25 🅿 🛗 ☒
🗝 All major cards

MURRAY RIVER

🏨🍴 LOXTON HOTEL/MOTEL
$$–$$$
45 EAST TERRACE, LOXTON
TEL 08/8584-7266
loxtonhotel.com.au
Basic rooms in the pub plus motel units. The bistro ($$) is very good.
ⓘ 55 🅿 🛗 🚭 ☒
🗝 All major cards

🏨🍴 RENMARK HOTEL/MOTEL
$$–$$$
MURRAY AVE., RENMARK
TEL 08/8586-6755
renmarkhotel.com.au
Carefully renovated three-story art deco hotel on the river. Counter meals, a good bistro ($$), and a dining room.
ⓘ 68 🅿 🛗 🚭 ☒
🗝 All major cards

◼ VICTORIA

MELBOURNE: DOWNTOWN

🏨 GRAND HYATT
$$$$$
123 COLLINS ST.
TEL 03/9657-1234

FAX 03/9650-3491
melbourne.grand.hyatt.com
Luxury hotel fitted out in flamboyant style. Four floors form the even more opulent Grand Club. All rooms have marble bathrooms and king-size beds. Excellent service.
ⓘ 544 🅿 🛗 🚭 ☒
🛎 🗝 All major cards

🏨 ART SERIES– THE BLACKMAN
$$$$–$$$$$
452 ST. KILDA RD.
TEL 03/9039-1444
FAX 03/9039-1445
artserieshotels.com.au
On fashionable St. Kilda Rd., this hotel is dedicated to Melbourne painter John Blackman and liberally decorated with artworks. A unique, stylish, and very comfortable boutique hotel.
ⓘ 209 🅿 🛗 🚭 🛎
🗝 All major cards

🏨 MELBOURNE MARRIOTT
$$$$–$$$$$
CORNER OF EXHIBITION & LONSDALE STS.
TEL 03/9662-3900
FAX 03/9663-4297
marriott.com.au
Luxury boutique hotel in the heart of Melbourne. Spacious rooms and suites, and lots of pampering for guests.
ⓘ 185 🅿 🛗 🚭 ☒ 🛎
🗝 All major cards

SOMETHING SPECIAL

🏨 THE WINDSOR
$$$$
103 SPRING ST.
TEL 03/9633-6000
FAX 03/9633-6001
thehotelwindsor.com.au
Built in 1883, this elegant property is an Australian landmark. The nation's constitution was drafted in one of its upstairs suites. The hotel has

exemplary old-world service, and though showing signs of age, its heritage charm is unrivaled. Afternoon tea here is a special treat.

[I] 180 [P] [⇄] [S] [⚡] [♥]
[⚐] All major cards

🏨 ALTO HOTEL ON BOURKE
$$$–$$$$
636 BOURKE ST.
TEL 03/8608-5500
FAX 03/9606-0766
altohotel.com.au
Near Southern Cross Station in a refurbished heritage building, this eco-friendly hotel has a range of smart accommodations, from small hotel rooms to three-bedroom apartments. Check online booking sites for best rates.

[I] 142 [P] [⇄] [S] [⚡] [♥]
[⚐] All major cards

🍴 TAXI DINING ROOM
$$$$$
LEVEL 2, TRANSPORT HOTEL, FEDERATION SQUARE, CORNER OF PRINCES BRIDGE & NORTHBANK ST.
TEL 03/9654-8808
transporthotel.com.au
Not a cab driver's diner, but a slick urban restaurant serving innovative modern fare with a dash of Japanese. Head upstairs away from the frenetic transport bar.

[⚐] 115 [⚡] [⚐] All major cards

🍴 FLOWER DRUM
$$$$–$$$$$
17 MARKET LANE
TEL 03/9662-3655
flower-drum.com
Elegant surroundings, wonderful Cantonese food, and a well-selected wine list. Reservations essential.

[⚐] 175 [⊙] Closed L Sun.
[S] [⚡] [⚐] All major cards

🍴 GROSSI FLORENTINO
$$$–$$$$
80 BOURKE ST.
TEL 03/9662-1811
grossiflorentino.com
This Melbourne institution, established for more than 100 years, serves wonderful Italian cuisine. The downstairs bar dishes up homemade pastas and good Italian coffee, while those seeking more elaborate fare can head upstairs to the formal restaurant.

[⚐] 150 [⊙] Closed Sun.
[⚡] [⚐] All major cards

🍴 CODA BAR & RESTAURANT
$$$–$$$$
141 FLINDERS LN.
(CORNER OF OLIVER LN.)
TEL 03/9650-3155
codarestaurant.com.au
A happening basement bar with tapas-style taste treats and more substantial mains.

[⚐] 80 [⊙] Closed Mon. & L Tues. [⚡] [⚐] All major cards

MELBOURNE SUBURBS

🏨 HOTEL URBAN ST. KILDA
$$$$
35–37 FITZROY ST., ST. KILDA
TEL 03/8530-8888
FAX 03/8530-8800
hotelurban.com.au
Stylish modern rooms close to the action in St. Kilda make this boutique hotel a favorite stay outside the city center.

[I] 80 [P] [⇄] [S] [⚡] [♥]
[⚐] All major cards

🏨 SEASONS HERITAGE MELBOURNE
$$$–$$$$
572 ST. KILDA RD., MELBOURNE
TEL 03/8506-8888
FAX 03/8506-8899
seasonsheritagemelbourne
.com.au
Halfway between the city center and St. Kilda, with a

tram out front. Value rooms range from small studios with kitchens to two-bedroom apartments. The building has three premium heritage suites.

[I] 142 [P] [⇄] [S] [⚡] [♥]
[⚐] All major cards

🍴 STOKEHOUSE
$$$–$$$$$
30 JACKA BLVD., ST. KILDA
TEL 03/9525-5555
stokehouse.com.au
Set in a stunning location with excellent bay views, this popular establishment has a less expensive downstairs café with light fare and a pricier modern Australian restaurant upstairs.

[⚐] 170 [⚐] All major cards

🍴 CAFFÉ E CUCINA
$$$$
581 CHAPEL ST., SOUTH YARRA
TEL 03/9827-4139
caffeecucina.com.au
This iconic Italian café on lively Chapel St. has fine food and exemplary service.

[⚐] 85 [⊙] Closed Sun. [⚡]
[⚐] All major cards

🍴 CHINTA RIA SOUL
$$
94 ACLAND ST., ST. KILDA
TEL 03/9525-4664
This ever popular, funky café in the heart of lively Acland St. serves excellent Malaysian cuisine at very reasonable prices.

[⚐] 90 [⊙] Closed L Sat.
[S] [⚡] [⚐] All major cards

🍴 BRUNETTI CARLTON
$–$$
180 LYGON ST., CARLTON
TEL 03/9347-2801
FAX 03/9347-9152
brunetti.com.au
On Lygon St. (Melbourne's Little Italy), this famous Italian cake shop offers all manner of sweet delights,

great coffee, and a few pasta and other dishes.

🔲 200 🔳 🔳 All major cards

OUTSIDE MELBOURNE: GREAT OCEAN ROAD

🏨 GREAT OCEAN ECOLODGE
$$$$$
635 LIGHTHOUSE RD.,
CAPE OTWAY, GREAT OTWAY
NATIONAL PARK
TEL 03/5237-9297
greatoceanecolodge.com
This friendly ecolodge in Cape Otway sits on 165 acres (67 ha) visited by kangaroos at dawn and dusk. The rooms are lovingly decorated, with hardwood floors and views out to the Otway Ranges or the kitchen gardens. Dine with other guests in the evening on delectable dishes made from local produce; breakfast and afternoon tea included. Be sure to join owner and conservationist Shayne Neal on the afternoon nature walk to see and learn about the local wildlife (including koalas!) and ongoing efforts to save endangered species.

🚪 5 🅿️ 🔳 All major cards

🏨 PEBBLE POINT
$$$
GREAT OCEAN ROAD,
THE TWELVE APOSTLES
TEL 03/5243-3579
pebblepoint.com.au
Be lulled to sleep by chirping frogs and undulating waves in your very own luxury tent, equipped with comfortable king bed, electricity for lights and fan/heater, and en suite bathrooms. There are no nearby restaurants, so come with your own supplies to cook at the communal gas barbecue or microwave. Access to the Great Ocean Walk—and a stroll to the Twelve Apostles—is just steps away.

🚪 5 tents 🅿️
🔳 All major cards

🏨 QUEENSCLIFF HOTEL
🍴 $$$
16 GELLIBRAND STREET,
QUEENSCLIFF
TEL 03/5258-1066
queenscliffhotel.com.au
Grand old Victorian hotel, built in opulent style in 1887 with wide sweeping verandas and ornamental iron lacework, located in a historic seaport, not far from the start of the Great Ocean Road. A little tired, but oozing charm.

🚪 15 🅿️ 🔳
🔳 All major cards

🏨 CLAERWEN RETREAT
$$–$$$$$
480 TUXION ROAD,
APOLLO BAY
TEL 03/5237-7064
claerwen.com.au
An attractive and tasteful place near the famed Twelve Apostles on the Great Ocean Road and the pleasant seaside town of Apollo Bay.

🚪 4 suites, 2 3-bedroom cottages, & 2 studios 🅿️ 🔳
🔳 AE, MC, V

BALLARAT

🏨 QUALITY INN HERITAGE
🍴 ON LYDIARD
$$$–$$$$$
15 LYDIARD ST. NORTH
TEL 03/5327-2777
heritageonlydiard.com.au
Modern rooms and suites in a superbly restored gold rush–era bank building. The wine bar serves great tapas.

🚪 13 🅿️ 🔳 🔳 🔳 🔳
🔳 All major cards

ECHUCA

🏨 RIVER GALLERY INN
$$$$
578 HIGH ST.
TEL 03/5480-6902

rivergalleryinn.com
This renovated 19th-century building has spacious, comfortable B&B rooms decorated with antique flair.

🚪 8 🅿️ 🔳 🔳
🔳 All major cards

🍴 OSCAR W'S
$$–$$$$
OLD ECHUCA WHARF
TEL 03/5482-5133
oscarws.com.au
This elegant restaurant is wonderfully situated on the town's historic wharf, overlooking a majestic gum-lined bend of the Murray River. The food is marvelous, the wine list superb, and in the afternoons the kookaburras come down from their trees to be fed.

🔲 100 🔳 🔳
🔳 All major cards

MILDURA

🍴 STEFANO'S
🏨 $$$$
GRAND HOTEL RESORT, 7TH ST.
TEL 03/5022-0881
stefano.com.au
Superb Italian cuisine and a fantastic wine list are offered up in the century-old hotel's wine cellar. The set menu makes the very best of fresh, local produce.

🔲 60 🕐 Closed L & Sun.
🔳 🔳 🔳 All major cards

■ TASMANIA

HOBART

SOMETHING SPECIAL

🏨 HENRY JONES ART HOTEL
$$$$$
25 HUNTER ST.
TEL 03/6210-7700
FAX 03/6210-7755
thehenryjones.com
Once a jam factory, this unique hotel on the waterfront has

won numerous tourism and architecture awards for its stunning makeover. Superb suite rooms, unusual artworks, and unrivaled character.

⚡ 56 🅿 ⮀ 🚭 🕒 🎾
🅲 All major cards

🏨 ISLINGTON HOTEL
$$$$$

321 DAVEY ST.
TEL 03/6223-3900
FAX 03/6234-9053
islingtonhotel.com
There are just suites at this converted 19th-century mansion. Beautiful gardens with a fine view of Mount Wellington. Breakfast included.

⚡ 11 🅿 🚭 🏊
🅲 All major cards

🏨 GRAND CHANCELLOR HOTEL
$$$$–$$$$$

1 DAVEY ST.
TEL 03/6235-4535
TEL 03/6223-8175
ghihotels.com
Luxury hotel on the wharf, with well-appointed, spacious guest rooms. Great water views and competitive rates.

⚡ 234 🅿 ⮀
🚭 🏊 🎾 🅲 All major cards

🏨 LENNA OF HOBART
🍴 **$$$–$$$$**

20 RUNNYMEDE ST.,
BATTERY POINT
TEL 03/6232-3900
lenna.com.au
A 19th-century building with old-world charm and a reputation for excellent cuisine at **Alexander's** restaurant.

⚡ 50 🅿 ⮀ 🚭
🅲 All major cards

🏨 THE OLD WOOLSTORE APARTMENT HOTEL
$$$–$$$$

1 MACQUARIE ST.
TEL 03/6235-5355

FAX 03/6234-9954
oldwoolstore.com.au
Great location near the waterfront in a converted Victorian-era warehouse. Spacious studio, one-, and two-bedroom apartments.

⚡ 242 🅿 ⮀ 🚭 🕒 🎾
🅲 MC, V

🍴 MURES UPPER DECK
$$$

VICTORIA DOCK
TEL 03/6231-1999
muresupperdeck.com.au
Excellent seafood in a great waterfront location. Cheaper meals downstairs.

🍴 160 🅿 🚭
🅲 All major cards

🍴 SMOLT
$$$

2 SALAMANCA SQ.
TEL 03/6224-2554
smolt.com.au
In prime position on Salamanca, cool modern lines and Mediterranean influences define this hip spot. Dishes from pizza and pasta to innovative mains and seafood platters.

🍴 60 🚭 🕒 🅲 All major cards

LAUNCESTON

🏨 COUNTRY CLUB
🍴 **TASMANIA**
$$$–$$$$

COUNTRY CLUB AVE.,
PROSPECT VALE
TEL 03/6335-5777 OR
1800-030-211
countryclubtasmania.com.au
Set in manicured gardens, this luxury club and casino has lots of amenities, including one of the best golf courses in Australia. The club is home to the formal **Terrace Restaurant.**

⚡ 104 🅿 ⮀ 🚭 🏊 🏊 🎾
🅲 All major cards

🏨 CLARION CITY PARK GRAND
$$$

TAMAR & WILLIAM STS.
TEL 03/6331-7633
cityparkgrand.com.au
The comfortable guest rooms have furnishings to match the inn's opulent Victorian style.

⚡ 31 🅿 🚭 🕒 Some rooms
🅲 All major cards

🍴 STILLWATER
$$$–$$$$$

RITCHIES MILL, PATERSON ST.
TEL 03/6331-4153
stillwater.net.au
On the Tamar River, casual by day, at night a formal restaurant offering adventurous modern Australian cooking.

🍴 65 🕒 Closed D Sun. & Mon. 🚭 🅲 All major cards

REST OF TASMANIA

🏨 BAY OF FIRES LODGE
$$$$$

BAY OF FIRES
TEL 03/6392-2211
bayoffires.com.au
Remote, eco-friendly lodge in Mt. William National Park, overlooking a stunning isolated beach. Guests hike to the lodge as part of a four-day package, including a night in tented accommodations.

⚡ 22 🅿 🚭 🕒 Some
🅲 MC, V

🏨 FREYCINET LODGE
🍴 **$$$$$**

COLES BAY
TEL 03/6225-7000
freycinetlodge.com.au
Environmentally sensitive resort of private cabins (with one or two bedrooms) overlooking Great Oyster Bay in Freycinet National Park. Basic rate includes breakfast. Dine on the premises at the **Bay Restaurant**, with fine views and seafood.

⚡ 60 🅿 🚭 🅲 All major cards

Shopping

There is never any shortage of kitsch offerings for tourists in Australia. Everything from stuffed koalas, made-in-Taiwan boomerangs, insulated beer-can holders (usually adorned with off-color blokey jokes), plastic kangaroos, coasters, and tacky T-shirts can be found in garish little shops from coast to coast. Most Aussie souvenirs—even the little Australian flags waved on Anzac Day—tend to be made somewhere in Asia. Happily, finding something a bit more tasteful, memorable, and authentic to take back home is fairly easy.

Aboriginal Art

Powerful and unique, Aboriginal art has become a highly prized commodity in the art world, with prices for significant works by top artists stretching into the tens of thousands of dollars. Sadly, big money and the fact that few laymen have a good understanding of Aboriginal art have drawn a lot of hucksters into the business. Consequently, buying Aboriginal art can be tricky. Your best bet is to stick to Aboriginal-owned and -operated galleries or to buy directly from the artists themselves.

The kinds of pieces offered vary from bark paintings to boomerangs, wood carvings, textiles, pottery, and didgeridoos. Good pieces will not be cheap, but then fine art never is. Expect to pay in the neighborhood of A$200 (U.S. $200) (and up!) for a nice didgeridoo, for example. Some Aboriginal-owned galleries include:

Darwin
Aboriginal Bush Traders
Lyons Cottage, Cnr. Knuckey St. &
The Esplanade
Tel 04/4832-9933
aboriginalbushtraders.com

Uluru
Maruku Arts and Crafts
Uluru–Kata Tjuta Cultural Centre
Tel 08/8956-2153
maruku.com.au

Kakadu
Injalak Arts and Crafts
Oenpelli
Tel 08/8979-0190
injalak.com

Alice Springs
DesArt
11/54 Todd St. Mall
Tel 08/8953-4736
desart.com.au
DesArt represents a number of other Aboriginal-owned galleries in central Australia and can help you contact reputable dealers.

If you are not going into the outback and still want to purchase Aboriginal art, try:

Sydney
The Artery
Shop 2, The Westbury,
Darlinghurst
Tel 02/9380-8234
artery.com.au

Melbourne
Dacou
35 Spring St (Cnr Flinders Lane)
Tel 03/9663-6368
dacoumelbourne.com.au

Arts & Crafts

Australia is rich in artistic talent and visitors can find interesting galleries and craft shops across the continent.

Sydney, as a last stop for most visitors, is a popular arts and crafts shopping destination. Two icons of Australian tourist art in Sydney are **Ken Done** (1–5 Hickson Rd., The Rocks, tel 02/8274-4599, kendone.com) and **Ken Duncan** (73 George St., The Rocks, tel 02/9241-3460, kenduncan .com). Done might be disdained by Australia's serious art community, but there's no denying

the appeal of his bright, color-splashed paintings. Duncan's panoramic landscape photographs are stunning, and can be enjoyed in books, posters, and postcards, as well as expensive prints.

The Rocks in Sydney also has a busy, touristy street market on weekends, and well-stocked art and craft galleries. **Craft NSW** (104 George St., The Rocks, tel 02/9241-5825, artsandcraftsnsw .com.au) is the outlet of the Society of Arts & Crafts of New South Wales representing local artisans. It sells jewelry, ceramics, weaving, fabric collage, glass, hand-knitted goods, silk painting, prints, and more.

In Adelaide, the **Jam Factory** (19 Morphett St., tel 08/8231-0005; and Rundle Mall Plaza, tel 08/8211-9777, jamfactory.com .au) offers glass, ceramics, wood, textiles, and jewelry from some of Australia's best artisans.

Clothing

Australia has some stylish outback clothing outfitters, and although they are making their mark overseas, their roots are still firmly in the outback, making reliable gear for stockmen, farmers, and stationhands as they have for generations. If you want authenticity, as well as excellent clothes, start with a pair of R. M. Williams boots or the Tasmanian-made Blundstone boots.

The South Australian–based **R. M. Williams** has been making boots and saddlery equipment for outback stockmen and riders since the 1930s. Their kangaroo leather boots are incredibly soft and fit like a glove. The company is also justly famous for its tough moleskin trousers and fashionable outdoor clothing. Its gear is readily available in all cities.

In Sydney, the main store is at 389 George St., tel 02/9262-2228; in Melbourne, it's at the Shot Tower, Shop 237 Melbourne Central, 300 Lonsdale St., tel 03/9663-7126. Visit *rmwilliams.com.au* for details on outlets around Australia (and overseas).

Blundstone boots have been a working-class icon since they were first produced in 1870, but they have a worldwide cachet, popping up as fashion musts on the streets of London and New York. For information on stores, contact the company's Hobart office *(tel 03/6721-2200, blundstone.com)*.

Although Australia is reckoned the world's driest inhabited continent, some of the world's best wet-weather gear is produced here. Both R. M. Williams and **Thomas Cook** *(thomascook.com.au)*, another long-established outfitter, make excellent oilskins, but the old classic stockman's oilskin is made by the Victoria-based **Driza-Bone**, which has been making them for more than a century. They are widely available around Australia. Information on retailers can be acquired by telephone at 03/9425-2298, by e-mail at *drizagpo@drizabone.com.au*, or at *drizabone.com.au*.

To round off the "Man from Snowy River" look and to ward off the fierce Australian sun, slap on an **Akubra** hat. Ruggedly made out of rabbit-fur felt, these hats are beloved by generations of bushmen, who use them for everything from carrying water to picking up a hot billy can out of a campfire. They even sometimes wear them on their heads. These, too, are widely available. Consult the company's website at *akubra.com.au*.

Other quintessentially Australian labels are **Explorer** socks, **Stubby** shorts, **Holeproof** underwear, and **Chesty Bonds** T-shirts and singlets. These can be found in most department stores.

Surfwear has become a significant export in recent years through companies such as **Billabong** *(billabong.com.au)*, **Ripcurl** *(ripcurl.com.au)* and **Quicksilver** *(quiksilver.com.au)*. Outlets can be found countrywide, but the home of surf gear is Torquay in Victoria (see p. 312).

Opals

Australia has 95 percent of the world's supplies of opal. Most of it is found in outback South Australia, near the town of Coober Pedy, with the New South Wales town of Lightning Ridge and the South Australian town of Andamooka accounting for much of the rest.

Almost every jeweler and souvenir shop in Australia seems to offer opals in one form or another, with special tax-free prices for tourists.

As with any precious stone, there are a number of factors that go into determining the value of an opal, such as clarity, color, shape, and pattern. The first criterion is the base color of the stone. A black opal is the most valuable, followed by a crystal (or almost transparent) opal, with milky opals bringing up the rear. The next thing to look for is the dominant color. Red-fire opal is the most valuable, followed by green, then blue. The pattern of colors on the stone is also important in determining its value. Harlequin opal, in which the colors are in large defined patches, is the most sought after. Pinfire opal, with its thousands of tiny specks of color, is generally less valuable.

The stones themselves come in three grades. The most valuable is solid opal, followed by doublets (a two-part stone consisting of precious opal glued to another, less valuable opal), then triplets (a three-part stone with a core of precious opal, a backing of a less valuable stone, and a transparent top piece). Accurately assessing opal is a job for experts. Stick to reputable jewelers, shop around, and compare prices (see also sidebar p. 31). In Sydney, the following shops offer more than most:

National Opal Collection
60 Pitt St.
Tel 02/9247-6344
nationalopal.com
Stocks opal jewelry and loose opals. They are unusual in mining and cutting their own stones, and have a shopfront museum with opalized fossils, a re-created opal mine, and more.

Opal Fields
119 George St., The Rocks
Tel 02/9251-3853
opalfields.com.au
Australian opal stones and jewelry featuring the collections of seven designers. Also a museum of opal fossils and specimens.

Wine

Australia is justifiably famous for its bold, fruity, and well-crafted wines, but with more than 2,000 winemakers around the country, navigating unknown labels can be a little confusing for visitors. A number of useful guides are on the market, two of the best being the Penguin *Good Australian Wine Guide* and James Halliday's *Australian Wine Companion*, which are available in most bookstores.

The major wine districts have helpful visitor centers:
Hunter Valley (see pp. 110–111)
Margaret River (see pp. 226–227)
McClaren Vale, Clare Valley, and Coonawarra (see pp. 263, 266)
Barossa Valley (see pp. 267–268).

Activities

Australia's sunny climate and open-air lifestyle lend themselves to a huge range of activities for visitors. Plan your holiday carefully and book ahead if you are specific about what you want to do. Otherwise, find help at a visitor information center. They will be able to tell you of the local possibilities and can probably book you a suitable option on the spot.

Camel-Trekking

Experience outback Australia as the original explorers did: from the back of a dromedary. You can camel-trek in Broome (see pp. 232–233), Silverton (see p. 117), and many other places around the country, but the Northern Territory has the biggest concentration of camel-trek operators. In Alice Springs, **Pyndan Camel Tracks** *(Jane Rd., tel 04/1617-0164, cameltracks .com)* does short treks around the desert, and **Camels Australia** *(Stuarts Well, Stuart Highway, tel 08/8956-0925, camels-australia .com.au)* has short treks and other wildlife at their property. **Uluru Camel Tours** *(tel 08/8956-3333, ulurucameltours.com.au)* at Yulara will take you around the Rock.

For a real camel adventure, check out **Outback Camel Company** *(tel 07/3850-7600, cameltreks.com.au)*, which runs treks and expeditions around the country, including a 28-day crossing of the Simpson Desert.

Cruising

Queensland's idyllic Whitsunday Islands are beautiful for yachts and cruising. For those visitors to Australia who like to do it themselves, charter boats can be arranged on the Whitsundays (see sidebar p. 162).

Tour operators offer daylong and multiday sailing cruises, some on well-known racing yachts of the past. Among them are:
Maxi Ragamuffin
Tel 07/4946-7777
Apollo (of Sydney–Hobart Yacht Race fame) Tel 1800-635-334

Diving

Exploring the Great Barrier Reef is a highlight of a visit to tropical Queensland, and if you do not know how to dive, there are numerous diving schools all along the Queensland coast eager to teach you, and some of the world's finest coral reefs in which to learn. As with anything, it is wise to shop around and be wary of cut-rate operators. Expect to pay in the neighborhood of A$400 (U.S. $400) for a five-day open-water certification course.

Cairns has a reputation for being the reef's diving capital, as well as typically being the first port of call for Great Barrier Reef visitors. A list of a few long-standing operators includes: **Deep Sea Divers Den** *(tel 07/4046-7333, diversden.com.au)*, **Pro Dive** *(tel 07/4031-5255, prodivecairns.com)*, **Tusa Dive** *(tel 07/4047-9100, tusadive.com)*. Airlie Beach and Townsville are other popular dive school locations.

If you are already a certified diver or simply want to do some snorkeling on the reef, finding a boat to take out to the reef is about as difficult as finding a casino in Las Vegas. They come in all shapes and sizes, from gleaming catamarans to yachts to powerboats, and cater to all budgets. Trips last from a day to several days.

The above-mentioned Tusa Dive is just one of the many well-established operators in Cairns.

Good diving can be found in other locations, of course, from Ningaloo Reef in Western Australia to the wrecks scattered around Tasmania's King Island. Consult local tourist authorities for advice

and recommendations (see also sidebar p. 168).

Four-wheel-drive Safaris

The Cape York Peninsula, the Northern Territory, and Western Australia's rugged and remote Kimberley offer some of Australia's best outback adventuring. Four-wheel-drive vehicles are necessary to get into the wildest and most interesting regions, and if you don't care to risk the driving yourself, numerous outfitters from Cairns to Darwin, Alice Springs, and Broome will take you. Standards vary, so shop around and consult local tourist authorities. One well-established outfitter is Cairns-based **Wilderness Challenge** *(tel 07/4035-4488, e-mail: info@wilderness-challenge.com.au, wilderness-challenge.com.au)*, which leads treks to the tip of Cape York and through the heart of the Kimberley. (See also sidebar p. 242.)

Surfing

Right from the moment Hawaiian surfer Duke Kahanomoku brought surfing to Australia (at Sydney's Freshwater Beach) in 1915, riding the breakers that roll into the island continent's 24,000 miles (39,000 km) of coastline has been an Australian passion.

If you do not know how to surf but would like to learn, there are plenty of surfing schools. Inquire at the local tourist information office or at surf and dive shops.

New South Wales: One of the best known beaches is Bondi (see pp. 96–97), but Manly and

Sydney's other northern beaches offer good surf, too. South of Sydney, probably the best is at Cronulla. Byron Bay, on the NSW north coast, is another very popular surfing hangout.

Southern Queensland: A string of surfing beaches stretches along the Gold Coast. As well as Surfers Paradise, try Burleigh Heads or Kirra. The Sunshine Coast also has good surfing right up to Noosa Heads.

Western Australia: You'll find some great surf around Margaret River, about 140 miles (224 km) south of Perth.

South Australia: The best known surfing beach in South Australia is far-flung Cactus Beach, west of Ceduna. There are more convenient places on both the east and west sides of the Fleurieu Peninsula, though.

Victoria: The Bells Easter Classic competition is held on Bells Beach, near Torquay on the spectacular Great Ocean Road, about 100 miles (160 km) southwest of Melbourne. Wilsons Promontory and the ocean side of the Mornington Peninsula also offer good surfing.

Tasmania: There is good surf around Marrawah on the west coast, and the beaches near St. Helens are just some of the surfing locations on the east coast, but the water around the island is cold.

White-water Rafting

Australia may be the world's driest inhabited continent, but when the rivers run here, they really run, with Tasmania, the Snowy Mountains, and the jungle-clad mountains near Cairns offering exhilarating wild water. Two of the better known wilderness operators are:

World Expeditions
Sydney Office
Level 5, 71 York St., Sydney

Tel 02/8270-8400 or
1300-720-000
worldexpeditions.com

Peregrine Adventure
Head Office
Level 4, 380 Lonsdale St.,
Melbourne
Tel 1300-791-485
peregrineadventures.com

By far the most remote and wildest rafting option is on Tasmania's Franklin River, a challenging two-week-long trek through some of the most remote wilderness on the planet. Both of the above operators run expeditions on the Franklin.

Further Information

Below is a list of organizations to contact for information about specific activities.

Bird-watching
Birdlife Australia
Suite 2-05, 60 Leicester St.,
Carlton, VIC 3053
Tel 03/9347-0757
birdlife.org.au

Canoeing
Australian Canoeing Inc.
1st Floor, Sports House,
6 Figtree Drive,
Sydney Olympic Park,
Homebush Bay, NSW
Tel 02/8116-9727
canoe.org.au

Cycling
Cycling Australia
Level 2, 280 Coward St.,
Mascot, NSW 2020
Tel 02/9339-5800
cycling.org.au

Ecotourism
Ecotourism Australia
Suite 3, 47 Brookes St.
Bowen Hills QLD 4006
Tel 07/3252-1530
ecotourism.org.au

Fishing
Recfish Australia
24 York St,
South Melbourne,
VIC 3205
Tel 04/1932-0843
recfishaustralia.org.au

Golf
Golf Australia
Level 3, 95 Coventry St.,
South Melbourne, VIC 3205
Tel 03/9626-5050
golfaustralia.org.au

Sailing
Yachting Australia
Level 1, 22 Atchison St.,
St. Leonards,
Sydney, NSW 2065
Tel 02/8424-7400
yachting.org.au

Surfing
Surfing Australia
PO Box 928,
Coolangatta,
QLD 4225
Tel 07/5599-3800
surfingaustralia.com

Tennis
Tennis Australia
Olympic Blvd.
Melbourne, VIC 3000
Tel 03/9914-4000
tennis.com.au

INDEX

Bold page numbers
indicate illustrations.
CAPS indicates
thematic categories.

A
Aboriginal culture **22, 209**
   art **181, 22,** 202–203,
      257–258, 386
   dance 176
   Dreamtime 208
   Dreamtime Culture Central,
      Queensland 150
   history 20–23, 133, 332–333
   literature 56
   music **57,** 59
   place-names 327
   rock art **32–33,** 176, 179,
      188–189, 190, 202–203, 327
   sacred places 206, 208
   Tjapukai Aboriginal Cultural
      Park, Cairns 168
   tourist experiences **11,**
      196–197, 209
Activities 388–389
Adelaide 252–258
   Adelaide Botanic Gardens 257
   Adelaide Cricket Ground 258
   Adelaide Festival Centre 256
   Art Gallery of South
      Australia 257
   Ayers House 257
   Elder Park 256
   festivals **272,** 272–273
   Government House 256
   hotels and restaurants 379–381
   Light's Vision 258
   Lion Arts Centre 256
   map 252–253
   Migration Museum 257
   North Adelaide 258
   North Terrace 254, 255
   Parliament House 255
   St. Peter's Cathedral **257,** 258
   shopping 256, 386
   South Australian Museum 257
   State Library 256–257
   Tandanya 257–258
   Zoo 257
Adelaide area 259–263, 266–271,
      274–279
   Adelaide Hills 260–263, 266, 381
   Angaston 268
   Barossa Valley **249,** 262, 263,
      265, 267–268, 273
   Clare Valley **264,** 266, 381
   Cleland Wildlife Park **260,** 261
   Coonawarra 266
   Coorong 275–276
   Encounter Bay 275
   Fleurieu Peninsula 262–263,
      381–382
   Flinders Ranges NP 209,
      277–279, **279,** 382
   Glenelg **259,** 259–260

Goolwa 275–276
Hahndorf 261–262
Heysen Trail 262, 279
Kangaroo Island 125, 205,
   268–271, **269, 271,**
   274, 382
Lower Murray River 276–277,
   277
Mannum 276–277
McLaren Vale 263, **263**
Mount Lofty Ranges 261, **263**
Murray River Valley 266
Naracoorte Caves Park 266
Penola 266
Port Adelaide 260
Quorn 278
Southern Vales 263
Victor Harbor **274,** 274–275
Wilpena Pound 278–279
wine regions 263, **263,**
   266–268
Adelaide Hills 260–263, 266, 381
Air travel 358, 359
Albany 225
Alice Springs **198,** 198–201, 286,
   377, 386
Alice Springs Desert Park,
   Alice Springs 199
Alien species 72, 352
Alpine country, Victoria 316–317
Amusement parks 145, 304
Angaston 268
Antarctica 126
Anzac Day 50, 134
Aquariums 92–93, 130, 167
Architecture **63,** 63–64, 121, 294
Argyle Diamond Mine **234,** 235
Arltunga 200
Arnhem Land **32–33,** 196–197,
   209
Art galleries see Museums
Art Gallery of Ballarat 320
Art Gallery of New South Wales,
   Sydney 82, **82**
Art Gallery of South Australia,
   Adelaide 257
Arthur's Seat SP 306
Arts 56–65
   Aboriginal **181, 202,** 202–203,
      257–258, 386
   architecture **63,** 63–64,
      121, 294
   cinema 60–61, 95, 132,
      145, 233, 235
   dance 59, 176
   festivals 272–273
   literature 56, 58–59, 225
   music **57,** 59–60, **60,** 109,
      109, 356
   painting 64–65, **65,** 117
   rock art **32–33,** 176, 179, 188–
      189, 190, 202–203, 327
   television 61–63, 363
   theater 59, 256
Atherton Tablelands 170–171, **171**
Australia (movie) 235
Australia Zoo, Sunshine Coast
   125, 167
Australian Capital Territory
   Canberra 65, 127–136, 371
   hotels and restaurants 371

map 129
National Trust 363
tourism website 366
Australian Institute of Sport,
   Canberra 130
Australian Museum, Sydney 89
Australian National Botanic Gardens,
   Canberra 130
Australian National Maritime
   Museum, Sydney 93
Australian Rules football 318–319,
   319, 357
Australian Stockman's Hall of Fame,
   Longreach 152–153
Australian War Memorial, Canberra
   134, 135–136
Ayers House, Adelaide 257
Ayers Rock see Uluru

B
Balladonia 245
Ballarat **63, 320,** 320–321, 384
Balmain, Sydney 95
Balmoral, Sydney 97
Bank hours 363
Barcaldine 152
Barossa Valley **249,** 262, 263, 265,
   267–268, 273, 381
Barrington Tops NP 120
Bass Strait Islands 354
Bathurst Island **196,** 197
Battery Point, Hobart 336
Bawaka Cultural Experiences 196
Bay of Fires 347
Beechworth 316–317
Bega 113
Bellingen 120
Belltrees Station 111
Ben Boyd NP 113
Bendigo 321
Bermagui 113
Bicentennial Tree **224,** 225
Bicycle Victoria 305
Bicycling 77, 216, 305, 389
Billabong Sanctuary, Townsville 167
Birding 68–69, 245–246, 389
Birdsville 176
Black Mountain, Canberra 130
Blackall 152
Blackall Range 147
Block Arcade, Melbourne 303
Blue Mountains **104,** 104–105, 369
Boat trips 361, 388, 389
   Brisbane River 143
   Coral Sea 167
   Franklin-Gordon Wild Rivers NP
      343, **343**
   Great Barrier Reef 160
   Hawkesbury River 118
   Murray River 276–277, 325
   Nitmiluk NP 195
   Sydney Harbour 79
   Tasmania 333
   Whitsunday Islands 162
   Yarra River 302
Bogong High Plains 316, 317
Bondi Beach, Sydney 77, **96,** 96–97
Boomerangs 23

Border Village 247
Botanic Garden, Perth 216
Boulder 241
Bradman, Sir Donald 91
Brampton Island 162
Bright 317
Brisbane **42–43, 140,** 140–143, 371–372
   map 141
Brisbane Botanic Gardens, Brisbane 142
Broken Hill **116,** 116–117
Broome **232,** 232–233, 378
Bruny Island 339
Bunbury 125, 226
Bunda Cliffs 247, **247**
Bungle Bungle NP 173, **236,** 236–237
Burke and Wills expedition 44–45
Burketown 178
Burley Griffin, Lake, Canberra **128,** 130–131
Burnie 346
Bus travel 360–361
Bushfires **106,** 106–107, **107**
Bushrangers **322,** 322–323
Byron Bay 121, **121**

C
Cable Beach, Broome 232, **232,** 233
Cabramatta, Sydney 77
Caiguna 245
Cairns 160, **166,** 167–168, 375, 386
Camels **198,** 199, **232,** 233, 388
Camping 367
Canberra 127–136
   Australian Institute of Sport 130
   Australian National Botanic Gardens 130
   Australian War Memorial **134,** 135–136
   Black Mountain 130
   Civic Centre **127,** 131–132
   hotels and restaurants 370–371
   Lake Burley Griffin **128,** 130–131
   map 131
   Museum of Australian Democracy 132
   National Film & Sound Archive 132
   National Gallery of Australia 65, 135
   National Library of Australia 131
   National Museum of Australia 132
   Parliament House 132–133
Cane toads 180
Canoe trips 195, 389
Canopy walkways 174, 225, 338
Cape York Peninsula 174–177, **175**
Capricorn, Tropic of 150–153
Car rentals 359–360
Carpentaria, Gulf of 177–179
Carseldine, Lee **90**
Cascade Brewery 337
Castlemaine 321

Caves 108, 227, 245, 280–281
Cellular phones 362
Central Mall, Melbourne **289**
Central Station, Fraser Island 149
Children, traveling with 361
Chinatown, Broome 233
Chinese Garden, Sydney 93
Christmas Island 124, 126
CHURCHES
   St. Andrew's Cathedral, Sydney 88
   St. Peter's Cathedral, Adelaide **257,** 258
Cinema 60–61, 95, 132, 145, 233, 235
Circular Quay, Sydney 74, 76, 84, **85**
City Botanic Gardens, Brisbane 142–143
City Hall, Brisbane 143
Civic Centre, Canberra **127,** 131–132
Clare Valley **264,** 266, 381
Cleland Wildlife Park **260,** 261
Climate 10, 26–27, 356
Clothing 362, 386–387
Cocklebiddy 245
Cocos Islands 124, 126
Coffs Harbour 120–121
Colonial Tramcar Restaurant, Melbourne 293
Conversions 362
Convict colonies *see* Prisons and prisoners
Coober Pedy **280,** 280–281, 286, 382
Cook, James 36, **37,** 38–39
Cooking lessons 218
Cooktown 175
Coolgardie 241
Cooloola NP 147–148
Cooma 114
Coonawarra 266
Coorong 275–276
Coot-tha, Mount, Brisbane 142
Cradle Mountain–Lake St. Clair NP 173, **344,** 344–345
Cricket **38–39, 90,** 90–91, 258
Crocodiles 70, **190,** 191, 197
Crown Casino, Melbourne 296
Currency 11, 363
Customs (border control) 357
Cycling *see* Bicycling
Cyclone Tracy 184

D
Daintree NP **30, 169,** 169–170, 173, 375–376
Daly Waters 288
Dance 59, 176
Dandenong Ranges NP 309
Darling Harbour, Sydney 77, 92–93
Darlinghurst, Sydney 77, 94–95
Darwin **184,** 184–187, 376–377, 386
   map 185
Day Dream Mine 117
Daydream Island 163–164
Daylesford 321

Devil's Marbles Conservation Reserve 287, **287**
Diamond mines **234,** 235
Dingoes 148, 149
Disabilities, travelers with 364
Diving **71,** 158, 168, 221, 388
Dolphins 226, **228,** 229
Dorrigo NP 120
Dreamtime 208
DRIVES
   Gibb River Road, Western Australia 238–239
   Great Ocean Road, Victoria 310–315
   Huon Valley, Tasmania 338–339
   Pacific Highway, New South Wales 118–121, **121**
   scenic loop drive, Tasmania 346–349
   Stuart Highway, South Australia 284–288
   Tropic of Capricorn, Queensland 150–153
Driving 237, 359–360
Drought 200
Drugs 357
Dunk Island 165, 167

E
Echuca **324,** 325, 384
Ecotourism 389
Eden 113
El Questro Wilderness Park 238–239
Elder Park, Adelaide 256
Electricity 362
Elizabeth Bay, Sydney 95
Elizabeth Farm 64
E-mail 362
Embassies and consulates 358, 364–365
Emerald 151
Emergencies 364
Encounter Bay 275
Environmental concerns 342, **342**
Esplanade, St. Kilda 304
Eucla **244,** 246
Eureka Stockade 46–48
Exmouth 231
EXPERIENCES
   Aborigines of Australia 209
   Adelaide festivals 273
   Adelaide markets 256
   Anzac Day 50
   Australian English language 19
   Australian Rules football 318
   Bay of Fires walk 347
   Biking Melbourne 305
   Birdsville horse races 176
   Brisbane boat trips 143
   bushwalking 205
   buying Aboriginal art 203
   buying opals 31
   camel treks 233
   Cape York Peninsula four-wheel-drive trip 174
   cattle mustering 281

cooking lessons 218
cruising Sydney Harbour 79
Dining by Tram, Melbourne 293
Eyre Bird Observatory
    bird-watching 245
getting close to Austalian
    wildlife 125
Great Barrier Reef cruises 160
Great Barrier Reef diving 168
Hawkesbury River
    houseboating 118
Henley-on-Todd regatta,
    Alice Springs 199
Lake Eyre fly-over 286
Melbourne photo walking
    tours 296
Mount Isa mine tour 178
Murray River houseboats 276
outback Australia 242
Overland Track, Tasmania 345
penguin viewing 307
Perth excursions 216
photo safari 296
platypus sightings 261
rail journeys 283
sea kayaking 167
seasonal work 267
Snowy River horseback
    riding 115
staying on a farm 136
surfing 315
swimming with whale sharks 231
taking a Priscilla tour 95
Tasmania fishing 353
Tasmanian devils 341
turtle nesting 147
Vegemite 25
volunteering 255
Whitsunday Islands sailing
    trips 162
wine courses 265
Exploration and discovery 33–39,
    43–45
    maps 34–35, 40
Eyre, Lake 286
Eyre Bird Observatory 245–246
Eyre Highway 243–248
Eyre Peninsula 125, 246

F
Fairfield Park Boathouse 305
Fairy penguins 307
Family vacations 361
Farm stays 136
Featherdale Wildlife Park, Sydney
    100, 125
Ferry trips 79, 333
Festivals 98, **99,** 176, **272,** 272–273,
    356–357
Finke Gorge NP 201
Fires **106,** 106–107, **107**
Fishing 113, 177, 178, **352,** 352–353,
    358, 389
Fitzgerald River NP 222
Fitzroy, Melbourne 296
Fitzroy Gardens, Melbourne 303
Five Rivers Lookout 238
Fleurieu Peninsula 262–263,
    381–382

Flinders Chase NP 205, 269, 270,
    271, **271**
Flinders Island 354
Flinders Ranges NP 209, 277–279,
    279, 382
Flinders Street Railway Station,
    Melbourne 298, **298**
Flora **66,** 70–72, **211, 222,** 222–
    223, **223**
Florence Falls **192,** 193
Food and drink **24,** 24–25, 218, 258,
    265, 357, 362
Football 318–319, **319,** 357
Fossils 173, 179–180
Four-wheel-drive trips 174, 242,
    355, 359, 388
Franklin-Gordon Wild Rivers NP
    343, **343**
Franklin River 342, 343, **343**
Fraser Island 148–149, **149,**
    172–173, 373
Fremantle **217,** 217–218
Freycinet NP 173, **346,** 348
Furneaux Islands 354

G
Gallipoli, Turkey **48,** 49–50
Gantheaume Point 233
GARDENS
    Adelaide 257
    Alice Springs 199
    Brisbane 142–143
    Canberra 130
    Melbourne 294, **295,** 299, 302,
        302, 303
    Perth 216
    Sydney 78, 84, 93, 98
Gay and lesbian travelers 362
Geeveston 338
Geography 26–31
Geraldton 228
Ghan (train) **282,** 282–283
Gibb River Road, Western Australia
    235, 238–239
Glass House Mountains 146
Glebe, Sydney 95
Glenelg **259,** 259–260
Gloucester Tree 224–225
Gold Coast **144,** 144–145, 315,
    372–373
Gold mining 28, **46–47,** 46–48,
    240–241, 320–321
Golf 359, 389
Goolwa 275–276
Gordon River 343
Gorge Scenic Drive, Beechworth 317
Government House, Adelaide 256
Government House,
    Melbourne 302
Government House, Sydney 84
Governor La Trobe's Cottage,
    Melbourne 302
Grafton 121
Grampians NP **326,** 326–327
Great Barrier Reef 154–165
    cruises 160
    diving and snorkeling 158, 168
    hotels and restaurants 373–374

islands 158–165
    map 155
    reef formation **156,** 156–157
    threats 159
    wildlife 70, 125, **154, 156–157,**
        157–158, **158, 163**
Great Dividing Range 308
Great Keppel Island 161
Great Northern Highway 222, 234
Great Ocean Road, Victoria 310–
    315, **314,** 384
    map 310–311
Great Ocean Walk 313
Great Sandy NP 149
Green Island 165
Gulf Developmental Highway 177
Gulf of Carpentaria 177–179
Gulf Track 178

H
Hahndorf 261–262
Hamelin Pool 229
Hamilton Island 163
Hartz Mountains NP 338
Hawkesbury River 118
Hayman Island 164
Healesville Sanctuary 125, 308
Health see Medicine and health
Henley-on-Todd regatta, Alice
    Springs 199, 356
Hellyer Gorge State Reserve 347
Henbury Meteor Craters 201
Hermannsburg community 201
Heron Island 160–161
Heysen Trail 262, 279
HIKING
    New South Wales 105,
        115, 205
    Queensland 145–146, 165, 205
    South Australia 262, 279
    Sydney 77, 205
    Tasmania 205, 340–341, 343,
        344–345, 347
    trails 205
    Victoria 205, 313, 316–
        317, 328
    Western Australia 205
Hinchinbrook Island 165
Hippies 120
History 32–55
    convicts 39–42
    exploration and discovery
        33–39, 43–45
    gold rushes 28, **46–47,** 46–48,
        240–241, 320–321
    government and politics 48–49,
        54–55
    immigration **51,** 52–53
    prehistory 32–33
    settlement 42–43
    World War I **48,** 49–50
    World War II 50–52, 186, 187
Hobart **334,** 334–337, 384–385
    map 335
Holidays 50, 134, 356–357, 363
Hook Island 163
Horse racing 111, 176, 297, **297**
Horseback riding 115

Hotels and restaurants
    accommodations 367
    farm stays 136
    restaurant variety 25, 367
    tipping 10, 364
    underground lodging 281
    Australian Capital Territory 371
    Melbourne 293
    New South Wales 105,
        369–371
    Northern Territory 376–377
    Queensland 371–376
    South Australia 281, 379–382
    Sydney 368–369
    Tasmania 385
    Victoria 293, 303, 312,
        382–384
    Western Australia 239,
        245–246, 378–379
Hotham, Mount **316,** 317
Houseboats 118, 276
Hunter Islands 354
Hunter Valley **110,** 110–111,
    369–370
Huon Valley, Tasmania 338–339
    map 339
Hyde Park, Sydney **76,** 89
Hydro Majestic Hotel, Medlow
    Bath 105

I

Ian Potter Centre: NGV Australia,
    Melbourne 298, 299
Immigration **51,** 52–53
Indian Pacific train 248
Inoculations 365
Insects 365
Insurance 357
Internet 362, 366
Introduced species 72, 352
Irwin, Steve 145

J

Jabiru 189
Jellyfish 69, 197
Jenolan Caves 108
Jewel Cave 227
Jim Jim Falls 191
Jindabyne 114–115

K

Kakadu NP 172, **172,** 173, **188,**
    188–191, **190,** 209
    hotels and restaurants 377
    shopping 386
Kalbarri NP 222, 228–229
Kalgoorlie **240,** 240–241, **243**
Kangaroo Island 125, 268–271, **269,**
    271, 274, 382
    Flinders Chase NP 205, 269,
        270, 271, **271**
Kangaroos 66–67, 67–68, **68**
Karumba 178
Kata-Tjuta **204,** 207–208
Katherine 194–195, 283, 288
Katoomba 104–105
Kayaking 167

Kelly, Ned **322,** 323
Keppel Bay Islands NP 161
Kiama 112–113
Killer Whale Museum, Eden 113
Kimberley region **66,** 218, **234,**
    234–235, 378–379
King Island 354
Kings Cross, Sydney 77, 94–95
Kings Park, Perth 216
Koalas **8,** 67–68, **125**
    sanctuaries 100, 125, 143
    viewing 9, 68, 120, 125,
        270, **271**
Koomurri Aboriginal Centre,
    Blue Mountains 105
Kosciuszko NP **101,** 114–115,
    173, 205
Kununurra 235
Kuranda 171
Kuranda Scenic Railway 170–171

L

Lady Elliott Island 159, 168
Lady Musgrave Island 159–160
Lake Gairdner NP 286
Lamington NP 145–146
Language 19, 54
Larrimah 288
Launceston 349, 385
Laura 176
Lava tubes 177
Lawn Hill NP 179–180, **179**
Leeuwin, Cape 227
Lesbian and gay travelers 362
Leura 105
Light, William 252–253
Light's Vision, Adelaide 258
Lindeman Island 163
Lion Arts Centre, Adelaide 256
Liquor laws 362
Litchfield NP **192,** 192–193
Literature 56, 58–59, 225
Living Desert Sculptures 117
Lizard Island **164,** 165, 168
Lizards 69
Lofty, Mount 261, **263**
Loggerhead turtles 154, **154**
Longreach 152–153
Lord Howe Island 122–124, **126,** 173
Lorne 312
Lost City 193
Luna Park, St. Kilda 304

M

MacDonnell Ranges 200–201, **201**
MacKillop, Mother Mary 266
Magnetic Island 164, 167, 374–375
Mail service 281, 361, 363
Main Yarra Trail, Victoria 305
Maldon 321
Mamu Rainforest Canopy
    Walkway 174
Manly 78
Manly Beach, Sydney 97
Mannum 276–277
Maps
    Adelaide 252–253
    Australian Capital Territory 129

Brisbane 141
Canberra 131
Darwin 185
exploration 34–35, 40
Gibb River Road 238–239
Great Barrier Reef 155
Great Ocean Road, Victoria
    310–311
Hobart 335
Huon Valley, Tasmania 339
Melbourne 300–301
New South Wales
    102–103, 119
Northern Territory 183
outlying territories 123
Perth 214–215
Queensland 138–139, 150–151
scenic loop drive, Tasmania
    346–349
South Australia 251, 285
Stuart Highway 285
Sydney 74–75
Sydney Harbour, Sydney 83
Tasmania 330–331, 339,
    348–349
Tropic of Capricorn 150–151
Victoria 290–291, 310–311
Western Australia 213,
    238–239
Margaret River **226,** 226–227
Markets 256, 294, 303
Mataranka 288
McLaren Vale 263, **263**
Meat pies 258
Medicine and health 20, 77,
    199, 365
Medlow Bath 105
Melbourne **4, 292,** 292–303
    bicycling 305
    Block Arcade 303
    boat trips 302
    Central Mall **289**
    cooking lessons 218
    Crown Casino 295–296
    festivals 356, 357
    Fitzroy 296
    Fitzroy Gardens 303
    Flinders Street Railway Station
        298, **298**
    Government House 302
    Governor La Trobe's
        Cottage 302
    horse racing 297, **297**
    hotels and restaurants 293, 303,
        382–384
    Ian Potter Centre: NGV
        Australia 298, 299
    Main Yarra Trail 305
    map 300–301
    Melbourne Gallery 295
    Melbourne Museum 295
    Melbourne Zoo 295
    NGV International 298, 299
    Old Treasury Building 303
    Prahran 296
    Queen Victoria Market
        294, 303
    Richmond 296
    Royal Botanic Gardens **295,**
        299, 302, **302**

shopping 303, 386, 387
Shrine of Remembrance 302
Southgate 299, 305
walks 296, 298–303
Williamstown 302
Young & Jackson Hotel 298
Melbourne Cup 297, **297**
Melville Island 197
Meteors 201
Migration Museum, Adelaide 257
Mildura 324–325, 384
Mindil Beach, Darwin 187
Mines and mining 28–31
    Argyle Diamond Mine
        234, 235
    Battery Hill Mining Centre 287
    Broken Hill 116–117
    gold mining **46–47,** 46–48,
        240–241, 320–321
    Mount Isa 178
    Olympic Dam mine 284, 286
    opals 280–281
    Ranger Uranium Mine 189
    sapphires 151–152
Mint, Sydney 89
Mirima NP 235
Mobile phones 362
Monasteries 219
Monastery Guesthouse,
        New Norcia 219
Money 11, 363
Monkey Mia 125, **228,** 229
Morning Glory
        phenomenon 177
Mornington Peninsula **306,**
        306–307
Mossman Gorge 169
Mount Buffalo NP 317
Mount Hypipamee NP 171
Mount Isa 178
Mount Lofty Ranges 261, **263**
Mount William NP 347
Mrs. Macquarie's Point,
        Sydney 82, 84
Mungo NP **29,** 325
Murray Bridge 276–277
Murray River 276–277, **277, 324,**
        324–325, 382
Murray River Valley 266
Museum of Australian Democracy,
        Canberra 132
MUSEUMS
    Art Gallery of Ballarat 320
    Art Gallery of New South
        Wales, Sydney 82, **82**
    Art Gallery of South Australia,
        Adelaide 257
    Australian Museum, Sydney 89
    Australian National Maritime
        Museum, Sydney 93
    Australian Stockman's Hall of
        Fame, Longreach 152–153
    Fremantle Arts Centre,
        Fremantle 218
    Goolwa Museum, Goolwa 275
    Ian Potter Centre: NGV
        Australia, Melbourne 298, 299
    Killer Whale Museum, Eden 113
    Melbourne Museum,
        Melbourne 295

Migration Museum,
    Adelaide 257
Mint, Sydney 89
Museum of Australian
    Democracy, Canberra 132
National Film & Sound Archive,
    Canberra 132
National Gallery of Australia,
    Canberra 65, 135
National Museum of Australia,
    Canberra 132
National Portrait Gallery 135
NGV International, Melbourne
    298, 299
Northern Territory Museum
    of Arts & Sciences, Darwin
    186–187
Powerhouse Museum,
    Sydney 92
Qantas Founders Museum,
    Longreach 153
Queensland Maritime Museum,
    Brisbane 142
South Australian Museum,
    Adelaide 257
Sovereign Hill, Ballarat **320,**
    320–321
Waltzing Matilda Centre,
    Winton 153
Western Australian Maritime
    Museum, Fremantle 218
Whale World, Albany 225
White's Mineral Art Gallery
    & Mining Museum, Broken
    Hill 117
Music **57,** 59–60, **60,** 109, **109**
Mutawinji NP 117

N
Nambung NP 173, 216
Naracoorte Caves Park 266
Narcotics 357
National Film & Sound Archive,
    Canberra 132
National Gallery of Australia,
    Canberra 65, 135
National Library of Australia,
    Canberra 131
National Museum of Australia,
    Canberra 132
National Portrait Gallery,
    Canberra 135
National Trust 363
New Norcia 219, **219**
New South Wales 101–126
    Blue Mountains **104,**
        104–105, 369
    Broken Hill **116,** 116–117
    drive 118–121
    hiking 105, 205
    hotels and restaurants 105,
        369–370
    Hunter Valley **110,** 110–111,
        369–370
    Jenolan Caves 108
    Kosciuszko NP **101,** 114–115,
        173, 205
    maps 102–103, 119
    national parks office 366

National Trust 363
Pacific Highway drive
    118–121, **121**
Snowy Mountains **101, 114,**
    114–115, 370
south coast **112,** 112–113, 370
surfing 389
Tamworth 109, **109**
tourism website 366
wine regions 111
see also Sydney
New Year's Eve 98, **99**
Newcastle 118
Newspapers 363
Newtown, Sydney 77, 95
NGV International, Melbourne
    298, 299
Nimbin 120
Ningaloo Marine Park 125, 168,
    230, 230–231, 379
Nitmiluk NP 194, **194,** 195
Noosa Heads 147
Noosa NP **146,** 147
Norfolk Island 124
Normanton 177
North Adelaide, Adelaide 258
North Terrace, Adelaide 254, 255
Northern Queensland 166–171,
    174–180
    Atherton Tablelands
        170–171, **171**
    Cairns 160, **166,** 167–168,
        375, 386
    Cape Tribulation
        169–170, 375–376
    Cape York Peninsula
        174–177, **175**
    Gulf of Carpentaria 177–179
    Lawn Hill NP 179–180, **179**
    Port Douglas 160,
        168–169, 375
    Townsville 166–167, 374–375
Northern Territory 181–210
    Alice Springs **198,**
        198–201, 286
    Arnhem Land **32–33,**
        196–197, 209
    Darwin 184–187
    hiking 205
    hotels and restaurants 376–377
    Kakadu NP 172, **172,** 173, **188,**
        188–191, **190,** 209, 377, 386
    Katherine 194–195, 283, 288
    Litchfield NP **192,** 192–193
    map 183
    national parks office 366
    National Trust 363
    Nitmiluk NP 194, **194,** 195
    shopping 386
    Tiwi Islands 197
    tourism website 366
    Uluru–Kata Tjuta NP 173, 204,
        204, 206–208, **207**
    Watarrka NP 210, **210,** 377–378
Northern Territory Museum of Arts
    & Sciences, Darwin 186–187
Northern Territory Wildlife Park, 193
Nourlangie 190
Nullarbor Plain 243–248

O
Old Treasury Building,
    Melbourne 303
Olgas *see* Kata-Tjuta
Olympic Dam mine 284, 286
Online services 362, 366
Opals 31, 280–281, 387
Orpheus Island 164
Otway, Cape 313
Outback 18–20, 237, 242, **355**
    schools 20, 153, 195, 199
Overland Track, Tasmania 205,
    344–345

P
Pacific Highway 118–121, **121**
Package tours 358
Paddington, Sydney 77, 94
Painting 64–65, **65**, 117
PARKS
    national parks 172–173, 366
    Arthur's Seat SP 306
    Barrington Tops NP 118, 120
    Ben Boyd NP 113
    City Botanic Gardens, Brisbane
        142–143
    Cleland Wildlife Park **260**, 261
    Cooloola NP 147–148
    Cradle Mountain–Lake St. Clair
        NP 173, **344**, 344–345
    Daintree NP **30, 169**, 169–170,
        173, 375–376
    Dandenong Ranges NP 309
    Dorrigo NP 120
    El Questro Wilderness Park
        238–239
    Elder Park, Adelaide 256
    Finke NP 201
    Fitzgerald River NP 222
    Flinders Chase NP 205, 269,
        270, 271, **271**
    Flinders Ranges NP 209,
        277–279, **279**, 382
    Fossil Mammal sites 173,
        179–180
    Franklin-Gordon Wild Rivers NP
        343, **343**
    Fraser Island 148–149, **149**,
        172–173, 373
    Freycinet NP 173, **346**, 348
    Grampians NP **326**, 326–327
    Great Sandy NP 149
    Hartz Mountains NP 338
    Hellyer Gorge State
        Reserve 347
    Kakadu NP 172, **172**, 173, **188**,
        188–191, **190**, 209, 377, 386
    Kalbarri NP 222, 228–229
    Keppel Bay Islands NP 161
    Kings Park, Perth 216
    Kosciuszko NP **101**, 114–115,
        173, 205
    Lake Gairdner NP 286
    Lamington NP 145–146
    Lawn Hill NP 178–180, **179**
    Litchfield NP **192**, 192–193
    Lord Howe Island 122–124,
        126, 173

Mirima NP 235
Mount Buffalo NP 317
Mount Hypipamee NP 171
Mount William NP 347
Mungo NP **29**, 325
Mutawinji NP 117
Nambung NP 173, 216
Naracoorte Caves Park 266
Ningaloo Marine Park 125, 168,
    230, 230–231, 379
Nitmiluk NP **194**, **194**, 195
Noosa NP **146**, 147
Point Nepean NP 307
Port Campbell NP 173
Purnululu NP 173, **236**,
    236–237
Rocky Cape NP 346
Royal NP 112, 172
Shark Bay NP 172
Southern Queensland national
    parks 145–146
Southwest NP **340**, 340–341
Springbrook NP 146
Tunnel Creek NP 239
Uluru–Kata Tjuta NP 173, 204,
    204, 206–208, **207**, 209
Walpole-Nornalup NP 222, 225
Watarrka NP 210, **210**,
    377–378
Wilsons Promontory NP 328
see also Zoos and wildlife parks
Parliament House, Adelaide 255
Parliament House, Brisbane 143
Parliament House, Canberra
    132–133
Passports 357
Paterson, A. B. "Banjo" 16, 56, **58**,
    115, 153
Pearling industry 232
Pemberton 224–225
Penal colonies *see* Prisons
    and prisoners
Penguins 307
Penola 266
Perth **107**, 214–216, 378
    map 214–215
Phillip Island 125, 307
Photography 208, 296, 363
Pichi Pichi railroad, Quorn 278
Pie floaters 258
Plants *see* Flora
Platypuses 261
Point Nepean NP 307
Poisonous animals 69, 197, 365
Pokolbin 110
Poms (British) 54
Port Adelaide 260
Port Arthur **38–39, 350**, 350–351
Port Campbell NP 173
Port Douglas 160, 168–169, 375
Port Fairy 315, 356
Port Lincoln 246
Port Macquarie 120
Post offices 281, 361, 363
Powerhouse Museum, Sydney 92
Prahran, Melbourne 296
Prehistory 32–33
Prisons and prisoners 39–42, 124,
    218, 350–351

Puffing Billy (train) 309, **309**
Purnululu NP 173, **236**, 236–237
Pyndan Camel Tracks,
    Alice Springs 199

Q
Qantas Founders Museum,
    Longreach 153
Queen Victoria Building, Sydney 88
Queen Victoria Market, Melbourne
    294, 303
Queenscliff 311–312
Queensland 137–180
    Brisbane **42–43**, 140–143,
        371–372
    cooking lessons 218
    Great Barrier Reef 70, 125,
        154–165, 168, 373–374
    hiking 205
    hotels and restaurants 371–376
    maps 138–139, 150–151
    national parks office 366
    National Trust 363
    Northern Queensland 160,
        166–171, 174–180,
        375–376, 386
    Southeast Queensland
        144–149
    surfing 389
    Tropic of Capricorn drive
        150–153
Queensland Maritime Museum,
    Brisbane 142
Queenstown 347–348
Quinkan Reserve Aboriginal rock
    art galleries 176
Quokkas 221
Quorn 278

R
Rabbits 72
Radio 363
Ranger Uranium Mine 189
Restaurants *see* Hotels and
    restaurants
Richmond, Melbourne 296
Richmond, Tasmania 348
Right whales 275, 313
Riversleigh Fossil Site 179–180
Rock art **32–33**, 176, 179, 188–189,
    190, 202–203, 327
Rockhampton 150
Rocks area, Sydney **73**, 76, 84–85
Rocky Cape NP 346
Rottnest Island **220**, 220–221, 379
Royal Botanic Gardens, Melbourne
    295, 299, 302, **302**
Royal Botanic Gardens, Sydney 78,
    84, 98
Royal Flying Doctor Service 20, 199
Royal NP 112, 172

S
Sailing 389
St. Andrew's Cathedral,
    Sydney 88
St. Clair, Lake 348

St. Kilda 296, 304, **304**
St. Peter's Cathedral, Adelaide **257**, 258
Salamanca Place, Hobart 336
Salt pans 286
Saltwater crocodiles 191, 197
Sandy Creek Falls 193
Sapphires 151–152
Scenic loop drive, Tasmania 346–349
map 348–349
Schanck, Cape 306, **306**
Schools, outback 20, 153, 195, 199
Scone 111
Scuba diving **71**, 158, 168, 221, 388
Sea kayaking 167
Seaplanes 79
Senior travelers 364
Seven Hills Winery, Clare Valley **264**, 266
Seven Mile Beach 113
Seven Spirit Bay 196–197
Shark Bay 172, **228**, 228–229
Sharks 70, **71**, 197, **230**, 230–231
Shipwrecks 312, 315
Shopping 386–387
Aboriginal art 203, 386
markets 256, 294, 303
opals 31, 387
opening hours 363
Shrine of Remembrance, Melbourne 302
Silverton **116**, 117
Simpson's Gap 200–201
Six Foot Track 108
Skiing **114**, 115, 316, **316**, 317
Snakes 69, 197, 365
Snorkeling 158, **164**, 221, 231
Snowy Mountains **101, 114,** 114–115, 370
Snowy River 115
South Australia
Aboriginal experiences 209
Adelaide 252–258, 272–273, 356, 357, 379–381, 386
Adelaide area 125, 205, 209, **249**, 259–263, 266–271, 274–279, 381–382
Coober Pedy **280**, 280–281, 286, 382
cooking lessons 218
entry from Western Australia 247–248
festivals **272**, 272–273, 356, 357
Ghan (train) **282**, 282–283
hiking 205
hotels and restaurants 281, 379–382
maps 251, 285
national parks office 366
National Trust 363
Stuart Highway drive 284–288
surfing 389
tourism website 366
wine regions 111, 263, **263**, 266–268
South Australian Museum, Adelaide 257

South coast, New South Wales **112**, 112–113, 370
South Coast Track, Tasmania 340–341
Southeast Queensland 144–149
Fraser Island 148–149, **149**, 172–173, 373
Gold Coast **144**, 144–145, 315, 372–373
national parks 145–146
Sunshine Coast 146–148, 373
Southern Vales 263
Southgate, Melbourne 299, 305
Southwest, Western Australia **224**, 224–225, 379
Southwest wilderness, Tasmania **340**, 340–341
Sovereign Hill, Ballarat **320**, 320–321
Spiders 69, 197, 365
Springbrook NP 146
Standley Chasm 201, **201**
Stanley 346–347
State Library, Adelaide 256–257
State Library of New South Wales, Sydney 89
State Parliament House, Sydney 89
Stations 18–20, **20–21**, 153, 195, 281
Steamboats 276–277, **277**, 325
Story Bridge, Brisbane 143
Stuart Highway 284–288
map 285
Sun Pictures, Broome 233
Sunburn 365
Sunshine Coast 146–148, 373
Super Pit, Kalgoorlie 241
Surf rescue **52–53**, 97
Surfers Paradise 144, **144**, 145
Surfing **15**, 226, 312, 315, 388–389
Swimming 69, 97, 226, 231, 364
Sydney 73–100
airport 359
Art Gallery of New South Wales 82, **82**
Asian culture 77
Australian Museum 89
Australian National Maritime Museum 93
Balmain 95
Balmoral 97
biking 77
boat trips 78, 79
bohemian Sydney 94–95
Bondi Beach 77, **96**, 96–97
Cabramatta 77
Chinese Garden 93
Circular Quay 74, 76, 84, **85**
cooking lessons 218
Darling Harbour 77, 92–93
Darlinghurst 77, 94–95
downtown Sydney **88**, 88–89
Elizabeth Bay 95
Featherdale Wildlife Park 100
gay and lesbian life **94**, 94–95
Glebe 95
Government House 84
hiking 77, 205

hotels and restaurants 368–369
Hyde Park **76**, 89
Hyde Park Barracks 89
Kings Cross 77, 94–95
Koala Park Sanctuary 100
Manly Beach 97
maps 74–75, 83
Mint 89
Mrs. Macquarie's Point 82, 84
New Year's Eve 98, **99**
Newtown 77, 95
Paddington 77, 94
Powerhouse Museum 92
Priscilla tours 95
Queen Victoria Building 88
Rocks area **73**, 76, 84–85
Royal Botanic Gardens 78, 84, 98
SEA LIFE Sydney Aquarium 92–93
St. Andrew's Cathedral 88
shopping 386, 387
State Library of New South Wales 89
State Parliament House 89
surfing 315
Sydney Fish Market 93
Sydney Harbour **16–17, 78,** 78–87, 98
Sydney Harbour Bridge 64, **78, 80–81,** 81, 85
Sydney Opera House **60**, 84, 86–87, **86–87**
Sydney Tower **88**, 89
Sydney Town Hall 88
Taronga Zoo 98, 100, **100**
transportation 77
walks 79, 82–85
WILD LIFE Sydney Zoo 93

T
Tahune Forest Reserve 338
Tamworth 109, **109**
Tandanya, Adelaide 257–258
Taronga Zoo, Sydney 98, 100, **100**
Tasmania 329–354
Aborigines 332–333
Bass Strait Islands 354
Cradle Mountain-Lake St. Clair NP 173, **344**, 344–345
environmentalism 342, **342**
ferry 333
Franklin-Gordon Wild Rivers NP 343, **343**
hiking 205
Hobart **334**, 334–337, 384–385
hotels and restaurants 384–385
Huon Valley drive 338–339
maps 330–331, 339, 348–349
Mount Wellington 337, **337**
national parks office 366
National Trust 363
Port Arthur **38–39, 350,** 350–351
scenic loop drive 346–349
Southwest wilderness **340**, 340–341

surfing 389
tourism website 366
trout fishing **352,** 352–353
wildlife viewing 125
wine regions 111
Tasmanian devils **329,** 341
Tasmanian tigers 347
Taxis 10
Telephones 362
Television 61–63, 363
Tennant Creek 287
Tennis 389
Theater 59, 256
Theme parks 145, 304
Thorsborne Trail 165, 205
Three Sisters 105
Thursday Island 176
Tidbinbilla Deep Space
    Communication Complex 132
Tidbinbilla Nature Reserve 132
Time zones 364
Tipping 10, 364
Tiwi people 197
Tjaynera Falls 193
Toads 180
Tolmer Falls 193
Torquay 312
Torres Straits Islands 176
Tourism offices 365–366
Townsville 166–167, 374–375
Trains 283, 361
    Ghan **282,** 282–283
    Indian Pacific train 248
    Kuranda Scenic Railway
        170–171
    Pichi Pichi railroad, Quorn 278
    Puffing Billy (train) 309, **309**
Trams 293
Transportation 358–361
    see also Boat trips; Trains
Travel insurance 357
Tree climbing 224–225
Tribulation, Cape 169–170,
    375–376
Tropic of Capricorn drive 150–153
    map 150–151
Trout fishing **352,** 352–353
Tunnel Creek NP 239
Turtles 147, **154**
Twelve Apostles 313, **313**
Twin Falls 191

U
Ubirr 190–191
Uluru **26–27,** 204, 206–207,
    207, 386
Uluru–Kata Tjuta NP 173, 204, **204,**
    206–208, **207,** 209
Undara Lava Tubes 177

V
Vegemite 25
Vegetation *see* Flora
Victor Harbor **274,** 274–275
Victoria 289–328
    alpine country 316–317
    bicycling 305
    bushfires 106

Dandenong Ranges NP 309
goldfields 320–321
Grampians NP **326,** 326–327
Great Ocean Road
    310–315, 384
hotels and restaurants 293, 303,
    312, 382–384
Main Yarra Trail 305
maps 290–291, 310–311
Melbourne **4,** 218, **289,**
    292–303, 305, 356, 357,
    382–384, 386, 387
Mornington Peninsula **306,**
    306–307
Murray River **324,** 324–325
national parks office 366
National Trust 363
St. Kilda 296, 304, **304**
surfing 389
Wilsons Promontory NP 328
wine regions 111, 308
Yarra Valley 308
Video 363
Visas 357
Volunteer opportunities 255, 364

W
WALKS
    Melbourne 296, 298–303
    Sydney 79, 82–85
Wallace, Kathleen **202**
Walpole-Nornalup NP 222, 225
Waltzing Matilda Centre,
    Winton 153
Wangi Falls 193
War memorials **134,** 135–136, 302
Warrnambool 313, 315
Watarrka NP 210, **210,** 377–378
Wave Rock 225
Weather 10, 26–27, 356
Websites, informational 366
Wellington, Mount 337, **337**
Western Australia 211–248
    Aboriginal experiences 209
    Boulder 241
    Broome **232,** 232–233, 378
    cooking lessons 218
    drives 238–239
    Eyre Highway 243–248
    Fremantle **217,** 217–218
    Gibb River Road 235, 238–239
    hiking 205
    hotels and restaurants 239,
        245–246, 377–379
    Kalgoorlie **240,** 240–241, **243**
    Kimberley region **66,** 218, **234,**
        234–235, 378–379
    maps 213, 238–239
    Margaret River **226,** 226–227
    national parks office 366
    National Trust 363
    New Norcia 219, **219**
    Ningaloo Marine Park 125, 168,
        230, 230–231, 379
    Nullarbor Plain 243–248
    Perth **107,** 214–216, 378
    Purnululu NP 173, **236,**
        236–237

roadhouses 245–246
Rottnest Island **220,**
    220–221, 379
Shark Bay 172, **228,** 228–229
Southwest **224,** 224–225, 379
surfing 315, 389
tourism website 366
wildflowers **222,** 222–223, **223**
wine regions 111, 227
Western Australian Maritime
    Museum, Fremantle 218
Whale sharks **230,** 230–231
Whale World, Albany 225
Whales 227, 275, 313, 315
White Cliffs 117
White-water rafting 389
White's Mineral Art Gallery &
    Mining Museum,
    Broken Hill 117
Whitsunday Islands 161–164
Wildflowers *see* Flora
Wildlife 66–72
    dangerous 69–70, 197, 365
    threats to 72, 180, 352
    see also Zoos and wildlife parks;
        specific animals
Williamstown, Melbourne 302
Wilpena Pound 278–279
Wilsons Promontory NP 328
Windsor Hotel, Melbourne 303
Wines and wineries 111, **264,**
    264–265, 387
    Adelaide area 263, **263,**
        266–268
    Hunter Valley **110,** 110–111
    Margaret River 227
    Victoria 111, 308
Winton **152,** 153
Winton, Tim 225
Wollongong 112, **112**
Woomera 284
World War I **48,** 49–50
World War II 50–52, 186, 187
Wyndham 209, 238
Wynyard 346

Y
Yallingup 227
Yarra Valley 308
Yellow Water 191
Young & Jackson Hotel,
    Melbourne 298

Z
Zeehan 347
Zoos and wildlife parks
    Adelaide 257
    Brisbane 125, 143
    Cleland Wildlife Park
        260, 261
    Healesville Wildlife Sanctuary
        125, 308
    Melbourne 295
    Monarto, Adelaide 277
    Sunshine Coast 125, 147
    Sydney 93, 98, 100, **100,** 125
    Territory Wildlife Park 193
    Tidbinbilla Nature Reserve 132

ILLUSTRATIONS CREDITS

National Geographic
TRAVELER
Australia

Published by the National Geographic Society

John M. Fahey, *Chairman of the Board and Chief Executive Officer*

Declan Moore, *Executive Vice President; President, Publishing and Travel*

Melina Gerosa Bellows, *Executive Vice President; Chief Creative Officer, Books, Kids, and Family*

Lynn Cutter, *Executive Vice President, Travel*

Keith Bellows, *Senior Vice President and Editor in Chief, National Geographic Travel Media*

Prepared by the Book Division

Hector Sierra, *Senior Vice President and General Manager*

Janet Goldstein, *Senior Vice President and Editorial Director*

Jonathan Halling, *Design Director, Books and Children's Publishing*

Marianne R. Koszorus, *Design Director, Books*

Barbara A. Noe, *Senior Editor, National Geographic Travel Books*

R. Gary Colbert, *Production Director*

Jennifer A. Thornton, *Director of Managing Editorial*

Susan S. Blair, *Director of Photography*

Meredith C. Wilcox, *Director, Administration and Rights Clearance*

Staff for This Book

Justin Kavanagh, *Project Editor*

Ruth Ann Thompson, *Designer*

Carl Mehler, *Director of Maps*

Mike McNey *&* Mapping Specialists, *Map Production*

Marshall Kiker, *Associate Managing Editor*

Gary Colbert, *Production Manager*

Galen Young, *Rights Clearance Specialist*

Production Services

Phillip L. Schlosser, *Senior Vice President*

Chris Brown, *Vice President, NG Book Manufacturing*

George Bounelis, *Vice President, Production Services*

Nicole Elliott, *Manager*

Rachel Faulise, *Manager*

Robert L. Barr, *Manager*

The information in this book has been carefully checked and to the best of our knowledge is accurate. However, details are subject to change, and the National Geographic Society cannot be responsible for such changes, or for errors or omissions.

First edition: Edited and designed by AA Publishing (a trading name of Automobile Association Developments Limited, whose registered office is Norfolk House, Priestley Road, Basingstoke, Hampshire, England RG24 9NY. Registered number: 1878835).

Drive maps drawn by Chris Orr Associates, Southampton, England

Cutaway illustrations drawn by Maltings Partnership, Derby, England

The National Geographic Society is one of the world's largest nonprofit scientific and educational organizations. Founded in 1888 to "increase and diffuse geographic knowledge," the member-supported Society works to inspire people to care about the planet. Through its on-line community, members can get closer to explorers and photographers, connect with other members around the world, and help make a difference. National Geographic reflects the world through its magazines, television programs, films, music and radio, books, DVDs, maps, exhibitions, live events, school publishing programs, interactive media, and merchandise. *National Geographic* magazine, the Society's official journal, published in English and 38 local-language editions, is read by more than 60 million people each month. The National Geographic Channel reaches 440 million households in 171 countries in 38 languages. National Geographic Digital Media receives more than 25 million visitors a month. National Geographic has funded more than 10,000 scientific research, conservation, and exploration projects and supports an education program promoting geography literacy. For more information, visit www.nationalgeographic.com.

For more information, please call 1800-NGS LINE (647-5463) or write to the following address:

National Geographic Society
1145 17th Street N.W.
Washington, D.C. 20036-4688 U.S.A.

For information about special discounts for bulk purchases, please contact National Geographic Books Special Sales: ngspecsales@ngs.org

For rights or permissions inquiries, please contact National Geographic Books Subsidiary Rights: ngbookrights@ngs.org

National Geographic Traveler: Australia (Fifth edition)
ISBN: 978-1-4262-1184-3

Printed in Hong Kong

13/THK/1

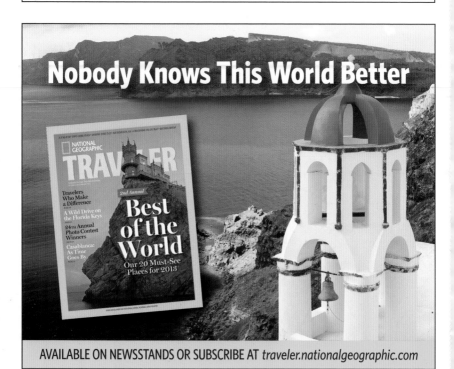